# Readings for

# AMERICAN GOVERNMENT

## *5*TH EDITION

# Theodore J. Lowi
CORNELL UNIVERSITY

# Benjamin Ginsberg
JOHNS HOPKINS UNIVERSITY

# David T. Canon
UNIVERSITY OF WISCONSIN-MADISON

# Anne Khademian
UNIVERSITY OF MICHIGAN

AND

# Kenneth R. Mayer
UNIVERSITY OF WISCONSIN-MADISON

# Readings for

# AMERICAN GOVERNMENT
## Freedom and Power
### 5TH EDITION

W • W • Norton & Company  New York • London

The text of this book is composed in New Baskerville
Composition by PennSet, Inc.
Manufacturing by Victor Graphics
Book design by Jack Meserole

Library of Congress Cataloging-in-Publication Data
Readings for American government : freedom and power / [edited
by]
Theodore J. Lowi . . . [et al.]. — 5th ed.
    p.    cm.
Includes bibliographical references.
**ISBN 0-393-97184-8 (pbk.)**
    1. United States—Politics and government.  I. Lowi, Theodore J.
II. Lowi, Theodore J. American government.
JK21.R35   1998
320.973—dc21                                                    97-39260

ISBN 0-393-97184-8 (pbk.)
W. W. Norton & Company, Inc., 500 Fifth Avenue, New York, N.Y. 10110
http://www.wwnorton.com
W. W. Norton & Company Ltd., 10 Coptic Street, London WC1A 1PU
1 2 3 4 5 6 7 8 9 0

# Contents

## for *American Government, 5th Edition*

# Contents

for *American Government, Brief 5th Edition*

## READINGS

# Preface

The readings contained in this volume are intended to enrich students' comprehension of the structure and operation of American government by providing a number of materials—articles, essays, and court cases—that illustrate the key concepts presented in the parallel chapter of the textbook. A headnote introducing each reading explains its significance and its precise relationship to the major concept presented in the core text.

The readings include classic pieces such as selections from major Federalist and Antifederalist writings and Tocqueville's *Democracy in America*, contemporary essays from important newspapers and magazines, and in a separate appendix, excerpts from major Supreme Court cases. By reprinting classic works in American government, we hope to acquaint students with some of the most profound thinking and writing on politics—thereby reinforcing the theoretical issues raised in the text. The contemporary essays are designed to provide students with lively and current illustrations of the phenomena and institutions discussed in the text; the court cases are selected for their importance in establishing the legal and institutional framework of American government. In every instance, we strongly urge students to read the headnote introducing each reading to gain an understanding of the significance of each piece and its relationship to the text, and to use the questions following each set of readings as an aid to studying the materials in both this reader and the text.

Also of note are "Debating the Issues: Opposing Views" essays, which appear in each chapter. The essays center on the topics introduced in the "Debating the Issues" boxes in the corresponding chapter in the text. Offering opposing views, the essays will help students think critically about important issues in American politics.

We encourage students to review and ponder the readings and cases in conjunction with the text and to use them as a learning tool. We are confident that these materials will assist students in learning more about issues of freedom and power in American government.

Theodore J. Lowi
Benjamin Ginsberg
David T. Canon
Anne Khademian
Kenneth R. Mayer

October 1997

# Readings for

## AMERICAN GOVERNMENT

# 1

# Freedom and Power

See Lowi and Ginsberg, pp. 6–7 or brief edition, pp. 12–13

## DEBATING THE ISSUES: FREEDOM AND POWER—THE ENDURING DEBATE

As the text notes, all governments must have, at the very least, the power to enforce public order and to collect public revenues. In the debates preceding the ratification of the United States Constitution, which creates the framework for the operation of the national government, the scope of these powers was directly at issue as the Federalists and Antifederalists battled over whether to create a strong central government or retain the confederated structure under which the country had operated since the Revolution. The arguments were advanced against the backdrop of state sovereignty: under the Articles of Confederation, states maintained their own militias and controlled the means by which revenues were generated for public purposes. Alexander Hamilton, a leading Federalist, argued that this structure left the federal government "in a kind of tutelage to the State governments," sapped of the energy and creativity required to sustain a union.

The following excerpts present the Federalist and Antifederalist positions on the potential gains and problems that would result from the emergence of a strong national government. The Federalist paper authored by Hamilton argues in favor of creating a strong central government with power to raise an army.

The author of the second selection is not known for certain: The Antifederalist writer styled himself "Brutus" and was responding to Hamilton's arguments in The Federalist No. 23. The Antifederalist writer warns against the aggregation of power in the national government that is certain to result from the delegation of such authority from the states to the national government.

A principle controversy surrounding ratification was whether the states or the national government should exercise military and fiscal powers. The Antifederalists warned that the remoteness of the national government could lead to abuses of power, and they preferred a balance that favored state governments. A government close to the people, they argued, would be more accountable. Moreover, as citizens worked to hold the government accountable through participation, they would generate a spirit of civic engagement necessary to sustain the American experiment in self governance. The Antifederalist position is again ascendant in the recent push in Congress to return authority over various federal programs (welfare, housing, environment) to state and local governments.

# Alexander Hamilton
## *The Federalist No. 23* *

The necessity of a Constitution, at least equally energetic with the one proposed, to the preservation of the Union is the point at the examination of which we are now arrived.

This inquiry will naturally divide itself into three branches—the objects to be provided for by a federal government, the quantity of power necessary to the accomplishment of those objects, the persons upon whom that power ought to operate. Its distribution and organization will more properly claim our attention under the succeeding head.

The principal purposes to be answered by union are these—the common defense of the members; the preservation of the public peace, as well against internal convulsions as external attacks; the regulation of commerce with other nations and between the States; the superintendence of our intercourse, political and commercial, with foreign countries.

The authorities essential to the common defense are these—to raise armies; to build and equip fleets; to prescribe rules for the government of both; to direct their operations; to provide for their support. These powers ought to exist without limitation, *because it is impossible to foresee or to define the extent and variety of national exigencies, and the correspondent extent and variety of the means which may be necessary to satisfy them.* The circumstances that endanger the safety of nations are infinite, and for this reason no constitutional shackles can wisely be imposed on the power to which the care of it is committed. This power ought to be coextensive with all the possible combinations of such circumstances; and ought to be under the direction of the same councils which are appointed to preside over the common defense. . . .

Whether there ought to be a federal government intrusted with the care of the common defense is a question in the first instance open to discussion; but the moment it is decided in the affirmative, it will follow that that government ought to be clothed with all the powers requisite to complete execution of its trust. And unless it can be shown that the circumstances which may affect the public safety are reducible within certain determinate limits; unless the contrary of this position can be fairly and rationally disputed, it must be admitted as a necessary consequence that there can be no limitation of that authority which is to provide for the defense and protection of the community in any matter essential to its efficacy—that is, in any matter essential to the *formation, direction,* or *support* of the NATIONAL FORCES.

Defective as the present Confederation has been proved to be, this principle appears to have been fully recognized by the framers of it; though they have not made proper or adequate provision for its exercise.

* Alexander Hamilton, *The Federalist No. 23*, ed. Clinton Rossiter (New York: NAL, 1961).

Congress have an unlimited discretion to make requisitions of men and money; to govern the army and navy; to direct their operations. As their requisitions are made constitutionally binding upon the States, who are in fact under the most solemn obligations to furnish the supplies required of them, the intention evidently was that the United States should command whatever resources were by them judged requisite to the "common defense and general welfare." It was presumed that a sense of their true interests, and a regard to the dictates of good faith, would be found sufficient pledges for the punctual performance of the duty of the members to the federal head.

The experiment has, however, demonstrated that this expectation was ill-founded and illusory; and the observations made under the last head will, I imagine, have sufficed to convince the impartial and discerning that there is an absolute necessity for an entire change in the first principles of the system; that if we are in earnest about giving the Union energy and duration we must abandon the vain project of legislating upon the States in their collective capacities; we must extend the laws of the federal government to the individual citizens of America; we must discard the fallacious scheme of quotas and requisitions as equally impracticable and unjust. The result from all this is that the Union ought to be invested with full power to levy troops; to build and equip fleets; and to raise the revenues which will be required for the formation and support of an army and navy in the customary and ordinary modes practiced in other governments.

If the circumstances of our country are such as to demand a compound instead of a simple, a confederate instead of a sole, government, the essential point which will remain to be adjusted will be to discriminate the OBJECTS, as far as it can be done, which shall appertain to the different provinces or departments of power; allowing to each the most ample authority for fulfilling the objects committed to its charge. Shall the Union be constituted the guardian of the common safety? Are fleets and armies and revenues necessary to this purpose? The government of the Union must be empowered to pass all laws, and to make all regulations which have relation to them. The same must be the case in respect to commerce, and to every other matter to which its jurisdiction is permitted to extend. Is the administration of justice between the citizens of the same State the proper department of the local governments? These must possess all the authorities which are connected with this object, and with every other that may be allotted to their particular cognizance and direction. Not to confer in each case a degree of power commensurate to the end would be to violate the most obvious rules of prudence and propriety, and improvidently to trust the great interests of the nation to hands which are disabled from managing them with vigor and success.

Who so likely to make suitable provisions for the public defense as that body to which the guardianship of the public safety is confided; which, as the center of information, will best understand the extent and urgency of the dangers that threaten; as the representative of the WHOLE, will feel itself most deeply interested in the preservation of every part; which, from the responsibility implied in the duty assigned to it, will be most sensibly impressed with the necessity of proper exertions; and which, by the extension of its authority throughout the States, can alone establish uniformity and concert in the plans and measures by which the common safety is to be secured? Is there not a manifest inconsistency in devolving upon the federal government the care of the general defense and leaving in the State governments the *effective* powers by which it is to be provided for? Is not a want of co-operation the infallible consequence of such a system? And will not weakness, disorder, and undue distribution of the burdens and calamities of war, an unnecessary and intolerable increase of expense, be its natural and inevitable concomitants? Have we not had unequivocal experience of its effects in the course of the revolution which we have just achieved?

Every view we may take of the subject, as candid inquirers after truth, will serve to convince us that it is both unwise and dangerous to deny the federal government an unconfined authority in respect to all those objects which are intrusted to its management. It will indeed deserve the most vigilant and careful attention of the people to see that it be modeled in such a manner as to admit of its being safely vested with the requisite powers. If any plan which has been, or may be, offered to our consideration should not, upon a dispassionate inspection, be found to answer this description, it ought to be rejected. A government, the constitution of which renders it unfit to be trusted with all the powers which a free people *ought to delegate to any government*, would be an unsafe and improper depository of the NATIONAL INTERESTS. Wherever THESE can with propriety be confided, the coincident powers may safely accompany them. This is the true result of all just reasoning upon the subject. And the adversaries of the plan promulgated by the convention would have given a better impression of their candor if they had confined themselves to showing that the internal structure of the proposed government was such as to render it unworthy of the confidence of the people. They ought not to have wandered into inflammatory declamations and unmeaning cavils about the extent of the powers. The POWERS are not too extensive for the OBJECTS of federal administration, or, in other words, for the management of our NATIONAL INTERESTS; nor can any satisfactory argument be framed to show that they are chargeable with such an excess. If it be true, as has been insinuated by some of the writers on the other side, that the difficulty arises from the nature of the thing, and that the extent of the country will not permit us to form a government in which such ample powers can safely be reposed, it would prove that we ought to contract our views, and resort to the expedient of separate confederacies, which will move within more practicable spheres. For the absurdity must continually stare us in the face of confiding to a government the direction of the most essential national interests, without daring to trust to it the authorities which are indispensable to their proper and efficient management. Let us not attempt to reconcile contradictions, but firmly embrace a rational alternative. . . . I trust, however, that the impracticability of one general system cannot be shown. I am greatly mistaken if anything of weight has yet been advanced of this tendency; and I flatter myself that the observations which have been made in the course of these papers have served to place the reverse of that position in as clear a light as any matter still in the womb of time and experience is susceptible of. This, at all events, must be evident, that the very difficulty itself, drawn from the extent of the country, is the strongest argument in favor of an energetic government; for any other can certainly never preserve the Union of so large an empire. If we embrace the tenets of those who oppose the adoption of the proposed Constitution as the standard of our political creed we cannot fail to verify the gloomy doctrines which predict the impracticability of a national system pervading the entire limits of the present Confederacy.

PUBLIUS

# "Brutus"
## *The Antifederalist*

In a confederated government, where the powers are divided between the general and the state government, it is essential . . . that the revenues of the country, without which no government can exist, should be divided between them, and so apportioned to each, as to answer their respective exigencies, as far as human wisdom can effect such a division and apportionment. . . .

No such allotment is made in this constitution, but every source of revenue is under the control of Congress; it therefore follows, that if this system is intended to be a complex and not a simple, a confederate and not an entire consolidated government, it contains in it the sure seeds of its own dissolution. One of two things must happen. Either the new constitution will become a mere *nudum pactum,* and all the authority of the rulers under it be cried down, as has happened to the present confederacy. Or the authority of the individual states will be totally supplanted, and they will retain the mere form without any of the powers of government. To one or the other of these issues, I think, this new government, if it is adopted, will advance with great celerity.

It is said, I know, that such a separation of the sources of revenue, cannot be made without endangering the public safety—"unless (says a writer) it can be shown that the circumstances which may affect the public safety are reducible within certain determinate limits; unless the contrary of this position can be fairly and rationally disputed, it must be admitted, as a necessary consequence, that there can be no limitation of that authority which is to provide for the defense and protection of the community, etc."[1]

The pretended demonstration of this writer will instantly vanish, when it is considered, that the *protection and defense* of the community is not intended to be entrusted *solely* into the hands of the general government, and by his own confession it ought not to be. It is true this system commits to the general government the protection and defense of the community against foreign force and invasion, against piracies and felonies on the high seas, and against insurrection among ourselves. They are also authorized to provide for the administration of justice in certain matters of a general concern, and in some that I think are not so. But it ought to be left to the state governments to provide for the protection and defense of the citizen against the hand of private violence, and the wrongs done or attempted by individuals to each other. Protection and defense against the murderer, the robber, the thief, the cheat, and the unjust person, is to be derived from the respective state governments. The just way of reasoning therefore on this subject is this, the general government is to provide for the protection and defense of the community against foreign attacks, etc. They therefore ought to have authority sufficient to effect this, so far as is consistent with the providing for our internal protection and defense. The state governments are entrusted with the care of administering justice among its citizens, and the management of other internal concerns; they ought therefore to retain power adequate to that end. The preservation of internal peace and good order, and the due administration of law and justice, ought to be the first care of every government. The happiness of a people depends infinitely more on this than it does upon all that glory and respect which nations acquire by the most brilliant martial achievements. And I believe history will furnish but few examples of nations who have duly attended to these, who have been subdued by foreign invaders. If a proper respect and submission to the laws prevailed over all orders of men in our country; and if a spirit of public and private justice, economy, and industry influenced the people, we need not be under any apprehensions but what they would be ready to repel any invasion that might be made on the country. And more than this, I would not wish from them. A defensive war is the only one I think justifiable. I do not make these observations to prove, that a government ought not to be authorised to provide for the protection and defense of a country against external enemies, but to show that this is not the most important, much less the only object of their care.

The European governments are almost all of them framed, and administered with a view to arms, and war, as that in which their chief glory consists. They mistake the end of government. It was designed to save men's lives, not to destroy them. We ought to furnish the world with an example of a great people, who in their civil institutions hold chiefly in view, the attainment of virtue, and happiness among ourselves. . . . The most im-

[1] *Federalist*, No. 23.

portant end of government then, is the proper direction of its internal police, and economy; this is the province of the state governments, and it is
evident, and is indeed admitted, that these ought to be under their control. Is it not then preposterous, and in the highest degree absurd, when
the state governments are vested with powers so essential to the peace and
good order of society, to take from them the means of their own
preservation?

The idea that the powers of Congress in respect to revenue ought to
be unlimited, because 'the circumstances which may affect the public
safety are not reducible to certain determinate limits' is novel, as it relates
to the government of the United States. The inconveniences which resulted from the feebleness of the present confederation was discerned,
and felt soon after its adoption. It was soon discovered, that a power to
require money, without either the authority or means to enforce a collection of it, could not be relied upon either to provide for the common defense, discharge the national debt, or for support of government.
Congress therefore, as early as February 1781, recommended to the states
to invest them with a power to levy an impost of five per cent ad valorem,
on all imported goods, as a fund to be appropriated to discharge the debts
already contracted, or which should hereafter be contracted for the support of the war, to be continued until the debts should be fully and finally
discharged. There is not the most distant idea held out in this act, that an
unlimited power to collect taxes, duties and excises was necessary to be
vested in the United States, and yet this was a time of the most pressing
danger and distress. The idea then was, that if certain definite funds were
assigned to the union, which were certain in their natures, productive, and
easy of collection, it would enable them to answer their engagements, and
provide for their defense, and the impost of five per cent was fixed upon
for the purpose.

This same subject was revived in the winter and spring of 1783, and after a long consideration of the subject, many schemes were proposed. The
result was, a recommendation of the revenue system of April 1783; this system does not suggest an idea that it was necessary to grant the United
States unlimited authority in matters of revenue. A variety of amendments
were proposed to this system, some of which are upon the journals of Congress, but it does not appear that any of them proposed to invest the general government with discretionary power to raise money. On the
contrary, all of them limit them to certain definite objects, and fix the
bounds over which they could not pass. This recommendation was passed
at the conclusion of the war, and was founded on an estimate of the whole
national debt. It was computed, that one million and an half of dollars, in
addition to the impost, was a sufficient sum to pay the annual interest of
the debt, and gradually to abolish the principal. Events have proved that
their estimate was sufficiently liberal, as the domestic debt appears upon
its being adjusted to be less than it was computed; and since this period a
considerable portion of the principal of the domestic debt has been dis-

charged by the sale of the western lands. It has been constantly urged by Congress, and by individuals, ever since, until lately, that had this revenue been appropriated by the states, as it was recommended, it would have been adequate to every exigency of the union. Now indeed it is insisted, that all the treasures of the country are to be under the control of that body, whom we are to appoint to provide for our protection and defense against foreign enemies. The debts of the several states, and the support of the governments of them are to trust to fortune and accident. If the union should not have occasion for all the money they can raise, they will leave a portion for the state, but this must be a matter of mere grace and favor. Doctrines like these would not have been listened to by any state in the union, at a time when we were pressed on every side by a powerful enemy, and were called upon to make greater exertions than we have any reason to expect we shall ever be again. . . .

I may be asked to point out the sources, from which the general government could derive a sufficient revenue, to answer the demands of the union. . . . There is one source of revenue, which it is agreed, the general government ought to have the sole control of. This is an impost upon all goods imported from foreign countries. This would, of itself, be very productive, and would be collected with ease and certainty. It will be a fund too, constantly increasing, for our commerce will grow with the productions of the country. And these, together with our consumption of foreign goods, will increase with our population. It is said, that the impost will not produce a sufficient sum to satisfy the demands of the general government; perhaps it would not. . . . My own opinion is, that the objects from which the general government should have authority to raise a revenue, should be of such a nature, that the tax should be raised by simple laws, with few officers, with certainty and expedition, and with the least interference with the internal police of the states. Of this nature is the impost on imported goods. And it appears to me that a duty on exports, would also be of this nature. Therefore, for ought I can discover, this would be the best source of revenue to grant the general government. I know neither the Congress nor the state legislatures will have authority under the new constitution to raise a revenue in this way. But I cannot perceive the reason of the restriction. It appears to me evident, that a tax on articles exported, would be as nearly equal as any that we can expect to lay, and it certainly would be collected with more ease and less expense than any direct tax. I do not however, contend for this mode; it may be liable to well founded objections that have not occurred to me. But this I do contend for, that some mode is practicable, and that limits must be marked between the general government, and the states on this head, or if they be not, either the Congress in the exercise of this power, will deprive the state legislatures of the means of their existence, or the states by resisting the constitutional authority of the general government, will render it nugatory. . . .

The next powers vested by this Constitution in the general government, which we shall consider, are those which authorize them to "borrow money on the credit of the United States, and to raise and support armies." I take these two together and connect them with the power to lay and collect taxes, duties, imposts and excises, because their extent, and the danger that will arise from the exercise of these powers, cannot be fully understood, unless they are viewed in relation to each other.

The power to borrow money is general and unlimited, and the clause so often before referred to, authorizes the passing [of] any laws proper and necessary to carry this into execution. Under this authority, Congress may mortgage any or all the revenues of the union, as a fund to loan money upon; and it is probable, in this way, they may borrow of foreign nations, a principal sum, the interest of which will be equal to the annual revenues of the country. By this means, they may create a national debt, so large, as to exceed the ability of the country ever to sink. I can scarcely contemplate a greater calamity that could befall this country, than to be loaded with a debt exceeding their ability ever to discharge. If this be a just remark, it is unwise and improvident to vest in the general government a power to borrow at discretion, without any limitation or restriction.

It may possibly happen that the safety and welfare of the country may require, that money be borrowed, and it is proper when such a necessity arises that the power should be exercised by the general government. But it certainly ought never to be exercised, but on the most urgent occasions, and then we should not borrow of foreigners if we could possibly avoid it.

The constitution should therefore have so restricted the exercise of this power as to have rendered it very difficult for the government to practice it. The present confederation requires the assent of nine states to exercise this, and a number of other important powers of the confederacy. It would certainly have been a wise provision in this constitution, to have made it necessary that two thirds of the members should assent to borrowing money. When the necessity was indispensable, this assent would always be given, and in no other cause ought it to be.

The power to raise armies is indefinite and unlimited, and authorises the raising [of] forces, as well in peace as in war. Whether the clause which impowers the Congress to pass all laws which are proper and necessary, to carry this into execution, will not authorise them to impress men for the army, is a question well worthy [of] consideration. If the general legislature deem it for the general welfare to raise a body of troops, and they cannot be procured by voluntary enlistments, it seems evident, that it will be proper and necessary to effect it, that men be impressed from the militia to make up the deficiency.

These powers taken in connection, amount to this: that the general government have unlimited authority and control over all the wealth and all the force of the union. The advocates for this scheme, would favor the world with a new discovery, if they would show, what kind of freedom or independency is left to the state governments, when they cannot command any part of the property or of the force of the country, but at the will of the Congress. It seems to me as absurd, as it would be to say, that I was free and independent, when I had conveyed all my property to another, and was tenant to him, and had beside, given an indenture of myself to serve him during life. . . .

BRUTUS

# From Coercion to Consent

*See Lowi and Ginsberg, pp. 14–23 or brief edition, pp. 9–13*

*A central debate between the Federalists and the Antifederalists concerns the appropriate balance between individual rights and collective interests. In the previous selections, the Federalists and Antifederalists debated the proper level at which governmental fiscal and security powers should be exercised. However, they both agreed that the government must exercise these powers at some level. The Antifederalists argued that greater individual freedom would be maintained if those powers were exercised by state governments, while the Federalists argued that it would be necessary for the national government to exercise greater power.*

*The following selections from Tracy Maclin and Amitai Etzioni take the debate one step further: at what point is government action an infringement on individual rights that are protected by the Constitution? How does the government—local, state, or national—balance the needs of collective safety against individual rights? These questions are raised in the context of "drug and gun sweeps" made by law enforcement officials in several Chicago public housing projects. Responding to an increased number of shootings and drug problems, city officials decided that extreme actions, including warrantless searches of apartments, were needed to reestablish collective security, even if it meant infringing on individual freedoms. Maclin argues that warrantless searches tip the balance too far toward collective security and infringe on basic protections for the individual against "illegal searches and seizures" as guaranteed in the Fourth Amendment to the Constitution. Etzioni argues that the collective public safety needs of the public housing residents (where on a given weekend night, as many as 200 shots are fired from windows of the projects) outweigh the individual rights of privacy. If citizens' residences have been turned into war zones, he argues, it makes little sense to talk about violating constitutional rights. Thus, the case of SWAT team sweeps of housing projects either reflects a justified use of government power to protect a fundamental freedom (the freedom to live in a relatively safe environment) or reflects an unwarranted intrusion of governmental power on a constitutional right (the freedom from illegal searches and seizures). As with most tradeoffs between freedom and power, there is no simple way to say which view is correct. How do you view the tradeoff between the need for collective security and individual rights? If you side with Etzioni, how would you determine what limits would be placed on the state?*

# Tracey Maclin
# "Public Housing Searches Ignore the Constitution"*

In 1760, the British government began a crackdown on illegal imports by American colonists. British customs officers, without judicial warrants or probable cause, searched homes and businesses looking for trade violations. A group of Boston merchants retained the lawyer James Otis to oppose this policy. In words that inspired revolutionary fervor, Otis declared that British search policy "places the liberty of every man in the hands of every petty officer."

Today, in response to a perceived increase in crime and violence, the Clinton administration has proposed police practices reminiscent of 18th —century British search tactics.

Responding to the pleas of residents of a crime-plagued Chicago housing project, the administration announced its support for warrantless searches of public housing apartments, frisking of suspicious persons, and the installation of metal detectors in the lobbies of buildings.

While the administration's proposals may please those calling for more "law and order," the options developed by the Clinton plan are inconsistent with the constitutional principles James Otis helped inspire.

The airwaves are jammed with the sound of politicians calling for more programs to get tough on criminals. Thugs and hoodlums are depriving innocent persons of their rights to safe housing, schools, and neighborhoods. Regarding warrantless sweeps of public housing projects, Housing and Urban Development Secretary Henry Cisneros dismissed the objections of civil liberties lawyers, whose "abstract analysis of people's rights," he said, is "swamped in real life by people's rights being denied."

The secretary's treatment of the Constitution leaves a lot to be desired. The Fourth Amendment guarantees everybody the right to be free from unreasonable searches and seizures by the government. It is a "made in America" freedom—a product of our battle against British law enforcement methods.

Unfortunately, the Fourth Amendment never has been popular, particularly during tough times. During the Prohibition era, the federal government routinely conducted illegal wiretaps to catch suspected bootleggers. In the 1960s and 1970s, state and federal officials continued this unlawful practice against alleged dissidents and political enemies.

The "war on drugs" involves officers going onto buses and trains and demanding to see the identification and tickets of passengers. The Supreme Court has said that police officers—acting without a warrant or any evidence of criminality—do not violate our privacy when they confiscate and search our garbage. News programs regularly show police officers, us-

* Tracey Maclin, "Public Housing Searches Ignore the Constitution" in the *Christian Science Monitor* (May 24, 1994). Copyright © 1994 by The Christian Science Publishing Society. Reprinted by permission of the author.

ing sledgehammers and accompanied by menacing dogs, raiding the homes of persons suspected of selling narcotics.

Looking for illegal drugs, a Boston police SWAT team using a no-knock warrant burst into the apartment of a 75-year-old minister, chased the minister through his home, and broke down a bedroom door to grab him. While being handcuffed, the minister died of what was later diagnosed as a heart attack. The police subsequently discovered they had raided the wrong apartment.

President Clinton now wants better security measures at the nation's public housing projects. Tenants will be encouraged to sign "consent clauses" that allow police to conduct unannounced searches of their apartments. Questioned at a press briefing, the acting associate attorney general conceded that consent clauses could "in some circumstances" be a mandatory condition of a tenant's lease. Housing officials have also been encouraged to conduct warrantless sweeps in the case of an "emergency." These measures, the public is assured, do no violence to Fourth Amendment freedoms.

Perhaps, to make it truly voluntary, tenants should be informed of their right to reject such "consent clauses" and to revoke consent that has been given previously. This is their right under the Constitution. On this point, however, the Clinton proposals are noncommittal. People with limited choices about where to live should not be presented with "take it or leave it" leases that require the sacrifice of rights that the rest of us enjoy.

Administration officials say that tenant support for warrantless searches and mandatory consent clauses are relevant criteria for deciding the legality of these measures. But these officials know that Fourth Amendment rights are personal; they cannot be waived by majority rule. If 99 percent of the tenants of a housing project favor police sweeps, they are free to open their doors any time they wish. Their desires, no matter how reasonable, should not control the Fourth Amendment rights of those who want to protect their privacy.

Now, administration officials favor immediate sweeps in emergency conditions, but leave it up to local authorities to define when emergency conditions exist. This sort of verbal back-and-forth will not satisfy constitutional norms. A warrantless search is permissible in an emergency, but the search must be directed at a specific target and supported by concrete evidence. Dragnet sweeps that encompass searching every apartment in a building do not meet these standards.

Requiring police officers to obtain warrants undoubtedly delays the process of searching. To some, this may seem too high a price to pay, but it is the price of liberty.

James Otis recognized as much when he observed: "A man's house is his castle; and while he is quiet, he is as well guarded as a prince in his castle."

# Amitai Etzioni
# "Balancing Act: Don't Sacrifice the Common Good to Personal 'Rights' "*

It is no accident that the issue of gun sweeps in Chicago's public housing recently caught the attention of the president of the United States and the national press. The question of the legitimacy of those sweeps has profound implications for the future of civility in American society.

We have become so inured to violence that the 15 shootings and eight fatalities during one weekend in the Robert Taylor Homes' neighborhood do not faze us. We tend to forget that in civil societies children can play outside, one and all walk the streets with impunity, and gunfire is the exception not the rule. Indeed, if anything resembling such conditions as are now common in inner-cities developed in one of our fancy suburbs, SWAT teams, if not the National Guard, would be called out.

The poor and largely black people of the Robert Taylor Homes are treated as "second-class" citizens, not because of the gun sweeps, as Congressman Henry Gonzalez (D-Texas) put it, but because they are denied the most elementary protection any state owes to its citizens: protection of life and limb.

But, argue civil libertarians, the Chicago Housing Authority violated the individual rights of residents with warrantless sweeps.

It is here that the national importance of the CHA's situation arises. We are now engaged in a nationwide debate about the nature of measures public authorities may use to enhance public safety.

The issues, even in the Robert Taylor Homes, encompass more than apartment searches; the same civil libertarians also try to block the use of photo IDs for residents and screening gates at public housing entrances, two other measures essential for the protection of residents from gangs and drug lords. Elsewhere, the ACLU and its ilk oppose schools that search lockers, neighborhoods that set up drug checkpoints, and so on.

In all these cases the underlying issue is a recognition that a civil society requires a balance between carefully observing individual rights and attending to the common good. Rights are not absolute; even the right to free speech, which many consider the most absolute, is clearly curbed by the notion that one may not shout fire in a crowded theater—because such shouts would endanger the public.

Someone could argue that this ruling violates the right of the shouter to express herself, but this limitation of free speech is a major component of America's constitutional tradition.

Indeed, while we hear frequent references to the Bill of Rights, much attention should also be given to the statement with which the founding

---

fathers opened the Constitution: "We the People of the United States, in order to form a more perfect Union . . . promote the general welfare . . . do ordain and establish this Constitution for the United States of America."

This dual attention to both individual rights and the common good is at the foundation of the American legal tradition.

Precisely for this reason the 4th Amendment reads, "The right of the people to be secure in their persons, houses, papers and effects, against unreasonable search and seizures, shall not be violated," of course implying that there are searches that are acceptable. The courts have long upheld warrantless searches that show themselves to be in the public interest.

In effect, every time you fly and often when you enter court buildings and legislative chambers, you pass through screening gates, backed by armed guards, that search you and your effects without warrants. This is exactly what the Robert Taylor Homes need.

In other cases, judges have allowed the use of warrantless searches of persons, school lockers and homes, under a "special needs" doctrine, defining the special needs as a compelling public interest. Steven Yarosh reviewed these cases for the Northwestern University Law Review and concluded in 1992 that "The CHA's warrantless housing sweeps do not appear to violate the 4th Amendment."

True, Judge Wayne Andersen recently ruled otherwise. But he objected to searches that take place 48 hours or later after the shootings. Forty-eight hours leaves police plenty of time to get warrants. Even this ruling, which might well be reversed, might be different next time if the searches would follow the shootings more closely. Hot pursuit is another legitimate reason for warrantless searches.

Let's leave these details to the lawyers. The big picture we must keep in sight is that civil liberties are endangered most directly when sweeps are not allowed to take place, when gangs are free to terrorize neighborhoods, and when public authorities stand by helplessly.

This is not to declare an open season on the Bill of Rights or suggest that anything goes for law enforcement, but under clearly established limitations we must give more leeway to provide disadvantaged citizens with what affluent Americans always insist on and still largely have in their neighborhoods: elementary public safety.

## Freedom and Power: The Problem

*See Lowi and Ginsberg, pp. 23–24 or brief edition, pp. 13–14*

*The debate over freedom and government power is not only about the locus of government power—with the states or at the national level—but how much power any government should exercise. Americans do not hesitate to demand government protection from risks: insurance when unemployed, income upon retirement, health care when sick, compensation when homes are destroyed by floods, and safety standards for consumer products, from cars to children's pa-*

jamas. We often see these protections as fundamental rights, or entitlements. Harvey Mansfield argues that the national government has grown obese in its efforts to meet these demands. The irony is that, because of the scope of entitlement programs, government is out of control. "The product of our society of entitlements is literally uncontrollable government. Uncontrollable government is not self-government." Mansfield argues that while government undeniably has a legitimate role in society, political leaders must define that role more clearly and have the courage to stop government from extensive meddling in our exercise of private freedoms.

## Harvey Mansfield, "The Election of 1996, and the Coming Choice Between Freedom and Entitlement"*

The results of the 1996 elections were a relief for Republicans, who expected to lose the presidency and thought they might lose the Congress, and a disappointment for Democrats, who took a presidential victory for granted and hoped for more. There was satisfaction for neither party.

Republicans could be glad that the 1994 realignment of Congress in their favor was confirmed; that Bill Clinton, in order to win, had moved to the right; and that a referendum against racial preferences passed in California. Yet the partisan euphoria of 1994 for the Republican Revolution is gone, and the country remains under divided government. Americans, especially women, seem uneasy about cutting, much less abandoning, their entitlements.

Despite the advantage of a popular President, Democrats made only small gains in the House and took small losses in the Senate; and the odds will be against them in the next congressional election. The advance of conservatism has left them as the party of the status quo, an uncomfortable situation for progressives even when they handle it skillfully, as Clinton has done. Divided government helps the Democrats' morale by providing limited victories, but it dooms their desires. Their plans become solely tactical, and they have delivered themselves over to a master tactician in Bill Clinton, whom they cannot admire and do not love.

To produce divided government, 15 percent of Clinton's voters crossed over to vote also for Republican congressmen. It's not clear whether this signifies moderation in the electorate—a desire to use the parties to check each other—or just an inability to decide. Party realignment as a whole remains an open question. Do Americans want a majority party or a stalemate?

* Harvey Mansfield, "The Election of 1996, and the Coming Choice Between Freedom and Entitlement" in *The American Enterprise* (January/February 1997), a Washington-based magazine of politics, business, and culture.

## PROFESSIONAL WRESTLING

Before looking at the campaign we must revisit Clinton's comeback from his defeat in 1994, which was an almost unprecedented repudiation of an incumbent President. Many observers, including me, thought it would be a devastating blow to the President—but it wasn't. As with the Arkansas governorship and his quest for the presidential nomination in 1992, Clinton shook off defeat, though with devices and deceptions that infuriate his enemies and make his defenders wince. He is as courageous as he is shameless.

The liberal initiatives of his first two years having failed, Clinton turned to alternatives that could be billed as conservative, such as deficit reduction and crime fighting. He would not waste his courage in a losing cause. The bombing in Oklahoma City in April 1995, it is agreed, began his climb back into contention. A manic attack on the federal government seemed to suggest there was grave risk in the Republican revolt against big government, and so Clinton discovered the theme of extremism to describe his opponents, a name they helped to paste on themselves with the boast of making a revolution.

Then, in the much-touted "train wreck" over the budget in late 1995, Clinton managed to make Congress alone bear the crash. Even though the shutdown of the federal government could have been prevented if Clinton had not vetoed their budget bills, Gingrich and the Republicans took the blame because they had said they were willing to see it happen. Later, on the campaign trail, Clinton was able to take credit for passage of the welfare reform act that he had mostly opposed and finally signed only after much hesitation. When nothing happens without the cooperation of two opponents, the political challenge is to take credit and lay blame—and every handclasp becomes a wrestling hold. Clinton proved the more adroit grappler.

## MASTER DEMAGOGUE BEATS LATE CONVERT

So Clinton's victory over Bob Dole was prepared by his victory over Gingrich, a more formidable foe. And Gingrich had a head of steam, while Dole started behind. This should give pause to critics of Dole's campaign. Dole was inept but Clinton was superb. He had said in his January 1996 State of the Union speech that the "era of Big Government is over," but in the campaign he showed he could still use big government to his advantage.

The "era" is over because large projects such as Clinton's health plan of 1993 are no longer possible. But Clinton found that small increments of big government do not awaken hostility. He put forth a variety of measures, such as targeted tax cuts, education and "training" ventures, and a mandatory 48-hour stay in the hospital for maternities—each proposal innocently modest but adding a little to the size and especially the scope of government. He did not grandly sum up his proposals; he advocated only more caring, not more government. On the contrary, he even boasted of reducing government, all the while attacking the Republicans for trying to slow the growth of spending on Medicare, education, and the environment. The era of big government is over, but apparently it is extremism to want to reduce it even marginally. This was demagoguery but it succeeded.

Meanwhile, Bob Dole proved to be a poor campaigner. He is an honorable man but his honor did not loosen his tongue or broaden his mind. He made a 15 percent across-the-board tax cut the centerpiece of his campaign, yet he could not find a way through Democratic criticism and voter cynicism to make this attractive idea even palatable. He who had always stood for "responsible" deficit reduction now proposed a tax cut which, Clinton claimed, would "blow a hole in the deficit." We could trust "Bob Dole" because of his previous record, Dole insisted, even though his new-found enthusiasm for tax cutting was a departure from his 40-year record. This was not convincing.

## What Dole Should Have Been Articulate About: "Entitlement"

Dole's failure was that he couldn't articulate the larger reasons behind his proposals, especially the tax cut. The main purpose of my tax cut, Dole should have said, is not to improve the economy or to leave more money in people's pockets—both worthy but lesser goals. The larger goal is to revive our constitutional form of government. To protect the Constitution and the self-government it provides, we must ensure that the government itself remains limited. When government tries to do too much, and the public sphere dominates the private, the result is a government too large to be directed by the people. Indeed, the product of our society of entitlements is literally "uncontrollable" government expenditures. Uncontrollable government is not self-government.

The New Deal and the Great Society created our entitlements not only by passing laws and establishing bureaucracies but also by making us think that rights formerly exercised by individuals should instead be understood as entitlements that a caring government must supply. Such a society has proved to suffer from two profound flaws, financial and moral: It costs too much, and it makes the people—all of them, not just welfare mothers—dependent.

The essence of big government is to insure us against all risk, a task that goes far beyond "promoting the general welfare." But insurance against risk is an infinite goal that government does not know how to accomplish. Worse, if government could somehow render our lives care-free by caring for all our needs, its success would put an end to our freedom and virtue by leaving us with nothing to do. Even blundering attempts to minimize risk endanger freedom and virtue by first raising expectations and then producing cynicism when life's unhappy surprises remain.

In short, the worst failing of big government is the way it has harmed the working and reputation of our self-government. This is what the party of government, the Democrats, has done.

One clear sign that a society of entitlement doesn't work, that infinite goals have uncontrollable costs, is our chronic federal deficit. Yet our most pressing problem is not how to close the deficit but how to reform entitlements. Every deficit fix will be fleeting so long as the pressure to secure entitlements is maintained. By itself, deficit reduction doesn't get to the root of the problem.

But neither does a tax cut, one might object. True, but the positive counterattraction of additional liberty and income is needed to balance the overweening desire for security, so that "reforming" entitlements (actually, shrinking and reducing them) does not appear harsh and authoritarian. Republicans should explain that more money in each citizen's pocket means more personal responsibility and better government. Republicans should be in favor of government *when it is limited*. And limitation has to do with control more than mere size. The best way to limit government is by principles, not percentage points.

Republicans should begin to specify what the federal government can do well. The need to provide voters with such clarifications explains why the libertarians the Republicans harbor, to say nothing of the militia movement, have cost the party more with the electorate than the Christian conservatives. While the majority of Americans agree with the Christian Right that something is wrong with our morality, they do not want to reduce government indefinitely. Just as the Christian Right has learned to speak more politically—compare Ralph Reed in the '90s with Jerry Falwell in the '80s—so Republicans must teach the libertarians that obese government, not all government, is the enemy.

These are things Dole could have said, but they also deserve study by many who called him "inarticulate" without saying what exactly it is that he should have articulated. The 1996 election suggests that conservative intellectuals still have some work to do.

## For the First Time Ever, the Sexes Choose Different Candidates

The most remarked-upon feature of the election was the gender gap. The rates at which men and women voted for Clinton differed by 11 points. Even black voters, who favor Democrats overwhelmingly, showed the same 11 point gap between men and women. Men actually favored Dole by a point, so Clinton was elected by women—apparently the first time the sexes have chosen different candidates. (On the other hand, the House Republicans did noticeably better with women voters than Dole did.)

The presidential gender gap was especially large in the case of unmarried women: unmarried women went for Clinton by 34 points, married women by five. (Among all married voters, both Dole and the House Republicans won a majority.)

It seems that women without husbands turn to government instead, inasmuch as surveys show that the gap comes not from feminist issues such as abortion but from women's predilection for caring, protective government.

Women, it appears, do not care for guns, violence, and conflict. They are turned off by partisanship: what men call a fight, women call a quarrel; what is argument to men is bickering to women. Women vote slightly more than men (in 1996 they were 52 percent of the voters), but they participate less in the heat of debate. A recent book-length study finds they have less knowledge of national politics than men, perhaps in the same way that, for lack of interest, they would also be less able to identify outstanding players in sports.

How strange that women seem to carry with them into politics the very stereotypes of tenderness they renounce when they leave home. Perhaps the stereotypes still capture something of the "essential" woman. Women did reject one stereotype in the 1996 election: their role as enforcers of morality, a role the suffragettes had once claimed they would fulfill. In women's eagerness to elect Clinton as father-protector (the role for him that feminist author Naomi Wolf reportedly urged on Dick Morris), they overlooked his reputation as a seducer. Of course, governmental caring may be "morality" of a sort, but it is the kind of morality that cares little for morals.

Dole was aware of the gender gap and struggled to overcome it. His party turned its convention into a festival of disabilities whose victims somehow managed to prevail without government help. But these Republican victims were not as convincing as the Democratic ones who followed and explained how grateful they were to government. The desire to maintain entitlements is the Democrats' version of conservatism.

With their appeal to women, and to black and Hispanic voters, Democrats may be reaching toward a new version of Jesse Jackson's Rainbow Coalition. This one would be founded on women rather than blacks, and it would avoid the divisive, puerile leftism characteristic of Jackson's attempt. This bloc would keep the idea of big government but, recognizing its defects, try to moderate its practice—as Clinton did after 1994, abandoning large commitments and continually offering small favors. Such a government would be as caring as an absent parent, as loving as an indulgent nanny.

## PUBLIC LIFE AND PRIVATE LIFE

To counter the menace of government-as-nanny, Republicans need to encourage women to be more accepting of risk. Taking a point from their religious conservative wing, Republicans should also remind men that male irresponsibility and abandonment often create in women the appetite for security that big government claims to satisfy.

Republicans must warn against tipping government too far toward caring and "compassion" at the expense of freedom and personal responsibility. They should point out that confusing the qualities desirable in private life with the qualities necessary to public life can be dangerous. They should note that caring within the home and risk-taking outside of it are both important; the key is to avoid confusing the two qualities (as the feminist slogan "the personal is political" does). Bringing family-like intimacy into politics is pretentious and oppressive.

Limited government cannot survive if we fail to cultivate the distinctions between the public and private spheres. *Vive la différence!*

---

*Like Mansfield, Faux draws distinctions between the public and private spheres. However, Faux's view of the private exercise of economic and social power (i.e., markets) is much less benign. He argues that market forces, now global in their influence, have depressed living standards for a majority of Americans and eroded the confidence we once had in our work in the economy. Faux supports a strong government role, and promotes something he calls a Progressive Contract focused on the political claims of working class. While government cannot eliminate all social ills or prevent people from making poor choices, it can, he argues, provide incentives, alternatives, and safety nets for people caught in poverty, unemployment, or economic insecurity. Faux concludes that a focus on economic security, rather than the traditional liberal politics of race, gender, environmentalism, or affirmative action, would provide a means to weave all of these concerns together into a more formidable political force than single-issue interest groups and coalitions.*

*Are the entitlement programs targeted by Mansfield the product of single-issue interest-group politics? If so, which alternative has the most potential to correct the "uncontrollable" entitlement programs that dominate government: Mansfield's suggestion to pare back the activities of government, or Faux's suggestion to build a more broad-based political coalition?*

# Jeff Faux
## "A Progressive Contract"*

The conservative tide has ebbed, for now. Newt Gingrich and his fellow social Darwinists, triumphant in 1994, were a millstone around Bob Dole's neck two years later. The electorate finally read the fine print in the Republican Contract With America, and turned it down. The contract was too risky, and the story about America that it told was too meanspirited.

---

* Jeff Faux, "A Progressive Compact" in *The Nation* (April 14, 1997). Reprinted with permission.

Progressives now have an opportunity to propose their own social contract. To win the political battles of the coming century, they must support their proposal with a narrative that unites the left, and unites the left with a political majority.

The progressive narrative must be relevant to the world—not as it was but as it is. The left has no chance to build a political majority on the implicit assumption that social justice means extending the benefits of an otherwise beneficent society to variously defined minorities who have been left behind by an affluent and bigoted majority. By definition, this is a politics of permanent marginalization.

So long as an expanding share of the population was enjoying the fruits of affluence, such a politics was perhaps the most practical and honorable course. But today the deregulation of the economy and its extension into the brutally competitive global marketplace is leaving a majority of Americans behind. Despite the incessant media hype about the performance of the current economic recovery, the long-term stagnation of living standards for most Americans has continued. Between 1989 and 1996, the real earnings of the three-quarters of the work force without a college degree dropped by more than 5 percent. Even for male college graduates, real earnings were no higher than they had been six years before. According to no less an authority than Alan Greenspan, the share of workers at large companies who fear being laid off rose from 25 percent in the depths of the 1991 recession to 46 percent in the midst of last year's "boom." In the winter of 1995-96, 61 percent of Americans polled considered themselves working or lower class, as opposed to 39 percent who defined themselves as middle or upper class. The brutal fact is that living standards cannot be maintained in a deregulated, privatized domestic economy under increasing pressure from an unregulated global marketplace. Thus, the continued deterioration of economic opportunities for the majority of Americans who work for a living is inevitable, and it represents the left's political opportunity.

The political claims of economic class are not morally superior to the claims of those disadvantaged by race, gender or sexual preference. But they have an inherently greater power to unify, and are therefore a sounder foundation upon which to base a majority politics. If, over the coming decade, the left can promote a new social contract that integrates its concern for social equity and environmental sanity with majoritarian demands for economic justice, it can once again make history in America.

To offer such a social contract, progressives must be willing to attack the center-right's excessive claims for America as a meritocracy, upon which the electorate's acceptance of growing inequality is based. We need to argue that the market should be constrained by the economic rights and obligations of citizenship. We need an explanation of how the world works that tells us that by virtue of being an American—not your race, your gender or your luck and talent in the marketplace—you have a set of rights and obligations that transcend your right and the right of others to buy low and sell high. The central point is the proposition that you, the citizen, are not alone in your increasingly desperate search for a safe niche in a world of all against all.

Thus, you have:

§ a right to a job that pays a livable wage—and an obligation to work;

§ a right to share in the social wealth left to you by those who have gone before—and an obligation to invest in a sustainable future for the next generation;

§ a right to profit from a business—and an obligation to support the community in which it operates;

§ a right to bargain collectively—and an obligation to cooperate in the creation of more productive workplaces;

§ a right to protection against certain risks (unemployment, sickness, an impoverished old age)—and an obligation to contribute to the pooling of those risks in social insurance.

The promotion of a new social contract is the key to unlocking the confusion sown by the center-right's misuse of terms like "family values," a slogan promoting the myth that we can solve social problems in a market economy without paying for them. Thus the national conversation has shifted from questions that we know how to answer to those that we do not, setting us up for the inevitable conclusion that government programs can't work.

Public policy cannot stop teenagers from experimenting with sex, drugs and alcohol, but it can provide alternative uses for their energies and a credible path to a healthy adulthood. Public policy cannot stop love from leaving marriage, but it can keep love from being crushed by unemployment, low wages and poverty. Public policy cannot eliminate the criminal urge, but it can keep people from mugging each other because they can't find a job, and can provide enough cops and streetlights to make neighborhoods physically secure.

If we are to forge a new social contract we must reject the dispiriting assumption that global forces have rendered the American people helpless to do anything but accommodate the faceless decisions of a dog-eat-dog international marketplace. Likewise, we must reject the romanticism that serious political change must await changes in the human heart. Or that while left activists may occasionally "think globally" they must confine themselves to "acting locally." A progressive strategy must dare to imagine itself victorious—in state capitals and ultimately in Washington. The national government remains the essential instrument available for countering the power of multinational capital.

This is obviously not an easy political task. Congress is controlled by conservative Republicans. The White House is occupied by a Democratic Administration that is at best indifferent to progressive concerns. An overwhelming majority of statehouses are still in the hands of Republican governors. And the Buchananite wing of the Republican Party is preparing more reactionary appeals that will be aimed at the non-college-educated majority—the majority *we* need if we are to have a successful left-of-center politics. Although the left must be committed to taking the struggle for electoral power seriously, the ultimate prize is not the next election, it is the next century.

Given this, there are several strategic tasks for progressives over the next four years.

To begin with, we should stop obsessing about our disappointment with Bill Clinton. By now it should be clear to all but the hopelessly naïve that Clinton will not lead the country or the Democratic Party—and certainly not the left—out of their respective predicaments. He abandoned his last opportunity to make history with domestic policy when he submitted a fiscal 1998 budget without any serious initiative to deal with the problems he identified in his 1992 campaign: eroding living standards, our irrational health care system, a bloated military budget. Next year is an election year, so any new initiatives are unlikely. And then Clinton will be a lame duck.

Nevertheless, the President has used his considerable political talents to keep conservatives from doing major long-term damage. Witness his leadership in defeating the balanced budget amendment, which looked like a sure thing after the Republicans gained seats in the Senate last year. His wilingness to use the bully pulpit to oppose racism and promote gender equity is no small contribution. Progressives should see Bill Clinton in the clear-eyed way that leading conservatives saw Richard Nixon and George Bush: as useful instruments for their own longer-term agenda. In a sense, Clinton has cracked open the door to a progressive social contract with his own rhetoric of "obligations," even though he is primarily concerned with stipulating the obligations of those at the bottom. Progressives should blow that door wide open with a vision of society in which obligations and rights are applied fairly to everyone—to those who sleep in the Lincoln Bedroom as well as those who sleep on the sidewalk.

It would help their confidence if liberal activists were less intimidated by media braying about popular support for Clinton's "centrism." As polling analyst Ruy Teixeira, a colleague of mine at the Economic Policy Institute, points out, Bill Clinton is only a "centrist" in terms of the political range of insider Washington politics and network media. When viewed through the prism of what the electorate says it wants, Clinton is to the right of the mainstream. The public opposes his cuts in Medicare to balance the budget, it is skeptical of his claims for free trade, it wants him to propose a comprehensive health care program and, while it despises welfare, it believes government should provide jobs, training and daycare for those who want to work but cannot find a job.

Thus there is a vacuum in the national discussion on these questions, which progressive political leaders and activists have an opportunity to fill. Since nothing of much use is going to be passed by this Congress and this Administration over the next two years, progressives ought to be building an independent case for large changes that support a common-sense social contract. In some areas, like health care, the strategic task is educational, i.e., nurturing support for the principle of universal coverage and cost containment. In others, the task is to shift the focus of the debate. Thus, for example, the scandal of the welfare system is not the insistence that poor people work but the politicians' refusal to provide enough jobs for people to live on. In the wake of that refusal, the inevitable result of spilling a million workers into an already oversupplied low-wage labor market will be more unemployment and lower wages for the near-poor. This is the classic way to divide the progressive constituency. The answer is not make-work; it is to create job opportunities by channeling investment into our cities and depressed rural areas, to rebuild our transportation and environmental infrastructure, to get the rats out of school basements and fix the roofs.

Some strategic issues will have to be fought now. Opposing the proposed expansion of NAFTA and the extension of trade concessions to China should be major priorities for progressives. These negative campaigns could motivate alliances among progressives and spur alternative proposals for a global economy with global rules that protect labor and the environment. The multinational elites should not have the conversation about the world's future all to themselves.

Putting eroding U.S. living standards at the center of a progressive politics will make some progressives uneasy. After all, even the poorest Americans live better than billions of others around the world. Why should we build a politics around the laid-off factory worker in Peoria rather than the ragged child in the streets of Lima? The answer is that the destitute of Peru and most other places in the world are trapped in an ideological model that is made in America. As the world's only superpower, the United States now generates the world's ideas of what is rational and fair more completely than at any time in this "American Century." Within the past decade, the social contracts of Western Europe and Latin America and the rest of North America have been devastated by the neoliberal "Washington Consensus," which, to paraphrase the late Michael Harrington, demands socialism for capital and free enterprise for labor. American progressives will do best for the worldwide struggle for social justice by reforming America first.

Another strategic issue for the left is the brutal competition among states and localities for business investment. Even more than the threat of outsourcing to foreign countries, this competitive atmosphere suppresses progressive politics in the most liberal of states, encouraging a race to the bottom as states shrink their tax base and outbid each other to provide corporate subsidies, tax giveaways and union-free environments. Regional compacts in which states agree to compete on the basis of quality of life and level of education rather than low taxes and docile labor ought to be promoted, along with changes in the federal code to tax extraordinary state subsidies to business.

Finally, the left now has an opportunity to become the champion of a national effort to reduce dramatically the influence of money in elections. The renting of the Lincoln Bedroom to fat-cat Americans, the acceptance of campaign funds from fat-cat foreigners and the stubborn resistance of politicians to do more than put a fig leaf over the problem have now aligned the stars for a national grass-roots get-the-money-out-of-politics movement that could unify and energize the left and provide new allies, much as the antiabortion crusade did for the right. Activists in Maine and elsewhere have shown that the public will support spending restrictions and even public financing. A constitutional amendment to overturn the Supreme Court's rigid equivalence of campaign donations with free speech could be the instrument for a national mass mobilization.

This agenda is not by any means a substitute for liberal concerns with affirmative action, environmental activism and social compassion. It is a way of finding the threads that can weave these issues together with the growing anxieties of the majority of working Americans. This requires, in turn, a greater sense of solidarity among the forces of the left. Thus, progressives must use the next few years to build up and link their political institutions. We have proved, painfully, that disconnecting ourselves from our allies does not lead to victory over our enemies. It is time for reconnection and mutual support. The rebuilding of the labor movement is not just the task of the A.F.L.-C.I.O. The expansion of the women's movement to reflect the non-college-educated is not just a problem for NOW. The revitalization of black and Latino networks is not just the responsibility of the N.A.A.C.P. and the Hispanic Caucus. The strengthening of environmental consciousness is not just the duty of the Sierra Club. Nor is the rebuilding of a populist Democratic Party just the job of Paul Wellstone or David Bonior or Maxine Waters. These are everyone's responsibilities.

The progressive story is a vision of community and mutual support. Its moral is that you are not alone. If we want to be credible to a majority of Americans, we will have to demonstrate that vision in our political behavior as well as our political ideas.

# Constructing a Government: The Founding and the Constitution

## The First Founding: Interests and Conflicts

*See Lowi and Ginsberg, pp. 30–34 or brief edition, pp. 17–19*

*Edmund Burke, a British statesman, is best known as the author of a political treatise entitled* Reflections on the Revolution in France, *published in 1790. Burke was appalled by the bloodshed and chaos he observed during the French Revolution, which he attributed to the misguided attempts of the French revolutionaries to introduce an entirely new social order, without respect for traditional rights and liberties.* Reflections on the Revolution in France *is a classic in conservative political philosophy.*

*Burke did not oppose the American Revolution, which took place while he was a member of British Parliament, with the vehemence he later exhibited during the French Revolution. Indeed, he suggested that the colonists' complaints had merit because the British government had disregarded their natural rights. In a speech before the House of Commons in 1770, Burke urged fellow members of Parliament to grant greater powers of self-government to the colonies. He pointed out that attempts to control the colonies from across the Atlantic, without any real understanding of the conditions under which the colonies operated, were doomed to failure. Every act of Parliament in governing the colonies was poorly thought out, with the result that the British government itself had to take the blame for the unrest that had resulted. He asserted: ". . . Your acts have not been listened to. . . . You have neither military nor civil power from the senseless manner in which you exercised them. A government without wisdom never will be without woe. All is shaken to the foundation by the entire absence of common sense."*

*By 1775, matters had gone from bad to worse. In the following excerpt from another speech given at that time, Burke urges the British government to attempt conciliation, restating his position that the situation called for "prudent management" rather than force of arms. In making out his case, he gives a detailed explanation of the American character—and the need to accommodate it—to convince his listeners that no other course of action would be likely to succeed.*

## Edmund Burke
## "On Conciliation" (March 22, 1775)*

The proposition is peace. Not peace through the medium of war; not peace to be hunted through the labyrinth of intricate and endless negoti-

---

* Edmund Burke, "On Conciliation" (March 22, 1775) in *Edmund Burke on the American Revolution*, Elliott Robert Barkan, ed. (Gloucester, MA: Peter Smith Publisher, Inc., 1972). Reprinted with permission.

ations; not peace to arise out of universal discord fomented from principle in all parts of the empire; not peace to depend on the juridical determination of perplexing questions or the precise marking [of] the shadowy boundaries of a complex government. It is simple peace, sought in its natural course, and in its ordinary haunts—it is peace sought in the spirit of peace, and laid in principles purely pacific. I propose, by removing the ground of the difference, and by restoring the *former unsuspecting confidence of the colonies in the mother country,* to give permanent satisfaction to your people; and (far from a scheme of ruling by discord) to reconcile them to each other in the same act, and by the bond of the very same interest which reconciles them to British government. . . .

[*Burke explains in detail the economic advantages that had accrued to the British through trade with the colonies in North America; two-thirds of all British export trade alone was conducted with the North American and West Indian colonies.*]

. . . America, gentlemen say, is a noble object. It is an object well worth fighting for. Certainly it is, if fighting a people be the best way of gaining them. Gentlemen in this respect will be led to their choice of means by their complexions and their habits. Those who understand the military art will of course have some predilection for it. Those who wield the thunder of the state may have more confidence in the efficacy of arms. But I confess, possibly for want of this knowledge, my opinion is much more in favour of prudent management than of force, considering force not as an odious, but a feeble instrument for preserving a people so numerous, so active, so growing, so spirited as this in a profitable and subordinate connection with us. . . .

[*Burke argues that force is not a desirable alternative since its effect is temporary and Britain has no great experience with using force as its sole means of governance.*]

. . . But there is still behind a third consideration concerning this object, which serves to determine my opinion on the sort of policy which ought to be pursued in the management of America, even more than its population and its commerce—I mean its *temper and character.*

In this character of the Americans, a love of freedom is the predominating feature which marks and distinguishes the whole; and as an ardent is always a jealous affection, your colonies become suspicious, restive, and untractable whenever they see the least attempt to wrest from them by force or shuffle from them by chicane what they think the only advantage worth living for. The fierce spirit of liberty is stronger in the English colonies probably than in any other people of the earth; and this from a great variety of powerful causes, which, to understand the true temper of their minds and the direction which this spirit takes, it will not be amiss to lay open somewhat more largely.

First, the people of the colonies are descendants of Englishmen. England, Sir, is a nation which still I hope respects, and formerly adored, her freedom. The colonists emigrated from you when this part of your character was most predominant, and they took this bias and direction the moment they parted from your hands. They are therefore not only devoted to liberty, but to liberty according to English ideas and on English principles. Abstract liberty, like other mere abstractions, is not to be found. Liberty inheres in some sensible object; and every nation has formed to itself some favourite point, which by way of eminence becomes the criterion of their happiness. It happened you know, Sir, that the great contests for freedom in this country were from the earliest times chiefly upon the question of taxing. . . . On this point of taxes the ablest pens and most eloquent tongues have been exercised; the greatest spirits have acted and suffered. . . .

[The British themselves have made it most clear that the people must have power over their own money.] The colonies draw from you, as with their life-blood, these ideas and principles. Their love of liberty, as with you, fixed and attached on this specific point of taxing. Liberty might be safe or might be endangered in twenty other particulars, without their [sic] being much pleased or alarmed. Here they felt its pulse, and as they found that beat they thought themselves sick or sound. . . . The fact is, that they did thus apply those general arguments; and your mode of governing them, whether through lenity or indolence, through wisdom or mistake, confirmed them in the imagination that they, as well as you, had an interest in these common principles.

They were further confirmed in this pleasing error by the form of their provincial legislative assemblies. Their governments are popular in a high degree, some are merely popular, in all the popular representative is the most weighty, and this share of the people in their ordinary government never fails to inspire them with lofty sentiments and with a strong aversion from whatever tends to deprive them of their chief importance.

If anything were wanting to this necessary operation of the form of government, religion would have given it a complete effect. Religion, always a principle of energy, in this new people is no way worn out or impaired, and their mode of professing it is also one main cause of this free spirit. The people are Protestants, and of that kind which is the most adverse to all implicit submission of mind and opinion. This is a persuasion not only favourable to liberty, but built upon it. . . . All Protestantism, even the most cold and passive, is a sort of dissent. But the religion most prevalent in our northern colonies is a refinement on the principle of resistance; it is the dissidence of dissent and the Protestantism of the Protestant religion. . . . The colonists left England when this spirit was high, and in the emigrants was the highest of all; and even that stream of foreigners, which has been constantly flowing into these colonies, has, for the greatest part, been composed of dissenters from the establishments of their several countries, and have brought with them a temper and character far from alien to that of the people with whom they mixed.

. . . It is [true] that in Virginia and the Carolinas they have a vast multitude of slaves. Where this is the case in any part of the world, those who are free are by far the most proud and jealous of their freedom. Freedom is to them not only an enjoyment, but a kind of rank and privilege. Not seeing there that freedom, as in countries where it is a common blessing and as broad and general as the air, may be united with much abject toil, with great misery, with all the exterior of servitude liberty looks amongst them like something that is more noble and liberal. I do not mean, Sir, to commend the superior morality of this sentiment, which has at least as much pride as virtue in it; but I cannot alter the nature of man. . . . In such a people, the haughtiness of domination combines with the spirit of freedom, fortifies it, and renders it invincible.

Permit me, Sir, to add another circumstance in our colonies, which contributes no mean part towards the growth and effect of this untractable spirit. I mean their education. In no country perhaps in the world is the law so general a study. The profession itself is numerous and powerful, and in most provinces it takes the lead. . . . [But] when great honours and great emoluments do not win over this knowledge [of law] to the service of the state, it is a formidable adversary to government. If the spirit be not tamed and broken by these happy methods, it is stubborn and litigious. *Abeunt studia in mores.*[1] This study renders men acute, inquisitive, dexterous, prompt in attack, ready in defence, full of resources. . . .

The last cause of this disobedient spirit in the colonies is hardly less powerful than the rest, as it is not merely moral, but laid deep in the natural constitution of things. Three thousand miles of ocean lie between you and them. No contrivance can prevent the effect of this distance in weakening government. Seas roll, and months pass, between the order and the execution, and the want of a speedy explanation of a single point is enough to defeat a whole system. . . . The Sultan gets such obedience as he can. He governs with a loose rein that he may govern at all. . . . This is the immutable condition, the eternal law, of extensive and detached empire.

Then, Sir, from these six capital sources: of descent, of form of government, of religion in the northern provinces, of manners in the southern, of education, of the remoteness of situation from the first mover of government— from all these causes a fierce spirit of liberty has grown up. It has grown with the growth of the people in your colonies, and increased with the increase of their wealth; a spirit that unhappily meeting with an exercise of power in England which, however lawful, is not reconcilable to any ideas of liberty, much less with theirs, has kindled this flame that is ready to consume us.

I do not mean to commend either the spirit in this excess or the moral causes which produce it. Perhaps a more smooth and accommodating spirit of freedom in them would be more acceptable to us. Perhaps ideas of liberty might be desired more reconcilable with an arbitrary and boundless authority. Perhaps we might wish the colonists to be persuaded that their liberty is more secure when held in trust for them by us (as their guardians during a perpetual minority) than with any part of it in their own hands. The question is, not whether their spirit deserves praise or blame, but—what, in the name of God, shall we do with it? . . . We are called upon to fix some rule and line for our future conduct which may give a little stability to our politics and prevent the return of such unhappy deliberations as the present. . . . Until very lately, all authority in America

[1] "Pursuits influence character."

seemed to be nothing but an emanation from yours. Even the popular part of the colony constitution derived all its activity, and its first vital movement, from the pleasure of the crown. We thought, Sir, that the utmost which the discontented colonists could do was to disturb authority; we never dreamt they could of themselves supply it, knowing in general what an operose business it is to establish a government absolutely new. . . . They have formed a government, sufficient for its purposes, without the bustle of a revolution or the troublesome formality of an election. Evident necessity and tacit consent have done the business in an instant. . . . The evil arising from hence is this: that the colonists, having once found the possibility of enjoying the advantages of order in the midst of a struggle for liberty, such struggles will not henceforward seem so terrible to the settled and sober part of mankind as they had appeared before the trial.

. . . In order to prove that the Americans have no right to their liberties, we are every day endeavoring to subvert the maxims which preserve the whole spirit of our own. To prove that the Americans ought not to be free, we are obliged to depreciate the value of freedom itself. . . .

. . . There are but three ways of proceeding relative to this stubborn spirit which prevails in your colonies and disturbs your government. These are: to change that spirit, as inconvenient, by removing the causes; to prosecute it as criminal; or, to comply with it as necessary. . . . [The first two ideas are unworkable in practice.]

The temper and character which prevail in our colonies are, I am afraid, unalterable by any human art. We cannot, I fear, falsify the pedigree of this fierce people, and persuade them that they are not sprung from a nation in whose veins the blood of freedom circulates. The language in which they would hear you tell them this tale would detect the imposition—your speech would betray you. An Englishman is the unfittest person on earth to argue another Englishman into slavery.

I think it is nearly as little in our power to change their republican religion as their free descent, or to substitute the Roman Catholic as a penalty, or the Church of England as an improvement. . . . The education of the Americans is also on the same unalterable bottom with their religion. You cannot persuade them to burn their books of curious science, to banish their lawyers from their courts of laws, or to quench the lights of their assemblies by refusing to choose those persons who are best read in their privileges. . . .

With regard to the high aristocratic spirit of Virginia and the southern colonies, it has been proposed, I know, to reduce it by declaring a general enfranchisement of their slaves. . . .

Slaves as these unfortunate black people are, and dull as all men are from slavery, must they not a little suspect the offer of freedom from that very nation which has sold them to their present masters?—from that nation, one of whose causes of quarrel with those masters is their refusal to deal any more in that inhuman traffic? An offer of freedom from England would come rather oddly, shipped to them in an African vessel, which is refused an entry into the ports of Virginia or Carolina, with a cargo of three hundred Angola negroes. . . .

If then the removal of the causes of this spirit of American liberty be, for the greater part, or rather entirely, impracticable; if the ideas of criminal process be inapplicable, or, if applicable, are in the highest degree inexpedient—what way yet remains? No way is open, but the third and last—to comply with the American spirit as necessary, or, if you please, to submit to it as a necessary evil.

## The Constitution

*See Lowi and Ginsberg, pp. 45–53 or brief edition, pp. 23–33*

*In Federalist Nos. 10 and 51, reprinted as an appendix to the text, James Madison observed that the strength of the new union—the division of its powers between state and federal governments and among different branches at the same level of government—lay in its ability to limit the power of factions, which, he observed, arise naturally where any collection of human beings occurs. The elaborate limiting of powers means, at the same time, that government tends to be fairly cumbersome and exasperatingly slow.*

*The two-hundredth anniversary of the Constitution was in 1987. As Americans pondered the meaning of that anniversary, they also thought about whether it was time to overhaul the system; after all, Thomas Jefferson once suggested that a constitution ought to be revised approximately once every twenty years. In the following article from a special issue of the* Los Angeles Times *celebrating the Constitution's birthday, commentator David Lauter examines the reasons the U.S. Constitution has survived for more than 200 years. Lauter explains that the Constitution has been a source of great stability for our nation, in part because it has been amended to address the changing social and political context. In periods of political change there is often a temptation to change the Constitution to reflect the policy goals of the new political majority. There is strong sentiment today among members of Congress and many citizens to amend the Constitution. Many of these efforts—to ratify amendments that require a balanced budget, impose congressional term limits, or protect the flag from desecration—no doubt reflect some of the inevitable frustrations of democratic governance.*

*Is the Constitution a sufficient base for governance? Why do you think it has endured, in contrast to the heavily amended state constitutions? What kinds of changes might make the Constitution a more workable basis for governing the United States? If state constitutions are a more responsive representation of public sentiment, should the Constitution be similarly flexible and responsive?*

## David Lauter
## "We the People: The American Constitution after 200 Years: Celebrating the Nation's Charter as Problem and Solution"*

The traveler wandered the rutted roads from New England south to the Carolinas and rode the mule-drawn canal barges west through the moun-

* David Lauter, "We the People: The American Constitution after 200 Years: Celebrating the Nation's Charter as Problem and Solution" in the *Los Angeles Times* (September 13, 1987). Reprinted with permission.

tains toward the Mississippi, all the while taking notes on the strange young country spread out before him.

When he returned to France, Alexis de Tocqueville wrote in 1835, "I have never been more struck by the good sense and the practical judgment of the Americans than in the manner in which they elude the numberless difficulties resulting from their federal Constitution."

A century-and-a-half later, the nation de Tocqueville viewed in adolescence has grown to adulthood. The Constitution, signed by its framers in Philadelphia on Sept. 17, 1787, is now the oldest written national charter of government in effect anywhere in the world. And Americans are still demonstrating a pragmatic genius for overcoming what de Tocqueville took to be the Constitution's "numberless difficulties."

Americans themselves complain ceaselessly about the inefficiencies and frustrations it entails, from the Fifth Amendment's protection of criminals to the seemingly archaic checks and balances that almost paralyze modern government. Critics of the Constitution yearn for the more streamlined decision making of parliamentary systems in which prime ministers have extraordinary freedom of action and are quickly replaced if they lose popular support.

Why, then, with all the manifest burdens it imposes, has the Constitution been so widely admired and so little changed in 200 years? Why did British Prime Minister William Gladstone declare, in 1878, that "the American Constitution is the most wonderful work ever struck off at a given time by the brain and purpose of man"?

The answer appears to be that the mechanisms designed by the Founding Fathers, while maddeningly slow and cumbersome, have proven remarkably effective at enabling the people of a huge and heterogeneous nation to preserve the pattern of "conflict within consensus" that historians identify as the unique feature of America's politics.

With one terrible exception, the Civil War, the constitutional process has enabled Americans to pass through periods of profound change, to disagree, struggle ferociously and sometimes violently over policies, yet ultimately reach decisions that most can support and almost all accept—without plunging into the abyss of fanaticism that has torn and destroyed so many societies.

## "INTENSE DISAGREEMENTS"

A constitution should "allow very intense disagreements to be handled without violence and without loss of legitimacy" of the nation's institutions, said UC Berkeley political scientist Raymond Wolfinger. By that measure, the Constitution has been a resounding success.

Unlike Marx and other more theoretical political thinkers, the framers of the Constitution started with human nature, which they saw as severely flawed and limited, then tried to design a government that would guarantee "the blessings of liberty" to the maximum extent possible within those limitations. After all, Madison wrote in the Federalist papers, "If men were angels, no government would be necessary. If angels were to govern men, neither external nor internal controls on government would be necessary."

Reinforcing such pragmatism, a tradition of almost-religious veneration has grown up around the Constitution. One 19th-Century President called it the "ark of the people's covenant" and said it must be "shield(ed) . . . from impious hands." Advocates of sundry causes claim the Constitution's support, and tourists line up in droves to see its first and last pages encased in bulletproof glass at the National Archives.

The American lexicon contains few political epithets more powerful than "unconstitutional."

## BENDING THE SYSTEM

To be sure, this veneration has not eliminated the frustrations inherent in the system. Nor has it always been strong enough to prevent abuses of the rights and values embodied in the Constitution and the Bill of Rights. In race relations particularly, as well as in periods of national crisis and in circumstances when public passions ran out of control, events have occurred that dishonored the Constitution's high ideals.

The importance of those ideals has become so ingrained in the nation's consciousness, however, that the system has shown a remarkable tendency to right itself and return to its intended course.

"Though written constitutions may be violated in moments of passion or delusion, yet they furnish a text to which those who are watchful may again rally and recall the people," Jefferson wrote to a friend in 1802, "they fix too for the people the principles of their political creed."

Within the framework of the Constitution, strong national leaders have tried to bend the system to their will—including Jefferson himself, who entered the White House with a restrictive view of presidential power but pushed his authority to the limit when the opportunity arose in 1803 to make the Louisiana Purchase and double the size of the nation.

Abraham Lincoln suspended portions of the Constitution during the Civil War. Theodore Roosevelt complained that the Constitution "permit(s) one set of people to hoist sails for their own amusement, and another set of people to put down anchors for their own purposes."

"The result from the standpoint of progress has not been happy," he said.

In contemporary times, writers, political scientists and practicing politicians all have advocated overhauls of the Constitution, arguing that the intricate system of checks and balances designed under 18th-Century theory will not do for the practice of the 21st.

## REVISION OF OLD CHARTER

Said political scientist Robert A. Dahl: "I'm increasingly doubtful that the Constitution is functioning really well. . . . I find it hard to engage in this year of celebrating the Constitution as if it were somehow a perfect document."

Indeed, over recent years, 32 states have called for a new Constitutional Convention to revise the old charter, mostly responding to popular frustration with the federal deficit. Two more states joining the call would suffice to bring a convention into being for the first time since the one that ended 200 years ago this week. While no such conventions have been held since the first one, the Constitution has been amended 26 times. The 10 amendments constituting the Bill of Rights were added in 1791, and later amendments introduced such far-reaching changes as ending slavery, creating national guarantees of due process and individual rights, granting women the vote and providing for direct popular election of senators.

Important as such changes have been and wracking as was the history that produced them, all can be seen as extending and intensifying the nation's commitment to the values and ideas underlying the original Constitution and, before it, the Declaration of Independence.

Many factors—including economic, regional and cultural differences —led to the cataclysm of the Civil War, for example. But one of the things that ultimately made a confrontation unavoidable was the inherent contradiction between the institution of slavery and the ideas of equality and fairness implicit in the Constitution.

Though the Founding Fathers had made clear their intention to create a national government superior to the states, they had sidestepped and compromised on what Madison called the "powder keg" of slavery— which many delegates even then saw in starkly moral terms.

In the end, more than 500,000 Americans died—more than in World War I and World War II combined—to meet the issue head-on. Henceforth, no state would have the right to abridge freedoms guaranteed to individuals by the national Constitution, and no institution or practice could stand permanently unchallenged if it contradicted the nation's fundamental values.

What accounts for the relative stability of the American system during two centuries in which the governments of so many other countries were ripped apart and radically changed not once but several times? Scholars point to several factors:

- A nation that seems always in the midst of rapid change in its social rules and economic relationships has been correspondingly conservative in changing the political framework within which those changes occur.

- A people who concentrate in overwhelming numbers on the pragmatic and immediate problems of their private lives have been highly resistant to the fanatical approaches to politics and religion that have shattered other societies. "The great middle-of-road-consensus impulse of Americans," one historian called it.

Indeed, American politics has tended to become most turbulent when large numbers of people believed that their personal lives—and hopes for the future—were threatened.

- A society that lacked an established church, a native aristocracy and a universal culture has clung to the Constitution as a symbol of unity.

"The Constitution has been to us what a king has often been to other nationalities," Harvard President A. Lawrence Lowell said in 1886.

The Constitution, of course, can neither be credited with all that has gone well in American history nor blamed for all failures. "There are other things in society" that help determine the fates of government and that can overwhelm even the most flexible of constitutions, as shown by the experience of numerous Latin American nations, political scientist Wolfinger pointed out.

## ISOLATED COUNTRY

America has been both wealthy and physically isolated. The nation's wealth—natural resources, abundant land and salubrious climate—tended to reduce social conflict by holding out the hope of improving standards of living for most citizens most of the time. Politics in America has most often—though not always—been fought out on a relatively narrow middle ground of shared assumptions, values and symbols, lacking the intense, class-based politics that in France, for example, have caused three revolutions and nine different systems in the last 200 years.

U.S. institutions also have been free to develop without the distortions caused by fear of external enemies.

The importance of such natural advantages cannot be underestimated: Even with them, World War I, which brought widespread jailing of socialists and pacifists, World War II, with its internment of Japanese-Americans, and the McCarthy-era assaults on civil liberties in the 1950s all hinted at how fragile constitutional liberties can be when war or other threats convulse a nation.

At the same time, the nation's wealth and size have posed unusual problems for the constitutional system. When the Constitution was written, many doubted that a republic could survive except in a geographically small unit.

In devising a system for a nation of continental proportions, "what's at stake is the difference between trying to turn the Queen Mary around and trying to turn a rowboat," UC Berkeley political scientist Nelson W. Polsby said.

The image of the Queen Mary is exactly what most of the Constitution's current critics seize on. Just like an ocean liner, they claim, the constitutional system is simply too slow to respond to the accelerating pace of life in the age of instant global communications, instant food and instant nuclear annihilation.

The system has been strained still further, many political scientists say, by the decline of effective political parties, which helped for many years to knit Presidents and Congress together and thereby counterbalance the system's tendency toward fractionation.

For all those reasons, "the fragmentation of power institutionalized in the system of checks and balances poses very severe questions for the constitutional system," political scientist James McGregor Burns said.

## SOURCE OF STABILITY

But the separation of powers, the inefficiency that so often makes government cumbersome, may, in fact, have been the greatest source of the Constitution's stability.

"Most of the founders believed the idea that, given power, men would abuse it," Degler said. Because of that belief, the governmental structure was built for distance, not for speed. To the Founding Fathers, a government that could handle day-to-day problems easily was less important than a government that could assure freedom and stability to generation after generation.

"Democratical states must always feel before they can see," George Washington wrote in 1785 to his Revolutionary War aide, the Marquis de Lafayette. "It is this that makes their governments slow, but the people will be right at last."

"The heterogeneity of the nation demands that we pay attention to the opinions of others," Polsby said. "It's a strength of our Constitution that a consensus is necessary to do large things."

The relationship between the Constitution and periods of national crisis has illustrated that point from the beginning.

While some states ratified the new charter quickly, in others the debates were long and arduous.

## NEW CONSENSUS

The unusual aspect of the debate, however, is that once it ended, so did serious opposition to the Constitution. Through the process of debate, a new consensus had been formed, and even those who had so strongly opposed the Constitution decided to accept it.

A more drawn-out, sometimes brutal process of consensus building centered on the nation's attempts, beginning in the late 19th Century, to strengthen the rights and protect the welfare of individuals by bridling the powers of massive corporations and their owners—"the malefactors of great wealth," as President Theodore Roosevelt called them.

As the Industrial Revolution transformed a country of villages, farms and small businesses into a nation of cities and giant factories, wrenching struggles took place—marked by political radicalism, riots, bloody confrontations, even anarchists' bombs.

Yet the period illustrates the way the system works for long-term stability, even at the price of near-term upheaval.

Over time, Congress and Presidents responded to the rising demand for economic and social reform; new laws were passed providing for collective bargaining of labor contracts, regulations of wages and hours, restrictions on child labor and similar reforms.

The establishment of an oversight role for the federal government in the realm of economics and commerce represented a dramatic change. Few nations have so fundamentally changed their economic systems except in a revolution or the aftermath of a war.

## UNIVERSAL PROBLEMS

"The underlying problems faced by human communities everywhere have to do with the intractable primordial differences that people have over race, religion and language," Berkeley's Polsby said.

"Religion was something they (the authors of the Constitution) solved right at the beginning," language has never yet become the serious social division for the United States that it is, for example, in Canada, and, he said, "we're on the road to doing something meaningful about race."

The Constitution no doubt will face challenges in the next 200 years, but having handled those three "primordial differences," perhaps it will continue to justify the boast of 19th-Century orator Sen. Henry Clay of Kentucky: "The Constitution of the United States was made not merely for the generation that then existed, but for posterity—unlimited, undefined, endless, perpetual posterity."

## DEBATING THE ISSUES: THE CONSTITUTION PROPERTY VERSUS PRAGMATISM

*See Lowi and Ginsberg, pp. 38–39 or brief edition, pp. 20–21*

*Despite the deference accorded to it today, the instrument drafted at the Constitutional Convention of 1787 did not command instant respect. The fight for ratification was bitter; as discussed later in the text, many were suspicious of the powers being vested in a national government.*

*The Federalist Papers, several of which are reprinted throughout these readings, are the most valuable exposition of the political theory of the Constitution available today. Written by Alexander Hamilton, James Madison, and John Jay, they contain a detailed outline of the arguments used to justify the new Constitution. They do not represent, however, a necessarily balanced view of the various arguments for and against the Constitution; they were written as political arguments to convince readers to support the new system. In The Federalist No. 15, reprinted below, Alexander Hamilton is at his best arguing for the necessity of a stronger central government than that established under the Articles of Confederation, pointing out the practical impossibility of engaging in concerted action when each of the thirteen states retains virtual sovereignty.*

*Opposed to the Federalists were such well-known patriots as Patrick Henry,*

> whose speech to the Virginia ratifying convention is reprinted below. Henry warned that the new Constitution was being pushed too quickly on the people, and that it was destined to "ruin and oppress" them. The part of his speech excerpted here outlines his concerns that there would be no effective checks on the power of federal officers and institutions.

# Alexander Hamilton
## *The Federalist No. 15* *

In the course of the preceding papers I have endeavored, my fellow-citizens, to place before you in a clear and convincing light the importance of Union to your political safety and happiness. . . . [T]he point next in order to be examined is the "insufficiency of the present Confederation to the preservation of the Union." . . . There are material imperfections in our national system and . . . something is necessary to be done to rescue us from impending anarchy. The facts that support this opinion are no longer objects of speculation. They have forced themselves upon the sensibility of the people at large, and have at length extorted . . . a reluctant confession of the reality of those defects in the scheme of our federal government which have been long pointed out and regretted by the intelligent friends of the Union. . . .

We may indeed with propriety be said to have reached almost the last stage of national humiliation. There is scarcely anything that can wound the pride or degrade the character of an independent nation which we do not experience. Are there engagements to the performance of which we are held by every tie respectable among men? These are the subjects of constant and unblushing violation. Do we owe debts to foreigners and to our own citizens contracted in a time of imminent peril for the preservation of our political existence? These remain without any proper or satisfactory provision for their discharge. . . . Are we in a condition to resent or to repel the aggression? We have neither troops, nor treasury, nor government. . . . Is public credit an indispensable resource in time of public danger? We seem to have abandoned its cause as desperate and irretrievable. Is commerce of importance to national wealth? Ours is at the lowest point of declension. Is respectability in the eyes of foreign powers a safeguard against foreign encroachments? The imbecility of our government even forbids them to treat with us. . . . Is private credit the friend and patron of industry? That most useful kind which relates to borrowing and lending is reduced within the narrowest limits, and this still more from an opinion of insecurity than from a scarcity of money. . . .

This is the melancholy situation to which we have been brought by those very maxims and counsels which would now deter us from adopting the pro-

* Alexander Hamilton, *The Federalist No. 15*, ed. Clinton Rossiter (New York: NAL, 1961).

posed Constitution; and which, not content with having conducted us to the brink of a precipice, seem resolved to plunge us into the abyss that awaits us below. Here, my countrymen, impelled by every motive that ought to influence an enlightened people, let us make a firm stand for our safety, our tranquility, our dignity, our reputation. Let us at last break the fatal charm which has too long seduced us from the paths of felicity and prosperity.

. . . While [opponents of the Constitution] admit that the government of the United States is destitute of energy, they contend against conferring upon it those powers which are requisite to supply that energy. . . . This renders a full display of the principal defects of the Confederation necessary in order to show that the evils we experience do not proceed from minute or partial imperfections, but from fundamental errors in the structure of the building, which cannot be amended otherwise than by an alteration in the first principles and main pillars of the fabric.

The great and radical vice in the construction of the existing Confederation is in the principle of LEGISLATION FOR STATES OR GOVERNMENTS, in their CORPORATE OR COLLECTIVE CAPACITIES, and as contradistinguished from the INDIVIDUALS of whom they consist. Though this principle does not run through all the powers delegated to the Union, yet it pervades and governs those on which the efficacy of the rest depends. Except as to the rule of apportionment, the United States have an indefinite discretion to make requisitions for men and money; but they have no authority to raise either by regulations extending to the individual citizens of America. The consequence of this is that though in theory their resolutions concerning those objects are laws constitutionally binding on the members of the Union, yet in practice they are mere recommendations which the States observe or disregard at their option. . . .

There is nothing absurd or impracticable in the idea of a league or alliance between independent nations for certain defined purposes precisely stated in a treaty regulating all the details of time, place, circumstance, and quantity, leaving nothing to future discretion, and depending for its execution on the good faith of the parties. . . .

If the particular States in this country are disposed to stand in a similar relation to each other, and to drop the project of a general DISCRETIONARY SUPERINTENDENCE, the scheme would indeed be pernicious and would entail upon us all the mischiefs which have been enumerated under the first head; but it would have the merit of being, at least, consistent and practicable. Abandoning all views towards a confederate government, this would bring us to a simple alliance offensive and defensive; and would place us in a situation to be alternate friends and enemies of each other, as our mutual jealousies and rivalships, nourished by the intrigues of foreign nations, should prescribe to us.

But if we are unwilling to be placed in this perilous situation; if we still will adhere to the design of a national government, or, which is the same thing, of a superintending power under the direction of a common council, we must resolve to incorporate into our plan those ingredients which may be considered as forming the characteristic difference between a league and a government; we must extend the authority of the Union to the persons of the citizens—the only proper objects of government.

Government implies the power of making laws. It is essential to the idea of a law that it be attended with a sanction; or, in other words, a penalty or punishment for disobedience. If there be no penalty annexed to disobedience, the resolutions or commands which pretend to be laws will, in fact, amount to nothing more than advice or recommendation. This penalty, whatever it may be, can only be inflicted in two ways: by the agency of the courts and ministers of justice, or by military force; by the COERCION of the magistracy, or by the COERCION of arms. The first kind can evidently apply only to men; the last kind must of necessity be employed against bodies politic, or communities, or States. . . . In an association where the general authority is confined to the collective bodies of the communities that compose it, every breach of the laws must involve a state of war; and military execution must become the only instrument of civil obedience. Such a state of things can certainly not deserve the name of government, nor would any prudent man choose to commit his happiness to it.

There was a time when we were told that breaches by the States of the regulations of the federal authority were not to be expected; that a sense of common interest would preside over the conduct of the respective members, and would beget a full compliance with all the constitutional requisitions of the Union. This language, at the present day, would appear as wild as a great part of what we now hear from the same quarter will be thought, when we shall have received further lessons from that best oracle of wisdom, experience. It at all times betrayed an ignorance of the true springs by which human conduct is actuated, and belied the original inducements to the establishment of civil power. Why has government been instituted at all? Because the passions of men will not conform to the dictates of reason and justice without constraint. . . .

In addition to all this . . . it happens that in every political association which is formed upon the principle of uniting in a common interest a number of lesser sovereignties, there will be found a kind of eccentric tendency in the subordinate or inferior orbs by the operation of which there will be a perpetual effort in each to fly off from the common center. This tendency is not difficult to be accounted for. It has its origin in the love of power. Power controlled or abridged is almost always the rival and enemy of that power by which it is controlled or abridged. This simple proposition will teach us how little reason there is to expect that the persons intrusted with the administration of the affairs of the particular members of a confederacy will at all times be ready with perfect good humor and an unbiased regard to the public weal to execute the resolutions or decrees of the general authority. . . .

If, therefore, the measures of the Confederacy cannot be executed without the intervention of the particular administrations, there will be little prospect of their being executed at all. . . . [Each state will evaluate every federal measure in light of its own interests] and in a spirit of interested and suspicious scrutiny, without that knowledge of national circumstances and reasons of state, which is essential to a right judgment, and with that strong predilection in favor of local objects, which can hardly fail to mislead the decision. The same process must be repeated in every member of which the body is constituted; and the execution of the plans, framed by the councils of the whole, will always fluctuate on the discretion of the ill-informed and prejudiced opinion of every part. . . .

In our case the concurrence of thirteen distinct sovereign wills is requisite under the Confederation to the complete execution of every important measure that proceeds from the Union. It has happened as was to have been foreseen. The measures of the Union have not been executed; and the delinquencies of the States have step by step matured themselves to an extreme, which has, at length, arrested all the wheels of the national government and brought them to an awful stand. Congress at this time scarcely possess the means of keeping up the forms of administration, till the States can have time to agree upon a more substantial substitute for the present shadow of a federal government. . . . Each State yielding to the persuasive voice of immediate interest or convenience has successively withdrawn its support, till the frail and tottering edifice seems ready to fall upon our heads and to crush us beneath its ruins.

PUBLIUS

# Patrick Henry
## "Speech at Virginia Ratifying Convention"
## (June 9, 1788)*

. . . A number of characters of the greatest eminence in this country, object to this Government, for its consolidating tendency. This is not imaginary. It is a formidable reality. If consolidation proves to be as mischievous to this country, as it has been to other countries, what will the poor inhabitants of this country do? This Government will operate like an ambuscade. It will destroy the State Governments, and swallow the liberties of the people, without giving them previous notice. . . . Sir, I ask you, and every other Gentleman who hears me, if he can retain his indignation, at a system, which takes from the State Legislatures the care and preservation of the interests of the people; 180 Representatives, the choice of the people of Virginia cannot be trusted with their interests. . . . So degrading an indignity—so flagrant an outrage to the States—so vile a suspicion is humiliating to my mind, and many others.

Will the adoption of this new plan pay our debts? This, Sir, is a plain question. It is inferred, that our grievances are to be redressed, and the evils of the existing system to be removed by the new Constitution. Let me inform the Honorable Gentleman, that no nation ever paid its debts by a change of Government, without the aid of industry. You never will pay your debts but by a radical change of domestic economy. At present you buy too much, and make too little to pay. Will this new system promote manufactures, industry and frugality? If instead of this, your hopes and designs will be disappointed; you relinquish a great deal, and hazard infinitely more, for nothing. Will it enhance the value of your lands? Will it lessen your burthens? Will your looms and wheels go to work by the act of adoption? If it will in its consequence produce these things, it will consequently produce a reform, and enable you to pay your debts. . . . I am a sceptic—an infidel on this point. . . . The evils that attend us, lie in extravagance and want of industry, and can only be removed by assiduity and economy. Perhaps we shall be told by Gentlemen, that these things will happen, because the administration is to be taken from us, and placed in the hands of the luminous few, who will pay different attention, and be more studiously careful than we can be supposed to be. . . .

[W]e can live happily without changing our present despised Government. Cannot people be as happy under a mild, as under an energetic Government? Cannot content and felicity be enjoyed in a republic, as well as in a monarchy, because there are whips, chains and scourges used in the latter? If I am not as rich as my neighbour, if I give my mite—my all—republican forbearance will say, that it is sufficient. . . . For better will it be for us to continue as we are, than go under that tight energetic Government.—I am persuaded of what the Honorable Gentleman says, that separate confederacies will ruin us. In my judgment, they are evils never to be thought of till a people are driven by necessity.—When he asks my opinion of consolidation—of one power to reign over America, with a strong hand; I will tell him, I am persuaded, of the rectitude of my honorable friend's opinion (Mr. *Mason*) that one Government cannot reign over so extensive a country as this is, without absolute despotism. Compared to such a consolidation, small Confederacies are little evils; though they ought to be recurred to, but in case of necessity. . . .

When we come to the spirit of domestic peace—The humble genius of Virginia has formed a Government, suitable to the genius of her people. I believe the hands that formed the American Constitution triumph in the experiment. . . . After all your reforms in Government, unless you consult the genius of the inhabitants, you will never succeed—your system can have no duration. . . . On this awful occasion [of the Revolution] did you want a Federal Government? Did federal ideas possess your minds? Did federal ideas lead you to the most splendid victories? I must again repeat the favorite idea, that the genius of Virginia did, and will again lead us to happiness. To obtain the most splendid prize, you did not consolidate. You accomplished the most glorious ends, by the assistance of the genius of your country. Men were then taught by that genius, that they were fighting for what was most dear to them. . . . Among all our troubles we have paid almost to the last shilling, for the sake of justice. We have paid as well as any State: I will not say better. To support the General Government, our own Legislature, to pay the interest of the public debts, and defray contingencies, we have been heavily taxed. To add to these things, the distresses produced by paper money, and by tobacco contracts, were sufficient to render any people discontented. These, Sir, were great temptations; but in the most severe conflict of misfortunes, this code of laws—this genius of Virginia, call it what you will, triumphed over every thing.

Some here speak of the difficulty in forming a new code of laws. Young as we were, it was not wonderful if there was a difficulty in forming and assimilating one system of laws. . . . My worthy friend said, that a republican form of Government would not suit a very extensive country; but that if a Government were judiciously organized and limits prescribed to it; an attention to these principles might render it possible for it to exist in an extensive territory. Whoever will be bold to say, that a Continent can be governed by that system, contradicts all the experience of the world. It is a work too great for human wisdom. Let me call for an example. Experience has been called the best teacher. I call for an example of a great extent of country, governed by one Government, or Congress, call it what you will. I tell him, that a Government may be trimmed up according to Gentlemen's fancy, but it never can operate—it will be but very short-lived. . . . I beseech Gentlemen to consider, whether they can say, when trusting power, that a mere patriotic profession will be equally operative and efficatious, as the check of self-love. In considering the experience of ages, is it not seen, that fair disinterested patriotism, and professed attachment to rectitude have never been solely trusted to by an enlightened free people?—If you depend on your President's and Senators [sic] patriotism, you are gone. . . . A good President, or Senator, or Representative, will have a natural weakness.—Virtue will slumber. The wicked will be continually watching: Consequently you will be undone. . . . In this system, there are only ideal balances. Till I am convinced that there are actual efficient checks, I will not give my assent to its establishment. The President and Senators have nothing to lose. . . . What powerful check is there here to prevent the most extravagant and profligate squandering of the public money? What security have we in money matters? Enquiry is precluded by this Constitution. I never wish to see Congress supplicate the States. But it is more abhorent to my mind to give them an unlimited and unbounded command over our souls—our lives—our purses, without any check or restraint. How are you to keep enquiry alive? How discover their conduct? We are told by that paper, that a regular statement and account of the receipts and expenditures of all public money, shall be published from time to time. Here is a beautiful check! What time? Here is the utmost latitude left. If those who are in Congress please to put that construction upon it, the words of the Constitution will be satisfied by publishing those accounts once in 100 years. They may publish or not as they please. Is this like the present despised system, whereby the accounts are to be published monthly?

The power of direct taxation was called by the Honorable Gentlemen the soul of the Government: Another Gentleman, called it the lungs of the Government. We all agree, that it is the most important part of the body politic. If the power of raising money be necessary for the General Government, it is no less so for the States. If money be the vitals of Congress, is it not precious for those individuals from whom it is to be taken? Must I give my soul—my lungs, to Congress? Congress must have our souls. The State must have our souls. This is dishonorable and disgraceful. These two coordinate, interferring unlimited powers of harassing the community, is unexampled: It is unprecedented in history: They are the visionary projects of modern politicians: tell me not of imaginary means, but of reality; this political solecism will never tend to the benefit of the community. It will be as oppressive in practice as it is absurd in theory. . . . I tell you, they shall not have the soul of Virginia. They tell us, that one collector may collect the Federal and State taxes. The General Government being paramount to the State Legislatures; if the Sheriff is to collect for both; his right hand for the Congress, his left for the State; his right hand being paramount over the left, his collections will go to Congress. We will have the rest. Deficiencies in collections will always operate against the States. Congress being the paramount supreme power, must not be disappointed. Thus Congress will have an unlimited, unbounded command over the soul of this Commonwealth. After satisfying their uncontrolled demands, what can be left for the States? Not a sufficiency even to defray the expense of their internal administration. They must therefore glide imperceptibly and gradually out of existence. This, Sir, must naturally terminate in a consolidation. If this will do for other people, it never will do for me.

. . . I shall be told in this place, that those who are to tax us are our Representatives. To this I answer, that there is no real check to prevent their ruining us. There is no actual responsibility. The only semblance of a check is the negative power of not re-electing them. This, Sir, is but a feeble barrier when their personal interest, their ambition and avarice come to be put in contrast with the happiness of the people. All checks founded on any thing but self-love, will not avail. This constitution reflects in the most degrading and mortifying manner on the virtue, integrity, and wisdom of the State Legislatures: it presupposes that the chosen few who go to Congress will have more upright hearts, and more enlightened minds, than those who are members of the individual Legislatures. To suppose that ten Gentlemen shall have more real substantial merit, than 170 [members of the Virginia legislature] is humiliating to the last degree. . . .

Congress by the power of taxation—by that of raising an army, and by their control over the militia, have the sword in one hand, and the purse in the other. Shall we be safe without either? Congress have an unlimited power over both: they are entirely given up by us. Let him candidly tell me, where and when did freedom exist, when the sword and purse were given up from the people? Unless a miracle in human affairs interposed, no nation ever retained its liberty after the loss of the sword and purse. Can you prove by any argumentative deduction, that it is possible to be safe without retaining one of these? If you give them up you are gone.

# 3

# The Constitutional Framework: Federalism and the Separation of Powers

## The Federal Framework

*See Lowi and Ginsberg, pp. 67–87 or brief edition, p. 42*

*Some of the most divisive and bitter political battles in our nation's history have been fought over interpretations of the constitutional principle of federalism: the division of powers and functions between the state governments and the national government. The struggle for desegregation and the civil rights of minorities, the legalization of abortion, the selective incorporation of the Bill of Rights into the Fourteenth Amendment, and the Civil War all ultimately forced the question: "Who has the authority to govern? The states, or the national government?" Our federal system is a delicate balance of power and shared responsibility between nation and states, each with constitutional authority to pass laws, levy taxes, and protect the interests and rights of citizens. It is a dynamic balance of power, easily destabilized by economic crises, political initiatives, and Supreme Court challenges, but often resolved by the question: "Who will pay the price for implementing and enforcing government policy?"*

*Arguments over this delicate balance of power animated debates over ratification of the Constitution. In* The Federalist *No. 39, James Madison conceded that the new Union would not be wholly federal in character, but would be a mixed system. In some respects, the new government would be national, exercising its powers directly on people in their individual capacities, while in other—and more important—respects its operation would be federal, since it was a government of limited authority, leaving "a residuary and inviolable sovereignty over all other objects" to the states. Madison argued that this combination of operations and functions would create the strength and flexibility required in the new government.*

*But the very specter of national powers disturbed many who feared encroachment on state sovereignty. In* The Federalist *No. 46, reprinted here, Madison went to great lengths to reassure the states that they would continue to wield a high degree of power, arguing that "the first and most natural attachment of the people will be to the governments of their respective states." While recognizing the potential for conflicts between state and federal governments, Madison concluded that the large measure of power retained by the states would be sufficient to overcome any efforts to usurp that power by the newly established national government.*

# James Madison
## *The Federalist No. 46**

I proceed to inquire whether the federal government or the State governments will have the advantage with regard to the predilection and support of the people. Notwithstanding the different modes in which they are appointed, we must consider both of them as substantially dependent on the great body of the citizens of the United States. . . . The federal and State governments are in fact but different agents and trustees of the people, constituted with different powers and designed for different purposes. The adversaries of the Constitution seem to have lost sight of the people altogether in their reasonings on this subject; and to have viewed these different establishments not only as mutual rivals and enemies, but as uncontrolled by any common superior in their efforts to usurp the authorities of each other. These gentlemen must here be reminded of their error. They must be told that the ultimate authority, wherever the derivative may be found, resides in the people alone, and that it will not depend merely on the comparative ambition or address of the different governments whether either, or which of them, will be able to enlarge its sphere of jurisdiction at the expense of the other. Truth, no less than decency, requires that the event in every case should be supposed to depend on the sentiments and sanction of their common constituents.

Many considerations . . . seem to place it beyond doubt that the first and most natural attachment of the people will be to the governments of their respective States. Into the administration of these a greater number of individuals will expect to rise. From the gift of these a greater number of offices and emoluments will flow. By the superintending care of these, all the more domestic and personal interests of the people will be regulated and provided for. With the affairs of these, the people will be more familiarly and minutely conversant. And with the members of these will a greater proportion of the people have the ties of personal acquaintance and friendship, and of family and party attachments; on the side of these, therefore, the popular bias may well be expected most strongly to incline.

The remaining points on which I propose to compare the federal and State governments are the disposition and the faculty they may respectively possess to resist and frustrate the measures of each other.

It has been already proved that the members of the federal will be more dependent on the members of the State governments than the latter will be on the former. It has appeared also that the prepossessions of the people, on whom both will depend, will be more on the side of the State governments than of the federal government. So far as the disposition of each towards the other may be influenced by these causes, the State governments must clearly have the advantage. But in a distinct and very important point of view, the advantage will lie on the same side. The pre-

---

* James Madison, *The Federalist No. 46*, ed. Clinton Rossiter (New York: NAL, 1961).

possessions, which the members themselves will carry into the federal government, will generally be favorable to the States; whilst it will rarely happen that the members of the State governments will carry into the public councils a bias in favor of the general government. A local spirit will infallibly prevail much more in the members of Congress than a national spirit will prevail in the legislatures of the particular States.

. . . What is the spirit that has in general characterized the proceedings of Congress? A perusal of their journals, as well as the candid acknowledgments of such as have had a seat in that assembly, will inform us that the members have but too frequently displayed the character rather of partisans of their respective States than of impartial guardians of a common interest; that where on one occasion improper sacrifices have been made of local considerations to the aggrandizement of the federal government, the great interests of the nation have suffered on a hundred from an undue attention to the local prejudices, interests, and views of the particular States. I mean not by these reflections to insinuate that the new federal government will not embrace a more enlarged plan of policy than the existing government may have pursued; much less that its views will be as confined as those of the State legislatures; but only that it will partake sufficiently of the spirit of both to be disinclined to invade the rights of the individual States, or the prerogatives of their governments.

Were it admitted, however, that the federal government may feel an equal disposition with the State governments to extend its power beyond the due limits, the latter would still have the advantage in the means of defeating such encroachments. If an act of a particular State, though unfriendly to the national government, be generally popular in that State, and should not too grossly violate the oaths of the State officers, it is executed immediately and, of course, by means on the spot and depending on the State alone. The opposition of the federal government, or the interposition of federal officers, would but inflame the zeal of all parties on the side of the State, and the evil could not be prevented or repaired, if at all, without the employment of means which must always be resorted to with reluctance and difficulty. On the other hand, should an unwarrantable measure of the federal government be unpopular in particular States, which would seldom fail to be the case, or even a warrantable measure be so, which may sometimes be the case, the means of opposition to it are powerful and at hand. The disquietude of the people; their repugnance and, perhaps, refusal to co-operate with the officers of the Union; the frowns of the executive magistracy of the State; the embarrassments created by legislative devices, which would often be added on such occasions, would oppose, in any State, difficulties not to be despised; would form, in a large State, very serious impediments; and where the sentiments of several adjoining States happened to be in unison, would present obstructions which the federal government would hardly be willing to encounter.

But ambitious encroachments of the federal government on the authority of the State governments would not excite the opposition of a single State, or of a few States only. They would be signals of general alarm.

Every government would espouse the common cause. A correspondence would be opened. Plans of resistance would be concerted. One spirit would animate and conduct the whole. The same combinations, in short, would result from an apprehension of the federal, as was produced by the dread of a foreign, yoke; and unless the projected innovations should be voluntarily renounced, the same appeal to a trial of force would be made in the one case as was made in the other.

The only refuge left for those who prophesy the downfall of the State governments is the visionary supposition that the federal government may previously accumulate a military force for the projects of ambition. The reasonings contained in these papers must have been employed to little purpose indeed, if it could be necessary now to disprove the reality of this danger. That the people and the States should, for a sufficient period of time, elect an uninterrupted succession of men ready to betray both; that the traitors should, throughout this period, uniformly and systematically pursue some fixed plan for the extension of the military establishment; that the governments and the people of the States should silently and patiently behold the gathering storm and continue to supply the materials until it should be prepared to burst on their own heads must appear to everyone more like the incoherent dreams of a delirious jealousy, or the misjudged exaggerations of a counterfeit zeal, than like the sober apprehensions of genuine patriotism. Extravagant as the supposition is, let it, however, be made. Let a regular army, fully equal to the resources of the country, be formed; and let it be entirely at the devotion of the federal government: still it would not be going too far to say that the State governments with the people on their side would be able to repel the danger.

Besides the advantage of being armed, which the Americans possess over the people of almost every other nation, the existence of subordinate governments, to which the people are attached and by which the militia officers are appointed, forms a barrier against the enterprises of ambition, more insurmountable than any which a simple government of any form can admit of.

Let us not insult the free and gallant citizens of America with the suspicion that they would be less able to defend the rights of which they would be in actual possession than the debased subjects of arbitrary power would be to rescue theirs from the hands of their oppressors. Let us rather no longer insult them with the supposition that they can ever reduce themselves to the necessity of making the experiment by a blind and tame submission to the long train of insidious measures which must precede and produce it.

The argument under the present head may be put into a very concise form, which appears altogether conclusive. Either the mode in which the federal government is to be constructed will render it sufficiently dependent on the people, or it will not. On the first supposition, it will be restrained by that dependence from forming schemes obnoxious to their constituents. On the other supposition, it will not possess the confidence of the people, and its schemes of usurpation will be easily defeated by the State governments, who will be supported by the people.

On summing up the considerations stated in this and the last paper, they seem to amount to the most convincing evidence that the powers proposed to be lodged in the federal government are as little formidable to those reserved to the individual States as they are indispensably necessary to accomplish the purposes of the Union; and that all those alarms which have been sounded of a meditated and consequential annihilation of the State governments must, on the most favorable interpretation, be ascribed to the chimerical fears of the authors of them.

PUBLIUS

## DEBATING THE ISSUES: CAN THE STATES DO IT BETTER?

*See Lowi and Ginsberg, pp. 82–83 or brief edition, pp. 56–57*

*The argument over the balance of power in our federal system is once again at the heart of numerous policy debates (reminiscent of the Federalists and Antifederalists). Many elected state officials, particularly governors, view the federal government as top-heavy and heavy-handed. What's more, the states labor under the burdens of adhering to federal one-size-fits-all rules and regulations for implementing health care, welfare, environmental, and transportation policies. Many mayors and governors argue that greater flexibility and state authority would not only save money but lead to more effective outcomes—more children getting health care, more welfare recipients obtaining jobs, and cleaner environments with lower costs for businesses. The recently enacted welfare reform legislation embraces this argument by using block grants that permit states to create more flexible welfare programs.*

*Not everyone is upbeat about this push toward state authority. John D. Donahue argues that the "devil in devolution" is the ability of a single state to undermine broad national concerns as it pursues its own interests. If every state acts in its own self-interest (and in the interests of its strongest political groups) to attract corporate headquarters or new factories, or to regulate the environment, the result is a "race to the bottom" as states compete to have the most lenient or attractive settings for business development. The de facto economic development policy that emerges is anything but a nationally focused plan with national interests at its core. Similarly, the Constitution's "full faith and credit" clause requires states to recognize the legal decisions of others states on issues such as marriage licenses, divorces, and driver's licenses. The result can be that one state, in effect, defines national moral and economic objectives.*

*Alan Ehrenhalt is more optimistic about the capacity of a state to take on more responsibility. He argues that the states are no longer the administratively backward and politically unrepresentative entities they once were. He argues that beginning in the 1970s many states became far more progressive than the federal government in their social and environmental policies. Rather than a race to the bottom, in other words, states set very high standards. States governments, concludes Ehrenhalt, are professional, well funded, and demographically representative. As a result, they are in a prime position to generate creative and workable policies.*

*Are there policies that are best left to the states? What are they? Are there national interests that require national policy standards? What are they? Does the Constitution provide guidance on trying to make these decisions?*

# John D. Donahue
## "The Devil in Devolution"*

The shift in government's center of gravity away from Washington and toward the states—a transition propelled by both popular sentiment and budget imperatives, and blessed by leaders in both major parties—reflects an uncommon pause in an endless American argument over the balance between nation and state. That argument got underway when the Framers gathered in Philadelphia to launch a second attempt at nationhood, after less than a decade's dismal experience under the feeble Articles of Confederation. The Constitution they crafted was a compromise between those who wanted to strengthen the ties among essentially autonomous states, and those who sought to establish a new nation to supersede the states as the locus of the commonwealth. While anchoring the broad contours of state and federal roles, the Framers left it to their successors to adjust the balance to fit the circumstances of the world to come and the priorities of future generations.

This moment of consensus in favor of letting Washington fade while the states take the lead is badly timed. The public sector's current trajectory—the devolution of welfare and other programs, legislative and judicial action circumscribing Washington's authority, and the federal government's retreat to a domestic role largely defined by writing checks to entitlement claimants, creditors, and state and local governments—would make sense if economic and cultural ties reaching across state lines were *weakening* over time. But state borders are becoming more, not less, permeable.

From a vantage point three-fifths of the way between James Madison's day and our own, Woodrow Wilson wrote that the "common interests of a nation brought together in thought and interest and action by the telegraph and the telephone, as well as by the rushing mails which every express train carries, have a scope and variety, an infinite multiplication and intricate interlacing, of which a simpler day can have had no conception."

Issues in which other states' citizens have no stakes, and hence no valid claim to a voice, are becoming rarer still in an age of air freight, interlinked computers, nonstop currency trading, and site-shopping global corporations. Our current enchantment with devolution will be seen one day as oddly discordant with our era's challenges.

The concept of "the commons" can help to cast in a sharper light the perils of fragmented decision-making on issues of national consequence. In a much-noted 1968 article in *Science*, biologist Garrett Hardin invoked the parable of a herdsman pondering how many cattle to graze on the village commons. Self-interest will lead the herdsman to increase the size of his herd even if the commons is already overburdened, since he alone benefits from raising an extra animal, but shares the consequent damage to the common pasture. As each farmer follows the same logic, overgrazing wrecks the commons.

Where the nation as a whole is a commons, whether as an economic reality or as a political ideal, and states take action that ignores or narrowly exploits that fact, the frequent result is the kind of "tragedy" that Hardin's metaphor predicts: collective value is squandered in the name of a constricted definition of gain. States win advantages that seem worthwhile only because other states bear much of the costs. America's most urgent public challenges—shoring up the economic underpinnings of an imperiled middle-class culture; developing and deploying productive workplace skills; orchestrating Americans' engagement with increasingly global capital—involve the stewardship of common interests. The fragmentation of authority makes success less likely. The phenomenon is by no means limited to contemporary economic issues, and a smattering of examples from other times and other policy agendas illustrate the theme.

## FAITH AND CREDIT

In the late 1700s, states reluctant to raise taxes instead paid public debt with paper money, with progressively little gold or silver behind it. Even states like Georgia, Delaware, and New Jersey that exercised some restraint in issuing paper money saw merchants lose confidence in their currencies, as the flood of bad money debased the reputation of American money in general. Half a century later defaults and debt repudiations by Pennsylvania, Arkansas, Florida, Illinois, and a few other states—which for the states concerned were unfortunate, but apparently preferable to the alternative of paying what they owed—polluted the common American resource of creditworthiness, and for a time froze even solvent states and the federal government out of international credit markets.

Presidential primaries, which are run state by state, provide another example. Each state prefers to be first in line to hold its primary (or at least early in the queue). In recent presidential election seasons—and especially the 1996 Republican primaries—states have wrecked the common resource of a deliberative primary process in a rational (but nonetheless tragic) pursuit of parochial advantage. California's primary in June 1992 had come too late to matter; anxious to avoid another episode of irrelevance four years later, it staked out March 26 for its vote. But several other states, whose *own* votes would be rendered superfluous once California's crowd of delegates was selected, rescheduled their primaries in response. A spiral of competitive rescheduling led to ugly squabbles as Delaware and Louisiana crowded New Hampshire's traditional first-in-the-nation franchise; a mass of state primaries ended up bunched right behind New Hampshire, and a grotesquely compressed primary season ensued. The outcome was clear by the first days of March, and California's primary—although held two months earlier than it had been in 1992—was just as irrelevant. Most voters perceived the 1996 primary season as a brief spasm of televised name-calling. Even supporters of the eventual nominee felt that Senator Dole, and the voters, had been ill served by the process.

Term limits for representatives and senators present a similar "commons" problem. Despite a flurry of term-limit legislation at the state level, anyone convinced that the United States should have a less-professionalized Congress may not want to count on state term-limit laws to accomplish the goal. If less-entrenched legislators make for better law—a plausible although not invulnerable proposition—then a citizen legislature is a common benefit for the nation as a whole. Yet an individual state is usually better off when represented by politicians with experience in the ways of Washington and a deep reserve of past favors on which to trade. Even if a majority of a state's citizens would like to see a Congress of fresh faces, they may well prefer to see *other* states restrict representatives and senators to a few years' service, while keeping their own old lions on the job.

The Constitution's "full faith and credit" clause, a court case in Hawaii, and the quadrennial uptick in political tawdriness brought an unusual sort of commons problem to center stage in 1996. The issue was whether the definition of "marriage" should be broadened to include same-sex unions. A handful of Hawaiian same-sex couples had asserted the right to have their relationships reckoned under state law as no different from heterosexual marriages, invoking provisions in the state constitution that bar sex discrimination in almost any form (including, the plaintiffs argued, restrictions on the gender of one's spouse). When a shift in the composition of Hawaii's supreme court made a seemingly lost cause suddenly viable, it dawned on advocates and opponents alike that if Hawaii legitimated same-sex marriage, those unions would have to be recognized nationwide. If any homosexual couple—at least those able to afford two tickets to Hawaii—could bypass more restrictive laws in their home states, the rapid result could be a national redefinition of what marriage means, without anyone outside Hawaii having any voice in the outcome.

National opponents of gay marriage staged a preemptive strike in the form of the Defense of Marriage Act, requiring the federal government to counter heterodoxy in Hawaii or anywhere else by declaring a *national* definition of marriage—one man, one woman, and that's that. Beyond excluding same-sex spouses from receiving benefits under any federal program, the act gave states the right to refuse recognition to other states' marriages. The Defense of Marriage Act raced through Congress and President Clinton quickly signed it (albeit without ceremony and literally in the middle of the night). Annoyed at being forced to alienate his gay supporters in order to stay wrapped in the family-values mantle, Clinton charged, no doubt correctly, that the bill's authors were driven by the partisan spirit of the election year. But whatever their motivations—and however one feels about same-sex marriage—they had a point: the definition of marriage in the United States should be settled by national deliberation.

There is an interesting historical irony here, however. Not so long ago, divorce was only a little more common, and only a little less out of the mainstream, than homosexual unions seem today. While the causes for its increase are many and complex, the pace was set in part by states' calculations of parochial advantage. Around the turn of the century legislators in several Western states—notably Nevada—passed liberal divorce legislation in part to encourage economic development. Unhappy couples facing onerous divorce laws in their home state could head West for a few weeks or months. There they could dissolve their union, while solidifying the local economy, in some striving desert town. Other states might have resisted the trend to more lenient divorce laws. But any couple—at least any able to afford a ticket to Reno—could bypass their home-state restrictions. If a legislature held the line it would only be subjecting its citizens to extra expense while sending money out of state.

The wholesale liberalization of American divorce laws is often seen as a mistake—if not from the perspective of men who can cast off unwanted obligations with minimal bother, at least from the perspective of women and, especially, young children who all too often are left economically stranded. Which raises a question: if states should be free to refuse recognition to marriages made elsewhere, on the grounds that another state's definition of marriage offends local morals, should they also be able to refuse to recognize out-of-state divorces? Suppose that Vermont, say, passed legislation toughening divorce laws and declaring Vermont marriages immune to dissolution by another state's laws. If the legislation survived constitutional challenge (which is doubtful, as it is for the Defense of Marriage Act's comparable provisions) there would be some definite advantages: more traditional states could wall themselves off as enclaves against unwelcome national trends; a potential spouse could signal the depth of his or her commitment by proposing a Vermont wedding. On the other hand, the United States would become a little bit less of a nation.

In one of the less glorious episodes in American history, this country attempted to define human slavery as an issue each state could settle on its own, according to its own economic and ethical lights. Northern states, however, eventually proved unwilling to accept the proposition that the moral commons could be so neatly subdivided. The Fugitive Slave Act required antislavery states to make room in their moral world for slaveholders to transport their "property" for use anywhere in the nation. The repercussions ultimately led to attempted secession, and then to the national abolition of slavery. The meaning of marriage may be another moral issue so basic that it must be dealt with through a national debate, protracted and painful as that will doubtless turn out to be.

## ENVIRONMENTAL REGULATION

Antipollution law is perhaps the most obvious application of the "commons" metaphor to policy-making in a federal system. If a state maintains a lax regime of environmental laws it spares its own citizens, businesses, and government agencies from economic burdens. The "benefits" of environmental recklessness, in other words, are collected in-state. Part of the pollution consequently dumped into the air or water, however, drifts away to do its damage elsewhere in the nation. If states held all authority over environmental rule-making, the predictable result would be feeble regulations against any kinds of pollution where in-state costs and benefits of control are seriously out of balance. Even in states whose citizens valued the environment—even if the citizens of *all* states were willing to accept substantial economic costs in the name of cleaner air and water—constituents and representatives would calculate that their sacrifice could not on its own stem the tide and reluctantly settle for weaker rules than they would otherwise prefer.

A state contemplating tough antipollution rules might calculate that its citizens will pay for environmental improvements that will be enjoyed, in part, by others. Even worse, by imposing higher costs on business than do other states, it risks repelling investment, and thus losing jobs and tax revenues to states with weak environmental laws. Congress explicitly invoked the specter of a "race for the bottom"—competitive loosening of environmental laws in order to lure business—to justify federal standards that would "preclude efforts on the part of states to compete with each other in trying to attract new plants." In a series of legislative changes starting in the early 1970s, the major choices about how aggressively to act against pollution were moved to the federal government. While aspects of enforcement remained state responsibilities—introducing another level of complications that continues to plague environmental policy—the trade-off between environmental and economic values moved much closer to a single national standard.

National regulation in a diverse economy does have a downside. States differ in their environmental problems, and in the priorities of their citizens. Requiring all states to accept the same balance between environmental and economic values imposes some real costs and generates real political friction. Yet even if the tilt toward national authority is, on balance, the correct approach to environmental regulation, there is reason to doubt we got all the details right. Moreover, logic suggests that the federal role should be stronger for forms of pollution that readily cross state borders, and weaker for pollution that stays put. But federal authority is actually weaker under the Clean Air Act and the Clean Water Act than under the "Superfund" law covering hazardous waste. Toxic-waste sites are undeniably nasty things. But most of them are situated within a single state, and stay there.

## CORPORATE CHARTERING

Few questions about the division of economic authority across our federal system have received as enormous an investment of intellectual energy as the state chartering of corporations. Since corporations can operate nationally, whatever their state of incorporation, state decisions on chartering have national implications. In the eighteenth and much of the nineteenth centuries, corporate charters were granted under far more stringent conditions than they are today, usually on the understanding that demonstrable public good would result from the corporation's activities. As corporations came to be seen less as agents of the public interest; as states came to presume, instead of demanding proof of, public benefits from business enterprise; and as some firms became sufficiently national to have meaningful choices about which state to call home, the specific terms of state chartering came to matter more. In 1896, New Jersey adopted aggressively liberal chartering rules, and became the legal home of choice for major corporations. New Jersey shifted to a somewhat tougher chartering law in 1913, however, and rapidly lost its hegemony to Delaware, which had altered its own incorporation provisions to mirror New Jersey's previous law. Delaware has tenaciously defended its dominant place in corporate chartering ever since.

Herbert Croly, the Progressive intellectual, considered state chartering a silly anachronism by 1909, arguing that "a state has in the great majority of cases no meaning at all as a center of economic organization and direction." Croly's call for national chartering was made "not because there is any peculiar virtue in the action of the central government, but because there is a peculiar vice in asking the state governments to regulate matters beyond their effective jurisdiction." States whose chartering rules appeal to managers win taxes, fees, and ample job opportunities for corporate attorneys, while the costs of unbalanced corporate law are spread widely, wherever the state has operations, sales, creditors, or investors. The commons scenario predicts a systematic weakening of the conditions of incorporation.

The phrase "race to the bottom" was introduced in 1933 by Supreme Court Justice Louis Brandeis—who also, interestingly enough, popularized the term "laboratories of democracy"—in connection with corporate chartering. Multistate companies, Brandeis said, sought charters "in states where the cost was lowest and the laws least restrictive. The states joined in advertising their wares. The race was one not of diligence but of laxity." The modern debate over the prudence of state chartering got underway in the early 1970s with an article by William L. Cary in the *Yale Law Journal* on the pernicious effects of interstate competition for corporate charters.

Some defenders of rivalrous state chartering argued that Delaware's advantage was not due to weak conditions of incorporation, but rather to its efficient procedures for chartering—streamlined administrative rule-making, courts dedicated to corporate law, a specialized private bar, and a tradition of depoliticizing corporate law made sustainable by the paucity of actual corporate *operations* within the state. But the more interesting rebuttal to the "race for the bottom" critics came from a group of scholars who emphasized the importance of market rationality in the crafting of corporate law. Ralph Winter, in an influential 1977 article, started by acknowledging that states compete to maximize their share of the nation's corporate charters, and that they do so primarily through loosening the conditions of chartering. But the race was to the *top*, not the bottom, Winter and like-minded analysts argued, because the goal toward which states raced, and the pace of their scramble, turn out to be set *not* by corporate managers but by investors.

The story goes like this: corporations must attract capital. Investors will be more likely to commit their funds to firms whose charters require managers to do right by investors. And that story seems sound, so far as it goes. But this is not quite the end of the conversation. Interstate competition promotes laws that favor investors not because legislators are directly solicitous of shareholders, but because investors have leverage over managers, and managers have leverage over state policymakers. By this same logic, interests with a weaker claim on managers' devotion have no reason to expect that interstate competition will generate favorable results. For example, the dynamics of state competition for corporate charters are unlikely to generate a national pattern of laws that strengthens the hand of employees within the firm.

## LEGALIZED GAMBLING

There has never been a time in America when a person determined to gamble could not find some action. Nor is *legal* gambling, for that matter, anything new. The Continental Congress fed and armed Washington's army, in part, with revenues from a lottery, and state-sanctioned games of chance financed the early growth of Harvard and other colleges. For much of this century, however, gambling has operated in the economic shadows. Except for the exotic enclave of Nevada, government's stance toward gambling ranged, until recently, from vigilant hostility to narrowly circumscribed tolerance.

This has changed with an astonishing speed and completeness. In 1988 Nevada and New Jersey were alone in allowing casino gambling. Eight years later there were around 500 casinos operating in 27 states, and some form of gambling was legal in all but two states. The total annual amount wagered legally in the United States is about $500 billion. (For a sense of scale, consider that America's entire annual output is in the range of $7,000 billion.)

Gambling brings some obvious benefits to the state that runs the lottery or hosts the casinos. It can generate relatively high-paying jobs even for workers without much training. It yields welcome revenues for the state treasury. (States took in $27 billion from lotteries in 1994, and had $9.8 billion in revenues left over after paying off winners and covering administrative costs. In 1994, taxes paid by casinos alone yielded $1.4 billion for states and localities.) Legalized gambling can also produce political benefits, most directly the rich lodes of campaign contributions available from a highly profitable industry that is so intensely dependent on political favor.

Yet there are costs as well. Some people will always gamble whether it is legal or not, but many more do so only when the law allows. Access to legal opportunities for gambling has been found to increase the number of people who develop a gambling problem. The consequences range from mild economic inconvenience to bankruptcy, embezzlement, divorce, and suicide. In 1995—ten years after their state launched a lottery, and four years after the first legal riverboat casino opened—nine out of ten Iowans indulged in gambling. One in twenty reported having a gambling problem, and Iowa social-service agencies were coping with a surge of collateral family and financial damage.

But shouldn't we leave it to officials in each state to tally up the expected costs and benefits and make decisions that sum to the right national policy? The logic of the commons makes this less than likely. If a state loosens its own restrictions on gambling, it gains the benefits in jobs, tax revenues, and political favor. It also suffers costs—but not *all* the costs. When citizens of *other* states buy the lottery tickets and visit the casinos, they leave their money behind when they return home, but take their gambling-related problems back with them. States that still ban gambling suffer much of the damage from the national trend toward legalization, but without sharing in the benefits.

Iowa, in fact, had maintained stringent antigambling laws until the mid-1980s. But as a growing number of Iowans played lotteries in neighboring states it became harder to resist proposals to revitalize a battered economy through riverboat casinos aimed at attracting out-of-state gamblers, especially from the prosperous, casino-free Chicago area. At first, Chicagoans did come, by the busload. But Illinois legislators, seeing gambling dollars heading down the interstate to Iowa, opted to allow riverboat gambling in their state, too. Iowa's initial liberalization law had tried to lower the risk of problem gambling by limiting the size of any one bet and the amount any person could gamble away in a single day. But when Illinois, Mississippi, and Louisiana introduced riverboats *without* any limits,

Iowa lifted its own restrictions. In a similar way, after Montana allowed slot machines in taverns in 1985 neighboring South Dakota called and raised, allowing slot machines in bars *and* convenience stores.

By 1996 the only two states with no legal gambling at all were Utah, whose Mormon culture was uniquely resistant to the national trend, and Hawaii, where it is a good deal harder than in most other states for citizens to escape local restrictions by doing their gambling in the state next door. The federal government's absolute deference to the separate states began to bend that same year with legislation establishing a commission to examine the broader national impacts of gambling. A Nevada congresswoman denounced the bill as "the nose under the tent of Federal interference with the right of states to regulate gambling." She was entirely correct. But it is questionable whether exclusive state control over so massive a change in the legal economy's scope, with such sweeping implications for our culture, ever made much sense.

Not every issue, to be sure, can be cast as a commons problem. And even where state officials *are* tempted to pursue narrow agendas at the expense of national interests, it is not automatically true that the shared loss exceeds the advantages of state autonomy, or that an acceptable way can be found of safeguarding common interests without straining the framework of our federal system. There are two basic strategies for overcoming the confusion of incentives that trigger the tragedy of the commons. One is to fragment the commons into private holdings where property rights are unambiguous. The other is to maintain a polity that commands both the capacity and the legitimacy to give force to common interests. The debate over the future of America's federal-state balance can be seen, in a sense, as pivoting on this strategic choice. Devolution seeks to simplify incentives by subdividing the commons into separate plots. Federal reform requires accepting the challenge of balancing multiple interests within the national commonwealth.

Fixing the federal government is an intimidating proposition in the late 1990s. The trajectory of fiscal and political trends suggests that devolution will remain the focus of politicians' promises and citizens' hopes for some time to come. But the inherent limits of a fragmented approach to national adaptation will eventually inspire America to reappraise the ascendancy of the states. Not too far into the new century we will again collect the resolve to confront together our common fate. And we will once more take up, in the two-century tradition of Americans before us, the echoing challenge of George Washington's 1796 farewell address: "Is there a doubt whether a common government can embrace so large a sphere? Let experience solve it."

# Alan Ehrenhalt
# "Out in the States, It's Not the 1930s Anymore"*

In case you haven't been reading the papers lately, let me catch you up on the news from Washington: Congress is about to entrust the fate of America's poor and elderly to a gang of 50 rapacious thieves who plan to abandon them, seize their allowance and blow it all on an orgy of waste and greed.

Well, perhaps nobody's said it quite that way. But if you listen closely to the arguments of those who criticize the devolution experiment now under way, you can't help detecting something scary just below the surface. It's a concern that the states lack a piece of crucial equipment for the new role they are about to assume. Not just computers, or caseworkers, or management expertise. Moral equipment. The underlying fear is that the states are deficient in compassion. That they are already lined up waiting for the gun to go off in the race to the bottom. "States' rights is about to reign again in America," columnist Carl Rowan proclaimed recently, "and millions of Americans are going to be hurt by it."

Can the states be trusted with the social safety net? The uncomfortable truth is that even those who find devolution intellectually appealing sometimes stop and ask themselves that question. But where did it come from? Why do we instinctively associate the federal government with Santa Claus and the states with Ebenezer Scrooge?

The answer, I think, has to do with a few images of modern American political history that most of us carry around in our heads. One is the still-powerful picture of FDR and the federal government moving into the social insurance business in the 1930s, at a moment when the political leadership of many states was practically boasting about its refusal to do anything to cushion the impact of the Depression on the lives of ordinary citizens. Another is the image of the U.S. Supreme Court having to impose desegregation on a collection of defiant Southern governors and legislatures in the 1960s. A third is the image of states all over the country allowing their air and water to become so dirty that by 1970 a conservative Republican president was arguing for federal environmental regulation.

By the end of the 1960s, indeed, it had become a cliché in polite liberal circles to suggest that the main generator of federal activism in American government was state dereliction of duty. "One glaring truth of the times," the political commentator Frank Trippett wrote in 1967, "is that most of the perplexing domestic problems confronting the country today would not exist if the states had acted." Few scholars of the federal system felt differently. In the face of palpable suffering, injustice and destruction, the states had been inert to the point of callousness.

The images we have of state governments in the old days are, for the

---

* Alan Ehrenhalt, "Out in the States, It's Not the 1930s Anymore" in *Governing* (December, 1995). Reprinted with permission. Copyright 1995.

most part, accurate ones. The question is whether or not they are the ones we need to be carrying around with us as we begin an entirely new round of governmental debate in the last few years of the century.

What most American states really lacked, for all those dreary decades of bad government, was not so much compassion as representation. The legislatures that balked at relief for the poor in the 1930s and ignored urban pollution in the 1960s were so hopelessly malapportioned that they offered no clue at all to what their states as a whole felt, thought or wanted. In most of them, a tiny rural oligarchy governed essentially without accountability, and was perfectly free to ignore the condition of the urban poor or the quality of big-city air.

All this shabby history is familiar enough. There's no need to dwell on it except to make the point that, up until 1970 or so, many of the states were burdened by a dysfunctional political system that carried its own set of problems beyond those of Congress or the federal government. That isn't true anymore. Cities, suburbs and rural counties all have the political representation they are mathematically entitled to. In Mississippi, African Americans make up 36 percent of the population; their numbers in the legislature are approaching 30 percent.

None of this is to deny that states can screw up pretty badly in meeting their responsibilities of the 1990s. Legislatures posture endlessly in partisan terms, write budgets with little concern for long-term capital needs and slither away from their revenue-raising responsibilities.

But when state legislatures screw up nowadays, it's not for the same reasons they used to. It's not because they are incapable of representing the views of the people. It's because, like Congress, they reflect the popular mood in all its short-sightedness and inconsistency. That's not in itself a reason to trust the states with a whole new array of governmental responsibilities. But it's not a reason to be afraid of them either.

Looking back in the broadest terms over the past 25 years of American government, it is very difficult to make the argument that the states have been less compassionate or less sensitive to human needs than the federal government has been. Some of them have carried generosity to a fault.

In most of the country during the past couple of decades, state legislatures have stood well to the left of Congress on a whole array of social welfare issues. In the 1970s, as reapportionment rooted out the old small-town Republican oligarchs in much of the East and Midwest, power passed to the Democrats and to a whole new generation of political professionals, educated in the 1960s and propelled into full-time legislative careers by an ideology of social activism and concern for the disadvantaged. Beginning in these years, legislatures started to attract a disproportionate number of members drawn directly from teaching, social work, public interest law and other professions in which compassion has never been in short supply.

This was the generation that, upon seizing power in Wisconsin in the early 1970s, proceeded in short order to enact consumer protection, strict environmental controls, huge increases in educational funding and a transfer of tax revenues from the suburbs to the inner cities. Wisconsin was far from alone. By the end of that decade, systematic expansion of the state "safety net" had been secured in virtually all of the large states of the East, Midwest and Pacific Coast.

In the early 1980s, after ornery voters had opted for strict property tax limitations by popular initiative in several of these states, their legislatures quickly stepped in and replaced most of the lost revenue out of state tax money. One can argue that this was an unwise decision and a major contributor to the structural budget deficits that began to emerge in California and Massachusetts, among other places, in the early 1990s. But it is hard to associate it with a shortage of generosity or compassion.

While the legislatures were doing all those things, state supreme courts were tilting even further in a liberal direction. In the 1980s, Massachusetts, California and New Jersey state courts all required the funding of abortions for poor women. Oregon's court granted free-speech protection to obscenity. During the 1980s, one scholarly study concluded a few years ago, state supreme courts around the country issued more than 200 decisions declaring state constitutions more protective of individual rights than the U.S. Constitution.

Of course, that was the 1980s. This is 1995. There is no reason to suppose that the Republican governors and legislatures sworn in this year will be equally solicitous of the disadvantaged or that the judges they appoint will be as concerned about individual rights. But all that suggests is that elections matter: When conservatives are elected to office, they will produce conservative public policies. And GOP leaders will be more attuned to the needs of the suburbanites who put them in power than to the city-dwellers who opposed them. That is a far cry from saying that state governments have some sort of constitutional predilection to be stingy or hard-hearted. They don't. Those days are over.

Which is not to say that states don't continue to vary enormously in the resources, energy and even the compassion they are willing to expend in behalf of their less fortunate residents. Just in the past decade, under what is supposed to be the redistributive effect of federal aid, rules and mandates, they have varied more than most people realize. At the moment, AFDC benefits for a family of four are $220 a month in Mississippi and $660 in New York. And this is with the federal government paying 80 percent of Mississippi's AFDC bill. The federal government has never done a particularly good job of equalizing benefits even in the social programs it has financed the most generously. There has always been a race to the bottom for those states that wanted to participate in it.

Now, with welfare and Medicaid no longer handled by Washington on an entitlement basis, the states will be even freer to seek their own levels. Some will inevitably turn out to be more compassionate—as well as more competent—than others. But turning responsibility back to the states in the last decade of the century doesn't mean turning it back to Ebenezer

Scrooge—or Harry Byrd or Herbert Hoover. Making sense of devolution in the 1990s requires updating our stereotypes about who the current players really are.

## The Second Principle: The Separation of Powers

*See Lowi and Ginsberg, pp. 87–93 or brief edition, pp. 59–61*

*The Founders carefully fragmented the powers of the national government between three branches, providing each with a means to check the power of the others. While the system is an effective check on the accumulation of power by any one branch, it is a cumbersome way to govern a nation. Conflict between the branches is inevitable, especially when one political party controls the Congress, and another the Presidency (divided government). The result, as pundits, politicians, and voters complain, is often gridlock. Indeed, in 1996 the federal government was completely shut down for several days because of disagreements between the White House and Congress over federal spending and tax cuts.*

*But is the separation of powers such a bad thing? Charles Jones argues that even though our system "always appears broken," it works as intended and better than we might think. Some of the most productive legislative periods in history occurred under divided government. More important, when party unity does speed legislation through the House or Senate, as occurred with portions of the "Contract with America" in the 104th Congress, the system of separated powers eventually slows the debate and forces more deliberate consideration of national policy.*

# Charles O. Jones
# "It Ain't Broke," from *Back to Gridlock**

The source of my title, is, of course, the pithy aphorism: "If it ain't broke, don't fix it." I would add this advisory: "If it is broke, choose your fixer carefully—and always get a second opinion." It is a quality of a separated powers system like ours that it always appears broken, thus encouraging professional fixers to ply their trade. Some political systems work with "clean" theories—the most pristine of which have proven to be very wrong. We dirty things up a bit by promoting access, propagating legitimate participation, and dispersing accountability, yet compelling agreement. None of it works very well, as Barber Conable has observed, "just as the founding fathers intended." The separated system doesn't show well along the way.

The stimulus to make changes in our political system often derives

* Charles O. Jones, "It Ain't Broke" from *Back to Gridlock: Government in the Clinton Years*, edited by James Sundquist (1995). Reprinted by permission of the Brookings Institution.

from a desire to have presidential government and strong political parties in the parliamentary mode. Congress gets in the way of achieving this end and is therefore the subject of much criticism and many reform proposals. The president should be strong, policy ambitious, and responsible so that he can form a government—well, at least those we agree with should be so endowed. The system at present is viewed as producing gridlock, a term applied when either the president or the House or the Senate exercises their constitutional prerogatives to check the other branch.

It is surely true that serious participation in a separated system is big-time politics. Not everyone is good at it—some, in fact, should seek other employment. Surely we know by now that partisanship is not sufficient. Consider how Madison and the lads disconnected the elections and varied the term lengths. House members who came in with the president are on their own in two years time. The one-third of the Senate elected with the president will never again see him on the ballot.

Therefore, most of the time presidents have to work hard to form cross-party coalitions, to convince members of Congress that what they want is good for them and their constituents. Ours is not a partisan, party-based system. Those who try to manage on a partisan basis typically fail. Nor do party members fall neatly into policy slots. And so cross-party coalitions on one issue may look very different from those on other issues. Building support is continuous. It requires that legitimate interests be heard and that deals then be made.

Otto von Bismarck is believed to have said: "If you like laws and sausages, you should never watch either one being made." That is fine for sausage, and probably for laws the way Bismarck made them. But that is nonsense for us. Take a look—a good look. Others do. Ours is the most watched system in the world, and should be. What you don't like can be changed only with your attention and participation—not with turning away. And instituting a system based on "clean" theory would do more harm than help.

One feature of a separated system that troubles critics is the potential for divided government or, as I prefer to label it, split-party government. If it is difficult to form a government in the parliamentary sense when one party has won the White House, the House of Representatives, and the Senate, then imagine the problems when each party wins a branch of government. First it is worth observing that such an outcome is a perfectly constitutional result, not a perversion. Then it is notable that voters have, in this age of modern, electronic communication, returned split-party government a majority of the time. When asked, they even profess a preference for that outcome.

Has split-party government resulted in gridlock? Not if measured by the production of major legislation, according to David R. Mayhew in his book *Divided We Govern*. There is no difference between single- and split-party government by his count. In fact, one of the most productive periods was 1973–74, when we believed at the time that government had virtually ceased to work because of Watergate.

My own detailed study of major legislation during the post–World War II period shows a rich variety of presidential-congressional interaction at all stages of lawmaking, with initiative coming from both parties and from all three elected institutions. Why should we not expect that variation in a scheme that propagates legitimate involvement by duly and independently elected representatives?

What about the system in the next century? I believe it will be more like it is and has been than what many want it to be. Reforms will be put in place, to be sure—many were in [the 104th] Congress. But present students of American politics will have no trouble recognizing their government twenty years from now. It will continue to be a separated system of diffused responsibility, broad access, institutional and federal-state competition, and cross-party alliances on issues. The strong party, presidency-centered advocates will be just as frustrated then as they are now, perhaps more so.

None of that is to say that the partisan balances will be the same. The 1994 elections resulted in a stunning reshuffling of power, displaying another variation in separated system politics. I will say something about those results since it is my belief that much is to be learned about the future from what is happening in the present.

One can sympathize with President Clinton as he struggles to find his place in the revised politics of the day. The president lost an election without being on the ballot—the only first-term elected Democrat in this century to lose both houses of Congress (Truman was not an elected president in 1946). He is experiencing what no Republican president could arrange over the past forty years—a Republican majority in the House. His present status and strategic options are defined by the congressional Republicans—not an enviable position. And so President Clinton has had to reshape a presidency that was not that well formed from the start, a challenge to cope with a rare form of split-party government.

But there is more that is historic. American political parties are criticized in presidential elections for offering, then ignoring, relatively flaccid party platforms. We surely don't expect to have explicit contracts with the voters during the state and local contests that make up a congressional midterm election.

In fact, despite the preference among many analysts for the strong party model of government, many were puzzled by Newt Gingrich's media extravaganza on September 27 when he brought House Republican candidates to Capitol Hill to sign the Contract with America. David Broder was one of the few commentators to recognize the effort as suited to party government: "Newt Gingrich . . . said at a press briefing, 'Our government operates on the party system. We are a team. And we're offering you a contract on what our team will do.' . . . That is a sound proposition. People need to be reminded that Congress writes the laws in a partisan setting . . . in which the opposing parties divide, not just for spite, but on philosophy, program and principle" (*Washington Post*, September 28, 1994, p. A23).

Most analysts were skeptical, if not mocking, of the exercise. E. J. Dionne reported: "Many Democratic strategists are gleeful because this document ties 'outsider' Republican candidates back into their congressional leadership and defines the Republicans as advocates of tattered Reagan-style tax cuts." Stanley Greenberg, Clinton's pollster, was quoted by Dionne as stating that the Republicans had made a mistake with the Contract in offering policy substance that was not popular (*Washington Post*, October 4, 1994, p. A17).

Paul Begala was quoted in the *New York Times* as very pleased with the Contract: "There is not a night I don't thank God for the contract" (October 9, 1994, p. A26). Editorial comment was scathing: "Reaganism in a rear-view mirror," "reckless," "deceptive," "duplicitous propaganda," "a gimmick." (*New York Times*, September 28, 1994, p. A20; *Washington Post*, September 28, 1994, p. A22).

Studies by my colleagues in political science will no doubt show that the Contract played a minor role with voters in the 1994 elections. In other respects, however, it was an historic development. A huge majority of Republican candidates signed the document and took it seriously. And tying "outsider" candidates into their congressional leadership is exactly what Gingrich and Co. had in mind as support for their consolidation of power in potential competition with new committee chairs.

Because much of reality is perceptual, the fact that House Republicans did much better than expected was bound to encourage talk of a mandate, that goofy concept for a separated system that is used in postelection analysis to make sense of what typically is not there. In this case the mandate was awarded to a leader who was very anxious to act.

The third historic aspect of the 104th Congress is in what was accomplished early. The House Republicans accomplished all of what they promised in the Contract—that is, to bring to a vote all of the legislative actions listed therein. More than that, they passed the overwhelming majority of the proposals brought to the floor within the time limit they set and with extraordinary party unity. Still more, they created an energy and momentum that is unprecedented for so early in a session. A president accomplishing this much in the first three months would have been labeled a political genius.

Is this a case of the effective working of the separated system? It is not. One-hundred-day deadlines are not well suited to our policy politics. Scorekeeping becomes an end in itself. There is a probable inverse relationship between a high score and good legislation. To say that the House Republicans achieved, even exceeded, the goals set in the Contract is not necessarily to point with pride to the results. Legislation by exhaustion is not recommended, nor is urgent large-scale testing of grand behavioral and structural theories of governing.

The House Republicans set an impressive agenda in this first one hundred days—one directed to basic questions about what government can do, which government ought to do it, as well as the capacity of the private sphere to solve public problems. It is surely the envy of any policy-ambitious president. But speculation abounds as to whether these will be the effects of political reform and policy change:

• Term limits will improve lawmaking.

• Denial of cash benefits will reduce teenage pregnancies.

• Block grants to the states will reduce bureaucracy.

• States are better at governing than is the nation.

• The item veto will reduce unnecessary expenditures.

• Cost-benefit analysis of regulations will limit government control.

• Capping punitive damages lowers medical care costs.

• "Loser pays" will reduce the number of frivolous lawsuits.

• Tax cuts are consistent with balancing the budget.

• A constitutional amendment will produce a balanced budget.

The quantity and complexity of legislation passed by the House and sent to the Senate in the first three months were awesome. The legislative pipeline was full even before the budget debates began. The House voted on final passage on twenty-six pieces of legislation—twenty-five wins and one loss.

Of these twenty votes on final passage, Republicans lost an average of 6 votes per bill (a range of 0 to 40, on term limits). They picked up an average of 83 Democratic votes (a range of 6 to 201). Party unity for House Republicans averaged 97 percent for the 26 votes (with a range of from 83 to 100 percent). Just one vote—term limits—fell below 90 percent unity. Republicans had 99 to 100 percent unity on 12 of the votes.

What is frightening about this record? Should we not be overjoyed that party government is here at last? It was precisely this type of lawmaking that concerned the Founders. Big questions have been answered by untested theories and with little time devoted to considering the consequences.

It is, indeed, a time for considering major shifts to achieve effectiveness of government at all levels. But in our system, devolution is to be achieved by evolution, not revolution.

That brings me to the reassurance offered by a separated system. Speaker Gingrich likes to compare this period with that in 1933. Indeed, the lamentable one-hundred-day timetable emanates from that time. Democratic presidents are fond of invoking the one-hundred-day promise; President Clinton being the most recent example with his economic and health care proposals. So far as I am aware, this is the first time a congressional leader has proposed such an ambitious program on this schedule. And he did it.

The argument for acting quickly is familiar. President Johnson summarized it well in his memoirs: "A president must always reckon that his mandate will prove short-lived." He might have added, "because it wasn't real anyway."

The separated system was sure to kick in. The House Republicans seized the initiative in setting the agenda and in formulating proposals that were fed to the other elected institutions. This is no small achievement—it is historic, as I have already pointed out.

Whereas the Senate will abide by this agenda for the most part, it will function precisely as designed. Counterproposals will be developed, action will be more deliberate, the minority party will be substantially more influential in forcing compromises, alternative theories will be propounded to those used as a basis for bills in the House, senators will take time to display their plumage.

And representatives of the two chambers will then meet in conference when passions have cooled.

I stress again the importance of the role played by Speaker Gingrich and the House Republicans. But a mandate for one of the three elected institutions is very different from one assigned to all three as led by the president (for example, 1932, 1964, and 1980). Just as the president is not the presidency and the presidency is not the government, just so the Speaker is not the House and the House is not the government (or even Congress).

What of the president's role in this version of the separated system? Of course, it depends on the person serving in the Oval Office. A president with limited domestic policy goals or one whose goals have been achieved (such as Eisenhower or Reagan in their final two years or Bush virtually from the start) can accommodate rather well to these political circumstances. They can concentrate on foreign and national security matters, employ the veto to curb congressional excesses, and participate in domestic initiatives where political gain might be realized.

\*   \*   \*

I close with these thoughts from a great and honored public servant:

Perhaps the dominant feeling about government today is distrust. The tone of most comment, whether casual or deliberate, implies that ineptitude and inadequacy are the chief characteristics of government. I do not refer merely to the current skepticism about democracy, but to the widely entertained feeling of the incapacity of government, generally, to satisfy the needs of modern society. But . . . we ask more from government than any society has ever asked. At one and the same time, we expect little from government and progressively rely on it more. We feel that the essential forces of life are no longer in the channels of politics, and yet we constantly turn to those channels for the direction of forces outside them. Generalizations like these elude proof because they are usually based on very subtle factors. But the large abstention from voting in our elections must certainly bespeak an indifference not without meaning. . . . We have not adjusted our thinking about government to the overwhelming facts of modern life, and so carry over old mental habits, traditional schoolbook platitudes and campaign slogans as to the role, the purposes, and the methods of government.

These words are a part of my reassurance. As contemporary as they sound, they were in fact delivered by Felix Frankfurter in a lecture sixty-five years ago this month. We ain't fixed yet, Mr. Justice, and probably never will be. But we ain't hopelessly broke either; and whatever we do by way of repairs, we need to be careful not to interfere too much with the current national conversation about government and its role in our lives. With regard to the structure of the separated system, be assured that the Founders built in sufficient protections to preserve even its most maddening features.

*See Lowi and Ginsberg, pp. 87–93 or brief edition, pp. 59–61*

*Like Charles O. Jones, Donald Robinson notes the value of a separated system for the purposes of checking the accumulation of power. Unlike Jones, though, Robinson focuses upon the "sense of paralysis and corruption" that accompanies divided government, and the "evidence that people may be getting a little impatient with this pattern of our politics." He proposes that we synchronize the elections of the President, the House, and the Senate to occur once every four years. This, he argues, would allow elected officials to act collectively to implement their campaign promises.*

*What do you think? Does our constitutional system inhibit effective governance? Should we amend the Constitution to allow for greater presidential authority to build public policies from electoral mandates?*

# Donald L. Robinson
# "[Does the System Need Fixing?] A Rationale,"
## from *Back to Gridlock*\*

The point of departure for reform[ing the constitutional system of separation of powers]—not just now but throughout American history and I suspect in the foreseeable future—must be people's suspicion and frustration with politics. Popular attitudes, deep and abiding in this culture, support a system that checks power. Public opinion sees advantages in such a system. Unless action is supported by large and durable majorities, it ought not to be taken. Thus, the Madisonian checks curtailed the New Deal and reigned in the Great Society. The same system saved Civil Rights in the 1980s. Now it protects the poor and the vulnerable, as well as the environment, from the mean-spirited and reckless legions in the House of Representatives.

\* Donald L. Robinson, "A Rationale" from *Back to Gridlock: Government in the Clinton Years*, edited by James Sundquist (1995). Reprinted by permission of the Brookings Institution.

At the same time we need to recognize that the status quo favors the rich and the well born, who are at great advantage by a system that stacks the odds against strong governmental and political action. Thus, when the left, from the 1930s through the 1960s, wanted to enact programs to redistribute wealth and opportunity, the system bent those programs out of shape. Now, when the populist right attempts to act on a presumed mandate to dismantle federal bureaucracy and strengthen the private sector and local governments, inertia again favors the status quo.

The American people generally approve of this moderating tendency of our political system. We want leadership, but we are also suspicious of it, and we resist the plebiscitary presidency.

Lately there is evidence that people may be getting a little impatient with this pattern of our politics. We are no longer as rich a nation as we used to be, comparatively, and we are certainly not as cocky. Our economy looks a little more vulnerable now that the dollar has fallen by 50 percent within five years against the yen; we look and feel vulnerable. Maybe we no longer can count on the abundance of this continent to ensure our position as the number one nation in the world.

Social relations also seem to be posing a more threatening challenge to our system. We wish we could protect our borders against illegal immigration. We are beginning to think we may need a stronger state than we have. At the same time, people want to hold the system more accountable. Of course, such a mood can fuel the politics of paranoia—an antidemocratic or anticonstitutionalist impulse. Thus, it behooves sensible people to ponder these moods and be ready with alternatives if the public begins to sense that panaceas like term limits and the item veto and Balanced Budget Amendments are not going to solve our problems.

Since its founding, the Committee on the Constitutional System has responded to this sense of systemic strain. We were galvanized originally in the beginning of the 1980s by a concern about deficits, which were opposed by everyone, and yet no one seemed to be able to do anything about them; and what was worse, there was no way to hold the government accountable for these deficits. There was a great deal of finger-pointing. The president was blaming Congress, Congress was blaming the president, and they were all blaming the Federal Reserve. There was no way for a voter who was concerned about deficits to punish those responsible.

In addition, we faced recurrent gridlock—a sense of paralysis and corruption, divided government. Thoughtful people banded together in the Committee on the Constitutional System to consider what could be done about these problems. There were relatively few academics involved. It was mostly people with experience in government who came together to form the committee and began to consider changes that were quite radical in the context of American history.

Now I want to relate what we have been doing to the worldwide movement around issues of constitutional form and democracy. Most of the world's constitutional systems have been parliamentary in form during the twentieth century. Many governments in Europe and nations under European influence were in crisis in the post–Second World War period, because they emphasized representation at the expense of authority and coherence and energy in government. Particularly in France and Italy, there was this sense that governments were representative to a fault and often near paralysis because they were unable to mobilize majorities to act.

The need, it was felt, was to strengthen the executive and to make it less vulnerable to majorities in the assemblies. One method was to give the prime minister power of dissolution, a whip hand, particularly in a two-party system. But many parliamentary systems withdrew from that alternative on the ground that strengthening the executive to that extent would make the prime minister too strong and invite extreme oscillations in public policy.

The trick was to keep the assembly representative (usually with a system of proportional representation)—to keep the prime minister on a short leash, vulnerable to motions of no confidence, but at the same time to find a way to give the regime strengthened executive power. The breakthrough, conceptually, came during the 1950s in France, when the Gaullists developed the model of the Fifth French Republic, which added a separately elected president to the parliamentary system of the Fourth Republic. There were other changes, too; but the essential change in the Fifth Republic was to add to the French parliamentary form of government a president, with authority in foreign affairs and able to intervene in emergencies and resolve great difficulties. A president could give government in France coherence, and energy, and the necessary authority to deal with crises.

A variant of the French form is seen in the German Federal Republic. Such "hybrid constitutionalism" (sometimes called "semi-presidentialism") is now the preferred model in Eastern Europe. The Eastern European regimes look not to the United States as the model of constitutional democracy, but instead to France and Germany. When they call on experts to come and offer counsel to them, frequently they seek folks from those Northern and Western European countries, rather than the United States.

The United States is not about to adopt a parliamentary system. We are immunized against it! We want checks and balances for the reasons I indicated earlier. At the same time, we are beginning to recognize that our government needs stronger political controls over the bureaucracy, a greater ability to act, and the voters' ability to hold the government accountable for what it does.

I have come to believe that the process adopted by parliamentary government—to think about what was wrong and adopt an institutional reform that moved it in the direction of the presidential system—is one that we ought to consider here. Perhaps there will be a convergence of constitutional forms. There is a great deal to be said for the accountability that a parliamentary system affords. Yet it lacks coherence and energy. There is much to be said for our system of separated powers, with its checks and balances. What we lack is the ability to hold executive power accountable, so that we can trust it to take leadership.

The reason we are skeptical about presidential leadership is that we are afraid we could not hold it accountable if we unleashed it from the system of separated powers. We will never trust a stronger presidency unless we are assured that we can hold it accountable. This is why, for example, we insist on retaining staggered elections. Staggered elections help to make the power of our system accountable.

One way to strengthen the president (an idea the Committee on the Constitutional System has explored a good deal) would be to coordinate the electoral cycles so that president, House, and Senate would be chosen together every four years. That would help to ensure that the government was empowered over a period of four years to enact a program, based on its electoral campaign. This idea is a good one if what we want to do is unleash presidential power for coherent leadership. But it is greeted with skepticism by the American people, because we are afraid to give presidential leadership so much power. And so, we have not had much luck in the Committee on the Constitutional System selling the idea of coordinated electoral cycles.

We will not have luck with the idea of coordinate electoral cycles until we build into the proposal some way to hold such a government to account, if within that four-year cycle it goes stray or otherwise violates the political promise in America. What we need is a system that would have enabled us, for example, in a year like 1930 or 1931, to judge that the government we put in place in 1928 was on the wrong track and needed to be reorganized.

Constitutional democracy is a quest. The jury is always out. There is certainly little impulse in the country at this time for even mild structural reform. But systems unravel quickly in this world, as we know from what happened to the Soviet Union and from seeing what is happening in Canada, Australia, and South Africa. Who could have predicted what has happened in South Africa?

We may soon, suddenly, want a government that can act—whether for left- or right-wing purposes, whether for communitarian or market-oriented goals. Americans, I trust, will never want direct, untrammeled democracy. The popular impulse must be tempered, and Americans deeply understand that. Until we are assured that referenda, for example, will not carry away our liberties, we are going to resist the impulse to move in the direction of referenda.

At the same time, we must not frustrate democracy overmuch. We need a government that can act effectively, and I hope we will insist on one we can hold accountable.

# 4

---

# The Constitutional Framework and the Individual: Civil Liberties and Civil Rights

## Civil Rights

*See Lowi and Ginsberg, pp. 129–158 or brief edition, pp. 83–95*

*In the next two selections, Abraham Lincoln and Martin Luther King, Jr. take opposing points of view about a central dilemma of how peaceful change may be achieved in a civil society: what happens when the fight for justice and equality comes into conflict with the rule of law? Are people ever justified in breaking laws for what they perceive to be the greater good? Is civil disobedience justified in some contexts? In a speech that was delivered 23 years before he became president, Lincoln argues that the laws must be followed—without adherence to laws we have no civil society. Change must come from working within the system. King disagrees, noting that people have a moral obligation to follow just laws, but they have an equally compelling duty to break unjust laws (through nonviolent means). In his "Letter From the Birmingham Jail," King outlines procedures for defining just and unjust laws and for resisting those laws that are unjust. It is perhaps ironic that despite Lincoln's admonitions about working within the system, under his leadership the bloodiest war in our nation's history was fought precisely because the central issues of states' rights and slavery could not be solved within the system. At the same time, King who argued for breaking unjust laws was actually instrumental in putting pressure on Congress ("the system") to change those laws that he and others in the Civil Rights movement identified as unjust.*

*The timeless nature of the debate between Lincoln and King is demonstrated by the current battle over abortion policy. Many pro-life activists invoke King's name to justify blocking access to abortion clinics. Pro-choice activists would probably side with Lincoln, and argue that pro-life forces, having lost the battle in the courts and legislatures, should not be able to take to the streets to impose their views unilaterally. How should King's and Lincoln's arguments be applied in this context? May King's method be applied to pro-life activists?*

# Abraham Lincoln
## "The Perpetuation of Our Political Institutions"*

In the great journal of things happening under the sun, we, the American People, find our account running, under date of the nineteenth century of the Christian era. We find ourselves in the peaceful possession, of the fairest portion of the earth, as regards extent of territory, fertility of soil, and salubrity of climate. We find ourselves under the government of a system of political institutions, conducing more essentially to the ends of civil and religious liberty, than any of which the history of former times tells us. We, when mounting the stage of existence, found ourselves the legal inheritors of these fundamental blessings. We toiled not in the acquirement or establishment of them—they are a legacy bequeathed us, by a *once* hardy, brave, and patriotic, but *now* lamented and departed race of ancestors. Theirs was the task (and nobly they performed it) to possess themselves, and through themselves, us, of this goodly land; and to uprear upon its hills and its valleys, a political edifice of liberty and equal rights; 'tis ours only, to transmit these, the former, unprofaned by the foot of an invader; the latter, undecayed by the lapse of time and untorn by usurpation, to the latest generation that fate shall permit the world to know. This task gratitude to our fathers, justice to ourselves, duty to posterity, and love for our species in general, all imperatively required us faithfully to perform.

How then shall we perform it? At what point shall we expect the approach of danger? By what means shall we fortify against it? Shall we expect some transatlantic military giant, to step the ocean, and crush us at a blow? Never! All the armies of Europe, Asia and Africa combined, with all the treasure of the earth (our own excepted) in their military chest; with a Buonaparte for a commander, could not by force take a drink from the Ohio, or make a track on the Blue Ridge, in a trial of a thousand years.

At what point then is the approach of danger to be expected? I answer, if it ever reach us, it must spring up amongst us. It cannot come from abroad. If destruction be our lot, we must ourselves be its author and finisher. As a nation of freemen, we must live through all time, or die by suicide.

I hope I am over wary; but if I am not, there is, even now, something of ill-omen, amongst us. I mean the increasing disregard for law which pervades the country; the growing disposition to substitute the wild and furious passions, in lieu of the sober judgment of Courts; and the worse than savage mobs, for the executive ministers of justice. This disposition is awfully fearful in any community; and that it now exists in ours, though grating to our feelings to admit, it would be a violation of truth, and an insult to our intelligence, to deny. Accounts of outrages committed by

* Abraham Lincoln, "The Perpetuation of Our Political Institutions" in *Abraham Lincoln: His Speeches and Writings*, ed. by Roy P. Basler (Cleveland: World Pub. Co., 1946).

mobs, form the everyday news of the times. They have pervaded the country, from New England to Louisiana; they are neither peculiar to the eternal snows of the former, nor the burning suns of the latter; they are not the creature of climate—neither are they confined to the slaveholding, or the non-slaveholding States. Alike, they spring up among the pleasure hunting masters of Southern slaves, and the order loving citizens of the land of steady habits. Whatever, then, their cause may be, it is common to the whole country.

It would be tedious, as well as useless, to recount the horrors of all of them. Those happening in the State of Mississippi, and at St. Louis, are, perhaps, the most dangerous in example and revolting to humanity. In the Mississippi case, they first commenced by hanging the regular gamblers; a set of men, certainly not following for a livelihood, a very useful, or very honest occupation; but one which, so far from being forbidden by the laws, was actually licensed by an act of the Legislature, passed but a single year before. Next, negroes, suspected of conspiring to raise an insurrection, were caught up and hanged in all parts of the State: then, white men, supposed to be leagued with the negroes; and finally, strangers, from neighboring States, going thither on business, were, in many instances, subjected to the same fate. Thus went on this process of hanging, from gamblers to negroes, from negroes to white citizens, and from these to strangers; till, dead men were seen literally dangling from the boughs of trees upon every road side; and in numbers almost sufficient, to rival the native Spanish moss of the country, as a drapery of the forest.

Turn, then, to that horror-striking scene at St. Louis. A single victim was only sacrificed there. His story is very short; and is, perhaps, the most highly tragic, of anything of its length, that has ever been witnessed in real life. A mulatto man, by the name of McIntosh, was seized in the street, dragged to the suburbs of the city, chained to a tree, and actually burned to death; and all within a single hour from the time he had been a freeman, attending to his own business, and at peace with the world.

Such are the effects of mob law; and such are the scenes, becoming more and more frequent in this land so lately famed for love of law and order; and the stories of which have even now grown too familiar, to attract any thing more than an idle remark.

But you are, perhaps, ready to ask, "What has this to do with the perpetuation of our political institutions?" I answer, it has much to do with it. Its direct consequences are, comparatively speaking, but a small evil; and much of its danger consists, in the proneness of our minds, to regard its direct as its only consequences. Abstractly considered, the hanging of the gamblers at Vicksburg was of but little consequence. They constitute a portion of population that is worse than useless in any community; and their death, if no pernicious example be set by it, is never matter of reasonable regret with anyone. If they were annually swept from the stage of existence by the plague or small pox, honest men would, perhaps, be much profited by the operation. Similar too, is the correct reasoning, in regard to the burning of the negro at St. Louis. He had forfeited his life, by the perpetration of an outrageous murder, upon one of the most worthy and respectable citizens of the city; and had he not died as he did, he must have died by the sentence of the law, in a very short time afterwards. As to him alone, it was as well the way it was, as it could otherwise have been. But the example in either case was fearful. When men take it in their heads today, to hang gamblers, or burn murderers, they should recollect, that, in the confusion usually attending such transactions, they will be as likely to hang or burn someone who is neither a gambler nor a murderer as one who is; and that, acting upon the example they set, the mob of tomorrow, may, and probably will, hang or burn some of them by the very same mistake. And not only so; the innocent, those who have ever set their faces against violations of law in every shape, alike with the guilty, fall victims to the ravages of mob law; and thus it goes on, step by step, till all the walls erected for the defence of the persons and property of individuals, are trodden down, and disregarded. But all this even, is not the full extent of the evil. By such examples, by instances of the perpetrators of such acts going unpunished, the lawless in spirit are encouraged to become lawless in practice; and having been used to no restraint, but dread of punishment, they thus become absolutely unrestrained. Having ever regarded Government as their deadliest bane, they make a jubilee of the suspension of its operations; and pray for nothing so much as its total annihilation. While, on the other hand, good men, men who love tranquility, who desire to abide by the laws, and enjoy their benefits, who would gladly spill their blood in the defence of their country; seeing their property destroyed; their families insulted, and their lives endangered; their persons injured; and seeing nothing in prospect that forebodes a change for the better; become tired of, and disgusted with, a Government that offers them no protection; and are not much averse to a change in which they imagine they have nothing to lose. Thus, then, by the operation of this mobocratic spirit, which all must admit is now abroad in the land, the strongest bulwark of any Government, and particularly of those constituted like ours, may effectually be broken down and destroyed—I mean the *attachment* of the People. Whenever this effect shall be produced among us, whenever the vicious portion of population shall be permitted to gather in bands of hundreds and thousands, and burn churches, ravage and rob provision-stores, throw printing presses into rivers, shoot editors, and hang and burn obnoxious persons at pleasure, and with impunity, depend on it, this Government cannot last. By such things, the feelings of the best citizens will become more or less alienated from it; and thus it will be left without friends, or with too few, and those few too weak, to make their friendship effectual. At such a time and under such circumstances, men of sufficient talent and ambition will not be wanting to seize the opportunity, strike the blow, and overturn that fair fabric which for the last half century has been the fondest hope of the lovers of freedom, throughout the world.

I know the American People are *much* attached to their Government; I know they would suffer *much* for its sake; I know they would endure evils long and patiently, before they would ever think of exchanging it for another. Yet, notwithstanding all this, if the laws be continually despised and disregarded, if their rights to be secure in their persons and property are held by no better tenure than the caprice of a mob, the alienation of their affections from the Government is the natural consequence; and to that, sooner or later, it must come.

Here then, is one point at which danger may be expected.

The question recurs, "how shall we fortify against it?" The answer is simple. Let every American, every lover of liberty, every well-wisher to his posterity, swear by the blood of the Revolution never to violate in the least particular the laws of the country; and never to tolerate their violation by others. As the patriots of seventy-six did to the support of the Declaration of Independence, so to the support of the Constitution and Laws, let every American pledge his life, his property, and his sacred honor; let every man remember that to violate the law is to trample on the blood of his father, and to tear the character of his own, and his children's liberty. Let reverence for the laws be breathed by every American mother to the lisping babe that prattles on her lap—let it be taught in schools, in seminaries, and in colleges; let it be written in Primers, spelling books, and in Almanacs; let it be preached from the pulpit, proclaimed in legislative halls, and enforced in courts of justice. And, in short, let it become the *political religion* of the nation; and let the old and the young, the rich and the poor, the grave and the gay, of all sexes and tongues, and colors and conditions, sacrifice unceasingly upon its altars.

While ever a state of feeling, such as this, shall universally, or even, very generally prevail throughout the nation, vain will be every effort, and fruitless every attempt, to subvert our national freedom.

When I so pressingly urge a strict observance of all the laws, let me not be understood as saying there are no bad laws, nor that grievances may not arise, for the redress of which, no legal provisions have been made. I mean to say no such thing. But I do mean to say that, although bad laws, if they exist, should be repealed as soon as possible, still while they continue in force, for the sake of example they should be religiously observed. So also in unprovided cases. If such arise, let proper legal provisions be made for them with the least possible delay; but, till then, let them, if not too intolerable, be borne with.

There is no grievance that is a fit object of redress by mob law. In any case that arises, as for instance, the promulgation of abolitionism, one of two positions is necessarily true; that is, the thing is right within itself, and therefore deserves the protection of all law and all good citizens; or, it is wrong, and therefore proper to be prohibited by legal enactments; and in neither case, is the interposition of mob law, either necessary, justifiable, or excusable. . . .

[*Lincoln observes that the legacy of the American Revolution has inspired men to distinguish themselves while rejecting the common path.*]

But this state of feeling *must fade, is fading, has faded*, with the circumstances that produced it.

I do not mean to say, that the scenes of the revolution *are now* or *ever will* be entirely forgotten; but that like everything else, they must fade upon the memory of the world, and grow more and more dim by the lapse of time. In history, we hope, they will be read of, and recounted, so long as the bible shall be read; but even granting that they will, their influence *cannot be* what it heretofore has been. Even then, they *cannot be* so universally known, nor so vividly felt, as they were by the generation just gone to rest. At the close of that struggle, nearly every adult male had been a participator in some of its scenes. The consequence was, that of those scenes, in the form of a husband, a father, a son or a brother, *a living history* was to be found in every family—a history bearing the indubitable testimonies of its own authenticity, in the limbs mangled, in the scars of wounds received, in the midst of the very scenes related—a history, too, that could be read and understood alike by all, the wise and the ignorant, the learned and the unlearned. But *those* histories are gone. They *can* be read no more forever. They *were* a fortress of strength; but, what invading foeman could *never do*, the silent artillery of time *has done*; the leveling of its walls. They are gone. They *were* a forest of giant oaks; but the all-resistless hurricane has swept over them, and left only, here and there, a lonely trunk, despoiled of its verdure, shorn of its foliage; unshading and unshaded, to murmur in a few more gentle breezes, and to combat with its mutilated limbs, a few more ruder storms, then to sink, and be no more.

They *were* the pillars of the temple of liberty; and now that they have crumbled away, that temple must fall, unless we, their descendants, supply their places with other pillars, hewn from the solid quarry of sober reason. Passion has helped us; but can do so no more. It will in future be our enemy. Reason, cold, calculating, unimpassioned reason, must furnish all the materials for our future support and defence. Let those materials be molded into *general intelligence, sound morality*, and, in particular, *a reverence for the constitution and laws*: and, that we improved to the last; that we remained free to the last; that we revered his name to the last; that, during his long sleep, we permitted no hostile foot to pass over or desecrate his resting place; shall be that which to learn the last trump shall awaken our WASHINGTON.

Upon these let the proud fabric of freedom rest, as the rock of its basis; and as truly as has been said of the only greater institution, *"the gates of hell shall not prevail against it."*

# Martin Luther King, Jr.
## "Letter from Birmingham Jail, 1963"*

*The "Negro Revolution" of the 1950s and early 1960s, which in the public mind had its beginning in the 1954 Supreme Court decision desegregating public schools, generally followed two paths: lawsuits pressed in state and federal courts, and the direct action programs of such organizations as the National Association for the Advancement of Colored People (NAACP), Congress of Racial Equality (CORE), and the Southern Christian Leadership Conference (SCLC). The Reverend Martin Luther King, Jr., who urged the tactic of passive resistance—Negroes, he said, should meet "physical force with an even stronger force, namely, soul force"—assumed the presidency of the SCLC and leadership of the new nonviolent protest movement. King and his followers chose Birmingham, Alabama, as the target of their antisegregation drive of 1963. King explained the choice: "If Birmingham could be cracked, the direction of the entire nonviolent movement in the South could take a significant turn." While King's group was pressing a boycott that crippled business and forced Birmingham businessmen to negotiate a desegregation agreement, Attorney General Robert F. Kennedy acted to secure the immediate registration of more than 2,000 Birmingham Negroes previously denied voting rights. Federal courts upheld the right of Negroes to nonviolent protest in Birmingham and elsewhere, but not before King had been arrested and jailed. The following letter (reprinted here in part), written from his cell on April 16, 1963, contained King's answer to charges by a group of eight Birmingham clergymen that he was in their city as an "outside agitator."*

Source: *Christian Century*, June 12, 1963.

My Dear Fellow Clergymen:

While confined here in the Birmingham City Jail, I came across your recent statement calling my present activities "unwise and untimely." Seldom do I pause to answer criticism of my work and ideas. If I sought to answer all the criticisms that cross my desk, my secretaries would have little time for anything other than such correspondence in the course of the day, and I would have no time for constructive work. But since I feel that you are men of genuine goodwill and that your criticisms are sincerely set forth, I want to try to answer your statement in what I hope will be patient and reasonable terms.

I think I should indicate why I am here in Birmingham, since you have been influenced by the view which argues against "outsiders coming in." I have the honor of serving as president of the Southern Christian Leadership Conference, an organization operating in every Southern state, with headquarters in Atlanta, Georgia. We have some eighty-five affiliate organizations across the South, and one of them is the Alabama Christian Movement for Human Rights. Frequently, we share staff, educational, and financial resources with our affiliates. Several months ago the affiliate here in Birmingham asked us to be on call to engage in a nonviolent direct-action program if such were deemed necessary. We readily consented, and when the hour came we lived up to our promise. So I, along with several members of my staff, am here because I was invited here. I am here because I have organizational ties here.

But more basically, I am in Birmingham because injustice exists here. Just as the prophets of the 8th century B.C. left their villages and carried their "thus saith the Lord" far afield, and just as the apostle Paul left his village of Tarsus and carried the gospel of Jesus Christ to the far corners of the Greco-Roman world, so am I compelled to carry the gospel of freedom beyond my own hometown. Like Paul, I must constantly respond to the Macedonian call for aid.

Moreover, I am cognizant of the interrelatedness of all communities and states. I cannot sit idly by in Atlanta and not be concerned about what happens in Birmingham. Injustice anywhere is a threat to justice everywhere. We are caught in an inescapable network of mutuality, tied in a single garment of destiny. Whatever affects one directly affects all indirectly. Never again can we afford to live with the narrow, provincial "outside agitator" idea. Anyone who lives inside the United States can never be considered an outsider anywhere within its bounds.

You deplore the demonstrations taking place in Birmingham. But your statement, I am sorry to say, fails to express a similar concern for the conditions that brought about the demonstrations. I am sure that none of you would want to rest content with the superficial kind of social analysis that deals merely with effects and does not grapple with underlying causes. It is unfortunate that demonstrations are taking place in Birmingham, but it is even more unfortunate that the city's white power structure left the Negro community with no alternative. . . .

You may well ask, "Why direct action? Why sit-ins, marches, etc.? Isn't negotiation a better path?" You are quite right in calling for negotiation. Indeed, this is the very purpose of direct action. Nonviolent direct action seeks to foster such a tension that a community which has constantly refused to negotiate is forced to confront the issue. It seeks so to dramatize the issue that it can no longer be ignored. My citing the creation of tension as part of the work of the nonviolent resister may sound rather shocking. But I readily acknowledge that I am not afraid of the word "tension." I have earnestly opposed violent tension, but there is a type of constructive, nonviolent tension which is necessary for growth. Just as Socrates felt that it was necessary to create a tension in the mind so that individuals could shake off the bondage of myths and half-truths and rise to the realm of creative analysis and objective appraisal, so must we see the need for nonviolent gadflies to create the kind of tension in society that will help men rise from the dark depths of prejudice and racism to the majestic heights of understanding and brotherhood.

The purpose of our direct-action program is to create a situation so crisis-packed that it will inevitably open the door to negotiation. I therefore concur with you in your call for negotiation. Too long has our beloved Southland been bogged down in a tragic effort to live in monologue rather than dialogue. . . .

We have waited for more than 340 years for our constitutional and God-given rights. The nations of Asia and Africa are moving with jetlike speed toward gaining political independence, but we still creep at horse-and-buggy pace toward gaining a cup of coffee at a lunch counter. Perhaps it is easy for those who have never felt the stinging darts of segregation to say "Wait." But when you have seen vicious mobs lynch your mothers and fathers at will and drown your sisters and brothers at whim; when you have seen hate-filled policemen curse, kick, and even kill your black brothers and sisters with impunity; when you see the vast majority of your 20 million Negro brothers smothering in an air-tight cage of poverty in the midst of an affluent society; when you suddenly find your tongue twisted as you seek to explain to your six-year-old daughter why she can't go to the public amusement park that has just been advertised on television, and see tears welling up when she is told that Funtown is closed to colored children, and see ominous clouds of inferiority beginning to form in her little mental sky, and see her beginning to distort her personality by unconsciously developing a bitterness toward white people; when you have to concoct an answer for a five-year-old son asking, "Daddy, why do white people treat colored people so mean?"; when you take a cross-country drive and find it necessary to sleep night after night in the uncomfortable corners of your automobile because no motel will accept you; when you are humiliated day in and day out by nagging signs reading "white" and "colored"; when your first name becomes "nigger," your middle name becomes "boy" (however old you are), and your last name becomes "John," and your wife and mother are never given the respected title "Mrs."; when you are harried by day and haunted by night by the fact that you are a Negro, never quite knowing what to expect next, and are plagued with inner fears and outer resentments; when you are forever fighting a degenerating sense of "nobodiness"—then you will understand why we find it difficult to wait. There comes a time when the cup of endurance runs over, and men are no longer willing to be plunged into an abyss of injustice where they experience the bleakness of corroding despair. I hope, sirs, you can understand our legitimate and unavoidable impatience.

You express a great deal of anxiety over our willingness to break laws. This is certainly a legitimate concern. Since we so diligently urge people to obey the Supreme Court's decision of 1954 outlawing segregation in the public schools, at first glance it may seem rather paradoxical for us consciously to break laws. One may well ask, "How can you advocate breaking some laws and obeying others?" The answer lies in the fact that there are two types of laws: just and unjust. I agree with St. Augustine that "an unjust law is no law at all." . . .

Let us consider some of the ways in which a law can be unjust. A law is unjust, for example, if the majority group compels a minority group to obey the statute but does not make it binding on itself. By the same token, a law in all probability is just if the majority is itself willing to obey it. Also, a law is unjust if it is inflicted on a minority that, as a result of being denied the right to vote, had no part in enacting or devising the law. Who can say that the legislature of Alabama which set up that state's segregation laws was democratically elected? Throughout Alabama all sorts of devious methods are used to prevent Negroes from becoming registered voters, and there are some counties in which, even though Negroes constitute a majority of the population, not a single Negro is registered. Can any law enacted under such circumstances be considered democratically structured?

Sometimes a law is just on its face and unjust in its application. For instance, I have been arrested on a charge of parading without a permit. Now there is nothing wrong in having an ordinance which requires a permit for a parade. But such an ordinance becomes unjust when it is used to maintain segregation and to deny citizens the First Amendment privilege of peaceful assembly and protest.

I hope you are able to see the distinction I am trying to point out. In no sense do I advocate evading the law, as would the rabid segregationist. That would lead to anarchy. One who breaks an unjust law must do so *openly, lovingly,* and with a willingness to accept the penalty. I submit that an individual who breaks a law that conscience tells him is unjust and who willingly accepts the penalty of imprisonment in order to arouse the conscience of the community over its injustice is in reality expressing the highest respect for law. . . .

I must make two honest confessions to you, my Christian and Jewish brothers. First, I must confess that over the past few years I have been gravely disappointed with the white moderate. I have almost reached the regrettable conclusion that the Negro's great stumbling block in his stride toward freedom is not the White Citizen's Counciler or the Ku Klux Klanner but the white moderate who is more devoted to "order" than to justice; who prefers a negative peace which is the absence of tension to a positive peace which is the presence of justice; who constantly says "I agree with you in the goal you seek, but I cannot agree with your methods"; who paternalistically believes he can set the timetable for another man's freedom; who lives by a mythical concept of time and who constantly advises the Negro to wait for a "more convenient season." Shallow understanding from people of goodwill is more frustrating than absolute misunderstanding from people of ill will. Lukewarm acceptance is much more bewildering than outright rejection.

I had hoped that the white moderate would understand that law and order exist for the purpose of establishing justice and that when they fail in this purpose they block social progress. I had hoped that the white moderate would understand that the present tension in the South is a necessary phase of the transition from an obnoxious negative peace, in which the Negro passively accepted his unjust plight, to a substantive and positive peace, in which all men will respect the dignity and worth of human personality. Actually, we who engage in nonviolent direct action are not the creators of tension. We merely bring to the surface the hidden tension that is already alive. We bring it out in the open where it can be seen and dealt with. Like a boil that can never be cured so long as it is covered up but must be opened with all its pus-flowing ugliness to the natural medicines of air and light, injustice must be exposed, with all the tension its exposure creates, to the light of human conscience and the air of national opinion before it can be cured. . . .

You speak of our activity in Birmingham as extreme. At first I was rather disappointed that fellow clergymen would see my nonviolent efforts as those of an extremist. I began thinking about the fact that I stand in the middle of two opposing forces in the Negro community. One is a force of complacency made up of Negroes who, as a result of long years of oppression, are so completely drained of self-respect and a sense of "somebodiness" that they have adjusted to segregation, and of a few middle-class Negroes who, because of a degree of academic and economic security and because in some ways they profit by segregation, have unconsciously become insensitive to the problems of the masses. The other force is one of bitterness and hatred, and it comes perilously close to advocating violence. It is expressed in the various black nationalist groups that are springing up across the nation, the largest and best-known being Elijah Muhammad's Muslim movement. Nourished by the Negro's frustration over the continued existence of racial discrimination, this movement is made up of people who have lost faith in America, who have absolutely repudiated Christianity, and who have concluded that the white man is an incorrigible "devil."

I have tried to stand between these two forces, saying that we need emulate neither the "do-nothingism" of the complacent nor the hatred of the black nationalist. For there is the more excellent way of love and nonviolent protest. I am grateful to God that, through the influence of the Negro church, the way of nonviolence became an integral part of our struggle.

If this philosophy had not emerged, by now many streets of the South would, I am convinced, be flowing with blood. And I am further convinced that if our white brothers dismiss as "rabble-rousers" and "outside agitators" those of us who employ nonviolent direct action and if they refuse to support our nonviolent efforts, millions of Negroes will, out of frustration and despair, seek solace and security in black nationalist ideologies—a development that would inevitably lead to a frightening racial nightmare. . . .

Let me take note of my other major disappointment. Though there are some notable exceptions, I have also been disappointed with the white church and its leadership. I do not say this as one of those negative critics who can always find something wrong with the church. I say this as a minister of the gospel, who loves the church; who was nurtured in its bosom;

who has been sustained by its spiritual blessings and who will remain true to it as long as the cord of life shall lengthen.

When I was suddenly catapulted into the leadership of the bus protest in Montgomery, Alabama, a few years ago, I felt we would be supported by the white church. I felt that the white ministers, priests, and rabbis of the South would be among our strongest allies. Instead, some have been outright opponents, refusing to understand the freedom movement and misrepresenting its leaders; all too many others have been more cautious than courageous and have remained silent and secure behind stained-glass windows.

In spite of my shattered dreams I came to Birmingham with the hope that the white religious leadership of this community would see the justice of our cause and with deep moral concern would serve as the channel through which our just grievances could reach the power structure. But again I have been disappointed.

I have heard numerous Southern religious leaders admonish their worshipers to comply with a desegregation decision because it is the *law*, but I have longed to hear white ministers declare, "Follow this decree because integration is morally *right* and because the Negro is your brother." In the midst of blatant injustices inflicted upon the Negro I have watched white churchmen stand on the sideline and mouth pious irrelevancies and sanctimonious trivialities. In the midst of a mighty struggle to rid our nation of racial and economic injustice I have heard many ministers say, "Those are social issues with which the gospel has no real concern," and I have watched many churches commit themselves to a completely otherworldly religion which makes a strange, unbiblical distinction between body and soul, between the sacred and the secular.

We are moving toward the close of the twentieth century with a religious community largely adjusted to the status quo—a taillight behind other community agencies rather than a headlight leading men to higher levels of justice. . . .

But the judgment of God is upon the church as never before. If today's church does not recapture the sacrificial spirit of the early church, it will lose its authenticity, forfeit the loyalty of millions, and be dismissed as an irrelevant social club with no meaning for the twentieth century. Every day I meet young people whose disappointment with the church has turned into outright disgust.

Perhaps I have once again been too optimistic. Is organized religion too inextricably bound to the status quo to save our nation and the world? Perhaps I must turn my faith to the inner spiritual church, the church within the church, as the true *ecclesia* and the hope of the world. But again I am thankful to God that some noble souls from the ranks of organized religion have broken loose from the paralyzing chains of conformity and joined us as active partners in the struggle for freedom. They have left their secure congregations and walked the streets of Albany, Georgia, with us. They have gone down the highways of the South on torturous rides for freedom. Yes, they have gone to jail with us. Some have been kicked out of their churches, have lost the support of their bishops and fellow ministers. But they have acted in the faith that right defeated is stronger than evil triumphant. Their witness has been the spiritual salt that has preserved the true meaning of the gospel in these troubled times. They have carved a tunnel of hope through the dark mountain of disappointment.

I hope the church as a whole will meet the challenge of this decisive hour. But even if the church does not come to the aid of justice, I have no despair about the future. I have no fear about the outcome of our struggle in Birmingham, even if our motives are at present misunderstood. We will reach the goal of freedom in Birmingham and all over the nation, because the goal of America is freedom. . . .

Before closing I feel impelled to mention one other point in your statement that has troubled me profoundly. You warmly commended the Birmingham police force for keeping "order" and "preventing violence." I doubt that you would have so warmly commended the police force if you had seen its angry dogs sinking their teeth into six unarmed, nonviolent Negroes. I doubt that you would so quickly commend the policemen if you were to observe their ugly and inhuman treatment of Negroes here in the City Jail; if you were to watch them push and curse old Negro women and young Negro girls; if you were to see them slap and kick old Negro men and young boys; if you were to observe them, as they did on two occasions, refuse to give us food because we wanted to sing our grace together. I cannot join you in your praise of the Birmingham Police Department.

It is true that the police have exercised discipline in handling the demonstrators. In this sense they have conducted themselves rather "nonviolently" in public. But for what purpose? To preserve the evil system of segregation. Over the past few years I have consistently preached that nonviolence demands that the means we use must be as pure as the ends we seek. I have tried to make clear that it is wrong to use immoral means to attain moral ends. But now I must affirm that it is just as wrong, or perhaps even more so, to use moral means to preserve immoral ends. Perhaps Mr. Connor and his policemen have been rather nonviolent in public, as was Chief Pritchett in Albany, Georgia, but they have used the moral means of nonviolence to maintain the immoral end of racial injustice. As T. S. Eliot has said, there is no greater treason than to do the right deed for the wrong reason.

I wish you had commended the Negro sit-inners and demonstrators of Birmingham for their sublime courage, their willingness to suffer and their amazing discipline in the midst of great provocation. One day the South will recognize its real heroes. . . . One day the South will know that when these disinherited children of God sat down at lunch counters they were in reality standing up for what is best in the American dream and for the most sacred values in our Judeo-Christian heritage, thereby bringing our nation back to those great wells of democracy which were dug deep by the founding fathers in their formulation of the Constitution and the Declaration of Independence.

# DEBATING THE ISSUES:
# AFFIRMATIVE ACTION

*See Lowi and Ginsberg, pp. 146–147 or brief edition, pp. 92–93*

The Civil Rights Act of 1964 ensured, at least on paper, that all Americans would enjoy equality of opportunity. But even after 1964, blacks continued to lag behind whites in socioeconomic status, because of enduring racism and gross inequalities in the distribution of income and the quality of education. Beginning in 1965, President Johnson tried to address these inequalities with a policy of affirmative action, which, as the text defines, is "a policy of compensatory action to overcome the consequences of past discrimination." By executive order, Johnson required all federal agencies and government contractors to submit written proposals to hire certain numbers of blacks, women, Asian-Americans, and Native Americans within various job categories. Throughout the 1970s and 1980s, affirmative action programs grew in the private sector and throughout higher education. Through such programs, employers and universities gave preferential treatment to minorities and women, either to make up for past patterns of discrimination or to pursue the general goals of diversity. These policies have created resentment in many whites who claim that they are the victims of reverse discrimination, and frustration in many blacks and other minorities who believe that the programs stand in the way of real progress toward an equal society. Affirmative action is without question one of the most controversial and difficult issues in American politics.

Shelby Steele, a research fellow at the Stanford University Hoover Institute, argues that affirmative action policies merely protect us from confronting and dealing with our vulnerabilities as white and black Americans. Steele argues that two stereotypes define the racial tensions in this country: "that whites are racist and blacks are inferior." Steele argues that, rather than confronting these stereotypes, affirmative action allows black Americans and black political leaders to claim victimization from racism, and whites to show deference to black victimization that takes a form of "virtuous activism." It is our fear of confronting who we are historically and what that means for the way we live together today that prevents us from going forward toward a society where all races are competitive. Deference through affirmative action for blacks and other minorities, Steele argues, is no substitute for a truly virtuous society.

Support for affirmative action programs, however, remains very strong. Representative Sheila Jackson Lee (D-Texas), offers a vigorous defense of affirmative action. Her argument is straightforward: minorities and women still lack equal opportunities in education, employment, housing, and voting. Individual and institutional discrimination continues to block equal levels of participation throughout society. Because discrimination is based upon race and gender, Jackson Lee argues, we must "fashion remedies that take race and gender into account."

Political scientist James Q. Wilson critiques affirmative action programs in the university setting. Preferential treatment, he argues, is not only unfair, it is detrimental to the achievements and intellectual strength of our universities. Wil-

*son argues that the best way to "mend not end" affirmative action is to apply it strictly to undergraduate college admissions, and end preferential treatment for admissions to professional and graduate programs. Three or four years of college, Wilson argues, will allow the brightest students who were denied a strong elementary and secondary education to "catch up." Beyond the undergraduate level, however, affirmative action programs run counter to core principles of excellence and merit. Even at the undergraduate level, Wilson argues, the guidelines for affirmative action programs in California run counter to the definition of compensation for past wrongs: Asian Americans, held in inland camps during World War II and the focus of blatant discrimination in California historically, are not included among underrepresented minority groups.*

*What do you think? Are affirmative action programs the way to achieve social equality? What other ways could the government promote the goal of ending discrimination? After reading Shelby Steele's argument, do you think government has a role to play in promoting greater racial and gender equality? Is there any way to balance the competing claims of whites and minority groups?*

# Shelby Steele
## "The Race Not Run"*

President Clinton, General Colin Powell and former Senator Bob Dole share a fascinating if dubious distinction: they have all pulled back from a principled disenchantment with preferential affirmative action into a qualified tolerance of it. Dole is the least tolerant of the three, yet even he has lost enthusiasm for legislation he himself introduced last year to end it, and while tacitly supporting the California Civil Rights Initiative he has distanced himself from it. In his 1995 autobiography Powell declared, "If it leads to preferential treatment . . . I am opposed," but by this summer's Republican convention he had emerged as one of affirmative action's most vocal proponents. All three claim it was principle that first led them to question the double standard inherent in race and gender preferences. But then, after signaling their doubts, each seemed to run into something. There were hesitations, long investigations and, finally, very calculated repositionings. Something chastened them into an embarrassing pragmatism, in which principle seemed premature and even extreme and in which the crafted statement seemed wiser than the grandstand.

I don't think it was some fresh encounter with American racism. Nor do I believe that people who support affirmative action do so because they believe discrimination is rampant in America. Preferential policies are most vigorously supported in institutions like universities, government agencies and corporations, where all agree that discrimination has sharply declined over the last thirty years. (With the glaring exception of Asians, when was the last time a person of color was discriminated against in ad-

* Shelby Steele, "The Race Not Run: Fear and the Roots of Affirmative Action" in *The New Republic*, (October 7, 1996). Copyright © 1996 by The New Republic, Inc. Reprinted with permission.

missions at an American university?) I am also unconvinced that "diversity" really justifies preferences for most people. It is simply not plausible that people can muster the sort of passion we see in many supporters of preferences for an idea as amorphous as diversity—an idea no two people define in the same way. Diversity is a word-cover, a term of high sentiment that we use when we don't know, or are unwilling to admit, what really motivates us.

So I don't think Clinton, Powell and Dole ran into diversity. I believe they hit what I have elsewhere called racial vulnerability—the fact that blacks and whites living today are remarkably vulnerable to their race's historical reputations and stereotypes. An unacknowledged dilemma for Americans of racial goodwill is that we can all be shamed by the same sad racial history that we work to overcome.

The main stereotypes are that whites are racist and blacks are inferior. A white or black child born in America today, utterly fresh to the world, will grow up under either the first Kafkaesque accusation or the second. They will not necessarily believe what history accuses them of—stereotypes are internalized as self-doubt rather than as belief. But even whites who are as free of racism as it is possible to be will be vulnerable to powerful doubts about their racial innocence when blacks accuse them of racism. In fact, this vulnerability may cause *more* anxiety in whites who have earnestly worked to put themselves beyond racism, since their investment in racial innocence is greater. Conversely, blacks are outraged at a book like *The Bell Curve* by Charles Murray and Richard J. Herrnstein because it triggers their vulnerability to the stereotype of inferiority.

It doesn't matter that the stereotype of black inferiority was never inherently true while the accusation of white racism essentially was. Racial vulnerability is *situational*, an outgrowth of integrated situations *today* in which the mere presence of the other race opens our vulnerability to stereotypes of our own. The sometimes awkward labor of integrated situations has to do with the pains we must take not to set off each other's vulnerabilities—an effort that ironically requires us to memorize the damning stereotypes of each other's group.

These are the racial vulnerabilities that I believe Clinton, Powell, Dole and millions of other Americans run into when they have to think seriously about group preferences. The affirmative action debate of the last few years is the *situation* that has triggered the racial vulnerabilities of many Americans. And no doubt it was suppressed for the two decades since its birth to keep this from happening. It is a measure of how fundamentally wrong group preferences are that this debate could no longer be evaded despite the vulnerabilities it has exposed us to.

Because we find our vulnerabilities unbearable, we *recompose* them into narratives we can live with. I don't say to myself that, as a black person, integrated situations trigger my vulnerabilities because I worry unconsciously that I might do something to *confirm* an ugly stereotype of blacks. I instead tell myself that such situations are ripe with racism and, thus, stacked against me.

Whites on the left tend to recompose their vulnerability to the stereotype of whites as racists into an exaggerated deference toward minorities. The white liberal does not say he feels vulnerable to being arbitrarily shamed by the charge of racism or that on some level he may doubt himself in that regard. He says instead that his racial goodwill, his inherent racial innocence, commits him to a politics in which deference to black victimization is a kind of virtuous activism. (Of course, not all whites respond to black accusations with uncritical deference. Some try to ignore them, and others relieve their anxiety with anger. But the anxiety itself is common to whites of all ideologies.)

One of the main reasons we make bad public policy around race—and a policy like group preferences that becomes more divisive with time is undoubtedly bad—is that we use these policies to confirm the recomposed version of ourselves rather than to overcome our actual vulnerabilities. Preferences gave liberal whites the chance to show deference to black victimization, and they give the black leadership the chance to keep asserting that racism is the main problem that blacks face. One recomposition symbiotically feeds the other through a preferential policy that is unfair on its face.

However, while there is some truth in these recompositions (deference sometimes *is* a display of real virtue, and victimization sometimes *does* explain black difficulty), the far greater truth is in the vulnerabilities that produce them. Neither race has yet done what is necessary to affirm itself against the accusations it is vulnerable to. An activism of deference will not affirm that whites are not racists (uncritical deference to the black "victim" is a form of racism). And the insistence that black difficulty is still the result of racism will not affirm blacks against the stereotype of inferiority.

These vulnerabilities are America's true racial challenge. A healthy democracy cannot abide white racism or the developmental inferiority imposed on blacks by America's history of racism. Yet even our thinking about race is controlled by a deferential language grounded in our recompositions. Words like "diversity," "multiculturalism," "inclusion" and "pluralism" say little more than that white deference answers minority victimization. And out of this disingenuous language universities, government agencies and corporations make all manner of race-based, preferential policies that again highlight white deference as the redemption of black victimization. Such policy amounts to a form of protectionism: it gives credence to our recompositions so we don't have to face our racial vulnerabilities.

Protectionism may be the truest purpose of affirmative action. By supporting it whites agree to see blacks as victims rather than as inferiors, and in return blacks agree to see whites as people of racial goodwill rather than as racists. Sadly, this quid pro quo, in which deference to the other race's vulnerability buys protection from one's own, is the only real contract that exists between blacks and whites on a policy level.

After almost thirty years of living with this contract, deference has become the American idea of social virtue. At the center of our national social conscience is the idea that virtue is served more by helping people hide from their vulnerabilities than by helping them to overcome them. Such a concept of virtue makes many good things bad. Merit, excellence, individual initiative, achievement are now dishonored in our society (at least in relation to minorities) because they are not deferential or protective. They buy whites no currency with blacks and blacks no currency with whites. In pursuing excellence or taking initiative we inevitably meet with setbacks and failures—experiences that seem to confirm ugly stereotypes of inferiority. Because these principles expose us to the stereotypes that make us vulnerable, we come to think of them as mean and oppressive—despite the fact that they are the only principles that can truly help us conquer our vulnerabilities. Our contract of mutual protection through deference forces us into a relativism that asks nothing much of anybody. What does it take to celebrate diversity? And yet, with the mere announcement that you favor it, you can win protection from the vulnerabilities that haunt you.

Political correctness, in all its myriad manifestations, is deferential relativism taken to the level of manners. It is the code that enforces mutual protection through deference in daily life. P.C. forces us to take each other's recompositions with grave seriousness and to ignore the real vulnerabilities behind them as a matter of good taste.

When President Clinton says of affirmative action "mend it, don't end it," he is going with relativism against difficult principle not only to buy protection from the likes of Jesse Jackson (a master at the manipulation of white vulnerability), but also to reaffirm this larger contract between blacks and whites. This contract keeps the various elements of his political base together—blacks, other minorities, women and liberals in general—all of whom now identify social virtue with deference.

So, in what has become one of the central ironies of contemporary liberalism, Clinton will show more deference to blacks than others yet do less than others to help them confront and overcome their vulnerabilities. He will choose protective policies like affirmative action over policies that put high expectations before deference, that require performance as a condition of special help, that support individuals rather than groups, and that show compassion by insisting on difficult principles. Were he to do anything else, he would not only look "mean" but would break his contract with a crucial segment of his constituency. If "mending" the old contract hid blacks from the challenge of their vulnerability, it also protected him from the risk of his.

And if Colin Powell were to challenge affirmative action, and therefore this larger contract, it would seem as if the most popular black man in America was ripping away the recomposition (racism and victimization) by which his own group protects its esteem. He would throw his people open to their historic vulnerability to the myth of black inferiority. In a culture where deference and self-protection are virtue, this would be mean and extreme. Running squarely into this, Powell, like Clinton before him, chose relativism over difficult principle. Affirmative action was okay because the playing field was "unlevel," he said, aligning himself with his race's recomposed version of its situation. ("Unlevel" meaning that racism still largely explains black difficulty.) And this brought the general back into the American racial contract after the denunciation of preferences in his autobiography had caused many to wonder where he stood.

Though Bob Dole articulately denounces group preferences, it is also true that he shelved his own piece of legislation (the Dole-Canady bill) to end them in the federal government and stepped back a little from the California Civil Rights Initiative, which would end them in California's state government. In these latter moves—these small retreats—he displayed the deference that he hoped would buy him some protection from his racial vulnerability—the stereotype that as a white male Republican he was probably racially intolerant. Clearly, the selection of Jack Kemp as his running mate was a part of this deferential display, since Kemp has great credibility in the black community. But Kemp will not work well as an offer of deference because he withdrew his support of affirmative action to join the ticket. The larger point is that a natural ideological opponent of affirmative action (with an honorable civil rights record) like Dole was racially vulnerable and therefore subject to the same contract as Clinton, Powell and all other Americans.

I think one reason the Republicans are having trouble transforming the '94 shift to the right into a presidential victory is that Dole and the much maligned Newt Gingrich were out of sync with the idea of social virtue as deference. In fact, the Republican revolution was, in many ways, an assault on this very idea of virtue. But without deferential virtue they had no protection from the stereotype that portrayed Republicans as racially intolerant. They had no way of joining the larger contract between blacks and whites, no way to buy favor. Barking principles at affirmative action rather than whispering deference, it looked as if they were mean and extreme, against equality itself.

Thus, their recent convention was a veritable fireworks display of deferential liberalisms—with words like "inclusion" and "diversity" finding their way into every major speech. Dole got good press coverage, and a public opinion boost, after this deferential convention, but without affirmative action he has no concrete way to join the contract and stave off negative stereotypes of white male Republicans. Reagan and Bush kept affirmative action out of play by quietly going along with it—a deferential gesture that kept stereotypes at bay and brought them into the contract. Dole is the first presidential candidate in over thirty years who, despite his belated shows of deference, has ended up outside this contract. He stands in new political territory.

We have to start over from a simple truth: all protection from racial vulnerability is illusion. All our recompositions only recycle the old stereotypes and expand our vulnerability to them. Today, after decades of deferential racial reform, blacks and whites are as vulnerable as ever to the legends of black inferiority and white racism. In truth, racial oppression would not have been oppression if it had not imposed developmental inferiority on blacks. And history makes it clear that whites are quite capable of blithely living with and practicing the most horrific kind of social evil. Oppression leaves no innocent people in its wake, its victims included. If whites have the guilt of oppression, blacks have the shame of subjugation. Instead of recomposing to assert an innocence we don't have, we ought to let the vulnerabilities themselves guide our policy-making on race. And, of course, the test of our sincerity in this will be whether we allow those difficult non-deferential principles, like excellence, hard work and honesty across racial lines, to have the same virtuous stature in reform as deference.

When Clinton, Powell and Dole were forced to take positions on preferences, they encountered fear. Affirmative action is based on an entrenched and familiar recomposition—white goodwill redeeming black victimization. What happens if we get rid of it? How will we know what to expect of each other? Having recomposed our fear for so long, we now believe in it more than ever. I often hear other blacks say that black students will never have the SAT scores of whites or Asians. I hear college professors say that without affirmative action blacks will all but disappear from higher education—as though we ought to make policy on the presumption of permanent black inferiority. Others say that it is more difficult for blacks to overcome the developmental inferiority imposed on us than for whites to overcome the racism that imposed it. This, I think, is arguable, but it makes no difference. We will not overcome history until blacks are competitive with all others and no longer the objects of positive or negative discrimination.

The fear that we are what history says we are is what waits on the other side of affirmative action. It would be a good sign of things to come if we could at least say so.

# Sheila Jackson Lee
# "Should Federal Affirmative Action Policies Be Continued? Pro"*

As most of you know, affirmative action is an issue of great importance to me. Thus, I am disheartened by the introduction of legislation which would roll back the clock on civil rights in this country. Under the guise of returning to the "original intent" of civil rights laws, this legislation would forbid the use of race and gender in governmental decisionmaking and curtail proven and widely accepted remedies for present and past discrimination.

* Reprinted from *Congressional Digest, The Pro & Con Monthly*, vol. 75, nos. 6–7 (June-July 1996), "Should Federal Affirmative Action Policies Be Continued?" Copyright © 1996 by The Congressional Digest Corp., Washington, DC 202-333-7332, http://www.congressionaldigest.com. Reprinted by permission.

I argue that there is still a need for affirmative action programs and that antidiscrimination laws are not sufficient to remedy the structural racial and gender discrimination which persists in our society today.

The sponsors of the Equal Opportunity Act of 1995 claim that the legislation will "put the Federal Government's own house in order" by prohibiting the Federal Government from granting preferences based on race, national origin, or sex in Federal procurement, Federal employment, and the administration of federally conducted programs. This legislation defines granting a preference as "any preferential treatment that includes but is not limited to any use of a quota, set-aside, numerical goal, timetable, or other numerical objective."

Goals and timetables should not be confused with quotas. Goals and timetables are targets set by employers for the employment of women and minorities, along with time frames for achieving the targets. Employers are encouraged to make good faith efforts, but there are no legal penalties if they make good faith efforts that are unable to meet the goals.

Federal affirmative action programs are not quotas nor are they preferences for unqualified persons. Quotas are illegal under current law. Affirmative action programs focus on giving everyone an equal opportunity to compete for good jobs, educational opportunity, and government contracts.

Goals are yardsticks to measure equal opportunity, not guarantees of results. Fashioned correctly, goals have legally and fairly provided equal opportunity for all Americans. They respect merit and hard work, while ensuring that everyone has a chance to participate. Federal courts, including the Supreme Court, have continuously supported the use of carefully crafted goals to broaden opportunities for all to compete for a share of the American dream.

Current standards for affirmative action were recommended in the late 1960s to the Nixon Administration by a group of several large corporations. These recommendations, accepted by President Nixon and implemented by Secretary of Labor George Schultz, included the "management-by-objectives" concepts of employment goals and timetables.

In recognizing the historical legacy of sexism, racism, and prejudice, Federal affirmative action programs are designed to help end the systematic exclusion of all women and minorities from opportunities in education, employment, and other areas of American society, and they have been successful.

The implementation of affirmative action programs has increased the proportion of women and minorities employed in the private and government sectors. According to the EEOC, from 1966 to 1993, the proportion of minorities in the private sector increased from 11.4 percent to 23.5 percent. From 1972 to 1992, the proportion of minorities employed in the Federal Government rose from 19.7 percent to 29 percent.

Affirmative action has been a significant factor in opening up employment opportunities for qualified women and minorities on college and university faculties and staffs, and in expanding educational opportunities for women and minority students. Without affirmative action, many talented students would never have attended college, and many gifted teachers and researchers would not have been hired.

While affirmative action policies have begun to expand opportunity for women and minorities, these programs are still critically needed to bring about equal opportunity in education and employment. Study after study concludes that in employment, education, housing, and voting, minorities and women do not have equal opportunity. Too often, individual or institutional discrimination, intentional or not, precludes minorities and women from participating in many levels of our society.

The U.S. Department of Labor's Glass Ceiling Commission report, released on March 16, 1995, shows that while white men are only 43 percent of the Fortune 2000 workforce, they hold 95 percent of senior management jobs. Today, women make up 23 percent of lawyers, but only 11 percent of partners in law firms. Women are 48 percent of all journalists, but hold only 6 percent of the top jobs in journalism. Women are 72 percent of elementary school teachers but only 29 percent of school principals. And while the number of women earning advanced degrees has increased dramatically in the past 20 years, women comprise only 40 percent of all college and university faculty in the United States and only 46 percent of all women faculty are tenured, compared with more than 70 percent of all men faculty. Women are only 14 percent of full professors and 12 percent of college presidents.

While women are over half of the adult population and nearly half of the workforce in this country, women remain disproportionately clustered in traditionally "female" jobs with lower pay and fewer benefits. Moreover, research on the status of girls in education found that the glass ceiling is constructed in kindergarten. Beginning in grade school, girls are systematically tracked away from the better-paying jobs in science and technology into "pink collar" occupations.

Minority women have lagged particularly far behind in both employment and education. Minority women also earn fewer college degrees than white women. And although white men constitute a minority of both the total workforce (47 percent) and of college-educated persons (48 percent), they dominate the top jobs in virtually every field. Moreover, white males' median weekly earnings in 1993 were 33 percent higher than those of any other group in America.

In 1990, African Americans accounted for 12.1 percent of the population but owned only 3.1 percent of the total businesses and 1 percent of receipts of all U.S. firms. Hispanic Americans accounted for 9 percent of the population, 3.1 percent of U.S. businesses, and 1.2 percent of all receipts.

The unfinished task of developing the Nation's collective and diverse brainpower is essentially preparation for effective competition in the global and technological markets of the next century. This is no time to roll back affirmative action.

Some have suggested that affirmative action programs that take race, national origin, or gender into account should be eliminated entirely and replaced by affirmative action programs to aid the economically disadvantaged (i.e., anti-poverty or "need-based" remedies). Programs to eliminate poverty and enhance opportunities for the economically disadvantaged are critically needed.

But affirmative action based on economic need cannot provide an adequate or workable substitute for programs aimed specifically at eliminating the past and present effects of discrimination based on race, national origin, or gender. In the workplace, discrimination cuts across all economic lines; women and members of racial or ethnic minorities who are not poor are nonetheless subject to the effects of sexual stereotyping and racial or ethnic prejudice.

As long as there is discrimination based on race or gender, we must fashion remedies that take race and gender into account. Race- and gender-conscious remedies have proved essential and remain essential. All Americans want a color- and gender-blind society. That is our goal. But serious discrimination persists and we cannot ignore it. As Lyndon Johnson said in 1965: "We seek not just freedom but opportunity, not just equality as a right and a theory but equality as a fact and as a result."

I am opposed to this legislation and I would urge my colleagues to resist the attempt to turn back the clock on civil rights in this country.

## James Q. Wilson
## "Sins of Admission"*

Affirmative action—by which I mean selecting persons based on their group membership—is not one program but many and has consequences that range from acceptable to intolerable. We understand these distinctions intuitively. When a television commercial displays white and black actors or when a political party endorses candidates from a variety of ethnic backgrounds, no one complains—even though this is, literally, affirmative action. But should someone suggest that the musicians in a major symphony orchestra or the players in the National Basketball Association be chosen to create a specific racial balance, most people would be outraged.

The difference, of course, has to do with the purposes of the organizations. Television commercials and party candidates are chosen chiefly to attract support from customers and voters. Everyone expects organizations trying to sell something to cater to the preferences of those who might buy. But top-ranked musicians and athletes are selected exclusively on the basis of merit.

* James Q. Wilson, "Sins of Admission: Good Affirmative Action and Bad" in *The New Republic* (July 8, 1996). Copyright © 1996 by The New Republic, Inc. Reprinted with permission.

The debate over affirmative action in contracts, university admissions and public employment is in large measure a debate over what set of standards ought to govern achievement in these enterprises. The strongest defenders of affirmative action argue that these organizations have a representative as well as a technical function, while the toughest critics claim that the latter greatly outweighs the former.

Consider undergraduate admissions. A plausible proposal might run as follows: given the growing importance of college education in the life of the nation and the uncertainty attached to conventional measures of merit, one might defend the modest use of racial preferences as a way of increasing participation of underrepresented groups in educated society without doing serious harm to the quality of the university. One might, by the same token, take into account other nonintellectual attributes like athletic or musical ability.

But as one moves up through the university experience—to medical and law schools and onto a faculty—academic ability becomes the dominant criterion. Excellence at teaching and research are overwhelmingly important tests for faculty recruitment; no one proposes that law or medical schools admit athletes or musicians. Furthermore, three or four years of college training ought to have given students with natural abilities but subpar elementary and secondary educations a chance to catch up.

This guideline—race and ethnicity as a factor for 18 year olds but not after—might provide a reasonable basis on which to "mend, not end" affirmative action. Unfortunately, preference programs, as administered today, make no such distinctions—affirmative action is at least as pervasive in admissions to law and medical schools as in college, if not more so.

UCLA's undergraduate admissions are based on two sets of criteria: academic (grades, test scores) and supplemental ("socio-economic or educational disadvantage"). For each, students are ranked from one (the highest) to six (the lowest). The admissions office admits between 40 and 60 percent of the student body strictly on academic grounds. The next group consists of people whose combined academic and supplemental ranking gives them a high total score. In this combined mark, being disadvantaged may count for more than being smart; a student can have an academic ranking as low as five and still get in if his or her disadvantage rating is at the top. The final group—the "read" group, meaning their files are closely read—are those whose rankings, academic and supplemental, are low.

In 1994, UCLA admitted 6,801 students as part of its academic-only criteria. Of these seventy-seven, or about 1 percent, were African Americans. The African American students admitted in the first, academic, group had an average SAT score nearly 300 points higher than blacks admitted in the latter two groups, and their high-school grades were half a grade higher. Among those not chosen on purely academic grounds, 19 percent were African Americans, and another 51 percent were Latino. These second two categories have effectively become ethnicity driven.

The evidence is equally clear for the fall of 1995. Eighty-one percent of

Asians and Caucasians admitted had academic rankings of one or two, but only 10 percent of the Asians and 1 percent of the Caucasians were in the top two supplemental ranks. For Mexican-American and African American applicants, less than 13 percent of those admitted had academic ranks of one or two, but more than 97 percent were in the top two supplemental ranks.

Once admitted, disparities remain. Among white and Asian American students, at least 80 percent graduate within five years. Among African American students, less than half do so. In the UCLA class admitted in 1990, Caucasians had an average grade of just over a "B" while African Americans averaged just above a "C."

A common defense of these disparities is that athletic ability or alumni connections already count in admissions and, therefore, race should, too. But this misses the point. Race, according to the Supreme Court, is a suspect classification subject to strict scrutiny. Athletic prowess (or musical ability, or rich parents) are not suspect classifications and do not require strict judicial scrutiny. If these traits were treated legally the same as race, then I could sue the Boston Red Sox for denying me my lifelong ambition of playing second base for them simply because I can't hit, an untalented violinist could sue the New York Philharmonic to get a seat in the string section, and rich parents could demand scholarships for their children. One cannot easily correct this problem by abandoning the judicial protection given race; to do that would permit colleges and employers to discriminate against blacks. To the extent race deserves special constitutional protection, it cannot be equated with other principles of classification.

The famous opinion of Justice Lewis Powell in the *Bakke* case, decided in 1978, is still supposedly the basis for racial preference in American law: race, despite its special status, can be a "plus factor" in admissions so long as it is not the decisive one. Yet, at the University of California today, strictly academic admissions would admit a 1 percent black student body (down from 7 percent currently), while the supplemental categories admit students of whom only a tiny fraction are white or Asian. The contrast between the two systems is not a "plus" factor. It is decisive.

The evidence from medical school is the same. Ellen and Jerry Cook— she teaches at the University of California at San Diego (UCSD)—have compared graduates of UCSD who applied to that university's medical school between 1987 and 1993. The *only* students admitted with MCAT scores below the sixtieth percentile or with college grades below 3.0 were from affirmative action groups. Furthermore, a separate study showed that students from poorer families received no advantage per se; the only criteria for preference was race and ethnicity. The result was that UCSD admitted students based on two different distributions of abilities—one curve consisted of almost all the affirmative action students, another (barely overlapping) curve consisted mostly of whites and Asians. This although both had access to the same undergraduate education.

Much the same pattern exists in law schools. If you have an LSAT score below the ninetieth percentile and college grades below 3.5, you are vastly more likely to be admitted into UCLA Law School if you are black or Hispanic than if you are white or Asian. One study, done unofficially by a student who cracked the law school's secrecy codes, suggests that the grades received by black students during their first year are significantly lower than those received by whites.

The costs of professional school racial preference are greater than those of undergraduate colleges in part because 18 year olds have a wider range of available opportunities. High-school students wanting to enter a good university have more choices than do those wanting to enter the considerably smaller number of good law or medical schools. By the same token, the costs to society of admitting less qualified students into these select institutions is greater.

In California, four Under-Represented Minority groups (URMs) are generically entitled to affirmative action: African Americans, Native Americans, Mexican-Americans and mainland Puerto Ricans. Let us suppose for a moment that African Americans belong there because of past discrimination and the legacy of slavery. But on what grounds are Mexican-Americans on the list and other Hispanics numerous in California— Guatemalans, El Salvadorans, Cubans—not? At one time Asians were the object of the bluntest possible discrimination in California—many could not own land or serve on a jury—and Japanese-Americans were exiled to inland camps during World War II. Yet Asians do not make the list and, indeed, lose space in universities owing to the preferences given to URMs. The Vietnamese came to this country poor after a war in which we were a major participant, but URM graduates applying for admission to California medical schools were 2.7 times as likely to be accepted as Vietnamese students despite the fact that the grades of most of the rejected Vietnamese were higher than those of most of the accepted URMs.

One argument often cited in favor of university affirmative action is its support among faculty. And, indeed, last year the UCLA faculty legislative assembly did vote by a margin of six to one to criticize the State Regents for abandoning racial preferences. (Although when the assembly's vote was sent out on a mail ballot to all faculty members, support for its position fell from six to one to three to two, and to even lower margins at other UC campuses.) But even this does not prove faculty support for racial preference, since some faculty may have objected to the *way* the Regents made their decision, rather than to the principle of color-blindness itself. In 1995 the California Association of Scholars polled faculty opinion in the nine California public universities. Designed by the Roper Center for Public Opinion Research, the central question was this: Should the university "grant preferences to women and certain racial and ethnic groups in admissions, hiring and promotions?" Most faculty said no.

Just as affirmative action is more costly for professional schools than undergraduate colleges, it is more problematic at some colleges than others. At Harvard, with its pick of the country's top high-school students, white and black, the racial gap on college entrance scores was modest. But the scarcity of academically prepared blacks means that the best universities skim off the top. The result is that other universities—including the very good public universities in California—take a chance admitting students who may be unprepared to tackle college-level work, and may not graduate at all.

Affirmative action has lost its moorings. Colleges legitimately want a diverse student body, but their definition of diversity is limited to ethnicity, excludes ideology and favors some but not other ethnic groups. Law and medical schools want to produce more attorneys and physicians of certain ethnicities, but they can only do this by denying—not modifying, but denying—equal access to more talented applicants, thereby lowering the quality of the professionals they produce. This inevitably has consequences for consumers of medicine and legal assistance.

As universities become more competitive overall while lowering the standards by which they admit certain students, they increasingly produce anger and frustration among those hardworking young people who have upheld demanding standards themselves and expect their universities to do the same. Even worse, the very professional schools that have long made a special claim to excellence have abandoned that claim—to the dismay of all those who once believed them.

# 5

# Congress: The First Branch

## House and Senate: Differences in Representation

*See Lowi and Ginsberg, pp. 176–178 or brief edition, pp. 104–106*

*In* The Federalist No. 10, *the most important of* The Federalist Papers *(also reprinted as an appendix to the text), James Madison outlined the theory of representation that was to serve as the foundation for the American political system. Madison argued that faction was inevitable in a democracy, and that the only way to mitigate the effects of faction was to set up a representative system through which the passions of the people could be "refine[d] and filter[ed] . . . by passing them through the medium of a chosen body of citizens, whose wisdom may best discern the true interest of their country."*

*This concept of a filter was critical to Federalist thought, and provided a key point of contention between the Federalists and the Antifederalists. The Antifederalists objected strongly to the idea that the views of the people ought to be screened by an elite representative body; they argued instead that representatives ought to mirror their constituents' views. Responding to the criticism about elite control, Madison propounded his views on a bicameral system in* The Federalist No. 57 *and* The Federalist No. 62. *Madison argued that the structure and composition of the House of Representatives would provide the necessary link to the people, while the structure and composition of the Senate would insure that intemperate actions proposed by the House would not be too readily adopted.*

*These institutional differences lead to differences in the way that law is made, as the text notes. Peter Carlson, writing in the* Washington Post Magazine *in 1990, described the resulting distinctions between the House and the Senate as follows: "The Senate is a gentleman's [sic] club. The House is a fraternity. The Senate is the* New York Times. *The House is the* New York Post. *The Senate is 'Washington Week in Review.' The House is 'The Morton Downey Show.'" Whatever the merit of this description, it is very clear from reading the following selections that the differences were designed into the system.*

## James Madison
### *The Federalist No. 57\**

[There is a] charge against the House of Representatives . . . that it will be taken from that class of citizens which will have least sympathy with the mass of the people, and be most likely to aim at an ambitious sacrifice of the many to the aggrandizement of the few.

* James Madison, *The Federalist No. 57*, ed. Clinton Rossiter (New York: NAL, 1961).

Of all the objections which have been framed against the federal Constitution, this is perhaps the most extraordinary. Whilst the objection itself is leveled against a pretended oligarchy, the principle of it strikes at the very root of republican government.

The aim of every political constitution is, or ought to be, first to obtain for rulers men who possess most wisdom to discern, and most virtue to pursue, the common good of the society; and in the next place, to take the most effectual precautions for keeping them virtuous whilst they continue to hold their public trust. The elective mode of obtaining rulers is the characteristic policy of republican government. The means relied on in this form of government for preventing their degeneracy are numerous and various. The most effectual one is such a limitation of the term of appointments as will maintain a proper responsibility to the people.

Let me now ask what circumstance there is in the constitution of the House of Representatives that violates the principles of republican government, or favors the elevation of the few on the ruins of the many? Let me ask whether every circumstance is not, on the contrary, strictly conformable to these principles, and scrupulously impartial to the rights and pretensions of every class and description of citizens?

Who are to be the electors of the federal representatives? Not the rich, more than the poor; not the learned, more than the ignorant; not the haughty heirs of distinguished names, more than the humble sons of obscure and unpropitious fortune. The electors are to be the great body of the people of the United States. They are to be the same who exercise the right in every State of electing the corresponding branch of the legislature of the State.

Who are to be the objects of popular choice? Every citizen whose merit may recommend him to the esteem and confidence of his country. No qualification of wealth, of birth, of religious faith, or of civil profession is permitted to fetter the judgment or disappoint the inclination of the people.

If we consider the situation of the men on whom the free suffrages of their fellow-citizens may confer the representative trust, we shall find it involving every security which can be devised or desired for their fidelity to their constituents.

In the first place, as they will have been distinguished by the preference of their fellow-citizens, we are to presume that in general they will be somewhat distinguished also by those qualities which entitle them to it, and which promise a sincere and scrupulous regard to the nature of their engagements.

In the second place, they will enter into the public service under circumstances which cannot fail to produce a temporary affection at least to their constituents. There is in every breast a sensibility to marks of honor, of favor, of esteem, and of confidence, which, apart from all considerations of interests, is some pledge for grateful and benevolent returns. . . .

In the third place, those ties which bind the representative to his constituents are strengthened by motives of a more selfish nature. . . . [A] great proportion of the men deriving their advancement from their influence with the people would have more to hope from a preservation of the favor than from innovations in the government subversive of the authority of the people.

All these securities, however, would be found very insufficient without the restraint of frequent elections. Hence, in the fourth place, the House of Representatives is so constituted as to support in the members an habitual recollection of their dependence on the people. Before the sentiments impressed on their minds by the mode of their elevation can be effaced by the exercise of power, they will be compelled to anticipate the moment when their power is to cease, when their exercise of it is to be reviewed, and when they must descend to the level from which they were raised; there forever to remain unless a faithful discharge of their trust shall have established their title to a renewal of it.

I will add, as a fifth circumstance in the situation of the House of Representatives, restraining them from oppressive measures, that they can make no law which will not have its full operation on themselves and their friends, as well as on the great mass of the society. . . . It creates between [the rulers and the people] that communion of interests and sympathy of sentiments of which few governments have furnished examples; but without which every government degenerates into tyranny. If it be asked, what is to restrain the House of Representatives from making legal discriminations in favor of themselves and a particular class of the society? I answer: the genius of the whole system; the nature of just and constitutional laws; and, above all, the vigilant and manly spirit which actuates the people of America—a spirit which nourishes freedom, and in return is nourished by it.

If this spirit shall ever be so far debased as to tolerate a law not obligatory on the legislature, as well as on the people, the people will be prepared to tolerate anything but liberty.

Such will be the relation between the House of Representatives and their constituents. Duty, gratitude, interest, ambition itself, are the cords by which they will be bound to fidelity and sympathy with the great mass of the people. It is possible that these may all be insufficient to control the caprice and wickedness of men. But are they not all that government will admit, and that human prudence can devise? Are they not the genuine and the characteristic means by which republican government provides for the liberty and happiness of the people? Are they not the identical means on which every State government in the Union relies for the attainment of these important ends? . . . What are we to say to the men who profess the most flaming zeal for republican government, yet boldly impeach the fundamental principle of it; who pretend to be champions for the right and the capacity of the people to choose their own rulers, yet maintain that they will prefer those only who will immediately and infallibly betray the trust committed to them?

PUBLIUS

# James Madison
## *The Federalist No. 62**

Having examined the constitution of the House of Representatives, and answered such of the objections against it as seemed to merit notice, I enter next on the examination of the Senate. . . .

The qualifications proposed for senators, as distinguished from those of representatives, consist in a more advanced age and a longer period of citizenship. . . . The propriety of these distinctions is explained by the nature of the senatorial trust, which, requiring greater extent of information and stability of character, requires at the same time that the senator should have reached a period of life most likely to supply these advantages; and which, participating immediately in transactions with foreign nations, ought to be exercised by none who are not thoroughly weaned from the prepossessions and habits incident to foreign birth and education. . . .

It is equally unnecessary to dilate on the appointment of senators by the State legislatures. . . . It is recommended by the double advantage of favoring a select appointment, and of giving to the State governments such an agency in the formation of the federal government as must secure the authority of the former, and may form a convenient link between the two systems.

The equality of representation in the Senate is another point which, being evidently the result of compromise between the opposite pretensions of the large and the small States, does not call for much discussion. . . . In a compound republic, partaking both of the national and federal character, the government ought to be founded on a mixture of the principles of proportional and equal representation. . . .

In this spirit it may be remarked that the equal vote allowed to each State is at once a constitutional recognition of the portion of sovereignty remaining in the individual States and an instrument for preserving that residuary sovereignty. So far the equality ought to be no less acceptable to the large than to the small States; since they are not less solicitous to guard, by every possible expedient, against an improper consolidation of the States into one simple republic.

Another advantage accruing from this ingredient in the constitution of the Senate is the additional impediment it must prove against improper acts of legislation. No law or resolution can now be passed without the concurrence, first, of a majority of the people, and then of a majority of the States. It must be acknowledged that this complicated check on legislation may in some instances be injurious as well as beneficial; and that the peculiar defense which it involves in favor of the smaller States would be more rational if any interests common to them and distinct from those of the other States would otherwise be exposed to peculiar danger. But as the

* James Madison, *The Federalist No. 62*, ed. Clinton Rossiter (New York: NAL, 1961).

larger States will always be able, by their power over the supplies, to defeat unreasonable exertions of this prerogative of the lesser States, and as the facility and excess of law-making seem to be the diseases to which our governments are most liable, it is not impossible that this part of the Constitution may be more convenient in practice than it appears to many in contemplation.

The number of senators and the duration of their appointment come next to be considered. . . . It will be proper to inquire into the purposes which are to be answered by a senate; and in order to ascertain these it will be necessary to review the inconveniences which a republic must suffer from the want of such an institution.

First. It is a misfortune incident to republican government . . . that those who administer it may forget their obligations to their constituents and prove unfaithful to their important trust. In this point of view a senate, as a second branch of the legislative assembly distinct from and dividing the power with a first, must be in all cases a salutary check on the government. It doubles the security of the people by requiring the concurrence of two distinct bodies in schemes of usurpation or perfidy, where the ambition or corruption of one would otherwise be sufficient. . . .

Second. The necessity of a senate is not less indicated by the propensity of all single and numerous assemblies, to yield to the impulse of sudden and violent passions, and to be seduced by factious leaders into intemperate and pernicious resolutions. . . . A body which is to correct this infirmity ought itself to be free from it, and consequently ought to be less numerous. It ought, moreover, to possess great firmness, and consequently ought to hold its authority by a tenure of considerable duration.

Third. Another defect to be supplied by a senate lies in a want of due acquaintance with the objects and principles of legislation. It is not possible that an assembly of men called for the most part from pursuits of a private nature continued in appointment for a short time and led by no permanent motive to devote the intervals of public occupation to a study of the laws, the affairs, and the comprehensive interests of their country, should, if left wholly to themselves, escape a variety of important errors in the exercise of their legislative trust. . . .

A good government implies two things: first, fidelity to the object of government, which is the happiness of the people; secondly, a knowledge of the means by which that object can be best attained. . . . The federal Constitution avoids this error; and what merits particular notice, it provides for the last in a mode which increases the security for the first.

Fourth. The mutability in the public councils arising from a rapid succession of new members, however qualified they may be, points out, in the strongest manner, the necessity of some stable institution in the government. Every new election in the States is found to change one half of the representatives. From this change of men must proceed a change of opinions; and from a change of opinions, a change of measures. But a continual change even of good measures is inconsistent with every rule of prudence and every prospect of success. The remark is verified in private life, and becomes more just, as well as more important, in national transactions.

. . . [If the nation's government changes too often], it forfeits the respect and confidence of other nations, and all the advantages connected with national character. . . . Every nation, . . . whose affairs betray a want of wisdom and stability, may calculate on every loss which can be sustained from the more systematic policy of its wiser neighbors. But the best instruction on this subject is unhappily conveyed to America by the example of her own situation. She finds that she is held in no respect by her friends; that she is the derision of her enemies; and that she is a prey to every nation which has an interest in speculating on her fluctuating councils and embarrassed affairs.

The internal effects of a mutable policy are still more calamitous. It poisons the blessings of liberty itself, it will be of little avail to the people that the laws are made by men of their own choice if the laws be so voluminous that they cannot be read, or so incoherent that they cannot be understood; if they be repealed or revised before they are promulgated, or undergo such incessant changes that no man, who knows what the law is today, can guess what it will be tomorrow. Law is defined to be a rule of action; but how can that be a rule, which is little known, and less fixed?

Another effect of public instability is the unreasonable advantage it gives to the sagacious, the enterprising, and the moneyed few over the industrious and uniformed mass of the people. Every new regulation concerning commerce or revenue, or in any manner affecting the value of the different species of property, presents a new harvest to those who watch the change, and can trace its consequences; a harvest, reared not by themselves, but by the toils and cares of the great body of their fellow-citizens. This is a state of things in which it may be said with some truth that laws are made for the *few*, not for the *many*.

In another point of view, great injury results from an unstable government. The want of confidence in the public councils damps every useful undertaking, the success and profit of which may depend on a continuance of existing arrangements. . . . In a word, no great improvement or laudable enterprise can go forward which requires the auspices of a steady system of national policy.

But the most deplorable effect of all is that diminution of attachment and reverence which steals into the hearts of the people towards a political system which betrays so many marks of infirmity, and disappoints so many of their flattering hopes. No government, any more than an individual, will long be respected without being truly respectable; nor be truly respectable without possessing a certain portion of order and stability.

PUBLIUS

## Constituency Service

*See Lowi and Ginsberg, p. 197 or brief edition, p. 117*

*Over the past few decades Congress has become a more professional and representative institution. Members hire large expert staffs to help them develop more informed legislation. They respond to thousands of constituent requests for assistance in dealing with government agencies from the Internal Revenue Service to the Immigration and Naturalization Service. They spend more time in their districts meeting with constituents, and work very hard to stay in close touch with important local interests. Yet the public dislikes Congress intensely, and there is no lack of proposals to reform the institution and "throw the bums out." Why?*

*Steven Stark argues that Congress simply tries too hard to meet the schizophrenic demands of the American public. On the one hand, Americans complain that government is too big and costs too much. We want a balanced budget and lower taxes. On the other hand, we still want a great deal from government, and we expect government to grapple with our biggest social problems; for example, discrimination, social security, disaster relief, health care, a clean environment, economic security, and safe airplanes. To Stark, institutional reforms such as reforming parliamentary procedures, imposing term limits, or ratifying a balanced budget amendment will not improve congressional performance. Members will still take on enormous challenges that they cannot realistically meet, in order to answer the demands of constituents seeking a riskless society that does not cost too much. Until both Congress and the nation accept a less-ambitious agenda and recognize that not every problem has a legislative solution, Stark concludes, we will continue to dislike the institution.*

# Steven Stark
# "*Too* Representative Government"*

"Suppose you were an idiot," Mark Twain wrote during the Gilded Age. "And suppose you were a member of Congress. But I repeat myself." "Do you pray for the senators?" someone asked the chaplain of the Senate in 1903. "No, I look at the senators and pray for the country," he replied.

The more things change, the more they remain the same. The 104th Congress began work in January [1995], and talk of institutional revolution is once again in the air. It's not just that the Republicans—finally in control of both Houses for the first time in four decades—have begun reforming the least popular branch by taking such measures as applying all federal employment laws to Congress, cutting House committee staffs by a third, and requiring a 60 percent majority in the House to approve tax increases. Many critics, such as Kevin Phillips and Lamar Alexander, have discussed a number of rather radical proposals for recasting the institution—everything from term limits to increasing the size of Congress

---

* Steven Stark, "Too Representative Government" from the *Atlantic Monthly* (May 1995). Reprinted by permission.

to cutting the length of the session in half to instituting national referenda.

One might argue that some of these changes would make Congress more effective, as would a few of the currently popular (but unlikely to pass) proposals for campaign-finance overhaul and restrictions on lobbying.

A number of scholars, former members of Congress, and other observers suggest, however, that even far-reaching reforms—not to mention the recent election results—are unlikely to quell the public's considerable discontent with Congress for long. In its attempts to lay the blame for that discontent at the feet of the Democrats, the new Republican majority is ignoring a fundamental reality that has come into being over the past generation: owing largely to the changing nature of representation, the expanding role of the federal government, and the influence of television, the public has arrived at new and often contradictory expectations of how Congress should act and what it should do. Until these contradictions are resolved, Congress is doomed to unpopularity and ineffectiveness, no matter who controls it.

There is, after all, an inevitable tension in any legislative system between deliberation and action, discretion and responsiveness. The job of a legislature is not only to get things done but also to air points of view and ensure the legitimacy of governmental action. These goals often conflict —as do the objectives of representing a constituency while exercising independent judgment, or looking out for both the national and the local interest. Throughout American history the pendulum has swung back and forth as legislators have tried to come to terms with these tensions. Today, however, voters apparently believe that the pendulum can be made to stop. In much the same way as the public seems to want a welfare state without picking up the tab, it wants the advantages of a legislative system without any of the costs.

Even if Congress adopts all the most ambitious reforms, this cannot be achieved. No matter how noble the goal, virtually any reform that seeks to change the makeup of Congress (such as term limits) or encourage debate or make members rely less on staff, so that they will draft their own bills and read those of others, will lead the institution to be even more dependent on special interests or to get less done. Almost any proposal that increases the institution's ability to act quickly, such as eliminating the filibuster or making it easier to "fast track" legislation, will tend to alienate those in the minority and cause some attempts at lawmaking to be less judicious and acceptable to the masses. Attempts to limit the length of the session will inevitably narrow the range of concerns that Congress can tackle. Although many of the current Republican proposals for institutional reform have surface appeal, chances are that they will eventually end up antagonizing at least as many voters as they please. And Congress will end up just as unpopular as it was when the Republicans took over, if not more so.

### THE WIRED CONGRESS

For the first four decades of the Republic, congressmen actually spent very little time in Washington. For the next century or so they had little contact with their districts once they were in Washington. (Senators, of course, were not even popularly elected until early in this century.) Theorists from Thomas Hobbes to Edmund Burke had debated the extent to which representatives should directly reflect the desires of their constituents, but that debate took place in a world in which a lot of groups couldn't vote, news was hard to come by, and no one really knew how to measure public opinion other than in an election. The difficulty of travel and the irregularity of mail delivery made communication between constituents and Congress problematic. Thus members inevitably had to exercise independent judgment on most issues, no matter where they stood philosophically on the representation question.

Today things have swung to the opposite extreme, and not just because the infamous lobbyists surround congressmen and senators. Daily polling, E-mail, 800 numbers, and call-in shows have exponentially increased the contact that representatives have with their constituents. "Many days I felt like nothing more than the end of a computer terminal," Elliott Levitas, a former representative from Georgia, told me in an interview. The danger today is not that representatives know too little about what the electorate feels but that they know too much. Like body temperature, public opinion can shift hourly without consequence. "The cooling-off process that used to exist isn't there any more," Dennis Eckart, a former representative from Ohio, says. "As a lover of democracy, I can appreciate that, but there was an advantage to having an electorate that couldn't figure out what was in a tax bill." What's more, polls are often misleading—in part because they can be manipulated, and in part because many issues are so complex that the public holds conflicting views of what it wants, and expects its representatives magically to resolve the conflict.

"Ultimately, there's very little clarity to all those poll numbers, even though a lot of analysts attach great significance to them," says Peter Smith, formerly a representative from Vermont and now the founding president of California State University at Monterey Bay. "Health care and welfare reform are abstractions, no matter what a poll says. People favor something in general. When you get down to specifics, however, they often don't." The debate last session over President Bill Clinton's health-care bill illustrated that principle once again.

The rise of constituency politics has also led the public to view legislators simply as instruments of its will. The political scientist David Mayhew, of Yale University, is not alone in having observed that the job of a federal legislator changed dramatically with the rise of New Deal and Great Society programs. Now an increasing number of constituents look to their legislator not only to obtain valuable pork-barrel projects for their state or district but also to help them obtain personal benefits from the government and its bureaucracies.

This development has been exacerbated by the fact that representatives have to serve more constituents today than they did in the past. Sixty-five representatives served four million Americans in the first Congress—a ratio of approximately 1:60,000. Today, with 435 representatives serving a population of more than 260 million, the ratio is approximately 1:600,000. Offices in home states have proliferated, and legislative aides have increasingly been transformed into caseworkers, thereby accounting for a healthy proportion of the increase in the size of those vilified congressional staffs. (The Republican reforms haven't even touched House and Senate personal-staff members, almost 40 percent of whom now work in district or state offices.) It should be no surprise, then, that voters increasingly view their legislators almost as personal therapists—a perspective that hardly encourages representatives to show any independence from the will of their districts, or to act in the national interest when it conflicts with local concerns. If legislators now seem excessively parochial and preoccupied with day-to-day responsiveness, that is what they are hearing the public demand.

While these changes have been occurring, Congress has also been attracting members of a different kind, whether Republican or Democrat. Virtually everyone agrees that today's representatives tend to be far better educated and informed, more professional, and less graft-ridden than their predecessors. Yet many also believe that something is missing from this generation in Congress—even from the new Republicans. "What happened is that as the quality of the legislature went up, its performance went down," says Theodore Lowi, a professor of government at Cornell University. "These people are much more individual entrepreneurs; they have far less respect for party institutions and hierarchy." Or, as the former representative Al Swift, of Washington, puts it, "We'd be better off with four hundred and ten followers and twenty-five leaders than the other way around."

The new entrepreneurial style is blamed in part for the lack of collegiality in Congress and the proliferation of committee and subcommittee assignments on the Hill, which have increased for senators and nearly doubled for representatives since the 1950s. (The number of committees and subcommittees has actually shrunk, owing to reorganizations; the Republican Contract with America has consolidated even more committees.) It also helps account, Lowi says, for the fact that Congress has become so sensitive to short-term public opinion: "They don't have the party to hide behind anymore. Because they're more individually accountable, they feel much more vulnerable and they react accordingly."

## CIRCULAR CURES

Reversing the trend toward a professional class of legislators is the goal of the term-limits movement. Mark Petracca, a political scientist at the University of California at Irvine, has written that legislative professionalization runs counter to the basic values of representative government, because "a profession entails a set of role relationships between 'experts' and 'clients' " which are fundamentally at odds with the way Congress is supposed to work. Yet the desire for a "citizen legislature," embodied in the term-limits movement, may be as quixotic as the search for a doctor who still makes house calls. "Sure, Congress has changed, but so has the country," says Ronald Peters, the director of the Carl Albert Congressional Research and Studies Center, at the University of Oklahoma. "Things have become less hierarchical than they once were almost everywhere. Part of this is generational, but a lot of it is just the way we've changed as a people. Legislators are more autonomous, but so is everyone else in the culture. This institution may be more professional, but all disciplines are becoming more professionalized. This is all part of a larger pattern, which in one sense couldn't be more representative."

The current cultural preoccupation with inclusion has also had important effects. Opening up the process to everyone—by such means as expansion of voting rights, more primaries and referenda, and encouraging access to government services—could be characterized as the major theme of our politics over the past third of a century, and there's obviously a lot to be said for it. The congressional response to Watergate, for example, often focused on the process of government, not its substance: lawmakers passed "sunshine laws" to force government to be more open and ethical, and in a spasm of reform wiped out many seniority privileges to make Congress more egalitarian. Even today, when complaints about Congress focus on how process reforms have still failed to address the institution's underlying problems, many of the popular ideas about how to change Congress—such as term limits and more referenda—continue to focus on process. The problems caused by being more democratic and process-oriented, both Republicans and Democrats seem to be saying, can be solved by being even more democratic and process-oriented.

The more a system values giving everyone a voice, however, the less it can value speed and effectiveness. All those voices have to be heard, and frequently they have to be accommodated. The correlate of enabling more women and members of minorities to be part of the legislature—a laudable goal—is that their concerns must be addressed, even though some of these concerns have traditionally been ignored by most legislatures. Irwin Gertzog, in his book *Congressional Women*, finds that women in Congress are far likelier than their male colleagues to stress such issues as the treatment of rape victims, the problems of displaced homemakers, and funding for diagnostic tests for breast cancer. "Congress succeeds much better as a representative body than it used to," says Michael Mezey, a professor of political science at DePaul University, "which means it's probably somewhat less successful as a lawmaking body."

Democratizing the internal rules of Congress has also made it harder to accomplish anything substantive. The more a culture moves toward democracy, however, the more it empowers those forces that have the ability to manipulate public opinion or provide access. The rise in the importance of media consultants, the press, and special-interest money is directly proportional to the growth of democracy in the culture and in Congress over the past thirty years. Read the polls or listen to talk radio and you will find that the complaints today are as much about these new forces and what they have done to the process as about anything else. The urge to destroy elites has simply created another class of them; the solution has become the problem. And the Republicans are doing next to nothing to stop that.

## THE BUCK STOPS NOWHERE

Congress once tended to pass relatively concrete, simple laws in relatively few areas, which meant that the results of any lawmaking were far easier to assess. For our first 140 years it dealt with economic issues primarily through tariffs and focused on the country's expansion, wars, and treaties. There was little money to spend, and the Constitution had been interpreted as allowing far less federal intrusion into the workings of the states than we know today. "Nineteenth-century Congresses actually worked better," Theodore Lowi says. "They just passed very limited, piecemeal laws." At the turn of the century the House had no staff members and the Senate only a few. (By 1991 the personal staffs of the two houses together numbered more than 11,000, and nearly another 3,500 people worked for the committees.)

The passage of a federal income tax early in this century was the first step toward the creation of the welfare state. Still, the concept of dealing with complicated economic and social-welfare problems on a systematic national basis really arose during the crisis presented by the Great Depression and then the Second World War. Congress's response in the 1930s and the three decades that followed was to cede to the executive branch (which had drafted most of the laws in the first place) the authority to solve most of these problems—and the creation of administrative agencies, along with the enlargement of administrators' responsibilities, was often part of the solution. The idea was that many problems were too complex or technical for a legislature and that a specialized agency such as the Federal Communications Commission, or an administrator such as the Secretary of Agriculture, could do a better job of solving them. These agencies were also created in an era when there was much intellectual support for the notion that decisions should be taken away from legislatures and given to experts, who knew better.

The typical congressional grant of authority to do this was quite brief, simple, and vague: "[to regulate] interstate and foreign commerce in communication by wire and radio"; to make agricultural marketing "orderly." In theory, Congress would strictly oversee the agency's performance. In reality, representatives were usually happy to pass the buck to someone else and leave the agency alone, except when they needed a favor. As it happened, legislators soon discovered that such a setup also allowed them to claim credit for a program and then, if things went awry, "run against the bureaucracy"—a bureaucracy they had created, to avoid having to deal with problems themselves. The buck stopped nowhere.

The Supreme Court put a stop to elements of Roosevelt's New Deal, on the grounds that the Constitution simply did not allow the federal government to act in many areas. Support for a further expansion of federal power, however, took hold in the public imagination in the 1950s and 1960s, with the civil-rights revolution, which ended up discrediting intellectual and legal arguments about "states' rights." Nelson Polsby, an expert on Congress and a professor of political science at the University of California at Berkeley, says, "It became an article of faith among liberals that you can't trust Mississippi, so you have to nationalize these things."

## 60,000 PAGES

For Lyndon Johnson's Great Society programs, in the mid-sixties, Congress was still using the New Deal agency as a model—with important differences. First, the traditional division between federal and state authority having been obliterated, Congress began moving into substantive areas, such as crime and housing, that had traditionally been beyond the purview of the federal government except in extreme emergencies. The early civil-rights laws were working, after all, and many of the nation's problems seemed rooted in its troubled racial past; a federal takeover seemed justified. Once involved in those areas, however, Congress kept expanding its grasp, eventually dictating to states on traditionally local questions—speed limits, for example. The result is that today Congress routinely passes laws dealing with local matters—crime, homelessness, education—and nobody even blinks at the loss of local control, which was once a cornerstone of our Jeffersonian public philosophy. As the former representative Al Swift puts it, "We've kind of blurred the distinction between a county sheriff and a congressman."

That's a recent and radical turn in our history, and one—"devolution" rhetoric to the contrary—that the Republicans show little sign of undoing. It is not simply that Speaker of the House Newt Gingrich may be misreading last year's election returns when he maintains that the public agrees it is time to dismantle much of the Great Society, or return programs to the states. The Contract With America, for example, promised a tougher anti-crime package, "strengthening rights of parents in their children's education," stronger child-pornography laws, and new rules to reform the welfare system, tort law, and product liability—efforts in many areas beyond what was seen as the purview of Congress when the Republicans last held both houses.

The 1960s blizzard of legislation came during an era when belief in the possibilities of governmental power may have been at a peak. In the 1965–1966 session alone nearly 20,000 bills were introduced. (The number in recent years has averaged fewer than 10,000 a session.) "If we can put a man on the moon, we can [fill in the blank]" seemed to characterize almost every politician's stump speech. Every problem, it seemed, had an effective legislative solution. Alan Ehrenhalt, the author of *The United States of Ambition*, finds that legislators of both parties still hold this belief. "Legislators are used to solving problems," he says. "Government tends to attract people who think government can solve problems. But once you get into things like crime, welfare, and education, you're trying to change human behavior, and that's much tougher to do. The New Deal was small potatoes compared to most of this stuff."

"Several things happen when the government gets into these areas," says James Q. Wilson, a professor of management and public policy at the University of California at Los Angeles. "First, no one really knows how to solve these problems. Second, the public itself is deeply conflicted about most of these issues; you rarely have a consensus from which to act. Third, these issues tend to be so complex that they overwhelm the process. And finally, when these measures fail to do much to solve something like crime—which is what inevitably happens—they greatly reinforce the general disillusionment with government. There's something to be said for sticking with what you know how to do."

During that legislative blizzard Congress was no longer just distributing money or dealing with problems in discrete areas (how to regulate the airwaves, or how to provide a supplemental income to senior citizens), and the grand problems it confronted, like poverty and crime, seemed to require a variety of coordinated strategies. "That was a key mistake," Theodore Lowi says. "Health and welfare are not holistic things; they're a collection of problems. The bills collapse of their own weight." Such bills also tend to be so elaborate that voters have difficulty understanding them—which means, at a minimum, that opponents have an easy time raising fears about them. Unsurprisingly, the public becomes more engaged when Congress is debating a seemingly straightforward issue like the Gulf War, in which voters can understand what is at stake.

Nonetheless, over time congressmen on both sides of the aisle began drafting longer, more comprehensive bills; the number of pages of law entered into the statute books during the relatively uneventful 1991–1992 session was two and a half times the number entered by the 1965–1966 Great Society Congress. With many legislators continually preoccupied by issues of openness and equal availability of services, access and due process became legislative focuses. That translated into greatly increased complexity and bureaucracy, not to mention a drain on the courts as litigants attempted to enforce their new rights. In 1936 there were 2,355 pages of regulations amplifying federal laws published in the Federal Register. By 1969 the number had risen to 20,464 pages; in the 1990s the register has been averaging about 60,000 pages a year.

## No Amendments Wanted

Trying to solve a national megaproblem with one huge bill is still an American obsession, as the recent health-care debate showed. Still, by the late 1960s the old model of legislating had begun to fall out of favor, at least in one respect. The criticism, advanced by Ralph Nader and others, was that administrative agencies such as the Interstate Commerce Commission and the Federal Communications Commission inevitably became controlled by the forces they were supposed to regulate. Moreover, distrust of authority was expanding along with voting rights, and there was a corresponding lack of trust in the opinions of experts vis-à-vis "the people." As David Schoenbrod, a professor at New York Law School, has related in *Power Without Responsibility* (1993), what followed was a series of congressional statutes (beginning with the Clean Air Act, in 1970), passed with bipartisan support, that started to abandon the concept of open-ended delegation to independent agencies. Instead these laws essentially ordered the agency in question to take action and gave "elaborate instructions about the goals that it should achieve and the procedures for promulgating them." These instructions often placed administrative obligations on the states, while Congress took credit for the benefits of the legislation.

As a result of this legislative model statutes not only became lengthier and more complicated but also began running up hidden costs, while parochial and elite interests inevitably asserted their influence with help from both sides of the aisle: it was Alaska's Republican senator Ted Stevens, after all, who got grant money for Alaska to try to convert the aurora borealis into electricity. (As Congress-watchers point out, by the past session Congress was appropriating money for a University of Georgia study of city pests, ordering the Department of Health and Human Services to hire "six medium sedans" for transport, and adding what amounted to a gang-rehabilitation program to a flood-relief bill.) And over time Congress confronted many scientific or technical questions—such as how to clean the air—that were far beyond the expertise of most congressmen. So legislators of both parties hired more staff members to deal with these questions, and stopped reading much of their own legislation. Because members needed to rely on experts to draft these extensive and specific statutes, they also became increasingly reliant on "special interests"—if not to write the bills, then at least to tell them what the bills said before a vote. Cutting committee staff, as the Republicans have done, will hardly solve this problem, particularly for newer members, who tend to know less about technical problems than their more experienced colleagues.

The effect of an interstate-highway-building program or a Voting Rights Act—two legislative success stories from the 1950s and 1960s—can be assessed fairly easily. But, as Bruce Ackerman and Susan Rose-Ackerman, professors at Yale Law School, ask in *The Uncertain Search for Environmental Quality*, how does a deliberative body measure precisely the relationship between clean water and public health, let alone determine whether clean water could be had more cheaply by another method?

What's more, even if a given approach makes sense now, things change over time. Once a bill gains a constituency—and all those that are enacted do, if only for economic reasons—it becomes very difficult to shift course.

The result has been a proliferation of vague or increasingly unworkable laws that judges cannot revise under current theories of statutory interpretation. (The same is not true of the common law.) These laws can also bankrupt the country, as the laws become ever more complex and costs mount. The Clean Air Act of 1970, complex as it was, filled forty-seven pages in the United States Code. The revision twenty years later filled more than 200 in the denser Congressional Record.

Having so many more constituents and areas of responsibility than it had in the past has also stymied Congress and shifted the way it operates. Besides muscling its way into areas once left to the states, Congress has spent an increasing amount of time over the past two decades on budgetary matters: the number of roll calls on budget questions in the House was almost six times as great in 1991 as it was in 1955—yet another trend that seems unlikely to change with Republican control. "The change in work load has affected the way Congress acts, which in turn has affected public perceptions," says Bruce I. Oppenheimer, a professor of political science at Vanderbilt University, who studies Congress. "In a time-constrained environment the opposition gains power. The filibuster wasn't used much before 1970, because it wasn't a very effective weapon. Who cared if you wasted time? Congress never ran out of time." In a legislative world where time is scarce, democratic values also tend to collapse and mistakes to become more common. One of the purposes of deliberation, after all, is to achieve consensus and avoid error. Tellingly, bills for many of the major legislative achievements of the past sixty years, though contentious, ended up passing with large majorities. For example, the Social Security Act passed in 1935 with seventy-seven votes in the Senate; the Civil Rights Act in 1964 won seventy-three.

Yet one of the distinguishing characteristics of recent sessions, particularly in the House, is that what little deliberation did once occur has been virtually eliminated. That, in turn, has increased partisanship. In recent years a bill has had about half the chance of passage that it had fifty years ago. In part to speed things up—which is, after all, what the public says it wants—bills introduced on the floor increasingly restrict amendments. Although the Republicans have promised to address that, so far there has been no significant change. Debates now typically take place with no one listening in the chamber, as anyone who has ever watched C-SPAN knows. Even the much-praised Senate and House exchanges before passage of the Gulf War resolution, in January of 1991, consisted primarily of members' rising to deliver prepared speeches to a body in which virtually every mind was already made up. And this year? The Republicans have added many new wrinkles to Congress, but careful deliberation does not appear to be among them.

## THE CAMERA AND CONGRESS

A different kind of congressional persona tends to flourish in the television age. Fifteen years ago Michael J. Robinson, a professor at Catholic University, wrote, "The increasingly greater reliance on the media for nomination, election, status in the Congress, and reelection is one sign of a new congressional character—one more dynamic, egocentric, immoderate, and, perhaps, intemperate." These telegenic figures, according to one source Robinson cited, were often more concerned with getting on television than with legislative mechanics—yet another reason for the lack of consensus, the emphasis on the illusion of results, and the expansion of staff to deal with the institution's real missions.

Because of its inherent biases, television has also subtly altered the way the public perceives Congress. C-SPAN, of course, has opened up the daily workings of Congress, but its effect is quite limited. C-SPAN's typical audience is minuscule compared with the audience that receives news about Congress from the major networks—which have greatly influenced the way print sources cover Congress.

The communications theorist Ernest Bormann once wrote that "television news coverage is, in many respects, an exercise in creative dramatics in which a cast of familiar characters assembles . . . and improvises a drama according to a stock scenario depending on the news event." By now the scenario involving Congress is very familiar. Because television is drawn to strong characters, it elevates the importance of the President and the speaker of the House vis-à-vis the institution of Congress. Because the medium is drawn to conflict, it denigrates the value of compromise, upon which legislatures depend, and plays up scandal or contentiousness. A recent study by S. Robert Lichter and Daniel R. Amundson, of the Center for Media and Public Affairs, has found that from 1972 to 1992 the proportion of network news stories concerning ethical lapses in Congress more than quadrupled, and the proportion of those portraying conflict between members nearly tripled from 1987 to 1992 (though, to be fair, conflict is up). Television is wedded to the dramatic gesture, and legislative bodies when legislating rarely act in a theatrical fashion. What's more, the legislative process is often messy and difficult; its lack of clear lines and packaging violates the whole spirit of scripted entertainment that has come to dominate the culture. The workings of Congress are complex and thus time-consuming to explain, and time is something that network television apparently cannot afford.

Changing the voters as much as the candidates, television creates a passive audience of viewer-voters who demand instant gratification and no loose ends. In a world where advertisers constantly proclaim, "You can have it all!" and "Just Do It!" voters have come to see government institutions as ones that should provide it all and just do it, Ross Perot–style. Commercial television also offers an implicit vision of the world in which it's not community or belief in an abiding principle that offers happiness but the acquisition of goods. No wonder, then, that as television became pervasive and the postwar consumer culture took root, voters came increasingly to view the purpose of Congress—if not of government—as guaranteeing their right to that happiness.

With Congress thus increasingly frustrated in its primary responsibility to develop and pass good laws, its members have turned to other tasks, many of them nurtured by television. Here, too, the Republicans have been no different from the Democrats. The memorable moments of the past three decades in Congress have naturally tended to come in front of the cameras—from the McCarthy hearings to Watergate to the Anita Hill–Clarence Thomas confrontation. Congress has been conducting investigations since the 1790s. Yet it is undeniable that congressional investigations have flourished in the television age, thereby appropriating more of Congress's time and attention. Unlike the typical lawmaking process, these hearings offer the broadcast media drama and compelling characters in a stately scene. And, as Daniel Boorstin pointed out nearly thirty-five years ago, in his book *The Image*, the real purpose of hearings is often difficult to discern. "In many cases," Boorstin wrote, "these committees have virtually no legislative impulse, and sometimes no intelligible legislative assignment."

And there is the confirmation process—another area that consumes increasing amounts of the Senate's energy, if only because the number of posts that require confirmation has risen from 149 to 310 since 1960. Confirmation fights are also part of our history, but dramatic confirmation *hearings* are mostly a media-age phenomenon. Here, too, the consensus is that the cameras have contorted the process into great TV drama but something of a well-documented travesty. In foreign policy, a stage that Presidents have long dominated, Congress has tried to share the television spotlight in recent decades, with the same mixed results and a commensurate loss of time to spend in other areas. In *War and Responsibility* (1993) the Stanford University law professor John Hart Ely argues that while Congress has appeared to try to take more responsibility for military action in recent decades, it has in fact happily abdicated to the President most of its powers in this area. This has allowed many members to claim credit when military ventures go well, but to hold accusatory hearings and press conferences before the cameras when they don't.

Congressional actions in the television age have thus come to join the category that Boorstin called "pseudo-events"—in which the illusion of results becomes far more significant in the culture than the results themselves. In legislative hearings that don't really look at legislation, in crime bills that almost everyone privately admits will do next to nothing to reduce crime, the appearance and the drama of the action overshadow the importance of the action itself. Pseudo-events, Boorstin said, are usually more interesting than real actions, and they therefore seem more compelling and often more real. He wrote,

Once we have tasted the charm of pseudo-events, we are tempted to believe they are the only important events. . . . And the poison tastes so sweet that it spoils our appetite for plain fact. Our seeming ability to satisfy our exaggerated expectations makes us forget that they are exaggerated.

## TAINTED PRESCRIPTIONS

In the end it is always easy to romanticize the past, just as it is tempting to exaggerate how much a shift in control will change Congress. A fifty-two-seat shift in the House is unusual in modern times, but it may mean only that the country is returning to the electoral patterns of a century ago, when party control of Congress often shifted back and forth by large margins, while the body drew its share of criticism. "There was no golden age of legislation," says the Yale political scientist David Mayhew.

Agreement is almost universal that Congress could take a number of steps both to purge itself of the effects of special-interest money and to make the legislative process operate more efficiently. After last November there is a perception of hope that the new majority will at least try to do the latter. (The Republican Party has never been enthusiastic about campaign-finance or lobbying reform.) But the Republicans, while in some ways addressing the expanding role of the federal government, appear only slightly more aware than the Democrats before them of the real polarities of sentiment that will have to be addressed before Congress can truly be reformed.

Few of the proposed structural reforms, moreover, would have the effect their proponents suggest. The notion, for example, that a national referendum would be any less susceptible than the legislative process to special-interest influence is ludicrous; and studies on term limits suggest that imposing a twelve-year limit would increase the mean turnover rate in the House by all of one percent per election (though it might, for better or worse, change the type of person elected to Congress). Sending Congress home for six months a year, or cutting down on staff, means that legislators would do less, more slowly; eliminating the filibuster and instituting referenda would be designed to get more or different laws on the books more quickly.

These reforms would not solve "the problem" with Congress, because voters and their representatives are terribly confused about what that is. Voters say they want less government at lower cost, but they apparently want it to do much of what it now does—or more. Polls tell us that among the major complaints about Congress are that it doesn't represent the voters well enough and that it becomes gridlocked—failing to solve the nation's lingering problems, such as health care and welfare reform. Yet over the past two generations Congress has become far more representative and responsive than it used to be, and it now addresses issues that previous legislatures never dreamed of. Nevertheless, as public disillusion

increases, the impulse has been to become even more closely tied to public opinion and to find new legislative ways of attacking megaproblems
more quickly and efficiently. The Republicans don't propose to turn all of
crime control or tort-law reform over to the states; they propose to enact
many of the sweeping reforms themselves, and do it better and faster than
the Democrats. So the demands and the contradictions spiral on, out of
control. The solutions are manifestations of the problem.

Ironically, what Congress may need is not more democracy but less,
and the will to address not bigger problems faster but smaller ones in
more-measured ways. Admittedly, much of the civil-rights legislation of the
1960s changed the country profoundly for the better, and subsequent efforts toward greater democracy and openness were implemented in good
faith. Now it is time to declare these efforts a success—we have democra-
tized the process!—and move on to developing a public philosophy to address some of the problems we have acquired from encouraging access to
national government.

In the populist rush to extend the spirit of democracy that, as Alexis de
Tocqueville reminded us 150 years ago, is part of the American character,
today's voters and leaders often forget that this is, in the end, a republic.
The founders feared the power of the mob and provided distance between
the rulers and the ruled, so that our representatives could deliberate
much like a jury and exercise collective judgment and even wisdom. Their
job, in the words of *The Federalist Papers*, was to "refine and enlarge" the
popular will. It is a hierarchical relationship; they are entrusted with
power. No parents or teachers worth their salt poll their children or pupils
constantly and then give in at the first sign of discontent—just as no legislators in their right minds would cut taxes while keeping government
benefits the same. Yet that's what pure representation will do for us a lot
of the time. Paradoxically, giving legislators the freedom to forget about
public opinion once in a while would do much to restore the voters' faith
in the integrity of their representatives. Similarly, few would quarrel with
the success of much of the New Deal—and even some of the Great Society—and many of our problems do require national solutions. But they
don't necessarily demand complicated, comprehensive solutions.

"If I could get legislators to do just one thing, it would be to take a
political Hippocratic oath," the author Alan Ehrenhalt says. "First, do no
harm. Just attack things you can do something about." Theodore Lowi
concurs. "Congress should narrow its agenda to a few things it knows how
to do," he says. "And it should quit writing these large bills which pretend
to address a problem but really don't, and create unforeseen problems in
their wake."

Those steps alone, it seems, would require a shift in sentiment, in both
parties and in the nation at large, not simply because they might mean the
passage of fewer complicated entitlement programs for the middle class,
but also because they would spell the end of the notion that there can
somehow be a risk-free society with a government solution to every problem. The public and the press would also be required to reevaluate

whether a buzz of legislative activity really constitutes a "golden age," and whether gridlock—which often means doing nothing because nothing can be done or because we don't know what to do—is always such a terrible thing. Yet such a change would even benefit liberalism. Congress would do less, but might well do better what it did, thereby increasing confidence in the national government generally. And the body might then have the will, occasionally, to act in the national interest by expanding government, even if that meant temporarily rejecting public opinion.

## DEBATING THE ISSUES: THE 104TH AND 105TH CONGRESSES: FROM REVOLUTION TO BUSINESS AS USUAL?

*See Lowi and Ginsberg, pp. 206–207 or brief edition, pp. 128–129*

*Immediately after the Republican rout in the 1994 midterm elections, political analysts began debating the historical significance of the election. Some drew parallels to the 1930 Democratic landslide, which presaged the realigning election of 1932 that swept Franklin Roosevelt and the Democrats into power for a generation. Others cautioned that Republicans should not become overconfident, however, because an equally compelling comparison could be made to the 1946 election in which Republicans regained control of the House and Senate for the first time in fourteen years, only to get trounced by Harry Truman and the Democrats in 1948. The parallels between 1946 and 1994 include an uncanny similarity in the policy agendas, similar grumblings (within the Democratic Party) about the lack of leadership from the White House, and the problems of divided government. Unlike the election of 1948, however, the Republican party maintained control of Congress in 1996. But are congressional Republicans still poised to turn policy and tradition on its head, or have they pulled back, chastened by the institutional challenges of governing and the public reaction to the 104th Congress?*

*Janet Hook and Jackie Koszczuk, both Congressional Quarterly journalists, offer insight into the difficulties Republicans faced as they assumed majority control. In Jaunary 1995, the Republicans had a clear agenda defined by the Contract with America. Their enthusiasm and momentum appeared to be unbounded, and House Republicans celebrated the vision and skill of their Speaker, Newt Gingrich (D-Georgia). Eighteen months later the party and its agenda were in disarray, following a failed confrontation with President Clinton over the budget and missteps by the leadership. Koszczuk argues that the Republican party had less of a mandate than it thought it had, and that internal divisions and a public backlash to the more extreme elements of the Republican agenda has forced the party to back off its sweeping agenda. It seems that Americans want a more centrist Congress, but not one that threatens to completely reject the welfare state.*

*Why has the Republican activism waned? Is the problem the institution of Congress itself? Would any political party operating within Congress meet the* same fate? Why? If voters supported the Contract with America in 1994, is it unfortunate that momentum for the agenda can be slowed, even stopped altogether? What changes in Congress might facilitate the broad policy changes that the Republican Party initially proposed?

## The Wall Street Journal
## "1946: Sobering Parallels for GOP"*

*Republicans this week take over both House and Senate after a long period of Democratic dominance. The last time this occurred was in 1946. As the accompanying headlines and excerpts from the* Wall Street Journal *and* New York Times *make clear, there are some uncanny parallels between the events of 1946–47 and 1994–95. That must have been a sobering thought for Republicans in their moment of triumph. The victory of '46, after all, led to a debacle in the presidential election of '48, just as the '94 landslide failed to put a Republican in the White House in '96.*

ARTHUR KROCK, "REPUBLICANS SURE OF CONTROL IN HOUSE MAKE GAINS IN NATION IN TURN TO RIGHT" IN THE *NEW YORK TIMES* (NOVEMBER 6, 1946). COPYRIGHT © 1946 BY THE NEW YORK TIMES COMPANY. REPRINTED WITH PERMISSION.

The voters in yesterday's elections for the full membership of the next House of Representatives, for one-third of the Senate and for Governors of many States, swung this nation sharply right in a left-veering world.

They placed the Republican party, the minority opposition in the United States for the last fourteen years, in control of the House by a majority of more than forty.

They put the government of twenty-five States, a majority of the Union, in Republican hands by adding Republican Governors in Ohio and Massachusetts to the twenty-three already belonging to that party.

They exchanged Democrats for Republicans in several key states—notably New York, Delaware, Massachusetts, Pennsylvania, Nevada, Idaho, and Ohio—with indications that the changes will amount to the ten necessary to give the Republicans control of the Senate. Also, a Wisconsin Senate seat changed from Progressive to Republican. . . .

JOHN D. MORRIS, "CHANGE ACCEPTED BY PARTY LEADERS" IN THE *NEW YORK TIMES* (NOVEMBER 7, 1946). COPYRIGHT © 1946 BY THE NEW YORK TIMES COMPANY. REPRINTED WITH PERMISSION.

Resignation, tinged in some instances with despair, pervaded the high command of the Democratic party today, while the jubilation of Republican leaders was noticeably modified by the realization of heavy responsibilities to come.

President Truman, returning to the White House after casting his vote in Missouri, was silent, but Robert Hannegan, Democratic national chairman, issued a statement after discussing the election results with the Chief Executive.

Reminding the Republicans of the "great responsibility" facing them as the majority party in the next Congress, Mr. Hannegan called for bipartisan efforts toward one basic objective which was the "strength and well-being" of the nation."

Carroll Reece, Republican national chairman, accepted the challenge of the responsibility and in turn called on the Democratic administration to acquiesce to the leadership of the Republican party.

While Democrats here generally accepted defeat without recriminations, Senator Claude Pepper of Florida, a leader of left-of-center forces, predicted "hard days ahead for people here and abroad."

He and Henry A. Wallace, former Secretary of Commerce, pleaded for "liberals" to continue their fight despite the setback at the polls.

ARTHUR KROCK, "THE NECESSITY AND DIFFICULTY OF SEMI-COALITION" IN THE *NEW YORK TIMES* (NOVEMBER 7, 1946). COPYRIGHT © 1946 BY THE NEW YORK TIMES COMPANY. REPRINTED WITH PERMISSION.

To perform the ordinary and essential functions of government a certain degree of cooperation between its executive and legislative branches, now that the Republicans have taken over control of Congress with a Democrat in the White House, has become a bipartisan instead of a Democratic problem. Beginning in the later years of President Roosevelt's administration, and culminating soon after President Truman took office, it was the split in the Democratic party in Congress that first reduced and then almost ended this cooperation. For the next two years the attitude of the Republican majority will determine its degree.

This is one of the very great changes produced by Tuesday's general elections. During his term heretofore Mr. Truman has dealt primarily with his own party, through its leaders, in Congress in proposing and seeking to legislate programs. Whenever he could bring the Democrats to vote for units in this program, which became less and less frequent, their numbers were sufficient to make it into law. Disagreeing Democrats were obliged to join the bulk of the Republicans in order to defeat administration measures or bury them in committee.

But when the Eightieth Congress assembles, the Republicans will be able to decide the fate of such measures unless they split as the Democrats have done. In that event an anti-administration coalition of members of the two major parties will still command the actions of Congress. But the responsibility to the country for Congress will rest on the Republicans, and not on the Democrats as it has for the last fourteen years.

That is why, in view of the difficulties of making a political bridge between a Republican majority and a Democratic President over which essential functions of government can travel, some long-headed Republican politicians hoped their gains would fall just short of majorities in the House and in the Senate. . . . But a landslide cannot be confined. . . .

VERMONT ROYSTER, "GOP PLAN: CUT TAXES, BALANCE BUDGET, REMOVE CONTROLS FROM BUSINESS" IN THE *WALL STREET JOURNAL* (NOVEMBER 7, 1946). REPRINTED WITH PERMISSION OF THE WALL STREET JOURNAL. COPYRIGHT © 1946 BY DOW JONES AND COMPANY, INC. ALL RIGHTS RESERVED.

Republican Party leaders have a blueprint of a positive program for the next session of Congress.

Implemented by the landslide in Tuesday's election, these specific and carefully thought-out plans call for:

A prompt ending of all wartime controls.

A return to conservative fiscal policy, with a balanced budget and lower taxes.

Abandonment of the philosophy of governmental interference with business and labor. . . .

This Tuesday's landslide, which ended 14 years of Democratic reign, did not catch the Republican leaders unprepared. They are ready to accept the full responsibility, as well as the authority, for the nation's legislation during the next two years.

The only thing not anticipated in the election was the sweeping nature of the G.O.P. victory. The election returns yesterday not only showed the Republicans in control of the House but in control of the Senate too.

The Republican leaders are prepared to rush through their program promptly. The only obstacle to its becoming law is the possibility of a veto from President Truman. But most G.O.P. leaders believe the President will accept the fact that the war-weary nation nation has changed its political thinking and will not resort to obstructionism. . . .

"REVIEW AND OUTLOOK: "THE MANDATE" IN THE *WALL STREET
JOURNAL* (NOVEMBER 7, 1946). REPRINTED WITH PERMISSION OF
THE WALL STREET JOURNAL. COPYRIGHT © 1946 BY DOW JONES AND
COMPANY, INC. ALL RIGHTS RESERVED.

One may hope that no Republican, at least none intelligent enough to deserve a responsible party voice, entertains any delusions that Tuesday's victory was due to any Republican display of high statesmanship, overwhelming wisdom or political consistency.

On the contrary the people turned against the Democrats because under a Democratic administration there had been a multiplication of controls, always arrogantly and often idiotically administered; because of an attempt to impose the "managed economy" with its assumption of super wisdom; because of the inevitable alliance that any such attempt must make with the forces of totalitarianism. There was an offensive mess and the electorate decided to be rid of those who made and preserved it. They turned to the Republicans because they had no other place to turn. They were under no delusion that the political dogs who rolled in the various ill-smelling portions of the mess always were of the Democratic breed. . . .

"WASHINGTON BUREAU: GOP SENATORS SET TO BALK 20% TAX SLASH
ADVOCATED BY REPUBLICAN LEADERS IN HOUSE" IN THE
*WALL STREET JOURNAL* (JANUARY 2, 1947). REPRINTED WITH
PERMISSION OF THE WALL STREET JOURNAL. COPYRIGHT © 1947 BY
DOW JONES AND COMPANY, INC. ALL RIGHTS RESERVED.

The Senate is likely to dash cold water on plans of the House Republican leaders to slash individual income taxes 20% "across the board."

The Senate Republicans and Democrats alike are cool to the 20% tax cut idea. They are determined first to reduce Federal expenditures, balance the budget and start liquidating the national debt. Then any remaining surplus would be used to lighten the taxpayers' load. . . .

JOHN D. MORRIS, "TRUMAN REJECTS RESIGNATION IDEA, PLANS
'NATIONAL WELFARE' POLICY", IN THE *NEW YORK TIMES*
(NOVEMBER 8, 1946). COPYRIGHT © 1946 BY THE NEW YORK TIMES
COMPANY. REPRINTED WITH PERMISSION.

With President Truman declining to give serious consideration to Senator J. William Fulbright's suggestion that Mr. Truman resign, Mr. Fulbright proposed today a constitutional amendment designed to eliminate future "lame duck" Presidents.

The Arkansas Democrat told a press conference he would introduce in the next Congress a resolution for an amendment to enable the House and Senate, by concurrent resolution, to call a national election at any time. Members of Congress as well as the President would have to go before the electorate for what would amount to a vote of confidence or no confidence in the tradition of British parliamentary law.

The people themselves and not the legislature, as in Britain, would still elect the executive head of the Government, it was emphasized by the Senator, a former Rhodes scholar. . . .

"REVIEW AND OUTLOOK: THE NEW CONGRESS" IN THE *WALL STREET JOURNAL* (JANUARY 6, 1947). REPRINTED WITH PERMISSION OF THE WALL STREET JOURNAL. COPYRIGHT © 1947 BY DOW JONES AND COMPANY, INC. ALL RIGHTS RESERVED.

Between the Congress just opening and its immediate predecessors there are a number of differences.

The most outstanding difference is that the new Congress has a Republican majority while its predecessors since the early 30's have been controlled by the Democrats. . . .

Perhaps a more important point is that the members of the new Congress return to Washington after a vacation during which most of them had the first real opportunity in some years to live in their home districts and to rub shoulders with the people there. The war Congresses were in almost continuous session and prolonged residence in Washington leaves one out of touch with the sentiment of the country outside Washington: the capital lives and thinks in an atmosphere which is likely to be one of its own making.

In the new Congress there will be an important group of new members. Freshmen members of the House and Senate do not head important committees and they are supposed to be seen rather than heard. Nevertheless they do vote, and if measures are not to their liking they can vote to change them. When their number is as large as it is in this Congress, they are a force to be reckoned with. . . .

VERMONT ROYSTER, "THE MAN WHO WILL RUN CONGRESS" IN THE *WALL STREET JOURNAL* (NOVEMBER 11, 1946). REPRINTED WITH PERMISSION OF THE WALL STREET JOURNAL. COPYRIGHT © 1946 BY DOW JONES AND COMPANY, INC. ALL RIGHTS RESERVED.

When last Tuesday's elections swept the Republican Party into control of Congress they also automatically—and somewhat inwittingly—handed the reins of government over to the Gentleman from Ohio. For Senator Robert A. Taft's voice was already the dominant one of the Party's Congressional councils, even above those more shrewd and experienced in the ways of politics.

It is no new phenomenon in our history for a President to lose his political initiative to a strong opposition leader in Congress. It has happened many times: to Cleveland, to Wilson, and most recently, to Herbert Hoover. The phenomenon in this case is Senator Taft himself, because he is not cut on the standard mold of a powerful party leader.

He is, in fact, the antithesis of a party wheelhorse. He is an independent-thinking man who rarely hesitates to disagree with anyone, including his own party associates, and he often does it publicly. His program for the Government is his own, and as a result he sometimes treads a lonesome path, pleasing neither to the liberals in his party nor to extreme conservatives. He has, therefore, made enemies in both camps.

Mr. Taft's biggest boom was the fact that when the Republicans began to gain power in the Congress he was the one party member who had a definite political philosophy and a program. Furthermore he had developed a strategical plan ready-cut to be put into action. As each new problem arose it was found that Mr. Taft had an answer thought out, and it gradually became easier and easier for his colleagues with no plan of their own simply to follow him. . . .

"GOP HOUSE AIDES ASK AUDIT OF PREDECESSORS" IN THE
*NEW YORK TIMES* (JANUARY 4, 1947). COPYRIGHT © 1947 BY THE
NEW YORK TIMES COMPANY. REPRINTED WITH PERMISSION.

Lindsay C. Warren, Controller General, disclosed tonight that the General Accounting Office which he heads was conducting an audit of the books of the disbursing and cashier's offices of the House of Representatives in the wake of the turnover of party control of that branch.

The audit, it was learned, was requested by Joseph W. Martin Jr., new Speaker of the House, after he had conferred with John Andrews, newly elected clerk of the House, and had instructed William F. Russell, elected today as sergeant-at-arms, not to take over the cashier's section of his office until the audit was complete. . . .

No audit, it was said, had been made during the last fifteen years.

Despite Republican economy plans, the nation cannot expect to pay off its public debt for a century, Joseph Martin, new Speaker, told the House as he took over his duties yesterday.

Mr. Martin (R., Mass.) listed repayment of public debt as one of his party's objectives while in control of Congress, but he indicated it will only attempt to pay off something over $2 billion annually.

"The debt into which this nation has been plunged is of such magnitude that it cannot be paid off in less than a century," he said. The debt now stands at $239 billion.

# Janet Hook
# "Republicans Step Up to Power in Historic 40-Year Shift"*

Euphoric about achieving power and giddy about making history, Republicans opened the 104th Congress Jan. 4—and then faced the hard work of governing. They tackled a legislative agenda that forces them to turn from concepts to details, from procedure to policy.

In the process, they have offered the first glimpse of what previously could be only imagined: what sort of Speaker Newt Gingrich will be, what manner of opposition Democrats will mount, what kind of place Congress will be now that Republicans are running the show.

Gingrich is emerging as a Speaker unlike any previously known to his colleagues: a self-styled intellectual for whom the office is not just a position of institutional power but a platform for revolutionary leadership.

House and Senate Democrats are starting out as a cautious minority, avoiding obstructionism and even embracing big parts of the GOP's popular legislative agenda.

And Congress as a whole has turned into a well-lit, busy stage on which Republicans and Democrats are reversing the partisan roles they have spent decades playing. If the first days of the new Congress are any indi-

* Janet Hook, "Republicans Step Up to Power in Historic 40-Year Shift" in *CQ Weekly Reports* ( January 7, 1995). Reprinted with permission.

cation, the entire institution will oscillate between the poles of cooperation and confrontation in the coming year.

The Republicans' agenda will for the first time face the rigors and uncertainties of the congressional process during the week of Jan. 9, as
House and Senate committees begin drafting bills to turn GOP political
slogans into legislative language.

That will test the conciliatory spirit and party unity that came easily to
Republicans on opening day of the 104th Congress, when they celebrated
their ascendancy, installed a raft of internal reforms in the House and
toasted their feisty new Speaker.

Differences between the parties—and among Republicans themselves
—will surely sharpen as House Republicans push for action on the 10-
plank "Contract With America," their policy manifesto.

"We all understand this is the easy part—the euphoria," said Rep.
Steve Gunderson, R-Wis. "We all know it's going to get harder. There will
be a lot of rough spots in this road."

## CONSENSUS ON THE CONCEPTS

With the inauguration of the new Congress, the clock began ticking:
House Republicans have promised a vote on all 10 planks of the Contract
With America, which includes dozens of legislative proposals, within 100
days. Although Republicans have promised only a vote in the House—and
not final action—the 100-day deadline is still an ambitious time frame.

The contract was drafted to skirt divisive social issues such as abortion
and school prayer, and to focus on politically popular issues about which
Republicans have few disagreements. GOP leaders are trying to start with
the ones they expect to be easiest to pass, such as the line-item veto and a
constitutional amendment to require a balanced budget.

Many of the proposals enjoy the support even of President Clinton,
who had a congenial meeting with GOP leaders at the White House
Jan. 5. "We can do a lot of business together for the benefit of the country," Clinton said after the meeting.

Gingrich, kicking off formal debate on the contract in Jan. 5 testimony
before the Ways and Means Committee, signaled some flexibility in carrying out the contract, which heretofore has been treated as sacrosanct.

"We don't think that we wrote in stone," said Gingrich, R-Ga. "We
thought we had in September some good ideas. But that was months ago.
The world changes."

Promises of cooperation and flexibility notwithstanding, divisions are
likely to emerge—among House Republicans, between moderates and
conservatives, newcomers and veterans, House and Senate Republicans—
as lawmakers put pen to paper.

While the balanced-budget amendment enjoys broad support, a group
of moderates in the House—and many Republicans in the Senate—object

to a proposal in the contract to include a requirement that income tax increases be approved by a three-fifths majority.

On the line-item veto, Senate Republicans are more cautious about giving new powers to the president than are House Republicans.

Freshmen are more enthusiastic about term limits than are more senior members, and House Republicans are more gung-ho than their Senate counterparts. There are also serious divisions among term limit proponents about whether the cap on House service should be six or 12 years.

Reaching a consensus will be even more difficult as Republicans tackle the complicated issue of overhauling welfare. Some moderate Republicans are uneasy about a contract proposal to deny cash benefits to certain welfare recipients while GOP governors are appealing for more state flexibility than some conservatives are advocating.

And efforts to cut the budget as deeply as Republicans say they want to will splinter the GOP in as many directions as there are constituent interests.

"We are dealing in concepts now, and we can agree on concepts," said E. Clay Shaw, Jr., R-Fla. "When we get into the details, different folks will have different ideas."

## END OF AN ERA

Whatever divisions among Republicans lurk beneath the surface, however, they were utterly invisible on opening day, which began at noon Jan. 4 and ended at 2:24 the next morning.

In the House, Republicans took majority control—230–204, with one independent—for the first time in 40 years. In the Senate, Republicans dominated, by 53–47, for the first time since 1986.

It was a day of uncommon attention to Congress, as the galleries and halls of the Capitol strained to accommodate all the visitors, reporters and television cameras on hand to witness or record history in the making.

The proceedings were riddled with symbols of one era ending and another beginning. Gingrich was introduced as Speaker for the first time by the House doorkeeper, whose job was soon to be abolished by Gingrich. He was sworn into office by Michigan Democrat John D. Dingell, the dean of the House and an emblem of the New Deal liberalism that Gingrich is dedicated to dismantling. The ceremony was attended by Gingrich's predecessor as Republican leader, Robert H. Michel of Illinois, a pillar of the conciliatory, traditional Republicanism that Gingrich aimed at destroying in his ascent to power.

As the House convened, the chamber was teeming with ebullient Republicans and grim Democrats—and lawmakers' children, cheerfully oblivious to the political significance of the events swirling around them. Gingrich's parents, wife and daughters watched proudly from the gallery as he realized the dream of his lifetime.

The vote to elect the new Speaker was taken the old-fashioned way, by calling the roll. After the predictable results were announced—Gingrich was elected over Democratic leader Richard A. Gephardt of Missouri by the traditional party line vote, 228–202—and the Speaker-elect was presented to the House, Republicans erupted into cheers of triumph that had been pent up through decades of powerlessness.

"Newt! Newt! Newt!" they chanted, like fans at a sporting event. "It's a whole Newt world!" shouted one person above the din.

Reaching for a dignified response in his party's darkest hour, Gephardt hailed America's ability to accommodate peacefully major transfers of power.

"With resignation but with resolve, I hereby end 40 years of Democratic rule of this House," Gephardt said, as he passed the gavel to Gingrich. "You are now my Speaker. Let the great debate begin."

## A CONCILIATORY TONE

Gingrich, in ascending to the Speakership, completed his implausible 16-year journey from the back benches of the House to its pinnacle of power, from being the enfant terrible of the Republican Party to its redeemer.

In a televised acceptance speech that introduced Gingrich to a wider audience across the country, he set a conciliatory tone that contrasted with his well-established reputation as a divisive partisan.

"If each of us will reach out prayerfully and try to genuinely understand the other," he told his colleagues, "if we'll recognize that in this building we symbolize America writ small, that we have an obligation to talk with each other, then I think a year from now we can look on the 104th [Congress] as a truly amazing institution."

It was a rambling, 35-minute address that spoke in many idioms—as Gingrich is wont to do. It ranged from bombast to personal reflection, from lofty intellectual constructs to arcane detail. It was a speech, largely extemporized, that could be given by no one but Gingrich—something that could not be said of many politicians' scripted speeches.

Sounding like the history professor he once was, Gingrich quoted Alexis de Tocqueville and unearthed obscure facts about the last Speaker from Georgia, Charles Frederick Crisp (Speaker 1891–95). Sounding like the Washington insider he is now, he sprinkled his speech with acknowledgments to House colleagues few television viewers would recognize.

But he did not sound like the tub-thumping partisan most people think he is. He called on Republicans to visit inner-city districts of black and Hispanic members. He condemned violence at abortion clinics (albeit indirectly). He hailed the Democratic Party's accomplishments in civil rights and social policy.

"The fact is that it was [President] Franklin Delano Roosevelt who gave hope to a nation that was in despair and could have slid into dictatorship,"

Gingrich said. "And the fact is every Republican has much to learn from studying what the Democrats did right."

Throughout the speech, Gingrich set an unusually personal tone: He spoke about his emotions of the moment; he mentioned that he and his father were adopted as children; he acknowledged the presence of his extended family, down to his nephews and nieces.

It was appropriate for a man whose election as Speaker was not just an institutional milestone but the end of a personal crusade. While most recent Speakers have been patient institutionalists who were slowly lifted to high office by the traditions of the House, Gingrich scrambled up the power structure with deliberateness and drive, smashing tradition along the way.

## FAMILIAR SCENES

The bipartisan spirit of Gingrich and Gephardt's speeches gave way to familiar partisan wrangling, as debate turned to GOP proposals to cut staff, ban proxy voting and make other changes in internal rules.

That tussle was the first real test of House Democrats' opposition strategy, which is still clearly a work in progress.

"We haven't begun to decide how we're going to cope in the minority," said Charles W. Stenholm, D-Texas.

A glimpse of internal dissent among Democrats emerged during the vote for Speaker: Two conservative Democrats, Gene Taylor and Mike Parker, both of Mississippi, voted "present" rather than endorse Gephardt.

Parker said the re-election of Gephardt as Democratic leader was like going to the captain of the *Titanic* and saying, "Let's go on a boat ride."

Democrats found little to oppose in the rules package itself, but they complained bitterly because Republicans were prohibiting any amendments to the package. The squabble was a stark reversal of roles for the two parties because for years in the minority, Republicans complained about precisely the same practice when Democrats shut out amendments.

Each side accused the other of hypocrisy—not a pretty sight for those who hoped the debate would help restore public confidence in Congress.

"If the current yes-you-did, no-I-didn't wallowing in hypocrisy continues, the voters will say a plague on both your houses," said Pat Williams, D-Mont.

Democrats criticized Republicans' reform agenda for not doing more to curb special interest influence in Congress. Democrats said they wanted to add a proposal to ban members from accepting gifts from lobbyists and to impose new limits on book royalties.

The book royalty proposal was an obvious slap at Gingrich, who in December was mired in controversy over a $4.5 million advance he had been offered to produce two books. It was a deal that met with criticism from fellow Republicans as well as Democrats, who said he was cashing in on his new position of power. Gingrich turned down the advance in favor of receiving royalties on future book sales, saying he did not want the controversy to eclipse the GOP agenda in Congress.

The Democrats' proposal to limit royalties and gifts provoked a vintage Gingrich barrage of partisan firepower just a few hours before his conciliatory acceptance speech. "To have the party, which has run this House like a machine, which was defeated after 40 years, which has been repudiated, to have the same gang in charge come back now . . . saying, 'Oh, we're not being fair, we're not for real reform. . . .' " Gingrich said. "Now they're for real reform. It does, at times, make one wonder about just how dumb they think the American people are."

But Gingrich made a point of promising in his acceptance speech that the House would consider campaign finance reform, lobbying reform and gift-ban legislation this spring.

### FOR THE GOP—AN EASY SELL

Opening day in the House also provided the first test of Republicans ability to hold their troops in line.

House Republican Whip Tom DeLay, R-Texas, said one of his first jobs as enforcer of the party line was to make sure Republicans—especially the many freshmen who had been elected on reform platforms—stuck with the GOP leadership in blocking Democratic efforts to offer a gift ban.

It was an easy sell, DeLay said, particularly because the Democrats linked it to the book royalty proposal that was so obviously directed at Gingrich.

"That made it real easy for the freshmen," said DeLay.

There was little question that Republicans would unanimously back most other House rules. However, there was one proposal for which unanimity could not be taken for granted: a proposed rule requiring a three-fifths majority to approve income tax increases.

Sherwood Boehlert, R-N.Y., said between 25 and 30 Republicans, mostly moderates, had concerns about including such a restriction in the constitutional amendment to balance the budget. A key question was whether they would swallow that reservation and support a similar restriction as a House rule.

They did: The rule passed with no Republican opposition—because the limit is almost meaningless in House rules, said Gunderson. The three-fifths requirement can be waived by a majority vote.

Even DeLay acknowledged that the limit was largely symbolic. "It doesn't make a whole lot of difference," he said. "So long as Gingrich is Speaker, there won't be a tax increase."

Whatever reservations members might have had, nothing mattered more than sticking together on that day of heady pride in being a Republican. "I want to show unity within the Republican Party today," said Boehlert. "There is a genuine team spirit today."

# Jackie Koszczuk
## "Members Move to Claim Center as Voters Demand Moderation"*

House Republicans may have read too much into the election that brought them to power two years ago, but they have a good grasp of the meaning of Nov. 5. It was not a revolution, it was a second chance. To ensure that the message was clear, voters narrowed the GOP majority sufficiently to discourage any residual bravado.

Now, the people who stormed the Capitol in the aftermath of the 1994 elections are searching for ways to function in the new, post-revolutionary order.

Voters have signaled that centrism and moderation will be rewarded, and neither was a defining strength of the first Republican-controlled House in four decades. Rather, returning lawmakers are looking for guidance to the final weeks of the 104th Congress, when they put their strong differences with President Clinton aside to push through initiatives that turned out to be popular with voters.

Republicans are also blowing the dust off the old House operating manual. Bipartisanship is making a comeback, at least in the early rhetoric of House leaders and the White House. And committees likely will be the centers of legislative activity, superseding all-Republican task forces created and controlled by the Speaker.

In 1994, when the GOP took control of the House, Speaker Newt Gingrich, R-Ga., and his top lieutenants rushed to Washington and claimed a broad mandate for their "Contract With America." Today, the post-election mood could not be more different.

Gingrich, whose politics and persona became a liability in many re-election campaigns, is being edged from center stage by an ascendant Trent Lott, the Republican Senate majority leader from Mississippi.

Although Gingrich called the election results "pretty amazing, a truly historic moment," that was not the overriding sentiment.

The mood was relief, not euphoria. Most Republican House members know how close they came to the abyss in the closing weeks of the campaign, how near they were to *not* becoming the first Republican majority since Herbert C. Hoover's day to win back-to-back House elections.

They can take heart that the election affirmed their basic philosophy of government: A national survey of voters showed that more Americans fear a Congress that is too liberal than one that is too conservative, a sign of the center-right tilt of the electorate. And Clinton was re-elected in large part because he moved away from the left in the direction of the House's conservative ideas.

"We've all learned a great deal," said Majority Leader Dick Armey of

* Jackie Koszczuk, "Members Move to Claim Center as Voters Demand Moderation" in *CQ Weekly Reports* (November 9, 1996). Reprinted with permission.

Texas. "The president pretty well ran on our themes. And I think that gives us a great deal of opportunity to work together and to move forward on the commonly shared legislative agenda."

But House Republicans are chastened by the backlash to the more extreme elements of their agenda and to bare-knuckled tactics like government shutdowns.

Chief Deputy Whip Dennis Hastert, R-Ill., described the new mood of the House this way: "We have to work together to get bipartisan support. That's how we will put our mark on history."

Ronald M. Peters Jr., director of the Carl Albert Congressional Research and Studies Center at the University of Oklahoma, said, "What Republicans ought to be aiming for is a long-term majority where the center of gravity lies with them. If they can do that, policy will flow in their direction."

## Less GOP Maneuvering Room

As a result of the election, the House GOP conference, the group of all House Republicans, is slightly more conservative than it was before. Although some of the more ardent members of the caucus' hard right were defeated, including 13 of the 74 freshmen, several moderates also lost. The new Republican freshmen are about as conservative as they were in 1994.

But there are fewer Republicans and more Democrats overall. The GOP leadership, which had little room to maneuver when the party ratio favored them 235–197 in the 104th Congress, is now in an even tighter squeeze with a likely ratio of 227–207 and one independent, according to unofficial results.

The new political dynamic could give Republican moderates power beyond their small number. "Any 10 people, if they band together, can prevent something from happening," said Rep. Michael N. Castle, R-Del.

That is the kind of role moderates played during political fights like raising the minimum wage last year. House Majority Leader Armey had been determined to stop the Democrat-led proposal until moderates threatened to cross party lines. The leadership was forced to bring a bill to the floor, where it passed.

The role of conservative Democrats, the self-described "Blue Dogs," could also grow as both parties court the center to avoid appearing extreme. The collective lesson of the last two elections seems to be that voters do not like extremes: Clinton was punished in the 1994 midterm election for policies that were too liberal, just as Republican lawmakers suffered a voter backlash in this election.

"We can spend the next two years jockeying for tactical position between the two parties, or we can solve some problems," said Rep. David E. Skaggs, D-Colo. "I would prefer to solve some problems."

"In order to resolve conflicts, the Republicans and Democrats are going to have to broaden their base," said William F. Connelly Jr., a politics professor at Washington and Lee University.

Tactically, the House Republicans learned last year that they cannot force Clinton to sign their legislation, and that the quickest way to get something done is to find middle ground with the president, as distasteful as that is for the conservative true believers. Clinton's overwhelming re-election victory assures that they will have to continue to do so.

Gingrich and Armey have already begun discussions about a new way of governing. Their staffs say there will be more bipartisan work at the committee level, with leaders holding more extensive briefings with committee chairmen, who were shoved aside during the contract stampede. Also, the approach will be more incremental, they say. The House is unlikely to crusade for the abolition of three Cabinet departments as it did in its first term.

"This will be a small-step Congress," said John J. Pitney, associate government professor at Claremont McKenna College in California. "It will not produce landmark legislation or remake America with policy changes."

The leadership also plans to air its proposals before a wider House audience and to attempt to sell its ideas to the public before bills hit the floor. That means including a wide spectrum of Republicans and also Democrats in the process.

Increased bipartisanship is not one of Gingrich's strengths. Democrats villainized him in an avalanche of campaign television advertising. And they pressed for the ethics probe being conducted by special counsel James M. Cole.

Lott, who works well with Democrats, is more likely to become Congress' liaison to the White House. Lott's political star is ascending. His Senate majority grew larger, not smaller, in the election. And he does not have the baggage of widespread unpopularity with the public that Gingrich does.

## CHANGING FORTUNES

Posing the greatest threat to the newly launched quest for bipartisanship is the ethics issue.

House Republicans have showed no sign of abating their multifront attack on Clinton's ethics. The controversy over large donations to the Democratic Party from foreigners, which erupted during the campaign, will be added to a long roster of issues pressed by Republicans. They include the Whitewater land deal, alleged White House abuses of FBI files and alleged cronyism in the Travel Office.

For their part, House Democrats have announced no ceasefire in their pursuit of ethics charges against Gingrich. Democrats have lodged numerous complaints, some of which were dismissed and some of which were deemed serious enough for further investigation by Cole.

"It's like two cars driving down the highway. There is the ethics investigation car and the policy car," said Burdett A. Loomis, a University of Kansas political scientist. "If the ethics investigation car veers into the policy car and smashes it, then little will happen. If you keep the cars separated, things can actually get done."

Initially, the two parties will also struggle for control of the agenda. House Republicans, who feel burned by Clinton for their bold attempts to balance the federal budget, are already determined to have the president move first and propose solutions to tough problems.

Foremost among those is the question of checking the rapid growth of the financially troubled Medicare program for the elderly—an issue that helped the Democrats tar the Republicans as heartless extremists in the campaign.

Armey said that once Clinton gets the annual report on the financial health of Medicare, the House will wait to see what he does. "His trustees will give a report," he said. "We would expect the president to examine that report and to make his recommendations to Congress."

Thomas E. Mann, a Brookings Institution political scientist, said, "We have neither the situation of the president in early 1993 or of Gingrich in early 1995, where it was absolutely clear where the initial program would come from. It will be a combination of initiatives from the White House and Congress."

General policy areas are being discussed by House leaders, including some holdovers from the previous, tumultuous Congress. They include: deficit reduction and balancing the budget, drug abuse and crime, health care, and banking and utility overhauls.

"The power is going to come from the center, but this is ultimately a Republican majority, and we are going to continue to pursue the same issues we pursued over the last two years," said Republican Christopher Shays of Connecticut.

Harold Rogers, R-Ky., said both Democrats and Republicans have been bloodied in the last two elections, making a course other than the strident partisanship that marked that period desirable for both sides.

"I think we learned our lessons, and they learned theirs. Both sides will be more measured," he said. "I think we will see a more moderated Congress."

# 6

# The President: From Chief Clerk to Chief Executive

## The Constitutional Basis of the Presidency

*See Lowi and Ginsberg, pp. 221–233 or brief edition, pp. 136–141*

*Wary of the power of the monarchy represented by Great Britain's rule, the founders of the American Constitution voiced grave concerns about the scope of power conferred upon a chief executive. Different proposals were suggested, including the idea that power should be distributed among two or more chiefs of state. Later, having accepted the idea of a single head of state, the problem lay in designing a system to insure that the chief executive could be an active and effective leader while restraining his or her ability to usurp more power than was warranted, given the republican structure of the American system.*

*Alexander Hamilton, author of several of* The Federalist Papers, *supported a strong central government headed by a single, powerful executive official. "Energy in the executive is a leading character in the definition of good government," he argued, and that energy could be sustained only by vesting authority in a single individual whose actions could then be carried out with "[d]ecision, activity, secrecy, and dispatch."*

## Alexander Hamilton
### *The Federalist No. 70\**

There is an idea, which is not without its advocates, that a vigorous executive is inconsistent with the genius of republican government. . . . Energy in the executive is a leading character in the definition of good government. It is essential to the protection of the community against foreign attacks; it is not less essential to the steady administration of the laws; to the protection of property against those irregular and high-handed combinations which sometimes interrupt the ordinary course of justice; to the security of liberty against the enterprises and assaults of ambition, of faction, and of anarchy. . . .

A feeble executive implies a feeble execution of the government. A fee-

* Alexander Hamilton, *The Federalist No. 70*, ed. Clinton Rossiter (New York: NAL, 1961).

ble execution is but another phrase for a bad execution; and a government ill executed, whatever it may be in theory must be, in practice, a bad government.

Taking it for granted, therefore, that all men of sense will agree in the necessity of an energetic executive, it will only remain to inquire, what are the ingredients which constitute this energy? How far can they be combined with those other ingredients which constitute safety in the republican sense? And how far does this combination characterize the plan which has been reported by the convention?

The ingredients which constitute energy in the executive are unity; duration; an adequate provision for its support; and competent powers.

The ingredients which constitute safety in the republican sense are a due dependence on the people, and a due responsibility.

Those politicians and statesmen who have been the most celebrated for the soundness of their principles and for the justness of their views have declared in favor of a single executive and a numerous legislature. They have, with great propriety, considered energy as the most necessary qualification of the former, and have regarded this as most applicable to power in a single hand; while they have, with equal propriety, considered the latter as best adapted to deliberation and wisdom, and best calculated to conciliate the confidence of the people and to secure their privileges and interests.

That unity is conducive to energy will not be disputed. Decision, activity, secrecy, and dispatch will generally characterize the proceedings of one man in a much more eminent degree than the proceedings of any greater number; and in proportion as the number is increased, these qualities will be diminished.

This unity may be destroyed in two ways: either by vesting the power in two or more magistrates of equal dignity and authority, or by vesting it ostensibly in one man, subject in whole or in part to the control and cooperation of others, in the capacity of counselors to him. . . .

[A]ttaching ourselves purely to the dictates of reason and good sense, we shall discover much greater cause to reject than to approve the idea of plurality in the executive, under any modification whatever.

Whenever two or more persons are engaged in any common enterprise or pursuit, there is always danger of difference of opinion. If it be a public trust or office in which they are clothed with equal dignity and authority, there is peculiar danger of personal emulation and even animosity. From either, and especially from all these causes, the most bitter dissensions are apt to spring. Whenever these happens, they lessen the respectability, weaken the authority, and distract the plans and operations of those whom they divide. If they should unfortunately assail the supreme executive magistracy of a country, consisting of a plurality of persons, they might impede or frustrate the most important measures of the government in the most critical emergencies of the state. And what is still worse, they might split the community into the most violent and irreconcilable factions, adhering differently to the different individuals who composed the magistracy. . . .

Upon the principles of a free government, inconveniences from the source just mentioned must necessarily be submitted to in the formation of the legislature; but it is unnecessary, and therefore unwise, to introduce them into the constitution of the executive. It is here too that they may be most pernicious. In the legislature, promptitude of decision is oftener an evil than a benefit. The differences of opinion, and the jarring of parties in that department of the government, though they may sometimes obstruct salutary plans, yet often promote deliberation and circumspection, and serve to check excesses in the majority. When a resolution too is once taken, the opposition must be at an end. That resolution is a law, and resistance to it punishable. But no favorable circumstances palliate or atone for the disadvantages of dissension in the executive department. Here they are pure and unmixed. There is no point at which they cease to operate. They serve to embarrass and weaken the execution of the plan or measure to which they relate, from the first step to the final conclusion of it. They constantly counteract those qualities in the executive which are the most necessary ingredients in its composition—vigor and expedition, and this without any counterbalancing good. In the conduct of war, in which the energy of the executive is the bulwark of the national security, everything would be to be apprehended from its plurality. . . .

[O]ne of the weightiest objections to a plurality in the executive, and which lies as much against the last as the first plan is that it tends to conceal faults and destroy responsibility. Responsibility is of two kinds— to censure and to punishment. The first is the more important of the two, especially in an elective office. Men in public trust will much oftener act in such a manner as to render them unworthy of being any longer trusted, than in such a manner as to make them obnoxious to legal punishment. But the multiplication of the executive adds to the difficulty of detection in either case. It often becomes impossible, amidst mutual accusations, to determine on whom the blame or the punishment of a pernicious measure, or series of pernicious measures, ought really to fall. It is shifted from one to another with so much dexterity, and under such plausible appearances, that the public opinion is left in suspense about the real author. . . .

It is evident from these considerations that the plurality of the executive tends to deprive the people of the two greatest securities they can have for the faithful exercise of any delegated power, *first*, the restraints of public opinion, which lose their efficacy, as well on account of the division of the censure attendant on bad measures among a number as on account of the uncertainty on whom it ought to fall; and, *second*, the opportunity of discovering with facility and clearness the misconduct of the persons they trust, in order either to their removal from office or to their actual punishment in cases which admit of it. . . .

I clearly concur in opinion, . . . with a writer whom the celebrated Junius pronounces to be "deep, solid, and ingenious," that "the executive power is more easily confined when it is one"; that it is far more safe there should be a single object for the jealousy and watchfulness of the people; and, in a word, that all multiplication of the executive is rather dangerous than friendly to liberty.

PUBLIUS

## DEBATING THE ISSUES: PRESIDENTIAL POWER: BROAD OR NARROW?

*See Lowi and Ginsberg p. 227 or brief edition, pp. 138–139*

*The Framers clearly intended Congress to be the premier branch of government, and it is only since the 1930s that the president has taken over that position. To many observers, the Republican takeover of Congress in 1994 signified a resurgence of the legislative branch's power. Historian Michael Beschloss argues that political power has "decisively shifted" to Congress, and that the Imperial Presidency is now over. House Speaker Newt Gingrich's ability to set the national agenda in 1995 supports this view. However, James Patterson, also a historian, argues that recent events are merely part of an ongoing struggle for power between the president and Congress. He notes that Gingrich and his Republican allies have actually sought to constrain Congress's power, through the line-item veto, term limits, a balanced budget amendment, and other procedural obstacles to an activist government. The president, concludes Patterson, retains substantial institutional and political resources, and the public will continue to look to the office for leadership.*

*Who is right? Has Congress regained some institutional strength vis-a-vis the president since 1994? What evidence can you identify to demonstrate the ascendancy of Congress, or the continued prominence of the presidency in governing the nation? Will the modified line item veto, which went into effect in January 1997, have an impact on the institutional balance of power? Will Newt Gingrich's scandals and embattled leadership, or President Clinton's various problems ranging from Paula Jones and campaign finance to the continuing Whitewater saga, have an impact on the balance of power?*

# Michael R. Beschloss, "The End of an Era"*

Listen closely, and you may hear the death rattle of the presidency we have known for 60 years. Seldom in recent history has the engine of political initiative in America so decisively shifted from White House to Congress.

* Michael R. Beschloss, "The End of an Era" in *Newsweek* (January 9, 1995). Copyright © 1995 by Newsweek, Inc. All rights reserved. Reprinted with permission.

This week Newt Gingrich's Republicans will begin enacting a hundred-day plan of the like once conceived only by presidents. Bob Dole has traveled to London in pursuit of his own foreign policy. Dick Gephardt, who holds the job Sam Rayburn once called "the president's man in the House," has declared his independence from Bill Clinton.

The resurgence of Congress may seem to be merely the temporary result of Clinton's repudiation by November voters. But it is more likely to prove the crowning blow to what Arthur Schlesinger Jr. in his 1973 book called "The Imperial Presidency"—the phenomenon in which an outsize share of political power came to be vested in one office.

The Founders deliberately limited presidential authority. Abraham Lincoln expanded his to fight the Civil War, but that was quickly dissipated by a parade of successors—Grant, Hayes, Garfield, Arthur—who deferred to Capitol Hill in a period Woodrow Wilson called "congressional government." Theodore Roosevelt and Wilson ruled in heroic fashion, but after them, the office shrank into its old template, shackled by a Congress grown adverse to presidential meddling in economics and world affairs.

World stage: The grandiose presidency owed its birth to the Great Depression, when Congress gave Franklin Roosevelt extraordinary power in domestic affairs, and World War II, when it did the same on the world stage. After VJ Day, the presidency might have receded to its modest origins. But by then, most Americans thought that FDR had done a better job than Congress of fighting depression and fascism.

The cold war injected new adrenaline into the presidency and swelled the executive branch. Citing Soviet advances in Europe and Asia, Harry Truman insisted on bipartisanship in foreign policy, but what he really wanted—and got—was congressional deference to the White House. The wildly increased postwar federal budget gave presidents new opportunities to impose their priorities on American life. During the liberal solstice of the 1960s, Americans exalted the president's ability to rise above the narrow bickering and petty compromises of congressional barons and earls: without the stewardship of President Lyndon Johnson, would we have seen the Civil Rights or Voting Rights acts?

During these years, the presidency acquired a mystique that Congress could not hope to match. Television gave presidents a potent means to impress the public, squeezing members of Congress to the periphery like Hollywood extras. Journalists and historians began writing about the "Leader of the Free World." A newly redesigned presidential seal appeared on matchbooks, cuff links, swizzle sticks and golf balls. West Wing functionaries invoked cliches like the "awesome burdens" of the "loneliest job in the world" to shake off annoyances. This lurch toward grandeur reached its zenith with Richard Nixon, who waged the most serious effort of any U.S. president to grab power, by means legal and not, culminating in Watergate.

That scandal did much to deflate the office—and as Congress took a lead role in forcing Nixon's resignation, it seemed to be reasserting itself. But after a few token reforms, Congress returned to its genteel ways. This was in keeping with its courtliness on foreign policy. Against LBJ's and Nixon's undeclared war in Indochina, the House and Senate could only muster piece-meal statutes against U.S. involvement and the dubious War Powers Act. That enabled Congress to demand removal of U.S. troops deployed without its consent, but also allowed presidents to dispatch troops for 90 days on their own authority.

Chief bogeyman: Today, our presidents can brandish no American-Soviet confrontation to provide cover for their domestic and foreign-policy mistakes. The entire executive branch is under attack—even by Bill Clinton. The president has now become flypaper for everything Americans hate about politics. In our current adoration for the grass roots, the chief bogeyman is the one who seems most distant from the people. Talk radio and hundreds of cable channels give voice and face time to thousands of competing leaders, from the 535 members of Congress to Rush Limbaugh.

This week the Congress is asserting itself in a way it did not dream of doing after Vietnam and Watergate. Are we embarking upon a new era of congressional government? The true test won't come until the same party seizes control of both the White House and Capitol Hill. It takes less hubris for Republicans in Congress to steal power from their nemesis Clinton than from a President Dick Cheney—or a President Bob Dole. Gingrich shrewdly notes that some elements of his program, such as the line-item veto and repeal of War Powers, may actually give more power to the president. There is also the possibility Americans will conclude the 104th Congress muffed its big chance, and demand that the next president clean up the mess.

# James Patterson
## "Not So Fast, Newt"*

Americans had barely left the polls last November before they were told that they had forged a new world of politics. *Congressional Quarterly* explained, "The electoral meteorite that slammed into the American political landscape November 8 represents the end of an era. The New Deal/cold war period, stretching back to Franklin D. Roosevelt and defining the nation for three generations, now is gone. And the voters have announced that they want their politics to march into the beckoning future and not hark back to the dead past."

Republicans plan to remake Congress so that it illuminates this "beckoning future." Newt Gingrich, like Henry Cabot Lodge in 1919 and Robert Taft in 1947, expects to exploit the apparent popular mandate of his

---

party in order to challenge the president and to establish Congress—and the states—as guiding lights of American government. Indeed, Gingrich talks like a parliamentarian ready to enact an ideological platform. "We are doing real things," he has said. "For the first time in many, many years, there is a political leadership that is doing after the election exactly what we said we were going to do before the election."

Many political developments, both short- and long-term, seem to justify these predictions. Republican members of Congress sit high in the saddle these days, and Gingrich is set to become the most powerful legislative leader in memory. A stroll through American history during this century, however, suggests that the always-tense relationship between the legislative and executive branches will continue, with neither succeeding in establishing supremacy. As in the past, they will have to share power and cooperate, for the Founding Fathers did a remarkably good job of requiring that the two institutions muddle through together.

The results of the 1994 elections appear to support the notion that some aspects of our politics have realigned, and that Congress—at least for the next two years—will be in the catbird seat. Republicans in the House can count several developments that historically have bolstered congressional resolve. One of these is the remarkably high number of relatively new members in the House; more than half of Gingrich's troops have arrived on Capitol Hill since 1992; seventy-three are newcomers. If we can generalize about much of anything in American politics, it is that new majorities are especially likely to hold together in the short run. Not since the post-Watergate babies of 1975—the most recent midterm shift of magnitude—have Americans seen so feisty a group as Gingrich and his spear-carriers. And the class of Watergate Democrats was considerably less united than Republicans (at least in the House) appear to be in 1995.

Longer-term historical trends further the likelihood that Clinton (and subsequent presidents) will face major obstacles to coalition-building on Capitol Hill. Among these is the volatility of voters and the consequent decomposition of partisan loyalties. Indeed, Democrats such as Bob Kerrey, David Boren and Jim Cooper proved almost as troublesome to Clinton during the past two years as Republicans did. These dramatic trends date from the 1890s and the progressive era. Temporarily stemmed by the New Deal, the changes have intensified since the 1950s. The spread of television, enabling individual candidates to run without much need for party support, has further weakened party solidarity. Not since Lyndon Johnson in 1965 (relying heavily on freshman Democrats) has a Democratic president been able to depend on fairly solid partisan backing in Congress.

This is another way of saying that FDR's powerful Democratic electoral coalition, while potent in congressional races for sixty years, has long been ineffective on Capitol Hill. Any notion that a liberal Congress has dominated since 1933 is a myth. Scholars choose different dates to mark its downfall, but we may begin as early as 1938, when Republicans gained eighty House seats. Although they remained a minority, they succeeded in defeating virtually all of FDR's domestic programs. For the remaining six years of his presidency Roosevelt had Democratic majorities in both houses, but lost battle after battle over domestic matters to an informal but determined conservative coalition of Republicans and (mostly) Southern Democrats. The Senate, he sneered in 1945, consisted largely of "a bunch of incompetent obstructionists."

Harry Truman did not fare much better. When he outlined his domestic program in September 1945, House Minority Leader Joseph Martin of Massachusetts exclaimed, "Not even President Roosevelt ever asked so much at one sitting. It is just a case of out-New Dealing the New Deal." Truman stayed on the defensive over a range of economic and labor issues in 1946, and he was strongly repudiated in the elections that fall. The president did not make a single political speech during the campaign, and Republicans gained fifty-five seats in the House and thirteen in the Senate to take control of Capitol Hill for the first time since 1930. Senator J. William Fulbright of Arkansas, a Democrat, went so far as to suggest after the election that Truman name a Republican as secretary of state and then resign so that the new secretary could take over. (That was the line of presidential succession at the time.) Truman ignored the suggestion, dismissing his critic as "Senator Half-bright." But, in the forthcoming Congress he took a battering from Republican partisans determined (like Gingrich today) to rechart the agenda of American domestic policy. The GOP overrode a presidential veto to pass the Taft-Hartley Act and three times approved a tax cut before producing one that also prevailed over Truman's veto. Even after Democrats reclaimed control of Congress in 1949—gaining seventy-five members in the House (the highest increase for the party in this century) and nine in the Senate—the conservative coalition still ruled. Aside from a housing bill approved in 1949, Truman's liberal agenda did not triumph.

Not much had changed by 1961, when the Democrats regained control of the presidency. House Democratic leaders managed to pack the Rules Committee, a core of conservative strength in the House, but otherwise struggled ineffectually during the Kennedy years. A federal aid to education bill failed in the new committee, as did President Kennedy's effort to establish a new Cabinet department of urban affairs. Lyndon Johnson labored mightily to resuscitate a liberal coalition, which enjoyed a splendid last hurrah on Capitol Hill in 1965. At that time Democrats controlled the House 295 to 140, and the Senate sixty-eight to thirty-two. But LBJ made a fateful choice: backing civil rights legislation in full knowledge that in time his stand was likely to destroy Democratic hegemony in the South. What he did not so clearly recognize was the extraordinary political impact of racial confrontation elsewhere in the nation. George Wallace did understand, as did Richard Nixon and many other Republicans. House GOP leader Gerald Ford asked in 1966, "How long are we going to abdicate law and order—the backbone of our civilization—in favor of a soft social theory that the man who heaves a brick through your window or tosses a fire bomb into your car is simply the misunderstood and underprivileged product of a broken home?" Conflicts over racially charged issues helped

Republicans gain forty-seven House seats in the pivotal 1966 elections. Thereafter these and other issues shattered Democratic Party unity and ushered in an era of successful congressional resistance to liberal Democratic programs that persists to this day. What is surprising is how long it took the trend toward independent voting and party decomposition to overturn Democratic control of the House.

The end of the cold war has further weakened presidents vis-à-vis Congress. All presidents from Truman through Ronald Reagan rallied congressional support by raising the specter of international communism. Truman, while assailing the "do-nothing" Republican Congress of 1947–48, secured major foreign policy measures from it, including financing for the Truman Doctrine and the Marshall Plan, backing in principle for the formation of NATO, and creation of the Defense Department and the CIA. In 1955 a Democratic Congress overwhelmingly approved the Formosa Resolution, which gave President Dwight D. Eisenhower a blank check in formulating military responses against China. In 1964 Congress approved the Tonkin Gulf Resolution unanimously in the House and with only two dissenting votes in the Senate.

During these especially anxious cold war years, liberals virtually fell over one another in celebration of the potential of the presidency. Without bold leadership from 1600 Pennsylvania Avenue, they said, the world might fall to communism. Theodore White in *The Making of the President 1960* spoke reverently of the "hush, an entirely personal hush" that surrounded presidential decisions concerning foreign affairs. The hush, he added, "was deepest in the Oval Office of the West Wing of the White House, where the president, however many his advisers, must sit alone."

By the late 1960s a few doubters, including Fulbright, tried to restore a significant congressional voice in foreign affairs, but this effort faltered in the cold war era. Indeed, Fulbright himself had been ready to surrender congressional authority. "For the existing requirements of American foreign policy," he said in 1961, "we have hobbled the president by too niggardly a grant of power." Senator Barry Goldwater agreed from the right. "The Constitution," he said in 1964, "gives the president, not the Congress, the primary war-making powers." There was "no question," he added, "that the president can take military action at any time he feels danger for the country."

The power of the presidency in foreign policy matters flourished even during the later years of the Vietnam War. Worried about America's economic standing in the world, the Democratic Congress in 1970 passed an Economic Stabilization Act that conferred extraordinary powers on President Nixon. The Congress trod with special care after Nixon's huge victory in 1972. Representative Carl Vinson of Georgia, a Democrat, grumbled in 1973 that the role of Congress "has come to be that of a somewhat querulous but essentially kindly uncle who complains while furiously puffing on his pipe but who finally, as everyone expects, gives in and hands over the allowance, grants the permission or raises his hand in blessing, and then returns to his rocking chair for another year of somnolence broken only by an occasional anxious glance down the avenue and a muttered doubt as to whether he had done the right thing."

The Imperial Presidency had become so well-entrenched by then that Democrats shrank at first from the idea of setting an impeachment process in motion. Among other things, they feared for the reputation of Congress if they attacked such a formidable institution as the presidency. In the end, of course, they acted, defying King Richard and greatly enhancing the visibility and prestige of the House, which had previously worked in the shadow of the Senate. With the vital aid of the Supreme Court, Congress began to puncture the mystique of the omnipotent executive, which had swollen to overblown proportions amid the tensions of the cold war.

Still, as long as the Soviets were perceived as a threat, the presidency remained a formidable institution. Americans denounced Washington— this was Jimmy Carter's message—but they still seemed to yearn for purposeful executive leadership. In the power vacuum following Nixon's resignation, James Reston identified this feeling by observing, "The White House is the pulpit of the nation, and the president is its chaplain." As if to prove the point, various presidents successfully ignored the War Powers Resolution that Congress had passed in 1973, over President Nixon's veto, to curb presidential adventurism abroad: Ford in 1975 sent troops into combat following the seizure by Cambodia of the American freighter *Mayaguez*, and subsequent presidents also flouted the resolution. The popularity of Ronald Reagan, as well as the wave of adulation that followed George Bush's decisive actions in the Gulf war, testify to the persistent popular yearning for bold presidential leadership.

The point, of course, is that the end of the cold war has curbed the ability of presidents to arouse this yearning, thereby tilting the balance of power toward Congress. President Clinton, stripped of the electoral coalition that had elevated FDR and elected Truman, cannot seek refuge behind the American flag. Instead, he confronts a different kind of yearning—that he do something to solve formidable social problems at home. This has always been a demanding assignment. From this perspective, Clinton (and his successors) seem more fated than ever to encounter frustrations on Capitol Hill, whatever party may control it.

This is but one perspective, however. To recite the long history of congressional resistance to presidential authority is not necessarily to conclude that Congress will permanently eclipse the White House or that special circumstances cannot revive the presidency.

It is in fact unlikely that Gingrich and his allies will be able to impose legislative supremacy on the nation. For one thing, they do not seem much interested in doing so in an institutional sense. They are reducing the number of committees and restricting terms of committee chairs. If they succeed in imposing term limits on themselves, they will deprive Congress of the experienced people—and the institutional memories—that have helped to empower the House and the Senate. If they enact a law authorizing a line-item veto for the president, they may surrender a measure of control over the appropriations process. What the Republicans ap-

*New Congress seems to want to go for Jeffersonian idea of states over federal*

pear to want is not a move toward legislative domination; rather, they seek to downsize the federal government and augment the authority of the states.

It is equally unlikely that Congress can change another reality of life on the Hill: the power of special interest groups. These, too, have a lengthy past, as anyone who read textbook accounts of the robber barons will remember. The proliferation of such groups expanded in the 1930s, when the New Deal finally turned the federal government into a source of benefits and entitlements; during World War II, when Washington exploded in size and power; and fantastically during the 1960s, when the war in Vietnam swelled the military-industrial complex and the Great Society increased the reach of the State. The growth of interest-group government has subjected Congress as an institution to fearsome public criticism. Nothing in the political history of the past century suggests that these interest groups will lose influence or that Congress as an institution can curb them in ways that will enhance its public reputation.

*Interest Groups = something to be ignored.*

Recent history indicates that the power of the media too, will persist and grow. Because it is much easier for reporters to cover a president than it is to follow 535 legislators, and because White House-watching has become a national sport, we may expect a continuing focus on everything that happens at 1600 Pennsylvania Avenue—sometimes to a president's advantage, sometimes not. But the media have also been casting an increasingly critical eye on Congress, helping to give it an image that since the 1970s has become even less flattering than that of the presidency. And television-driven congressional campaigns seem likely to incite even heavier mud-slinging than that which plastered so many candidates in 1994. So long as television cameras crowd the halls of Capitol Hill we may expect to watch Congress, like the president, get cut down to size as an institution.

Can Gingrich, an unusually purposeful leader, restore some congressional influence? Surely, for the unity of his party is indeed unusual. Clinton has already yielded some control of his agenda by caving in and calling for tax cuts that mimic Gingrich's Contract with America. But Gingrich will face formidable constraints. As in the past, the House and the Senate often will go their separate ways. Senate Democrats have the numbers to filibuster against especially objectionable proposals. Individual representatives and senators, elected in highly personal campaigns, will continue to resist party discipline when constituent pressures intervene. And Gingrich's special mandate may not last long. Ever since Speaker Joe Cannon was stripped of his dictatorial powers by angry colleagues in 1910, senior committee chairs have dominated legislative proceedings. President Woodrow Wilson complained that America had a "government by the standing committees of Congress." Some speakers—Nicholas Longworth in the 1920s, Sam Rayburn in the 1940s and 1950s, Jim Wright in the 1980s—have managed to exert substantial personal influence. So have Senate Majority Leaders Joseph Robinson in the 1930s and Lyndon Johnson in the 1950s. Robert Taft may have been the most influential of all— he and his GOP colleagues managed to enact their own legislation. But these are exceptions to a pattern of congressional leadership that has been dispersed since 1910 and that has if anything grown still more decentralized since the 1950s. The major bursts of domestic legislation in modern American history have come in the early 1930s and the mid-1960s and have emanated from the White House. The House speakers during both periods played small roles in this process. Robinson, the Senate majority leader until 1937, did much to aid Roosevelt's efforts, but Mike Mansfield, Democratic leader in the mid-1960s, mainly carried out executive decisions. And these were eras of Democratic control of both the White House and Capitol Hill. No modern president who has faced opposition majorities in Congress has rolled over in submission. It would be a remarkable first if Clinton does so.

Reports of the demise of an active, effective presidency are also premature. Have we forgotten already the extraordinary boost that Reagan gave to the prestige of the institution before the Iran-contra scandals? Or his success in setting a new domestic agenda that affects us still? The history of executive-congressional relations since the 1930s indicates that special *political* climates largely determine a president's ability to dominate Congress. These climates have appeared twice during this era—in the 1930s, when economic catastrophe produced widespread popular demands for presidential leadership, and in the 1960s, when (conversely) a booming economy helped to foster near-utopian notions that the State could design a new age of economic opportunity. Roosevelt and Johnson, savvy and dynamic leaders, seized the day. There are no significant new *institutional* developments that stand in the way of effective presidential leadership if and when favorable political climates of this sort reappear.

No one would be foolhardy enough to imagine such a reappearance in the next two years. The short run will favor Gingrich, as earlier tidal waves in off-year elections favored Lodge and Taft. Still, the election of 1994 did not reveal major changes in party identification or political ideology. Voters rejected only two incumbent Democratic senators. Although Americans clearly rebuked the Washington political establishment, they did not make it clear that they will accept specific GOP programs. Indeed, nearly three-quarters of voters never heard of Gingrich's Contract with America. Given the volatility of the American electorate, voters can surprise us at any time, maybe even in 1996.

There remains, finally, a reservoir of popular yearning for effective presidential leadership. The events of the past century—and particularly of the years since 1932—have focused ever-rising attention on the White House. Chief among these developments have been the expansion of the national security state and the rise of ever-more complex domestic problems. These have seemed to demand a large administrative apparatus centered in the executive branch. The attention given to the White House, all the more riveting in the mass media age, will not diminish. It is often a president's worst enemy, since it accentuates the already large expectations that Americans have developed about leadership since the 1930s. Excepting Eisenhower and Reagan—presidents who did not promise much in the way of new domestic programs—no modern president has managed for long to satisfy these expectations, let alone to build a popular mandate for domestic legislation. And LBJ, who did so manage in the short run, promised far more than he could deliver, thus unleashing devastating recriminations on himself and his party.

We have lived since then amid these recriminations. The gap between popular expectations and the perception of government performance, especially powerful since 1966, continues to be a central reality of American politics. Polls since then have shown that the American people do not trust their leaders. This disenchantment seems unlikely to change, at least in the near future, for it rests in part on a distrust of the State that has deep historical roots. Moreover, many of the expectations are excessive. The federal government cannot do much—at least not quickly—about social problems such as crime, illegitimacy and drug abuse. It does not know how to promote economic growth, which has languished for twenty years. Loud dissatisfaction about the performance of the federal government— aimed at the president as well as Democratic members of the House—inspired the reaction of last November and has aroused the aspirations of Gingrich and others who would resuscitate the states.

It is doubtful, however, that these dissatisfactions have weakened the institutional power of the presidency vis-à-vis that of the legislative branch. The voters in 1994, after all, took aim not only at the Clinton administration but also at Congress, whose reputation has suffered in recent years. Clinton himself, never popular with the electorate, may not survive in office beyond 1996. But, Americans are likely to blame him personally and Congress, not the institution of the presidency, for whatever deadlock lies in store. However jaded the voters may have sounded in 1994, many will continue to hope in their hearts that a strong president will succeed in curbing the deadlock.

# Presidential Government

*See Lowi and Ginsberg, pp. 239–270 or brief edition, pp. 147–162*

*In 1948, Arthur M. Schlesinger, Professor of History at Harvard University, asked 55 leading historians to rate the presidents from Washington to Truman on a five-point scale from "Great" to "Failure." Several similar polls have been conducted since then, the most recent sponsored by* The Times Magazine *in 1996. Arthur Schlesinger, Jr., son of the first author of the presidential rating study and special assistant to President Kennedy, examines the 1996 results for clues as to what makes a great president, and what the rating prospects are for President Clinton. What makes a "great" president? Not necessarily the personal characteristics of intelligence, loyalty, or maturity, Schlesinger argues, but a vision for the country that rings true with the circumstances of the people they lead, and the stamina and courage to lead the country on an educational journey toward that vision. All presidents are victims of, or the beneficiaries of, their times. Wars often create heroes, and scandals and economic downturns can tear presidencies asunder. But what a president does with those circumstances, ir-*

*respective of popularity ratings, is the key, he argues, to finding greatness as a leader.*

*Has President Clinton defined a vision of America? Has he pursued that course while in office? How would you rate Clinton on a scale of great, near great, average, below average, and failure? Who do you think has been our best president? Why? What criteria would you use?*

# Arthur M. Schlesinger, Jr.
## "The Ultimate Approval Rating"*

William Jefferson Clinton now faces his rendezvous with history. Debarred by the 22d Amendment from pursuing a third term, he must make his mark between now and Jan. 19, 2001. This may not be easy. The 22d Amendment, by turning re-elected Presidents into lame ducks, reduces their political potency. Second terms tend to be times of trouble: Ask Franklin D. Roosevelt, Eisenhower, Nixon, Reagan. On the other hand, lame-duckery, by liberating Presidents from the demands of re-election, does allow them to run political risks for national benefits.

*[margin note: means Pres doesn't worry about reelection So goes for more risky stuff.]*

Clinton brings to the bar of history a rare combination of talents and infirmities. He is a man of penetrating intelligence. He has impressive technical mastery of complicated issues. He has genuine intellectual curiosity and listens as well as talks. He is a skilled and resilient politician. When the spirit moves him, he is capable of real eloquence, and the spirit moves him most of all when he confronts the supreme American problem—race relations. Racial justice appears to be his most authentic concern.

On the other hand, he lacks self-discipline. His judgment of people is erratic. His political resilience strikes many as flagrant opportunism. His reactions are instinctively placatory. He rushes to propitiate the audience before him, often at his own expense. His scandals and cover-ups are ripe for exploitation by a vindictive opposition.

Who can tell how this combination of talents and infirmities will play out? Clinton's second term offers at once the potential of greatness and the potential of humiliation. As he ponders how to secure his place in history, he will inevitably think about those among his predecessors whom posterity ranks highest. What were the qualities that made them great? And who indeed are our great Presidents?

The game of ranking Presidents is a popular pastime among scholars. My father, Arthur M. Schlesinger, for 40 years a professor at Harvard and a more eminent historian than his son, started it all nearly half a century ago. In 1948 he invited 55 leading historians to render their verdicts. The scholars' ratings, published in *Life* magazine just before Truman con-

---

* Arthur Schlesinger, Jr., "The Ultimate Approval Rating" in *New York Times Magazine* (December 12, 1996). Copyright © 1996 by The New York Times Company. Reprinted with permission.

founded the prophets and won re-election, excited interest and controversy. In 1962 *The Times Magazine* prevailed upon my father to repeat the poll. Again much interest and much controversy.

The Schlesinger polls asked historians to place each President (omitting W. H. Harrison and Garfield because they died so soon after taking office) in one of five categories: Great, Near Great, Average, Below Average and Failure. The standard was not lifetime achievement but performance in the White House. The scholars were to decide for themselves how Presidential performance was to be judged. It was supposed that historians would know greatness—or failure—when they saw it, as Justice Potter Stewart famously said of pornography.

Presidents might well have wondered (and some did): Who are historians to arrogate to themselves the judging of Presidential performance? The Presidential office, said Calvin Coolidge in an unwonted lyrical outburst, "remains a great mystery. . . . Like the glory of a morning sunrise, it can only be experienced—it cannot be told." John F. Kennedy said to me: "How the hell can you tell? Only the President himself can know what his real pressures and real alternatives are. If you don't know that, how can you judge performance?" Some of his greatest predecessors, he continued, received credit for doing things when they could have done nothing else; only detailed inquiry could disclose what difference Presidents made by their individual contributions. War, he observed, made it easier for a President to achieve greatness. But would Lincoln have been judged so great a President if he had had to face the almost insoluble problem of Reconstruction?

Many polls have been taken, and there have been nine Greats and Near Greats in nearly all the reckonings. Lincoln, Washington and Franklin D. Roosevelt are always at the top, followed always, in varying order, by Jefferson, Jackson, Polk, Theodore Roosevelt, Wilson and Truman. Occasionally John Adams and Cleveland join the top nine. The Failures have always been Grant and Harding, with Buchanan, Pierce, Fillmore, Taylor and Coolidge always near the bottom.

The choice of best and worst Presidents has remained relatively stable through the years. There is much fluctuation in between. Some Presidents—particularly John Quincy Adams, Buchanan, Andrew Johnson and Cleveland—have declined in later polls, but the most striking change has been the rise of Eisenhower from 22d place in the Schlesinger 1962 poll to 12th in David Porter's 1981 poll, to 11th in the poll taken by Robert Murray and Tim Blessing in 1982 and to 9th in Steve Neal's Chicago Tribune poll the same year.

Over the years it has been periodically suggested that I replicate my father's polls. But the difficulty of making judgments about some of the Presidents since Eisenhower stumped me—in the cases of Kennedy and Ford, because of the brevity of their time in office; in the cases of Lyndon Johnson, Nixon and Bush, because their domestic and foreign records are so discordant. Scholars might be inclined to rate Johnson higher in domestic than in foreign affairs and do the reverse for Nixon and Bush. And the most recent Presidents always seem more controversial. Still, the passage of time encourages new perspectives. So in 1996 The Times Magazine took a new poll.

The question of disjunction still nags in the cases of Johnson, Nixon and Bush. "I find three cases which one could describe as having dichotomous or schizoid profiles," Walter Dean Burnham says. "On some very important dimensions, both Wilson and L. B. Johnson were outright failures in my view, while on others they rank very high indeed. Similarly with Nixon. . . ." Alan Brinkley says, "There are Presidents who could be considered *both* failures *and* great or near great (e.g. Wilson, Johnson, Nixon)." James MacGregor Burns observed of Nixon: "How can one evaluate such an idiosyncratic President, so brilliant and so morally lacking? . . . So I guess to average out he would be average."

Yet the 1996 poll still shows a high degree of scholarly consensus. Lincoln, with a unanimous Great vote, comes in first in 1996. Washington and F.D.R., as usual, are next; each had one Near Great vote. The big three are followed, as usual, by the Near Greats—Jefferson, Jackson, Polk, Theodore Roosevelt, Wilson and Truman.

Most Presidents fall in the Average class. Recent Presidents, too close for the cool eye of history, are most likely to rise or fall in polls to come. Carter currently has one Near Great and two Failures, with the rest of his votes in between. Some admire his accomplishment in putting human rights on the world's agenda; others deplore his political ineptitude and the absence of any clear direction in his handling of domestic affairs.

Reagan, on the other hand, has seven Near Great votes, including some from liberal scholars impressed by his success in restoring the prestige of the Presidency, in negotiating the last phases of the cold war and in imposing his priorities on the country. But he also receives nine Below Averages and four Failures from those who consider his priorities—his attack on government and his tax reductions that increased disparities between rich and poor while tripling the national debt—a disaster for the Republic.

Reagan's score actually comes out a shade below that of Bush, who receives no Near Greats but more Averages than Reagan and only one Failure. Bush's skill in putting together the coalition that won the gulf war outweighs for many his seeming lack of purpose in domestic policy.

The list of failures shows a slight shift from past polls. Harding and Grant are, as usual, favorite Failures. Do they really deserve it? They are marked down because of the scandal and corruption that disgraced their Administrations. But they were careless rather than villainous. Their sin was excessive loyalty to crooked friends. "Harding was not a bad man," as Theodore Roosevelt's daughter, Alice Roosevelt Longworth, put it. "He was just a slob." Scandal and corruption are indefensible, but they may injure the general welfare less than misconceived policies.

The belated national sensitivity to racial injustice may explain why two Presidents receive more Failure votes this time than in earlier polls: James Buchanan, whose irresolution encouraged the secession of the Confederate states; and Andrew Johnson, who, while a Unionist, was a stout believer in white supremacy. It seems reasonable to suggest that Buchanan, Andrew Johnson, Hoover and Nixon—the one President who resigned to escape impeachment—damaged the Republic more than did the hapless Grant and the feckless Harding.

Nine men, we have seen, continue to lead the list as they did in the first Schlesinger poll. What do Washington, Jefferson, Jackson, Polk, Lincoln, Theodore Roosevelt, Wilson, Franklin Roosevelt and Truman have in common? What do they tell us about the qualities necessary for success in the White House?

Intelligence is helpful, though Reagan—with seven Near Greats—showed that an influential President need not have much. Maturity? The British ambassador thought Theodore Roosevelt was an arrested 11-year-old. Loyalty? This can be a Presidential defect: remember Grant and Harding. Private virtues do not guarantee public effectiveness.

More to the point is the test proposed 125 years ago by our most brilliant historian, Henry Adams. The American President, he wrote, "resembles the commander of a ship at sea. He must have a helm to grasp, a course to steer, a port to seek." The course and the port constitute the first requirement for Presidential greatness. Great Presidents possess, or are possessed by, a vision of an ideal America. Their passion is to make sure the ship of state sails on the right course.

If that course is indeed right, it is because they have an instinct for the dynamics of history. "A statesman may be determined and tenacious," de Gaulle said, "but if he does not understand the character of his time, he will fail." Great Presidents have a deep connection with the needs, anxieties, dreams of the people. "I do not believe," said Wilson, "that any man can lead who does not act . . . under the impulse of a profound sympathy with those whom he leads."

Franklin Roosevelt said that our great Presidents were "leaders of thought at times when certain ideas in the life of the nation had to be clarified." So Washington embodied the idea of the Federal union, Jefferson and Jackson the idea of democracy, Lincoln union and freedom, Cleveland rugged honesty. Theodore Roosevelt and Wilson, said F.D.R., were both "moral leaders, each in his own way and his own time, who used the Presidency as a pulpit."

To succeed, Presidents must have a port to seek and must convince Congress and the electorate of the rightness of their course. Politics in a democracy is ultimately an educational process, an exercise in persuasion and consent. Every President stands in Theodore Roosevelt's "bully-pulpit." National crisis widens his range of options but does not automatically make the man. The crisis of rebellion did not spur Buchanan to greatness, nor did the Depression turn Hoover into a bold and imaginative leader. Their inadequacies in face of crisis allowed Lincoln and the second Roosevelt to show the difference that individuals can make to history.

Some of the top nine made their mark without benefit of first-order crisis. Presidents like Jackson and Theodore Roosevelt forced the nation through sheer power of personality to recognize incipient problems— Jackson in vindicating the national authority against the Bank of the United States; the first Roosevelt in vindicating the national authority against the great corporations. As the historian Elting Morison described this quality of noncrisis leadership: "Theodore Roosevelt could get the attention of his fellow citizens and make them think. He knew . . . how to startle the country into informing debate; and how to move people into their thinking beyond short-run self-interest toward some longer view of the general welfare."

*[handwritten margin note: Can still be a great Pres without crisis but more difficult]*

We hear much these days about the virtues of the middle of the road. But none of the top nine can be described as a middle-roader. Middle-roading may be fine for campaigning, but it is a sure road to mediocrity in governing. The middle of the road is not the vital center: it is the dead center. Clinton would be wise to eschew it if he wants to improve his ratings. The Greats and the Near Greats all took risks in pursuit of their ideals. They all provoked intense controversy. They all, except Washington, divided the nation before reuniting it on a new level of national understanding.

Every President would like to be loved by everyone in the country, but Presidents who sacrifice convictions to a quest for affection are unlikely to make it to the top. Harding was an immensely popular President. His death provoked an outpouring of national grief that observers thought unmatched since the death of Lincoln. Yet scholars are unanimous in pronouncing him a Failure.

Presidents who seek to change the nation's direction know they will alienate those who profit from the status quo. Great Presidents go ahead anyway. "Judge me," F.D.R. said, "by the enemies I've made." Truman's approval rating at the end of his Presidency was down to 31 percent. Look where he ranks now.

How does Clinton stand in the eyes of historians? Some think it premature to judge, but two vote him Near Great and two more a Failure, and he ends up Average. The second term gives him his opportunity to move up—or down.

Now he confronts history—and the second-term curse. The months ahead will see a struggle for, and within, the President's soul. Some advisers will tell him that he won re-election because he kidnapped the welfare bill and other Republican policies. Others will tell him that he won because he had a solid record on the economy—increased employment, reduced deficits, stable prices, a higher minimum wage—and because he championed Medicare, education, the environment and other liberal programs against Republican assault. Like any practical political leader, he will strive to hold his party together, which means he will do some things to gratify the right and other things to gratify the left.

There will be storms ahead. Whitewater, Kenneth Starr, Paula Jones and the Indonesian philanthropists lie in wait. When harried, Clinton must throttle his impulse to dissemble. Otherwise Congressional squalls may throw him off course, drive his craft to the rocks and make his second term a voyage into misery.

Yet he is not without resources, besides his Houdini-like agility in getting out of tight spots. His opposition has its own troubles. Republicans, too, are divided over the meaning of the election. The Christian Coalition thinks the Republicans lost because the candidates did not wage cultural warfare with sufficient zeal. Northern moderates think that right-wing extremism on abortion, gun control, amending the Constitution and shutting down the Government turned off independent voters. This split gives Clinton an opportunity to court Republican moderates and to seize control of the Washington agenda.

What are the issues that will determine Clinton's place in history? Prediction is hazardous in these unpredictable times, but one may doubt that draconian budget-balancing measures and amendments will insure him a high ranking. He already has a creditable fiscal record in reducing deficits for four successive years. Our deficit today is the smallest, as a percentage of the budget, of any of the leading industrial economies. He need not punish the poor and helpless further.

In domestic policy, better possibilities present themselves. In 1900 the United States was the most literate nation in the world; today, according to the United Nations, it is the 45th. A crusade against illiteracy, accompanied by the establishment of national educational standards, would justify the title Education President.

Another key issue is campaign finance reform. The parade of dubious figures from exotic places bearing bags of "soft" money properly provokes outrage. Let President Clinton rally the country behind a bill that would drastically reduce the power of private money in elections.

Education and campaign finance reform appeal across party lines. So do—or should—civil rights, redemption of our cities, cleaning up the health care mess, protection of the environment, rehabilitation of the nation's infrastructure and jobs for people thrown off welfare. Reversing what may become our gravest internal threat—the growing inequality of wealth and opportunity—would encounter more hostility, but even a losing battle would prepare the way for reform later and would assure more respect from history.

If harassment and gridlock block domestic reform, Clinton will be tempted to escape from Trent Lott, Dick Armey and Newt Gingrich into the more glamorous realm of foreign policy—Air Force One tickets to romantic places, bands playing, crowds cheering, royal-cousin chats with heads of state. Historians tend to look down on isolationists, and in the absence of war Clinton may have his best opportunities for making a mark by making peace. Peace making has already developed as a major theme in his foreign policy. It's one he would be wise to pursue. Despite setbacks, he must press on in Bosnia, in Ireland, in the Middle East. He must, after the uncouth handling of Boutros Boutros-Ghali, mend our relations with the United Nations. He must argue against the reduction of our diplomatic budget in favor of our often misspent defense and intelligence budgets.

To make a mark on history, let Clinton liberate himself from polls and focus groups. Let him put his first-rate intelligence to work on the hard issues. Playing it safe, taking it easy, sticking to the middle of the road may make for a more comfortable second term. But following this course would put Clinton alongside William Howard Taft and Rutherford B. Hayes on the ratings list. Only boldness and creativity, even if at times foiled and frustrated, will earn him a place among the nine immortals.

# 7

# The Executive Branch: Bureaucracy in a Democracy

## The Bureaucratic Phenomenon

*See Lowi and Ginsberg, pp. 277–283 or brief edition, pp. 162–170*

*In 1887, Woodrow Wilson (then a professor of government) argued that government bureaucracies would perform more effectively if organized and operated more like American businesses, or organizations in the private sector. The sentiment remains today. Perhaps with greater emphasis upon performance and customer (citizen) satisfaction, government bureaucracies would issue our car registrations more promptly, police officers would respond more quickly, income tax returns would be processed more rapidly, the rights of citizens would be protected more thoroughly, pollution would be controlled more rigorously, and diplomacy would be conducted more effectively. The catch is, we want this all done in a very efficient manner, with limited tax dollars and minimal intrusion in our lives, yet we want government bureaucracies to be held strictly accountable for the authority being exercised.*

*James Q. Wilson argues that the Registry of Motor Vehicles (or any government bureaucracy) will most likely never service their clientele as expeditiously as the neighborhood McDonald's (or any private bureaucracy) services their customers. In order to understand "what government agencies do and why they do it," Wilson argues that we must first understand that government bureaucracies operate in a political marketplace, rather than an economic one. The annual revenues and personnel resources of a government agency are determined by elected officials, not by the agency's ability to meet the demands of its customers in a cost-efficient manner. The government agency's internal structure and decision-making procedures are defined by legislation, regulation, and executive orders, while similar decisions in a private business are made by executive officers and management within the organization. It is critical that the goals given to a government agency to implement can be vaguely stated, contested by competing political interests, and even contradictory, while the basic goal of a private business has always been to maximize profit. While we should not approach the reform of government agencies the way we might a private bureaucracy, Wilson notes we should nevertheless try to make government bureaucracies operate more effectively and efficiently.*

# James Q. Wilson
## From *Bureaucracy: What Government Agencies Do and Why They Do It**

By the time the office opens at 8:45 A.M., the line of people waiting to do business at the Registry of Motor Vehicles in Watertown, Massachusetts, often will be twenty-five deep. By midday, especially if it is near the end of the month, the line may extend clear around the building. Inside, motorists wait in slow-moving rows before poorly marked windows to get a driver's license or to register an automobile. When someone gets to the head of the line, he or she is often told by the clerk that it is the wrong line: "Get an application over there and then come back," or "This is only for people getting a new license; if you want to replace one you lost, you have to go to the next window." The customers grumble impatiently. The clerks act harried and sometimes speak brusquely, even rudely. What seems to be a simple transaction may take 45 minutes or even longer. By the time people are photographed for their driver's licenses, they are often scowling. The photographer valiantly tries to get people to smile, but only occasionally succeeds.

Not far away, people also wait in line at a McDonald's fast-food restaurant. There are several lines; each is short, each moves quickly. The menu is clearly displayed on attractive signs. The workers behind the counter are invariably polite. If someone's order cannot be filled immediately, he or she is asked to step aside for a moment while the food is prepared and then is brought back to the head of the line to receive the order. The atmosphere is friendly and good-natured. The room is immaculately clean.

Many people have noticed the difference between getting a driver's license and ordering a Big Mac. Most will explain it by saying that bureaucracies are different from businesses. "Bureaucracies" behave as they do because they are run by unqualified "bureaucrats" and are enmeshed in "rules" and "red tape."

But business firms are also bureaucracies, and McDonald's is a bureaucracy that regulates virtually every detail of its employees' behavior by a complex and all-encompassing set of rules. Its operations manual is six hundred pages long and weighs four pounds. In it one learns that french fries are to be nine-thirty-seconds of an inch thick and that grill workers are to place hamburger patties on the grill from left to right, six to a row for six rows. They are then to flip the third row first, followed by the fourth, fifth, and sixth rows, and finally the first and second. The amount of sauce placed on each bun is precisely specified. Every window must be washed every day. Workers must get down on their hands and knees and pick up litter as soon as it appears. These and countless other rules designed to reduce the workers to interchangeable automata were incul- cated in franchise managers at Hamburger University located in a $40 million facility. There are plenty of rules governing the Registry, but they are only a small fraction of the rules that govern every detail of every op- eration at McDonald's. Indeed, if the DMV manager tried to impose on his employees as demanding a set of rules as those that govern the Mc- Donald's staff, they would probably rebel and he would lose his job.

It is just as hard to explain the differences between the two organiza- tions by reference to the quality or compensation of their employees. The Registry workers are all adults, most with at least a high-school education; the McDonald's employees are mostly teenagers, many still in school. The Registry staff is well-paid compared to the McDonald's workers, most of whom receive only the minimum wage. When labor shortages developed in Massachusetts during the mid-1980s, many McDonald's stores began hiring older people (typically housewives) of the same sort who had long worked for the Registry. They behaved just like the teenagers they re- placed.

Not only are the differences between the two organizations not to be explained by reference to "rules" or "red tape" or "incompetent work- ers," the differences call into question many of the most frequently men- tioned complaints about how government agencies are supposed to behave. For example: "Government agencies are big spenders." The Wa- tertown office of the Registry is in a modest building that can barely handle its clientele. The teletype machine used to check information sub- mitted by people requesting a replacement license was antiquated and prone to errors. Three or four clerks often had to wait in line to use equip- ment described by the office manager as "personally signed by Thomas Edison." No computers or word processors were available to handle the preparation of licenses and registrations; any error made by a clerk while manually typing a form meant starting over again on another form.

Or: "Government agencies hire people regardless of whether they are really needed." Despite the fact that the citizens of Massachusetts prob- ably have more contact with the Registry than with any other state agency, and despite the fact that these citizens complain more about Registry ser- vice than about that of any other bureau, the Watertown branch, like all Registry offices, was seriously understaffed. In 1981, the agency lost 400 workers—about 25 percent of its work force—despite the fact that its workload was rising.

Or: "Government agencies are imperialistic, always grasping for new functions." But there is no record of the Registry doing much grasping, even though one could imagine a case being made that the state govern- ment could usefully create at Registry offices "one-stop" multi-service cen- ters where people could not only get drivers' licenses but also pay taxes and parking fines, obtain information, and transact other official business. The Registry seemed content to provide one service.

In short, many of the popular stereotypes about government agencies and their members are either questionable or incomplete. To explain why government agencies behave as they do, it is not enough to know that they are "bureaucracies"—that is, it is not enough to know that they are big, or complex, or have rules. What is crucial is that they are *government* bureaucracies. As the preceding chapters should make clear, not all government bureaucracies behave the same way or suffer from the same problems. There may even be registries of motor vehicles in other states that do a better job than the one in Massachusetts. But all government agencies have in common certain characteristics that tend to make their management far more difficult than managing a McDonald's. These common characteristics are the constraints of public agencies.

The key constraints are three in number. To a much greater extent than is true of private bureaucracies, government agencies (1) cannot lawfully retain and devote to the private benefit of their members the earnings of the organization, (2) cannot allocate the factors of production in accordance with the preferences of the organization's administrators, and (3) must serve goals not of the organization's own choosing. Control over revenues, productive factors, and agency goals is all vested to an important degree in entities external to the organization—legislatures, courts, politicians, and interest groups. Given this, agency managers must attend to the demands of these external entities. As a result, government management tends to be driven by the *constraints* on the organization, not the *tasks* of the organization. To say the same thing in other words, whereas business management focuses on the "bottom line" (that is, profits), government management focuses on the "top line" (that is, constraints). Because government managers are not as strongly motivated as private ones to define the tasks of their subordinates, these tasks are often shaped by [other] factors.

\* \* \*

## REVENUES AND INCENTIVES

In the days leading up to September 30, the federal government is Cinderella, courted by legions of individuals and organizations eager to get grants and contracts from the unexpended funds still at the disposal of each agency. At midnight on September 30, the government's coach turns into a pumpkin. That is the moment—the end of the fiscal year—at which every agency, with a few exceptions, must return all unexpended funds to the Treasury Department.

Except for certain quasi-independent government corporations, such as the Tennessee Valley Authority, no agency may keep any surplus revenues (that is, the difference between the funds it received from a congressional appropriation and those it needed to operate during the year). By the same token, any agency that runs out of money before the end of the fiscal year may ask Congress for more (a "supplemental appropriation") instead of being forced to deduct the deficit from any accumulated cash reserves. Because of these fiscal rules agencies do not have a material incentive to economize: Why scrimp and save if you cannot keep the results of your frugality?

Nor can individual bureaucrats lawfully capture for their personal use any revenue surpluses. When a private firm has a good year, many of its officers and workers may receive bonuses. Even if no bonus is paid, these employees may buy stock in the firm so that they can profit from any growth in earnings (and, if they sell the stock in a timely manner, profit from a drop in earnings). Should a public bureaucrat be discovered trying to do what private bureaucrats routinely do, he or she would be charged with corruption.

We take it for granted that bureaucrats should not profit from their offices and nod approvingly when a bureaucrat who has so benefited is indicted and put on trial. But why should we take this view? Once a very different view prevailed. In the seventeenth century, a French colonel would buy his commission from the king, take the king's money to run his regiment, and pocket the profit. At one time a European tax collector was paid by keeping a percentage of the taxes he collected. In this country, some prisons were once managed by giving the warden a sum of money based on how many prisoners were under his control and letting him keep the difference between what he received and what it cost him to feed the prisoners. Such behavior today would be grounds for criminal prosecution. Why? What has changed?

Mostly we the citizenry have changed. We are creatures of the Enlightenment: We believe that the nation ought not to be the property of the sovereign; that laws are intended to rationalize society and (if possible) perfect mankind; and that public service ought to be neutral and disinterested. We worry that a prison warden paid in the old way would have a strong incentive to starve his prisoners in order to maximize his income; that a regiment supported by a greedy colonel would not be properly equipped; and that a tax collector paid on a commission basis would extort excessive taxes from us. These changes reflect our desire to eliminate moral hazards—namely, creating incentives for people to act wrongly. But why should this desire rule out more carefully designed compensation plans that would pay government managers for achieving officially approved goals and would allow efficient agencies to keep any unspent part of their budget for use next year?

Part of the answer is obvious. Often we do not know whether a manager or an agency has achieved the goals we want because either the goals are vague or inconsistent, or their attainment cannot be observed, or both. Bureau chiefs in the Department of State would have to go on welfare if their pay depended on their ability to demonstrate convincingly that they had attained their bureaus' objectives.

But many government agencies have reasonably clear goals toward which progress can be measured. The Social Security Administration, the Postal Service, and the General Services Administration all come to mind.

Why not let earnings depend importantly on performance? Why not let agencies keep excess revenues?

*   *   *

But in part it is because we know that even government agencies with clear goals and readily observable behavior only can be evaluated by making political (and thus conflict-ridden) judgments. If the Welfare Department delivers every benefit check within 24 hours after the application is received, Senator Smith may be pleased but Senator Jones will be irritated because this speedy delivery almost surely would require that the standards of eligibility be relaxed so that many ineligible clients would get money. There is no objective standard by which the tradeoff between speed and accuracy in the Welfare Department can be evaluated. Thus we have been unwilling to allow welfare employees to earn large bonuses for achieving either speed or accuracy.

The inability of public managers to capture surplus revenues for their own use alters the pattern of incentives at work in government agencies. Beyond a certain point additional effort does not produce additional earnings. (In this country, Congress from time to time has authorized higher salaries for senior bureaucrats but then put a cap on actual payments to them so that the pay increases were never received. This was done to insure that no bureaucrat would earn more than members of Congress at a time when those members were unwilling to accept the political costs of raising their own salaries. As a result, the pay differential between the top bureaucratic rank and those just below it nearly vanished.) If political constraints reduce the marginal effect of money incentives, then the relative importance of other, nonmonetary incentives will increase. . . .

That bureaucratic performance in most government agencies cannot be linked to monetary benefits is not the whole explanation for the difference between public and private management. There are many examples of private organizations whose members cannot appropriate money surpluses for their own benefit. Private schools ordinarily are run on a nonprofit basis. Neither the headmaster nor the teachers share in the profit of these schools; indeed, most such schools earn no profit at all and instead struggle to keep afloat by soliciting contributions from friends and alumni. Nevertheless, the evidence is quite clear that on the average, private schools, both secular and denominational, do a better job than public ones in educating children. Moreover, as political scientists John Chubb and Terry Moe have pointed out, they do a better job while employing fewer managers. Some other factors are at work. One is the freedom an organization has to acquire and use labor and capital.

## ACQUIRING AND USING THE FACTORS OF PRODUCTION

A business firm acquires capital by retaining earnings, borrowing money, or selling shares of ownership; a government agency (with some exceptions) acquires capital by persuading a legislature to appropriate it. A business firm hires, promotes, demotes, and fires personnel with considerable though not perfect freedom; a federal government agency is told by Congress how many persons it can hire and at what rate of pay, by the Office of Personnel Management (OPM) what rules it must follow in selecting and assigning personnel, by the Office of Management and Budget (OMB) how many persons of each rank it may employ, by the Merit Systems Protection Board (MSPB) what procedures it must follow in demoting or discharging personnel, and by the courts whether it has faithfully followed the rules of Congress, OPM, OMB, and MSPB. A business firm purchases goods and services by internally defined procedures (including those that allow it to buy from someone other than the lowest bidder if a more expensive vendor seems more reliable), or to skip the bidding procedure altogether in favor of direct negotiations; a government agency must purchase much of what it uses by formally advertising for bids, accepting the lowest, and keeping the vendor at arm's length. When a business firm develops a good working relationship with a contractor, it often uses that vendor repeatedly without looking for a new one; when a government agency has a satisfactory relationship with a contractor, ordinarily it cannot use the vendor again without putting a new project out for a fresh set of bids. When a business firm finds that certain offices or factories are no longer economical it will close or combine them; when a government agency wishes to shut down a local office or military base often it must get the permission of the legislature (even when formal permission is not necessary, informal consultation is). When a business firm draws up its annual budget each expenditure item can be reviewed as a discretionary amount (except for legally mandated payments of taxes to government and interest to banks and bondholders); when a government agency makes up its budget many of the detailed expenditure items are mandated by the legislature.

All these complexities of doing business in or with the government are well-known to citizens and firms. These complexities in hiring, purchasing, contracting, and budgeting often are said to be the result of the "bureaucracy's love of red tape." But few, if any, of the rules producing this complexity would have been generated by the bureaucracy if left to its own devices, and many are as cordially disliked by the bureaucrats as by their clients. These rules have been imposed on the agencies by external actors, chiefly the legislature. They are not bureaucratic rules but *political* ones. In principle the legislature could allow the Social Security Administration, the Defense Department, or the New York City public school system to follow the same rules as IBM, General Electric, or Harvard University. In practice they could not. The reason is politics, or more precisely, democratic politics.

\* \* \*

## PUBLIC VERSUS PRIVATE MANAGEMENT

What distinguishes public from private organizations is neither their size nor their desire to "plan" (that is, control) their environments but rather the rules under which they acquire and use capital and labor. General Motors acquires capital by selling shares, issuing bonds, or retaining earnings; the Department of Defense acquires it from an annual appropriation by Congress. GM opens and closes plants, subject to certain government regulations, at its own discretion; DOD opens and closes military bases under the watchful guidance of Congress. GM pays its managers with salaries it sets and bonuses tied to its earnings; DOD pays its managers with salaries set by Congress and bonuses (if any) that have no connection with organizational performance. The number of workers in GM is determined by its level of production; the number in DOD by legislation and civil-service rules.

What all this means can be seen by returning to the Registry of Motor Vehicles and McDonald's. Suppose you were just appointed head of the Watertown office of the Registry and you wanted to improve service there so that it more nearly approximated the service at McDonald's. Better service might well require spending more money (on clerks, equipment, and buildings). Why should your political superiors give you that money? It is a cost to them if it requires either higher taxes or taking funds from another agency; offsetting these real and immediate costs are dubious and postponed benefits. If lines become shorter and clients become happier, no legislator will benefit. There may be fewer complaints, but complaints are episodic and have little effect on the career of any given legislator. By contrast, shorter lines and faster service at McDonald's means more customers can be served per hour and thus more money can be earned per hour. A McDonald's manager can estimate the marginal product of the last dollar he or she spends on improving service; the Registry manager can generate no tangible return on any expenditure he or she makes and thus cannot easily justify the expenditure.

Improving service at the Registry may require replacing slow or surly workers with quick and pleasant ones. But you, the manager, can neither hire nor fire them at will. You look enviously at the McDonald's manager who regularly and with little notice replaces poor workers with better ones. Alternatively, you may wish to mount an extensive training program (perhaps creating a Registration University to match McDonald's Hamburger University) that would imbue a culture of service in your employees. But unless the Registry were so large an agency that the legislature would neither notice nor care about funds spent for this purpose—and it is not that large—you would have a tough time convincing anybody that this was not a wasteful expenditure on a frill project.

If somehow your efforts succeed in making Registry clients happier, you can take vicarious pleasure in it; in the unlikely event a client seeks you out to thank you for those efforts, you can bask in a moment's worth of glory. Your colleague at McDonald's who manages to make customers happier may also derive some vicarious satisfaction from the improvement but in addition he or she will earn more money owing to an increase in sales.

In time it will dawn on you that if you improve service too much, clients will start coming to the Watertown office instead of going to the Boston office. As a result, the lines you succeeded in shortening will become longer again. If you wish to keep complaints down, you will have to spend even more on the Watertown office. But if it was hard to persuade the legislature to do that in the past, it is impossible now. Why should the taxpayer be asked to spend more on Watertown when the Boston office, fully staffed (naturally, no one was laid off when the clients disappeared), has no lines at all? From the legislature's point of view the correct level of expenditure is not that which makes one office better than another but that which produces an equal amount of discontent in all offices.

Finally, you remember that your clients have no choice: The Registry offers a monopoly service. It and only it supplies drivers' licenses. In the long run all that matters is that there are not "too many" complaints to the legislature about service. Unlike McDonald's, the Registry need not fear that its clients will take their business to Burger King or to Wendy's. Perhaps you should just relax.

If this were all there is to public management it would be an activity that quickly and inevitably produces cynicism among its practitioners. But this is not the whole story. For one thing, public agencies differ in the kinds of problems they face. For another, many public managers try hard to do a good job even though they face these difficult constraints.

## Bureaucracy in a Democracy

*See Lowi and Ginsberg, pp. 317–319*

*The primary political impediment to bureaucratic reform is illustrated by Morris P. Fiorina's assessment of the competition between Congress and the president to control the bureaucracy. Fiorina argues that Congress is responsible for bureaucratic inefficiency. Simply put, members of Congress benefit from the way in which the bureaucracy is designed and operated. Citizens reward politicians at election time for their assistance in securing a delayed social security check, for cutting through the red tape to secure veterans' benefits, or for speeding the processing of a passport. A bureaucracy that is as complex as the congressional committee system facilitates the ability of members to take credit for bringing about responsiveness from the bureaucracy for constituents.*

*Presidents, on the other hand, want to centralize bureaucratic power and make it more responsive to their policy priorities and more effective in implementing public programs. Yet presidents do not have the power, Fiorina argues, to bring about reforms without the support of Congress. The National Performance Review (NPR) is the most recent manifestation of presidential efforts to improve bureaucratic performance and responsiveness to the executive branch, but congressional support is essential if reforms are to take hold—an unlikely outcome, if Fiorina's analysis is correct.*

# Morris P. Fiorina
## "Congressional Control of the Bureaucracy: A Mismatch of Incentives and Capabilities"*

Recent political commentary contains numerous references to "out of control," "irresponsible," or "runaway" bureaucracy, and already this concern has had important effects. It has stimulated various reform proposals (zero-based budgeting, sunset laws, revenue and spending limits), helped elect Jimmy Carter, and made it increasingly difficult to tell traditional liberals from conservatives. . . .

It is one thing to note that the bureaucracy is an important branch of the federal government, that it can develop and use political resources, that its expertise gives it an advantage in dealing with other branches of the government; it is quite another to claim that the bureaucracy is out of control. On its face, the claim may appear patently true, but on a deeper level it is mostly false.

## WHAT IS CONTROL OF THE BUREAUCRACY?

The bureaucracy is not out of control because the Congress controls the bureaucracy, and the Congress gives us the kind of bureaucracy it wants. If some modern day James Madison were to conceive a plan that would guarantee an efficient, effective, centrally directed bureaucracy, Congress would react with fear and loathing. To be sure, particular members may wish to terminate particular agencies, but if the choice were between the existing bureaucratic world and the utopian bureaucratic world just conjured up, Congress would cast a nearly unanimous vote for the status quo. The parent loves the child, warts and all.

## ■ Theoretical and Actual Control

Obviously, I am playing on ambiguities in the concept of "control." First, we must distinguish between *theoretical* (formal or legal) control and *actual* (politically feasible) control. The Constitution divides formal control over the bureaucracy between the president and Congress, and the courts have come to play an important role as well. While nominally the president heads the bulk of the federal apparatus, his practical authority is rather modest. Civil Service and advise and consent requirements circumscribe his appointment powers. The president's personal agency, the Office of Management and Budget (OMB), is indisputably powerful, but once matters escape its clutches and get into the congressional arena, renegade

* Morris P. Fiorina, "Congressional Control of the Bureaucracy: A Mismatch of Incentives and Capabilities" in *Congress Reconsidered*, Second Edition, ed. by Lawrence C. Dodd and Bruce I. Oppenheimer (Washington, D.C.: CQ Press, 1981).

agencies may defy their formal master. Lacking the rifle of the item veto, the president can only threaten the cannon of the general veto, and denizens of Washington can judge when he dares not fire the cannon.

Congress, on the other hand, has the formal power of life and death over the bureaucracy. Congress can abolish an agency or reorganize it, change its jurisdiction or allow its program authority to lapse entirely. Congress can cut its appropriations and conduct embarrassing investigations. A hostile Congress unconcerned about the consequences of its actions could decimate the federal establishment.

Of course, Congress seldom exercises its formal powers. In fact, such seemingly radical ideas as sunset laws and zero-based budgeting are merely attempts to insure that existing congressional powers are used more frequently or at least that their use is contemplated more frequently. As numerous observers have remarked, procedural changes alone are insufficient to increase control over the bureaucracy; to achieve their purpose such changes must also provide incentives to exercise that control.

## ■ Coordinated and Uncoordinated Control

There is a second, more important ambiguity in the concept of "control." What kind of control do we want? Control for what? Imagine a naval fleet in which each vessel is under the absolute control of a chief officer. But suppose that these captains themselves are responsible to no higher authority and have no particular interest in communicating with each other. Well-meaning observers who watch such a fleet maneuver might judge the fleet to be out of control. They might even recommend measures intended to enhance control of the fleet's operation. Yet each commanding officer would greet such recommendations with skepticism; looking about his ship he sees no evidence of lack of control.

Like the individual ships in the preceding analogy, the *parts* of the federal bureaucracy typically are well-behaved in the sense that they are responsive to the captains in the congressional committees and subcommittees that determine their fates. But the *whole* of the bureaucracy is out of control, as is Congress.

Thus, the second distinction is that between *coordinated* and *uncoordinated* control, or alternatively, *centralized* and *decentralized* control. When I remark that the Congress controls the bureaucracy, I use the term in the second sense. Congress controls the parts, but there is little overall coordination. Particular congressional committees control the agencies they want to in the manner they want to. But those who address the problem of "control of the bureaucracy" have centralized or coordinated control in mind. How can the disparate parts of the bureaucracy be integrated? How can they be made to work in harness to achieve major policy goals?

The causes and consequences of decentralized control of the bureaucracy constitute the agenda for this essay. . . . In a nutshell, I will argue that the Congress has the power but not the incentive for coordinated control of the bureaucracy, while the president has the incentive but not the power. This mismatch between the incentives and capabilities of the relevant political actors is at least as important as informational overload, imbalance in expertise, and the internal processes of bureaucracies in explaining the absence of coordinated control of the federal bureaucracy. . . .

### DIFFERING INCENTIVES FOR CONTROL

Put most simply, the goals of the president lead him to prefer centralized control of the bureaucracy, while the goals of members of Congress lead them to favor decentralized control. Given the Congress's somewhat stronger position than the president's vis-à-vis the instruments of control, decentralized control prevails.

### ■ Presidential Goals

What are the goals of the typical president? Re-election comes most immediately to mind, but place in history is a close second. Fortunately for analytical purposes, the two goals often appear to be consistent. The president is the nation's chief official and responsible for major policy directions. Presumably, the president will attain re-election as well as a prominent place in the history books by dealing successfully with important national problems: attaining peace with honor, lowering unemployment, controlling inflation, ending crime in the streets, achieving racial equality. . . .

### ■ Congressional Goals

Members of Congress are in a different situation. Most of them simply wish to stay where they are, although House members are always on the lookout for a stray Senate seat, and numerous senators find personally compelling reasons to offer themselves as presidential candidates. With a few exceptions, place in history is an unrealistic goal for members of Congress. Each representative is a paltry one vote of 435. Unlike the president, a representative cannot credibly claim responsibility for putting the economy back on its feet or healing the wounds of a civil war. At best, several generations may remember him or her as the person who brought several sewage treatment plants to the district. Senators are in a somewhat better position, but even so they are merely one vote of 100, and how many twentieth-century senators can plausibly be said to have achieved a prominent place in history? No, for the member of Congress life is in the here and now. ("Now" is literally "now" for representatives whose lives are organized into two-year cycles.) The primary goal of members is figuring out how to survive the next election.

And survive they do! Since the Second World War about 90 percent of all incumbents have chosen to run for re-election and on average 90 percent of those have succeeded. Moreover, they have been getting even more successful in recent years. How have they managed, given the erosion of traditional partisan sources of support and the increase in public cynicism toward government institutions and incumbents?

## ■ The Congressional Role

The key to this puzzle is a mid-century change in the congressional role. As the scope of the federal government has expanded, the federal bureaucracy has enjoyed a concomitant expansion. Citizens in turn "enjoy" more opportunities to interact with their public servants, whether in an effort to take advantage of federal programs or to evade federal regulations. In this situation the member of Congress is ideally situated. Traditionally, if one has problems with the bureaucracy, one writes one's representatives in Congress who have a long history of intervening in bureaucratic decisionmaking for the benefit of constituents. With the expansion of federal activity, the member of Congress's role as an intervenor—an ombudsman—has become more important. Objectively, there is a greater demand for members' services, and sensible incumbents have done little or nothing to stem that demand. In fact, some members, particularly the more junior ones, stimulate the demand for ombudsman services, seeing such activities as a means to reach those individuals in their districts who would otherwise oppose them on policy, ideological, or party grounds. In short, members are increasingly de-emphasizing their role as formulators of national policies—a controversial role, after all—and emphasizing their role as ombudsmen who strike fear into the hearts of incompetent or arbitrary bureaucrats.

In turn, citizens increasingly tolerate members' positions on major national policies. What does it matter if one's representative is a conservative or liberal, Republican or Democrat? One vote of 535 can't make much difference. But as subcommittee chairman or ranking minority member, the representative in Congress has been a whiz at getting water treatment plants and mass transit feasibility studies. Moreover, he or she kept the old coke ovens from being shut down by EPA and tracked down umpteen lost social security and veterans' checks. Why give up the incumbent's seniority and experience just because of disagreements about the MX or national health care?

How have members of Congress managed to carry out ombudsman activities so successfully? Simple. Congress has powerful instruments of control over the bureaucracy, and there is ample evidence that the threat of those instruments is seldom far from bureaucratic minds. The effectiveness of those instruments is made all the more real by the establishment and maintenance of the elaborate committee-reciprocity system already mentioned. Members of Congress are given the opportunity to exercise disproportionate influence over segments of the federal bureaucracy that are of special concern to them. If an agency is causing problems for a member's constituents, the member need not organize a coalition of 51 or 218 members to discipline that agency. All that's needed is agreement from a couple of subcommittee colleagues. One can hardly blame an agency for paying special attention to "suggestions" from an interested member of Congress. . . .

## CONSEQUENCES OF THE STATUS QUO

The status quo in the last quarter of the twentieth century is not comforting. Citizens increasingly find themselves in contact with a bureaucratic establishment, often federal or at least federally stimulated. This bureaucratic establishment is somewhat unresponsive as bureaucracies are wont to be; at times it may be downright capricious. And every day it seems to extend a little further into citizens lives. But whether the bureaucracy is in the right or in the wrong, citizens know that they can count on one powerful ally in their attempts to triumph over bureaucratic procedures and/or dictates: their members of Congress. Increasingly, citizens view members as powerful, benevolent friends in an ever more threatening, impersonal world. Citizens receive solace; members of Congress get votes.

Meanwhile, in Washington, Congress maintains a federal bureaucracy deliberately organized to make it permeable to congressional intervention—not only to the chamber as a whole, but to subgroups and even individuals. So long as an agency cooperates when members make specific requests, it is unlikely to suffer long-term losses no matter how poor its performance. Perversely, the more inefficient and/or unreasonable its performance, the greater the political resource it constitutes. It is no great exaggeration to say that if OSHA did not exist, Congress might find it necessary to invent it.

And the president? He is something of the odd man out. His personal appointees become the captives of the subgovernments they were appointed to control. He finds himself circumscribed at every step. In the first flush of victory, throwing a net around "runaway" agencies addicted to cement pouring seems like a fine idea. But then Congress tells him that he can forget about a national energy policy if he doesn't learn to keep his nose out of where it doesn't belong. To obtain his goals the *president* must actively use a coordinated bureaucracy to achieve some positive purpose. But to achieve *their* goals *members* often can do no more than fend off perceived bureaucratic assaults on their constituents. This asymmetry would put the president in a weaker position than Congress even if his formal control powers were comparable.

The described state of affairs has several important consequences for the operation of the federal government in the foreseeable future. First, *in terms of organization and administration,* we can expect more of what we've got in the way of inefficient, "out of control" bureaucracy. Congress has no electoral incentive to work toward coordinated control. Quite the opposite is the case. Congress is making increasing use of instruments that keep the bureaucracy more closely tied to decentralized congressional control such as the congressional veto and sunset provisions. I think it is accurate to say that we are currently experiencing an increase in uncoordinated control and a decrease in coordinated control. Moreover, the dynamics of current trends have a self-perpetuating aspect. The more that members of Congress are perceived as, and elected as, ombudsmen, the greater their incentive to maintain the status quo, and the greater their reluctance to agree to proposals that would make major changes in the direction of coordinated control.

Second, *in terms of policy*, we can identify certain biases that arise from conflicting presidential and congressional goals. A president may look fondly on proposals to replace the jerry-built structure of income security programs with a guaranteed annual income accomplished entirely through the tax laws. Or perhaps he might contemplate razing the educational grant structure and implementing a voucher system. In theory such programs hold the promise of reducing gaps and conflicts in the existing program structure while requiring fewer administrative procedures and allowing greater individual freedom of choice. They are naturals for presidents on the prowl for places in history.

But members of Congress have a different bias. Even if such massive program shifts resulted in no net changes in their constituents' welfare— admittedly an unlikely possibility—they would decrease the political resource base of members. If benefits are distributed automatically, constituents will expect them as their due and not treat them as the gift of their benevolent representatives in Congress. And if costs are imposed automatically, as with the collection of taxes, fewer citizens will seek the aid of members in efforts to avoid those costs. Of course, one should grant the possibility that the congressional biases are preferable to the presidential biases—as those interests vested in existing programs believe. Weighing biases, unfortunately, is much more difficult than identifying them.

Finally, *in terms of political responsibility*, we can expect continued abdication by the U.S. Congress. In Theodore Lowi's compelling analysis, elected officialdom delegates power to the bureaucracy but provides vague or nonexistent standards for the exercise of that power. Again the persistent theme appears. The bureaucracy can be out of control only because those charged with the responsibility to control it choose not to. Why do they so choose?

Lowi sees the roots of the problem in acceptance of a public philosophy that exalts flexibility over uniformity and dependability, a philosophy that holds that every problem should be bargained and brokered rather than settled according to a fixed rule of law. Perhaps. But why should this philosophy have such a hold on our decisionmakers? Lowi blames a generation of pluralist social scientists who laid the intellectual groundwork in the classrooms of academia. That is rather heavy stuff for a discipline that has been remarkably irrelevant to the conduct of political affairs. Still, ideas may take hold where we least expect.

Perhaps a more plausible explanation lies in the goals held by individual members of Congress. They adopt (or appear to adopt) a public philosophy based on pluralist tenets largely because it rationalizes what their political self-interest dictates. Woll makes the case nicely:

A major reason for the power of the bureaucracy in policy formulation is the frequent lack of congressional incentives to adhere to the Schechter rule* and establish explicit standards for administrative action. This is particularly true in the regulatory realm, an area involving political conflict that legislators often wish to avoid. Congress is always willing to deal *rhetorically* with problems requiring regulation and with the area of regulatory reform, but real decisions on the part of the legislature will undoubtedly raise the ire of powerful pressure groups on one side or the other that are affected by government regulation.

Why take political chances by setting detailed regulations sure to antagonize some political actor or another? Why not require an agency to do the dirty work and then step in to redress the grievances that result from its activities? Let the agency take the blame and the member of Congress the credit. In the end everybody benefits. Members successfully wage their campaigns for re-election. And while popularly vilified, bureaucrats get their rewards in the committee rooms of Congress.

A public philosophy that holds that the bureaucracy should be granted the flexibility to deal with complex issues may seem to be the best way for an assembly of generalists to make public policy in a post-industrial society. But the entire justification of the committee-reciprocity system rests on the specialized expertise it purportedly fosters. Can we have it both ways? Can we *afford* to have it both ways? . . .

In the past, a great deal of imagination has gone into proposals for the reform of Congress. I hope that imagination still exists because, in the final analysis, an out of control bureaucracy reflects an out of control Congress. We might just as well avoid preoccupation with the symptoms and focus directly on the cause.

## The Bureaucratic Phenomenon

*See Lowi and Ginsberg pp. 277–283*

*The frustration of presidential efforts to make the bureaucracy responsive to executive-branch priorities are borne out in Jonathan Rose's historical assessment of the U.S. civil service. Created in 1883 by the Pendleton Act, the civil service was intended to prevent particular administrative positions from being filled routinely with political loyalists after each presidential election. Although presidents complained of the burdensome responsibility to appoint political supporters to hundreds of bureaucratic positions, the exercise of patronage was nevertheless*

* This refers to a 1935 Supreme Court ruling in *A.L.A. Schechter Poultry Corp. v. United States*, in which the Court limited Congress's power to delegate its legislative authority to Executive branch agencies. Since then, the Court has backed away from this ruling and allows broad delegations of power.

*a key means by which the chief executive could ensure loyalty within the bureaucracy.*

*As the federal government grew, particularly during the New Deal, the civil service grew with it. Currently, more than 99 percent of all bureaucratic positions in the federal government are excluded from presidential appointment. Yet a bureaucracy staffed by neutral experts is a bureaucracy perhaps less responsive to presidential priorities and less loyal to the president. Presidents come and go every four to eight years, while the civil service is a permanent feature of the federal government. Supporters of stronger presidential government have long advocated reforms to bring the bureaucracy and its civil servants under tighter presidential control. Contrast this chronology of civil service reform presented by Rose, however, with the most recent reform arguments presented by Vice President Al Gore.*

# Jonathan Rose
# "From Spoils to Merit: 195 Years of the U.S. Civil Service"*

One day in 1977, U.S. President Jimmy Carter noticed an unsavory smell in the White House. He quickly discovered its source: a mouse had crawled into an Oval Office wall and died there. Because Carter was about to receive a foreign diplomat, an aide asked the General Services Administration (GSA) to remove the mouse immediately.

But officials of the GSA—the agency that manages federal property—insisted that they had already exterminated all the mice inside the Executive Mansion. Therefore, the officials reasoned, the dead mouse must have come from outside—from the White House grounds, which were administered by the Department of the Interior. An aide contacted Interior officials, but they replied that they were responsible only for federal lands. Interior had no jurisdiction over a dead mouse indoors.

## POWERFUL COMPLAINT

Fuming, President Carter summoned GSA and Interior bureaucrats to his smelly office. "I can't even get a damn mouse out of my office," complained the Chief Executive of the world's most powerful nation.

After a while, the officials agreed on a strategy for removing the offending rodent. They created a special interagency task force and put it under White House supervision.

Most Presidents have told similarly bizarre stories about coping with

* Jonathan Rose, "From Spoils to Merit: 195 Years of the U.S. Civil Service" in *Scholastic Update* (September 20, 1985). Copyright © 1985 by Scholastic Inc. Reprinted by permission of Scholastic, Inc.

the U.S. civil service—a group they have battled to control throughout our nation's history. For the most part, the bureaucracy has won the battles. A President can issue as many orders as he likes, but his directives must follow guidelines laid down by bureaucrats. And the bureaucrats may or may not choose to carry out those directives.

A glance back at the history of the federal bureaucracy will show you its eery power to go its own way. It does so, it must be added, while its members keep working for what they feel to be the nation's best interests.

In the early days of the republic, the civil service was small and relatively manageable. As the first Secretary of State, Thomas Jefferson in 1790 headed a "bureaucracy" of exactly seven employees: four clerks, one translator, and two overseas diplomats.

Early Presidents were able to control bureaucrats through the "spoils system." They awarded government jobs to their political supporters, who in turn were loyal and obedient, although not always competent.

Andrew Jackson, our seventh President, is often blamed for creating the spoils system in 1829. Earlier, however, George Washington and John Adams had handed out many offices to their friends in the Federalist Party.

When Republican Thomas Jefferson entered the White House in 1801, he confronted a civil service staffed by hostile Federalists. Jefferson simply did what Jackson would do 28 years later. He fired many of his enemies and replaced them with bureaucrats who shared his political views.

## EXPANDING ECONOMY

Jefferson was the first of many Presidents who tried to halt the growth of the bureaucracy. But he was no more successful than those who came after him. An expanding economy and Jefferson's own Louisiana Purchase, which doubled the land area of the U.S., created hundreds of new jobs for federal officials. By 1824, Jefferson was warning: "We have more machinery of government than is necessary, too many parasites living on the labor of the industrious."

John Quincy Adams, elected President that year, tried to govern without the spoils system. He fired only 12 employees in four years and kept in office several political opponents.

Adams's integrity was noble but politically suicidal. The President's opponents used their official powers to undermine him. Because he would not dole out government jobs to his backers, he could not build a political party. The result: He was defeated by Andrew Jackson in 1828.

Jackson himself replaced no more than 20 percent of all federal employees with his own supporters. Even these friendly officials did not always carry out Jackson's wishes, however. So, Jackson undertook the first major reorganization of the bureaucracy.

## MAKING JOBS ROUTINE

Before Jackson, officeholders were relatively free to act on their own initiative. Jackson's reforms put limits on those freedoms. Each government post was assigned a standard routine—the essence of a modern bureaucracy. Such a routine can frustrate creativity and innovation, but it makes each job so simple that it can be carried out by any reasonably able person. And it ensures that government goals won't change radically every time a new official is appointed.

Abraham Lincoln was a far more ruthless practitioner of the spoils system than Andrew Jackson. When he entered the White House in 1861, he replaced nearly 90 percent of all Presidential officers, and he appointed many Union generals solely for political reasons. Reportedly, Lincoln once pressured an officeholder to pay a kickback to the Republican Party—a common political practice at that time.

If this seems shocking, remember that Lincoln was fighting a desperate civil war. By doling out patronage to an array of politicians, he guaranteed their loyalty to the Union and held the nation together.

## LINCOLN'S LAMENT

But even Lincoln was demoralized by endless demands for political plums. He said he felt like "a man so busy letting rooms in one end of his house that he cannot stop to put out the fire that is burning the other."

The Pendleton Act of 1883 finally curbed the spoils system. The law "classified" some federal offices, requiring them to be filled by competitive examinations. Also, the law protected holders of classified offices from being removed for failing to support the party in power.

The Pendleton Act protected only future appointments, however, and at first it applied to no more than 10 percent of the civil service. But the merit system was gradually extended until, today, it covers at least 85 percent of all federal bureaucrats. Ronald Reagan has only about 2,000 jobs available to fill with supporters—fewer than Andrew Jackson had a century and a half ago.

Protected by the merit system, the civil service became more honest but also more difficult to reorganize. In 1905, President Theodore Roosevelt appointed the Keep Committee to streamline the machinery of government. But the U.S. Congress and the Cabinet refused to follow the committee's recommendations.

Their resistance wasn't unusual. Bureaucracies are hard to reform. Reform usually strips some bureaucrats of certain responsibilities, and they will fight doggedly to hang on to the powers that those responsibilities give them. William Gibbs McAdoo, Secretary of the Treasury under Woodrow Wilson, is said to have "kicked like a steer" when his department was asked to surrender control of health services and the construction of post offices.

By 1930, the civil service had grown to 600,000 employees. Franklin D. Roosevelt, then the Democratic governor of New York, was demanding a "halt to this steady process of building commissions and regulatory bodies." But when Roosevelt became President three years later, he embarked on the greatest expansion of the federal bureaucracy in the nation's history.

## INEVITABLE GROWTH

Under the circumstances, growth was almost inevitable. To combat the Great Depression, Roosevelt created an "alphabet soup" of new agencies: the National Recovery Administration (NRA), the Agricultural Adjustment Administration (AAA), the Works Progress Administration (WPA), and many others. Armies of experts and office workers were hired to staff these departments.

Then, in 1941, the U.S. entered World War II. Defense agencies took on many more employees, including thousands of unpaid volunteers called "dollar-a-year men." The civil service ballooned to more than 1.4 million workers in 1941 and to more than 3.8 million in 1945.

Roosevelt found this mammoth bureaucracy very difficult to control. At one point, the Navy Department decided to begin a $2 billion shipbuilding program. The department didn't bother to inform Roosevelt, the Commander-in-Chief of the armed forces. He found out about the plan one morning while reading a newspaper.

## TRUMAN'S ANGER

Roosevelt's successor, Harry S. Truman, had similar problems. "I thought I was the President," Truman once snapped, "but when it comes to these bureaucracies, I can't make 'em do a damn thing."

Sitting in the Oval Office, Truman chuckled when he contemplated the fate of his successor, former General Dwight D. Eisenhower. "He'll sit here," Truman said, "and he'll say, 'Do this! Do that!' And nothing will happen. Poor Ike—it won't be a bit like the Army. He'll find it very frustrating."

Eisenhower was indeed frustrated by the federal bureaucracy, as was his fellow Republican, Richard Nixon. The Ramspeck Act of 1940 allowed the President to extend the coverage of civil service protection, and Harry Truman used this authority to ensure that future Republican Presidents would not be able to dismiss Democratic appointees.

The Democratic administrations of Roosevelt, Truman, John F. Kennedy, and Lyndon Johnson greatly expanded social welfare programs and the bureaucracy that handled these programs. By the time Richard Nixon reached the White House in 1969, these programs and bureaucrats were firmly entrenched and largely beyond Presidential control. Nixon tried and failed to abolish the Office of Economic Opportunity, the agency that ran Johnson's "War on Poverty." While Nixon denounced "forced busing" of school children, his own Justice Department filed lawsuits to enact busing plans for school desegregation.

## STAFFING THE WHITE HOUSE

The President can bypass these bureaucracies only by relying on his own personal bureaucracy—the White House staff. Abraham Lincoln had one secretary, whom he paid out of his own pocket. Herbert Hoover, President from 1929–33, had three secretaries.

In 1939, Congress created the Executive Office of the President to help Franklin Roosevelt manage the huge New Deal bureaucracy. The White House staff quickly mushroomed to 1,664 employees under President Kennedy in the early 1960s, to 5,395 under President Nixon 10 years later.

Nixon used his "counter-bureaucracy" to carry out bold policy initiatives that the civil service might not approve. He did not trust the State Department bureaucracy with the delicate job of pursuing Soviet-American detente—a relaxation of tensions—while he made overtures to the People's Republic of China. So he delegated that task to Henry Kissinger, his adviser on national security affairs.

## THE "PLUMBERS"

As bureaucracies often do, Nixon's staff expanded out of control. It created a secret "special investigations unit," nicknamed the "plumbers," to plug information leaks. In 1972, in Washington, DC, members of this group burglarized the Democratic Party's national headquarters at the Watergate office complex. An investigation into the burglary uncovered other illegal actions by the White House staff and by Nixon himself. The damning revelations forced Nixon out of office.

The 1962 Cuban Missile Crisis, when the U.S. and the Soviet Union stood at the brink of nuclear war, graphically illustrates the dangers of an unmanageable bureaucracy. On October 27, the Soviets offered to remove their missiles from Cuba—if President Kennedy withdrew U.S. Jupiter missiles from Turkey.

Kennedy was furious. Twice in the past six months he had ordered the removal of the out-of-date Jupiter missiles, but the bureaucrats in charge had done nothing. Now Kennedy could not dismantle those missiles without appearing to be knuckling under to Soviet pressure. Fortunately, the situation was defused on October 28, when the Russians agreed to bring home their Cuban missiles.

The very next morning, an interdepartmental task force was set up to remove the Jupiter missiles. This time, the task force chairman promised, there would be no bureaucratic delays. "Those missiles are going to be out of there by April 1 if we have to shoot them out," the chairman promised. The missiles were removed from Turkey—but not until April 15.

## DEBATING THE ISSUES: THE FEDERAL BUREAUCRACY— WHO SHOULD CONTROL IT?

*See Lowi and Ginsberg, pp. 312–313*

*The most recent reform effort to make government agencies both more accountable to citizens yet efficient and effective in performance is the "reinventing government" movement. Like many past reform efforts, supporters of reinvention draw upon the language and practice of business to inform bureaucratic improvements. Citizens are to be treated like valued customers; just as many American corporations are streamlining their operations, bureaucratic power should be decentralized, providing more authority to employees on the front line so that they can serve their "customers" more effectively; and excessive layers of management should be eliminated.*

*Under the leadership of Vice President Al Gore, Jr., a commission entitled the National Performance Review (NPR) issued a report in 1993 suggesting ways to "reinvent" federal agencies that embraced these principles. The report is a radical departure from past reform efforts in its emphasis upon empowering public sector employees to be entrepreneurial and creative in their efforts to serve citizens, rather than emphasizing tighter centralized control over their actions; yet the report is clearly in the tradition of presidential efforts to make bureaucracy more responsive and accountable to a presidential agenda. With the empowerment of bureaucrats in the executive branch automatically comes a reduction of the power exercised by elected officials in Congress. This tension, and the basic principles of the NPR report are apparent in a speech given by Gore entitled, "The New Job of the Federal Executive."*

*Political scientist Donald Kettl offers an analysis of the NPR report and its recommendations for the way in which government programs are managed. He reminds the reader of the critical importance of the political context within which any bureaucratic reform takes place. Prescriptions for bureaucratic reform based upon the operation of private sector organizations might make logical sense, but politics cannot be removed from the administration of government. Hence, any effort to reform the administration of government, such as the NPR, will require the political support of elected officials in Congress, of bureaucrats affected by the changes, and of the American public. Control, in other words, will not be readily transferred to the executive branch for more entrepreneurial implementation efforts.*

# Al Gore, Jr.
## "The New Job of the Federal Executive"*

In March 1993, President Clinton asked me to lead a review of the performance of the federal government. I enlisted the support of a core of very capable career federal employees to help craft a vision of what the federal government should be like. I presented this report to the President in September 1993. With his hearty endorsement of the report, I have been working vigorously to implement its recommendations to create a government that works better and costs less.

A key finding in that report was that only 20 percent of the American people trust the federal government to do the right thing most of the time. Thirty years ago, 76 percent trusted the government. Reducing this "trust deficit" is an important initiative of the Clinton/Gore administration. But this is possibly an even more important issue for career public servants—and their leaders—who face the public on a day-to-day basis.

Overcoming the trust deficit is an important impetus as to why the job of the federal executive must change. But it is only part of the reason. During the past few years, there have been significant changes in what the federal executive does and how he or she does it. The report I presented to the President last September will accelerate these changes. I would like to discuss why and how these changes came about and share my vision of the new job of the federal executive.

Two relatively recent developments have dramatically shifted the premises on which traditional public and private sector management theory has been based: (1) a new understanding of how best to employ human capacity; and (2) the new role of information technology in transforming the manager's job.

### A SHIFT IN THE UNDERSTANDING OF HUMAN CAPACITY

First, let me talk about the shift in our understanding of human capacity. In the early 1900s, Frederick Taylor—the father of work measurement—advocated the use of hierarchies and the specialization of functions as the path to high productivity and efficiency. Similarly, organizational theorist Chester Barnard defined the role of the executive in the 1930s as being the central coordinator of an organization.

Yet, in today's environment, these approaches now seem to limit productivity rather than promote it, in part because hierarchical structures and specialization of tasks cannot meet the communication needs of a complex and rapidly changing environment. Today, we recognize that Taylor's theories about "scientific management" are no longer applicable

* Al Gore, Jr., "The New Job of the Federal Executive" in *Public Administration Review* (July/August 1994, vol. 54, no. 4). Reprinted with permission.

in the information age, and that Chester Barnard's definition of the role of the executive is likewise outdated.

Were they wrong—the way alchemists were wrong to think lead could be turned into gold? I don't think so. In fact, you could argue that they were right for their time. In the 1930s, it would have been difficult for executives—whether President Franklin Roosevelt, or the CEO of General Motors—to influence what was going on in their organizations without using a hierarchical approach.

The old hierarchies were based in part on a sharp division between those who worked with their heads by thinking and those who worked with their muscles. But before very long, the best managers realized that the single most valuable asset in their organizations was the unused brain power and creativity of the men and women who were being asked only to use their muscles. And so, today, we have developed different ideas about human capacity. We have discovered that people who work primarily with their hands are capable of having new ideas. Individuals within organizations are capable of producing more than had been previously thought possible by those who assumed that the division between thinking and muscle work was the basis for organization. It is the job of the executive to uncover this untapped potential.

I remember at a meeting last November, a big man got up to speak. He was a line worker at Corning Glass, named Dick Allen. In the old days, he told me, when something went wrong with his machine, two engineers would come onto the factory floor and look into it. He knew they were engineers for two reasons. First, they wore ties. And second, they never talked to him. A lot of times he knew what was wrong. "I can remember," he said, "going home nearly every evening—or morning, depending on what shift I was on—and describing to my wife all the things that were wrong with Corning and all of my brilliant ideas of how to fix it. But I had no way at the factory to deliver those ideas." Well, the culture of the times dictated that he keep his thoughts to himself and let the "men with ties" work it out.

Then Corning changed its philosophy. Now the engineers still come onto the factory floor. But the very first thing they do is ask Dick Allen what's wrong. They've found out that if anyone knows, it's likely to be him. And of course the engineers are right. But, this requires an entirely new model of leadership that is based on the notion that workers can make major, positive contributions to improving the understanding of the workplace and the understanding of how to enhance productivity.

INTRODUCTION OF THE INFORMATION AGE

The information age has brought about a second development that has caused revolutionary changes in management theory. Information technology gives the new manager a set of tools that did not exist even a decade ago. Computers, and their interconnection through telecommunications, have made possible flatter organizations, wider spans of control and much faster information sharing. The key change has been increased communications between the bottom and the top of an organization.

It is now possible for a president—whether of a company or a country—to decentralize, yet at the same time keep field operations fully informed and accountable for results. It is this concept—accountability—that links the federal manager of the Clinton era to the role of federal managers in earlier eras. They are both accountable—to the law, to the Congress, to the President, and to the public. But the information age allows the new federal manager to communicate effectively across very large organizations. And information technology also allows this to be done without sacrificing accountability.

## THE EFFECTS OF THESE DEVELOPMENTS ON THE ROLE OF FEDERAL EXECUTIVES

These two new developments have combined to transform the job of the federal executive. It is now possible to transform the nature of management in the federal government. So, what is the new job of the federal executive? I see it embodying seven characteristics:

### ■ Developing a Clear Vision

In the old way of doing things, federal executives were expected to know best, and they often created special offices at the top of their organizational charts to manage change and create innovation—largely apart from the rest of the organization. They would call it the "office of strategic planning." In the new way, federal executives need to involve all employees in developing a clear vision and a shared sense of mission.

In this administration, we want managers and employees to work together to paint a clear vision and articulate a compelling mission. A shared vision—supplemented with clearly understood goals and shared values among everyone in the organization, from top to bottom—can be the basis of intelligent decisions. This approach results in the empowerment of all employees—managers as well as workers—to innovate and ensure a high level of performance. It ensures that everyone "buys into" the vision and is part of the process for creating it, so that goals can be developed together.

I've seen this in action. A couple of weeks ago, for example, I visited the Department of Veterans Affairs. I met Joe Thompson, the New York Regional Office Director. He described how he helped create a vision for his staff. He took his benefit determination staff to nearby Veterans' hospitals and let them meet actual customers face to face. As a team, these employees then developed a vision of how they wanted to change the process from a 23-step sequential process to one that was run by a set of small teams serving specific beneficiaries. This new 8-step process has resulted in savings of 20 percent in processing costs and has cut waiting time for veterans who want to see a claims counselor from 30 minutes to 3 minutes. The veterans like it better because they deal with a recognizable, familiar human being from the beginning to the end of the process. The employees like it better because they are able to see their work from the beginning to the end, not as an isolated fragment in a disconnected whole.

## ■ Creating a Team Environment

In the old way, federal executives were expected to keep staff working within organizational boundaries. In the new way, federal executives will need to help staff cross boundaries to work effectively with other organizations. The federal executive of the Eisenhower era found, according to Professor Bernstein, that "much of his work is designed to protect his agency and the integrity of its programs."

This can no longer be seen as the path to success. As organizational theorists Gifford and Elizabeth Pinchot have observed, teamwork is now the other hallmark of success. "Bureaucracy keeps teams isolated, focused on their task assigned from above." In intelligent organizations, teams and their members must reach out through voluntary collaboration to create a more integrated organization. This administration is committed to doing just that. For example, the fiscal year 1995 budget creates a government-wide approach to job training, a cross-agency attack on homelessness, an innovative approach to ecosystems management, and a governmentwide approach to implement new information technology, just to name a few examples.

Recently the Commerce Department created a cross-organizational team to promote export assistance. The department has piloted several centers around the country to create a "one stop" center for businesses seeking markets overseas for their products. Under the old approach, a company would go from agency to agency to get the information and support they needed. In the center recently opened in Baltimore, the U.S. Department of Commerce, the Export-Import Bank, the Small Business Administration, and the Maryland state government are co-located. A business can now get information on overseas markets as well as apply for financial assistance. Representatives from these agencies are cross-trained and actually visit businesses to become familiar with their special needs.

## ■ Empowering Employees

In the old way, federal executives were expected to circumscribe discretion with rules because employees were not to be trusted. In the new way, federal executives must empower their employees to achieve the goals of the organization, within statutory constraints and the agreed-upon vision of the organization.

Recently, I had the privilege of introducing a woman named Joan Hyatt to President Clinton. She and some of the field staff at the Occupational Safety and Health Administration (OSHA) proposed cutting its 400-page field manual down to 93 pages. Ms. Hyatt told the President, "This is our field operations manual. . . . [It] tells us exactly what kind of documentation we need to provide. It also tells us how to put one foot in front of the other and walk down the aisle of a workplace to do our inspections." The revised manual, she said, will allow OSHA's workplace inspectors to spend more of their time assuring American workplaces are safe and much less of their time doing paperwork. OSHA found—like many of America's most successful corporations have found—that those who are closest to the problem are often in the best position to make dramatic improvements.

## ■ Putting Customers First

In the old way, federal executives were expected to protect and enlarge their operations and to satisfy higher levels of management. In the new way, federal executives will need to work to satisfy their customers. In the past, federal executives were presumed to know what the citizen wanted. The idea of a customer survey would have seemed ridiculous to federal executives. Moreover, if you saw one customer, you could safely assume you had seen them all. Rules were standardized to ensure uniformity and equality. This rigid approach was nominally intended to provide quality service, but over time it failed to keep up with customers' evolving needs.

In September 1994, President Clinton signed a customer service executive order that creates an entirely new relationship between the federal government and its customers. It calls on agencies to set and publicly post standards so that people can know exactly what they should expect. For example, the Miami Customs Service Office has set standards for clearing shipments into the United States. It made major shippers, like American Airlines, partners in its enforcement strategy. It showed shippers how to conduct self-enforcement. Customs is now able, in Miami, to focus on high-risk targets and spot check others. As a result, customers are no longer inconvenienced by delays, and cargo moves much more quickly through the port. Interdiction is up because the law enforcement effort is now targeted more appropriately to where it is needed.

## ■ Communicating with Employees

In the old way, federal executives were expected to communicate one level up and one level down. In the new way, federal executives will need to communicate through every layer in their agencies. As organizations added layers and as work became more specialized, the old communications channels and approach became ineffective. Executives became disconnected from front line workers because they were insulated by all the layers in between. Craziness crept into the system—like the military specifications for chocolate chip cookies at the Department of Defense, or a 23-step process for determining a veterans' eligibility for benefits—and the executives all of the sudden seemed powerless to reestablish a sense of coherence within the organization and to ensure a focus on the mission.

In the new way, executives will need to communicate directly to front line employees to find out what they are really doing, then the executives will need to broadcast clear vision statements throughout the organization, and accept responsibility as executives for maintaining a high level of awareness—on the part of every employee—of the vision, the goals and the values upon which the organization is based.

## ■ Cutting Red Tape

In the old way, federal executives were expected to tell their subordinates what the executive needed. In the new way, the federal executive will need to ask subordinates what they need to get their job done. How do we change these things? One way is to do more of what Secretary of Education Dick Riley is doing. He hands out wallet size "reinvention permission slips" to every single employee in his department. It says: "Ask yourself: (1) is it good for my customers? (2) is it legal and ethical? (3) is it something I am willing to be accountable for? (4) is it consistent with my agency's mission? (5) am I using my time wisely? (6) is the answer YES to all of these questions? (7) If so, don't ask permission. You already have it. Just do it!" That is a pretty powerful message from the secretary of a department to front line employees.

Similarly, Bureau of Reclamation Commissioner Dan Beard has handed out to his managers what he calls "forgiveness coupons" designed to encourage them to take risks—and they can redeem them if necessary —and sometime it is necessary, but the point is to encourage them to try something new, to innovate, to take some chances, to try to change. Mistakes are then recognized as opportunities to learn. Organizations that do not learn, do not change. Organizations that do not change eventually do not work. Because the world changes, change is a fact of life. And the best way for an organization to change is to learn about the change to which they must adapt.

How do organizations learn? The computer world provides an apt metaphor. There are two major architectures for computers. One is the large central processing unit, which is characterized by most mainframe computers. In these computers, a problem is sent out to the field of memory surrounding the central processor for bits of information and then brought back to the center to process it. When the problem is solved, the answer is then parceled back out to the memory. It takes a lot of time to go back and forth three times. It also consumes a lot of energy. The other, newer architecture—called massively parallel computing—takes a different approach. It breaks up a problem into lots of tiny processing units and distributes them throughout the memory field. So, when a task has to be performed, the work is done simultaneously in little bits throughout the memory field and then the answer is assembled at the center. It is a much more efficient approach.

Similarly, the same improvements in efficiency, when it comes to solving problems, can be gained by an organization. In the old way, a manager assumed that his or her task was to reach out into the organization for little bits of information, to bring them all to the center, to try to figure them all out, and then to parcel the answers to the employees who were waiting for guidance from above. This approach takes a long time to solve the complex, new problems that organizations now face. If, in contrast, a manager asks all of the employees to think about the part of the problem that he or she is most familiar with, and participate collectively in an organizationwide effort to solve that problem, and then assemble all of the answers to change the organization, then an organization can change much more rapidly and learn much more quickly.

## ■ Creating Clear Accountability

In the old way, federal executives were expected to use hierarchical arrangements, with checks and controls over every input, elaborate reporting mechanisms, and extensive use of rules and regulations. In the new way, federal executives will be expected to concentrate on performance and carefully measure results—outcomes and outputs, not just inputs.

Focusing on process and conformity may once have made sense, but no longer. That approach built an ever-increasing overhead in paperwork, redundant reporting, and immersion in checking details that slowed down performance and diverted professionals from the intent of the law.

President Clinton and I believe that, in order to succeed, we must clearly articulate our intent and continue to encourage flexibility when it comes to how our goals are achieved. For example, recently the president and five agency heads signed performance agreements. These agreements lay out, in written form, a publicly available vision of the agencies' goals and missions. This is a powerful tool for communicating with every employee in an organization.

## ■ Hurdles in Accepting the Challenge of Change

The best way for the federal executive to fulfill the traditional role of implementing the will of the President is to share those expectations explicitly—openly and publicly—with every single employee in the organization so that everyone can work simultaneously on ensuring that the job is well done. But, in order to perform their role successfully, federal executives must surmount two major hurdles.

The first is cynicism—specifically a belief that this new set of changes is not real. I know that some managers out there think to themselves, "this too shall pass." But the movement to reinvent government is grounded in very big changes that are remaking all sectors of the economy. If federal executives let cynicism stand in the way of change, they will face more and more hostility from an ever more cynical public and from restless employees who understand why this change is good for the work force as well as for the American people.

The second obstacle is culture. Many federal employees find security in the existing work culture. It has set forth the status and reward structure to which they have long since accommodated themselves. This structure limits individual accountability and protects against change. But because this existing culture no longer serves the public interest as well as it should, our challenge is to create a new one. Specifically our challenge is to create a work environment that: (1) promotes and rewards innovation, (2) preserves accountability and respect for the law, (3) puts customers first, and (4) provides employees with a feeling of security, recognition, and personal accomplishment.

## CONCLUSION

And so, I offer this challenge to federal executives throughout the federal government. This administration supports the changes you have asked for. But we cannot achieve them simply by issuing a report. This can only be done by individuals who lead by example. We are relying on you to lead this charge. My report to the president last fall is a blueprint for change. But it is only a beginning.

Over time, old ways of thinking will fade and will be replaced by a new culture that promotes innovation and quality. A new face of government will appear—of leaders with vision, of employees newly empowered and newly motivated, and of customers newly satisfied. Recall how a few decades ago the phrase "made in Japan" was synonymous with poor quality. And now "made in Japan" is synonymous with very high levels of quality. We need to create a future in which the phrase "good enough for government work" is said in an admiring tone. It can be done. It will be done.

However, this new vision of a reformed national government will lie fallow without the federal executive also seeing this as his or her own personal vision. Executives are the key. Today, I see that as my challenge—to help federal executives make this new vision theirs.

Recently I returned to the Pentagon to help the secretary of defense celebrate some heroes of reinvention. I met a woman named Wilett Bunton, a Defense Department employee who told me last summer in an open meeting in the Pentagon courtyard how entangled in red tape the federal travel system is. Others heard her comment last summer and, using the new empowerment that the National Performance Review recommends, they went about changing it. Wilett gave me a new insight into perhaps the most important job of a federal executive. She said that, because of the reinvention efforts underway, including dramatic changes in the travel system, "We're not the same people we were six months ago." The new job of a federal executive is to help other federal employees believe, "We're not the same people we were six months ago" and to make the public believe we're not the same government we were either.

# Donald Kettl
# "National Performance Review: An Analysis"*

Vice President Al Gore's National Performance Review (NPR), with a report issued in September 1993, promised nothing less than a revolutionary reinvention of the federal government. Critics dismissed it as hollow rhetoric, and some scholars criticized it as dangerous. In its first year, however, the NPR has produced impressive results and a genuine start on changing the culture of government simplification of some rules and procedures, especially by eliminating the onerous Federal Personnel Manual and the much-hated SF-171 job application form; a reform of the procurement process; improved top-level coordination of the government's management; and the stimulation of widespread innovation by federal managers through "reinvention labs."

## THE SHORT TERM

The NPR produced more than almost anyone, including perhaps the reinventors themselves, believed possible. Even when the movement produced sketchy results, the problems it attacked usually were the right ones. To get the NPR moving, however, the reinventers made short-term tactical decisions to get quick wins. The quick wins, though, have come at the cost of building the foundation for lasting success. As a result, the NPR is not now self-sustaining. It has shown great potential, but the risk is that the NPR will become just a short-term political tactic instead of a lasting reform. Two problems, in particular, have plagued the NPR.

■ Preoccupation with Savings over Performance Improvement

Of course, a government that works better can cost less, as the NPR report's subtitle suggests. Streamlining procurement can save money, while a more customer-focused government can tailor programs more carefully to citizens' needs. In practice, however, seeking big savings in short order can undermine the broader effort for management improvement and increase costs in the long run. The largest single chunk of the NPR's prom-

* Donald Kettl, "National Performance Review: An Analysis" in the *La Follette Policy Report* (Fall 1994). Vol. 6, No. 2, La Follette Institute, University of Wisconsin—Madison.

ised $108 billion savings was to come from downsizing the federal work force ($40.4 billion). The downsizing was to be the product of the NPR's management improvements. The Clinton administration's eagerness for quick savings, however, led officials to shrink employment first and let the management improvements follow.

On one level, the focus on budget savings quickly alienated many government workers. The NPR had built a strong pro-bureaucrat case. It told public employees that the government's performance problems were the fault of the system, not of its workers. It also held out the promise of much greater flexibility for managers ("empowerment") and a reduction in red tape. The prospect of reducing federal employment by 272,900 workers, however, quickly preoccupied many managers, and, for many government workers, soon became the defining reality of the NPR.

On another level, the savings proved far easier to promise than to deliver. The administration has had recurring disputes with members of Congress and the Congressional Budget Office about the savings from individual proposals. These disputes diminished congressional support for the NPR and delayed pieces of the legislative program, especially the bill that provided buyout payments to employees who agreed to leave the federal service.

Moreover, the savings proved the hardest element of the NPR to judge. Some long-term savings required short-term investments, like the buyouts. Some short-term savings risked increasing long-term costs, especially if downsizing in the absence of a "reinvented" workplace led the wrong employees to leave or weakened government management. Beyond counting federal workers who left the government, putting hard numbers on the NPR's other savings required extraordinary feats of budgetary analysis. That complexity not only increased the difficulty of assessing the NPR's savings but also sometimes surrounded the NPR with debate of such technical detail as to undermine their political value. In the meantime, of course, the downsizing led many bureaucrats not to enlist in the NPR's revolution, but to hope that the NPR would soon go away. And since the public assumes that the NPR has long since produced the promised savings, the reinventers face the task of living up to the pledge as the task of achieving it—without undermining the rest of the movement—becomes ever greater.

## ■ Lack of an Explicit Strategy for Dealing with Congress

NPR officials initially believed that they could accomplish most of their reforms without seeking congressional approval. The lesson of the first year, however, is that virtually no reform that really matters can be achieved without at least implicit congressional support. The NPR has not yet developed a full strategy for winning it.

Congress embraced the broad downsizing initiative and, in fact, increased the reduction from 252,000 to 272,900 employees. For months, however, members stalled the buyout bill required to produce the savings, in part because of uncertainty about whether it would cost or save money in the short run. The House, meanwhile, voted to exempt the Veterans Health Administration, with 212,000 employees, from the downsizing, so as not to threaten veterans' health care. The Senate then voted to exempt federal criminal justice activities, so as not to jeopardize the war on crime. Many members of Congress supported the NPR in the whole, but then tugged at its individual threads in ways that threatened to unravel it.

In the beginning, the NPR had concentrated on launching its report. It had not developed a strategy for implementing its recommendations beyond trying to enlist legions of bureaucrats throughout the agencies in the cause and hoping that the power of the ideas would defuse opposition. Members of Congress had everything to gain from embracing the broad principles of reinvention and then protecting their constituents and favorite programs behind the scenes in committee rooms and little-noticed riders to complex bills.

In sum: The NPR, in its first year, accomplished far more than cynics suggested might be possible. It has launched a broad reform movement in the right direction, and it has been asking the right questions. Nevertheless, and this is the NPR's critical problem, the short-term accommodations it made to get the movement going weakened its chances for long-term success. It is not now a self-sustaining revolution, and considerable work needs to be done to move the invasion from a beachhead to a breakout, and then from a breakout to a conquest.

## THE LONG TERM

For the NPR to endure, it will need to build congressional support. That will require striking a different kind of bargain between the executive branch and Congress. The NPR's recommendations need congressional support while Congress needs a strategy for meaningful oversight. Both the president and Congress have a strong interest in attaining this uneasy balance. The stakes for the executive branch, both political and managerial, are clear. Moreover, especially in Congress's Governmental Affairs and Government Operations Committees,* there is fresh interest in defining a new congressional role in management. Without finding a new kind of bargain between the branches, it would be easy for the congressional micro-politics of the NPR to nibble away its key elements. Launching the reinvention revolution was the easy part. Sustaining the revolution will require much harder, and far less glamorous work. It will require considerable creativity, far more than either the reinventers or their critics have

* These are, respectively, the Senate and House committees with the formal responsbility of overseeing the management and administrative operations of the Executive branch. In 1995, the House changed the name of its committee from Government Operations to Government Reform and Oversight.

demonstrated, in recognizing and solving the four critical underlying problems that lie beyond the beachhead.

## ■ Tensions

There really is no such thing as *the* NPR. It has, in fact, been a three-front campaign: to shrink the size and cost of the government; to spread a new gospel of reinvention in areas like procurement reform and customer service; and to encourage an army of reinventers throughout the federal government. Its outside game, however, based on shrinking the government, undercut its efforts to transform the government's inside workers because it alienated many public employees. Long-term success requires the NPR to ensure that, on each of its fronts, its strategies complement—not disrupt—each other.

## ■ Capacity

The NPR report argued the need to bulldoze away overbearing forces of supervision, authority, and oversight. The report, however, was far weaker on what ought to spring up in their place. The overwhelming lesson of the last generation of policy experimentation in the United States is that government programs do not manage themselves. Rather, success depends on finding the institutions, processes, money, technology, and especially people—that is, the capacity—to do the job.

Will a reinvented government transform itself into a leaner government, faster on its feet and better able to adapt to the dizzying pace of change? Or will the legacy of reinvention be an even more hollow government with far less capacity to do its job, a government managed by employees with even less incentive to do their jobs well? The former would produce a truly revolutionary change. The latter would perpetuate the cycle of raised expectations, disappointing results, increased inefficiency, and public cynicism. Long-term success requires the NPR not only to explain what it wants to sweep away but, more important, to define what ought to spring up in the place of dysfunctional systems. Strengthening government capacity will require more than adherence to the broad themes of employee empowerment and customer service.

## ■ Ideas

The NPR built on ambitious ideas about cutting red tape, putting customers first, empowering employees, and cutting back to basics. Far less clear, however, was what those concepts actually meant. When do procedural due process and proper administrative safeguards become red tape? Who are the government's customers and how can they be served? Does customer service contradict other public goals? What would it take to empower employees, and what risks would empowerment create? Who decides what the basics are? In *Reinventing Government*, a driving spirit of the NPR, David Osborne and Ted Gaebler make the case that government should "steer, not row." But in what direction should government steer, and how good are the ideas that serve as its compass? The lessons from reinventions abroad and from private sector reform in the United States is that a clear sense of purpose and sharp guiding principles are critical to success. Long-term success requires the NPR to define, far more sharply, its purpose and guiding principles if it is to escape the quicksand of fuzzy rhetoric.

## ■ Glue

The NPR builds on a philosophy of "empowering" government workers to make better decisions. It argues for a more "entrepreneurial" philosophy, with a competition prescription replacing monopoly-based command-and-control management. In short, the NPR seeks to shift power from Congress to the bureaucracy and, within the bureaucracy, from top to bottom levels. If empowered bureaucrats behave entrepreneurially, what glue will prevent government from disintegrating into a vast network of quasi-independent operators? What processes will ensure democratic accountability to elected officials? What processes will ensure that the public interest dominates private behavior? Long-term success requires the NPR to build a force at the center of government, perhaps in the Office of Management and Budget, to focus government on results and to avoid having the reform spin off into scores of different, unconnected directions. It also requires that the NPR focus sharply on striking a new kind of bargain with Congress over government management.

Even more fundamentally, achieving the NPR's promise will require more clearly linking the question of what government ought to do with how government ought to do it. The NPR, in the report's own words, "focused primarily on how government should work, not on what it should do." The burden of a century of public management research, however, is that the distinction is artificial: the *how* powerfully shapes the *what* because means embody ends; from the beginning, the *how* has to be driven by the *what.*

To a greater degree than even political noncombatants stop to recognize, and certainly far more than government officials ever acknowledged, many public performance problems are often the product of what government sets out to do. Government in fact does many things very well, from delivering social security checks to providing weather satellite maps. Often, when things work badly, it is because it tries to do things that are very hard or impossible, like preventing drug abuse, training unemployed workers, cleaning up toxic waste, or providing welfare without creating dependence.

## The Challenge

Improving performance on one level requires focusing government most clearly on what it does well and figuring out how to do those things better. The problem is that no one (and this includes the NPR) has thought clearly about what those things are. On another level, if we seek to do things well that are hard to do, we must be frank about the degree of difficulty and focus sharply on how to tackle the impossible. Many of the most basic questions to which the NPR has addressed itself revolve around such issues. If we choose to attack these problems at a superficial level, by focusing on the number of bureaucrats that can be eliminated or the dollars that can be saved, we will both miss the real issues and even further undercut government's ability to perform well.

The National Performance Review accomplished, in just its first year, far more than anyone thought possible. It energized employees, it attracted citizens, it drew media attention to government management, and it made the point that management matters. In the blush of success, however, the NPR failed to build the foundation for success in the long haul. It borrowed bits and pieces of management reform from both the public and private sectors and pasted them together in a patchwork that, while initially attractive, could not hold together. In the process, the NPR missed the most important lesson that other successful reforms teach: in the long run, management, matched to mission, matters most. The movement launched in September 1993, however promising, was not self-sustaining. Making it stick requires hard work on tough questions—work that, for the most part, has not begun.

# The Federal Courts: Least Dangerous Branch or Imperial Judiciary?

## Judicial Review

*See Lowi and Ginsberg, pp. 331–345 or brief edition, pp. 183–190*

*The power of judicial review—the authority of the federal courts to determine the constitutionality of state and federal legislative acts—was established early in the nation's history in the case of* Marbury v. Madison *(1803). While the doctrine of judicial review is now firmly entrenched in the American judicial process, the outcome of* Marbury *was by no means a sure thing. The doctrine had been outlined in* The Federalist No. 78, *and had been relied upon implicitly in earlier, lower federal court cases, but there were certainly sentiments among some of the Founders to suggest that only Congress ought to be able to judge the constitutionality of its acts.*

## *Marbury v. Madison* (1803)\*

[*The facts leading up to the decision in* Marbury v. Madison *tell an intensely political story. Efforts to reform the federal judiciary had been ongoing with the Federalist administration of President Adams. Following the defeat of the Federalist party in 1800, and the election of Thomas Jefferson as president, the Federalist Congress passed an act reforming the judiciary. The act gave outgoing President Adams authority to appoint several Federalist justices of the peace before Jefferson's term as president began. This would have enabled the Federalist party to retain a large measure of power.*

*Marbury was appointed to be a justice of the peace by President Adams, but his commission, signed by the president and sealed by the secretary of state, without which he could not assume office, was not delivered to him before President Jefferson took office March 4, 1803. Jefferson refused to order James Madison, his secretary of state, to deliver the commission. Marbury, in turn, filed an action in the U.S. Supreme Court seeking an order—called a writ of mandamus—directing the secretary of state to compel the delivery of the commission.*

*The Constitution grants the Supreme Court original jurisdiction in only a limited number of cases—those involving ambassadors, public ministers, and those*

\* *Marbury v. Madison, 5 U.S. 137, 1803.*

*in which a state is a party; in the remaining cases, the Court has authority only as an appellate court. When it acts according to its original jurisdiction, the Court exercises initial authority over a controversy, just like a trial court, as distinguished from the more limited authority it exercises when a case is presented as an appeal from a lower court's decision.*

*In 1789, Congress passed legislation setting up the federal courts, called the Judiciary Act of 1789. That legislation gave the Supreme Court the original authority to "issue writs of mandamus in cases warranted by the principles and usage of law. . . ." Thus, the ultimate question in* Marbury v. Madison *was whether Congress could, by statute, enlarge the original jurisdiction of the Court.*

*The Court first considered whether Marbury's appointment was complete—and therefore irrevocable—before Jefferson took office. Under the law, the appointment was deemed complete when the president signed the commission and the secretary of state sealed it; the appointment was a completed fact at that time, and was not dependent upon delivery. Therefore, the Court found that Marbury was entitled to his commission. The Court then decided that by withholding the commission, Secretary of State Madison was violating Marbury's legal rights. The remaining question was whether the Supreme Court could issue an order compelling the delivery of the commission.]*

CHIEF JUSTICE MARSHALL delivered the opinion of the Court.

. . . It is, then, the opinion of the Court.

1st. That by signing the commission of Mr. Marbury, the President of the United States appointed him a justice of peace for the county of Washington, in the District of Columbia; and that the seal of the United States, affixed thereto by the Secretary of State, is conclusive testimony of the verity of the signature, and of the completion of the appointment, and that the appointment conferred on him a legal right to the office for the space of five years.

2d. That, having this legal title to the office, he has a consequent right to the commission; a refusal to deliver which is a plain violation of that right, for which the laws of his country afford him a remedy.

It remains to be inquired whether,

3d. He is entitled to the remedy for which he applies. This depends on,

1st. The nature of the writ applied for; and,

2d. The power of this court. . . .

This . . . is a plain case for a mandamus, either to deliver the commission, or a copy of it from the record; and it only remains to be inquired,

Whether it can issue from this court.

The act to establish the judicial courts of the United States authorizes the Supreme Court "to issue writs of mandamus in cases warranted by the principles and usages of law, to any courts appointed, or persons holding office, under the authority of the United States."

The Secretary of State, being a person holding an office under the authority of the United States, is precisely within the letter of the description, and if this court is not authorized to issue a writ of mandamus to such an officer, it must be because the law is unconstitutional, and therefore absolutely incapable of conferring the authority, and assigning the duties which its words purport to confer and assign.

The constitution vests the whole judicial power of the United States in one Supreme Court, and such inferior courts as congress shall, from time to time, ordain and establish. This power is expressly extended to all cases arising under the laws of the United States; and, consequently, in some form, may be exercised over the present case; because the right claimed is given by a law of the United States.

In the distribution of this power it is declared that "the Supreme Court shall have original jurisdiction in all cases affecting ambassadors, other public ministers and consuls, and those in which a state shall be a party. In all other cases, the Supreme Court shall have appellate jurisdiction." . . .

To enable this court, then, to issue a mandamus, it must be shown to be an exercise of appellate jurisdiction, or to be necessary to enable them to exercise appellate jurisdiction. . . .

It is the essential criterion of appellate jurisdiction, that it revises and corrects the proceedings in a cause already instituted, and does not create that cause. . . . [Y]et to issue such a writ to an officer for the delivery of a paper, is in effect the same as to sustain an original action for that paper, and, therefore, seems not to belong to appellate, but to original jurisdiction.

The authority, therefore, given to the Supreme Court, by the act establishing the judicial courts of the United States, to issue writs of mandamus to public officers, appears not to be warranted by the constitution; and it becomes necessary to inquire whether a jurisdiction so conferred can be exercised.

The question, whether an act, repugnant to the constitution, can become the law of the land, is a question deeply interesting to the United States; but, happily, not of an intricacy proportioned to its interest. It seems only necessary to recognize certain principles, supposed to have been long and well established, to decide it.

That the people have an original right to establish, for their future government, such principles, as, in their opinion, shall most conduce to their own happiness is the basis on which the whole American fabric has been erected. The exercise of this original right is a very great exertion; nor can it, nor ought it, to be frequently repeated. The principles, therefore, so established, are deemed fundamental. And as the authority from which they proceed is supreme, and can seldom act, they are designed to be permanent.

This original and supreme will organizes the government, and assigns to different departments their respective powers. It may either stop here, or establish certain limits not to be transcended by those departments.

The government of the United States is of the latter description. The powers of the legislature are defined and limited; and that those limits may not be mistaken, or forgotten, the constitution is written. To what purpose are powers limited, and to what purpose is that limitation committed to writing, if these limits may, at any time, be passed by those intended to be restrained? The distinction between a government with limited and unlimited powers is abolished, if those limits do not confine the persons on whom they are imposed, and if acts prohibited and acts allowed, are of equal obligation. It is a proposition too plain to be contested, that the constitution controls any legislative act repugnant to it; or, that the legislature may alter the constitution by an ordinary act.

Between these alternatives there is no middle ground. The constitution is either a superior paramount law, unchangeable by ordinary means, or it is on a level with ordinary legislative acts, and, like other acts, is alterable when the legislature shall please to alter it.

If the former part of the alternative be true, then a legislative act contrary to the constitution is not law: if the latter part be true, then written constitutions are absurd attempts, on the part of the people, to limit a power in its own nature illimitable.

Certainly all those who have framed written constitutions contemplate them as forming the fundamental and paramount law of the nation, and, consequently, the theory of every such government must be, that an act of the legislature, repugnant to the constitution, is void.

This theory is essentially attached to a written constitution, and, is consequently, to be considered, by this court, as one of the fundamental principles of our society. It is not therefore to be lost sight of in the further consideration of this subject.

If an act of the legislature, repugnant to the constitution, is void, does it, notwithstanding its invalidity, bind the courts, and oblige them to give it effect? Or, in other words, though it be not law, does it constitute a rule as operative as if it was a law? This would be to overthrow in fact what was established in theory; and would seem, at first view, an absurdity too gross to be insisted on. . . .

It is emphatically the province and duty of the judicial department to say what the law is. Those who apply the rule to particular cases, must of necessity expound and interpret that rule. If two laws conflict with each other, the courts must decide on the operation of each.

So if a law be in opposition to the constitution; if both the law and the constitution apply to a particular case, so that the court must either decide that case conformably to the law, disregarding the constitution; or conformably to the constitution, disregarding the law; the court must determine which of these conflicting rules governs the case. This is of the very essence of judicial duty.

If, then, the courts are to regard the constitution, and the constitution is superior to any ordinary act of the legislature, the constitution, and not such ordinary act, must govern the case to which they both apply.

Those, then, who controvert the principle that the constitution is to be considered, in court, as a paramount law, are reduced to the necessity of maintaining that courts must close their eyes on the constitution, and see only the law.

This doctrine would subvert the very foundation of all written constitutions. It would declare that an act which, according to the principles and theory of our government, is entirely void, is yet, in practice, completely obligatory. It would declare that if the legislature shall do what is expressly forbidden, such act, notwithstanding the express prohibition, is in reality effectual. It would be giving to the legislature a practical and real omnipotence, with the same breath which professes to restrict their powers within narrow limits. It is prescribing limits, and declaring that those limits may be passed at pleasure.

That it thus reduces to nothing what we have deemed the greatest improvement on political institutions, a written constitution, would of itself be sufficient, in America, where written constitutions have been viewed with so much reverence, for rejecting the construction. But the peculiar expressions of the constitution of the United States furnish additional arguments in favour of its rejection.

The judicial power of the United States is extended to all cases arising under the constitution.

Could it be the intention of those who gave this power, to say that in using it the constitution should not be looked into? That a case arising under the constitution should be decided without examining the instrument under which it arises?

This is too extravagant to be maintained.

In some cases, then, the constitution must be looked into by the judges.

. . . [I]t is apparent, that the framers of the constitution contemplated that instrument as a rule for the government of courts, as well as of the legislature.

Why otherwise does it direct the judges to take an oath to support it? This oath certainly applies in an especial manner, to their conduct in their official character. How immoral to impose it on them, if they were to be used as the instruments, and the knowing instruments, for violating what they swear to support!

The oath of office, too, imposed by the legislature, is completely demonstrative of the legislative opinion on this subject. . . .

Why does a judge swear to discharge his duties agreeably to the constitution of the United States, if that constitution forms no rule for his government? If it is closed upon him, and cannot be inspected by him?

If such be the real state of things, this is worse than solemn mockery. To prescribe, or to take this oath, becomes equally a crime.

It is also not entirely unworthy of observation, that in declaring what shall be the supreme law of the land, the constitution itself is first mentioned; and not the laws of the United States generally, but those only which shall be made in pursuance of the constitution, have that rank.

Thus, the particular phraseology of the constitution of the United States confirms and strengthens the principle, supposed to be essential to all written constitutions, that a law repugnant to the constitution is void;

and that courts, as well as other departments, are bound by that instrument.

## Influences on Supreme Court Decisions

*See Lowi and Ginsberg, pp. 345–360 or brief edition, pp. 190–196*

*In the last 30 years, the process of Senate confirmation of judges nominated to the Supreme Court has become increasingly public and, in some highly controversial cases, contentious. This is in part because the Court has been asked to resolve especially difficult issues such as abortion, affirmative action, and civil rights. Groups opposed to a nominee have used the confirmation process to generate grass-roots public opposition, a tactic used to defeat Robert Bork's nomination. Nobody was pleased with how Clarence Thomas's nomination was handled; the Senate hearings that investigated Anita Hill's charges of sexual harassment were widely regarded as a debacle both by Thomas's supporters and opponents. Robert A. Katzmann, who served as Senator Daniel P. Moynihan's (D-NY) special counsel on Ruth Bader Ginsburg's confirmation, argues that nominees must be judged on the broad elements of their record—a judgment that cannot be reached solely through public hearings.*

# Robert A. Katzmann
# "Developing Confirmation Guidelines"*

More than a year ago, concerned about recent contentious confirmation battles over Supreme Court nominees, Senator Joseph Biden declared that "a new era must dawn." He offered two essentials for a smooth confirmation process. First, the president should genuinely consult with the Senate in searching for a nominee. And, second, he must offer a nominee who is philosophically acceptable to a substantial bipartisan majority of the Senate. Senator Biden's prescriptions largely followed, President Clinton nominated and, last August, the Senate approved Ruth Bader Ginsburg as our 107th Justice by a vote of 96–3.

From what we know, President Clinton undertook the most searching of inquiries, and, in the end, the White House produced a short list of highly qualified men and women (who may yet join the court). The chief executive consulted widely with senators from both parties. Indeed, Senator Biden credited Senator Daniel Patrick Moynihan with recommending Judge Ginsburg to him and to the president (and New York's senior senator has in turn acknowledged the pivotal role of my colleague Stephen Hess).

For all those hoping to avoid the bruising battles of the recent past,

---

* Robert A. Katzmann, "Developing Confirmation Guidelines" in the *Brookings Review* (Fall 1993). Reprinted with permission.

Judge Ginsburg must have seemed like manna from heaven. By dint of her experience as a pioneering litigator, scholar, and jurist, she was the very definition of what Americans could hope for in a Supreme Court nominee.

In the weeks before the hearings, Judge Ginsburg met with the senators on the Judiciary Committee (and more than a score of others), and as the steady request for information indicated, the committee diligently approached its task.

The hearings themselves can be considered part of an evolving effort of the senators and the nominee to determine the kinds of questions and answers they can appropriately expect of each other. That a consensus does not yet exist on this point reflects the fact that until the relatively recent hearings on Robert Bork, senatorial inquiry into a nominee's philosophy was mostly perfunctory.

As I have written in these pages, the uncertainty about proper questions and answers highlights a constitutional tension. The Constitution calls for a role for the president and the Senate in the appointment of judges. But the founders also sought to create a system in which the independence of the judiciary would be secured. With life tenure, judges were to be free to make unpopular decisions. The founders appreciated the danger of placing judges in positions that threatened their impartiality or forced them to prejudge issues. What all that means is that the confirmation process must be finely tuned to consider a variety of interests. The president, the Senate, and the public must have enough information about the nominee to make an informed evaluation. But the process must also protect the integrity of the judiciary.

In his remarks last year, Senator Biden put the hearings in their proper context. They "cannot alone provide a sufficient basis for determining if a nominee merits a seat on our Supreme Court." Further, "as they did before there were confirmation hearings, Senators—and the public—should make their determination about a nominee based on his or her record. . . . Thus, the hearings can be the crowning jewel of this evaluation process —a final chance to clear up confusion or firm up a soft conclusion—*but they cannot be the entire process itself.*"

Judge Ginsburg further advanced the discussion by setting forth her views as to the kinds of questions she could answer. She noted in her opening statement that her writings as a law teacher, lawyer, and judge were the most reliable indicator of her attitude, outlook, approach, and style.

Acknowledging the legitimacy of the Senate's efforts to question her, Judge Ginsburg observed that she would "act injudiciously" were she to "say or preview" how she would cast her vote on questions the Supreme Court may be called on to decide. "Judges in our system," she said, "are bound to decide concrete cases, not abstract issues; each case is based on particular facts and its decision should turn on those facts and the governing law, stated and explained in light of the particular arguments the parties or their representatives choose to present." In the hearings, Judge

Ginsburg was more than willing, masterfully so, to explain how she approaches problems and makes decisions. Nor did she hesitate to respond to queries about her writings.

By the hearings' end, it was clear that the Judiciary Committee would continue in the years ahead to press on with the effort to determine the proper boundaries of questions and answers. The grand gift of the Ginsburg confirmation process was that it restored comity. In that spirit, the time may be ripe for the committee to convene a study group, perhaps including former participants and students of the process, to reflect on the lessons learned from the Ginsburg experience, and in so doing fashion a benchmark that would guide future exchanges.

## DEBATING THE ISSUES: INTERPRETING THE CONSTITUTION AND ORIGINAL INTENT

*See Lowi and Ginsberg, pp. 364–365 or brief edition, pp. 198–199*

*Debates over the federal judiciary's role in the political process often focus on the question of how judges should interpret the Constitution. Should judges apply the document's literal meaning and the inferred intent of the Framers, or should they use a broader interpretive framework that incorporates their own attitudes and opinions? This debate intensified during Earl Warren's tenure as Chief Justice (1953–1969), because of Supreme Court decisions that expanded the scope of civil liberties and criminal rights far beyond what strict constructionists thought the Constitution's language authorized.*

*Edwin Meese III, former attorney general for the Reagan administration, and Rhett DeHart, a special counsel to Meese, adopt the strict constructionist position and view with alarm the "judicial activism" of the past 40 years. When unelected judges "read their personal views and prejudices into the Constitution," they argue, rather than adhere to their constitutionally circumscribed role of interpreting the law, we must ask, "will we have government by the people?" They cite as "judicial excesses" the sanctioning of preferences and quotas for affirmative action programs, the establishment of a "right" to public welfare assistance, and the judicial overthrow of a state public referendum. The authors recommend several reforms to halt their definition of an activist judiciary, including a call for Congress to be more vigorous in its oversight of the judiciary and to more clearly limit and delineate judicial power.*

*Stuart Taylor discusses original intent in the context of a public debate over the proper role of judges, between Edwin Meese and former Supreme Court Justice William Brennan. Taylor criticizes the original intent doctrine as fraught with inconsistencies, even as he faults Brennan for his willingness to rule on the basis of his own moral convictions rather than the letter of the law. Taylor advocates the judicial search for middle ground, recognizing that the meaning of the Constitution must change over time, while at the same time the language of the Constitution necessarily bounds judicial power.*

*Michael Kelly writes of what he views as a dangerous trajectory from the conservative opposition to judicial decisions to the impeachment of justices whose policy goals are at odds with the congressional majority and their supporters. Impeachment of justices has long been reserved to those committing "treason, bribery, or other high crimes and misdemeanors." In fact, over the 221 years since the Constitution become law, only 13 people have been impeached from the judiciary. In the summer of 1997, Representative Tom De Lay (R-Tx and majority whip) identified three justices as potential candidates for impeachment given their decisions in three unrelated cases that represented what Meese and Dehart would call judicial activism.*

*What do you think? Should justices be held to a strict construction of the Constitution? What about when they are dealing with issues not even imagined during the writing of the Constitution? How does strict constructionism differ from an effort to broaden the Constitution to meet the needs of a changing society in practice?*

# Edwin Meese III and Rhett DeHart
# "The Imperial Judiciary . . . And What Congress Can Do About It"*

Under the modern doctrine of judicial review, the federal judiciary can invalidate any state or federal law or policy it considers inconsistent with the U.S. Constitution. This doctrine gives unelected federal judges awesome power. Whenever these judges exceed their constitutional prerogative to interpret law and instead read their personal views and prejudices into the Constitution, the least democratic branch of government becomes its most powerful as well.

America's Founding Fathers created a democratic republic in which elected representatives were to decide the important issues of the day. In their view, the role of the judiciary, although crucial, was to interpret and clarify the law—not to make law. The Framers recognized the necessity of judicial restraint and the dangers of judicial activism. James Madison wrote in *The Federalist Papers* that to combine judicial power with executive and legislative authority was "the very definition of tyranny," and Thomas Jefferson believed that allowing only the unelected judiciary to interpret the Constitution would lead to judicial supremacy. "It is a very dangerous doctrine to consider the judges as the ultimate arbiters of all constitutional questions," said Jefferson. "It is one which would place us under the despotism of an oligarchy."

Unfortunately, the federal judiciary has strayed far beyond its proper functions, in many ways validating Jefferson's warnings about judicial power. In no other democracy in the world do unelected judges decide as

* Edwin Meese III and Rhett Dehart, "The Imperial Judiciary . . . And What Congress Can Do About It" in *Policy Review* (January–February, 1997). Reprinted with permission.

many vital political issues as they do in America. We will never return the federal government to its proper role in our society until we return the federal judiciary to its proper role in our government.

Supreme Court decisions based on the Constitution cannot be reversed or altered, except by a constitutional amendment. Such decisions are virtually immune from presidential vetoes or congressional legislation. Abraham Lincoln warned of this in his First Inaugural Address when he said:

"[T]he candid citizen must confess that if the policy of the government, upon vital questions, affecting the whole people, is to be irrevocably fixed by decisions of the Supreme Court . . . the people will have ceased to be their own rulers, having, to that extent, practically resigned their government into the hands of that eminent tribunal."

When the most important social and moral issues are removed from the democratic process, citizens lose the political experience and moral education that come from resolving difficult issues and reaching a social consensus. President Reagan explained how judicial activism is incompatible with popular government:

"The Founding Fathers were clear on this issue. For them, the question involved in judicial restraint was not—as it is now—will we have liberal courts or conservative courts? They knew that the courts, like the Constitution itself, must not be liberal or conservative. *The question was and is, will we have government by the people?*" [Emphasis added.]

## JUDICIAL EXCESSES

When federal judges exceed their proper interpretive role, the result is not only infidelity to the Constitution, but very often poor public policy. Numerous cases illustrate the consequences of judicial activism and the harm it has caused our society. Activist court decisions have undermined nearly every aspect of public policy. Among the most egregious examples:

### ■ Allowing Racial Preferences and Quotas

In *United Steelworkers of America v. Weber* (1979), the Supreme Court held for the first time that the Civil Rights Act of 1964 permits private employers to establish racial preferences and quotas in employment, despite the clear language of the statute: "It shall be an unlawful employment practice for any employer . . . to discriminate against any individual because of his race, color, religion, sex, or national origin." Had the Court decided *Weber* differently, racial preferences would not exist in the private sector today. The *Weber* decision is a classic example of how unelected government regulators and federal judges have diverted our civil-rights laws from a color-blind ideal to a complex and unfair system of racial and ethnic preferences and quotas that perpetuate bias and discrimination.

## ■ Creating a "Right" to Public Welfare Assistance

In *Goldberg v. Kelly* (1970), the Supreme Court sanctioned the idea that welfare entitlements are a form of "property" under the Fourteenth Amendment. The Court's conclusion: Before a government can terminate benefits on the grounds that the recipient is not eligible, the recipient is entitled to an extensive and costly appeals process akin to a trial. Thanks to the Court, welfare recipients now have a "right" to receive benefits fraudulently throughout lengthy legal proceedings, and never have to reimburse the government if their ineligibility is confirmed. The decision has tied up thousands of welfare workers in judicial hearings and deprived the truly needy of benefits. By 1974, for example, New York City alone needed a staff of 3,000 to conduct *Goldberg* hearings.

## ■ Hampering Criminal Prosecution

In *Mapp v. Ohio* (1961), the Supreme Court began a revolution in criminal procedure by requiring state courts to exclude from criminal cases any evidence found during an "unreasonable" search or seizure. In so holding, the Court overruled a previous case, *Wolf v. Colorado* (1949), which had allowed each state to devise its own methods for deterring unreasonable searches and seizures. The Supreme Court in effect acted like a legislature rather than a judicial body. As a dissenting justice noted, the *Mapp* decision unjustifiably infringed upon the states' sovereign judicial systems and forced them to adopt a uniform, federal procedural remedy ill-suited to serve states with "their own peculiar problems in criminal law enforcement."

In fact, nothing in the Fourth Amendment or any other provision of the Constitution mentions the exclusion of evidence, nor does the legislative history of the Constitution indicate that the Framers intended to require such exclusion. Instead we ought to explore other means of deterring police misconduct without acquitting criminals, such as permitting civil lawsuits against reckless government officials and enforcing internal police sanctions against offending officers with fines and demotions.

Since *Mapp v. Ohio*, the exclusionary rule has had a devastating impact on law enforcement in America. One recent study estimated that 150,000 criminal cases, including 30,000 cases of violence, are dropped or dismissed *every year* because the exclusionary rule excluded valid, probative evidence needed for prosecution.

## ■ Lowering Hiring Standards for the U.S. Workforce

In *Griggs v. Duke Power Co.* (1971), a plaintiff challenged a company's requirement that job applicants possess a high-school diploma and pass a general aptitude test as a condition of employment. The lawsuit argued that because the diploma and test requirements disqualified a disproportionate number of minorities, those requirements were unlawful under the Civil Rights Act of 1964 unless shown to be related to the job in question.

The Court ruled that under the Act, employment requirements that disproportionately exclude minorities must be shown to be related to job performance, and it rejected the employer's argument that the diploma and testing requirements were implemented to improve the overall quality of its work force. Moreover, the Court held that "Congress has placed on the employer the burden of showing that any given requirement must have a manifest relationship to the employment in question."

In fact, the Act explicitly authorizes an employer to use aptitude tests like the one challenged in *Griggs*. This insidious court decision has lowered the quality of the U.S. workforce by making it difficult for employers to require high-school diplomas and other neutral job requirements. It also forced employers to adopt racial quotas in order to avoid the expense of defending hiring practices that happen to produce disparate outcomes for different ethnic groups.

■ "Discovering" a Right to Abortion

In *Roe v. Wade* (1973), the Court considered the constitutionality of a Texas statute that prohibited abortion except to save the life of the mother. Although the Court acknowledged that the Constitution does not explicitly mention a right of privacy, it held that the Constitution protects rights "implicit in the concept of ordered liberty." The Court ruled that "the right of personal privacy includes the abortion decision," and it struck down the Texas statute under the Due Process Clause of the Fourteenth Amendment. The Court then went on, in a blatantly legislative fashion, to proclaim a precise framework limiting the states' ability to regulate abortion procedures.

The dissenting opinion in *Roe* pointed out that, in order to justify its ruling, the majority had to somehow "find" within the Fourteenth Amendment a right that was unknown to the drafters of the Amendment. When the Fourteenth Amendment was adopted in 1868, there were at least 36 state or territorial laws limiting abortion, and the passage of the Amendment raised no questions at the time about the validity of those laws. "The only conclusion possible from this history," wrote the dissenting justices, "is that the Drafters did not intend to have the Fourteenth Amendment withdraw from the States the power to legislate with respect to this matter."

One of the most pernicious aspects of the *Roe* decision is that it removed one of the most profound social and moral issues from the democratic process without any constitutional authority. For the first two centuries of America's existence, the abortion issue had been decided by state legislatures, with substantially less violence and conflict than has attended the issue since the *Roe* decision.

■ Overturning State Referenda

In *Romer v. Evans* (1996), the U.S. Supreme Court actually negated a direct vote of the people. This case concerned an amendment to the Colorado constitution enacted in 1992 by a statewide referendum. "Amendment 2" prohibited the state or any political subdivisions therein from adopting any policy that grants homosexuals "any minority status, quota preference, protected status, or claim of discrimination." The Court ruled that the amendment was unconstitutional because it did not bear a "rational relationship" to a legitimate government purpose and thus violated the Equal Protection Clause of the Fourteenth Amendment.

The state of Colorado contended that this amendment protected freedom of association, particularly for landlords and employers who have religious objections to homosexuality, and that it only prohibited *preferential treatment* for homosexuals. But the Court rejected these arguments and offered its own interpretation of what motivated the citizens of Colorado, claiming that "laws of the kind now before us raise the inevitable inference that the disadvantage imposed is born of animosity toward the class of persons affected."

The dissenting opinion argued that Amendment 2 denies equal treatment only in the sense that homosexuals may not obtain "preferential treatment without amending the state constitution." Noting that under *Bowers v. Hardwick* (1986), states are permitted to outlaw homosexual sodomy, the dissent reasoned that if it is constitutionally permissible for a state to criminalize homosexual conduct, it is surely constitutionally permissible for a state to deny special favor and protection to homosexuals. The Court's decision, the dissent charged, "is an act not of judicial judgment, but of political will."

It is hard not to regard the *Romer* decision as the pinnacle of judicial arrogance: Six appointed justices struck down a law passed by 54 percent of a state's voters in a direct election, the most democratic of all procedures. In one of the most egregious usurpations of power in constitutional history, the Court not only desecrated the principle of self-government, but appointed itself the moral arbiter of the nation's values.

TURNING THE TIDE

Fortunately, Congress has a number of strategies at its disposal to confine the judiciary to its proper constitutional role:

*1. The Senate should use its confirmation authority to block the appointment of activist federal judges.*

When a president appoints judges who exceed their constitutional authority and usurp the other branches of government, the Senate can properly restrain the judiciary by carefully exercising its responsibilities under the "advise and consent" clause of Article II, Section 2 of the Constitution.

Normally, the Senate Judiciary Committee conducts a hearing on the president's nominees. Those nominees who are approved by the committee or submitted without recommendation go to the full Senate for a confirmation vote.

Unfortunately, the confirmation process in recent years has been relatively perfunctory. The Senate has been reluctant to closely question a nominee to ascertain the candidate's understanding of the proper role of the judiciary. The Senate committee hearing provides an excellent opportunity to discern a judicial candidate's understanding of a constitutionally limited judiciary. It also provides a public opportunity for judicial watchdog organizations to testify in support of or against a particular nominee.

The Constitution established Senate confirmation to ensure that unqualified nominees were not given lifelong judgeships. In carrying out this important responsibility, senators should ascertain a prospective judge's commitment to a philosophy of judicial restraint and fidelity to the Constitution. In so doing, they should carefully review all the opinions, legal articles, and other materials authored by the candidate, the personal background report prepared by the Federal Bureau of Investigation, and the testimony of judges and other attorneys who have had ample opportunities to view a candidate's work.

In the name of efficiency, the full Senate sometimes votes to confirm judicial nominees in bundles. This practice should cease. Senators should vote on each nominee individually, in order to remind the prospective judge and the public of the awesome responsibility of each new member of the judiciary and to hold themselves accountable for every judge they confirm to the federal bench.

### 2. Congress should strip the American Bar Association of its special role in the judicial selection process.

The American Bar Association (ABA) has shown itself to be a special-interest group, every bit as politicized as the American Civil Liberties Union or the National Rifle Association. In the 104th Congress, for example, the ABA officially supported federal funding for abortion services for the poor, racial and ethnic preferences, and a ban on assault weapons; and it opposed a ban on flag-burning, reform of the exclusionary rule and of death-penalty appeals, and a proposal to restrict AFDC payments for welfare mothers who have additional children. Hence it should be removed from any official role in evaluating judicial nominees. It would still be free to testify before the Senate Judiciary Committee concerning potential judges, but it would not have any special status or authority.

The Senate will always need the impartial assessment of judges and lawyers who have a detailed knowledge of the work and background of a judicial candidate. In place of the ABA, the Senate should appoint a special fact-finding committee in each of the 94 federal judicial districts. These lawyers would be selected for their objectivity, ideological neutrality, and understanding of the constitutional role of the judiciary. They would obtain the detailed information the Senate needs to evaluate a candidate, and would give that information directly to the Judiciary Committee without subjective comments or evaluation.

### 3. Congress should exercise its power to limit the jurisdiction of the federal courts.

Congress has great control over the jurisdiction of the lower federal courts. Article III, Section 1, of the Constitution provides that "[t]he judicial power of the United States, shall be vested in one supreme Court, *and in such inferior Courts as the Congress may from time to time ordain and establish.*" [Emphasis added.] It is well-established that since Congress has total discretion over whether to create the lower federal courts, it also has great discretion over the jurisdiction of those courts it chooses to create. In fact, Congress has in the past withdrawn jurisdiction from the lower federal courts when it became dissatisfied with their performance or concluded that state courts were the better forum for certain types of cases. The Supreme Court has repeatedly upheld Congress's power to do so.

Congress also has some authority to limit the jurisdiction of the Supreme Court and to regulate its activities. Article III of the Constitution states that the Supreme Court "shall have appellate jurisdiction, both as to law and fact, *with such Exceptions, and under such Regulations as the Congress shall make.*" [Emphasis added.] Although we recognize that the scope of Congress's power to regulate and restrict the Supreme Court's jurisdiction over particular types of cases is under debate, there is a constitutional basis for this authority.

In the only case that directly addressed this issue, the Supreme Court upheld Congress's power to restrict the Court's appellate jurisdiction. In *Ex Parte McCardle* (1869), the Court unanimously upheld Congress's power to limit its jurisdiction, stating:

"We are not at liberty to inquire into the motives of the legislature. We can only examine into its power under the Constitution; *and the power to make exceptions to the appellate jurisdiction of this court is given by express words.* What, then, is the effect of the repealing act upon the case before us? We cannot doubt as to this. Without jurisdiction, the court cannot proceed at all in any case." [Emphasis added.]

Although some respected constitutional scholars argue that Congress cannot restrict the Supreme Court's jurisdiction to the extent that it intrudes upon the Court's "core functions," there is no question that Congress has more authority under the Constitution to act than it has recently exercised.

The 104th Congress displayed an encouraging willingness to assert its authority over the jurisdiction of the lower federal courts. For example, the Prison Litigation Reform Act of 1995 reduced the discretion of the federal courts to micromanage state prisons and to force the early release of prisoners. The Act also makes it more difficult for prisoners to file frivolous lawsuits. (An incredible 63,550 prisoner lawsuits were filed in federal court in 1995 alone.) Congress also passed the Effective Death Penalty Act of 1995. This Act limited the power of the federal courts to entertain endless habeas corpus appeals filed by prisoners on death row, significantly expediting the death-penalty process.

Other issues are due for some congressional muscle-flexing to restrain an activist judiciary:

## ■ Private-School Choice

Some radical groups like the American Civil Liberties Union argue that the government would violate the First Amendment's Establishment Clause if it gave a tuition voucher to a family who uses it at a religious school. Under current Supreme Court precedents, school vouchers are almost certainly constitutional. Nevertheless, some federal judges have indicated that they would invalidate private-school choice plans under the Establishment Clause. Moreover, if more activist justices are named to the Supreme Court, a liberal majority could crush one of the most promising educational initiatives in recent years by judicial fiat. To ensure that the issue of private-school choice is decided through the democratic process, Congress should consider restricting the Court's jurisdiction over this issue.

## ■ Judicial Taxation

"Judicial taxation" refers to federal court orders that require a state or local government to make significant expenditures to pay for court-ordered injunctions. For example, one federal judge ordered the state of Missouri to pay for approximately $2.6 billion in capital improvements and other costs to "desegregate" the school districts of St. Louis and Kansas City, which in recent years had lost many white students. To attract white students back into the system, a federal judge required Kansas City to maintain the most lavish schools in the nation, and actually ordered the city to raise property taxes to pay for his court-ordered remedies.

There's a name for tax increases imposed by appointed, life-tenured federal judges: taxation without representation. Under the Constitution, only Congress can lay and collect taxes; our Founding Fathers would be appalled at the thought of federal judges doing so. In *Federalist No. 48*, James Madison explained that in our democratic system, "the legislative branch alone has access to the pockets of the people." To codify this principle, Congress should consider restricting the federal courts' authority to order any government at any level to raise taxes under any circumstance.

## ■ Use of Special Masters

Federal judges sometimes appoint "special masters" to micromanage prisons, mental hospitals, and school districts. In the past, these special masters have been appointed to carry out the illegitimate excursions of judges into the province of the legislative and executive branches. Moreover, the use of special masters has been a form of taxation, in that state and local governments are required to pay their salaries and expenses—which have often been extravagant. In some cases, special masters have hired large staffs to help execute the court order. Congress should outlaw special masters; without them, federal judges would be constrained by the limits on their time and resources from managing prisons or other institutions.

## ■ Same-Sex Marriage

No area of the law has been more firmly reserved to the states than domestic relations. Nevertheless, the Court's reasoning in *Romer v. Evans* suggests the possibility that some federal judges will "discover" a constitutional right to homosexual marriage, and thus remove the issue from the democratic process.

The Hawaii Supreme Court recently indicated that it would soon recognize homosexual marriages, which all other states would then have to recognize under the Full Faith and Credit Clause of the Constitution (Article IV). This possibility motivated Congress to pass the Defense of Marriage Act, which authorized any state to refuse to recognize a same-sex marriage performed in another state. The Act does not, however, prevent the federal judiciary from usurping this issue. Congress should consider going one step further to remove the jurisdiction of the lower federal courts over same-sex marriages to ensure that this cultural issue is decided by the legislative process in each state.

*4. The states should press Congress to amend the Constitution in a way that will allow the states to ratify constitutional amendments in the future without the approval of Congress.*

One reason judicial activism is so dangerous and undemocratic is that reversing or amending federal court decisions is so difficult. When a decision by the Supreme Court or a lower federal court is based on the Constitution, the decision cannot be reversed or altered except by a constitutional amendment. Such constitutional decisions are immune from presidential vetoes or congressional legislation.

The existing means of amending the Constitution, however, are seldom effective in halting judicial activism. The amendment procedure set forth in Article V of the Constitution is difficult and lengthy for good reason: to avoid hasty changes spurred by the passions of the moment. But history has shown that even the most egregious court decisions— particularly those that affect the balance of power between the national government and the states—have been impervious to correction by constitutional amendment. One reason for this is that Congress, which must initiate such amendments, is loath to give up federal power.

The amendment procedure of the U.S. Constitution led Lord Bryce to conclude in his 1888 study, *The American Commonwealth,* that "[t]he Constitution which is the most difficult to change is that of the United States." This difficulty has encouraged judicial activism and allowed the unelected federal courts to "twist and shape" the Constitution, as Jefferson predicted, as an "artist shapes a ball of wax." The reason that the difficult amendment procedure encourages judicial activism is simple: Life-tenured judges are less likely to show restraint when the possibility that their rulings will be rejected is slight.

Consequently, one strategy to rein in the federal judiciary is to revise the amendment procedure in Article V of the Constitution to allow the states to amend the Constitution without Congress's approval and without a constitutional convention.

Here's how it would work: When two-thirds of state legislatures pass resolutions in support of a proposed amendment to the Constitution, Congress would have to submit it to all the states for ratification. The proposal would then become part of the Constitution once the legislatures of three-fourths of the states ratify it. Congress's role would be purely ministerial. This process would give the states equal power with Congress to initiate an amendment and would further check the power of the federal courts and of Congress.

### 5. Congress should stop the federalization of crime and the expansion of litigation in federal court.

Whenever Congress enacts a new federal criminal statute or a statute creating a cause-of-action in federal court, it enlarges the power and authority of the federal courts and provides more opportunities for judicial activism. At the same time, the federalization of crimes that have traditionally concerned state and local governments upsets the balance between the national government and the states. The following steps can help reduce the federalization of the law and once again restore balance to the federal-state relationship.

### ■ Recodify the U.S. Code

In the present federal criminal code, important offenses like treason are commingled with insignificant offenses like the unauthorized interstate transport of water hyacinths. The Federal Courts Study Committee found that the current federal code is "hard to find, hard to understand, redundant, and conflicting." Ideally, Congress would start with a blank slate, recodifying only those offenses that truly belong under federal jurisdiction. Due to the highly political nature of crime, such an undertaking might require the creation of an independent commission, modeled after the recent commission for closing unneeded military bases.

■ Require a "Federalism Assessment" for Legislation

This idea would require that all federal legislation offer a justification for a national solution to the issue in question, acknowledge any efforts the states have taken to address the problem, explain the legislation's effect on state experimentation, and cite Congress's constitutional authority to enact the proposed legislation.

■ Create a Federalism Subcommittee Within the Judiciary Committees of the House and Senate

First proposed by President Reagan's Working Group on Federalism, federalism subcommittees would attempt to ensure compliance with federalism principles in all proposed legislation.

Judicial activism has harmed virtually every aspect of public policy in America. Liberalism has accomplished much of its agenda in the last 30 years not through the electoral process, but instead in the federal courts. Conservatives will never be able to shape public policy until they can curb activist judges. Congress can and should move to do so.

# Stuart Taylor, Jr.
# "Who's Right about the Constitution?
# Meese v. Brennan"*

An activist jurisprudence, one which anchors the Constitution only in the consciences of jurists, is a chameleon jurisprudence, changing color and form in each era.

The Constitution . . . is a mere thing of wax in the hands of the judiciary, which they may twist and shape into any form they please.

If the policy of the Government upon vital questions affecting the whole people is to be irrevocably fixed by decisions of the Supreme Court, the instant they are made . . . the people will have ceased to be their own rulers.

The Court . . . has improperly set itself up as . . . a super-legislature . . . reading into the Constitution words and implications which are not there, and which were never intended to be there. . . . We want a Supreme Court which will do justice under the Constitution—not over it.

Sounds like Ed Meese, doesn't it? Well, the first quotation is the attorney general's. But the second comes from Thomas Jefferson, the third from

Abraham Lincoln, and the fourth from Franklin D. Roosevelt. When Meese assails government by judiciary, he is in good company.

Meese has denounced major Supreme Court rulings of the past 60 years and called for judges to look to "the original meaning of constitutional provisions" as "the only reliable guide for judgment." No attorney general in the past four decades has set out so deliberately to reduce the power of the judiciary or to screen the ideological credentials of new appointees.

Champions of liberal judicial activism have launched a ferocious counterattack. Justices William J. Brennan Jr. and John Paul Stevens retorted with pointed critiques of Meese's so-called "jurisprudence of original intention." Brennan said it was "arrogance cloaked as humility" for anyone "to pretend that from our vantage we can gauge accurately the intent of the Framers on application of principle to specific, contemporary questions." The real animus of advocates of this "facile historicism" he said, is a "political" agenda hostile to the rights of minorities.

Meese is certainly vulnerable to this sort of attack. He seems less a constitutional philosopher than a constitutional window-shopper, seeking to dress up his conservative political agenda as a principled quest for truth. His notion that judges can answer the hard questions raised by the Constitution without being "tainted by ideological predilection," simply by plugging in the intent of the Framers, is at best simpleminded and at worst disingenuous. When the Framers' intentions *are* clear, but contrary to a result Meese wants, he ignores them. While calling for restraint in the exercise of judicial power—especially enforcement of civil liberties—he pushes to aggrandize executive power.

Along the way, he has said some revealing things. "You don't have many suspects who are innocent of a crime," he told *U.S. News & World Report.* "That's contradictory. If a person is innocent of a crime, then he is not a suspect." This from a man who was himself suspected of several federal crimes until a special prosecutor cleared him last year—a man who then billed the government $720,824.49 for his defense lawyers. (He later confessed to a "bad choice of words.")

Meese also assailed as "intellectually shaky" and "constitutionally suspect" the Court's 60-year-old doctrine that most of the Bill of Rights, originally applicable only to the national government, was applied to the states by the 14th Amendment. Eminent Supreme Court justices criticized the doctrine too, but that was decades ago. When a Supreme Court ruling has "been affirmed and reaffirmed through a course of years," Lincoln said in 1857, "it then might be, perhaps would be, factious, nay even revolutionary, not to acquiesce in it as a precedent."

Nevertheless, the standard liberal retort to Meese is superficial. It caricatures his position as more extreme than it is. It ignores the long and honorable history of political attacks on judicial usurpation of power. Most important, its scorn for the "original intention" approach begs the question of where—if not from those who wrote and ratified the Constitution and its amendments—unelected judges get a mandate to override the will of the political majority by striking down democratically enacted laws.

For all his fumbling, Meese has spotlighted some of the real problems with the freewheeling judicial activism sometimes practiced by people like Brennan. Among these is a tendency to "find" in the Constitution rights (such as abortion rights) and social policies that can honestly be found neither in the language of the document, nor in the records left by those who wrote it, nor in any broad national consensus that has evolved since then. This is bad constitutional law even when you like the policies, as I sometimes do.

Meese deserves credit for bringing the deepest questions of constitutional law out of the law journals and into the newspapers. He surely has a political motive. But liberals who believe in democracy (anybody out there after two Reagan landslides?) should welcome the debate.

Too often liberals have taken the elitist view that ordinary voters are the natural enemies of civil liberties, and that only judges can be trusted to protect them. It is a shortsighted approach. As Justice Robert Jackson said four decades ago, "Any court which undertakes by its legal processes to enforce civil liberties needs the support of an enlightened and vigorous public opinion." Today most people confine their thinking about the Constitution to whether they like the policies the Court has decreed. The larger question of when courts should displace the ordinary policy-making role of elected officials gets little attention from anyone but law professors. Meese has begun to remind the public that in enforcing constitutional rights, federal judges are by definition restraining majority rule.

Within proper limits this is a noble function. Those who wrote the Constitution and its amendments saw them as bulwarks against oppression of minorities by a tyrannical majority. They specified certain fundamental rights shared by all Americans. They created special protections for minorities, especially blacks. They laid down these principles in majestic generalities meant to have continuing relevance in a changing society— freedom of speech, equal protection of the laws, due process of law. The federal courts—precisely because they are not answerable to the voters— are the logical bodies to enforce these rights against the majority.

Here, however, lies a difficult dilemma to which no wholly satisfactory solution exists. The Constitution being what the judges say it is, how can the judges be prevented from usurping the powers of elected officials and making political decisions? Meese's admonition to stick to original intent is only a starting point. The Constitution does tell judges to enforce certain broad principles such as "freedom of speech," but if these principles are to be enforced at all in a changing society, judges must supply much of their meaning.

The trouble is that judges of all political stripes have gone beyond applying the Constitution's principles to new circumstances. They have written their own moral and political values into it, pretending to have found them there. Sometimes they have "interpreted" the Constitution to forbid things explicitly allowed by its language.

Take Brennan, a hero to liberals—deservedly so—and Meese's principal foil in the current debate. In his speech belittling "original intention" theorists, Brennan denied writing his own views into the Constitution. "It is, in a very real sense, the community's interpretation that is sought," he said. "Justices are not platonic guardians appointed to wield authority according to their personal moral predilections."

But he gave these words a hollow ring when he explained why he always votes to strike down death penalty laws. He said they violate "the essential meaning" of the Eighth Amendment's prohibition against cruel and unusual punishment by denying "the intrinsic worth" of the murderers who are executed. Now, Brennan knows perfectly well that those who wrote that amendment had no intention of banning the death penalty, which was common at the time and was explicitly recognized in the Fifth and 14th Amendments.

So whence comes his mandate for invalidating the death penalty? "I hope to embody a community striving for human dignity for all, although perhaps not yet arrived," he explained. Translation: my moral convictions on this issue are so strong I would override the laws adopted by the people's elected representatives any way I could. Brennan admitted that most of his fellow countrymen and justices think the death penalty constitutional. As Judge Robert Bork has put it: "The truth is that the judge who looks outside the Constitution looks inside himself and nowhere else."

Well, what's so bad about that? If elected officials don't have the decency to end the death penalty (or antiabortion laws, or minimum-wage laws, or whatever else offends you), why shouldn't the judges do it?

The most important answer is that judicial legislation erodes democratic self-government. It converts judges into an unelected and illegitimate policymaking elite. Indeed, its more radical exponents evince a deep antipathy for the democratic process. But as Felix Frankfurter said, "Holding democracy in judicial tutelage is not the most promising way to foster disciplined responsibility in a people."

Defenders of judicial activism like to point out the vagueness of the Constitution's words and the futility of the quest for consensus on original intention. "And even if such a mythical beast could be captured and examined, how relevant would it be to us today?" asks Harvard law professor Laurence Tribe. He dismisses as a dangerous fallacy the notion that judges can be significantly restrained by the Constitution's text or history. The Supreme Court, he says, "just cannot avoid the painful duty of exercising judgment so as to give concrete meaning to the fluid Constitution."

Well, perhaps. But why can't the Court do something many law professors barely deign to discuss? When the Constitution's language and history provide little or no guidance on a subject, why can't it leave the law-making to legislatures? Those who work so hard to prove that the Constitution cannot supply the values for governance of modern society seem to think it follows that judges must do it, with a little help from their friends in academia. But their argument rebounds against the legitimacy of judicial review itself. Bork poses a question for which they have no good answer: "If the Constitution is not law—law that, with the usual areas of ambiguity around the edges, nevertheless tolerably tells judges what to do and what not to do— . . . what authorizes judges to set at naught the majority judgment of the American people?"

The activist approach of amending the Constitution in the guise of interpreting it goes hand in hand with a certain lack of candor about the enterprise. A judge who acknowledged that his goal was to strike down democratically adopted laws by rewriting the Constitution would risk impeachment. So we hear a lot about "finding" in the Constitution rights that had somehow gone unnoticed for more than a century.

There is no reason to suppose that unelected judges, using theories concocted by unelected law professors, will make better policies over time than elected officials. Nor that they will make more liberal policies. Judicial activism is not a game played only by liberals. Conservative judges rode roughshod over progressive and New Deal legislation for several decades ending about 1937. "Never . . . can the Supreme Court be said to have for a single hour been representative of anything except the relatively conservative forces of its day," Robert Jackson wrote in 1941.

Franklin Roosevelt changed that, ushering in an era of liberal judicial activism. Now the tables are turning again. Reagan and Meese are filling up the lower federal courts with conservatives and hoping to do the same with the Supreme Court. "I dream of a conservative Supreme Court striking down most federal legislation since the New Deal as unconstitutional," writes conservative columnist Joseph Sobran. Liberals may soon rediscover the virtues of judicial restraint, and find themselves urging a Reaganized judiciary to practice what Meese has been preaching.

Brennan and other liberal activist judges deserve the applause they have won for thrusting upon the nation some policies that were also triumphs of constitutional principle. Desegregation is one example. Protection of the rights of poor criminal defendants is another.

But liberal activism has gone to dubious extremes. Take the case of the man who approached a policeman in Denver and said he'd killed someone. The policeman told him about his rights to remain silent and have a lawyer. The man said he understood and proceeded with his confession, leading police to the scene where he said he had killed a 14-year-old girl. The sometime mental patient later told a psychiatrist that the voice of God had ordered him to confess. The Colorado Supreme Court threw out the confession on the ground that it was compelled by mental illness, and therefore involuntary. If he is ever tried, neither the confession nor, presumably, the other evidence ("fruits" of the confession) will be admissible. And he may go free.

Such judicial excesses are giving constitutional rights a bad name. Ed Meese is not alone in his outrage at judges who free criminals on the basis of technical rules that protect only the guilty, especially where they have little to do with deterring police abuse. The more this sort of thing happens, the greater the danger that the considerable public backlash may build to radical reaction.

There will always be cases in which judges must let criminals go free, and must defy public opinion, to vindicate the constitutional rights of innocent and guilty alike. Their ability to do so suffers when they squander the reservoir of goodwill they need for such occasions. "Liberty lies in the hearts of men and women," Learned Hand wrote. "When it dies there, no constitution, no law, no court can save it."

Judicial creation of new constitutional rights can also be mistaken even when much or most of the public approves. The best example is *Roe v. Wade*, the 1973 decision creating a constitutional right to abortion and striking down all state antiabortion laws. Abortion is one of the toughest moral issues around. If I were a legislator I might vote (with misgivings) to allow free access to abortion in the early stages of pregnancy, as the Supreme Court did. But the Court is not a legislature, and there is no plausible basis in the Constitution for it to take this issue away from the states, some of which had already legalized abortion before *Roe*.

Justice Harry Blackmun's opinion "found" a right to abortion within the vague, general "right to personal privacy." He said these rights were in the Constitution somewhere, though he was not sure where—probably the 14th Amendment's generalized protection of "liberty," maybe the Ninth Amendment. Blackmun (appointed by Richard Nixon) made no pretense that the Framers of these amendments intended to legalize abortion. History shows clearly that they did not. They were not thinking about abortion at all, although it was a familiar practice, illegal in some states, when the 14th Amendment was adopted. Nor do the words of the Constitution provide a shred of support for the detailed regulations the Court has drafted over time to curb state regulation of abortion.

Right-to-lifers are not the only people who deplore *Roe v. Wade*. Many liberal scholars—defenders of the pioneering Warren Court decisions so despised by Meese—have said the Burger Court went too far down the road of naked judicial legislation in that case. Among them are Archibald Cox, now retired from Harvard Law School, Dean John Hart Ely of Stanford Law School, and Dean Benno Schmidt of Columbia Law School, soon to be president of Yale. The abortion issue poses an excruciating clash between two moral imperatives: a woman's right to personal autonomy and protection of the unborn. Why every detail of local, state, and national policy on such a fundamental moral issue should depend on the personal philosophies of five or six judges escapes them, and me.

The disregard for the written Constitution that *Roe v. Wade* embodies is also a two-edged sword. President Reagan said in his debate with Walter Mondale that an unborn child is a living human being "protected by the Constitution, which guarantees life, liberty, and the pursuit of happiness to all of us." Well, there he goes again, quoting the Declaration of Independence and calling it the Constitution. But he was close enough: the 14th Amendment says no state may "deprive any person of life, liberty, or property, without due process of law." For those who believe a fetus is a "person" and abortion is murder, as Reagan does, it is possible to conclude that judges should strike down any state laws that allow it. Far-fetched? Well, what if a state excluded homosexuals or handicapped children from the protection of its murder laws?

None of this means Meese's own approach to constitutional interpretation is adequate. It isn't. For starters, there is little evidence he has given the subject much thought. Beyond the high-sounding, platitudinous stuff about the Framers in the speeches his aides have written for him, he has had little specific to say about what he thinks their intentions were, or how broadly these intentions should be read. There is enormous room for disagreement here. The most important constitutional phrases, like "equal protection of the laws," are sweeping, vague, and only dimly illuminated by history.

Meese has tiptoed away from some of the few specific things he has said, including his attack on the doctrine that most of the Bill of Rights applies to the states through the 14th Amendment. It appeared in the written text of his July 9 speech to the American Bar Association. For some reason he omitted this point when he read the speech aloud. Moments afterward, reporters bearing tape recorders asked Meese whether he thought the Court had gone too far in applying the Bill of Rights to the states. "No," he responded. "I, well, I think this is something that's been done in 1925 and since, and so I don't think, ah, ah, I think, I do not have any particular quarrel at this stage of the game with what the Court has done in the intervening 60 years." Will the real Ed Meese please stand up?

Meese has stuck to his guns in denouncing as "infamous" major decisions upholding the rights of criminal defendants. One of his least favorites is *Mapp v. Ohio* (1961), which extended to the states the "exclusionary rule" barring use of evidence seized in violation of the Fourth Amendment. Meese has said *Mapp* helps only "the guilty criminal," and has suggested abandoning the exclusionary rule in state and federal cases alike.

But Meese seems to have forgotten *Boyd v. U.S.*, which Justice Louis Brandeis said "will be remembered as long as civil liberty lives in the United States." The 1886 decision was the Supreme Court's first major Fourth and Fifth Amendment ruling. Unlike modern rulings, it was explicitly based on a detailed study of the Framers' intentions. *Boyd* held that the Framers intended the Fourth Amendment's ban on "unreasonable searches and seizures" to prohibit *all* governmental attempts to obtain a person's private papers or other property—even by warrant or subpoena—and to forbid their use as evidence to convict him. Innocence or guilt was irrelevant to this determination. The Court's confident assertion that this was the Framers' intention was based on a reading of their natural rights philosophy, on 18th–century case law, and on the fury at sweeping British searches that helped fuel the American Revolution.

If *Boyd* were the law today, it would place far greater restrictions on police than any imposed by the Warren Court, which Meese has denounced for its "expansive civil libertarianism." The modern Court, unwilling to restrict official power so severely, has abandoned this broad vision. Its use of the exclusionary rule as a limited deterrent to police abuses is a pale remnant of the expansive rights the Court saw in the Fourth Amendment 99 years ago.

Meese's contention that the exclusionary rule helps only guilty criminals is demonstrably false. Of course, exclusion of improperly obtained but reliable evidence helps only the guilty in the immediate case at hand. But if officials knew they could search everyone indiscriminately and use any evidence they found, a lot of innocent people would be victims of illegal searches. The only way to take the profit out of police abuses is to bar use of the evidence found. This means letting some guilty criminals go free. It is one thing to say this is too high a price to pay in cases in which police inadvertently cross the line between marginally legal and marginally illegal searches. It is quite another to let officials use any and all illegally obtained evidence, as Meese would.

Meese's selectiveness in applying original intention is not limited to criminal law issues. If he really believed the Framers' specific intentions are "the only reliable guide for judgment," he would have to condemn *Brown v. Board of Education*, the landmark 1954 decision desegregating public schools. Anybody who did that today would be assailed as a segregationist crank. Meese recently applauded *Brown* as a case study in finding the original intention of the post-Civil War 14th Amendment. "The Supreme Court in that case was not giving new life to old words, or adapting a 'living,' 'flexible' Constitution to new reality," he declared. "It was restoring the original principle of the Constitution."

That's nice, but it's not true. The Congress that wrote the amendment had no intention of outlawing segregation, as Raoul Berger, Alexander Bickel, and others have demonstrated. The same Congress segregated its own Senate gallery and the District of Columbia schools, and rejected various desegregation bills. What the Court saw nearly 90 years later was that state-enforced segregation, relegating blacks to inferior schools and other facilities, had made a mockery of the 14th Amendment's central purpose: to put blacks and whites on an equal footing before the law. So the Court gave "new life to old words," to use Meese's mocking phrase, and threw out segregation.

The same Congress that drafted the 14th Amendment also passed some special welfare programs for recently freed slaves and other blacks in the South. These were, in modern parlance, affirmative action programs involving racial preferences, for blacks—sort of like the government hiring quotas that Meese has declared in violation of the 14th Amendment. Congress specifically excluded whites from some of these programs. Among them were federally funded, racially segregated schools for blacks only—a single program that contradicts the Meese view of the 14th Amendment's original intention on segregation and affirmative action alike. These programs were passed over the Meese-like objections that they discriminated against whites and included some blacks who were not personally victims of discrimination. But Meese's Justice Department, checking its slogans about judicial restraint at the door, has urged the Supreme

Court to strike down every local, state, and federal government affirmative action program in the nation that prefers black employees over whites. Right or wrong, Meese's position on affirmative action is at war with his preachings about strict adherence to original intention.

The same is true of his position on a lot of issues. Many of the powers that his Justice Department exercises daily—reaching into every community with its wiretaps, its informers, its subpoenas—would have horrified the Framers. They feared centralized power more than anything but anarchy. They sought to limit severely the national government's law enforcement powers, leaving to state and local authorities jurisdiction over the all but genuinely interstate crimes.

What would Meese do about the strong historical evidence that the Framers intended to deny the government the power to issue paper money, which they saw as a threat to propertied interests? What about their intent to bar the president from launching military expeditions without congressional approval, except to repel attacks on United States territory?

And what about the First Amendment's religion clauses, as expounded by Joseph Story, a 19th-century justice whom Meese sometimes quotes on original intention? "The real object," Story said, "was not to countenance, much less to advance, Mahometanism, or Judaism, or infidelity, by prostrating Christianity; but to exclude all rivalry among Christian sects." Meese buys the "infidels" part when he says the Framers would have found "bizarre" the notion that government may not favor religion over nonreligion. He ignores the rest, of course. Any official who argued today that only Christians are protected by the religion clauses would be drummed out of office, and properly so.

The broader point is that sticking to the Framers' immediate goals as closely as Meese sometimes suggests is neither possible nor desirable. If *Brown v. Board of Education* was right, and it was, then a "jurisprudence of original intention" worthy of respect cannot mean enforcing constitutional rights only in the specific ways envisioned by the Framers. Such an approach would doom these rights to wither with the passage of time. The Framers' central purpose of preventing abuse of minorities would be strangled by narrow-minded attention to their more immediate concerns. As for the possibility of updating the Constitution by the formal amendment process, this takes a two-thirds majority in each house of Congress and approval by three-fourths of the states. Such majorities could rarely be mustered to deal with new threats to the rights of minorities.

New technologies such as wiretapping threaten liberties the Framers enshrined in ways that they could not have imagined. And the changing nature of society poses threats that the Framers did not foresee to the constitutional principles they established. Take libel law. Million-dollar libel suits by public officials were not prevalent in the 18th century, and it is fairly clear that the Framers did not intend the First Amendment (or the 14th) to limit private libel suits as the modern Court has done. But they did intend to protect uninhibited, robust, and wide-open debate about public affairs. And it seems to me proper for the Supreme Court to effectuate that broad purpose, in this litigious era, by imposing some curbs on libel suits.

Am I slipping into the kind of judicial revision of the Constitution I just rejected? I don't think so. There is a middle ground between narrow adherence to original intention and freewheeling judicial legislation. As Chief Justice John Marshall said in a famous 1819 decision, the Constitution is not a code of "immutable rules," but rather the "great outlines" of a system intended "to endure for ages to come, and, consequently, to be adapted to the various crises of human affairs." But it is for elected officials, as he said, to do most of the adapting. Judges should invalidate democratically enacted laws only, in John Ely's words, "in accord with an inference whose starting point, whose underlying premise, is fairly discoverable in the Constitution."

This approach will often set only loose outer boundaries around the Court's options in deciding specific issues. It requires judges in close cases to draw fine lines. And it does not pretend to purge their moral and political convictions entirely from the process. But its recognition that the Constitution imposes some bounds on judicial power—limits fleshed out more clearly by the accumulation of precedent—would channel the growth of the law in a more principled and therefore more legitimate direction.

At the outer limits of legitimacy are those cases in which the justices read into vague constitutional phrases like "due process" an emerging social consensus that seems contrary to the particular intentions of the Framers. This goes beyond applying old principles to new circumstances, and gets into tinkering with the principles or creating new ones. I think the Supreme Court should do it in a few rare cases, nudging society to progress in the common law tradition of gradually evolving principles against a background of continuity.

*Brown v. Board of Education* was such a case. It struck at the heart of a great evil. Though departing from the particular plans of the Framers, it honored their deeper, nobler intentions. And though overriding the democratic process, it crystallized an emerging national consensus that legally compelled racial segregation was unacceptable in modern America. That is the difference between judicial activism and judicial statesmanship, and why most of the fiercest critics of judicial activism don't dare criticize *Brown* today.

But the Court should attempt to lead only where the nation is prepared to follow. The creation of new constitutional values is a slippery slope, down which the courts should not travel too far too fast. At the bottom lies the kind of uninhibited and essentially lawless judicial legislation that Bork has justly assailed. The urge to do good is powerful, the urge to court greatness intoxicating. Judges should resist the sincere, but arrogant, assumption that they know best. Brandeis's words, aimed at Ed Meese's ideological predecessors, should also be heeded by his ideological adversaries: "The greatest danger to liberty is the insidious encroachment by men of zeal, well-meaning but without understanding."

# Michael Kelly
## "TRB: Judge Dread"*

The Republicans are not happy. They suffer from feelings of loss and inadequacy. This confuses and frustrates them. After all, they fared pretty well in 1996; they kept the Hill and lost the White House in a race where one of the most agile campaigners of all time ran against one of the least agile. The national agenda is, more or less, their agenda. Their great nemesis Bill Clinton is, again, beset by scandal. And yet it's just no fun anymore. Things are not going the way they should. Trent Lott has caved to the Democrats, and now Fred Thompson's committee will be looking into Republican fund-raising improprieties as well as Democratic illegalities, which wasn't the idea at all. Nothing much else is happening. The revolution is in the doldrums. Nobody's got a plan; nobody's got a direction. God only knows where Newt is, probably locked in his office to work on his design for a perpetual motion machine.

It is precisely at moments like these that Republicans get the sort of brilliant ideas that have won them the sobriquet of The Stupid Party. Once again, they do not disappoint. On March 11, House Majority Whip Tom DeLay unveiled to *The Washington Times* the party's dazzling new scheme for getting the revolution back on track: congressional Republicans will begin attempting to impeach liberal federal judges. DeLay told the Times that "articles of impeachment are being written right now" against a Texas judge and that two other judges are being considered for impeachment. "As part of our conservative efforts against judicial activism, we are going after judges," DeLay said. "Congress has given up its responsibility in [overseeing] judges and their performance on the bench, and we intend to revive that and go after them in a big way."

DeLay's idea would be frightening even if it were only the expression of one man's fatheadedness, but it is not. The right has once again fingered judicial activism as the cause of its woes. The right-wing National Legal Foundation is calling for the impeachment of six out of the nine Supreme Court justices for failing to vote properly in support of Colorado's prohibition against anti-discrimination laws for homosexuals. Far-right writer Pat Buchanan last week denounced "the lawlessness of the federal courts" in "frustrating the will of a conservative majority." Mid-right writer William Kristol adopted much the same position, urging conservatives on March 12 to mobilize behind "the battle cry: 'No new liberal judges.' "

The cry is already in full bellow on the Hill. Senator Orrin Hatch, chairman of the Judiciary Committee, is presiding over a slowdown of confirmations that amounts almost to a stoppage. Under great pressure from younger and more perfervid senators, Hatch has said his committee will not confirm any nominees deemed to be excessively activist. On November 15, in an assertion of breathtaking sweep, Hatch declared: "a judicial activist is not qualified to sit on the federal bench."

What Hatch is saying here is that a liberal activist jurist—which Republicans vaguely and inconsistently define as one who believes in exercising a very broad and final authority over the law, to the point of overruling the legislative will of the people—is definitionally unfit to serve.

Hatch is backing up this extraordinary expansion of senatorial privilege with action, or rather inaction. His committee is sitting on twenty-six nominations that the White House has sent up since January. More than twenty of the nominations are actually renominations, people named but not confirmed in the last Congress; in some cases these nominations have been held up for more than two years. Hatch's position already stretches the limits of the doctrine of separation of powers. Now DeLay proposes to destroy this fundamental precept entirely. It is hard to imagine a surer scheme for producing a constitutional crisis than for the party that controls Congress to conduct a campaign of impeachment against judges whose views represent those of the other party.

This was never intended by the Framers, nor has it ever been attempted. The Constitution allows Congress to impeach, to convict and to remove from office a federal judge for "treason, bribery, or other high crimes and misdemeanors." It merely requires a simple majority in the House to impeach and a two-thirds majority in the Senate to convict on the impeachment. But it has always been understood that this power is to be used against serious, almost always criminal, malfeasance. In 221 years, only thirteen judges have been impeached. Only once—in the 1804 impeachment (but not conviction) of Supreme Court Associate Justice Samuel Chase—has this occurred because a judge rendered a politically incorrect judicial decision.

DeLay has no patience with Congress's silly old prudishness about abusing its power and corrupting the Constitution. He is explicitly calling for Congress to use the impeachment process against judges who are not accused of any criminal conduct, but who have simply made rulings that go against conservative philosophy or Republican interests. The judge in Texas that DeLay mentioned is a case in point. He is U.S. District Judge Fred Biery. His high crime? In January, he ruled that two Republican winners in the 1996 elections, candidates for county sheriff and county commissioner, could not be sworn in, because their elections had been illegally decided by 800 absentee votes cast by long-departed military personnel from Laughlin Air Force Base. The two other judges under consideration for impeachment are Harold Baer Jr., a Clinton appointee to the U.S. District Court in New York, and Chief U.S. District Judge Thelton Henderson, in San Francisco. Their crimes? Baer threw out evidence and a confession in a drug case because he said the police had insufficient cause to search the defendant's car. (Under pressure from Clinton, he reversed himself.) Henderson blocked implementation of California's Proposition 209, a voter referendum to ban preferences by race and sex in state employment and in admissions to state colleges.

As these latter two cases indicate, conservatives do have a case against those judges who practice judicial activism as a means of fulfilling their own ideological fancies. As legislatures and popular votes have increasingly disfavored the left's positions, the left has at times used judges to achieve what could not be gained in a democratic fashion. But there are two remedies available for this: the Supreme Court, which may overrule these judges, and the electoral process, by which the citizens may reject a president whose judicial appointments annoy them. Congressional Democrats and Republicans have already corrupted the confirmation process, turning it into an endless round of Borking and counter-Borking. But the damage that has done to the rule of the Constitution is as nothing compared to what DeLay's bright idea would unleash.

# 9

# Public Opinion

## The Marketplace of Ideas

*See Lowi and Ginsberg, pp. 374–381 or brief edition, pp. 210–216*

*Are the media to blame for America's cynical and antagonistic view of politics? Critics of the media argue that the airwaves are full of negative commentators bent on exposing every public official's moral warts; network news coverage of campaigns reduces complex issues to trivial, quick sound bites. For every critic who claims that the media has a liberal slant, another alleges a conservative bias. Nobody, it seems, is happy with media coverage of politics.*

*The problem, Michael Nelson argues, is not the media. It is also not the politicians, the political process, or the political parties. The problem is that Americans hold tightly to fundamental, but contradictory, values about the way in which the American political system should work. First, we believe that government ought to function according to a higher law or "ultimate standard of right." Second, Americans believe that government ought to function according to "popular sovereignty"—it ought to do what the people want. Nelson argues that the problem is these two values can and often do conflict: What the people want is not always the same as the principles set out in higher law. Consequently, when government inevitably fails to meet both standards, we do not blame our governing principles or ourselves, but rather the politicians, the institutions within which they exercise their authority, or the media.*

## Michael Nelson
## "Why Americans Hate Politics and Politicians"*

Do psychiatrists still use word-association techniques with their patients? You know what I mean: Dr. Jungfreud says "food" and the patient says "mother," the doctor says "girls" and the patient says "mother," the doctor says "father" and the patient says "mother," and quickly they realize that the patient has a hangup with his mother. Modern psychiatric practices notwithstanding, I sometimes do a little word association on the first day of my introductory American government classes at Rhodes College. The first word I say is "politics" and back come the replies from the students (not "mother"): "corrupt," they say, "dirty," "games-playing," "ego trip," "a waste." (The nicest thing I heard the last time I did this was "bor-

* Michael Nelson, "Why Americans Hate Politics and Politicians" from *Virginia Quarterly Review* (Autumn 1994). Reprinted by permission.

ing.") Here is what they say in response to "politician": "selfish," "ambitious," "mediocre," "unprincipled."

* * *

Why do Americans hate politics and politicians? There is no scarcity of answers to this question. 1993 being the 30th anniversary of President John F. Kennedy's assassination and the 25th anniversary of the assassinations of his brother Robert and of Martin Luther King, Jr., much was made of the despair about politics that spread among the American people in the wake of those brutal deaths. Other explanations of our distrust and cynicism are grounded in the lies and half-truths the government told about the Vietnam war and about Watergate and all its many offspring: Koreagate, Irangate, Iraqgate, and, most recently, Whitewatergate, to name but a few. The media is another likely suspect—remodeled network evening news programs that treat politics and government with a sneer, now joined by new-style trash TV news shows and radio talk shows (Rush Limbaugh, can you hear me?) that are overtly hostile to politics and politicians. On top of all that, professional political consultants use the media to air their increasingly negative campaign ads, the cumulative effect of which, some argue, is to convince Americans that all the candidates in all our elections are bums.

Still other explanations of our cynicism and indifference may be found in two recent and very thoughtful books by journalists. E. J. Dionne of *The Washington Post*, in the book whose title I have adapted for this essay— *Why Americans Hate Politics*—blames the poverty of our prevailing political ideologies. "Liberalism and conservatism are framing political issues as a series of false choices. . . ." he writes. "On issue after issue, there is consensus [among the public] on where the country should move or at least on what we should be arguing about; [but] liberalism and conservatism make it impossible for that consensus to express itself." Most Americans agree, for example, that to help lift the underclass out of poverty will require some combination of government help *and* greater personal responsibility. But, Dionne argues, conservatives don't want to admit the need for government help and liberals don't want to tell poor people to take responsibility for their lives, so nothing is done. The progress of welfare reform in Washington will provide a good test of how far the political process has come on this issue.

Another journalist, Alan Ehrenhalt, turns his gaze to the politicians in a book called *The United States of Ambition*. Ehrenhalt argues that running for and serving in political office has become so time consuming and demanding that only people who are willing to become fulltime politicians can do it. Pernicious effects flow from this modern fact of political life. The talent pool from which leaders are drawn has narrowed—it now excludes the business or professional person (much less the blue collar or pink collar worker) who could spare some time for public service but not abandon a career or job to do so. The talent pool also includes many more liberals than conservatives, according to Ehrenhalt. Liberals, after all, like government and are more likely to be drawn to it on a fulltime basis. And with politics as their vocation, those who are elected in the modern era feel compelled to do everything they can to stay in office.

All of these explanations of why Americans hate politics and politicians have three things in common. First, they all point the blame away from the American people and fix it on somebody else—politicians, political consultants, the media, liberals, conservatives, assassins, and so on. (How convenient for us.) Second, they are all ahistorical, grounded almost entirely in recent events and developments. Third, they are all partial explanations—accurate, especially in explaining why antipolitical feelings are higher now than ever, but accurate only to a degree. In truth, there has never been a time when Americans were pro-politics and pro-politicians. Historically, the United States has lagged far behind other Western democracies in the development and extent of its welfare state. The American approach has been to regulate businesses rather than nationalize them. Political ideologies that exalt government—from fascism to communism—simply have not taken root in American soil; the United States is the only Western country in which Socialists were never able to form a leading political party. We seem to be antipolitical in our very bones.

## II

Clearly another piece needs to be added to the great jigsaw puzzle that, once assembled, can reveal why Americans hate politics and politicians. This new piece would be a picture of us—of "we the people"—and not just of us in this generation but us through all the generations that, taken together, constitute the history of the United States. The label on the new piece would read: "American political culture."

American political culture consists of our longstanding, widely-shared, and deeply-felt values about how the political system ought to work (our process values) and the ends it ought to serve (our purpose values). It has become fashionable to speak of multiculturalism, and in many areas of American life it is accurate to do so as well. But when it comes to the purposes the political system ought to serve, almost everything that Americans in all their hyphenated variety have ever valued can be grouped under the headings "liberty" and "equality." One can argue—as Americans have for more than two centuries—about what these values mean and how they should be applied in specific situations. But liberty and equality are the banners under which such battles invariably are fought.

More pertinent to the question of why Americans hate politics and politicians are the process values of our political culture, our values concerning how the American political system ought to work, the rules of the game.

Deeply rooted in American political culture—that is, in us—is the belief that government ought to work in accordance with "higher law," some ultimate standard of right.

\*   \*   \*

"Higher law" philosophy certainly prevailed in the America of 1776, when, as the historian Gordon Wood has shown, "the traditional covenant theology of Puritanism combined with the political science of the eighteenth century [Enlightenment] into an imperatively persuasive argument for revolution." (If that seems densely academic, does this sound more familiar? "We hold these *truths* to be *self-evident.*" That is higher law philosophy in a nutshell.) And it endures in the modern practice of inscribing our ideals into public policy.

\*   \*   \*

But Americans' political process values include more than higher law. They also believe that the political system ought to operate in accordance with "popular sovereignty," a value that consists of the related beliefs that the only legitimate basis of political authority is the consent of the governed ("government of the people," to quote another greatest hit from American history) and that government is supposed to work in accordance with what the public wants ("government by the people"). The belief in popular sovereignty not only infuses virtually every political writing of the founding period, but it forms the philosophical foundation of the Constitution itself: "We the people . . . do ordain and establish this Constitution of the United States of America." . . . Since 1787, the belief in popular sovereignty has manifested itself in an endless and, by the standards of other Western nations, radical series of democratic reforms: universal suffrage; primaries, initiatives, referendums, recalls; and direct election of senators, presidential electors, and, in many states, judges, school boards, sheriffs, clerks, trustees, and commissioners—the American people are asked to speak authoritatively in so many ways. Popular sovereignty also underlies Americans' widely shared expectations of members of Congress and other legislators, whom we insist should vote in accordance with our wishes, not with their own considered judgments as to what is best.

Matters grow especially interesting when these two process values from the political culture are laid alongside each other, which is what most of us do, without thinking very much about it, in our own minds. Let's review the bidding. As Americans, we believe that government is supposed to work according to higher law—a fixed, external, eternal standard of right that is embodied in the Constitution. We also believe that it is supposed to work according to what the people want—popular sovereignty. An obvious problem arises. Which standard is supposed to prevail when what the higher law seems to require and what the people want are not the same? Never fear—Americans take pride in being great problem-solvers. And one of the most effective strategies for dealing with problems is to pretend that they do not exist. That is what we have done in this case. Listen, for example, to that great American problem-solver, Andrew Jackson:

I believe that man can be elevated; man can become more and more endowed with divinity; and as he does he becomes more God-like in his character and capable of governing himself. Let us go on elevating our people, perfecting our institutions, until democracy shall reach such a point of perfection that we can acclaim with truth that the voice of the people is the voice of God.

*Vox populi, vox dei*—the voice of the people *is* the voice of God. How convenient the doctrine that allows us to believe that popular sovereignty will never conflict with the higher law.

And the doctrine endures, as reflected in comparative studies of civic competence and social trust in a number of Western democracies. To a far greater extent than Britons, Germans, Austrians, Netherlanders, Mexicans, Italians, and the French, Americans have been found to feel personally competent to participate intelligently in politics and to trust each other to do the same. In short, we see no contradiction between government of the people and by the people, and government for the people.

Americans also revere the Constitution. Ask a random sample of Europeans (as political scientists have done) what they are proudest of about their country and they are likely to mention its physical beauty or cultural achievements; ask Americans the same question and they will describe their form of government—democracy, freedom, "all men are created equal," etc. When Americans travel to Washington with their families (which most who can afford to do so eventually do), they are making pilgrimages of a sort. They visit the city's sacred shrines to Lincoln, Washington, Jefferson, Kennedy, and our fallen soldiers. They gaze upon its sacred texts—the Constitution and the Declaration of Independence—at the National Archives. They visit its temples of law and democracy—the Supreme Court, the Capitol, the White House. Their attitude is serious, even reverential; their gaze open-mouthed.

Why, then, do Americans hate politics and politicians? We hate them because we have left ourselves no alternative. When things go wrong, as most people think they have in the political system, we have no one else to blame. We can not blame the Constitution for what is wrong—far from it, it is our embodiment of higher law. And we certainly are not about to blame ourselves. And so we blame the only people who are left—the politicians. And they, wanting to please us, are only too happy to confirm us in our beliefs by pointing their own fingers of blame at each other.

\* \* \*

## Measuring Public Opinion

*See Lowi and Ginsberg, pp. 229–234 or brief edition, pp. 393–410*

*Assessing public opinion in a democracy of 250 million people is no easy task. George Gallup, who is largely responsible for the development of modern opinion polling, argued that public opinion polls enhanced the democratic pro-*

*cess by providing elected officials with a picture of what Americans think about current events. Despite Gallup's vigorous defense of his polling techniques and the contribution of polling to democracy, the public opinion poll remains controversial. While some express concern about the representativeness of "the public" through sampling techniques, others argue that opinion polls can be overemphasized by elected officials who should exercise informed, independent judgment rather that respond to rapid and short-term fluctuations in public opinion.*

# George Gallup
## "Polling the Public"*

We have a national election every two years only. In a world which moves as rapidly as the modern world does, it is often desirable to know the people's will on basic policies at more frequent intervals. We cannot put issues off and say "let them be decided at the next election." World events do not wait on elections. We need to know the will of the people at all times.

If we know the collective will of the people at all times the efficiency of democracy can be increased, because we can substitute specific knowledge of public opinion for blind groping and guesswork. Statesmen who know the true state of public opinion can then formulate plans with a sure knowledge of what the voting public is thinking. They can know what degree of opposition to any proposed plan exists, and what efforts are necessary to gain public acceptance for it. The responsibility for initiating action should, as always, rest with the political leaders of the country. But the collective will or attitude of the people needs to be learned without delay.

### THE WILL OF THE PEOPLE

How is the will of the people to be known at all times?

Before I offer an answer to this question, I would like to examine some of the principal channels by which, at the present time, public opinion is expressed.

The most important is of course a national election. An election is the only official and binding expression of the people's judgment. But, as viewed from a strictly objective point of view, elections are a confusing and imperfect way of registering national opinion. In the first place, they come only at infrequent intervals. In the second place, as Bryce pointed out in *The American Commonwealth*, it is virtually impossible to separate issues from candidates. How can we tell whether the public is voting for the man or

* George Gallup in *Public Opinion in a Democracy*. Published under the University Extension Fund, Herbert L. Baker Foundation, Princeton University, 1939.

for his platform? How can we tell whether all the candidate's views are endorsed, or whether some are favored and others opposed by the voters? Because society grows more and more complex, the tendency is to have more and more issues in an election. Some may be discussed; others not. Suppose a candidate for office takes a position on a great many public issues during the campaign. If elected, he inevitably assumes that the public has endorsed all his planks, whereas this may actually not be the case. . . .

## THE ROLE OF THE ELECTED REPRESENTATIVE

A second method by which public opinion now expresses itself is through elected representatives. The legislator is, technically speaking, supposed to represent the interests of all voters in his constituency. But under the two-party system there is a strong temptation for him to represent, and be influenced by, only the voters of his own party. He is subject to the pressure of party discipline and of wishes of party leaders back home. His very continuance in office may depend on giving way to such pressure. Under these circumstances his behavior in Congress is likely to be governed not by what he thinks the voters of his State want, but by what he thinks the leaders of his own party in that State want. . . .

Even in the event that an elected representative does try to perform his duty of representing the whole people, he is confronted with the problem: What is the will of the people? Shall he judge their views by the letters they write him or the telegrams they send him? Too often such expressions of opinion come only from an articulate minority. Shall the congressman judge their views by the visitors or delegations that come to him from his home district?

## PRESSURE GROUPS AND THE WHOLE NATION

Legislators are constantly subject to the influence of organized lobbies and pressure groups. Senator Tydings, in a lecture here in Princeton, pointed out recently that the United States is the most fertile soil on earth for the activity of pressure groups. The American people represent a conglomeration of races, all with different cultural backgrounds. Sections and groups struggle with one another to fix national and international policy. And frequently in such struggles, as Senator Tydings pointed out, "self-interest and sectionalism, rather than the promotion of national welfare, dominate the contest." Senator Tydings mentions some twenty important group interests. These include labor, agriculture, veterans, pension plan advocates, chambers of commerce, racial organizations, isolationists and internationalists, high-tariff and low-tariff groups, preparedness and disarmament groups, budget balancers and spending advocates, soft-money associations and hard-money associations, transportation groups and states righters and centralizationists.

The legislator obviously owes a duty to his home district to legislate in its best interests. But he also owes a duty to legislate in the best interests of the whole nation. In order, however, to carry out this second duty he must *know* what the nation thinks. Since he doesn't always know what the voters in his own district think, it is just that much more difficult for him to learn the views of the nation. Yet if he could know those views at all times he could legislate more often in the interest of the whole country. . . .

## THE CROSS-SECTION SURVEY

This effort to discover public opinion has been largely responsible for the introduction of a new instrument for determining public opinion—the cross-section or sampling survey. By means of nationwide studies taken at frequent intervals, research workers are today attempting to measure and give voice to the sentiments of the whole people on vital issues of the day.

Where does this new technique fit into the scheme of things under our form of government? Is it a useful instrument of democracy? Will it prove to be vicious and harmful, or will it contribute to the efficiency of the democratic process?

The sampling referendum is simply a procedure for sounding the opinions of a relatively small number of persons, selected in such manner as to reflect with a high degree of accuracy the views of the whole voting population. In effect such surveys canvass the opinions of a miniature electorate.

Cross-section surveys do not place their chief reliance upon numbers. The technique is based on the fact that a few thousand voters correctly selected will faithfully reflect the views of an electorate of millions of voters. The key to success in this work is the cross section—the proper selection of voters included in the sample. Elaborate precautions must be taken to secure the views of members of all political parties—of rich and poor, old and young, of men and women, farmers and city dwellers, persons of all religious faiths—in short, voters of all types living in every State in the land. And all must be included in correct proportion. . . .

## RELIABILITY OF OPINION SURVEYS

Whether opinion surveys will prove to be a useful contribution to democracy depends largely on their reliability in measuring opinion. During the last four years the sampling procedure, as used in measuring public opinion, has been subjected to many tests. In general these tests indicate that present techniques can attain a high degree of accuracy, and it seems reasonable to assume that with the development of this infant science, the accuracy of its measurements will be constantly improved.

The most practical way at present to measure the accuracy of the sampling referendum is to compare forecasts of elections with election results.

Such a test is by no means perfect, because a preelection survey must not only measure opinion in respect to candidates but must also predict just what groups of people will actually take the trouble to cast their ballots. Add to this the problem of measuring the effect of weather on turnout, also the activities of corrupt political machines, and it can easily be seen that election results are by no means a perfect test of the accuracy of this new technique. . . .

Many thoughtful students of government have asked: Why shouldn't the Government itself, rather than private organizations, conduct these sampling surveys? A few political scientists have even suggested the establishment of a permanent federal bureau for sounding public opinion, arguing that if this new technique is a contribution to democracy, the government has a duty to take it over.

The danger in this proposal, as I see it, lies in the temptation it would place in the way of the party in power to conduct surveys to prove itself right and to suppress those which proved it to be wrong. A private organization, on the other hand, must stand or fall not so much on what it reports or fails to report as on the accuracy of its results, and the impartiality of its interpretations. An important requirement in a democracy is complete and reliable news reports of the activities of all branches of the government and of the views of all leaders and parties. But few persons would argue that, for this reason, the government should take over the press, and all its news gathering associations. . . .

## CLOTURE ON DEBATE?

It is sometimes argued that public opinion surveys impose a cloture on debate. When the advocates of one side of an issue are shown to be in the majority, so the argument runs, the other side will lose hope and abandon their cause believing that further efforts are futile.

Again let me say that there is little evidence to support this view. Every election necessarily produces a minority. In 1936 the Republicans polled less than 40 percent of the vote. Yet the fact that the Republicans were defeated badly wasn't enough to lead them to quit the battle. They continued to fight against the New Deal with as much vigor as before. An even better example is afforded by the Socialist Party. For years the Socialist candidate for President has received but a small fraction of the total popular vote, and could count on sure defeat. Yet the Socialist Party continues as a party, and continues to poll about the same number of votes.

Sampling surveys will never impose a cloture on debate so long as it is the nature of public opinion to change. The will of the people is dynamic; opinions are constantly changing. A year ago an overwhelming majority of voters were skeptical of the prospects of the Republican Party in 1940. Today, half the voters think the G.O.P. will win. If elections themselves do not impose cloture on debate, is it likely that opinion surveys will?

## Possible Effect on Representative Government

The form of government we live under is a representative form of government. What will be the effect on representative government if the will of the people is known at all times? Will legislators become mere rubber stamps, mere puppets, and the function of representation be lost?

Under a system of frequent opinion measurement, the function of representation is not lost, for two reasons. First, it is well understood that the people have not the time or the inclination to pass on all the problems that confront their leaders. They cannot be expected to express judgment on technical questions of administration and government. They can pass judgment only on basic general policies. As society grows more complex there is a greater and greater need for experts. Once the voters have indicated their approval of a general policy or plan of action, experts are required to carry it out.

Second, it is not the province of the people to initiate legislation, but to decide which of the programs offered they like best. National policies do not spring full-blown from the common people. Leaders, knowing the general will of the people, must take the initiative in forming policies that will carry out the general will and must put them into effect.

Before the advent of the sampling referendum, legislators were not isolated from their constituencies. They read the local newspapers; they toured their districts and talked with voters; they received letters from their home State; they entertained delegations who claimed to speak for large and important blocs of voters. The change that is brought about by sampling referenda is merely one which provides these legislators with a truer measure of opinion in their districts and in the nation. . . .

## How Wise Are the Common People?

The sampling surveys of recent years have provided much evidence concerning the wisdom of the common people. Anyone is free to examine this evidence. And I think that the person who does examine it will come away believing as I do that, collectively, the American people have a remarkably high degree of common sense. These people may not be brilliant or intellectual or particularly well read, but they possess a quality of good sense which is manifested time and again in their expressions of opinion on present-day issues. . . .

It is not difficult to understand why the conception of the stupidity of the masses has so many adherents. Talk to the first hundred persons whom you happen to meet in the street about many important issues of the day, and the chances are great that you will be struck by their lack of accurate or complete knowledge on these issues. Few of them will likely have sufficient information in this particular field to express a well founded judgment.

But fortunately a democracy does not require that every voter be well informed on every issue. In fact a democracy does not depend so much on the enlightenment of each individual, as upon the quality of the collective judgment or intelligence of thousands of individuals. . . .

It would of course be foolish to argue that the collective views of the common people always represent the most intelligent and most accurate answer to any question. But results of sampling referenda on hundreds of issues do indicate, in my opinion, that we can place great faith in the collective judgment or intelligence of the people.

## The New England Town Meeting Restored

One of the earliest and purest forms of democracy in this country was the New England town meeting. The people gathered in one room to discuss and to vote on the questions of the community. There was a free exchange of opinions in the presence of all the members. The town meeting was a simple and effective way of articulating public opinion, and the decisions made by the meeting kept close to the public will. When a democracy thus operates on a small scale it is able to express itself swiftly and with certainty.

But as communities grew, the town meeting became unwieldy. As a result the common people became less articulate, less able to debate the vital issues in the manner of their New England forefathers. Interest in politics lagged. Opinion had to express itself by the slow and cumbersome method of election, no longer facilitated by the town meeting with its frequent give and take of ideas. The indifference and apathy of voters made it possible for vicious and corrupt political machines to take over the administration of government in many states and cities.

The New England town meeting was valuable because it provided a forum for the exchange of views among all citizens of the community and for a vote on these views. Today, the New England town meeting idea has, in a sense, been restored. The wide distribution of daily newspapers reporting the views of statesmen on issues of the day, the almost universal ownership of radios which bring the whole nation within the hearing of any voice, and now the advent of the sampling referendum which provides a means of determining quickly the response of the public to debate on issues of the day, have in effect created a town meeting on a national scale.

How nearly the goal has been achieved is indicated in the following data recently gathered by the American Institute of Public Opinion. Of the 45,000,000 persons who voted in the last presidential election, approximately 40,000,000 read a daily newspaper, 40,000,000 have radios, and only 2,250,000 of the entire group of voters in the nation neither have a radio nor take a daily newspaper.

This means that the nation is literally in one great room. The newspapers and the radio conduct the debate on national issues, presenting both information and argument on both sides, just as the townsfolk did in person in the old town meeting. And finally, through the process of the sampling referendum, the people, having heard the debate on both sides of every issue, can express their will. After one hundred and fifty years we return to the town meeting. This time the whole nation is within the doors.

## Shaping Public Opinion

*See Lowi and Ginsberg, pp. 382–392 or brief edition, pp. 216–221*

*Perhaps the most challenging critique of the public opinion poll is that it can be manipulated to "transform opinion from a politically potent, often disruptive, force into a more docile, plebiscitary phenomenon." This is the argument made by political scientist Benjamin Ginsberg: he argues that the survey instrument and public opinion interact in ways that alter the character of public opinion. The spontaneity of opinion and its connection to action is replaced by a more passive response to questions of inquiry defined by the pollster. The dangerous result, Ginsberg argues, is the potential for government management of public opinion, using it to legitimize and support government agendas, rather than as a force for change or a means to insure the responsiveness and accountability of government leaders.*

*What do you think? Do public-opinion polls represent the voice of the people? Are there alternatives to polling for bringing the voice of the people to the political process?*

# Benjamin Ginsberg
# "How Polling Transforms Public Opinion"*

The "will of the people" has become the ultimate standard against which the conduct of contemporary governments is measured. In the democracies, especially in the United States, both the value of governmental programs and the virtue of public officials are typically judged by the extent of their popularity. . . .

Much of the prominence of opinion polling as a civic institution derives from the significance that present-day political ideologies ascribe to the will of the people. Polls purport to provide reliable, scientifically derived information about the public's desires, fears and beliefs, and so to give concrete expression to the conception of a popular will. The availability of accurate information certainly is no guarantee that governments will actually pay heed to popular opinions. Yet, it has always been the belief of many students and practitioners of survey research that an accurate picture of the public's views might at least increase the chance that governments' actions would be informed by and responsive to popular sentiment.

Unfortunately, however, polls do more than simply measure and record the natural or spontaneous manifestation of popular belief. The data reported by opinion polls are actually the product of an interplay between opinion and the survey instrument. As they measure, the polls interact with opinion, producing changes in the character and identity of the views receiving public expression. The changes induced by polling, in turn, have the most profound implications for the relationship between public opinion and government. In essence, polling has contributed to the domestication of opinion by helping to transform opinion from a politically potent, often disruptive, force into a more docile, plebiscitary phenomenon.

### PUBLICIZING OPINION

Over the past several decades, polling has generally come to be seen as the most accurate and reliable means of gauging the public's sentiments. Indeed, poll results and public opinion are terms that are used almost synonymously. But, despite this general tendency to equate public opinion with survey results, polling is obviously not the only possible source of knowledge about the public's attitudes.

[A] presumption in favor of the polls . . . [however] stems from both the scientific and representative character of opinion polling. Survey research is modeled after the methodology of the natural sciences and at least conveys an impression of technical sophistication and scientific objectivity. Occasional press accounts of deliberate bias and distortion of survey findings only partially undermine this impression.

At the same time, the polls can claim to offer a more representative view of popular sentiment than any alternative source of information is likely to provide. Group spokespersons sometimes speak only for themselves. The distribution of opinion reflected by letters to newspapers and public officials is notoriously biased. Demonstrators and rioters, however sincere, are seldom more than a tiny and unrepresentative segment of the populace. The polls, by contrast, at least attempt to take equal account of all relevant individuals. And, indeed, by offering a representative view of public opinion the polls have often served as antidotes for false spokespersons, correctives for mistaken politicians, and guides to popular concerns that might never have been mentioned by the individuals writing letters to legislators and newspaper editors.

Nevertheless, polling does more than offer a scientifically derived and representative account of popular sentiment. The substitution of polling for other means of gauging the public's views also has the effect of changing several of the key characteristics of public opinion. Critics of survey research have often noted that polling can affect both the beliefs of individuals asked to respond to survey questions and the attitudes of those who subsequently read a survey's results. However, the most important effect of the polls is not a result of their capacity to change individuals' beliefs. The major impact of polling is, rather, on the cumulation and translation of individuals' private beliefs into collective public opinion. Four fundamental changes in the character of public opinion can be traced to the introduction of survey research.

## CHANGING THE CHARACTER OF PUBLIC OPINION

First, polling alters both what is expressed and what is perceived as the opinion of the mass public by transforming public opinion from a voluntary to an externally subsidized matter. Second, polling modifies the manner in which opinion is publicly presented by transforming public opinion from a behavioral to an attitudinal phenomenon. Third, polling changes the origin of information about public beliefs by transforming public opinion from a property of groups to an attribute of individuals. Finally, polling partially removes individuals' control over the subject matter of their own public expressions of opinion by transforming public opinion from a spontaneous assertion to a constrained response.

Individually and collectively, these transformations have profound consequences for the character of public opinion and, more important, for the relationship of opinion to government and policy. To the extent that polling displaces alternative modes of gauging popular sentiment, these four transformations contribute markedly to the domestication or pacification of public opinion. Polling renders public opinion less dangerous, less disruptive, more permissive and, in some instances, more amenable to governmental control.

Polling does not make public opinion politically impotent. Nor, as the recent failure of the Reagan administration's efforts to "disinform" the American public on the government's policies toward Iran and Central America indicate, does the availability of polling guarantee that governments will be able to successfully manipulate public beliefs for an indefinite length of time. Nevertheless, polling helps to diminish the danger that public opinion poses to those in power and helps to increase the potential for government management of mass beliefs.

## FROM VOLUNTARISM TO SUBSIDY

In the absence of polling, the cost and effort required to organize and publicly communicate an opinion are normally borne by one or more of the individuals holding the opinion. . . . The polls, by contrast, organize and publicize opinion without necessitating any initiative or action on the part of individuals. . . .

This displacement of costs from the opinion-holder to the polling agency has important consequences for the character of the opinions likely to receive public expression. In general, the willingness of individuals to bear the costs of publicly asserting their views is closely tied to the intensity with which they hold those views. . . . So long as the costs of asserting opinions are borne by opinion-holders themselves, those with relatively extreme viewpoints are also disproportionately likely to bring their views to the public forum.

The polls weaken this relationship between the public expression of opinion and the intensity or extremity of opinion. The assertion of an opinion through a poll requires little effort on the part of the opinion-holder. As a result, the beliefs of those who care relatively little or even hardly at all, are as likely to be publicized as the opinions of those who care a great deal about the matter in question. Similarly, individuals with moderate viewpoints are as likely as those taking extreme positions to publicly communicate their opinions through a survey. The upshot is that the distribution of public opinion reported by the polls generally differs considerably from the distribution that emerges from forms of public communication initiated by citizens. . . .

This difference between polled and voluntarily expressed opinion can have important implications for the degree of influence or constraint that public opinion is likely to impose upon administrators and policymakers. The polls, in effect, submerge individuals with strongly held views in a more apathetic mass public. The data reported by the polls are likely to suggest to public officials that they are working in a more permissive climate of opinion than might have been thought on the basis of alternative indicators of the popular mood. A government wishing to maintain some semblance of responsiveness to public opinion would typically find it less difficult to comply with the preferences reported by the polls than to obey the opinion that might be inferred from letters, strikes, or protests. Indeed, relative to these other modes of public expression, polled opinion could be characterized as a collective statement of permission.

Certainly, even in the era of polling, voluntary expressions of public opinion can still count heavily. In recent years, for example, members of Congress were impressed by calls, letters, and telegrams from constituents—and threats from contributors—regarding President Reagan's various tax reform proposals. Of course, groups like the National Rifle Association are masters of the use of this type of opinion campaign. Nevertheless, contradiction by the polls tends to reduce the weight and credibility of other sources of public opinion. This effect of polling can actually help governments to resist the pressure of constituent opinion. Constituency polls, for example, are often used by legislators as a basis for resisting the demands of political activists and pressure groups in their districts.

Polling is especially useful when voluntary expressions of public opinion indicate severe opposition to a government and its programs. The relatively permissive character of polled opinion can allow a government faced with demonstrations, protests, and other manifestations of public hostility a basis for the claim that its policies are compatible with true public opinion and opposed only by an unrepresentative group of activist malcontents. A notable contemporary illustration of this role of the polls is the case of the "silent majority" on whose behalf Richard Nixon claimed to govern. The notion of a silent majority was the Nixon administration's answer to the protestors, who demanded major changes in American foreign and domestic policies. Administration spokespersons frequently cited poll data, often drawing upon Scammon and Wattenberg's influential treatise, *The Real Majority* (1970) to question the popular standing of the activist opposition. According to the administration's interpretation, its activist opponents did not represent the views of the vast majority of "silent" Americans who could be found in the polls but not on picket lines, marches, or in civil disturbances. . . .

## FROM BEHAVIOR TO ATTITUDE

Prior to the advent of polling, public opinion could often only be inferred from political behavior. Before the availability of voter survey data, for example, analysts typically sought to deduce electoral opinion from voting patterns, attributing candidates' electoral fortunes to whatever characteristics of the public mood could be derived from election returns. Often, population movements served as the bases for conclusions about public preferences. Even in recent years, the movement of white urbanites to the metropolitan fringe, dubbed "white flight," has been seen as a key indicator of white attitudes toward racial integration. Particularly, however, where the least articulate segments of the populace were concerned, governments often had little or no knowledge of the public's mood until opinion manifested itself in some form of behavior. Generally, this meant violent or disruptive activity. . . .

## FROM ASSERTION TO RESPONSE

In the absence of polling, individuals typically choose for themselves the subjects of any public assertions they might care to make. Those persons or groups willing to expend the funds, effort, or time needed to acquire a public platform, normally also select the agenda or topics on which their views will be aired. The individual writing an angry letter to a newspaper or legislator generally singles out the object of his or her scorn. The organizers of a protest march typically define the aim of their own wrath. Presumably, 19th-century mobs of "illuminators" determined of their own accord the matters on which the larger public would be enlightened.

The introduction of opinion surveys certainly did not foreclose individuals' opportunities to proffer opinions on topics of their own choosing. Indeed, in the United States, a multitude of organizations, groups, and individuals are continually stepping forward to present the most extraordinary notions. Nevertheless, the polls elicit subjects' views on questions which have been selected by an external agency—the survey's sponsors— rather than by the respondents themselves. Polling thus erodes individuals' control over the agenda of their own expressions of opinion. With the use of surveys, publicly expressed opinion becomes less clearly an assertion of individuals' own concerns and more nearly a response to the interest of others.

The most obvious problem stemming from this change is that polling can create a misleading picture of the agenda of public concerns. The matters which appear significant to the agencies sponsoring polls may be quite different from the concerns of the general public. Discrepancies between the polls' agenda and the general public's interests were especially acute during the political and social turmoil of the late 1960s and early 1970s. Though, as we saw, polling was used by the government during this period to help curb disorder, the major commercial polls took little interest in the issues which aroused so much public concern. The year 1970, for example, was marked by racial strife and antiwar protest in the United States. Yet, the 1970 national Gallup Poll devoted only 5 percent of its questions to American policy in Vietnam and only 2 of 162 questions to domestic race relations.

But, whatever the particular changes polling may help to produce in the focus of public discourse, the broader problem is that polling fundamentally alters the character of the public agenda of opinion. So long as groups and individuals typically present their opinions on topics of their own choosing, the agenda of opinion is likely to consist of citizens' own needs, hopes, and aspirations. A large fraction of the opinion which is publicly expressed will involve demands and concerns that groups and individuals wish to bring to the attention of the government. Opinions elicited by the polls, on the other hand, mainly concern matters of interest to government, business, or other poll sponsors. Typically, poll questions have as their ultimate purpose some form of exhortation. Businesses poll to help persuade customers to purchase their wares. Candidates poll as part of the process of convincing voters to support them. Governments poll as part of the process of inducing citizens to obey. Sometimes several of these purposes are combined. In 1971, for example, the White House Domestic Council sponsored a poll dealing with a host of social issues designed both to assist the administration with policy planning and to boost the president's reelection efforts.

In essence, rather than offer governments the opinions that citizens want them to learn, the polls tell governments—or other sponsors—what they would like to learn about citizens' opinions. The end result is to change the public expression of opinion from an assertion of demand to a step in the process of persuasion.

## MAKING OPINION SAFER FOR GOVERNMENT

Taken together, the changes produced by polling contribute to the transformation of public opinion from an unpredictable, extreme, and often dangerous force into a more docile expression of public sentiment. Opinion stated through the polls imposes less pressure and makes fewer demands upon government than would more spontaneous or natural assertions of popular sentiment. Though opinion may be expressed more democratically via the polls than though alternative means, polling can give public opinion a plebescitary character—robbing opinion of precisely those features that might maximize its impact upon government and policy. . . .

## GOVERNMENT: FROM ADVERSARY TO MANAGER OF OPINION

Because it domesticates public opinion, polling has contributed to one of the 20th century's major political transformations—the shift from an adversarial to a managerial relationship between government and popular opinion. . . .

On a day-to-day basis, the 20th-century state depends upon considerable support, cooperation, and sacrifice from its citizens in forms ranging from military service and large tax payments, through popular adherence to a multitude of rules and regulations. The scope and technical complexity of the modern state's activities, moreover, render governmental administration extremely sensitive to popular opposition. In the short term, opposition can often be forcibly quelled and a populace forcibly compelled to obey its rulers' edicts, pay taxes, and serve in the military. But, over long periods, even many of those governments commanding both the requisite armed might and appropriate lack of scruples have come to appreciate the wisdom of the Napoleonic dictum that one "may do anything with a bayonet but sit on it." By cultivating favorable public opinion, present-day rulers hope to persuade their citizens to voluntarily obey, support, and make whatever sacrifices are needed to further the state's goals. In the twentieth century, management of public opinion has become a routine public function in the democracies as well as in the dictatorships. Typically, the censor has been supplanted, or at least joined, by the public relations officer as the governmental functionary most responsible for dealing with public opinion. . . .

Polling is the spearhead of this vast opinion-management apparatus. Opinion surveys provide governments with more or less reliable information about current popular sentiment, offer a guide to the character of the public relations efforts that might usefully be made, and serve as means of measuring the effect of "information programs" upon a target population. Though it cannot guarantee success, polling allows government a better opportunity to anticipate, regulate, and manipulate popular attitudes. Ironically, some of its early students believed that polling would open the way for "government by opinion." Instead, polling has mainly helped to promote the governance of opinion.

## DEBATING THE ISSUES: THE POWER
## OF PUBLIC OPINION

*See Lowi and Ginsberg, pp. 408–409*

*As the earlier readings argue, public opinion polls and voting provide law makers with imperfect indications of public opinion. Even a medium such as talk radio is criticized for shaping public opinion, rather than providing a forum for the expression of public opinion. One alternative, according to Amitai Etzioni, is the "electronic town meeting." A version of "teledemocracy," he argues, would provide a forum for deliberation among the public on important policy issues, rather than forcing an immediate public response to important policy questions through public opinion polls, for example. After explaining his research on a version of teledemocracy that would incorporate the advantages of town hall meetings and the representative process, Etzioni notes that it is not realistic to allow all citizens to determine directly the details of policies. Instead, small groups of voters would meet via teleconference to discuss an issue and then elect representatives who would express their views to the next level of discussion, and so on. After seven meetings, more than one million Americans would have participated in the process. Issues that did not require extensive compromise and debate could be voted on directly through a telephone call-in process. Etzioni does not recommend the elimination of alternative means of determining public opinion, but suggests that teledemocracy would supplement the information gleaned from current methods. Etzioni's suggested method for increased democratic deliberation parallels that of House Speaker Newt Gingrich whose vision of an enhanced democratic process includes a "lap-top [computer] for every American." How does the argument for increasing access to the deliberative process contrast with the intention of the Founding Fathers? What would George Gallup and Benjamin Ginsberg say?*

*Anthony Lewis, a political columnist for the* New York Times, *is apprehensive about the use of teledemocracy. Acknowledging that a new technological age has dawned, he urges Americans to consider the concerns of the Farmers: the capacity for majority opinion to tyrannize minorities, and the uninformed and easily manipulated views often expressed in public opinion. Representative government, Lewis argues, was designed to check these flaws of democracy based upon broad, direct participation; the concerns still have salience today and should not be easily supplanted.*

# Amitai Etzioni
## "Teledemocracy"*

The idea of technologically enhanced national "town meetings" has been around at least since Buckminster Fuller proposed it a generation ago. And it is not likely to go away just because Ross Perot dropped out of the presidential race. The idea deserves serious examination, because if the 1992 election campaign has taught us anything, it is that most Americans feel alienated from national politics as currently practiced, and there is a need to find ways to reinvolve them. Simply changing the cast of characters may not do the trick. Public-opinion polls show a deep sense of disaffection that reaches well beyond the candidates themselves.

There are long-established precedents for the idea of adding some elements of direct democracy to our representative government. Twenty-three states currently grant their citizens the right to pass directly on items of legislation and even to modify state constitutions by putting amendments on a ballot. (California leads the pack.) In addition, numerous measures, such as school bonds and public-works funding, are regularly decided on by referenda of the electorate. Indeed, the number of initiatives and referenda has been increasing. A preponderance of the four hundred or so such measures introduced since the Progressives, in the first decades of this century, made them a hallmark of government reform have been introduced in the past twenty years, according to the political scientist Aaron Wildavsky.

To be sure, there is a big difference between adding some direct democracy to our representative system and replacing Congress with TV shows and push buttons. Electronic town meetings, though hardly a cure for all the ills of our democracy, could be arranged in ways that would avoid several of the pitfalls against which critics correctly warn. Or so I will argue.

Twenty years ago I spent a third of a million dollars—a hefty sum in the early 1970s—of your (taxpayer) money, granted to me by the National Science Foundation, conducting experiments with electronic town meetings. Indeed, they are the subject of an article I published in *Policy Science* in 1972. I have good reason to believe that Ross Perot and his staff did not read my writings on the subject; their model lacked all of the features that I argued were needed to render electronic town meetings even approximately democratic.

To be frank, the NSF team started with the same simplistic notion that seemed to animate Perot: given new developments in cable and interactive television and in telepolling (which allowed incoming calls to be tallied automatically, without anybody's even answering the phone), we could engineer an electronic system that would enable large numbers of people to have the kind of active political participation that town meetings afforded

* Amitai Etzioni, "Teledemocracy" in the *Atlantic Monthly* (October 1992). Reprinted with permission.

the citizens of New England towns (and that, before them, the citizens of the Greek polis enjoyed). We sold a Columbia University professor of engineering, Stephen Unger, on the idea, and he joined the NSF team.

Having just outgrown the sixties and their notion of direct or participatory democracy, we were clear about one major principle: it would be undemocratic to replace elected representatives and legislatures with computerized voting or any other kind of electronic wizardry. One main reason, which became known by the NSF team as the Burke argument (after the political philosopher Edmund Burke), is that large groups need two or more layers of representation, rather than direct representation, in order to work out consensus-based public policies. History has proved that large groups are unable to agree on policies by means of the kind of dialogue possible in a town meeting, where fewer than two thousand people tend to be involved. In a layered system the voters grant their elected representatives "mandates," a kind of generalized guidance that reflects what the voters seek: Get us out of Vietnam. Focus on domestic issues. Do something about competitiveness. The voters neither feel compelled nor wish to be engaged in the specifics.

For the system to work at all, citizens must allow their representatives to engage in give-and-take, within the confines of their mandates, in order to find a shared public policy. If the various mandates have no overlap, no honest give-and-take is possible. Either a stalemate will occur until some parts of the electorate give in, or politicians will fudge, claiming that they are acting within the confines of their mandates while they are actually violating them. Each of these situations, in turn, will lead to policies that lack the support of the public and that contribute to its alienation. A case in point is the Maastrict Treaty, which provides for eventual political unification in Europe. The politicians signed the treaty without a mandate from their people. As a result, voters in Denmark rejected the treaty, and many others are grumbling.

Telepolling, like other forms of direct democracy en masse, provides only limited room for give-and-take. It can be made to work for a few isolated items that can be straightforwardly voted up or down (such as hospital bonds), but not for complex issues of the kind we typically face. Given such issues, direct democracy produces few if any opportunities to work out compromises that most people can feel comfortable ratifying.

For this reason, telepolling should be used to supplement the existing representative government. At the same time, if it was properly conducted, it could serve between elections as a continuous source of information to the legislature about the preferences of the populace.

The National Science Foundation team experimented in New Jersey with a system both layered and containing mandates. Systems like it could be employed nationwide to bring teledemocracy a step closer to real democracy. Our experiment was conducted with the help of the League of Women Voters, which was attempting to decide, as it does once a year, which issues to give priority. We organized the league's members into groups of ten, and they conducted their "town meetings" by means of conference calls. Each group chose its own priorities and selected a representative to take that agenda to the next level for discussion. We then held conference calls with groups of ten representatives, who decided among themselves which views and preferences to carry to the third and final level, at which statewide policy decisions were made. A survey established that the members were highly satisfied with the results. Every member was able to participate in the decision-making process, and yet the elected representatives were free, within an area indicated by those who elected them, to work out a league-wide consensus.

Such a model could be applied to a nationwide audience, drawing on the magical power of exponential curves: if representatives were layered in the suggested manner, millions of participants could very quickly be included. Indeed, suppose that various experts addressed the country on Sunday from 10:00 to 11:00 A.M. about whether the United States should cut back the military by 50 percent over five years. The conference buzz would start with groups of fourteen citizens, each having an hour to discuss and vote. Each group would elect one representative to participate in conference-call discussions with thirteen representatives of other groups. Each group of representatives would in turn elect an individual to speak for them, and so on in a rising pyramid. If this process occurred seven times, by six o'clock in the evening 105 million adults could be reached, which is more than the 91 million who voted in the 1988 presidential election.

The technical problems we encountered in our experiments were minor. We discovered that it takes some practice to get used to a conference by telephone. For example, you have to find ways to let it be known that you wish to speak (raising your hand obviously will do little good). And it is not always easy to tell who is the chair, the person who facilitates the dialogue and must control those who hog time. We dealt with the first problem by making use of the fact that the receiver button can be briefly clicked without disconnecting the line. The resulting signal can be recorded on a panel attached to the chair's phone, showing that you are in the queue to speak. Costlier possibilities come to mind, but they might require that U.S. phone companies do what the government of France has already done: equip each citizen's phone with a small computer attachment. The second problem resolved itself, for during a short dry run most chairs quickly learned to assert themselves.

*Sesame Street* teaches children about democratic elections in the following manner: You have three dollars to spend. Some people want crayons, others juice. You vote on what to buy. If the majority wants crayons, you get crayons. Such a simplistic explanation may do for young children, but adults who think of democracy as a voting machine miss an important feature of town meetings: such meetings expose people to conflicting arguments and make them think about their preferences before they vote.

The last thing a democracy needs is for people to vote their raw feelings, their first impulses, before they have had a chance to reflect on them and discuss them with others. Hence it is highly undesirable to expose people to a new idea, policy, or speech and ask them to vote on it immediately—which is precisely what most media polling currently does. A much more democratic model would result if at least a day's delay were required before the vote was taken, to enable people to discuss the matter with their families, neighbors, and co-workers.

We conducted such an experiment in three high-rise buildings in Queens, New York. These buildings, which contained about eleven hundred families, shared a cable system, and a studio in the basement of one of them enabled a person to address all the TV sets in the buildings. We provided the residents with questionnaires on which they marked their views on selected local issues. We then broadcast a panel discussion on TV. Next we created an opportunity for dialogue: residents were invited to walk over to the studio and address the community about the issues on the table. This was followed by a second brief questionnaire. Unfortunately, owing to various technical difficulties, I cannot state unequivocally that the results were beneficial. The data suggest, however, that people moved from more extreme positions toward the middle, and that they moved either toward a consensus or, on one issue, toward two positions from a much wider, confused spread.

A minor but not trivial problem is that when citizens speak up in a live town meeting, they get immediate feedback on how their views are received. As a result, they continually adjust what they are saying, moderating their views (or expounding upon them) when faced with a negative reception and speaking more firmly (or more conciliatorily) if faced with a sea of heads nodding in approval. This feedback is largely lacking in conference calls and other communication by electronic means. So the NSF team provided levers that participants in a lab could move on a continuum from "agree" to "disagree," thus affecting a small amber light that would shine brightly when a majority pulled their levers toward "agree," and would dim if many pulled in the opposite direction. This device provided speakers with some instant feedback. To provide a similar feature on a nationwide or community-wide basis, we would probably, again, have to move toward phone-system technology similar to that in France.

Once we put our minds to it, other shortcomings of the electronic town meeting could be fixed. Take, for example, ballot-box stuffing. Even when much less than national policy is at stake, call-in polls have been grossly manipulated. Richard Morin, the polling director for *The Washington Post*, reports two such incidents. In one, *USA Today* asked its readers in June of 1990 if Donald Trump symbolized what was right or wrong with the United States. Eighty-one percent of the 6,406 people who called in said that he was great, 19 percent a skunk. It turned out that 72 percent of the calls came from two phone numbers. In another 1990 poll 21 percent of the callers on the issue of abortion voted at least twice.

This problem can be fixed. People could be required to punch in a Social Security number and two other identifying details, perhaps birth date and mother's maiden name. Computers could flag instances in which either the identifying information did not match the Social Security number or the same Social Security number was used more than once. And penalties like those now in place for election fraud could be extended to the electronic ballot box. The system would not be foolproof, but neither is the other system—as historians of the city of Chicago and biographers of Lyndon B. Johnson will tell you.

Those who complain that teledemocracy allows people to make only simple yes and no choices should note that the system can be as complicated as citizens wish. There are no technical obstacles to providing callers with three phone numbers instead of two (for "maybe" as well as "yes" and "no"), or with decision trees, in which, for example, they reach the "yes" line and are then offered a menu of choices, such as "only if the cost is less than $10 billion," or "less than $20 billion," and so on. Such a system would be at least as subtle as a vote that takes place on the electronic board of the House of Representatives or on a paper ballot loaded with local initiatives.

Several of the sharpest critics of teledemocracy focus on the fact that it is highly unrepresentative. James Fishkin, a political philosopher at the University of Texas, discussed this issue in the journal *The Responsive Community*, in an article about "America on the Line," a CBS program that aired after the 1992 State of the Union address. The network invited viewers to call in their reactions; seven million people tried to call, and three hundred thousand got through. When their reactions were compared with those of a scientific sample of public opinion taken at the same time. Fishkin reports, significant differences were noted. For instance, whereas 53 percent of the callers believed that America was worse off than it had been a year earlier, only 32 percent of the representative sample felt that way. Others have pointed out that those who are most likely to participate in a teledemocratic exchange are those who are educated, are politically active, or feel passionately about an issue.

All this would be a problem if one expected electronic town meetings to replace public-opinion polls and the ballot box. It is much less problematic, however, if teledemocracy is *added* to other means of public expression, each of which has its own defects—defects that can to some extent be compensated for by combining the various means. Take public-opinion polls, which play a major role in selecting candidates for office and affect policy between elections. Although the sampling methods used are accurate, and result in a cross-section of the public that is superior to anything to be hoped for in telepolling, the results can be deeply skewed by the phrasing of the questions. Even small changes in wording often lead to major changes in the public's response. Moreover, polltakers allow no time for deliberation or dialogue, and provide no information to those they query about the issues the pollsters are raising. Finally, those who show up at traditional ballot boxes do not themselves constitute a scientifically accurate cross-section of the public. They are more educated, more politically active, more affluent, and often more passionate about the issues than those who do not vote.

A key point is that actual voting allows citizens to have a say only once every two years at most. Present-day government, which directly affects numerous issues, from abortion to unemployment, from school busing to security of savings, requires ways to read the public mind between elections.

Electronic town meetings might reduce but would not expunge the deep sense of citizen disaffection, because they would address only part of the problem. The American political system suffers not only from a lack of opportunities to participate but also from the strong influence that special-interest groups wield upon national and state legislatures. Congress often knows quite well what the public prefers, but special-interest groups are a major source of the vast funds that members of Congress need for their election campaigns. Until this unholy alliance is severed, teledemocracy's primary contribution might well be to make it even clearer to the public that legislators often do not respond to the public will.

# Anthony Lewis
# "Not a Rose Garden"*

After the election, Republicans charged that the press was biased against George Bush. A conservative think tank produced a solemn report to the same effect.

Well, ladies and gentlemen, look at the press now and think again. Reporters and commentators are savaging Bill Clinton. They are doing what comes naturally to a free press: criticizing those in authority.

The battering the new President is taking arises from two episodes of his first 10 days in office: the forced withdrawal of his nominee for Attorney General, and his forced compromise on homosexuals in the armed forces. Those episodes carry important lessons on the problem of governing in contemporary America.

We have moved rapidly in this country toward a form of mass-participatory democracy. The American public learns instantly what happens in Washington, and members of that public massively and almost as instantly tell their leaders what they think.

The public awareness and response are a product of technology but also of something else: the discontent with government that was so evident in the 1992 election campaign. The sour feelings that brought Ross Perot 19 percent of the vote are still there, and focused on the new President.

The idea of participatory democracy is quite different from the political system that the founders of this country meant to create. James Madison and the other Framers of the Constitution feared the whim—the tyranny—of passing majorities. They tried to construct a system insulated from the winds of public passion.

But here we are, in a new age and a new reality with which every President will have to deal, starting with Bill Clinton. Doing so means not just yielding to instant public emotions but working to keep alive the Framers' constitutional design for a more reflective, more considered form of government.

The danger of mass participatory democracy is that it can be manipulated: shaped by ideologues and demagogues. That was the concern when Ross Perot proposed his "electronic town hall," which he said would make "the White House and Congress, like a ballet," pirouette around the stage. And the danger has been evident in these first days of the Clinton Administration.

The negative public reaction to Zoë Baird's past use of illegal aliens for child care—the telephone calls to senators—seemed genuine. Sensitized by the scandals of recent years, the public did not want an Attorney General who had violated a law.

But the protests against President Clinton's plan to end the ban on gay men and women in the services were different. To a considerable degree they were orchestrated by the religious right and conservative extremists.

Randall Terry of Operation Rescue, the group that tries to terrorize women out of having abortions, turned to the homosexual issue. He said, "We're avalanching [Congress] with phone calls and letters," because "sodomy is against God's law." The extreme-right talk show hosts on Thug Radio also denounced the Clinton plan.

So it is important to have some perspective on manifestations of public emotion. Randall Terry, Pat Robertson and others in the religious right opposed Bill Clinton in the election, as did the talk show hosts. They lost.

In such turbulent and dangerous conditions, it is harder than ever to be an effective President. And quite plainly Bill Clinton was insufficiently prepared for the storm. He misjudged the public temper, and he failed to pay due deference to Congressional egos.

One necessary corrective is obvious. President Clinton needs some aides with political sensitivity. He had picked one of the best, Harold Ickes, to be deputy chief of staff but held off when Mr. Ickes was attacked for having had as a legal client an unsavory labor union. Judging lawyers by their clients is a particularly poor form of guilt by association. If the President needs Mr. Ickes—and he does—he should give him the job.

But in the end what will be required in this new political world will be more of the old bully pulpit of Presidential leadership. If Bill Clinton wants to cut the deficit, if he wants to reform health care, he can overcome the opposition of vested interest only by persuading us.

# 10

# Elections

## Political Participation

*See Lowi and Ginsberg pp. 419–429 or brief edition, pp. 243–244*

*The votes are cast, the tallies are in, the winning candidate claims victory and a mandate to govern—the people have spoken! But just what have the people said when they have cast a plurality of votes for one candidate? In the first chapter of his book* The Responsible Electorate, *the political scientist V. O. Key, Jr., argued that the voice of the people is nothing more than an echo of the cacophony and hubbub of candidates and parties scrambling for popular support. "Even the most discriminating popular judgment," wrote Key, "can reflect only ambiguity, uncertainty, or even foolishness if those are the qualities of the input into the echo chamber."*

*Hence, what was the logic of the voting decision? Why do people vote as they do? Key, writing thirty years ago, believed that voting decisions are more logical than is often believed, that voters look beyond the "images and cultivation of style," to "substance of politics." His reading of the evidence led to his famous conclusion that "voters are not fools," and that the electorate makes collective decisions based on a concern for public policy, the performance of government, and the personalities of the candidates.*

## V. O. Key, Jr.
## "The Voice of the People: An Echo" from
### *The Responsible Electorate**

In his reflective moments even the most experienced politician senses a nagging curiosity about why people vote as they do. His power and his position depend upon the outcome of the mysterious rites we perform as opposing candidates harangue the multitudes who finally march to the polls to prolong the rule of their champion, to thrust him, ungratefully, back into the void of private life, or to raise to eminence a new tribune of the people. What kinds of appeals enable a candidate to win the favor of the great god, The People? What circumstances move voters to shift their preferences in this direction or that? What clever propaganda tactic or slogan led to this result? What mannerism of oratory or style of rhetoric produced another outcome? What band of electors rallied to this candidate to save the day for him? What policy of state attracted the devotion of another bloc of voters? What action repelled a third sector of the electorate?

The victorious candidate may claim with assurance that he has the answers to all such questions. He may regard his success as vindication of his beliefs about why voters vote as they do. And he may regard the swing of the vote to him as indubitably a response to the campaign positions he took, as an indication of the acuteness of his intuitive estimates of the mood of the people, and as a ringing manifestation of the esteem in which he is held by a discriminating public. This narcissism assumes its most repulsive form among election winners who have championed intolerance, who have stirred the passions and hatreds of people, or who have advocated causes known by decent men to be outrageous or dangerous in their long-run consequences. No functionary is more repugnant or more arrogant than the unjust man who asserts, with a color of truth, that he speaks from a pedestal of popular approbation.

It thus can be a mischievous error to assume, because a candidate wins, that a majority of the electorate shares his views on public questions, approves his past actions, or has specific expectations about his future conduct. Nor does victory establish that the candidate's campaign strategy, his image, his television style, or his fearless stand against cancer and polio turned the trick. The election returns establish only that the winner attracted a majority of the votes—assuming the existence of a modicum of rectitude in election administration. They tell us precious little about why the plurality was his.

For a glaringly obvious reason, electoral victory cannot be regarded as necessarily a popular ratification of a candidate's outlook. The voice of the people is but an echo. The output of an echo chamber bears an inevitable and invariable relation to the input. As candidates and parties clamor for attention and vie for popular support, the people's verdict can be no more than a selective reflection from among the alternatives and outlooks presented to them. Even the most discriminating popular judgment can reflect only ambiguity, uncertainty, or even foolishness if those are the qualities of the input into the echo chamber. A candidate may win despite his tactics and appeals rather than because of them. If the people can choose only from among rascals, they are certain to choose a rascal.

Scholars, though they have less at stake than do politicians, also have an abiding curiosity about why voters act as they do. In the past quarter of a century [since the 1940s] they have vastly enlarged their capacity to check the hunches born of their curiosities. The invention of the sample survey—the most widely known example of which is the Gallup poll—enabled them to make fairly trustworthy estimates of the characteristics and behaviors of large human populations. This method of mass observation revolutionized the study of politics—as well as the management of political campaigns. The new technique permitted large-scale tests to check the validity of old psychological and sociological theories of human behavior. These tests led to new hunches and new theories about voting behavior, which could, in turn, be checked and which thereby contributed to the extraordinary ferment in the social sciences during recent decades.

The studies of electoral behavior by survey methods cumulate into an imposing body of knowledge which conveys a vivid impression of the variety and subtlety of factors that enter into individual voting decisions. In their first stages in the 1930's the new electoral studies chiefly lent precision and verification to the working maxims of practicing politicians and to some of the crude theories of political speculators. Thus, sample surveys established that people did, indeed, appear to vote their pocketbooks. Yet the demonstration created its embarrassments because it also established that exceptions to the rule were numerous. Not all factory workers, for example, voted alike. How was the behavior of the deviants from "group interest" to be explained? Refinement after refinement of theory and analysis added complexity to the original simple explanation. By introducing a bit of psychological theory it could be demonstrated that factory workers with optimistic expectations tended less to be governed by pocketbook considerations than did those whose outlook was gloomy. When a little social psychology was stirred into the analysis, it could be established that identifications formed early in life, such as attachments to political parties, also reinforced or resisted the pull of the interest of the moment. A sociologist, bringing to play the conceptual tools of his trade, then could show that those factory workers who associate intimately with like-minded persons on the average vote with greater solidarity than do social isolates. Inquiries conducted with great ingenuity along many such lines have enormously broadened our knowledge of the factors associated with the responses of people to the stimuli presented to them by political campaigns.

Yet, by and large, the picture of the voter that emerges from a combination of the folklore of practical politics and the findings of the new electoral studies is not a pretty one. It is not a portrait of citizens moving to considered decision as they play their solemn role of making and unmaking governments. The older tradition from practical politics may regard the voter as an erratic and irrational fellow susceptible to manipulation by skilled humbugs. One need not live through many campaigns to observe politicians, even successful politicians, who act as though they regarded the people as manageable fools. Nor does a heroic conception of the voter emerge from the new analyses of electoral behavior. They can be added up to a conception of voting not as a civic decision but as an almost purely deterministic act. Given knowledge of certain characteristics of a voter—his occupation, his residence, his religion, his national origin, and perhaps certain of his attitudes—one can predict with a high probability the direction of his vote. The actions of persons are made to appear to be only predictable and automatic responses to campaign stimuli.

\* \* \*

Conceptions and theories of the way voters behave do not raise solely arcane problems to be disputed among the democratic and antidemocratic theorists or questions to be settled by the elegant techniques of the analysts of electoral behavior. Rather, they touch upon profound issues at the heart of the problem of the nature and workability of systems of popular government. Obviously the perceptions of the behavior of the electorate held by political leaders, agitators, and activists condition, if they do not fix, the types of appeals politicians employ as they seek popular support. These perceptions—or theories—affect the nature of the input to the echo chamber, if we may revert to our earlier figure, and thereby control its output. They may govern, too, the kinds of actions that governments take as they look forward to the next election. If politicians perceive the electorate as responsive to father images, they will give it father images. If they see voters as most certainly responsive to nonsense, they will give them nonsense. If they see voters as susceptible to delusion, they will delude them. If they see an electorate receptive to the cold, hard realities, they will give it the cold, hard realities.

In short, theories of how voters behave acquire importance not because of their effects on voters, who may proceed blithely unaware of them. They gain significance because of their effects, both potentially and in reality, on candidates and other political leaders. If leaders believe the route to victory is by projection of images and cultivation of styles rather than by advocacy of policies to cope with the problems of the country, they will project images and cultivate styles to the neglect of the substance of politics. They will abdicate their prime function in a democratic system, which amounts, in essence, to the assumption of the risk of trying to persuade us to lift ourselves by our bootstraps.

Among the literary experts on politics there are those who contend that, because of the development of tricks for the manipulation of the masses, practices of political leadership in the management of voters have moved far toward the conversion of election campaigns into obscene parodies of the models set up by democratic idealists. They point to the good old days when politicians were deep thinkers, eloquent orators, and farsighted statesmen. Such estimates of the course of change in social institutions must be regarded with reserve. They may be only manifestations of the inverted optimism of aged and melancholy men who, estopped from hope for the future, see in the past a satisfaction of their yearning for greatness in our political life.

Whatever the trends may have been, the perceptions that leadership elements of democracies hold of the modes of response of the electorate must always be a matter of fundamental significance. Those perceptions determine the nature of the voice of the people, for they determine the character of the input into the echo chamber. While the output may be governed by the nature of the input, over the longer run the properties of the echo chamber may themselves be altered. Fed a steady diet of buncombe [bunkum], the people may come to expect and to respond with highest predictability to buncombe. And those leaders most skilled in the propagation of buncombe may gain lasting advantage in the recurring struggles for popular favor.

The perverse and unorthodox argument of this little book is that voters are not fools. To be sure, many individual voters act in odd ways indeed; yet in the large the electorate behaves about as rationally and responsibly as we should expect, given the clarity of the alternatives presented to it and the character of the information available to it. In American presidential campaigns of recent decades the portrait of the American electorate that develops from the data is not one of an electorate strait-jacketed by social determinants or moved by subconscious urges triggered by devilishly skillful propagandists. It is rather one of an electorate moved by concern about central and relevant questions of public policy, of governmental performance, and of executive personality. Propositions so uncompromisingly stated inevitably represent overstatements. Yet to the extent that they can be shown to resemble the reality, they are propositions of basic importance for both the theory and the practice of democracy.

To check the validity of this broad interpretation of the behavior of voters, attention will center on the movements of voters across party lines as they reacted to the issues, events, and candidates of presidential campaigns between 1936 and 1960. Some Democratic voters of one election turned Republican at the next; others stood pat. Some Republicans of one presidential season voted Democratic four years later; others remained loyal Republicans. What motivated these shifts, sometimes large and sometimes small, in voter affection? How did the standpatters differ from the switchers? What led them to stand firmly by their party preference of four years earlier? Were these actions governed by images, moods, and other irrelevancies; or were they expressions of judgments about the sorts of questions that, hopefully, voters will weigh as they responsibly cast their ballots? On these matters evidence is available that is impressive in volume, if not always so complete or so precisely relevant as hindsight would wish. If one perseveres through the analysis of this extensive body of information, the proposition that the voter is not so irrational a fellow after all may become credible.

## How Voters Decide

*See Lowi and Ginsberg, pp. 441–444 or brief edition, pp. 253–255*

*Voters are alienated by the negative campaigning and dirty politics that characterize so many electoral campaigns ranging from city council to the presidency. Given the perceived level of "mudslinging," it is difficult to imagine that campaigning has ever been more vicious than it is today. However, as Eileen Shields West makes clear, comparative history reveals that campaigning today is positively tame by the standards of nineteenth-century political etiquette. Just to put things in perspective, try to imagine Bob Dole claiming that "murder, robbery, rape, adultery and incest will be openly taught and practiced" if Bill Clinton is reelected in 1996, as Thomas Jefferson's opponents warned would surely happen if that "mean-spirited, low-lived fellow, the son of a half-breed Indian squaw, sired by a Virginian mulatto father" was elected. One of the big differences in campaigning in the two political eras is that today's media at least*

> attempt to report news objectively while nineteenth-century newspapers were propaganda machines for their favorite candidates. West is not trying to argue that campaigning today is substantive and issue-based; however, it is useful to put things in a historical context.

# Eileen Shields West
## " 'Give 'em Hell' These Days Is a Figure of Speech"*

This has been the year of the Seven Democratic Dwarfs and alleged wimpery, of demands for medical and military records, of titillated talk about monkey business afloat and lamentation at the cruelty of one campaign aide for blowing the whistle on oral plagiarism committed on TV. The race for the Presidency is getting too nasty, some people aver, and there is a tendency to blame it on what is seen as a tasteless and permissive age.

But whatever is wrong with American political campaigns, they have not become more salacious or more savage. Quite the reverse. "What respectable person today," political expert Paul Boller Jr. asks, "would think of calling one of the candidates for the highest office in the land a carbuncled-faced old drunkard? Or a howling atheist?" Or, for that matter, "a pickpocket, thief, traitor, lecher, syphilitic, gorilla, anarchist, murderer"? Nobody, of course. When the Senate minority leader, Robert Dole, asked Vice President George Bush to stop lying about his (Dole's) political record, the country's pundits acted as if Dole had practically frothed at the mouth.

But in the good (or bad) old days, Dole's comment would have been the height of politesse. Starting with the Founding Fathers (Washington excepted), candidates for the Presidency or their cohorts verbally assaulted each other in ways today not only unspeakable but virtually unthinkable. Verbal violence during Presidential campaigns was as American as apple pie. President Martin Van Buren, for example, was charged with wearing corsets and taking more baths than a real man should. As late as 1888, trying to give folks back home an idea of what a Yankee political campaign was like, Britain's Lord Bryce described it as a "tempest of invective and calumny. . . . Imagine all the accusations brought against all the candidates for the 670 seats in the English Parliament," he wrote, "concentrated on one man, and read . . . daily for three months."

Starting in the election of 1800 ( John Adams versus Thomas Jefferson) campaign songs appeared, too. By 1840, when plebeian beginnings in a log cabin appealed to the mob, the first full-scale campaign songbook helped the Whig candidate, William Henry Harrison, the hero of the Battle of Tippecanoe, defeat Van Buren by transforming Harrison from a Vir-

---

* Eileen, Shields West, " 'Give 'em Hell' These Days Is a Figure of Speech" in the *Smithsonian* (October 1988). Reprinted with permission from the author.

ginia aristocrat (who owned a Georgian mansion and sipped gentle-man's whiskey) into a popular, log-cabin-dwelling, hard-cider-swigging hill-billy.

## "HE'S A LITTLE SQUIRT-WIRT-WIRT"

The tunefully reinforced image caught on and, try as they might, the Dem-ocrats could never discredit it, nor expunge another song-inspired in-ference that their own hapless candidate, President Van Buren, was a pantywaist. Democratic protests were drowned out by rousing choruses of "Old Tip he wears a homespun coat / He has no ruffled shirt-wirt-wirt / But Mat has the golden plate / And he's a little squirt-wirt-wirt." The wirt-wirts were embellished by spitting (usually tobacco juice) through the singer's teeth. It was that kind of campaign year. Out in Illinois a lawyer named Lincoln, running for the state legislature, could (and did) reach over to rip open his Democratic opponent's tightly buttoned cloth coat to reveal the ruffled silk shirt and velvet vest hidden beneath.

By then, political campaigning had become a staple of American en-tertainment. Politics is "the only pleasure an American knows," Alexis de Tocqueville wrote. "Even the women frequently attend public meetings and listen to political harangues as a recreation from their household la-bors." Men, and presumably women too, though they were 80 years from the vote, were mightily interested in the goings-on of the 1840 campaign, which notably contributed to what Lord Bryce would call the "boom-ing" quality of American politics. The "boom," Bryce thought, struck the "imagination of those who in country hamlets read of the doings in the great city." American elections, Bryce held, were largely a matter of "booming."

More eligible voters (80 percent of about 2.4 million) cast their ballots in the 1840 campaign than had ever voted in a Presidential election, sweeping Harrison into office. It wasn't the public's fault that he was 68 years old, delivered an interminable Inaugural speech without a hat or coat, then died of pneumonia a month later. And though the rudeness of booming is now deplored, during the last half of the 19th century, when booming and outrageous incivility were at their peak, 75 to 85 percent of the electorate voted.

That figure compares sadly with all our recent elections when barely 50 percent of the eligible voters managed to get to the polls to choose the President. Every four years the experts sit around wondering why this is so. But most agree with political writer David Broder that Presidential cam-paigns, "whether or not they appeal to the mind at all, they don't stir peo-ple at the gut level the way they used to."

More than anything else, television gets blamed for what it has done to candidates and conventions, where the press seems to outnumber the pol-iticians a thousand to one, and everybody grows accustomed to candidates trying to say as little as possible in answer to the same questions, asked again and again. Whatever the cause, a trip back to some of the most vicious campaigns—a time when libel suits were rare and incivility was in fine flower—provides a useful and diverting perspective.

By 1800, the aura that had somewhat protected the justly sacrosanct figure of George Washington had already given way to savage partisanship. His two terms were followed by one term for John Adams, a plump, brilliant but sometimes silly man who loved grand titles and was secretly mocked by enemies as "His Rotundity." The system of electoral votes, since modified, played strange tricks in the early Presidential races, especially since the candidate who came in second became Vice President. During his term (1797–1801), Adams was derided as the "President by three votes," because in 1796 he received only 71 electoral votes (to rival Jefferson's 68). When the Federalists chose to run Adams again, with Gen. Charles Cotesworth Pinckney of South Carolina as his running mate, the new Republican Party ran Jefferson with Aaron Burr.

## "Head Itching for a Crowny"

The agrarian, egalitarian Republicans (who gradually became what history knows as Jeffersonian Democrats) swiftly spread a rumor that President Adams planned to marry one of his sons to the daughter of George III in order to start an American dynasty with economic ties to England. Comic rumor even had it that George Washington himself got Adams to change his mind by donning his Revolutionary uniform and threatening to run him through with his patriot's sword. "See Johnny at the helm of State," Jeffersonians chorused, "Head itching for a crowny, / He longs to be, like Georgy, great, / And pulls Tom Jeffer downy!"

Adams had a sharp tongue. He once referred to Alexander Hamilton, his party's brilliant Secretary of the Treasury, as the "bastard brat of a Scotch pedlar." But under Republican onslaughts he often managed to stay cool. When it was put about that he had sent Pinckney to England in a U.S. frigate to procure four pretty girls as mistresses—for them both—Adams genially replied: "I do declare upon my honor, if this be true General Pinckney has cheated me out of my two."

Other Federalists fought back, questioning Jefferson's courage during the Revolution, mocking him as a dilettante inventor who dreamed up nothing but "Gim-Krackery." But that was the high road compared to this biographical précis of the sage of Monticello: "Tom Jefferson . . . a mean-spirited, low-lived fellow, the son of a half-breed Indian squaw, sired by a Virginia mulatto father . . . raised wholly on hoe-cake made of coarse-ground Southern corn, bacon and hominy, with an occasional . . . fricasseed bullfrog." Were he elected, an editorial in the Federalist *Connecticut Courant* warned readers, "Murder, robbery, rape, adultery and incest will be openly taught and practiced."

In a land still largely agrarian, the Republicans had won the support of country folk and (thanks largely to Jefferson's friend James Madison) were better organized. Even so, history records a neck-and-neck election result and bitter finagling because of the peculiar ground rules regarding the Presidency and the electoral votes. The two Republicans each got 73, Adams 65. This forced a runoff vote in the House of Representatives between Burr and Jefferson. On the 36th ballot, Jefferson was chosen. Federalists promptly cried "President by No Votes!" But the political power of the Northeast had been broken, at least for the moment. Years later a New York congressman mourned those good old days, "when a Federalist could knock a Republican down in the streets [of New York] and not be questioned about it."

In 1816 Gen. Andrew Jackson, surely one of the most combative men in American history, uncharacteristically wrote President-elect James Monroe, saying "Now is the time to exterminate the monster called party spirit." It was true that during the War of 1812, partisan loyalties, and to some extent sectional interests, had been submerged in a national desire to fight off the British. Americans felt good about themselves, as we would put it today, in part because of Jackson's astounding victory in the Battle of New Orleans. What has come to be known as the Era of Good Feelings was about to begin.

Largely thanks to Jackson, it did not last long. By 1824 he had run for President himself and got the most popular votes, only to be robbed, he thought, by the pesky Electoral College. In a runoff of the three leading candidates, the House of Representatives found itself having to choose between John Adams' diplomat son, John Quincy Adams; Secretary of the Treasury William Crawford; and Jackson. Henry Clay, Speaker of the House, had been eliminated and now used his influence to elect Adams.

What really stuck in Jackson's craw was, to him, the certain evidence that a deal had been struck between Adams and Clay, who was speedily appointed the new Secretary of State. Jacksonian anger at this "corrupt bargain," made, as he mildly put it, "by the Judas of the West" (Clay was from over the mountains in Kentucky), fueled the campaign of 1828. Adams' National Republicans, heirs to the old Federalists, stood for stronger central government, more federal expenditure and a higher tariff, but the issues took a backseat to a personality struggle between Adams, seen as an effete representative of Eastern power and privilege, and Old Hickory, a brawling, rough-tongued, frontier war hero, clearly a man of the people. The confrontation also helped create a new populist party, the Jackson Party, which swiftly became the new national Democratic Party. It also fueled a campaign almost too silly, too scurrilous to be believed.

Adams was a brilliant and dedicated public servant who rose at 5 each morning and worked pretty much without ceasing until 5 in the afternoon. But Democrats accused him of being a gambler because he once bought a secondhand billiard table for the White House. "When we find the fathers and mothers of our country . . . persuading young men from practices which lead to destruction," one Jacksonian editor soberly moralized, "we greatly fear that the too frequent answer will be, 'Why, the President plays billiards!' "

That was the polite part. They also asserted that the President and his wife had had premarital relations, and freely labeled him "The Pimp" on the strength of their unfounded charge that, during his term as ambassador to Russia (1809–14), Adams had procured an American girl for Czar Alexander I. Jackson was more vulnerable than Adams in this area, because he had been obliged to remarry his beloved wife Rachel when it turned out that her divorce (a scandal in itself) was not legal. He had to bear editorials and rhetorical speeches asking: "Ought a convicted adulteress and her paramour be placed in the highest offices of this free and Christian land?" Famous for a hot temper and for executing men during his military campaigns, he ground his teeth and listened as gleeful Adams supporters sang: "Oh, Andy! Oh Andy, / How many men have you hanged in your life? / How many weddings make a wife?"

Beside such things, routine charges that his mother was a "COMMON PROSTITUTE, brought to this country by the British soldiers!" perhaps set the celebrated duelist's adrenaline flowing. Nothing deterred the rolling wave of Jackson people from street demonstrations, barbecues and, above all, innumerable plantings of Jackson's symbol, the hickory pole, in parks and on street corners all over the country. On November 4, 1828, just before the election, Jackson's people tore up the sidewalk in front of Tammany Hall and the pro-Adams *New-York Spectator* sneered, "The pole was erected amid loud yells . . . the beer-barrels were rolled out; and it required no vivid imagination to distinguish in the uproar the yell of the hyæna, the cry of the panther and the whoop of the Winnebagoes."

The turnout was heavy, three times larger than in 1824. Old Hickory won by a comfortable margin. His Inauguration party, with common folk overrunning the White House, breaking furniture, spitting tobacco juice in corners and leaving muddy footprints on the carpets, is regarded as a classic symbol of democracy triumphant. But it was not only Jackson's victory, but his practices as President which insured that savage campaign partisanship would continue in Presidential politics. Jackson increased the power of the Presidency enormously. Unlike Adams, Jackson threw his cronies into office, ushering in a full-scale spoils system that used patronage mercilessly for political purposes, thus strengthening the hold of Democrats on power and preference. So much for exterminating the monster called party spirit.

The scene shifts past the Civil War, when the issues of slavery and the survival of the Union were agonizing and profound. By 1884 Reconstruction was over, America was exploding westward, business was booming and it was open season on campaign madness again. Republicans (a far different party from that of 1800) favored a protective tariff higher than the Democrats, but otherwise there was little difference between the party platforms. It was time for a campaign of pure theater or, as one critic has put it, a contest between the "copulative habits of one and the prevaricative habits of the other."

The one was Democrat Grover Cleveland, a Buffalo lawyer who, in three years, had leapfrogged from being his city's mayor to the governorship of New York to Presidential candidacy. The other was Republican James Blaine from Maine, an ex-Congressman and former Secretary of State.

Cleveland was a bit rough around the edges, a man reputed to wash down his dinner with beer and then relieve himself out of the window of his law office. (He had once been sued, in fact, by a passer-by who got in the way.) Cleveland was stoutly honest, though, and as a politician he had made many of the right enemies. His campaign slogan, "A Public Office is a Public Trust," stood in marked contrast to Blaine, a charming, sophisticated and sometimes funny man who campaigned as the "Plumed Knight," but who was also justly known as "Slippery Jim," a dishonest politician.

Blaine was a veteran legislator and skilled campaigner, of course, and his partisans soon were successfully poking fun at plodding Cleveland's inexperience and mushroomlike arrival on the political scene. Then on July 21, the gods seemed to deliver the Presidency to Blaine on a silver platter. There, under a banner headline on the front page of the Buffalo *Telegraph* was the shocking revelation that Governor Cleveland had an illegitimate, 10-year-old son by Maria Halpin, a widow who had sewed collars for a living. Some of Cleveland's advisors rushed to Albany, expecting denial. But Cleveland had always told his associates, "Whatever you say, tell the truth," and that was exactly what he did now. Many years before, he admitted, he'd cavorted with Halpin, and had since supported the child, though he was never sure it was really his. When advisers wrung their hands at the political implications of the affair, he is said to have added, "I don't believe the American people want a gelding in the White House."

Republicans exulted and paraded around in knightly armor sporting brightly colored plumes, gleefully singing "Ma! Ma! Where's my Pa? Gone to the White House—Hah! Hah! Hah!" The president of Amherst College told his students that only voters with corrupt morals could support Cleveland, who was charitably characterized as a "coarse debauchee who would bring harlots to Washington."

How the campaign might have turned out if Cleveland's amorous proclivities had remained the major issue, no one knows. Just in time, letters turned up new evidence that Blaine had been engaged in some shady bond deals, one with the unheeded postscript: "Burn this letter." Blaine denied wrongdoing, while cartoonists like Thomas Nast pilloried him as a creature drenched in loot, wearing three very bedraggled plumes. It was the turn of Democrats to chant: "Blaine! Blaine! Jay Gould Blaine! The Continental Liar from the state of Maine!"

Cleveland won by a whisker—23,000 votes out of a total of 9.7 million cast for both candidates—and chortling Democrats sang: "Hurray for Maria! Hurray for the Kid! / I voted for Cleveland, and I'm damned glad I did!"

The election of 1896 was an amazing show, too. It was not scandalous, but rather a study in contrasting character and political style which illustrated the hold that Presidential campaigning had upon the American public. It also marked the permanent arrival in American politics of the prominent as well as powerful campaign manager in the person of Cleveland businessman Mark Hanna, who had helped his unprepossessing protégé, Republican William McKinley, become Governor of Ohio.

McKinley was a high-tariff man and wanted to campaign, as much as he wanted to campaign at all, on that issue. But his Democratic opponent, a 36-year-old Nebraska Congressman named William Jennings Bryan, wouldn't let him. As a Western agrarian and Populist with a golden voice, Bryan had a bimetallist bee in his bonnet. These were depression years and bimetallists, especially Bryan, believed with a crusading fervor that the poor would have more money and the economy would look up if the country went off the gold standard.

## Speeches at the Rate of 30 a Day

McKinley believed that bimetallism, which called for unlimited coinage of silver, was nonsense and initially he refused to campaign about it. Quite a few conservative Democrats agreed and quit the party. To take his problem to the people, Bryan ran a whistle-stop campaign so successful that it forced succeeding Presidential candidates to follow suit. He traveled 18,000 miles, gave more than 600 speeches, sometimes at a rate of 30 a day, brought his message to five million people and laid a rhetorical mark on the American language with the ringing phrase: "You shall not press down upon the brow of labor this crown of thorns. You shall not crucify mankind upon a cross of gold."

McKinley was unimpressed, but Hanna grew nervous and urged his candidate to go on the road. McKinley refused to budge from his porch. "I might as well put up a trapeze on my front lawn and compete with some professional athlete," he said, "as go out speaking against Bryan." In the end, however, he agreed to have delegations come to him in Canton and said he would speak out for gold.

With a little help from Hanna, gold standard supporters began to appear. They wore gold neckties and gold hatbands and some rode gold-trimmed bicycles. They brought McKinley gifts: cheese, butter, watermelons and even live American eagles. Each delegation chairman would read a statement. McKinley would smile and listen, "like a child looking at Santa Claus." Then, his mother at his side, he stood on a chair in a long double-breasted coat with a carnation in his buttonhole and offered some pithy remark. One such message, succinct and economically sound: "Free silver will degrade your money."

By November 3 he and Hanna had outdone Bryan. Where the neat lawn had been, there was plain brown earth, looking "as if a herd of buffalo had passed that way." The white picket fence and grape arbor had long since been demolished by souvenir hunters. And the front porch threatened to collapse. But some 750,000 visitors had trooped past McKinley's home.

Democrats decried the special excursion rates the railroads had been induced to charge for a trip to Canton. Hanna was cartooned as pig-eyed and bloated, wearing a suit checkered with dollar signs. But the election turned out two million more voters than in 1892 and Bryan was decisively defeated.

"My relatives told me about the fun of packing up a wagon to hear William Jennings Bryan speak," the 60-ish national columnist and political commentator Hugh Sidey once told me. "It was like a neighborhood barn raising. Even when Franklin Roosevelt came through on the train in 1934, a lot of our neighbors went down in their Model A Fords, hoisted their kids up to see and brought a picnic lunch, instead of going to the movies."

### TRUMAN VERSUS REPUBLICAN "BLOODSUCKERS"

The excitement of such campaigns is now mainly a fading memory, and like Sidey's, most of the recollections are secondhand. Yet FDR was not the last President to go to the people in this way. That honor belongs to Harry Truman and the legendary "Give 'em hell, Harry" whistle-stop campaign of 1948, when Truman, refusing to believe newspapers, experts and straws in the wind, took off around the country, his rimless spectacles glittering, and let Tom Dewey and the "no-account, do-nothing, Republican, Eightieth Congress" have it.

Sometimes making 14 short speeches a day from the back platform of the train, he called the Republicans "bloodsuckers." Noting that they had "already stuck a pitchfork in the farmer's back," he told the folks in Missouri and Kansas and Iowa, "I wonder how many times you have to be hit on the head before you find out who's hitting you." All the rich Republicans would do, he said, was "let a little trickle down off the table like the crumbs that fell to Lazarus."

The press and the pundits wrote Truman off entirely. Though Alice Roosevelt Longworth said Dewey looked like the "bridegroom on a wedding cake," *Life* referred to him simply as "The next President," while the *Kiplinger Magazine* devoted an issue to what Dewey would do when, not if, he was elected. On the campaign train, one day, campaign adviser Clark Clifford tried to hide a copy of *Newsweek*, which had just polled 50 leading political commentators, reporting that not a single "expert" had picked Truman. But the President got hold of the copy anyway. He was not dismayed. "He looked at me," Clifford recalls, "and said, 'You know, not one of those 50 fellows has enough sense to pound sand in a rat hole!' "

And then came television.

## DEBATING THE ISSUES: DO ELECTIONS AND VOTING MATTER?

*See Lowi and Ginsberg, pp. 420–421 or brief edition, pp. 266–277*

*The votes are cast, the tallies are in, the winning candidate claims victory and a mandate to govern—the people have spoken! But just what have the people said when they cast a plurality of the votes for one candidate? In his book,* The Responsible Electorate, *political scientist V. O. Key, Jr., argued that the voice of the people was nothing more than an echo of the cacophony and hubbub of candidates and parties scrambling for popular support. "Even the most discriminating popular judgment," writes Key, "can reflect only ambiguity, uncertainty, or even foolishness if those are the qualities of the input into the echo chamber." So how are we to interpret elections? Most political commentators implicitly reject the notion that elections are random and confused outcomes, searching instead for the collective meaning of elections and the mandate given by the electorate. Needless to say, the interpretations of the mandate are wide ranging.*

*Consider the two interpretations of President Clinton's victory in 1996 by Will Marshall and Joshua Muravhcik. For Marshall, Clinton won for what he did right (correctly and politically). By reclaiming what Marshall identifies as the progressive center, and rejecting the politics of the far left, Clinton was able to appeal to a broad base of voters concerned about crime, the quality of life for their children, fiscal discipline, smaller government, and of course economic security. Marshall argues that Clinton could lead a more explicitly defined progressive effort by building upon key strategies such as the reform of popular entitlement programs, and government reform for budget savings that can be reinvested in new progressive programs. The dominance of the far left in Democratic politics, Marshall argues, has long inhibited the opportunity for progressive reforms that, if successful, could possibly parallel those of two past Democratic presidents, Woodrow Wilson and Franklin D. Roosevelt.*

*For Joshua Maravchik, however, it wasn't the progressive nature of Clinton's agenda, but rather its very Republican-ness that won him the election. From family values to law-and-order to balancing the budget, Maravchik argues that Clinton performed an amazing "about face" from an early liberal agenda of racial and gender preferences, tax hikes, defense cuts, and a foray into developing a national health care system, to a centrist ideology that broke with Democratic orthodoxy. This more centrist Clinton, he argues, appealed to voters, but the Republicans in Congress facilitated the victory by appearing more "right-wing" than conservative. Their "anti-government zeal" presented the party as the radicals, a position once assumed by the left, and presented Clinton the opportunity to capitalize on the center. Clinton's success is not the Democratic Party's, however. Maravchik also suggests why the Republicans were able to hold Congress in 1996, but argues that whatever party can develop and serve a "mature conservatism" will succeed following the election of 2000.*

# Will Marshall
# "Why Did Clinton Win?"*

Bill Clinton's re-election not only broke the Republicans' so-called "lock" on presidential elections, it foreshadowed the emergence of a new progressive majority in America. For left-leaning Democrats, however, there's a big hitch: The new progressivism aims not, as they would like, at European-style social democracy, but at a new political synthesis that decentralizes decisions, injects choice and competition into the public sector, respects the prerogatives of civil society, and replaces welfare-state paternalism with a government that equips people to take care of themselves.

In trouncing an estimable opponent, Clinton joined Woodrow Wilson and Franklin Roosevelt as the only Democratic presidents in this century to win back-to-back elections. The parallels are intriguing: Wilson and FDR were pivotal figures who transformed their dispirited and rudderless party into a vital instrument of reform and national leadership. Clinton also has a historic opportunity to change the course of U.S. politics by converting Democrats from a party that defends narrow interests and outdated programs into a modernizing force in the nation's public life.

The election vindicated Clinton's "New Democrat" renovation of the progressive agenda, a project that is expanding the party's appeal even as it raises hackles among liberal elites. Clinton set the tone for a mold-breaking campaign by declaring, in January, that the "era of big government is over." Boosted by a strong economy, which he linked to White House policies of fiscal restraint and trade expansion, Clinton stressed such social and moral concerns as drugs and tobacco, juvenile crime and television sex and violence. In August, Clinton overrode fierce liberal opposition to sign a landmark bill fulfilling his key 1992 campaign pledge to "end welfare as we know it."

Liberals are certainly right to point as well to Clinton's defense of Medicare, education, and environmental protection as key factors in his success. What they ignore, however, is the predicate Clinton himself never failed to mention on the hustings—that he would protect these programs within the constraints of fiscal discipline. In short, Clinton's winning formula in 1996 was a canny synthesis of traditional Democratic commitments and New Democrat innovations. While the former appeals to core Democratic constituencies, the latter has greatest potential for enlarging the party's base.

In a postelection study for the Democratic Leadership Council (DLC), Mark Penn, a key Clinton strategist and pollster, found that voters recognized and explicitly endorsed Clinton's New Democrat agenda.

* Will Marshall, "Why Did Clinton Win?" in *The American Prospect* (March/April 1997). Reprinted by permission from *The American Prospect* 31 (March/April). Copyright 1997 The American Prospect, P.O. Box 383080, Cambridge, MA 02138. All rights reserved.

It is specifically this distinction between Clinton and what the people view as traditional Democratic ways of doing business that made voters—many of whom had not voted for Democratic presidential candidates in the past—willing to vote for him in 1996, even as they were voting against Democratic House candidates.

Though drawn to Clinton's new ideas, voters were warier of congressional Democrats, whom they saw as more likely to cling to old-time liberalism. Although voters described Clinton as a different kind of Democrat, by a margin of 57 to 37 percent, they also said, by a margin of 54 to 41, that the Democratic Party is pretty much the same. Penn notes that on issues where Clinton successfully staked out the center—balancing the budget, crime, and welfare—Clinton's approval rating was nine or ten percentage points higher than that of House Democrats. He concludes:

Had the Democrats moved with the President toward more mainstream positions, they would have retaken the House. Their lesson for the future is clear: earn credibility by proving fiscal responsibility and centrist moderation. Only by establishing these more centrist credentials will the Democrats acquire the credibility they need to be heard on the rest of their issues, such as education, the environment and protection of entitlements.

## The Left's Interpretation

No sooner were the ballots counted when a new left-labor group, the Campaign for America's Future, came out spinning. Its postmortem, based on a poll by former Clinton pollster Stan Greenberg, held that Clinton won primarily because he defended Medicare, education, and the environment: his "centrist" stands on other issues were secondary.

To a certain extent, this is true—but only because Clinton succeeded in defining the ground on which the election was contested. The real key to Clinton's victory was his strategy of seizing the political center abandoned long ago by liberal activists and elites and more recently by the new Republican majority in Congress. This forced Bob Dole to the right while reassuring independents and suburbanites unnerved by the Gingrich "revolution" that they could vote for a Democratic president without giving him a mandate for going back to big government liberalism.

Had Clinton heeded his leftish critics, had he failed to endorse the goal of a balanced budget, had he saved the roundly despised welfare system, had he ceded crime and other social and family concerns to his conservative opponents, the Republicans once again would have waged a presidential campaign on familiar and favorable terrain. Democrats' defense of Medicare and domestic programs would have appeared in an entirely different light—as more evidence that the party remains bent simply on preserving the bureaucratic status quo. Instead, Senator Dole grew visibly frustrated as the old GOP attack lines and supply-side elixir failed to work their customary magic. Republicans tried to cast Clinton as a conventional liberal, but the public simply wouldn't buy it.

Clinton's preemption of issues that Republicans used to control elicited predictable squawking on the left about abandoning principles and "moving to the right." In fact, Clinton and the New Democrats are bringing the party home to a politics grounded in the moral outlook as well as the economic aspirations of the "forgotten middle class."

Sooner or later, the party's left will have to resolve its ambivalence on questions of values. Opinion surveys and election results alike confirm that Americans are worried at least as much about social as economic problems. Nonetheless, the labor-left axis insists that the party should dwell exclusively on the tried-and-true themes of class warfare, now rechristened as "economic populism." Afraid of being accosted at the cash machine by some remorseless juvenile with a Tech-9? Concerned that the breakdown of marriage and family is yielding a bitter harvest of damaged and vulnerable children? These, we are instructed, are Republican issues; real Democrats talk about stagnant wages, job insecurity, and corporate perfidy.

And we really should talk about these things. But the left's economic reductionism and pessimism can only narrow the party's appeal. This approach discounts Clinton's success in restoring economic confidence and links the party's success to economic misery. It trivializes citizens' well-founded concerns about the social and moral climate in which they raise their children. And it patronizes working Americans by casting them as victimized proles moved only by appeals to class resentment and material self-interest.

## THE EMERGING COALITION

If a new progressive majority is aborning, what are its critical elements? Where is its social base?

By blunting traditional GOP advantages, Clinton was able to win back for Democrats key voter groups like independents, married voters with children, and middle-class families in general, Penn reports. For example, Clinton scored significant gains among people with annual incomes between $30,000 and $75,000—precisely the average working families whose past defections from the party fueled the GOP ascendancy in presidential politics after 1968.

The enormous margin Clinton rolled up among women voters provides a striking illustration of the New Democrat synthesis at work. Women—suburban and younger women especially—strongly endorsed Clinton's defense of key federal programs against the GOP onslaught. At the same time, they backed fiscal discipline, vigorous anticrime efforts, and especially Clinton's table-turning discourse on family values, in which he emphasized ways in which government can help parents shield their children from harmful influences, from drugs to school disorder to the marketing of sex and violence.

In addition, Clinton tallied big gains among Asian and Hispanic voters, perhaps in reaction to the Republican Party's restrictive stands on social benefits for legal immigrants and on immigration generally. "In thinking about the future, the Democratic party needs to continue to consolidate its support among the middle class and to energize support among its new key constituencies—namely, youth, women and Hispanics," concludes Penn.

To build a new progressive majority, it is imperative that Democrats build a constituency in the new economy. Just as industrial workers formed the backbone of the New Deal coalition, the party needs to attract the knowledge workers who are emerging as the dominant force in the information economy. Dubbed "wired workers" by Morley Winograd and Dudley Buffa, they transcend the old "white collar, blue collar" dichotomy. Whether they work in factories or offices, wired workers use computers, have more flexibility in deciding how to do their jobs, and often work in unstructured settings and as part of teams.

According to recent research by Winograd and Buffa, wired workers now constitute 51 percent of California's workforce and 31 percent of its electorate, and their ranks are growing rapidly. In many respects, wired workers look like the quintessential New Democrats: They are optimistic about their economic prospects; they are for choice and competition in education and against race and gender preferences; they are impatient with the ideological ax-grinding of the left-right debate; and, they favor a smaller, nonbureaucratic form of government activism that equips people to help themselves.

Whereas the left's economic story mainly conveys fear of change and animosity toward U.S. businesses—usually depicted with all the subtlety of a Snidely Whiplash cartoon—progressives must craft a new narrative that appropriates the new symbols, lexicon, and techniques of the information age. Democrats must remain especially attentive to the inequities and insecurities generated by today's rapid economic changes. But basic electoral math dictates that a new progressive majority must include upwardly mobile Americans as well as those caught in the downdraft of the global economy.

In short, Democrats need to develop a new political economy, a new social compact, and new ways of governing tailored to the new conditions of postindustrial America. From its stress on marketled growth and open trade to its attempts to redesign government and anchor social policy in the mainstream values of work, family, and mutual responsibility, the Clinton administration has made the first, tentative steps in the right direction. It has established important beachheads in the struggle to bring about structural changes in government and the nation's policy agenda. These include:

- Expanding public support for the working poor, through a $21 billion increase in the earned income tax credit.

- Cutting in half the federal deficit as well as slowing spending growth.

- Injecting choice and competition in public education through charter schools.
- Helping communities defend themselves through community policing and more police on the streets.
- Replacing the *federal* entitlement to welfare with an obligation to work.
- Stimulating community initiative and economic development in the inner cities.
- Reinventing government, including a sharp reduction in the federal workforce.
- Linking increased college aid to national service through the AmeriCorps initiative.
- Expanding trade and assisting emerging democracies.

The party's challenge now is to steadily enlarge these beachheads—to move these progressive innovations from the margins of a big, bureaucratic government to the center of a leaner yet more dynamic public enterprise that enables people and communities to tackle their own problems.

In *Building the Bridge: 10 Big Ideas To Transform America*, the Progressive Policy Institute elaborates a new progressive governing philosophy and offers large policy prescriptions for dramatically transforming how government works to advance public purposes in the information age. Here, for example, are three tasks that progressives should tackle in the second Clinton term:

First, wean U.S. businesses from dependence on government subsidies. In a January 1994 study for PPI, economist Robert Shapiro identified and challenged the rationale for hundreds of billions of dollars in federal subsidies for U.S. industries. Former Secretary of Labor Robert Reich subsequently endorsed the study and called for ending "corporate welfare." An odd-couple pairing of environmental activists and the free market Cato Institute next joined the chorus. This is an issue on which new and old Democrats can agree and perhaps even win the support of honest conservatives who don't conflate being pro-market with being pro-business.

President Clinton and congressional Democrats should adopt Shapiro's practical suggestion for creating an independent panel, modeled on the highly successful military base-closing commission, to examine industry subsidies—both direct spending and indirect tax subsidies—and present Congress with a list of eliminations and cutbacks for an up-or-down vote. PPI estimates such an effort could yield as much as $20 billion a year in savings, which should be split evenly between new public investments and deficit reduction.

Second, adopt a "reform and invest" strategy that links government reform to empowering U.S. workers. David Osborne, whose seminal work inspired the Clinton-Gore "reinventing government" initiative, proposes that the effort be pushed to a second, more radical stage. Drawing on the success of government reform efforts in Britain and Australia, he calls for converting large federal agencies that deal directly with the public—such as the Patent Office and the U.S. Forest Service—into semi-autonomous "performance based organizations" (PBOs). Agencies would get the flexibility they need to improve performance in return for being held accountable for results. Osborne estimates that PBOs could achieve productivity gains of 3 percent a year (a common benchmark in the private sector), saving the federal government $25 billion a year.

That would be more than enough to finance President Clinton's array of educational initiatives: tax credits for a thirteenth and fourteenth year of schooling, deductions for college tuition, and his previously proposed "GI Bill" for American workers that was derailed by right-wing opposition in the last Congress. That measure would consolidate federal job training programs for dislocated workers and convert the money into vouchers workers could use to buy education, training, or other employment services from private vendors. To encourage all workers to develop their own intellectual capital and manage their own job security, Osborne further proposes that Washington create "Career Opportunity Accounts"—tax-free savings accounts that would be used to upgrade skills.

Third, lay the groundwork for entitlement reform. Eventually, Democrats will have to get serious about reforming Social Security and Medicare so that these massive programs don't default on their obligations to future retirees, impose a crushing tax burden on tomorrow's workers, or crowd out other urgent public needs.

Yet talk of structural reform induces self-righteous conniptions among the party's old guard, which seems equally incapable of acknowledging structural flaws in the programs or imagining any change that would not strip them of their universal or "solidaristic" character. Is it conceivable that poor people could actually reap more in retirement benefits if some portion of their Social Security taxes were invested in private savings accounts? We may never know, because their self-appointed tribunes are too worried that someone on Wall Street might make money too.

Die-hard defense of troubled entitlement programs also conflicts with an urgent progressive goal: increased public investment in education, health care, antipoverty initiatives, and infrastructure. Since the early 1970s, the exponential growth of Social Security, Medicare, and Medicaid has dramatically squeezed these so-called "discretionary" accounts of government. In the President's last budget, for example, nondefense discretionary spending was frozen at $275 billion, while the entitlement programs were allowed to rise from $875 billion to $1.2 trillion in 2002. Of course, the contradiction between shielding entitlements from reform and expanding public investment disappears if, in lieu of constraining the former's growth, liberals declare themselves ready to raise taxes substantially, slash defense spending, or expand the federal deficit.

As usual, the public takes a more practical and nuanced view of the issue than the ideologues. Penn's survey found that people are surprisingly receptive to major entitlement reform: Given a choice between "staying within the existing system" or implementing "more structural changes" that include "getting the private sector involved" in Medicare and "letting people control portions of their own retirement savings" in Social Security, they overwhelmingly chose the more dramatic structural changes.

How to square this public realism with liberal assertions that unyielding defense of the current structure and benefits of Medicare and Social Security is the Democrats' political trump card? One obvious explanation is that Americans know that the entitlement programs have to be modernized in order to be preserved for the long haul. They want Democrats to do the job, because they quite reasonably don't trust Republicans.

The new progressive agenda includes much more. A top priority is moving stepwise toward a universal system of private medical insurance. Another imperative is to convert our public school system from a public monopoly that offers wildly varying quality to a pluralistic system that offers uniformly high standards within a setting of school choice and diversity. In *Building the Bridge*, PPI also offers new ideas for reducing inner-city poverty, revamping America's archaic criminal justice system, fortifying families, launching a "second generation" of environmental activism, restructuring our defense and foreign policy institutions, and more.

As this list suggests, the end of big government need not mean the end of big ideas. At this pivotal moment, what America needs is not a politics of modest ambitions, crimped vision, and incrementalism, but a contemporary version of the "bold, persistent experimentation" that was FDR's greatest legacy.

# Joshua Muravchik
## "Why the Republicans Lost, and Won"*

What was it that made the Republicans such hapless contenders in last November's race for the presidency?

One short answer is: peace and prosperity. In 1996, the combined rate of unemployment and inflation was as low as it has been in 30 years. Fifty-five percent of the voters interviewed in exit polls on November 5 estimated the general state of the economy as good or excellent, and these people went heavily for Clinton, as did those who said their own personal financial situation had improved. As for peace, Clinton's two biggest international gambles, Haiti and Bosnia, had paid off, allowing him a plausible claim of success with virtually no American casualties. Nowhere in the world were Americans dying under enemy fire.

Under such benign economic and international circumstances, said the conservative commentator Fred Barnes, "President Clinton's defeat of Bob Dole [was] inevitable." But was it? Throughout much of 1995, when

---

* Joshua Muravchik, "Why the Republicans Lost, and Won" in *Commentary* (January 1997). Reprinted with permission.

the economy was no less robust, and the nation no less at peace, Dole had *led* Clinton in the polls. And notwithstanding the favorable circumstances of 1996, Clinton retained important areas of vulnerability, especially on the "character issue." On election day, when asked if they believed "Bill Clinton is honest and trustworthy," 54 percent of voters said no; asked how a Clinton victory would make them feel, 52 percent replied either "concerned" or "scared." Exit polls also revealed that nearly half of those who voted for Clinton did so with reservations.

If peace and prosperity did not defeat Bob Dole, there is another short answer to hand: the manifest shortcomings of the Republican candidate himself. In the words of the columnist Charles Krauthammer, "But for Dole (and Kemp), it was winnable."

Without a doubt, Bob Dole had personal shortcomings aplenty. And it was also true, as a *New York Times* analysis noted, that Dole's "third run for the presidency was plagued by missteps, indecision, and strategic blunders so fundamental that they bordered on amateurish." Yet were Dole's undeniably mediocre rhetorical skills worse than those of other contemporary presidential candidates—George Bush, for instance, or Jimmy Carter, or Richard Nixon, or even Lyndon Johnson? Losing campaigns, moreover, almost always look poorly organized, for the simple reason that *most* campaigns are poorly organized, what with so much to be done in so short a time by teams of people who hardly know one another. Besides, whatever the weaknesses of Dole and his staff, he did win the Republican nomination, and he won it by beating all the other declared aspirants. However poor a campaigner he may have been, he was better than they.

In the end, whatever weight one attributes to the favorable economic and international circumstances that benefited Clinton, or to the deficiencies of Dole and his campaign, no presidential race can ever be adequately accounted for without reference to those things that lie at the heart of politics: issues and ideologies. As in past elections, November's exit polls showed again that ideology is a more reliable predictor of voting behavior than economic circumstances. Even those reporting an improved financial situation were less likely to vote for Clinton than those calling themselves liberal; conversely, even those whose situation had deteriorated were less likely to vote for Dole than those identifying themselves as conservative.

The ideological key to the 1996 presidential election was twofold. First, Clinton as President had moved sharply to the Center. To be sure, there may have been more appearance than reality in this. The Clinton campaign claimed, for example, that the President had increased defense spending "three times in three years," when in reality he had slashed spending by $127 billion in his first year and then grudgingly restored small bits under strong pressure. "He is of course a shocking liar," wrote Michael Kelly, the newly installed editor of the *New Republic*, adding, "Fourteen of the accomplishments of which Clinton bragged in his acceptance speech at the Democratic convention were actually GOP measures."

But to say that there was more appearance than reality in Clinton's behavior is not to say that there was no reality. Here, a bit of history is in order. In 1992, Clinton had won a large plurality of self-identified "moderate" voters by campaigning as a centrist or "new kind of Democrat." But no sooner had he won than he executed a shift to the Left, ordering that his administration be staffed according to rigid rules of racial and gender preferences and proposing steep defense cuts, a new government jobs program for college students, a lifting of the ban on homosexuals in the military, tax hikes, and above all a convoluted program of national health insurance that would have assimilated a further 13 percent of the U.S. economy to the federal government.

When all this resulted in the great Republican triumph of 1994, Clinton turned around again in one of the most amazing political makeovers in memory. His about-face began with the 1995 State of the Union address in which he proclaimed a "middle-class bill of rights." Banal as that may sound, it was a departure from liberal Democratic orthodoxy, as expressed canonically by Mario Cuomo in his famous address to the Democratic convention of 1984 when he described America as "a tale of two cities," one rich and one poor, "the lucky and the left out, the royalty and the rabble."

A year later, in his 1996 State of the Union speech, Clinton made a still sharper break with Democratic orthodoxy by declaring that "the era of big government is over." By then he had rehired his old strategist, Dick Morris, who helped hone the tactic of "triangulation": positioning Clinton midway between the Republicans and the Democrats in Congress. Soon the President was abandoning earlier budget proposals that had assumed deficits of hundreds of billions of dollars and was embracing first the principle of a balanced budget and then the Republican deadline for it of the year 2002.

The most remarkable of Clinton's moves focused not on the economy but on an area long ceded to conservatives: social issues, or, as they are now more often called, "values" or "family-values" issues. This is the area in which George Bush had clobbered Michael Dukakis in 1988, and Clinton absorbed the lesson. In 1995–96, he set about making these issues his own, speaking up for school uniforms, V-chips, and restrictions on teen smoking; signing the welfare-reform bill (which aimed to stem the tide of illegitimacy) and the defense-of-marriage act (which denied automatic legal recognition to homosexual wedlock); proposing an extension of the family-leave act for new parents; and above all taking a hard line on law and order.

Politically, law-and-order was perhaps the most powerful of all the social issues, and also the one that had long been the virtually exclusive property of the Republican party. Clinton's "initial strike" on this front, reported *Time* magazine in its blow-by-blow post-election account of the campaign,

was a series of crime ads to be aired seventeen months before the election. . . . "The idea," as [one aide] said, "was, 'This is not the guy you think you know.' "

Throughout the campaign, Clinton boasted incessantly that he had put 100,000 new policemen on the beat (his Justice Department confessed that the actual number was 17,000), and in the end he won the endorsement of the Fraternal Order of Police. By October 1996, a small plurality of voters said they preferred the Democrats to the Republicans on the issue of crime.

All in all, Clinton's transformation, striking in its audacity, was even more striking in its success. By the time his makeover was complete, Fred Barnes was writing that Clinton had "become in many ways a more conservative president than Ronald Reagan"; on the other side, the liberal apparatchik Richard N. Goodwin was lamenting in the *New York Times* that "the venerable principles of the [Democratic] party . . . have been abandoned." True, Clinton paid a price for his maneuver in the coin of credibility. Not only did a majority of voters doubt his honesty, but when asked whether they expected Clinton would "stay in the political Center" after the election or would "move in a more liberal direction," they were nearly evenly divided. But still they reelected him. In November, moderates, who constitute a little under half of the electorate, favored Clinton over Dole by 57 percent to 33 percent, by far the most uneven division in the two decades for which we have such data.

Why was the moderate vote so lopsided? To explain that, we need to look at the second side of the ideological story of this election, which is that while Clinton was claiming the Center, the Republicans were disdaining it.

Upon assuming the role of Speaker of the House in 1994, following the historic GOP victory that he had helped to engineer, Newt Gingrich declared: "I am a genuine revolutionary. [Democrats] are genuine reactionaries. We are going to change the world." Later, Gingrich would wax bitter at Democrats who called him an extremist; but it was he who had used the term revolutionary, and in America, revolutionaries are extremists.

The congressional Republicans, who had been swept to power on a wave of popular reaction against the Clintons' health-care proposal, were guilty of overinterpreting their mandate. True, the voters had rejected any contemplated enlargement of the welfare state; but to oppose government expansion, or even to believe that the government was already too large, is not the same thing as welcoming drastic cutbacks, or being anti-government. Americans are especially loath to contemplate reductions in the one area in which government has grown the most drastically: namely, the so-called entitlements of Social Security, Medicare, and the like. (An exception is welfare, which most voters are ready to see reduced, but it is a relatively small federal program.) This is a reality Clinton would exploit against the Republicans, at first haltingly and then mercilessly.

Though they succeeded in passing much of their "Contract with America," the congressional Republicans soon found themselves deadlocked with the administration over the budget. Convinced that the voters shared their anti-government passions, they hit upon the tactic of forcing a shutdown until Clinton came to terms. But their actions were soon revealed to be highly unpopular. By the time the GOP threw in the towel, Clinton's approval ratings were registering a marked improvement.

The Republicans' anti-government zeal got them into trouble again over federal law enforcement. In the controversies over the deadly raid against the armed compound of the Branch Davidian religious cult at Waco, Texas, and the shoot-out between FBI agents and white supremacists at Ruby Ridge, Idaho, GOP legislators managed to convey the unfortunate impression that they believed the real villains of the story were the federal officials involved. This had further reverberations when, as federal indictments charge, two or three individuals associated with the so-called militia movement commemorated the Waco tragedy by bombing the federal building in Oklahoma City in April 1995. Clinton seized the opportunity to project himself as a pillar of national unity and lawfulness, and opinion polls recorded an immediate spike in his public approval.

But Oklahoma City and Ruby Ridge did more than give Clinton an opportunity to act "presidential." They also signaled that the Right had supplanted the Left as the home of radical misfits and violent extremists. Of course, the militia groups were no more Republican than the Weathermen had been Democratic, but in each case a faint penumbra of shame was cast across one side of the political spectrum. It deepened in this case when certain Republican figures like Pat Robertson and Patrick J. Buchanan echoed the ravings of the radical Right in their own warnings against the "new world order."

Nor did it help that Republican legislators blocked Clinton's proposed anti-terrorism measures on the grounds that enhanced powers of surveillance by the authorities would endanger civil liberties. By striking this constraining stance toward federal law enforcement, the GOP continued the process of squandering some of its most valuable political capital—its standing as the party of law and order. That waste had already begun in 1993 and 1994 when, under the impetus of the gun lobby, Republican legislators in both houses opposed the ban on assault weapons by margins of more than three to one, almost the exact inverse of the position taken by the electorate. Thus did Republican leaders help pave the way for Clinton's capture of the crime issue.

Nor was crime the only "values" issue the Republicans flubbed. On several others they failed to exploit weaknesses in the Democrats' position while magnifying their own. Since, for example, an important bloc of Republican constituents is not just opposed to abortion but sees it as murder, the party is bound to take a strong stand on the matter, even if doing so is an electoral liability. But Dole might well have elicited the sympathy of a majority by seizing on Clinton's veto of the congressional ban on partial-birth abortions, a procedure repugnant even to many Americans who believe that abortion should be legal. Instead, after the Republican convention beat back a small compromise with the party's pro-choice minority, the campaign shied away from abortion altogether.

Another such issue was education. The Republicans' advantage here was their support for school choice, a popular idea. But Dole got off-track in his acceptance speech when he chose to attack teachers' unions. The attack seemed gratuitous, and anyway fell flat: most people think teachers' unions have a positive influence on education.

Then there was affirmative action. The November victory of the California Civil Rights Initiative, which passed by 54 to 46 percent, suggests that this issue could have helped the Republicans. Opponents of the California measure, which outlaws racial preferences, accused its supporters of racism; in truth, however, the case against affirmative action rests solidly on the great "dream" of Martin Luther King, Jr. that Americans be judged by "the content of their character" and not "the color of their skin." Yet not only did the Republicans fail to argue compellingly for a return to these first principles, they made things harder for themselves by taking a harsh approach to immigrants and thus lending plausibility to the charge that they were motivated by bigotry rather than by a devotion to equal rights.

True, once Clinton decided to compete for the values issues, the Republicans were hard put to match him program for program. Not only is Republican philosophy skeptical of government programs in general, but this is an area particularly ill-suited to government-engendered solutions. That, however, makes simple acts of moral advocacy and example all the more important. Nancy Reagan's "Just-Say-No" initiative, Dan Quayle's critique of Murphy Brown, William J. Bennett's crusade against violence and obscenity in popular culture have demonstrated how public figures can use their platforms effectively for moral purposes. Possibly the best moment of Bob Dole's own campaign was his May 1995 polemic against the glorification of "mindless violence and loveless sex" in Hollywood movies. But this was virtually a one-shot effort. Dole's failure to stress such themes during the next year and a half remains a great mystery.

Could the Republicans have recouped some of the ground lost on the values issues by reasserting their well-earned stance as the paragons of national security? Perhaps. Although foreign policy was of little interest to voters in this election, Clinton provided an opening by his hollow response to Saddam Hussein's thrust into Iraqi Kurdistan. But instead of castigating Clinton for his fecklessness, Jack Kemp inexplicably said that Clinton should have tried "diplomacy first," and Dole bizarrely called for more consultation with the UN.

Finally, Dole compromised his effectiveness, and also squandered his advantage on the "character issue," by his decision to push for a $550-billion tax cut. Ever since 1995, when the House Republicans insisted on pursuing a (much smaller) across-the-board cut, the Democrats and their allies in organized labor had been claiming that this was a "tax cut for the rich," to be financed out of Republican-demanded "cuts" in Medicare. This was demagogic: the Democrats knew that the Republicans were proposing only to cut Medicare's rate of growth, and that this was inevitable under any circumstances. Still, the attack bit, because a large proportion of the tax benefits would have gone to the better-off and because the federal budget is all one pot: the size of cuts in Medicare or other programs is indeed affected by a reduction in tax revenues. And the attack was given added force by Dole's announcement in July of a much more sweeping cut. Now, just as the Democrats had long been seen as pandering to special interests, the Republicans were seen as pandering wholesale.

Dole expressed frustration late in the race that voters would chose someone like Clinton over someone like himself: "Where's the outrage?" One answer was given by the economist Herb Stein, a Dole supporter, in July:

The voters know that his advisers are urging Mr. Dole to recommend a big tax cut because they are desperate about the election, not because it represents his policies and principles. Can Mr. Dole afford to be seen doing that? The biggest thing he has going for him against Mr. Clinton is that voters think he sticks by his beliefs, that he tries to do the right thing even though it's hard. Should he sacrifice that public estimation of him now?

When Dole took to claiming that he was more trustworthy, he sounded merely egotistical. To demonstrate true superiority of character, he might have talked turkey to the American people about the national debt and the mismatch between taxes and entitlements. He might have spoken of the need for shared sacrifice before the aging of the baby-boom generation makes our problems all the more dire. At the very least this would have made for an arresting contrast with Bill Clinton's smooth bromides. Perhaps the electorate would not have wanted to hear painful truths, but polls did show that voters were more keen for deficit reduction than for tax cuts. By October, however, between Dole's tax proposal and Clinton's adoption of Gingrich's deadline for a balanced budget, the Republican advantage as the party most trusted to reduce the deficit had shrunk from a 21-percent margin in mid-1995 to a mere 3 percent.

In sum, the Republican party came across less as conservative than as right-wing, thus creating the impression that the Center was up for grabs. And the Center was precisely where Bill Clinton was strenuously, and effectively, positioning himself.

Still, that too is far from the whole story of the 1996 elections, and may be even less than half of it. For the Center of American politics has itself shifted rightward in recent years. Moreover, Clinton victory or no Clinton victory, so far it shows no signs of shifting back. Exhibit A for this are the November election returns for the House and Senate. There, the Republicans confirmed that in some underlying sense, they have become the majority American party.

Even their vulnerabilities confirm this fact. It is because the majority party sets the agenda that the opposition party can fall back on counterpunching—which in politics, as in boxing, is often a winning tactic. Nixon, Reagan, and Bush won presidential elections largely by making an issue of Democratic foibles, and Bill Clinton won in 1996 largely by doing the same to the Republicans. But what a single candidate can do at the presidential level is very hard to replicate in mass at the congressional level.

Although the Republican majority in the new Congress is narrow, there are reasons to think that it will endure. Two years from now, in 1998, the GOP will enjoy the advantage that traditionally accrues in off-year elections to the party not in the White House, an advantage especially strong during a President's second term. In addition, there is not likely soon to be another election in which the prospects for the Democrats will be as favorable as they were in 1996.

In recent decades, congressional incumbents have won reelection more than 90 percent of the time. An insurgent's best chance is against an incumbent who has served only one term and is not yet a fixture in the eyes of voters and donors. Thanks to their epochal victory in 1994, the Republicans had a whopping 70 freshmen Representatives in that vulnerable position last November. Naturally, these were the races especially targeted by Democratic funders and organized labor. But in the end, 59 of the 70 survived.

Democratic candidates last year had another advantage that will not come around again, namely, Bill Clinton's substantial margin over Bob Dole; during the last weeks of the race, Clinton was comfortable enough in his lead to campaign in Republican strongholds and help boost the rest of the Democratic ticket. The Democrats also had the benefit of the unhappy performance of the Republican-led Congress of 1995 and 1996, a performance highlighted by the two shutdowns of the federal government. "If the GOP can keep control after [such] monumental stupidity," the columnist Ben Wattenberg wrote, "their base is strong." Clearly, it is.

There are also demographic reasons for believing that Republican dominance is fairly secure, at least in the near term: the class composition of the American electorate has evolved from mainly blue-collar to increasingly college-educated and white-collar, a source of growing strength for Republicans. And finally, the electorate also continues to tilt ideologically toward conservatism. Several public-opinion surveys suggest that a plurality of voters, though unhappy with specific policies, favor the long-term direction signaled by the Republicans and, no less significantly, fear that a Democratic-controlled Congress would be too liberal. In November exit polls, 33 percent of voters described themselves as conservatives, as against only 20 percent who said they were liberals. Asked whether government "should do more to solve problems" or "is doing too many things better left to business and private individuals," a majority, 52 to 41 percent, said that government was doing too much.

The big question remains what will become of the Democratic party. If, after Clinton, the Democrats revert to the Left-liberalism that has characterized their politics for a quarter-century, then the Republicans will continue to benefit from a wide margin of safety. There are signs that this may happen, in particular in the newly assertive role being played by organized labor. With the forced retirement of Lane Kirkland as president of the AFL-CIO and his replacement by John Sweeney, who recently enrolled in the Democratic Socialists of America, the unions have taken a dramatic turn. Having once fought to keep the Democratic party in the Center, labor will now be tugging it to the Left, just as the trade unions tug the Labor party in Britain. The advantage can only redound to the Republicans.

On the other hand, novice Democratic candidates for Congress this year mostly imitated Clinton, and others in the party may be spurred by his successful example. ("We're all New Democrats now," said House minority leader Richard Gephardt.) If the party should indeed remake itself in Clinton's 1996 centrist image, then the Republicans will face a more serious challenge. It is, however, a challenge they can meet—not by presenting themselves as right-wingers, harsh on social issues, reckless on budgetary issues, and isolationist or opportunist on international issues, but instead by competing forcefully for the Center that is theirs to define. This does not mean abandoning conservatism; quite the contrary, it means consolidating it.

Decades ago, Irving Kristol branded the GOP the "stupid party" for restricting itself to promises to clean up after the messes made by Democratic profligacy, and failing to articulate an alternative political vision. Today, there are signs that the American electorate, after a long era of self-indulgence, hungers for such a vision, whose essence is a return to responsibility, moral no less than fiscal (and, one hopes, international as well). That is the basis for a mature conservatism, and the party that becomes its vehicle will probably assure its dominance in the post-Clinton era.

Republicans lost election but kept a majority — strong base.

# 11

# Political Parties

## The Two-Party System in America

*See Lowi and Ginsberg, pp. 478–489 or brief edition, pp. 274–284*

*As the text discusses, the appeal of the political parties as a source of particpation and identification continues to decline among American voters. Ross Perot's success as a third-party candidate for president in 1992 and the growing number of Americans who reject both political parties and choose not to vote (see Robert Reich's article), have led many political observers to argue that the time is ripe for a third party to emerge. The two-party system, it is argued, limits voter choice and inhibits rather than facilitates the changes in governance many voters demand.*

*Debate over the utility of a two-party system is not new. In 1950, the Committee on Political Parties within the American Political Science Association (the professional organization for political scientists) put forth the definitive defense of the two-party system. A "responsible two-party system," it argued, was essential to ensure a broad base of political support for the winning party—a necessary characteristic of democratic governance. In the Committee's view, third parties not only contradicted political tradition in the United States, but if they could not offer a strong challenge to the party in power, they could not offer voters a meaningful choice at the ballot box. A strong opposition, instead, was more likely under a two-party system. The Republican Party's congressional victory in 1994 represented the role a strong opposition party can play and the importance of a clear alternative agenda—The Contract with America. As several authors argue herein, the 1996 congressional election represented a continued American voter preference for a more conservative agenda held out by the Republican Party.*

*Is the two-party system alive and well? Do the parties offer a vehicle for bringing a majority of voters together beyond a broad policy agenda? Should any institutional changes be made to encourage third parties?*

# American Political Science Association
## "A Report of the Committee on Political Parties: Toward a More Responsible Two-Party System"*

### THE NEED FOR GREATER PARTY RESPONSIBILITY

■ The Role of the Political Parties

**1. *The Parties and Public Policy*** Throughout this report political parties are treated as indispensable instruments of government. That is to say, we proceed on the proposition that *popular government in a nation of more than 150 million people requires political parties which provide the electorate with a proper range of choice between alternatives of action.* The party system thus serves as the main device for bringing into continuing relationship those ideas about liberty, majority rule and leadership which Americans are largely taking for granted.

For the great majority of Americans, the most valuable opportunity to influence the course of public affairs is the choice they are able to make between the parties in the principal elections. While in an election the party alternative necessarily takes the form of a choice between candidates, putting a particular candidate into office is not an end in itself. The concern of the parties with candidates, elections and appointments is misunderstood if it is assumed that parties can afford to bring forth aspirants for office without regard to the views of those so selected. Actually, the party struggle is concerned with the direction of public affairs. Party nominations are no more than a means to this end. In short, party politics inevitably involves public policy in one way or another. *In order to keep the parties apart, one must consider the relations between each and public policy.*

This is not to ignore that in the past the American two-party system has shown little propensity for evolving original or creative ideas about public policy; that it has even been rather sluggish in responding to such ideas in the public interest; that it reflects in an enlarged way those differences throughout the country which are expressed in the operation of the federal structure of government; and that in all political organizations a considerable measure of irrationality manifests itself.

Giving due weight to each of these factors, we are nevertheless led to conclude that the choices provided by the two-party system are valuable to the American people in proportion to their definition in terms of public policy. *The reasons for the growing emphasis on public policy in party politics are to be found, above all, in the very operations of modern government.* With the ex-

* American Political Science Association,"A Report of the Committee on Political Parties: Toward a More Responsible Two-Party System" in the *American Political Science Review*, Volume 44.3, Part 2 (September 1950).

traordinary growth of the responsibilities of government, the discussion of public affairs for the most part makes sense only in terms of public policy.

**2. *The New Importance of Program***   One of the most pressing requirements of contemporary politics is for the party in power to furnish a general kind of direction over the government as a whole. *The crux of public affairs lies in the necessity for more effective formulation of general policies and programs and for better integration of all of the far-flung activities of modern government.*

Only large-scale and representative political organizations possess the qualifications needed for these tasks. The ascendancy of national issues in an industrial society, the impact of the widening concern of government with problems of the general welfare, the entrance into the realm of politics of millions of new voters—all of these factors have tended to broaden the base of the parties as the largest political organizations in the country. *It is in terms of party programs that political leaders can attempt to consolidate public attitudes toward the work plans of government.*

Modern public policy, therefore, accentuates the importance of the parties, not as mere brokers between different groups and interests, but as agencies of the electorate. Because it affects unprecedented numbers of people and because it depends for its execution on extensive and widespread public support, modern public policy requires a broad political base. That base can be provided only by the parties, which read people touched by no other political organization.

**3. *The Potentialities of the Party System***   *The potentialities of the two-party system are suggested, on the one hand, by the fact that for all practical purposes the major parties monopolize elections; and, on the other, by the fact that both parties have in the past managed to adapt themselves to the demands made upon them by external necessities.*

Moreover, in contrast with any other political organization today in existence, the major parties even now are forced to consider public policy at least broadly enough to make it likely for them to win elections. If public esteem of the parties is much less high than it might be, the depressed state of their reputation has resulted in the main from their past indifference to broadly conceived public policy. This indifference has fixed in the popular mind the idea of spoils, patronage and plunder. It is hence not astonishing when one hears a chosen representative assert for the public ear that in his state "people put principles above party." Much of the agitation for nonpartisanship—despite the impossibility of nonpartisan organization on a national level—is rooted in the same attitudes.

Bad reputations die hard, but things are no longer what they used to be. Certainly success in presidential campaigns today is based on broad national appeals to the widest possible constituencies. To a much greater extent than in the past, elections are won by influences and trends that are felt throughout the country. *It is* therefore *good practical politics to reconsider party organization in the light of the changing conditions of politics.*

It appeared desirable in this report to relate the potentialities of the party system to both the conditions that confront the nation and the expected role of the parties. *Happily such an effort entails an application of ideas about the party system that are no longer unfamiliar.*

Consideration of ways and means of producing a more responsible party system leads into the hazards of political invention. This is a challenge that has usually been accepted with misgivings by political scientists, who are trained to describe what is and feel less well qualified to fashion innovations. We hope that our own effort will stimulate both other political scientists and participants in practical politics to attempt similar undertakings on their own account. Only by a continuous process of invention and adjustment can the party system be adapted to meet the needs of our day.

## ■ What Kind of Party System Is Needed?

There is little point to talking about the American party system in terms of its deficiencies and potentialities except against a picture of what the parties ought to be. Our report would be lacking in exactness without an indication of the sort of model we have in mind.

Americans are reasonably well agreed about the purposes served by the two major parties as long as the matter is discussed in generalities. When specific questions are raised, however, agreement is much more limited. We cannot assume, therefore, a commonly shared view about the essential characteristics of the party system. But we can and must state our own view.

In brief, our view is this: *The party system that is needed must be democratic, responsible and effective*—a system that is accountable to the public, respects and expresses differences of opinion, and is able to cope with the great problems of modern government. Some of the implications warrant special statement, which is the purpose of this section.

## ■ A Stronger Two-party System

1. *The Need for an Effective Party System*   In an era beset with problems of unprecedented magnitude at home and abroad, it is dangerous to drift without a party system that helps the nation to set a general course of policy for the government as a whole. In a two-party system, when both parties are weakened or confused by internal divisions or ineffective organization it is the nation that suffers. When the parties are unable to reach and pursue responsible decisions, difficulties accumulate and cynicism about all democratic institutions grows.

*An effective party system requires, first, that the parties are able to bring forth programs to which they commit themselves and, second, that the parties possess sufficient internal cohesion to carry out these programs.* In such a system, the party program becomes the work program of the party, so recognized by the party leaders in and out of the government, by the party body as a whole, and by the public. This condition is unattainable unless party institutions have been created through which agreement can be reached about the general position of the party.

Clearly *such a degree of unity within the parties cannot be brought about without party procedures that give a large body of people an opportunity to share in the development of the party program.* One great function of the party system is to bring about the widest possible consent in relation to defined political goals, which provides the majority party with the essential means of building public support for the policies of the government. Democratic procedures in the internal affairs of the parties are best suited to the development of agreement within each party.

**2. The Need for an Effective Opposition Party**   The argument for a stronger party system cannot be divorced from measures designed to make the parties more fully accountable to the public. *The fundamental requirement of such accountability is a two-party system in which the opposition party acts as the critic of the party in power, developing, defining and presenting the policy alternatives which are necessary for a true choice in reaching public decisions.*

Beyond that, the case for the American two-party system need not be restated here. The two-party system is so strongly rooted in the political traditions of this country and public preference for it is so well established that consideration of other possibilities seems entirely academic. When we speak of the parties without further qualification, we mean throughout our report the two major parties. The inference is not that we consider third or minor parties undesirable or ineffectual within their limited orbit. Rather, we feel that the minor parties in the longer run have failed to leave a lasting imprint upon both the two-party system and the basic processes of American government.

In spite of the fact that the two-party system is part of the American political tradition, it cannot be said that the role of the opposition party is well understood. This is unfortunate because democratic government is greatly influenced by the character of the opposition party. The measures proposed elsewhere in our report to help the party in power to clarify its policies are equally applicable to the opposition.

*The opposition most conducive to responsible government is an organized party opposition,* produced by the organic operation of the two-party system. When there are two parties identifiable by the kinds of action they propose, the voters have an actual choice. On the other hand, the sort of opposition presented by a coalition that cuts across party lines, as a regular thing, tends to deprive the public of a meaningful alternative. When such coalitions are formed after the elections are over, the public usually finds it difficult to understand the new situation and to reconcile it with the purpose of the ballot. Moreover, on that basis it is next to impossible to hold either party responsible for its political record. This is a serious source of public discontent. . . .

## The Weakening of Party Organization

*See Lowi and Ginsberg, pp. 501–513 or brief edition, pp. 289–301*

*According to Morris Fiorina, strong political parties provide electoral accountability and discipline in government. The decline of the party organization, however, has removed an important vehicle for direct political participation for voters, and has eliminated the motivation for elected members of the parties to define broad policy objectives. Instead, policies are aimed at serving the narrow interests of various single-issue groups that now dominate politics. Without strong parties, American politics is suffering a "decline in collective responsibility."*

*In the effort to reform political parties of the late 1800s—often referred to as "machines" that dominated the electoral process in many cities with corrupt tactics—it is important to consider whether we have eliminated the primary means by which a large electorate can gain assess to and hold accountable elected officials at the ballot box. If the American system of governance is truly democratic, there must be some means to collectively translate the public's interest into government action, and some means to check the actions of elected officials. Fiorina argues that the political parties have long played this role, bringing people into the political process and defining broad policy agendas to which voters can respond. If political parties don't facilitate this critical process, then what?*

# Morris P. Fiorina
## "The Decline of Collective Responsibility in American Politics"*

Though the Founding Fathers believed in the necessity of establishing a genuinely national government, they took great pains to design one that could not lightly do things *to* its citizens; what government might do *for* its citizens was to be limited to the functions of what we know now as the "watchman state." . . .

Given the historical record faced by the Founders, their emphasis on constraining government is understandable. But we face a later historical record, one that shows two hundred years of increasing demands for government to act positively. Moreover, developments unforeseen by the Founders increasingly raise the likelihood that the uncoordinated actions of individuals and groups will inflict serious damage on the nation as a whole. The byproducts of the industrial and technological revolutions impose physical risks not only on us, but on future generations as well. Re-

* Morris P. Fiorina, "The Decline of Collective Responsibility in American Politics," reprinted by permission of *Daedalus,* Journal of the American Academy of Arts and Sciences, from the issue entitled, "The End of Consensus?" Summer 1980, Volume 109, Number 3.

source shortages and international cartels raise the spectre of economic ruin. And the simple proliferation of special interests with their intense, particularistic demands threatens to render us politically incapable of taking actions that might either advance the state of society or prevent foreseeable deteriorations in that state. None of this is to suggest that we should forget about what government can do *to* us—the contemporary concern with the proper scope and methods of government intervention in the social and economic orders is long overdue. But the modern age demands as well that we worry about our ability to make government work *for* us. The problem is that we are gradually losing that ability, and a principal reason for this loss is the steady erosion of *responsibility* in American politics. . . .

Unfortunately, the importance of responsibility in a democracy is matched by the difficulty of attaining it. In an autocracy, individual responsibility suffices; the location of power in a single individual locates responsibility in that individual as well. But individual responsibility is insufficient whenever more than one person shares governmental authority. We can hold a particular congressman individually responsible for a personal transgression such as bribe-taking. We can even hold a president individually responsible for military moves where he presents Congress and the citizenry with a *fait accompli.* But on most national issues individual responsibility is difficult to assess. If one were to go to Washington, randomly accost a Democratic congressman, and berate him about a 20-percent rate of inflation, imagine the response. More than likely it would run, "Don't blame me. If 'they' had done what I've advocated for *x* years, things would be fine today." . . .

American institutional structure makes this kind of game-playing all too easy. In order to overcome it we must lay the credit or blame for national conditions on all those who had any hand in bringing them about: some form of *collective responsibility* is essential.

The only way collective responsibility has ever existed, and can exist given our institutions, is through the agency of the political party; in American politics, responsibility requires cohesive parties. This is an old claim to be sure, but its age does not detract from its present relevance. In fact, the continuing decline in public esteem for the parties and continuing efforts to "reform" them out of the political process suggest that old arguments for party responsibility have not been made often enough or, at least, convincingly enough, so I will make these arguments once again in this essay.

A strong political party can generate collective responsibility by creating incentive for leaders, followers, and popular supporters to think and act in collective terms. First, by providing party leaders with the capability (e.g., control of institutional patronage, nominations, and so on) to discipline party members, genuine leadership becomes possible. Legislative output is less likely to be a least common denominator—a residue of myriad conflicting proposals—and more likely to consist of a program actually intended to solve a problem or move the nation in a particular direction. Second, the subordination of individual officeholders to the party lessens their ability to separate themselves from party actions. Like it or not, their performance becomes identified with the performance of the collectivity to which they belong. Third, with individual candidate variation greatly reduced, voters have less incentive to support individuals and more incentive to support or oppose the party as a whole. And fourth, the circle closes as party-line voting in the electorate provides party leaders with the incentive to propose policies that will earn the support of a national majority, and party back-benchers with the personal incentive to cooperate with leaders in the attempt to compile a good record for the party as a whole.

In the American context, strong parties have traditionally clarified politics in two ways. First, they allow citizens to assess responsibility easily, at least when the government is unified, which it more often was in earlier eras when party meant more than it does today. Citizens need only evaluate the social, economic, and international conditions they observe and make a simple decision for or against change. They do not need to decide whether the energy, inflation, urban, and defense policies advocated by their congress-man would be superior to those advocated by [the president]—were any of them to be enacted!

The second way in which strong parties clarify American politics follows from the first. When citizens assess responsibility on the party as a whole, party members have personal incentives to see the party evaluated favorably. They have little to gain from gutting their president's program one day and attacking him for lack of leadership the next, since they share in the president's fate when voters do not differentiate within the party. Put simply, party responsibility provides party members with a personal stake in their collective performance.

Admittedly, party responsibility is a blunt instrument. The objection immediately arises that party responsibility condemns junior Democratic representatives to suffer electorally for an inflation they could do little to affect. An unhappy situation, true, but unless we accept it, Congress as a whole escapes electoral retribution for an inflation they *could* have done something to affect. Responsibility requires acceptance of both conditions. The choice is between a blunt instrument or none at all. . . .

In earlier times, when citizens voted for the party, not the person, parties had incentives to nominate good candidates, because poor ones could have harmful fallout on the ticket as a whole. In particular, the existence of presidential coattails (positive and negative) provided an inducement to avoid the nomination of narrowly based candidates, no matter how committed their supporters. And, once in office, the existence of party voting in the electorate provided party members with the incentive to compile a good *party* record. In particular, the tendency of national midterm elections to serve as referenda on the performance of the president provided a clear inducement for congressmen to do what they could to see that their president was perceived as a solid performer. By stimulating electoral phenomena such as coattail effects and mid-term referenda, party transformed some degree of personal ambition into concern with collective performance. . . .

## The Continuing Decline of Party in the United States

### ■ Party Organizations

In the United States, party organization has traditionally meant state and local party organization. The national party generally has been a loose confederacy of subnational units that swings into action for a brief period every four years. This characterization remains true today, despite the somewhat greater influence and augmented functions of the national organizations. Though such things are difficult to measure precisely, there is general agreement that the formal party organizations have undergone a secular decline since their peak at the end of the nineteenth century. The prototype of the old-style organization was the urban machine, a form approximated today only in Chicago. . . .

[*Fiorina discusses the reforms of the late nineteenth and early twentieth century discussed in the text.*]

In the 1970s two series of reforms further weakened the influence of organized parties in American national politics. The first was a series of legal changes deliberately intended to lessen organized party influence in the presidential nominating process. In the Democratic party, "New Politics" activists captured the national party apparatus and imposed a series of rules changes designed to "open up" the politics of presidential nominations. The Republican party—long more amateur and open than the Democratic party—adopted weaker versions of the Democratic rules changes. In addition, modifications of state electoral laws to conform to the Democrtic rules changes (enforced by the federal courts) stimulated Republican rules changes as well. . . .

A second series of 1970s reforms lessened the role of formal party organizations in the conduct of political campaigns. These are financing regulations growing out of the Federal Election Campaign Act of 1971 as amended in 1974 and 1976. In this case the reforms were aimed at cleaning up corruption in the financing of campaigns; their effects on the parties were a by-product, though many individuals accurately predicted its nature. Serious presidential candidates are now publicly financed. Though the law permits the national party to spend two cents per eligible voter on behalf of the nominee, it also obliges the candidate to set up a finance committee separate from the national party. Between this legally mandated separation and fear of violating spending limits or accounting regulations, for example, the law has the effect of encouraging the candidate to keep his party at arm's length. . . .

The ultimate results of such reforms are easy to predict. A lesser party role in the nominating and financing of candidates encourages candidates to organize and conduct independent campaigns, which further weakens the role of parties. . . . [I]f parties do not grant nominations, fund their choices, and work for them, why should those choices feel any commitment to their party?

■ Party in the Electorate

In the citizenry at large, party takes the form of a psychological attachment. The typical American traditionally has been likely to identify with one or the other of the two major parties. Such identifications are transmitted across generations to some degree, and within the individual they tend to be fairly stable. But there is mounting evidence that the basis of identification lies in the individual's experiences (direct and vicarious, through family and social groups) with the parties in the past. Our current party system, of course, is based on the dislocations of the Depression period and the New Deal attempts to alleviate them. Though only a small proportion of those who experienced the Depression directly are active voters today, the general outlines of citizen party identifications much resemble those established at that time.

Again, there is reason to believe that the extent of citizen attachments to parties has undergone a long-term decline from a nineteenth-century high. And again, the New Deal appears to have been a period during which the decline was arested, even temporarily reversed. But again, the decline of party has reasserted itself in the 1970s. . . .

As the 1960s wore on, the heretofore stable distribution of citizen party identifications began to change in the general direction of weakened attachments to the parties. Between 1960 and 1976, independents, broadly defined, increased from less than a quarter to more than a third of the voting-age population. Strong identifiers declined from slightly more than a third to about a quarter of the population. . . .

Indisputably, party in the electorate has declined in recent years. Why? To some extent the electoral decline results from the organizational decline. Few party organizations any longer have the tangible incentives to turn out the faithful and assure their loyalty. Candidates run independent campaigns and deemphasize their partisan ties whenever they see any short-term electoral gain in doing so. If party is increasingly less important in the nomination and election of candidates, it is not surprising that such diminished importance is reflected in the attitudes and behavior of the voter.

Certain long-term sociological and technological trends also appear to work against party in the electorate. The population is younger, and younger citizens traditionally are less attached to the parties than their elders. The population is more highly educated; fewer voters need some means of simplifying the choices they face in the political arena, and party, of course, has been the principal means of simplification. And the media revolution has vastly expanded the amount of information easily available to the citizenry. Candidates would have little incentive to operate campaigns independent of the parties if there were no means to apprise the citizenry of their independence. The media provide the means.

Finally, our present party system is an old one. For increasing numbers of citizens, party attachments based on the Great Depression seem lacking in relevance to the problems of the late twentieth century. Beginning with the racial issue in the 1960s, proceeding to the social issue of the 1970s, and to the energy, environment, and inflation issues of today, the parties have been rent by internal dissension. Sometimes they failed to take stands, at other times they took the wrong ones from the standpoint of the rank and file, and at most times they have failed to solve the new problems in any genuine sense. Since 1965 the parties have done little or nothing to earn the loyalties of modern Americans.

## ■ Party in Government

If the organizational capabilities of the parties have weakened, and their psychological ties to the voters have loosened, one would expect predictable consequences for the party in government. In particular, one would expect to see an increasing degree of split party control within and across the levels of American government. The evidence on this point is overwhelming. . . .

The increased fragmentation of the party in government makes it more difficult for government officeholders to work together than in times past (not that it has ever been terribly easy). Voters meanwhile have a more difficult time attributing responsibility for government performance, and this only further fragments party control. The result is lessened collective responsibility in the system.

What has taken up the slack left by the weakening of the traditional [party] determinants of congressional voting? It appears that a variety of personal and local influences now play a major role in citizen evaluations of their representatives. Along with the expansion of the federal presence in American life, the traditional role of the congressman as an all-purpose ombudsman has greatly expanded. Tens of millions of citizens now are directly affected by federal decisions. Myriad programs provide opportunities to profit from government largesse, and myriad regulations impose costs and/or constraints on citizen activities. And, whether seeking to gain profit or avoid costs, citizens seek the aid of their congressmen. When a court imposes a desegregation plan on an urban school board, the congressional offices immediately are contacted for aid in safeguarding existing sources of funding and in determining eligibility for new ones. When a major employer announces plans to quit an area, the congressional offices immediately are contacted to explore possibilities for using federal programs to persuade the employer to reconsider. Contractors appreciate a good congressional word with DOD procurement officers. Local artistic groups cannot survive without NEA funding. And, of course, there are the major individual programs such as social security and veterans' benefits that create a steady demand for congressional information and aid services. Such activities are nonpartisan, nonideological, and, most important, noncontroversial. Moreover, the contribution of the congressman in the realm of district service appears considerably greater than the impact of his or her single vote on major national issues. Constituents respond rationally to this modern state of affairs by weighing nonprogrammatic constituency service heavily when casting their congressional votes. And this emphasis on the part of constituents provides the means for incumbents to solidify their hold on the office. Even if elected by a narrow margin, diligent service activities enable a congressman to neutralize or even convert a portion of those who would otherwise oppose him on policy or ideological grounds. Emphasis on local, nonpartisan factors in congressional voting enables the modern congressman to withstand national swings, whereas yesteryear's uninsulated congressmen were more dependent on preventing the occurrence of the swings. . . .

[*The result is the insulation of the modern congressional member from national forces altogether.*]

The withering away of the party organizations and the weakening of party in the electorate have begun to show up as disarray in the party in government. As the electoral fates of congressmen and the president have diverged, their incentives to cooperate have diverged as well. Congressmen have little personal incentive to bear any risk in their president's behalf, since they no longer expect to gain much from his successes or suffer much from his failures. Only those who personally agree with the president's program and/or those who find that program well suited for their particular district support the president. And there are not enough of these to construct the coalitions necessary for action on the major issues now facing the country. By holding only the president responsible for national conditions, the electorate enables officialdom as a whole to escape responsibility. This situation lies at the root of many of the problems that now plague American public life.

## SOME CONSEQUENCES OF THE DECLINE OF COLLECTIVE RESPONSIBILITY

The weakening of party has contributed directly to the severity of several of the important problems the nation faces. For some of these, such as the government's inability to deal with inflation and energy, the connections are obvious. But for other problems, such as the growing importance of single-issue politics and the growing alienation of the American citizenry, the connections are more subtle.

## ■ Immobilism

As the electoral interdependence of the party in government declines, its ability to act also declines. If responsibility can be shifted to another level or to another officeholder, there is less incentive to stick one's neck out in an attempt to solve a given problem. Leadership becomes more difficult, the ever-present bias toward the short-term solution becomes more pronounced, and the possibility of solving any given problem lessens.

. . . [P]olitical inability to take actions that entail short-run costs ordinarily will result in much higher costs in the long run—we cannot continually depend on the technological fix. So the present American immobilism cannot be dismissed lightly. The sad thing is that the American people appear to understand the depth of our present problems and, at least in principle, appear prepared to sacrifice in furtherance of the long-run good. But they will not have an opportunity to choose between two or more such long-term plans. Although both parties promise tough, equitable policies, in the present state of our politics, neither can deliver.

## ■ Single-Issue Politics

In recent years both political analysts and politicians have decried the increased importance of single-issue groups in American politics. Some in fact would claim that the present immobilism in our politics owes more to the rise of single-issue groups than to the decline of party. A little thought, however, should reveal that the two trends are connected. Is single-issue politics a recent phenomenon? The contention is doubtful; such groups have always been active participants in American politics. The gun lobby already was a classic example at the time of President Kennedy's assassination. And however impressive the antiabortionists appear today, remember the temperance movement, which succeeded in getting its constitutional amendment. American history contains numerous forerunners of today's groups, from anti-Masons to abolitionists to the Klan—singularity of purpose is by no means a modern phenomenon. Why, then, do we hear all the contemporary hoopla about single-issue groups? Probably because politicians fear them now more than before and thus allow them to play a larger role in our politics. Why should this be so? Simply because the parties are too weak to protect their members and thus to contain single-issue politics.

In earlier times single-issue groups were under greater pressures to reach accommodations with the parties. After all, the parties nominated candidates, financed candidates, worked for candidates, and, perhaps most important, party voting protected candidates. When a contemporary single-issue group threatens to "get" an officeholder, the threat must be taken seriously. . . .

Not only did the party organization have greater ability to resist single-issue pressures at the electoral level, but the party in government had greater ability to control the agenda, and thereby contain single-issue pressures at the policy-making level. Today we seem condemned to go through an annual agony over federal abortion funding. There is little doubt that politicians on both sides would prefer to reach some reasonable compromise at the committee level and settle the issue. But in today's decentralized Congress there is no way to put the lid on. In contrast, historians tell us that in the late nineteenth century a large portion of the Republican constituency was far less interested in the tariff and other questions of national economic development than in whether German immigrants should be permitted to teach their native language in their local schools, and whether Catholics and "liturgical Protestants" should be permitted to consume alcohol. Interestingly, however, the national agenda of the period is devoid of such issues. And when they do show up on the state level, the exceptions prove the rule; they produce party splits and striking defeats for the party that allowed them to surface.

In sum, a strong party that is held accountable for the government of a nation-state has both the ability and the incentive to contain particularistic pressures. It controls nominations, elections, and the agenda, and it collectively realizes that small minorities are small minorities no matter how intense they are. But as the parties decline they lose control over nominations and campaigns, they lose the loyalty of the voters, and they lose control of the agenda. Party officeholders cease to be held collectively accountable for party performance, but they become individually exposed to the political pressure of myriad interest groups. The decline of party permits interest groups to wield greater influence, their success encourages the formation of still more interest groups, politics becomes increasingly fragmented, and collective responsibility becomes still more elusive.

## ■ Popular Alienation from Government

For at least a decade political analysts have pondered the significance of survey data indicative of a steady increase in the alienation of the American public from the political process. . . . The American public is in a nasty mood, a cynical, distrusting, and resentful mood. The question is, Why?

If the same national problems not only persist but worsen while ever-greater amounts of revenue are directed at them, why shouldn't the typical citizen conclude that most of the money must be wasted by incompetent officials? If narrowly based interest groups increasingly affect our politics, why shouldn't citizens increasingly conclude that the interests run the government? For fifteen years the citizenry has listened to a steady stream of promises but has seen very little in the way of follow-through. An increasing proportion of the electorate does not believe that elections make a difference, a fact that largely explains the much-discussed post-1960 decline in voting turnout.

Continued public disillusionment with the political process poses several real dangers. For one thing, disillusionment begets further disillusionment. Leadership becomes more difficult if citizens do not trust their leaders and will not give them the benefit of a doubt. Policy failure becomes more likely if citizens expect the policy to fail. Waste increases and government competence decreases as citizens disrespect for politics encourages a lesser breed of person to make careers in government. And "government by a few big interests" becomes more than a cliché if citizens increasingly decide the cliché is true and cease participating for that reason.

Finally, there is the real danger that continued disappointment with particular government officials ultimately metamorphoses into disillusionment with government per se. Increasing numbers of citizens believe that government is not simply overextended but perhaps incapable of any further bettering of the world. Yes, government is overextended, inefficiency is pervasive, and ineffectiveness is all too common. But government is one of the few instruments of collective action we have, and even those committed to selective pruning of government programs cannot blithely allow the concept of an activist government to fall into disrepute.

Of late, however, some political commentators have begun to wonder whether contemporary thought places sufficient emphasis on government *for* the people. In stressing participation have we lost sight of *accountability?* Surely, we should be as concerned with what government produces as with how many participate. What good is participation if the citizenry is unable to determine who merits their support?

Participation and responsibility are not logically incompatible, but there is a degree of tension between the two, and the quest for either may be carried to extremes. Participation maximizers find themselves involved with quotas and virtual representation schemes, while responsibility maximizers can find themselves with a closed shop under boss rule. Moreover, both qualities can weaken the democracy they supposedly underpin. Unfettered participation produces Hyde Amendments and immobilism.

## Weakening of Party Organization

*See Lowi and Ginsberg, pp. 501–513 or brief edition, pp. 289–301*

*The negative campaigning dominating the airwaves is perhaps more troubling to many Americans than the vast sums of money elected officials must raise to win an election. Campaign finance laws regulate the amount of money any individual, group, or corporation can give, where the money can or cannot come from, how politicians raise the money, and how it is spent. Yet congressional investigations and daily media accounts reveal regulatory softness, intricate evasions of these restrictions, and enormous contributions connected to legislative votes and agendas for both political parties. Dan Hamburg, former U.S. Representative from California, reflects on his time "inside the money chase." His perpetual fund-raising experience left him less than enchanted with the democratic process, and ultimately concerned with the significance of American citizenship and of American government as a force in society.*

*What do you think? Does the need to raise money keep members of Congress connected to the people? Or does the "money chase" distort democracy? What reforms would you suggest?*

# Dan Hamburg
## "Inside the Money Chase"*

My wife and I have a favorite saying: "It's not the money." To me, getting money to make my first run for Congress in 1992 was simply something I needed to do to win. I certainly never intended to become the least bit impressed with it or driven by it. After getting elected, I was sure I could be a freewheeling progressive. Joining what I believed would be legions of my kind in the new Congress and a Democratic administration, we would begin to put the country right.

When I ran for Congress, I had never raised more than $15,000 for a political race. But I knew that Congressional seats didn't come cheap. I contacted an old supporter, Bonnie Raitt, and asked her to help me raise money for my campaign. To my elation, she said yes and I was off and running.

Bonnie, along with Holly Near, did several concerts for me in early 1992, raising a total of about $60,000. It turned out, incredibly, that no one challenged me in the spring primary. I remember thinking that the money would now flow like wine. It was exciting. I had already caught money fever. By June, I was broke, my campaign management team having taken virtually all the money for their salaries and ancillary expenses. My Sacramento-based campaign manager put it this way: "As a candidate, you have two jobs: carry the message and raise money." It was time to raise more. I was learning my job.

I raised another $800,000 or so for the general election. Bonnie helped raise another chunk with a blockbuster concert with Jackson Browne on the driving range of a Napa country club golf course. Where did the rest of the money come from? Environmentalists. Labor. Women. Peace and justice organizations. That was my mantra whenever anybody asked me where the money was coming from. I said it with pride, as if cool people got cool money and everything was cool.

Pretty quickly I lost track of where much of the money was coming from. I was far too busy trying to cover the sprawling seven-county district and raise the money needed to keep an ever-expanding campaign team in place. Some money came from wealthy individuals who were known to me simply as "major donors," some from state and national parties, some from Democratic incumbents who just wanted to make sure the party continued to hold the majority in the House. About a third of the roughly $900,000 raised for the 1992 campaign came from PACs. At one point, at the urging of Democratic Representative Bill Brewster, I found myself talking to the N.R.A. about giving me money because my opponent had voted to restrict sales of automatic weapons. Finally, they offered me no money, but agreed not to fund my opponent either.

* Dan Hamburg, "Inside the Money Chase" in *The Nation* (May 5, 1997). Reprinted with permission.

By the time I won the general election that November, the campaign was in debt about $80,000 and I was personally in debt another $40,000. But hell, I'd raised nearly a million and now I was the incumbent, so no sweat! It took nearly all of 1993 to clear my '92 campaign expenses. It turned out that in off-years (years in which there is not a House election) much of the fundraising had to be done at in-district events in which supporters pay and gather around to hear the celebrity/politician expound on the political wars in D.C.

In September 1993, I went to see the President and Vice President at the White House. This was a small meeting, with about eight members of Congress, Bill Clinton and Al Gore, George Stephanopoulos and David Gergen. The day before, I had been at the annual picnic of the Operating Engineers, a union that "maxed out" to me ($5,000 each for primary and general elections). At the picnic, several of the union leaders had gone over a problem they were having—getting the go-ahead for a freeway-widening project in the district. I said I'd do what I could. The next day, there I was at the White House arguing for more money for "infrastructure," including, of course, the project the Operating Engineers were pushing.

This is the kind of thing members of Congress do routinely. After all, this is how the system is supposed to work. The member goes out into the district, talks to the constituents, finds out what they need and then fights to get it, especially if it's for a group that's good for $10,000 the next time election season comes around. I knew lots of reasons that the widening project was a bad idea, at best unnecessary. In fact, I had voted against it as a county official several times. But it wasn't hard to conjure up reasons to be for it either: primarily, jobs and campaign money.

Once, when I complained to my administrative assistant (and '92 campaign fundraising director) about how much time it was taking and how demeaned I felt constantly sticking my hand out for money, her response was, "If you Congressmen didn't have to grovel for money, your heads would be even fatter." I really thought about that. Is fundraising some kind of leveling device, forcing the pol to go to the people? I concluded that if it is, the leveling needs to happen in other ways. There's nothing inherently character-building or constituent-serving about having to call people on the phone again and again to get them to cut you a check or come to a fundraiser at $250, $500 or $1,000 a ticket, stand around in some tastefully remodeled Victorian on the Hill and eat hors d'oeuvres and drink wine with people with whom your connection is a check.

A "successful politician" is a politician with a healthy bankroll. Behaviors that we might think of as degrading to the profession or "detrimental to democracy" are to the politician both legitimate and necessary. All the rewards come with raising tons of money—pundits laud your "prolific fundraising," colleagues have confidence in your viability (i.e., re-electability), staff members need not fear for their jobs.

Most large individual donations come from wealthy business-people. Campaign rules disallow corporate giving to individual candidates. So unless they give through a PAC, individuals must write non-tax-deductible personal checks, for which they expect a service. For example, the Congressional district I represented has lots of wineries. Wealthy vintners routinely give large checks to candidates, often to candidates from both parties. When the Clinton Administration considered raising taxes on alcohol to help cut the deficit in 1993, the wine and beer industries screamed bloody murder. Raise taxes on the sustenance of Joe and Jane Sixpack? Blasphemy! Raise taxes on the nectar of yuppiedom? Quel horror! Besides, it would cost jobs and tarnish one of the few bright spots in U.S. trade.

Members of Congress who represent competitive districts spend hours each week, and during campaign season hours each day, making fundraising calls from private offices on Capitol Hill. "Making your calls" is a basic responsibility of the job. But the problem doesn't end there. Despite all the whitewash, the fact is that campaign funds are routinely solicited from federal offices.

When I entered Congress, I was advised that while it was illegal to make fundraising calls from my Congressional office, it was legal to accept return calls. Of course, even this phony line is frequently crossed. Politicians as seemingly at odds as Phil Gramm and Al Gore have claimed that it's O.K. to use Senate and even White House offices to make fundraising calls so long as they used their own, or their campaign committee's, credit cards. Gore came up with yet another angle when he claimed that it's O.K. to make such calls from official quarters so long as the recipient was not receiving the call on federal property. The relevant point here, of course, is that public officials should not be soliciting funds from offices owned by the taxpayers.

California Assembly Speaker Jesse Unruh once said, "If you can't take their money and then vote against them, you should get out of politics!" Unruh was no ingénue, but that comment seems ridiculously naïve now. For one thing, money shapes what even makes it to the floor for a vote. Proposals that are perceived by the moneyed interests as truly threatening, such as single-payer health insurance, are quickly squelched by committee chairs fattened up by industry. Sure, the Progressive Caucus gets a few hours once a year to argue for a budget that would slash military spending, but it's a very pro forma exercise. Progressives may take a nick out of the system once in a while, pass an amendment to build three Trident subs instead of four, but that's about it. Money buys power. Why else would it be that only the poor are getting kicked off the government dole?

On a less grand level, here's how it works: A company, say United Parcel Service, has problems with an arcane section of a bill dealing with air transit fees that's coming before your committee. You know there may be some opposition to the bill by the Teamsters, but they haven't pressed their case. The U.P.S. lobbyist meets you at the door of your office as you're returning from the floor (lobbyists have an uncanny knack for finding members and waylaying them). He states his case. He's a nice guy, he sounds authoritative on the subject. You're inclined to say, "Fine, I'll be glad to support your position," or at least, "I can't say how I'll vote but I think what you say has a lot of merit." The fact that this person has handed you two checks for $5,000 over the past months certainly helps seal the deal. The vast majority of your constituents will never know what has happened; the consequences will be well hidden.

Many entrenched politicians are not only able to fund their own re-election campaigns and intimidate potential opponents, they establish their own PACs to give money to other members. This is another way, besides the seniority system, that established politicians influence less-established politicians. It's also another way that money controls politics. Several times I went to the floor of the House to seek out members, whose names I would have typed on an index card, who were known to have money to hand out. These members might be ideological allies or might simply have ambitions to move up through the system by handing out $1,000 checks.

It was no secret in the House that Charlie Rose of North Carolina in-tended to challenge Dick Gephardt for Democratic majority leader. His plan was to run against Gephardt during the party organizational period just before the 104th Congress commenced. I had an important bill before one of Rose's subcommittees, so I felt the need to have him as a friend. After all, he could kill my bill on a whim anytime he desired. Instead, Charlie took me under his wing and helped guide my bill toward passage. He also gave me $1,000 from his personal PAC to help me in an unex-pected primary I faced in the spring of '94, a race in which my challenger spent at least $250,000.

The next time I asked Charlie for money it was for the November gen-eral election. In the meantime, I had decided to support Gephardt to con-tinue as majority leader, mostly because of his strong stance opposing NAFTA and his generally more liberal politics. I also knew that I was fac-ing another million-dollar race. When I approached Charlie for money, his response was, "Son, you better get on over with your friend Gephardt. You won't see any more money coming from me." I felt so awkward and silly. Here I was a grown man, a Congressman, getting blown off for a lousy $1,000.

The issue of campaign finance points to a deeper problem in U.S. pol-itics: the subservience of the political system to the economic system. The real government of our country is economic, dominated by large corpo-rations that charter the state to do their bidding. Fostering a secure envi-ronment in which corporations and their investors can flourish is the paramount objective of both parties. Campaign finance works to place and keep in office those who willingly reproduce this culture. The covenant be-tween the citizen and the law, as recapitulated through the electoral proc-ess, has lost its meaning. Campaign finance is a useful way of looking into a larger question: In an era of increasing economic globalism, when the state itself is fast becoming a subordinate entity, what is the relevance of being an American citizen?

# DEBATING THE ISSUES:
# THE STATE OF THE PARTIES:
# DECAYING OR REVITALIZED?

*See Lowi and Ginsberg, pp. 490–491 or brief edition, pp. 298–299*

*Do the two major political parties offer voters sufficient alternatives? Perhaps more important, are they able to govern in a manner that takes the country forward toward values and priorities deemed essential to American society?*

*Robert Reich, former Secretary of Labor under the first Clinton administration, is pessimistic about the current status of both parties, and frustrated by suggestions that the Democratic Party should become more Republican, or centrist in its policy. The future of the Democratic Party, he argues, lies with a progressive agenda based upon the "moral principles" of American capitalism. The American economy is growing, Reich acknowledges, but a significant number of Americans have been losing ground since the late 1970s, reflecting a growing income inequality between the richest Americans and everyone else. Unemployment may be low in 1997, but more and more people are working at low-wage jobs with little if any benefits such as health care and retirement support. The "political dimension" of this trend is also troubling. People in the bottom half of the income distribution vote less and less. If the Democratic Party is to succeed in the future, Reich argues, it must bring these people to the polls by speaking to their basic concerns.*

*Michigan Governor John Engler has no doubt about the strength and vitality of the Republican Party. The evidence lies not only in the growing number of governors and elected state officials, as well as the Republican majority in Congress, but with the strength of the economy and the success of social welfare programs. Yes, America is quite strong at present, but the credit goes to state governors who have cut taxes, reformed welfare, and cut regulations to encourage growth. More specifically, Engler argues that the credit goes to Republican governors and state legislatures. The Republican Party's success is a "rout" of liberalism, based at the grass roots of the country and manifest in the successful policies that have toppled what Engler argues were the failed liberal policies of the past.*

*An interesting point of contrast in this debate is the source of party strength identified by each author. For Reich, the definition of a progressive moral agenda and hence the revitalization of the Democratic Party implicitly comes from party leadership. For Engler, the strength is the emphasis upon state and local government, where party politics traditionally thrived in the form of ward, city, county, and state-wide committees. Which strategy do you think would be most effective for exercising the collective sovereignty discussed by Fiorina? Why?*

# Robert B. Reich
## "Up from Bipartisanship"*

Conventional political opinion holds that Democrats should henceforth engage in an orgy of bipartisanship. According to this view, Americans are converging at a new center somewhat right of the old center; they want their leaders to work constructively together; and they desire only incremental change—witness the rejection of health care in 1994 and the Contract with America in 1995. The President successfully co-opted the issues of crime, welfare, and fiscal responsibility, leaving Republicans with little to say. Now, it is supposed, Democrats should cement their claim on the center. They should agree with Republicans on a plan to balance the budget, extend NAFTA to Latin America and Asia, ensure the short-term solvency of the Medicare trust fund, make a respectable start on reforming Medicare and Social Security for the long term (which may entail "privatizing" part or all of either one), adjust the Consumer Price Index so that it no longer overstates inflation (a move that helps balance the budget and eases the pressure on Social Security); cut capital gains taxes somewhat; and provide tax breaks for post-secondary education. When necessary to assuage particularly vocal constituencies on any of these issues, they should create bipartisan commissions or panels that will make expert recommendations with which "opinion leaders" and pundits in Washington and New York will agree. All the while, they should do symbolic things that cost very little but exhort the private sector to take action. Hold bipartisan conferences with business leaders. Engage in bipartisan praise of charitable acts—of companies hiring former welfare recipients, of religious and civic groups cleaning up their communities, of individuals who "make a difference." In short, Democrats should become moderate Republicans.

This conventional view does reflect a public weariness with partisan wrangling and ideological posturing. Party affiliation is waning. Washington "gridlock" has bred cynicism. Agreements reached at the end of the 104th Congress to raise the minimum wage, to ensure the continued eligibility for health insurance of workers who had lost theirs when they lost their job, and to "reform" welfare improved the public image of both Congress and the President, and contributed to the victories of incumbents last November at both ends of Pennsylvania Avenue. And it is axiomatic that when the federal government is in the hands of a Democratic president and a Republican Congress in which Democrats have enough votes to sustain a veto or to block legislation in the Senate, some agreement ultimately must be reached if anything is to get done.

The question comes down to where agreement is reached—how much ground Democrats must concede in order to achieve bipartisanship, on what issues they actively and visibly seek compromise—or, alternatively,

* Robert Reich, "Up from Bipartisanship" in *The American Prospect* (May/June 1997). Reprinted with permission.

where and how hard Democrats fight, and how willing they are to hold their ground. The conventional view that bipartisanship is good in and of itself, especially if it congeals around moderate Republicanism, is misleading and dangerous—misleading because it ignores a large and growing portion of the potential electorate who are economically stressed and politically disaffected, dangerous because in so doing it could render the Democratic Party irrelevant and leave this segment of the American population even more disaffected, economically isolated, and susceptible to demagoguery.

## FEEBLE CENTER

When Arthur Schlesinger, Jr., wrote his book, *The Vital Center*, in 1949, the center was resolutely liberal. Today, the supposed national consensus is on terms dictated by the center-right. Half a century ago, Schlesinger could write that since Roosevelt, "One has been able to feel that liberal ideas had access to power in the United States, that liberal purposes were dominating national policy." The vital center, Schlesinger observed, was a liberal center, because it not only empowered the individual both by providing opportunity but also by shielding the individual from brutal social forces.

For all the magnificent triumphs of individualism, we survive only as we remain members of one another. The individual requires a social context, not one imposed by coercion, but one freely emerging in response to his own needs and initiatives. Industrialism has inflicted savage wounds on the human sensibility; the cuts and gashes are to be healed only by a conviction of trust and solidarity with other human beings.

This was the liberal center of a half century ago, not today.

Begin with the economic stress. The national economy is growing at a healthy clip, and we are currently blessed by a combination of low unemployment and low inflation. The so-called "misery index," a combination of both measures, is at its lowest level in 30 years. But it is important to note the unevenness of this benign picture. Most of the growth is going to people at the top, whose incomes have soared. Average wages are rising, but the median wage is barely inching upward, and even this measure hides the fact that a substantial portion of the workforce is still losing ground—following a trend that began in the late 1970s.

Nor do wages tell the whole story. Employer-provided health and pension benefits are declining or disappearing at a rapid rate, particularly for lower-income workers with only high school degrees. Job insecurity is high, especially among those with low or no special skills. Overall levels of unemployment may be low relative to recent history, but more than 10 percent of the adult population of the United States remain either unemployed, or working in part-time jobs when they would prefer full-time jobs, or too discouraged even to look for work—and this percentage reaches 14 percent among those whose formal educations end with high school.

The long-term trend toward income inequality has slowed, largely because labor markets have tightened and a larger portion of the poor or near-poor have found jobs. Such is to be expected at this stage of an economic expansion. But, according to data from the Census and the Bureau of Labor Statistics, earnings inequality among people who have jobs continued to widen through the fourth quarter of 1996 (the last date for which we have data). This is not a statistical fluke; it has nothing to do with how we measure productivity improvements or changes in the cost of living. Every rung on the economic ladder is farther apart than it was 4, 8, or 16 years ago. On few other economic issues is there as much unanimity among researchers. The enduring expansion is surely helping those in the bottom half of the workforce, but the structural trends lying just behind the business cycle—trends having more to do with technological change and global trade and investment than with fiscal and monetary policies—continue to exert powerful centrifugal forces. Unless these deeper trends are addressed, America will maintain its course toward a two-tiered society of have-mores and have-lesses.

Consider now the political dimension. Those in the bottom half of the income distribution are voting less. Data comparing the midterm elections of 1994 with 1990, and the presidential elections of 1992 with 1996, confirm the trend. According to the Census, fully 60 percent of Americans with family incomes over $50,000 voted in the 1994 midterm elections, marking a very slight increase in participation of this group from the previous midterm election in 1990, in which 59 percent voted. By contrast, just 27 percent of those with incomes under $15,000 turned out in 1994, markedly lower than the 34 percent of them who voted in 1990. In the presidential election of 1996, a lower percentage of the voting population turned out than at any time since 1924—seven million fewer people than in the presidential election of 1992. Preliminary evidence suggests that almost all of the new nonvoters were from households earning less than $50,000 a year; three-quarters of them had ended their formal education with high school.

When lower-income people do vote, they tend to vote for Democratic candidates. Those who failed to vote in 1994 but were lured back to the voting booths in 1996 comprised fully a fifth of the electorate last November, and they voted three to one for Clinton. If the same portion of the electorate that voted in the 1992 presidential election had been lured back in 1996, there is a high probability that Democrats would have reclaimed the House of Representatives, if not Congress as a whole.

The telling point is that Democrats did not lure them back. I am not aware of any surveys explaining unambiguously why the nonvoters of 1996 stayed away from the voting booths, but it seems a fair guess that they refrained from voting because they assumed it would make little or no difference to their lives. Lower-wage Americans, in particular, are voting less because they see less reason to vote. Their disconnection from politics and government became vividly apparent to me over the four years I was Secretary of Labor, during the first Clinton administration, when I undertook a kind of free-floating "focus group" across America. I spoke with thousands of people working in factories, hospitals, offices, retail shops, coal mines, telemarketing centers, and in the fields. The vast majority of these people earned below the median wage, and were under significant economic stress. Many were struggling to keep themselves and their families out of poverty. Most worked more than 40 hours a week, whether at one job or several. Only a minority of the people I met had health insurance or an employer-provided pension. Their concerns were almost always the same: having enough money to pay the rent or mortgage, meet the car payments, and buy clothes and food (prices were rising faster than their wages, they often said); coping with the possibility that a member of their family would require hospitalization or otherwise become seriously ill; finding safe and affordable child care services for their younger children when they had to be at work, or taking care of their children when they became sick; and getting their children a good education, which they understood was the necessary prerequisite to a good job. A large majority worried about themselves and their spouses keeping their jobs.

As the economy improved during the four years, fewer people told me there were "no jobs" to be had, but in every other respect the stories I heard did not change. The people I met were "coping," but they felt they were on the verge of adversity. Almost always they asserted they were managing on their own and without help; many were proud of what they were achieving against high odds. They did not think they were entitled to handouts. Nor did they trust large institutions to help them—be they companies, unions, political parties, or state and federal governments. Sometimes they blamed corporations or government for their predicament; occasionally they blamed immigrants, welfare recipients, or foreign trade. But for the most part, they did not impute blame. The stresses they felt were, in their view, the result of impersonal forces over which they had no control, and with which they had to deal on their own. Politics was irrelevant to their lives. They saw no connection between the actions (or inactions) of Washington leaders or their representatives in state capitols, and these mounting stresses. They perceived little difference between the parties.

I do not claim that my sample—although large and often in-depth— was either representative or necessarily sincere. After all, the people with whom I spoke usually knew I was the Secretary of Labor. But what I heard bore strong resemblance to the results of polls and focus groups that political consultants shared with me during these four years. Moreover, the fact that so many low-income Americans would tell me, in my official capacity, that they did not feel that government was helping them deal with the daily challenges they faced, suggests that my sample may, if anything, have understated the actual extent of their disconnection from political life.

One conclusion that can safely be drawn is that the party of nonvoters is larger than either the Democratic or the Republican parties. Another conclusion, almost as safe, is that if Democrats move toward bipartisanship in pursuit of traditionally moderate-Republican goals, the party of nonvoters will continue to gain converts from erstwhile Democrats who see even less reason to go to the polls. The political consequences are not difficult to predict: The major beneficiaries of this continuing erosion will be congressional Republicans, whose majorities would swell after the 1998 midterm elections—putting them in a strong position to pillory the White House for the 22 months leading up to the presidential election of 2000.

Meanwhile, the rightward drift of the White House will have further eroded support among traditional Democrats. Al Gore will not stand a chance. The formidable bloc of lower-wage non-voters will attract the attention of political opportunists hailing from the extreme right or left, who sense possibilities for mobilizing these potential voters by stirring latent resentments. Pat Buchanan tried with some degree of success, even as the economy was expanding. Should the economy turn sour between now and 2000—a not unlikely possibility—the resulting stresses on lower-wage workers could well invite a combustible mix of xenophobia, nativism, and racism, unless these disaffected voters have a more constructive alternative toward which to turn.

The only way to begin to win them back is to address their everyday problems, and do so in a manner that distinguishes Democrats from Republicans. This does not mean Democrats must abandon the center, or disavow moderation. To the contrary, the new progressive strategy must maintain the center ground while reclaiming the traditional Democratic base of lower-wage workers. It should not require choices between "new" Democrat and old, between the suburban middle class and the down-scale, between "family values" and the economy, or between the "free market" and government. These distinctions are lost on most working people. Any successful progressive coalition must embrace both the middle class as well as those below it, address economic stresses that are inextricably related to stresses on family life, and shift the conversation away from the size of government and away from false choices between central planning and free markets, which are Republican obsessions that have only distracted attention from the practical problems of ordinary people. The strategy must instead contain a few bold initiatives that will clearly reduce economic stresses on working families.

Importantly, the new progressive strategy should be based not in ideology or class but in common morality. Here too, I draw on my informal focus groups. Again and again, average working people talked to me about the economy and their families in moral terms. The two central responsibilities of adulthood, they asserted, were working and parenting, and the two are closely related. A willingness to work hard in order to support one's family and a desire to be a good parent are the preconditions upon which all else depends. To the extent that the rest of society has a responsibility as well, it is to help people achieve these two ends. Even though most of those with whom I spoke felt that they could not count on the rest of society to adequately support them in these ways, they readily agreed that society should be supportive. Indeed, they asserted that they owed such support to others less fortunate than they.

## A New Progressive Center

This moral core of American capitalism is seldom if ever articulated, but I felt its force in many of the controversies of the last few years—notably, the struggle to raise the minimum wage, the debate over the Family and Medical Leave Act, the campaign to eradicate sweatshops within our borders, the movement against child labor abroad, the public response to mass layoffs by profitable companies, and the 1996 budget battle over education and training. In each of these instances, a large majority of Americans supported public action, not because they would personally benefit from it but because they were morally offended by the consequences of inaction. Raising the minimum wage was the clearest case in point. In poll after poll, between 75 and 85 percent of Americans consistently were in favor. Only a tiny fraction of these supporters would directly or indirectly benefit from the proposed raise; in fact, were it to go into effect, many would end up paying marginally higher prices for certain goods or services. Yet there was a strong consensus that people who work full-time should receive a wage sufficient to lift them and their families out of poverty. A higher minimum wage was a step toward this goal. A similar broad majority supported the Family and Medical Leave Act, on the ground that someone should not lose a job because a sick child or elderly parent requires their attention.

Others of the issues I listed ignited public indignation, which in turn compelled remedial action by the private sector. And here too, public concern was rooted in morality rather than self-interest. Our discovery of sweatshops in Los Angeles and New York—in which immigrants (legal and illegal) were paid pennies an hour and subjected to dangerous working conditions—precipitated a consumer movement against sweatshops, and forced mass retailers and large manufacturers to establish monitoring systems to inspect the cutting and sewing shops with which they dealt. The revelations about the employment of very young children in South Asia had a similar effect. The spate of large-scale layoffs by profitable companies—culminating in AT&T's stunning announcement in January 1996 that it would lay off 40,000 workers despite its positive balance sheet and the bonuses it subsequently awarded its top executives—generated sufficient outrage as to briefly make "corporate irresponsibility" a political issue even in the Republican primaries, perhaps slowing the downsizing trend. (By the spring of 1996 I was regularly receiving phone calls from chief executives seeking to reassure the administration that the large "restructuring" they were contemplating would result in few if any job losses.) And the frantic eagerness of Republican appropriators to add funding for education and job training, just before the November elections, reflected polls evincing sharp public disapproval of Republican-sponsored cuts in this area.

Behind the struggle over welfare "reform" lurked the same core ideas about work and responsibility. Most people around the country with whom I spoke expressed opposition to the very idea of welfare, and polls underscored the deep-seated antipathy. Welfare recipients are considered "undeserving" poor, in contrast to the working poor (whose wages should be raised) or to people who have lost their jobs through no fault of their own and receive unemployment compensation. Some of the distinction may reflect racism and the false assumption that most welfare recipients are young black women. But my conversations, confirmed by a number of polls, suggested that the major reason for the public's negative view of welfare is that it conflicts with the moral premise that able-bodied people should be working. That premise now applies even to mothers with young children, which marks something of a change in attitudes. As the proportion of working mothers with children under age six rose dramatically— from less than 20 percent of mothers with young children in 1960 to over 50 percent by the early 1980s—public expectations seem to have shifted. If a majority of mothers with young children worked, the public seemed to be saying, what was the moral justification for giving welfare to some who apparently chose not to?

I stress this core set of beliefs about the morality of work, and the reciprocal social obligations it generates, because I think it offers a way for Democrats both to talk convincingly about where we need to move as a society and also to focus on several issues that will engage the party of nonvoters. For starters, begin where the minimum wage and Family and Medical Leave Act ended, and consider the next set of minimum standards at work. One might require from employers a minimum level of health insurance for an employee and a dependant. No large bureaucracy would be needed to implement such a requirement. Government would need only to specify the contents of the minimum health insurance, just as government specifies the minimum wage. No single business would be put in competitive jeopardy because all businesses would bear the same minimum cost per employee, as is true of the minimum wage. Much of the cost would be passed on to consumers in any event. Even if the minimum health insurance package ended up adding another two dollars an hour to payrolls, the effective minimum wage plus minimum health would still be lower than the real minimum wage of the late 1960s (in 1997 dollars).

A related step might be to assure safe and affordable day care for preschoolers, along with meaningful family medical leave from work for parents of school-age children bedridden with common childhood infirmities like the flu, a bad cold, or the chickenpox. Working parents in my free-floating focus group returned to these problems again and again. It is simply not true that working parents easily can rely on extended families or their own parents to provide child care. They worry that the only child care they can afford is neither safe nor adequate. Democrats should press for a refundable child care tax credit, providing lower-wage working parents with up to $2,000 per year in child care expenses, and middle-income working parents a direct credit off their taxes up to $2,000. Moreover, the Family and Medical Leave Act, as currently designed, covers only "serious" health conditions requiring medical treatment and visits to the doctor. In more common situations, parents now have no protection against job loss. Yet recent studies show that one in six working parents with young children stays home with a sick child for an average of four weeks or more per year, often thereby jeopardizing their jobs. Expand the FMLA to cover common child ailments keeping parents home. Expand it also to provide for paid maternity leave of up to six weeks. Most women executives or professionals already receive paid maternity leave; the United States is the only industrialized nation that does not extend this benefit to all working women.

Move now to welfare, and to the implicit societal obligation lying behind its "reform"—which must be to ensure that anyone who loses welfare benefits and who needs a job can find one. The moral logic here extends beyond the welfare population, to all people who want and need work in our society. On this point, the vast majority of the public agree: It is not enough that someone be ready and willing to work. There should be a job. That monetary policy is now engineered to lift short-term interest rates when the official rate of unemployment sinks much lower than 5.5 percent presents a logical inconsistency with this principle that has not deeply permeated the public's consciousness. And that is precisely the point. Democrats should use welfare reform as a way to revive the debate over the best means of assuring "full employment."

If the Federal Reserve Board is certain that long-term interest rates will soar if it cuts short-term rates any more than it already has, then we are left with only two choices. Either the private sector voluntarily must create additional private-sector jobs for all those who cannot find other employment—a highly implausible outcome—or government must create public-service jobs for them. Spotty "work-fare" programs for former welfare recipients will not be adequate, because the pool of unemployed adults extends far beyond those on welfare. Ultimately, we will need a new Works Progress Administration, the cost of which might plausibly be borne by businesses in the form of a very small (1 percent) corporate tax earmarked for public-service jobs where no private-sector jobs are available.

Another minimum requirement: Profitable companies intent on shedding workers should be required to provide six months of severance pay, so that employees can find and train for new jobs. Few events are as traumatic to working families as the sudden loss of a job. Unemployment insurance covers only about a third of job losers. And here too, my "focus group" spoke repeatedly in moral terms: Common decency demands that loyal workers not be treated like disposable pieces of machinery.

The third moral principle at the core of American capitalism is that people should be able to make the most of their talents and abilities. Public support for education has been a feature of American life since the early nineteenth century, culminating in the great "high school" movement of the early decades of the twentieth century and the vast extension of state-supported higher education in the two decades after the Second World War. But not since the GI Bill and the National Defense Education Act in the 1950s has the federal government taken a bold lead. The President recently stated that education and training will be the central focuses of his second administration, but the problem is one of scale. The federal government is still a bit player in elementary and secondary education, providing only 8 cents of every dollar devoted to it. The federal share of elementary and secondary education costs has actually declined in the last quarter century. Half of the revenues supporting K–12 education come from local property taxes, the distribution of which has become ever more skewed toward affluent townships. The start of another demographic wave is further straining state and local resources. During the next decade an additional three million children will enter our nation's primary schools, and high school enrollments will increase 15 percent. Simply to maintain current levels of services will require an estimated 190,000 additional teachers, 6,000 more schools, and approximately $15 billion in additional operating expenditures. Nothing so far proposed in the federal budget comes close to dealing with this challenge.

Voluntary national standards are a starting place, not an ending place. Significant resources are needed, and the federal government must step into the breach. Democrats must also talk straight-forwardly about what to do with schools that don't measure up. Putting them under "state receivership" will not necessarily guarantee improvements. School "choice" is a fine concept so long as the poorest children or those who are the most difficult to teach or to discipline do not end up dumped together in the worst schools. Parents are clearly worried about their schools, and lower-income parents have the most to worry about. One possibility: In return for sharp increases in federal assistance, the states, school districts, principals, and teachers should agree to achieve specific improvements in performance. A second possibility, which also deals with the problem of finding safe and affordable child care for school-age children of parents who work: Extend the school day to 5:30 p.m. The conventional school day ending at 3 p.m. is a vestige of an agrarian economy in which children were needed in the afternoon on the farm. But it has become a major burden to working families. Federal funding should be conditioned on all-day operations. A third possibility, rendered only marginally more possible by the President's proposed $1,500-a-year educational tax credit: A thirteenth and fourteenth year of education for all, centered on computer literacy, problem solving, and basic work skills. The new economy demands it. The extra federal funds needed to accomplish these three goals—tens of billions of dollars a year—should come directly out of "corporate welfare" in the federal budget. Eliminate the tax loopholes and spending subsidies going to specific companies and industries, and earmark the savings for education.

In sum, build on the three moral principles at the core of American capitalism: Someone who works diligently should have a minimally decent job including minimum health care, child care, and severance pay in the event of a layoff; anyone who wants and needs a job should get one, including a public-service job if none is available in the private sector; anyone who wants to get ahead should have a good school, meeting national standards, which operates full-day, and extends through fourteenth grade.

This is hardly a radical or even a terribly liberal agenda. It is not particularly redistributionist, nor does it rely heavily on the state. Nor does it challenge values that most Americans hold dear. On the contrary, it helps make them a reality. It holds companies accountable to employees and communities, not by exhortation, but through minimum standards and contributions which improve the odds that prosperity will be widely shared.

Most Americans value a society whose ground rules allow ordinary people to work hard and to parent well, without having to sacrifice the one for the other, or to worry that their loyalty to their job will not be reciprocated. Alas, that ideal is far from today's prevailing social reality and far from today's political center, with its simple celebration of entrepreneurship, fiscal balance, and small government. With the right so squarely in the saddle, this is the wrong moment to seek a bipartisan consensus for its own sake. To combine the best of the liberal legacy with a new progressivism, we need nothing so much as a new partisanship.

# John Engler
## "The Liberal Rout"*

There is a story the late publisher Henry Regnery liked to tell about one of his first conversations with Russell Kirk, the founder of postwar American conservative thought and a native of Michigan. In 1952, Kirk submitted a major book manuscript to Regnery and suggested that it be titled *The Conservative Rout*. Regnery talked him out of it. That title seemed too gloomy, too fatalistic. What if conservative ideas made a comeback?

* John Engler, "The Liberal Rout" in *Policy Review* (January/February 1997). Reprinted with permission.

Would not *The Conservative Mind* be a better title in the long run? And so it was.

Were Kirk and Regnery alive today, they might revisit the word "rout" —and this time apply it instead to liberalism. Apologists for the most liberal ideals of FDR, JFK, and LBJ are in serious retreat on the eve of the 21st century.

Bill Clinton had enough liberal credentials to win the nomination (and renomination) of the Democratic party. But his re-election in 1996 can hardly be viewed as a victory for the left wing of his party. The Man from Hope remains at best a "plurality president," having failed to win a majority of votes in both 1992 and 1996. After Democrats finished off the champagne on Election Night last November, they were no doubt sobered by the realization that, beyond the Oval Office, the Democratic Party is now much weaker than it was in November 1992 when Bill Clinton was first elected. The composition of the nation's legislatures and governorships shows why: In 1997, there are 11 more GOP senators than in 1992, prior to Clinton's election. What's more, Americans returned a more conservative Senate to Washington than occupied that chamber during the last Congress. Not since the 1920s have so many Republicans filled the U.S. Senate.

Americans expressed their confidence in most of the conservative freshmen from the Class of '94 by sending them back to the House. At press time, several elections were undecided, but this much is clear: Today there are about 50 more House Republicans than in 1992. Only twice since the onset of the New Deal (in 1947–49, during the 80th Congress, and during the last Congress) have there been more GOP representatives on Capitol Hill.

Today there are 14 more Republican governors than in 1992. More Americans are represented by Republican governors than ever before in our nation's history—192 million. That's 74 percent of the American people. In state senates, there are 172 more Republicans today than in 1992. And in the lower chambers of state legislatures, there are 228 more Republicans today than in 1992. These numbers suggest that a major realignment of American politics is underway. Even before the votes were counted, *New York Times* reporter R. W. Apple remarked, "No matter who wins the presidency on Tuesday, no matter who gains or loses control of Congress, the returns, like the conduct of candidates great and small these many months, will confirm the nation's drift to the right."

So what of President Clinton's re-election? Two factors helped the silver-tongued Arkansan retain control of the White House, and both have to do with the conservative temper of the 1990s. The first concerns Bill Clinton's political instincts and his skill as a campaigner. In response to the 1994 elections—a debacle for liberal Democrats across the nation— Clinton recast himself to fit the *Zeitgeist* and campaigned on the premise that "the era of Big Government is over." Sounding positively Reaganesque, he offered the most conservative rhetoric of any Democratic president this century. (One wonders whether Clinton has recently graced the walls of the Oval Office with portraits of Grover Cleveland and Martin Van Buren—the only Democratic presidents in history who both preached and practiced the virtues of a limited federal government.)

With the help of consultant Dick Morris and a bevy of polls and focus groups, Clinton succeeded in marketing himself as a centrist considerably to the right of his liberal friends and his liberal past. He ran on such conservative themes as deficit-cutting, targeted tax cuts, job growth, welfare reform; school uniforms, youth curfews, and more cops on the street. An English observer recently mused, "If you imagine a president committed to a balanced budget, welfare reform, and a stronger death penalty, would you say conservatism was losing?"

The second factor has little to do with Bill Clinton himself, yet it played an enormous role in his re-election. Few commentators noticed, but the campaign themes of 1996 were determined largely by politics and policies in the states, where conservative ideas have long been ascendant. It was the achievements of the nation's 32 Republican governors and their legislatures, not those of the White House, that made a majority of Americans believe the nation was on the right track. Their record of reform helped Bill Clinton win re-election. The Man from Hope adroitly, if shamelessly, took credit for the many impressive accomplishments of GOP administrations from Albany to Sacramento, and from Lansing to Austin.

## CUTTING TAXES AND SPENDING

One of the critical debates before American voters in the 1990s has been the proper size and scope of government at every level. All sides have reached a consensus that government should serve citizens better, limit its role in society, and give taxpayers more value for their dollar.

Quietly, without fanfare, Republican governors and legislatures beyond the glare of Washington politics have been balancing budgets, cutting taxes, and making government more responsive to the people. Over the past four years, while Bill Clinton has consistently refused to support the Balanced Budget Amendment to the Constitution, every GOP governor has been submitting a balanced budget to his or her legislature on an annual basis.

In just one year, Connecticut governor John Rowland turned a $174-million deficit into a $74-million surplus. Ohio governor George V. Voinovich has held state spending to its lowest rate of growth in four decades, and turned a $1.5-billion deficit in 1991 into an $800-million surplus. Similarly, in Minnesota and Michigan, respectively, Governor Arne Carlson and I each inherited deficits of $1.8 billion. Governor Carlson not only erased that deficit; he turned it into a $824-million surplus for 1996. In Michigan, we transformed a $1.8-billion deficit into a surplus of more than $1 billion. Today Michigan's "rainy day" fund is among the largest in the nation.

At the same time they were submitting balanced budgets, most GOP governors and legislatures were—guess what?—cutting taxes. Liberal Democrats have ignored an overwhelming body of evidence that tax cuts help create new jobs and fill the treasury at the same time. Yet the examples are legion. In recent years, many governors have seen significant growth in jobs after enacting significant tax cuts, including Massachusetts's William Weld, New Jersey's Christine Todd Whitman, Pennsylvania's Tom Ridge, Virginia's George Allen, Idaho's Phil Batt, and Arizona's Fife Symington.

Since 1991, Michigan has cut taxes more often than any other state— 21 times. These 21 tax cuts have resulted in a savings of $6.5 billion to taxpayers. The average family of four has been able to keep $2,000 more in their wallets every year; it is they, not government bureaucrats, who get to choose whether to save or spend the money.

The economic results of these tax cuts have been nothing short of spectacular. They have helped create more than a half-million new jobs. Remember that Michigan used to be thought of as a Rust Belt state suffering high unemployment rates. From the late 1970s to the early 1990s—in fact, for 192 months in a row—our unemployment rate was consistently above the national average. By contrast, it has been at or below the national average for the past 34 consecutive months. As of this writing, Michigan's unemployment rate has been below 5 percent every month in 1996, while the U.S. rate has hovered above 5 percent. That makes Michigan's unemployment rate for 1996 the best since 1969. The Michigan experience shows that significant tax reductions do help cut the deficit, balance the budget, and turbocharge the economy.

Last September, the Cato Institute released a study that compared the 10 states that raised taxes the most during the 1990s with the 10 states that cut taxes the most. Just what were the economic and fiscal results of these "laboratories of democracy"?

The 10 tax-cutting states economically out-performed the 10 tax-hiking states. Measured in current dollars, the economies of the tax cutters grew by 33 percent from 1990 to 1995, while the economies of the tax hikers lagged behind, with 27 percent growth. More striking is the contrast in job growth. The top 10 tax-cutting states gained 1.84 million new jobs between 1990 and 1995, while the top 10 tax-hiking states created zero net new jobs over that same period.

Income for a family of four grew by $1,600 more in the tax-cutting states than the tax-hiking ones. The tax-cutting states have experienced more vigorous population growth in the 1990s: 7.4 percent, compared with just 4.2 percent average growth in the tax-hiking states. The tax-cutting states have not only balanced their budgets; but they also now enjoy a budget reserve that amounts on average to 7.1 percent of state expenditures. The tax-hiking states, by contrast, have a budget reserve on average of only 1.7 percent. As a result, Moody's bond ratings are higher for states that cut taxes than for states that raised them.

Expanding economies, robust job growth, rising personal income, vigorous population growth, historically large "rainy day" funds—no wonder

Clinton could claim that it looks like morning in America. But odds are that it is only dawning brightly if you live in a fiscally conservative state. Bill Clinton owes his re-election in part to the policies of these GOP governors.

## REGULATORY REFORM

The top tax-cutting states are doing relatively well, no doubt about it. But the United States is currently experiencing its slowest economic recovery this century. Bureaucratic strangulation is a major factor in the long-term slowdown of the national economy. In 1965, there were about 17,000 pages in the Federal Register. Just since 1992, the volume of federal rules and regulations has grown by 231,000 pages—the most prodigious growth rate since Jimmy Carter. It appears that Messrs. Clinton and Gore are not so much reinventing government as simply inventing it—and doing so prodigiously. Richard Vedder at Washington University's Center for the Study of American Business estimates that government regulations now cost our nation a staggering $1.3 trillion each year.

Most governors believe government should be less intrusive. Many are aggressively attacking unnecessary rules and regulations wherever they can. In California last year, Governor Pete Wilson abolished some 4,000 useless and outdated rules and regulations. In Kansas, Governor Bill Graves imposed a six-month moratorium on new government regulations, then eliminated 530 of the most burdensome and obsolete ones. In the past year, we in Michigan have rescinded more than 2,000 rules and regulations.

With Republicans in control of the 105th Congress and GOP governors at the helm in about two-thirds of the states, the Clinton administration will be thwarted in its attempts to promulgate new rules and regulations. GOP governors support the efforts of congressional Republicans to reform the federal regulatory system and impose cost-benefit analysis before the Federal Register grows any larger.

## WELFARE REFORM

The so-called Great Society turned out to be neither great nor good for society. By the 1990s, it was clear that the federal welfare system was discouraging work, financial independence, and the formation of families. Yet Bill Clinton twice vetoed welfare reform and held his nose last August when he signed the third bill Congress sent to his desk. Four years into his presidency, Clinton had done little to fulfill his 1992 campaign pledge "to end welfare as we know it"—but he was happy to take credit for the success of the states while masking his party's hostility to transferring power out of Washington.

Shortly after Clinton signed the welfare-reform bill, Health and Human Services Secretary Donna Shalala told the *New Yorker* magazine, "Everyone agrees that [Clinton] signed [welfare reform] and he has to fix it, and to fix it we need to elect a Democratic president and Democratic Congress in 1996, so we can repeal the parts of the bill we hate."

There's more than a little irony to the fact that for three years, Clinton talked the talk of welfare reform while refusing to sign a bill. New York senator Daniel Patrick Moynihan aptly observed of Clinton's decision to sign this legislation 14 weeks before the election, "If it were 14 weeks after the election, he'd say no."

Once again, the governors deserve the credit for leading the welfare-reform movement. They understood that the welfare system could not be transformed unless it was linked to personal responsibility and accountability. Throughout the 1990s, many governors have applied for and received federal waivers to loosen Washington's grip on the welfare system. Waivers are cumbersome, bureaucratic procedures, but they have at least enabled the states to begin finding innovative solutions to the social and economic problems caused by dependency. The results have been dramatic. States with Republican governors for at least the last four years have already seen the number of people receiving Aid to Families with Dependent Children (AFDC) decrease by an average of 16 percent since 1993.

No GOP governor has garnered more national attention for his welfare reforms than Wisconsin's Tommy Thompson. Building on the highly successful "Work Not Welfare" program, his administration in 1996 launched "Wisconsin Works," or "W-2." This program requires welfare recipients to participate in employment and job training to receive benefits. Since Wisconsin implemented these and other reforms, its welfare caseload has decreased by 33 percent.

Common-sense welfare reforms have also been implemented by, among others, New Hampshire's Steve Merrill, Connecticut's John Rowland, New York's George Pataki, Illinois's Jim Edgar, Iowa's Terry Branstad, Tennessee's Don Sundquist, Mississippi's Kirk Fordice, Texas's George W. Bush, Utah's Mike Leavitt, and Arizona's Fife Symington.

Our experience with welfare reform in the Great Lakes State has also been encouraging. Michigan requires welfare recipients to seek work, receive job training, or perform community service for at least 20 hours a week. Since we implemented our program "To Strengthen Michigan Families" in 1992:

• The AFDC caseload has dropped for 30 consecutive months;

• The number of welfare recipients in Michigan has fallen to its lowest level in a quarter-century;

• 101,652 families no longer receive cash benefits because they are working and earning paychecks;

- Almost one in three Michigan welfare recipients on AFDC is working; nationally, only one in 11 is working. In our state, moreover, about half of all two-parent families on welfare are working.

The success of Michigan and other states shows that the 104th Congress was right to try to get Washington out of the way of welfare reform. Some, like Virginia under Governor Allen, have passed time limits for benefits so that welfare cannot become a way of life. Others, like California, require beneficiaries to stay in school and earn educational credentials, a crucial step toward achieving independence. Still others, such as Massachusetts under Governor Weld, have ended the financial incentive to have additional children while on welfare by requiring teen mothers under the age of 18 to live at home. Whatever the particulars of reform, the 50 laboratories of democracy will continue to find innovative solutions to help the poor help themselves. Washington should just stay out of the way.

## EDUCATION REFORM

As William Bennett and Lamar Alexander have frequently noted, education in America is the constitutional responsibility of our states, the social responsibility of our communities, and the moral responsibility of our families. Our nation does not need a $31-billion federal Department of Education. This agency contributes 7 percent of the funding of our nation's schools while mandating about 50 percent of the paperwork. And for all that meddling, not one bureaucrat in the Education Department teaches our students to be more competent in math, science, English, history, and government. It is time to return the money held hostage in Washington to the states and their citizens. After all, it's their money.

The national leaders in education reform have been the states, not Washington bureaucrats. More parental involvement, higher standards, greater discipline, increased autonomy for teachers, more choice for students and their families—these are the keys to improving our public schools and making them the best in the world.

Governors have long understood that. They have led the burgeoning charter-school movement, which is injecting competition into the nation's public schools. Now there are hundreds of these innovative schools around the nation—including 116 in California, 114 in Arizona, and 74 in Michigan. In my state alone, charter public schools are serving more than 10,400 students. And contrary to union propaganda, they are not elitist. In Michigan, for example, one in every three charter public schools was founded by African-American educators; more than 50 percent of the enrollment in charter schools is African American or at-risk students. As a result, charter public schools serve more than twice the minority population that conventional public schools do. Michigan's first charter school, in the heart of Detroit, was so popular that its 300 slots drew more than

5,000 applications. One child was so eager to be admitted that he applied more than 100 times!

Even more sweeping plans have been enacted in Wisconsin and Ohio, giving students in the lowest-performing and least-disciplined schools the opportunity to choose better schools for their children. Bureaucrats and special interests can no longer keep our nation's children chained to a monopoly of mediocrity. The states will be in the vanguard of educational liberation, ensuring educational options for all families.

## Free the States!

Observers of all political persuasions agree: Liberalism is suffering a rout. America is choosing to go right and return to its conservative roots. In the 1990s, Republican governors have worked closely with legislatures to spearhead needed reform. Year after year, it is the governors who are slashing deficits and balancing the budget; who are cutting taxes and eliminating red tape; who are restoring personal responsibility to and reducing dependency on the welfare system; who are making public schools more accountable to parents and their communities.

In 1996, Bill Clinton was able to parlay the governors' accomplishments into a successful reelection bid. But more enduring than any cleverly run campaign is the legacy of state-driven reform. For the foreseeable future, the domestic reforms that are most needed and most attuned to the conservative temper of the American people will continue to come from the nation's governors, working with their respective legislatures. They have a proven record of success. And they are more accountable to the people than any Beltway bureaucrat. Thus it is critical that Washington do the right thing for our nation.

Our message is: Free the states! Unshackle us from overweening federal control. Let us in the states govern as the U.S. Constitution meant us to govern. This is already beginning to happen, of course. During the past two years, the Republican-led 104th Congress ushered in a new spirit of cooperation with the governors and began the process of returning power to the states. All indications are that the Republican-led 105th Congress will try to devolve even more power, consistent with the Tenth Amendment.

But what of the Democrat in the White House? Although Bill Clinton is a former governor and has lately learned to speak like a conservative, deep down he probably has little sympathy for the states and their drive for reform. Therefore those of us beyond the Beltway dare not take devolution for granted. We know all about the false starts of the past.

In 1935, when the New Deal was taking root, Supreme Court justice Louis Brandeis told a top aide to Roosevelt, "This is the end of this business of centralization, and I want you to go back and tell the president that we are not going to let this government centralize everything. It's come to an end. As for your young men, you call them together and tell them to get out of Washington—tell them to go home, back to the states. That is where they must do their work."

Amen to that.

Let us hope that enough people in the Washington establishment see the wisdom of these words. Let us also hope that, during the presidential campaign four years from now, there will be candidates who do not merely speak like conservatives, but who truly believe in conservative ideas and know how to implement conservative policies consistent with the best in our nation's tradition.

# 12

## Groups and Interests

### The Character of Interest Groups: Who Is Represented?

*See Lowi and Ginsberg, pp. 520–523 or brief edition, pp. 307–311*

*In the United States the right to associate freely with others—and particularly to pursue political ends—has long been viewed as the cornerstone of American democracy. Respect for that right, in fact, stood in marked contrast to political systems in Europe at the time the Constitution was granted, which often suppressed political associations that were perceived as posing threats to the existing regime.*

*Alexis de Tocqueville argued that the right to associate provides an important check on the power of majorities in democratic regimes, where that power places minority interests in constant jeopardy. Tocqueville pointed out that allowing citizens to associate in a variety of groups with a variety of crosscutting interests enables compromises to be reached, as each interested group attempts to build support among shifting coalitions.*

### Alexis de Tocqueville
### "Political Association in the United States"*

Better use has been made of association and this powerful instrument of action has been applied to more varied aims in America than anywhere else in the world. . . .

The inhabitant of the United States learns from birth that he must rely on himself to combat the ills and trials of life; he is restless and defiant in his outlook toward the authority of society and appeals to its power only when he cannot do without it. The beginnings of this attitude first appear at school, where the children, even in their games, submit to rules settled by themselves and punish offenses which they have defined themselves. The same attitude turns up again in all the affairs of social life. If some obstacle blocks the public road halting the circulation of traffic, the neighbors at once form a deliberative body; this improvised assembly produces an executive authority which remedies the trouble before anyone has thought of the possibility of some previously constituted authority beyond

* Alexis de Tocqueville, "Political Association in the United States" in *Democracy in America*, ed. by J. P. Mayer and Max Lerner, tr. by G. Lawrence. English translation copyright © 1965 by Harper & Row, Publishers, Inc. Reprinted with permission.

that of those concerned. Where enjoyment is concerned, people associate to make festivities grander and more orderly. Finally, associations are formed to combat exclusively moral troubles: intemperance is fought in common. Public security, trade and industry, and morals and religion all provide the aims for associations in the United States. There is no end which the human will despairs of attaining by the free action of the collective power of individuals. . . .

The right of association being recognized, citizens can use it in different ways. An association simply consists in the public and formal support of specific doctrines by a certain number of individuals who have undertaken to cooperate in a stated way in order to make these doctrines prevail. Thus the right of association can almost be identified with freedom to write, but already associations are more powerful than the press. When some view is represented by an association, it must take clearer and more precise shape. It counts its supporters and involves them in its cause; these supporters get to know one another, and numbers increase zeal. An association unites the energies of divergent minds and vigorously directs them toward a clearly indicated goal.

Freedom of assembly marks the second stage in the use made of the right of association. When a political association is allowed to form centers of action at certain important places in the country, its activity becomes greater and its influence more widespread. There men meet, active measures are planned, and opinions are expressed with that strength and warmth which the written word can never attain.

But the final stage is the use of association in the sphere of politics. The supporters of an agreed view may meet in electoral colleges and appoint mandatories to represent them in a central assembly. That is, properly speaking, the application of the representative system to one party. . . .

In our own day freedom of association has become a necessary guarantee against the tyranny of the majority. In the United States, once a party has become predominant, all public power passes into its hands; its close supporters occupy all offices and have control of all organized forces. The most distinguished men of the opposite party, unable to cross the barrier keeping them from power, must be able to establish themselves outside it; the minority must use the whole of its moral authority to oppose the physical power oppressing it. Thus the one danger has to be balanced against a more formidable one.

The omnipotence of the majority seems to me such a danger to the American republics that the dangerous expedient used to curb it is actually something good.

Here I would repeat something which I have put in other words when speaking of municipal freedom: no countries need associations more—to prevent either despotism of parties or the arbitrary rule of a prince—than those with a democratic social state. In aristocratic nations secondary bodies form natural associations which hold abuses of power in check. In countries where such associations do not exist, if private people did not artificially and temporarily create something like them, I see no other dike to hold back tyranny of whatever sort, and a great nation might with impunity be oppressed by some tiny faction or by a single man. . . .

In America the citizens who form the minority associate in the first place to show their numbers and to lessen the moral authority of the majority, and secondly, by stimulating competition, to discover the arguments most likely to make an impression on the majority, for they always hope to draw the majority over to their side and then to exercise power in its name.

Political associations in the United States are therefore peaceful in their objects and legal in the means used; and when they say that they only wish to prevail legally, in general they are telling the truth. . . .

The Americans . . . have provided a form of government within their associations, but it is, if I may put it so, a civil government. There is a place for individual independence there; as in society, all the members are advancing at the same time toward the same goal, but they are not obliged to follow exactly the same path. There has been no sacrifice of will or of reason, but rather will and reason are applied to bring success to a common enterprise.

## Strategies: The Quest for Political Power

*See Lowi and Ginsberg, pp. 331–352 or brief edition, pp. 316–329*

*The power of an interest group depends in large part upon its access to members of Congress, and the ability to influence the decision-making of members. Since the late 1960s, environmental interest groups enjoyed access to members of the Democratic Party who were strong advocates for the environment. Following the 1994 Republican Party victory, Margaret Kriz labels the environmental lobby the "conquered coalition."\* Faced with new party leaders, committee chairs, committee membership, and a majority party agenda much less sanguine about rigorous regulation of the environment (particularly at the expense of business), environmentalists have been forced to rethink their legislative strategy. Kriz argues that these groups must refocus their efforts away from the direct lobbying of Congress toward broader grass-roots participation in state and local governments, and try to influence the activities of federal agencies responsible for the implementation of environmental laws. As the text points out, interest groups must have viable political strategies to leave their mark on the public policy record. The capacity for significant change in the political system, however, provides an essential check on the capacity for any one interest to dominate the national debate.*

\* The term "conquered coalition" is a pun referring to the "Concord Coalition," a group established by former Senator Warren Rudman (R-NH) and Paul Tsongas, candidate for the Democratic presidential nomination in 1992, aimed at seeking budget deficit reduction.

# Margaret Kriz
# "The Conquered Coalition"*

Expectations were running high on Nov. 16 as Vice President Albert Gore Jr. was to give his first speech on environmental issues since the Republican Party's landslide victory in the midterm elections.

Long before the election, Gore had agreed to be the featured speaker at a gala dinner to celebrate the Environmental Law Institute's 25th anniversary and to honor Senate Majority Leader George J. Mitchell, D-Maine, who's retiring at the end of this term.

Now Gore faced more than 800 environmental activists, lawyers and others who were crowded into the grand ballroom of the Washington Hilton, nibbling salmon and Ben & Jerry's ice cream and swapping the latest rumors on who's in and who's out.

Those who were expecting Gore to issue a rousing call-to-arms, however, were quickly disappointed by his subdued performance. After running through the now-standard jokes about his Achilles tendon operation, Gore made a passing reference to the election's impact on environmental policies and programs, observing only that "those of us who care deeply about this struggle must redouble our efforts."

Mitchell, on the other hand, warned of disaster in his impassioned address. If conservatives implement policies of "unrestrained economic growth and disregard for the natural environment," he said, the nation could become as environmentally devastated as Eastern Europe. "No matter what happened in the election," he said, "we've got to stand up and fight for the protection of the American environment."

The two speeches were evidence of the formidable struggle that's going on within the environmental movement in the aftermath of the Nov. 8 elections. Environmental activists in government and in national advocacy organizations are spending long hours debating how they should react to the Republican takeover of Capitol Hill.

One thing they all seem to agree on, however, is that the elections transfigured the politics of environmental policy and could force a radical reexamination of federal environmental laws.

Environmental activists argue that the elections were not a referendum on the American public's commitment to environmental protection and therefore shouldn't be seen as a mandate for Republicans to overhaul environmental and natural resource programs.

But they admit that they will have far fewer friends in the next Congress than they have now. In the Senate, one of their allies, John H. Chafee, R-R.I., will become the chairman of the Environment and Public Works Committee if he survives a strong conservative challenge. And the

Appropriations Subcommittee on Energy and Water Development is likely to be chaired by Mark O. Hatfield, R.-Ore., one of the original authors of the 1973 Endangered Species Act.

Chafee and Hatfield, however, are likely to have precious few Republican Senators on their side to help them protect the nation's environmental laws.

More dramatic are the changes in the House, where such environmental pit bulls as George Miller, D-Calif., the chairman of the Natural Resources Committee, and Henry A. Waxman, D-Calif., the chairman of the Energy and Commerce Subcommittee on Health and the Environment, will move to the minority. (Another, Rep. Mike Synar, D-Okla., lost his Democratic primary election earlier in the year.)

In their places will be Republicans who voted "green" only 7 per cent of the time in the 103rd Congress, according to the League of Conservation Voters.

Republican leaders in the House say that their top priority during the first 100 days of the 104th Congress will be their "Contract With America," a 10-point legislative agenda that promises, among other things, to protect the nation from environmental regulations run amok.

The contract, which says nothing about environmental protection, places a new importance on defending private property rights. Some key Republicans on Capitol Hill, in fact, are trying to set up new subcommittees on regulatory reform specifically to safeguard property rights.

The contract would also require regulators to balance the economic costs of a new regulation against its benefits. And it would stop the federal government from adopting environmental programs that have to be implemented and paid for by the states.

During the past two years, lobbyists for the nation's largest environmental organizations fought tooth and nail to block all property-rights, cost-benefit analysis and "unfunded mandates" proposals, which they said were being used by conservatives and business interests to overturn existing environmental controls.

In the process, however, the environmental activists unwittingly helped to kill legislation that would have also strengthened existing environmental laws.

"It is very convenient to say that the environmental bills failed because the Republicans blocked them," Peter L. Scher, the staff director of the Senate Environment and Public Works Committee, said in an interview. "But that's legitimate complaints about the way these laws operate and that these problems are not going to go away."

Two years after they celebrated President Clinton's election with an environmental inaugural ball and bold promises to strengthen federal environmental policies, environmental activists pushed only one major new law through Congress: the California Desert Protection Act. The chairman of the House Energy and Commerce Subcommittee on Energy and Power, Philip R. Sharp, D-Ind., who's retiring at the end of this term, recently described the 103rd Congress as "the nadir of the political influence of the environmental movement in the Congress."

Little wonder that some of the nation's leading environmental organizations are rethinking their past political stands and legislative tactics. In devoting too many resources to building their images and lobbying firepower in Washington, they now recognize, they didn't tend to their grass roots. A sign of the neglect: declining membership rolls.

Virtually everyone in the environmental movement is looking for new political strategies, and some are seeking to work with the Republicans to shape a more moderate approach to environmentalism.

First and foremost, however, the nation's big environmental organizations want to regain the trust of the American public. Having barely survived the earthquake, they're looking for new ways to rebuild the House of Green.

## THE FORK IN THE ROAD

Ever since the environmental movement came of age with the birth of the Environmental Protection Agency (EPA) in 1970, Democrats have controlled the House and usually controlled the Senate. Even when the Republicans seized the Senate in 1980, a team of powerful moderate Republicans were there to defend federal environmental protection laws.

Today, all that's changed. Conservative Republicans in the House and Senate have taken charge; moderates are few and far between. And environmental leaders on and off Capitol Hill are understandably baffled about how to react.

"The heyday of the old-style environmental movement is over," Robert W. Hahn, a resident scholar at the American Enterprise Institute for Public Policy Research (AEI), said in an interview.

Environmental activists are considering two different strategies to respond to the Republican landslide. They can attack the GOP's new leaders as radical ideologues who are out of touch with the American mainstream, they said. Or they can work with the Republicans to develop less punitive environmental controls. But the smart money says that most environmental groups will do a lot of the former and only some of the latter.

The wheels are already in motion within several environmental organizations to wage a negative campaign that portrays the new Republican leaders as modern incarnations of former Interior Secretary James G. Watt. During the early years of the Reagan Administration, Watt's ultraconservative policies and antagonistic rhetoric triggered a public backlash that helped the environmental groups to attract millions of dollars in contributions and thousands of new members.

In a similar way, the environmentalists aim to capitalize on the rise to power of the pro-industry lawmakers who are taking the reins of several key environmental committees. Their primary targets will be Alaska Republicans Frank H. Murkowski, who's in line to be the chairman of the Senate Energy and Natural Resources Committee, and Don Young, who's in line to be the chairman of the House Natural Resources Committee. Environmental activists are tagging them as right-wing extremists.

The environmental activists are also calling attention to several of the more radical Republican proposals that in the 1980s were particularly unpopular with the American public. Some Republicans have suggested, for example, that the federal government sell off some national parks as well as some lands controlled by the Bureau of Land Management.

Lobbyists for environmental organizations warn that they will declare war on Congress if the Republicans try to implement that plan or try to fulfill their promises to dramatically rewrite the Endangered Species Act and the wetlands protection provisions of the 1972 Clean Water Act. They're also launching a massive public relations effort to educate the American public about the GOP's property-rights campaign.

In particular, they're taking aim at legislation introduced in the 103rd Congress by Sen. Phil Gramm, R-Texas, that would have required the federal government to compensate property owners when an environmental regulation reduces the value of their land. Environmental activists argue that Gramm's proposal would force the government to compensate corporations that are required by law to install pollution control equipment.

"The property-rights people are not unbeatable," said Brock Evans, the National Audubon Society's senior vice president for national issues. "I'd love to force their agenda into the public eye."

Such a politically combative posture could have the added benefit of boosting the ailing bottom lines of many environmental groups. During the past five years, the nation's 10 largest environmental organizations have seen their memberships fall off and revenues decline or stagnate.

Since 1990, for example, Greenpeace has seen a 40 per cent drop in membership, the Wilderness Society a 35 per cent decrease and the National Wildlife Federation a 14 per cent decrease. In October, the Sierra Club announced that it was cutting its 1995 budget by $4 million and eliminating 40 jobs.

Some argue that the Republicans' strong rhetoric could be just what the doctor ordered to revive the sagging environmental movement. "The next Congress is going to be almost as good for the environmentalists' direct-mail solicitations as James Watt was," Robert N. Stavins, an associate professor of public policy at Harvard University's John F. Kennedy School of Government, said in an interview.

But Carl Pope, the executive director of the Sierra Club, warned that the cure might be worse than the illness. The potential fund-raising benefit "certainly doesn't help enough to make up for the damage done by having two Republican Senators from Alaska in charge of the nation's land use policies," Pope said. "It's not good news."

## Seize and Desist

While some environmental activists are eager to go on the attack, others want to negotiate with the new Republican leaders of Congress to "reinvent" more-moderate environmental policies.

Officials of the Environmental Defense Fund (EDF), for example, say that the Republican victory is a sign that the American public, while supporting a clean environment, wants less government control and more incentive-based regulations.

"The message from the election is that people are angry about the government and they're tired of programs that don't work," Fred Krupp, the EDF's executive director, said in an interview. "They're concerned about the intrusiveness of government."

Krupp said that the public—and a majority of Capitol Hill lawmakers—want government-industry partnerships and regulations that provide incentives, tax credits and market-based systems for protecting the environment.

Krupp's organization is the environmental movement's most enthusiastic supporter of such approaches. The EDF helped to craft the market-based acid rain reduction system that President Bush included in his proposal to rewrite the 1990 Clean Air Act, and it supports similar techniques for cutting other types of pollution.

"These are the ideas that will capture the center," Krupp said. "I can see both Republicans and Democrats now being open to using more economic incentives and less command-and-control-style regulations. We need to mandate tough results, but we can afford to be far more flexible about the means."

An increasing number of environmental leaders are also voicing tentative support for industry-friendly environmental controls. "We have to look at a whole new generation of market-based incentives," said Jay D. Hair, the president of the National Wildlife Federation, "but we're always going to need some semblance of command and control."

EPA administrator Carol Browner championed flexible regulations and negotiated agreements with industry during the 103rd Congress. She was instrumental, for example, in getting environmental activists to sit down with representatives of the chemical and insurance industries to craft compromise legislation to overhaul the superfund program.

Browner said that the issues of property rights, risk assessment and unfunded mandates need to be addressed head-on next year, before any other environmental legislation can be handled. "Certainly these issues cast a shadow over environmental legislation," she said in an interview.

In the past, environmental activists sought to dismiss the three issues by disparaging them as the "unholy trinity," and later as "the three pigs" of the right wing. No more.

"We accommodate the ideologues on the Right when we say we're going to draw a line along these code words and show our teeth every time we hear them," Jim Maddy, the director of the League of Conservation

Voters, said. "We shouldn't have done it in the last Congress, and we'd be even more foolish to do it in the next Congress."

Instead, some environmental activists are looking for ways to acknowledge the validity of the public concerns about the three issues and to recast the debate with an environmental slant.

"We're for property rights, but not irrational property-rights legislation," G. Jon Roush, the president of the Wilderness Society, said. "There's room for some rationality, and environmentalists should not deny that. We shouldn't let people cast us in the position of being regulatory zealots. We have to seize the center."

## FIGHTING FOR THE WHITE HAT

Even before the Republicans won control of Congress, no one had to measure the coat of the woolly caterpillar to conclude that the environmental community was in for a long, cold winter.

In the weeks before the election, a wind shift was apparent throughout the nation's capital. Environmental activists who once belittled their colleagues for working with industry lobbyists to rewrite the superfund law suddenly were preaching the virtues of such cooperation.

Melancholy Democratic aides on Capitol Hill began quoting from President Nixon's 1970 State of the Union address, in which he described clean air and open spaces as "the birthright of every American."

Storm-weary Democratic House leaders alerted lobbyists for environmental organizations to don their flak jackets in preparation for Republican attacks in 1995.

The truth was, the 103rd Congress was almost a total loss for the environmental movement, and the 104th doesn't look much better.

What went wrong? For one thing, environmental organizations lost many of their most respected leaders to the Clinton Administration as Gore helped to pepper the executive branch with his supporters. The environmental activists left behind were spread thin. Rather than focus on one or two major campaigns on Capitol Hill, however, they promoted dozens of large and small legislative programs.

Many environmental organizations pursued their own pet projects and were unable or unwilling to help one another. Several of the biggest were more interested in getting credit for their own accomplishments than in getting behind a united agenda, according to insiders.

In trying to protect their past gains, environmental activists also fell into the trap of defending big government and its cumbersome regulatory structures. They were loath to accept, for example, that the laws protecting endangered species and wetlands have been unevenly enforced, have hurt some landowners and need to be reformed. They were also unwilling to admit that federal drinking water programs were strangling local governments with high costs and unnecessary red tape.

The environmental movement's unyielding defense of several troublesome laws hurt its cause, argued Myron Ebell, the Washington representative of the American Land Rights Association, a conservative advocacy group. "As long as those laws are on the books," he said, "the environmentalists are going to lose ground and we are going to gain converts, because those laws cause people pain."

When lobbyists for environmental organizations pushed a legislative initiative, they often wanted Congress to impose the traditional command and control methods of regulation. In their proposals to strengthen the Clean Water Act, for example, they sought to punish farmers who pollute rivers with chemical-laden runoff from their fields. Farm groups wanted to develop incentive programs that would gradually phase in new farming practices.

"What governor is going to ask the legislature to authorize a program that imposes penalties and jail terms on farmers and ranchers?" asked Tom Curtis, the director of the National Governors' Association's natural resources group. "That would not have been politically salable. The environmentalists are so caught up in the notion that you've got to stick it to the regulated community if they don't comply."

In the battle over rewriting the Clean Water Act and the 1974 Safe Drinking Water Act, the environmental activists also found themselves clashing with the nation's mayors and governors. "In the early '70s, it was the environmentalists on one side and it was industry on the other side," said Scher of the Environment and Public Works Committee. "The whole dynamic is very different now."

And Congress listens when governors and mayors come to Capitol Hill to oppose ambitious environmental laws that must be implemented and paid for by local governments.

When votes were counted in the House and Senate, the environmentalists found themselves totally outgunned. Not only did they lack the stature they once had as the only voice for the public interest, but they also lacked the grass-roots muscle needed to push their legislative proposals over the top.

Administration officials and Democrats in Congress begged environmental organizations, for example, to unleash a grass-roots blitz to pressure Congress into passing their rewrite of the Safe Drinking Water Act. But the extra help never came.

"We've done a miserable job of organizing our supporters into a political force," said Maddy of the League of Conservation Voters. "Organizing is unglamorous and expensive. To organize, you need thousands of poorly paid young people. Environmentalists are a little bit like bureaucrats. They prefer a smaller number of highly paid specialists."

In the final calculation, lobbyists for environmental organizations came across as representatives of just another special interest rather than protectors of a sacred public trust.

"There are new constituencies that have an arguable claim to the white hat," AEI's Hahn said. "They're vying for power with the environmentalist community, and they're winning."

## "OUR TIME TO MAKE HAY?"

What route the national environmental organizations take next year will depend a great deal on the agenda and tactics adopted by Congress's new Republican leaders.

The early statements of House conservatives seem to foreshadow a year of ideological warfare between the environmental community and Congress. The environmental movement engaged in a similar struggle with the Reagan Administration in the early 1980s, when Watt and EPA administrator Anne Gorsuch Burford tried to roll back several major environmental laws.

"We could have a return to the Reaganesque environmental policy," said Jonathan H. Adler, the associate director of environmental studies at the Competitive Enterprise Institute. "The problem with that type of a policy is it sows the seeds of its own defeat because it is purely negative."

The new Republican leaders, like the environmental activists, have two options for the next Congress: They can try to quickly rewrite major environmental laws, which would trigger battles and possibly gridlock on Capitol Hill, or they can work with some compromise-minded environmental groups and with free-market-oriented think tanks to develop new approaches to protecting the environment.

House Republicans undoubtedly will try to fulfill their promises under their Contract With America by bringing legislation to promote private-property rights and risk assessment to the floor.

"We will do everything to ensure that property rights is on an equal level as environmentalism," said Nancie G. Marzulla, the president and chief legal counsel of Defenders of Property Rights. "We are going to win big in the 104th Congress. This is our time to make hay."

But the Republican leadership, which will have its hands full with other parts of the GOP's wish list, isn't likely to give other environmental legislation as high a priority.

Even if they wanted to dismantle 25 years of environmental legislation, Republicans don't have a comfortable majority in either chamber of Congress. Just as Democrats in the 103rd Congress didn't have the votes to strengthen the environmental laws, Republicans in the 104th probably won't have the votes to gut the programs, according to lobbyists for both sides. Only moderate proposals that capture Congress's elusive center are likely to become law.

In addition, the new Republican leaders may be reluctant to take up the environmental laws, which tend to be complex and overwhelming. With nearly half of all House Members in their first or second terms, the collective learning curve will be especially steep.

Consequently, Adler and other conservative activists are pushing the Republican leaders to consider a longer-term, free-market approach to environmental policy that would, among other things, promote private-sector incentives and move more control over environmental protection laws to the states.

Adler said that there's plenty of room for compromise, recalling the unlikely coalition of conservative and environmental groups opposed to legislation that would have allowed local governments to require all local garbage to be processed at a designated facility. The coalition argued that the measure would hinder market-driven recycling efforts and create a government monopoly.

Among those joining that campaign were representatives of Clean Water Action, the Competitive Enterprise Institute, the National Taxpayers Union and the Atlantic chapter of the Sierra Club.

Maddy predicted that the House Speaker-in-waiting Newt Gingrich of Georgia and other Republican leaders may be willing to work with environmental organizations to make needed changes to the Safe Drinking Water Act and the superfund. "Gingrich doesn't want dirty air and dirty water to become his 'gays in the military,' " Maddy said, referring to the public relations debacle that Clinton faced shortly after his election.

But all hell could break loose if conservatives try to eviscerate federal laws that protect endangered species, public lands and wetlands, he said.

"It's the public lands issues where we will fight the hardest for a filibuster," Maddy said. "Failing that, we'll hold midnight vigils around the White House begging for a veto."

And Republicans on Capitol Hill may not have a large window of opportunity to pass environmental legislation before the debate is overwhelmed by the onset of the 1996 presidential campaign, the National Wildlife Federation's Hair predicted.

The 1996 race is also certain to affect the White House's handling of environmental protection legislation, Hair said. "I would guess they'll put effort into anything that will raise the popularity of the President," he said. "And if it is perceived that the environment won't do that, they won't play that card."

Instead of turning automatically to Congress, representatives of national environmental groups say that they'll increasingly look to federal departments and agencies to strengthen environmental protection programs. They're also forming coalitions with smaller environmental organizations to tackle regional problems. The National Wildlife Federation, for example, is putting more resources into a program to improve water quality in the Great Lakes region. American Rivers and other national groups have joined with environmental activists in the Midwest and the South to create the Mississippi River Basin Alliance.

Environmental activists hope that working with the regional groups on regional problems will help them rebuild their grass-roots support and their power base in Congress.

For the environmental movement, the journey into 1995 comes with no road maps and no guarantees. Its top activists may try to shape government policy by reverting to the movement's old alarmist tactics or by settling for something less than the punitive environmental laws of the past. No matter which way they turn, however, the future is politically uncharted terrain.

## Groups and Interests: The Dilemma

*See Lowi and Ginsberg, pp. 552–553 or brief edition, pp. 329–330*

*In a large democracy, we face a dilemma. On the one hand, there must be meaningful ways for citizens to participate in the national political process. In addition to voting, citizens need means to express their opinions and petition the government. With the decline of political party identification and member-ship, Americans increasingly rely upon interest groups as a means to express their views and bring pressure to bear on government decision-making. On the other hand, it is costly to organize a group to provide meaningful representation of an interest. Citizens and economic interests most able to organize and partic-ipate can express their preferences for government policy more loudly than oth-ers, and can misrepresent the "public" interest for their own benefit. If money is so central to the process of governing and the policy priorities of elected officials, those groups with the most access and money to elected officials will play a dominant role.*

*Central to the debate over the influence exercised by particular groups is the role played by lobbyists who represent these groups and who help to raise money for candidates. Thomas Hale Boggs, Jr., a lobbyist, argues that lobbyists are essential to the successful functioning of the American democratic system. According to Boggs, lobbyists "fill the information vacuum": they garner facts and information that legislators need in order to make informed decisions. Lob-byists also "help to identify and mobilize grass-roots constituents who agree with [a] client's position . . . [and] build coalitions among . . . diverse groups." Boggs agrees that lobbyists may be too influential in raising money for candidates, but he argues that the answer to that problem lies in reforming campaign finance altogether and not in limiting the influence of lobbyists.*

# Thomas Hale Boggs, Jr.
## "All Interests Are Special"*

Shakespeare's "kill all the lawyers" has been replaced with "kill all the lob-byists." Journalists at most major publications have joined the chorus. In a recent editorial, for example, [the *New York Times*] described the "threat that corporate influence and big-time lobbying represent to enlightened populism."

I agree that the system needs to be changed. Campaign finance re-form, stricter lobbying disclosure rules and post-employment restrictions for Government officials and employees would serve the democracy well. But few commentators ever stop to consider the legitimate role lobbyists play in policy-making.

Critics charge that the use of lobbyists by special interests is unfair, that if members of Congress respond to the influence of special interests, they

---

* Thomas Hale Boggs, Jr., "All Interests Are Special" in the *New York Times* (Feb-ruary 16, 1993). Copyright © 1993 by The New York Times Company. Reprinted with permission.

are somehow acting contrary to the benefit of their constituents as a whole.

All interests are special and every individual and organization seeks to advance its own special interests. In the last quarter of 1992 alone, the House Clerk listed more than 6,000 registered lobbyists, who were supported by tens of thousands of additional personnel. These individuals fight for the interests of 40,000 registered clients, including religious organizations, foreign governments, the Boy Scouts, doctors, gambling organizations, trial lawyers, consumers, environmental protectionists, baseball players—the list goes on and on.

To cite a few of my firm's activities, is it unfair to: Lobby for Federal assistance to Chrysler to save thousands of jobs? Seek a regulatory structure to keep newspaper publishers from being forced out of business by legal monopolies? Help defeat a constitutional amendment on flag burning? Seek legislation making it easier for homeless people to vote?

Lawyer-lobbyists advocate the position of their clients. Our first role is to determine the proper forum—the courts, Congress or a regulatory agency—in which the client can seek to achieve its goals.

When the issue involves Congress, we prepare substantive materials explaining the issue and the likely impact on the member's district: How many jobs are at stake? What's the likely impact on the local economy? We help to identify and mobilize grass roots constituents who agree with our client's position. We build coalitions among these diverse groups.

Facts are the first source of a lobbyist's power. Forty-three percent of House members have served less than five years. Newspapers cannot give them the substantive detail they need. Congressional staffs are overworked and underpaid. Lobbyists help fill the information vacuum.

The second source of the lobbyist's power is money. In 1992 House races, including uncontested seats, major party candidates spent $369,000 on average. That's less than $1 per voter. Citizens see more advertising for hamburgers and beer than for political candidates. The problem with the campaign finance system lies not in the amount spent but in the incursion on a member's time that fund-raising entails. In a $500,000 campaign, the member may have to make 4,000 phone calls at two calls per contribution to get an average contribution of $250.

Lobbyists help by raising money from clients, colleagues and allies. And the help brings influence, connections and returned phone calls. But anyone can give or raise money. A lawyer cannot become a truly effective lobbyist without strategic skills and information, which can be shared with the member of Congress.

The first source of power—facts—is essential to the democratic process. The second—fund-raising—we all could do without. Meaningful campaign finance reform would reduce this source of power.

To take the fund-raising burden away from the candidate, and with it the need to rely on lobbyists' assistance, we should strengthen the parties and make them the primary recipients and distributors of campaign funds. We could begin with a transition period when candidates could raise a fixed amount, which would be matched by the party. As the parties grew stronger, candidate fund-raising could be phased out.

Many observers advocate public financing and permanent campaign-spending limits—ill-advised proposals, in my opinion. Public financing requires spending limits, and such limits would protect incumbents blessed with name recognition, franking privileges and free media time. Voters need more information, not less. Candidates, particularly challengers, spend money to get their message to the people.

Other reforms are needed. Lobbying disclosure rules only require the reporting of meetings with a member of Congress to influence him or her about pending legislation, along with very limited information about the legislation involved. The rules should be amended to include contacts with executive branch officials. A central repository should be maintained with uniform reporting requirements for all types of contacts. More detail should be required on the subject involved.

Some limitation on post-government employment lobbying should be maintained. But the restriction cannot be so Draconian as to limit the talent available to the legislative and executive branches.

A third source of lobbying power has waned with time. In the 1980s, lobbyists were needed to bridge the gap of divided government. On occasions when gridlock was overcome, lobbyists usually played a significant role in bringing factions of the two parties together. Conversely, lobbyists in the 80s could use gridlock by championing partisanship in order to obtain the opposition of the White House or Congress to the proposals of the other branch.

But the American people spoke clearly in November [1992]: no more gridlock. Public officials and lobbyists alike should get that message.

The system has some problems. Too much time is spent raising money, and lobbyists play too important a function in that regard. But the democratic process works best when all "special interests" are heard and all information is available to policymakers. Lobbyists serve an important role in the process.

## DEBATING THE ISSUES:
## PACS AND POLITICS

*See Lowi and Ginsberg, pp. 550–551 or brief edition, pp. 328–329*

*In Federalist No. 10 (see appendix), James Madison wrote of the "mischief of factions." It was natural, he argued, for people to organize around a principle or interest they held in common, and the most common motivation for organizing such factions was property—those who had it versus those who did not, and creditors versus debtors. The danger in such efforts, however, was the possibility of a majority faction usurping the rights of a minority. In a small direct* democracy, where a majority of the people could share a common passion, the threat was very real. However, expand the geographic size of the country, re-place direct democracy with a system of elected representatives, and the threat diminished. The likelihood of any one faction appealing to a majority of citizens in a large republic governed by representatives from diverse geographic regions was remote. Factions were eminent where liberty thrived, but the mischief of factions could be checked by the multiplicity of factions in a diverse country, and by a system of representation based upon varied constituencies. From the competition of diverse minority interests, compromise and balanced public pol-icy could arise.

Was Madison right? In the following excerpt from The Governmental Process, David Truman answers with an emphatic "yes!" Despite the popular criticism of "special" interests that seem to taint the political process with their dominant influence, Truman argues that such groups have been a common feature of American government since the time of the Founders—indeed, the formation of special interests was the topic of Federalist No. 10. What the critics of group influence fail to recognize, however, is the fact that people have "multiple or overlapping membership" in groups so that "no tolerable normal person is totally absorbed in any group which he participates." There is balance, in other words, to the views any one member brings to the organization and ultimately to the political process. Furthermore, the potential for a group to form is always present, and "[s]ometimes it may be this possibility of organization that alone gives the potential group a minimum of influence in the political process." Just because someone is not a member of an organized group, in other words, does not obviate the influence they can bring to bear on the political process. The result, as Madison argued, is a balanced approach to the diverse interests who must compromise to form public policy.

Jonathan Rauch disagrees. He views with pessimism the ever-expanding number of interest groups in the political process. Whether groups claim to rep-resent narrow economic interests or a broader public interest, Rauch does not see balance and compromise as the result of their competition in the political arena. Rather, he sees a nation suffering from "hyperpluralism," or the explosion of groups making claims on government power and resources. When elected officials attempt to reduce budget deficits or to establish new priorities and re-focus expenditures, they are overwhelmed by the pressures of a wide range of groups. The very powerful protests from groups such as the American Association of Retired People have long prevented significant reforms in the Social Security and Medicare programs, for example. As a result, government programs are never terminated or restructured; tough budget cuts or tax changes are rarely made; and a very rich democratic nation and its government become immobile.

# David B. Truman
# "The Alleged Mischiefs of Faction" from
## *The Governmental Process**

Most accounts of American legislative sessions—national, state, or local—are full of references to the maneuverings and iniquities of various organized groups. Newspaper stories report that a legislative proposal is being promoted by groups of business men or school teachers or farmers or consumers or labor unions or other aggregations of citizens. Cartoonists picture the legislature as completely under the control of sinister, portly, cigar-smoking individuals labeled "special interests," while a diminutive John Q. Public is pushed aside to sulk in futile anger and pathetic frustration. A member of the legislature rises in righteous anger on the floor of the house or in a press conference to declare that the bill under discussion is being forced through by the "interests," by the most unscrupulous high-pressure "lobby" he has seen in all his years of public life. An investigating committee denounces the activities of a group as deceptive, immoral, and destructive of our constitutional methods and ideals. A chief executive attacks a "lobby" or "pressure group" as the agency responsible for obstructing or emasculating a piece of legislation that he has recommended "in the public interest."

\* \* \*

Such events are familiar even to the casual student of day-to-day politics, if only because they make diverting reading and appear to give the citizen the "low-down" on his government. He tends, along with many of his more sophisticated fellow citizens, to take these things more or less for granted, possibly because they merely confirm his conviction that "as everybody knows, politics is a dirty business." Yet at the same time he is likely to regard the activities of organized groups in political life as somehow outside the proper and normal processes of government, as the lapses of his weak contemporaries whose moral fiber is insufficient to prevent their defaulting on the great traditions of the Founding Fathers. These events appear to be a modern pathology.

### GROUP PRESSURES AND THE FOUNDING FATHERS

Group pressures, whatever we may wish to call them, are not new in America. One of the earliest pieces of testimony to this effect is essay number 10 of *The Federalist*, which contains James Madison's classic statement of the impact of divergent groups upon government and the reasons for

* David Truman, "The Alleged Mischiefs of Faction" from *The Governmental Process* Published by Alfred A. Knopf © 1963. Reprinted by permission of the author.

their development. He was arguing the virtues of the proposed Union as a means to "break and control the violence of faction," having in mind, no doubt, the groups involved in such actions of the debtor or propertyless segment of the population as Shays's Rebellion. He defined faction in broader terms, however, as "a number of citizens, whether amounting to a majority or minority of the whole, who are united and actuated by some common impulse of passion, or of interest. . . ."

\* \* \*

[Madison's] analysis is not just the brilliant generalization of an armchair philosopher or pamphleteer; it represents as well the distillation from Madison's years of acquaintance with contemporary politics as a member of the Virginia Assembly and of [the Continental] Congress. Using the words "party" and "faction" almost interchangeably, since the political party as we know it had not yet developed, he saw the struggles of such groups as the essence of the political process. One need not concur in all his judgments to agree that the process he described had strong similarities to that of our own day.

The entire effort of which *The Federalist* was a part was one of the most skillful and important examples of pressure group activity in American history. The State ratifying conventions were handled by the Federalists with a skill that might well be the envy of a modern lobbyist. It is easy to overlook the fact that "unless the Federalists had been shrewd in manipulation as they were sound in theory, their arguments could not have prevailed."

\* \* \*

Alexis de Tocqueville, perhaps the keenest foreign student ever to write on American institutions, noted as one of the most striking characteristics of the nation the penchant for promoting a bewildering array of projects through organized societies, among them those using political means. "In no country in the world," he observed, "has the principle of association been more successfully used or applied to a greater multitude of objects than in America." De Tocqueville was impressed by the organization of such groups and by their tendency to operate sometimes upon and sometimes parallel to the formal institutions of government. Speaking of the similarity between the representatives of such groups and the members of legislatures, he stated: "It is true that they [delegates of these societies] have not the right, like the others, of making the laws; but they have the power of attacking those which are in force and of drawing up beforehand those which ought to be enacted."

Since the modern political party was, in the Jackson period, just taking the form that we would recognize today, De Tocqueville does not always distinguish sharply between it and other types of political interest groups. In his discussion of "political associations," however, he gives an account of the antitariff convention held in Philadelphia in October of 1831, the form of which might well have come from the proceedings of a group meeting in an American city today:

Its debates were public, and they at once assumed a legislative character; the extent of the powers of Congress, the theories of free trade, and the different provisions of the tariff were discussed. At the end of ten days the Convention broke up, having drawn up an address to the American people in which it declared: (1) that Congress had not the right of making a tariff, and that the existing tariff was unconstitutional; (2) that the prohibition of free trade was prejudicial to the interests of any nation, and to those of the American people especially.

Additional evidence might be cited from many quarters to illustrate the long history of group politics in this country. Organized pressures supporting or attacking the charter of the Bank of the United States in Jackson's administration, the peculations surrounding Pendleton's "Palace of Fortune" in the pre-Civil War period, the operations of the railroads and other interests in both national and state legislatures in the latter half of the last century, the political activities of farm groups such as the Grange in the same period—these and others indicate that at no time have the activities of organized political interests not been a part of American politics. Whether they indicate pathology or not, they are certainly not new.

*   *   *

The political interest group is neither a fleeting, transitory newcomer to the political arena nor a localized phenomenon peculiar to one member of the family of nations. The persistence and the dispersion of such organizations indicate rather that we are dealing with a characteristic aspect of our society. That such groups are receiving an increasing measure of popular and technical attention suggests the hypothesis that they are appreciably more significant in the complex and interdependent society of our own day than they were in the simpler, less highly developed community for which our constitutional arrangements were originally designed.

Many people are quite willing to acknowledge the accuracy of these propositions about political groups, but they are worried nevertheless. They are still concerned over the meaning of what they see and read of the activities of such organizations. They observe, for example, that certain farm groups apparently can induce the Government to spend hundreds of millions of dollars to maintain the price of food and to take "surplus" agricultural produce off the market while many urban residents are encountering painful difficulty in stretching their food budgets to provide adequately for their families. They observe that various labor organizations seem to be able to prevent the introduction of cheaper methods into building codes, although the cost of new housing is already beyond the reach of many. Real estate and contractors' trade associations apparently have the power to obstruct various governmental projects for slum clearance and low-cost housing. Veterans' organizations seem able to secure and protect increases in pensions and other benefits almost at will. A church apparently can prevent the appropriation of Federal funds to public schools unless such funds are also given to the schools it operates in competition with the public systems. The Government has declared that stable and friendly European governments cannot be maintained unless Americans buy more goods and services abroad. Yet American shipowners and seamen's unions can secure a statutory requirement that a large proportion of the goods purchased by European countries under the Marshall Plan* must be carried in American ships. Other industries and trade associations can prevent the revision of tariff rates and customs regulations that restrict imports from abroad.

In all these situations the fairly observant citizen sees various groups slugging it out with one another in pursuit of advantages from the Government. Or he sees some of them co-operating with one another to their mutual benefit. He reads of "swarms" of lobbyists "putting pressure on" congressmen and administrators. He has the impression that any group can get what it wants in Washington by deluging officials with mail and telegrams. He may then begin to wonder whether a governmental system like this can survive, whether it can carry its responsibilities in the world and meet the challenges presented by a ruthless dictatorship. He wants to see these external threats effectively met. The sentimental nonsense of the commercial advertisements aside, he values free speech, free elections, representative government, and all that these imply. He fears and resents practices and privileges that seem to place these values in jeopardy.

A common reaction to revelations concerning the more lurid activities of political groups is one of righteous indignation. Such indignation is entirely natural. It is likely, however, to be more comforting than constructive. What we seek are correctives, protections, or controls that will strengthen the practices essential in what we call democracy and that will weaken or eliminate those that really threaten that system. Uncritical anger may do little to achieve that objective, largely because it is likely to be based upon a picture of the governmental process that is a composite of myth and fiction as well as of fact. We shall not begin to achieve control until we have arrived at a conception of politics that adequately accounts for the operations of political groups. We need to know what regular patterns are shown by group politics before we can predict its consequences and prescribe for its lapses. We need to re-examine our notions of how representative government operates in the United States before we can be confident of our statements about the effects of group activities upon it. Just as we should not know how to protect a farm house from lightning unless we knew something of the behavior of electricity, so we cannot

* The U.S. European Recovery Plan after World War II.

hope to protect a governmental system from the results of group organization unless we have an adequate understanding of the political process of which these groups are a part.

\* \* \*

There are two elements in this conception of the political process in the United States that are of crucial significance and that require special emphasis. These are, first, the notion of multiple or overlapping membership and, second, the function of unorganized interests, or potential interest groups.

The idea of overlapping membership stems from the conception of a group as a standardized pattern of interactions rather than as a collection of human units. Although the former may appear to be a rather misty abstraction, it is actually far closer to complex reality than the latter notion. The view of a group as an aggregation of individuals abstracts from the observable fact that in any society, and especially a complex one, no single group affiliation accounts for all of the attitudes or interests of any individual except a fanatic or a compulsive neurotic. No tolerably normal person is totally absorbed in any group in which he participates. The diversity of an individual's activities and his attendant interests involve him in a variety of actual and potential groups. Moreover, the fact that the genetic experiences of no two individuals are identical and the consequent fact that the spectra of their attitudes are in varying degrees dissimilar means that the members of a single group will perceive the group's claims in terms of a diversity of frames of reference. Such heterogeneity may be of little significance until such time as these multiple memberships conflict. Then the cohesion and influence of the affected group depend upon the incorporation or accommodation of the conflicting loyalties of any significant segment of the group, an accommodation that may result in altering the original claims. Thus the leaders of a Parent-Teacher Association must take some account of the fact that their proposals must be acceptable to members who also belong to the local taxpayers' league, to the local chamber of commerce, and to the Catholic Church.

\* \* \*

We cannot account for an established American political system without the second crucial element in our conception of the political process, the concept of the unorganized interest, or potential interest group. Despite the tremendous number of interest groups existing in the United States, not all interests are organized. If we recall the definition of an interest as a shared attitude, it becomes obvious that continuing interaction resulting in claims upon other groups does not take place on the basis of all such attitudes. One of the commonest interest group forms, the association, emerges out of severe or prolonged disturbances in the expected relationships of individuals in similar institutionalized groups. An association continues to function as long as it succeeds in ordering these disturbed relationships, as a labor union orders the relationships between management and workers. Not all such expected relationships are simultaneously or in a given short period sufficiently disturbed to produce organization. Therefore only a portion of the interests or attitudes involved in such expectations are represented by organized groups. Similarly, many organized groups—families, businesses, or churches, for example —do not operate continuously as interest groups or as political interest groups.

Any mutual interest, however, any shared attitude, is a potential group. A disturbance in established relationships and expectations anywhere in the society may produce new patterns of interaction aimed at restricting or eliminating the disturbance. Sometimes it may be this possibility of organization that alone gives the potential group a minimum of influence in the political process. Thus . . . the Delta planters in Mississippi "must speak for their Negroes in such programs as health and education," although the latter are virtually unorganized and are denied the means of active political participation.*

\* \* \*

Obstacles to the development of organized groups from potential ones may be presented by inertia or by the activities of opposed groups, but the possibility that severe disturbances will be created if these submerged, potential interests should organize necessitates some recognition of the existence of these interests and gives them at least a minimum of influence.

More important for present purposes than the potential groups representing separate minority elements are those interests or expectations that are so widely held in the society and are so reflected in the behavior of almost all citizens that they are, so to speak, taken for granted. Such "majority" interests are significant not only because they may become the basis for organized interest groups but also because the "membership" of such potential groups overlaps extensively the memberships of the various organized interest groups. The resolution of conflicts between the claims of such unorganized interests and those of organized interest groups must grant recognition to the former not only because affected individuals may feel strongly attached to them but even more certainly because these interests are widely shared and are a part of many established patterns of behavior the disturbance of which would be difficult and painful. They are likely to be highly valued.

\* \* \*

It is thus multiple memberships in potential groups based on widely held and accepted interests that serve as a balance wheel in a going political system like that of the United States. To some people this observation may appear to be a truism and to others a somewhat mystical notion. It is neither. In the first place, neglect of this function of multiple memberships in most discussions of organized interest groups indicates that the

* Until the 1960s, most southern blacks were denied the right to vote.

observation is not altogether commonplace. Secondly, the statement has no mystical quality; the effective operation of these widely held interests is to be inferred directly from verbal and other behavior in the political sphere. Without the notion of multiple memberships in potential groups it is literally impossible to account for the existence of a viable polity such as that in the United States or to develop a coherent conception of the political process. The strength of these widely held but largely unorganized interests explains the vigor with which propagandists for organized groups attempt to change other attitudes by invoking such interests. Their importance is further evidenced in the recognized function of the means of mass communication, notably the press, in reinforcing widely accepted norms of "public morality."

\* \* \*

Thus it is only as the effects of overlapping memberships and the functions of unorganized interests and potential groups are included in the equation that it is accurate to speak of governmental activity as the product or resultant of interest group activity. As [political scientist Arthur F.] Bentley has put it:

There are limits to the technique of the struggle, this involving also limits to the group demands, all of which is solely a matter of empirical observation. . . . Or, in other words, when the struggle proceeds too harshly at any point there will become insistent in the society a group more powerful than either of those involved which tends to suppress the extreme and annoying methods of the groups in the primary struggle. It is within the embrace of these great lines of activity that the smaller struggles proceed, and the very word struggle has meaning only with reference to its limitations.

To assert that the organization and activity of powerful interest groups constitutes a threat to representative government without measuring their relation to and effects upon the widespread potential groups is to generalize from insufficient data and upon an incomplete conception of the political process. Such an analysis would be as faulty as one that, ignoring differences in national systems, predicted identical responses to a given technological change in the United States, Japan, and the Soviet Union.

# Jonathan Rauch
## "The Hyperpluralism Trap"\*

Anyone who believes Washington needs to get closer to the people ought to spend a little time with Senator Richard Lugar, the Indiana Republican.

\* Jonathan Rauch, "The Hyperpluralism Trap" in the *New Republic* (June 6, 1994).
Copyright © 1994 by The New Republic Inc. Reprinted with permission.

"Take a look at the people coming into my office on a normal Tuesday and Wednesday," Lugar said in a speech not long ago. "Almost every organization in our society has a national conference. The typical way of handling this is to come in on a Monday, rev up the troops, give them the bill number and send them up to the Hill. If they can't get in on Tuesday, strike again on Wednesday. I regularly have on Tuesday as many as fifteen constituent groups from Indiana, all of whom have been revved up by some skillful person to cite bills that they don't understand, have never heard of prior to that time, but with a score sheet to report back to headquarters whether I am for or against. It is so routine, it is so fierce, that at some point you [can't be] immune to it."

This is the reality of modern government. The rhetoric of modern politics, alas, is a little different. Take today's standard-issue political stemwinder, which goes something like this: "I think perhaps the most important thing that we understand here in the heartland . . . is the need to reform the political system, to reduce the influence of special interests and give more influence back to the kind of people that are in this crowd tonight by the tens of thousands." That stream of boilerplate is from Bill Clinton (from his election-night speech), but it could have come from almost any politician. It's pitched in a dominant key of political rhetoric today: *standard populism*—that is, someone has taken over the government and "we" must take it back, restore government to the people, etc. But who, exactly, are those thousands of citizens who troop weekly through Senator Lugar's suite, clutching briefing packets and waving scorecards? Standard populism says they are the "special interests," those boils on the skin of democracy, forever interposing themselves between the American people and the people's servants in Washington.

Well, fifty years ago that analysis may have been useful, but not anymore. In America today, the special interests and "the people" have become objectively indistinguishable. Groups are us. As a result, the populist impulse to blame special interests, big corporations and political careerists for our problems—once a tonic—has become Americans' leading political narcotic. Worse, it actually abets the lobbying it so righteously denounces.

Begin with one of the best known yet most underappreciated facts of our time: over the past three or four decades we have busily organized ourselves into interest groups—lobbies, loosely speaking—at an astonishing rate. Interest groups were still fairly sparse in America until about the time of World War II. Then they started proliferating, and in the 1960s the pace of organizing picked up dramatically.

Consider, for instance, the numbers of groups listed in Gale Research's *Encyclopedia of Associations.* The listings have grown from fewer than 5,000 in 1956 to well over 20,000 today. They represent, of course, only a small fraction of America's universe of interest groups. Environmental organizations alone number an estimated 7,000, once you count local clean-up groups and the like; the Washington *Blade*'s resource directory lists more than 400 gay groups, up from 300 at the end of 1990. Between 1961 and

1982 the number of corporate offices in Washington increased tenfold. Even more dramatic was the explosion in the number of public-interest organizations and grass-roots groups. These barely existed at all before the 1960s; today they number in the tens of thousands and collect more than $4 billion per year from 40 million individuals, according to political scientist Ronald Shaiko of American University.

Well, so what? Groups do many good things—provide companionship for the like-minded, collect and disseminate information, sponsor contests, keep the catering industry solvent. Indeed, conventional political theory for much of the postwar period was dominated by a strain known as pluralism, which holds that more groups equals more representation equals better democracy. Yet pluralism missed something. It assumed that the group-forming process was self-balancing and stable, as opposed to self-feeding and unstable. Which is to say, it failed to grasp the danger of what American University political scientist James Thurber aptly calls hyperpluralism.

In economics, inflation is a gradual increase in the price level. Up to a point, if the inflation rate is stable, people can plan around it. But if the rate starts to speed up, people start expecting more inflation. They hoard goods and dump cash, driving the inflation still faster. Eventually, an invisible threshold is crossed: the inflation now feeds on its own growth and undermines the stability of the whole economic system.

What the pluralists missed is that something analogous can happen with interest groups. People see that it pays to organize into groups and angle for benefits, so they do it. But as more groups make more demands, and as even more hungry groups form to compete with all the other groups, the process begins to feed on itself and pick up momentum. At some point there might be so many groups that they choke the political system, sow contention and conflict, even erode society's governability. That's hyperpluralism. And if it is less destabilizing than hyperinflation, it may be more insidious.

The pattern is most visible in smaller social units, such as local school districts, where groups colonize the curriculum—sex education for liberals, values instruction for conservatives, recycling lessons for environmentalists, voluntary silent prayer for Christians. But even among the general population the same forces are at work. Fifty years ago the phrase "the elderly" denoted a demographic category; today, thanks largely to federal pension programs and the American Association of Retired Persons (AARP), it denotes a giant and voracious lobby. In the 1930s the government set up farm-subsidy programs, one per commodity; inevitably, lobbies sprang up to defend each program, so that today American agriculture is fundamentally a collection of interest groups. With the help of group organizers and race-based benefits, loose ethnic distinctions coalesce into hard ethnic lobbies. And so on.

Even more depressing, any attempt to fight back against the proliferating mass of subdivision is foiled by the rhetoric of standard populism and its useful stooge: the special interest. The concept of a "special interest" is at the very core of standard populism—the "them" without which there can be no "us." So widely accepted is this notion, and so useful is it in casual political speech, that most of us talk routinely about special interests without a second thought. We all feel we know a special interest when we see one, if only because it is a group of which we are not a member. Yet buried in the special interest idea is an assumption that is no longer true.

The concept of the special interest is not based on nothing. It is, rather, out of date, an increasingly empty relic of the time of machine politics and political bosses, when special interests were, quite literally, special. Simply because of who they were, they enjoyed access that was available to no one else. But the process of everyone's organizing into more and more groups can go only so far before the very idea of a special interest loses any clear meaning. At some point one must throw up one's hands and concede that the hoary dichotomy between special interests and "us" has become merely rhetoric.

According to a 1990 survey conducted for the American Society of Association Executives, seven out of ten Americans belong to at least one association, and one in four Americans belongs to four or more. Practically everyone who reads these words is a member of an interest group, probably several. Moreover, formal membership tallies omit many people whom we ordinarily think of as being represented by lobbies. For example, the powerful veterans' lobbies enroll only perhaps one-seventh of American veterans, yet the groups lobby on behalf of veterans as a class, and all 27 million veterans share in the benefits. Thus the old era of lobbying by special interests—by a well-connected, plutocratic few—is as dead now as slavery and Prohibition. We Americans have achieved the full democratization of lobbying: influence-peddling for the masses.

The appeal of standard populism today comes precisely from the phony reassurance afforded by its real message: "Other people's groups are the special interests. Less for them—more for you!" Spread that sweet manure around and the natural outgrowth is today's tendency, so evident in the Clinton style, to pander to interest groups frantically while denouncing them furiously. It is the public's style, too: sending ever more checks to the AARP and the National Rifle Association and the National Federation of Independent Business and the National Wildlife Federation and a million others, while railing against special interests. Join and join, blame and blame.

So hyperpluralism makes a hash of the usual sort of standard populist prescription, which calls for "the people" to be given more access to the system, at the expense of powerful Beltway figures who are alleged to have grown arrogant or corrupt or out of touch. Activists and reformers who think the answer to democracy's problems is more access for more of the people need to wake up. Uncontrolled access only breeds more lobbies. It is axiomatic that "the people" (whatever that now means) do not organize to seek government benefits; lobbies do. Every new door to the federal treasury is an opportunity for new groups to queue up for more goodies.

Populists resolutely refuse to confront this truth. Last year, for example, Republicans and the editors of *The Wall Street Journal* campaigned fiercely—and successfully—for new congressional rules making it easier for legislators and groups to demand that bottled-up bills be discharged from committee. The idea was to bring Congress closer to "the people" by weakening the supposedly high-handed barons who rule the Hill. But burying the Free Christmas Tree for Every American Act (or whatever) in committee—while letting members of Congress say they *would* have voted for it—was one of the few remaining ways to hold the door against hungry lobbies clamoring for gifts.

A second brand of populism, *left-populism*, is even more clueless than the standard brand, if that's possible. Many liberals believe the problem is that the wrong groups—the rich, the elites, the giant corporations, etc.— have managed to out-organize the good guys and take control of the system. One version of this model was elaborated by William Greider in his book *Who Will Tell the People*. The New Deal legacy, he writes, "rests upon an idea of interest group bargaining that has gradually been transformed into the random deal-making and permissiveness of the present. The alterations in the system are decisive and . . . the ultimate effects are anti-democratic. People with limited resources, with no real representation in the higher levels of politics, are bound to lose in this environment." So elaborate is the Washington machine of lobbyists, consultants, P.R. experts, political action committees and for-hire think tanks, says Greider, that "powerful economic interests," notably corporations and private wealth, inevitably dominate.

What's appealing about this view is the truism from which it springs: the wealthy enjoy a natural advantage in lobbying, as in almost everything else. Thus many lobbies—even liberal lobbies—are dominated by the comfortable and the wealthy. Consider the case of environmental groups. Anyone who doubts they are major players in Washington today need only look at the massive 1990 Clean Air Act, a piece of legislation that business gladly would have done without. Yet these groups are hardly battalions of the disfranchised. "Readers of *Sierra*, the magazine of the Sierra Club, have household incomes twice that of the average American," notes Senior Economists Terry L. Anderson of the Political Economy Research Center. And *The Economist* notes that "in 1993 the Nature Conservancy, with $915 million in assets, drew 73 percent of its income from rich individuals." When such groups push for emissions controls or pesticide rules, they may be reflecting the priorities of people who buy BMWs and brie more than the priorities of people who buy used Chevies and hamburger. So left-populism's claim to speak for "the people" is often suspect, to say the least.

The larger problem with left-populism, however, is its refusal to see that it is feeding the very problem it decries. Left-populism was supposed to fix the wealth-buys-power problem by organizing the politically disadvantaged into groups: unions, consumer groups, rainbow coalitions and so on. But the strategy has failed. As the left (the unions, the environmentalists) has organized ever more groups, the right (the bosses, the polluters) has followed suit. The group-forming has simply spiraled. This makes a joke of the left-populist prescription, which is to form more "citizens' groups" on the Naderite model, supposedly reinvigorating representative democracy and giving voice to the weak and the silenced. Greider proposes giving people subsidies to spend on political activism: "Giving individual citizens the capacity to deploy political money would inevitably shift power from existing structures and disperse it among the ordinary millions who now feel excluded."

Inevitably, it would do no such thing. Subsidies for activism would perforce go straight into the waiting coffers of (what else?) interest groups, new and old. That just makes matters worse, for if one side organizes more groups, the other side simply redoubles its own mobilization ad infinitum. That escalating cycle is the story of the last three decades. The only winner is the lobbying class. Curiously, then, left-populism has come to serve the very lobbying elites—the Washington lawyers and lobby shops and P.R. pros and interest group execs—whom leftists ought, by rights, to loathe.

The realization that the lobbying class is, to a large extent, both entrepreneurial and in business for itself has fed the third brand of populism, *right-populism*. In the right-populist model, self-serving political careerists have hijacked government and learned to manipulate it for profit. In refreshing contrast to the other two brands of populism, however, this one is in touch with reality. Washington *is* in business for itself, though not only for itself. Legislators and lobbies have an interest in using the tax code to please their constituents, but they also have an interest in churning the tax code to generate campaign contributions and lobbying fees. Luckily for them, those two imperatives generally coincide: the more everyone hunts for tax breaks, the more lobbying jobs there are. Right-populism has tumbled to the fact that so-called public interest and citizens' groups are no more immune to this self-serving logic of lobbying— create conflict, reap rewards—than is any other sort of professional lobby.

Yet right-populism fails to see to the bottom of the problem. It looks into the abyss but flinches. This is not to say that term limits and other procedural fine-tunes may not help; such reforms are no doubt worth trying. But even if noodling with procedures succeeded in diluting the culture of political careerism, it would help (or hurt) mainly at the margins. No, tinkering with the process isn't the answer. What we must do is go straight at the beast itself. We must attack and weaken the lobbies—that is, the *people's* lobbies.

It sounds so simple: weaken the lobbies! Shove them aside, reclaim the government! "It's just that simple," twinkles Ross Perot. But it's not that simple. Lobbies in Washington have clout because the people who scream when "special interests" are attacked are Medicare recipients defending benefits, farmers defending price supports, small businesses defending subsidized loans, racial groups defending set-asides and so on. Inherently, challenging these groups is no one's idea of fun, which is why politicians so rarely propose to do it. The solution is to strip away lobbies' protections and let competition hammer them. In practice, that means:

*Balance the federal budget.* It is a hackneyed prescription, but it is the very first thing we should do to curtail the lobbies' ability to rob the future. Deficits empower lobbies by allowing them to raid the nation's scarce reserves of investment capital. Deprived of that ability, they will be forced to compete more fiercely for money, and they'll be unable to steal from the future.

*Cut the lobbies' lifelines.* Eliminate subsidies and programs, including tax loopholes, by the hundreds. Killing a program here or there is a loser's game; it creates a political uproar without actually making a noticeable difference. The model, rather, should be the 1986 tax reform measure, which proved that a wholesale housecleaning really is possible. Back then, tax loopholes were cleared away by the truckload. The trick was—and is—to do the job with a big package of reforms that politicians can tout back home as real change. That means ditching whole Cabinet departments and abolishing virtually all industry-specific subsidies. Then go after subsidies for the non-needy—wholesale, not retail.

*Promote domestic perestroika.* Lobbies live to lock benefits in and competition out, so government restraints on competition should be removed—not indiscriminately, but determinedly. President Carter's deregulation of transportation industries and interest rates, though imperfectly executed, were good examples. Air travel, trucking and rail shipping are cheaper *and* safer. The affected industries have been more turbulent, but that's exactly the point. Domestic competition shakes up interest groups that settle cozily into Washington.

*Encourage foreign competition.* This is most important of all. The forces that breed interest groups never abate, and so fighting them requires a constant counterforce. Foreign competition is such a counterforce. Protection invariably benefits the industries and groups with the sharpest lobbyists and the fattest political action committees; stripping away protection forces them to focus more on modernizing and less on lobbying.

No good deed, they say, goes unpunished. We sought to solve pressing social problems, so we gave government vast power to reassign resources. We also sought to look out for ourselves and bring voices to all of our many natures and needs, so we built countless new groups to seek government's resources. What we did not create was a way to control the chain reaction we set off. Swarming interest groups excited government to perpetual activism, and government activism drew new groups to Washington by the thousands. Before we knew it, society itself was turning into a collection of ravenous lobbies.

Why was this not always a problem? Because there used to be control rods containing the chain reaction. Smoke-filled rooms, they were called. On Capitol Hill or in Tammany Hall, you needed to see one of about six people to have any hope of getting what you wanted, and those six people dispensed (and conserved) favors with parsimonious finesse. Seen from today's vantage, smoke-filled rooms and political machines did a creditable job of keeping a lid on the interest group frenzy—they just didn't do it particularly fairly. That's why we opened up access to anyone who wants to organize and lobby, and opened up power to subcommittee chairs and caucus heads and even junior legislators. In doing so, we abolished the venal gatekeepers. But that was only the good news. The bad news was that we also abolished the gate.

No, we shouldn't go back to smoke-filled rooms. But the way forward is harder than it ever was before. The maladies that now afflict government are ones in which the public is wholly, enthusiastically implicated. Still, there are sprigs and shoots of encouragement all around. There was the surprisingly strong presidential bid of former Senator Paul Tsongas, which built something of a constituency for straight talk. There's the rise of a school of Democrats in Congress—among them Senator Bob Kerrey and retiring Representative Tim Penny—who are willing to drag the White House toward sterner fiscal measures. There was the Clinton-led triumph of NAFTA last year. Those developments show promise of a political movement that is counter-populist yet also popular. Maybe—is it too much to hope?—they point beyond the desert of populism.

# 13

# The Media

## News Coverage

*See Lowi and Ginsberg, pp. 566–575*

*The media have undergone dramatic changes in the past few decades, a transformation Adam Gopnik attributes to differences in how reporters cover their stories. Whereas journalists once achieved success via access, they can now pursue an alternative track that depends on "a willingness to stage visible, ritualized displays of aggression." The access culture arose in the second half of the nineteenth century, as journalism evolved into its modern form. Before that time—Gopnik traces this development—as politicians beginning with Garfield began to recognize that reporters needed access to do their jobs, the access was provided with the understanding that there were certain stories that were off limits—FDR's disability and JFK's peccadillos, to give two famous examples. There are disadvantages to this model, to be sure, but there are also positive aspects: access-based reporting, argues Gopnik, allowed for more complex and contextual judgments, whereas attack journalism depends more on simplistic explanations that distort public debate rather than inform it. The journalistic ethic of "objectivity," he concludes, serves mostly to prevent reporters from realistically evaluating the debates and events they write about. Consider Gopnik's argument. Does the access culture facilitate the democratic process?*

## Adam Gopnik
## "Read All About It"*

There's a wonderful moment in Ian Fleming's 1961 novel "Thunderball" that captures the way a certain kind of high-end journalism once worked in America. Ernst Blofeld and SPECTRE—the Special Executive for Counterintelligence, Terrorism, Revenge, and Extortion—have stolen a couple of atomic bombs from NATO and are holding the free world for ransom. This is supposed to be top secret, but when James Bond is in the Bahamas, where the bombs are (M figured this out instantly, on a hunch), he picks up the *Times* and notices that Arthur Krock, the leading columnist of his day, has "a heavyweight column about the security aspects of the NATO alliance." The *Times*, Bond speculates grimly, must know all about the missing bombs. It was part of the credibility of the story, in other words (and Fleming, himself a newspaperman, had a peerless sense of how to make local details sell the fantasy), that the *Times*, knowing that SPECTRE and Ernst Blofeld had stolen two atomic bombs and were threatening the entire world, would prudently decide not to panic the public by publishing the news, while allowing Arthur Krock to signal the paper's knowledge to other insiders in a sapient, elliptical column.

Nowadays, the *Times* would put a profile of Blofeld on the front page above the fold ("Controversial Mastermind from Gdynia"), while Anna Quindlen would write a column about the pain of women executioners stuck on SPECTRE's Mommy track—stranded in Revenge, and never promoted to Extortion and Counterintelligence. But in the old days that was how the dispensation of access and collusion between the press and the government really worked: you would find out about Operation Thunderball and would be expected not to write about it. In exchange for access, the reporter would show discretion.

The difference between James Bond's era and our own is pretty apparent. When Tom Clancy introduces a journalist into one of his novels, you can be sure that the only person in the book more unreliable will be a liberal woman. (If the journalist *is* a liberal woman, you will be looking at a portrait of pure evil.) A media that in its upper, more self-conscious reaches—in the *Times*, that is, and in the Washington *Post* and the news magazines and on the big networks—once dealt in quiet signals now sounds loud and acts mean. However you feel about Bill Clinton, no other American President since the eighteen-seventies has been hung up by his thumbs so soon, and left there to hang for so long. To read about the Roosevelts in the White House, with their intimates sleeping upstairs, and the reporters knocking away the Speed Graphic of any photographer who tried to show that F.D.R. was in a wheelchair, and then to contemplate our own moment, with Maureen Dowd announcing on the front page of the *Times* that the President on a trip to Oxford had "returned today for a sentimental journey to the university where he didn't inhale, didn't get drafted, and didn't get a degree," is to consider a change not only in tone, or even in kind, but in worlds. . . .

In the past twenty years, the American press has undergone a transformation from an access culture to an aggression culture: the tradition, developed after the Civil War, in which a journalist's advancement depended on his intimacy with power, has mutated into one in which his success can also depend on a willingness to stage visible, ritualized displays of aggression. The reporter used to gain status by dining with his subjects; now he gains status by dining on them. But because his aggression still has to thrive within the old institutions of the commercial press, whose whole point and historical achievement was the suppression of political thought in the interests of an ideal (or at least an appearance) of objectivity, the new culture has forced on the reporter a double life. The media now relish aggression while still being prevented, by their own self-enforced codes, from letting that aggression have any relation to serious political argument, let alone to grown-up ideas about conduct and morality. Aggression has become a kind of abstract form, practiced in a void of ideas, or even of ordinary sympathy. In a grim paradox, the media in America, because their aggression has been kept quarantined from good ideas, have become surprisingly vulnerable to bad ideas. Having turned themselves into a forum for the sort of craziness that was previously kept to the margins of American life, the media have nothing left to do but watch the process, and act as though it were entertaining; the jaded tone and the prosecutorial tone are masks, switched quickly enough so that you can appear active and neutral at the same time. Or, to put it another way, the cynicism and the sanctimony turn out to be a little like electricity and magnetism—two aspects of a single field, perpetuating themselves in a thought-free vacuum.

One of the overlooked turning points in the history of American journalism occurred in the spring of 1864, after General Meade, the hero of Gettysburg, publicly humiliated a reporter he happened to dislike. In retaliation, as Shelby Foote relates, the Northern press for the rest of the war carried out a complete and successful blackout of his activities, except when his name was connected with a defeat, reducing the hero of Gettysburg to a nonperson. (Every American kid knows, or used to, who *lost* Gettysburg, and how nobly. General Lee knew how to spin.)

The Meade blackout may mark the moment when the American press first realized its power as a more or less unified body, and the consequences of that realization are the subject of "The Press Gang: Newspapers and Politics, 1865–1878," a vivid and entertaining new book by Mark Wahlgren Summers. The book retells a series of absurd episodes in the history of the post-Appomattox press, but Summers has a serious point to make. Briefly, it is that the Civil War produced a largely new profession: "reporting" in the modern sense, in which the reporter not only gets news from a variety of sources but is expected to string it all together into a "story." (Before the war there had mostly been "correspondents," or glorified letter writers, and political news had been taken directly from congressional records.) Once the war was over, many reporters ended up in Washington, in part because the Associated Press had agreed to supply its subscribers with common reports from all locales except Washington (and, of all places, Albany). You had to send your own reporters to the capital, because that was where the competition was.

Papers in the eighteen-seventies were in transition from their prewar role as unapologetic party organs, funded largely by subscriptions and political money, to their modern role as commercial enterprises funded by advertising. The reporters had learned during the war that they had much more power than anyone had previously thought. Now the press, sensing that power, and freed from neat party affiliations, became the vehicle for a kind of free-floating belligerence that would not return until our own time. The favorite targets of the Washington pack were President Grant and Reconstruction: Grant because he was vacillating, weak, and distant; Reconstruction because, like most well-intentioned government social programs, its successes were diffuse and its failures obvious. (Anyone who is inclined to feel nostalgic for the post-Civil War era, before the press was reined in by its owners, ought to recall, as Summers does, that one of its most important contributions to American life was the dissemination of the mythology of Reconstruction, with its vicious carpetbaggers and dim-witted scalawags, which lasted until the day before yesterday.)

Summers also points out that it was James A. Garfield who was perhaps the first American politician to act effectively on the insight that reporters needed access as much as they enjoyed aggression, and that the way to save yourself from the second was to provide the first. The system that Garfield helped invent, in which information was, in effect, exchanged for protection, remained in place for almost a hundred years, both in the national capital and in the local capitals that looked to it for an example. It became the expected thing for an ambitious politician to cultivate reporters, to feed them soup and stories. American journalists, who had previously been just a cut above circus roustabouts, now joined the establishment— or many of them did—and learned, or were taught, an elaborate protocol of "professionalism," objectivity, and self-censorship: "All the News That's Fit to Print." Presidents fed White House correspondents; first basemen fed sportswriters; and Broadway press agents and, later, movie stars fed columnists. The fix was always in: you got access, but at the cost of absolute honesty.

In its upper reaches, the access culture produced results that can look preposterous now. To read, for instance, fifty years of the letters of Walter Lippmann (as compiled in "Public Philosopher," edited by John Morton Blum), the most widely revered American journalist of the first half of this century, is to see how bizarrely intermingled observers and their subjects could become. . . .

Lippmann, in his letters, tenderly thanks Cabinet members for their attentions, proffers advice to generals, offers campaign counsel to candidates (sometimes to two candidates in the same race), and even meets with Polish and Indian ambassadors, for instance, and reports back to the C.I.A.'s Allen Dulles on the results. Lippmann's columns were offered as the ruminations of an independent-minded public man rather than as what they were—a complicated series of signals and compromises, broadcast from one end of the establishment to the other.

The old collusion has been much mocked and put upon, and it is easy to say what was wrong with it. For a journalist not to print what he or she knew to be true—whether it was that F.D.R. had to have help to take his pants off or that J.F.K. needed help to keep his on—was to enter into a conspiracy to suppress truth. Yet, in view of what the new order has brought about, it's hard not to feel a twinge of nostalgia for the old system. One good thing about an establishment is that it *establishes* things. NATO, the United Nations, the Marshall Plan—to read Lippmann's letters or the memoirs of James Reston is to see how the process that built consensus for all these things worked. When Kennedy confided something to Reston— for instance, that Khrushchev had "savaged" him at their 1961 Vienna summit—Reston may have kept it from his readers the next day, but he didn't put it out of his mind. Discretion about small things seemed a small price to pay for understanding about big ones.

At the lower level, where ordinary reporters worked, the system had its points, too. Anyone who has ever tried to get a long interview with a contemporary ballplayer and then reads, say, the sportswriter Fred Lieb's manically detailed account of Lou Gehrig's wedding reception and married life will be stunned at how much access was once *available*. Whether this was, on the whole, a good or bad thing is hard to decide. Morally, though, knowing vaguely disreputable things about someone which you refuse to print seems indisputably superior to printing vaguely disreputable things about someone just because you happen to know them.

The best thing to be said for the access culture was that, almost inadvertently, it produced something truly first-rate, and that was the worldly tradition in American reporting. The old system gave American reporters an efficient, unsentimental education in American realities. Liebling in Providence and Mencken in Baltimore, to name only giants, learned rapidly that corruption and collusion and ambiguity were part of the daily run of democratic life. But they learned, too, that reforming the system was not always a self-evident consequence of exposing its shortcomings. (Liebling's first venture into investigative journalism, as he recounts it, a little ruefully, in "The Wayward Pressman," ended up revealing that the state lunatic asylum operated on the cheap but in the process ruined a frightened and inept Indian technician who had been hired as a pathologist.) Nobody can describe Mencken as "soft" or "in the tank," but his experience made him cautious about judging from a distance what was and was not a sin. When Mencken, for all his reputation as a hatchet man, tried to define his credo, he wrote that the man he had come to mistrust most was the one whose "distinguishing mark is the fact that he always attacks his opponents, not only with all arms, but also with snorts and objurgations— that he is always filled with moral indignation—that he is incapable of imagining honor in an antagonist, and hence incapable of honor himself." The kind of man he admired most was one who had "a serene spirit, a steady freedom from moral indignation, an all-embracing tolerance," he wrote. "Such a man is not to be mistaken for one who shirks the hard knocks of life. On the contrary, he is frequently an eager gladiator, vastly enjoying opposition. But when he fights he fights in the manner of a gentleman fighting a duel, not in that of a longshoreman cleaning out a waterfront saloon. That is to say, he carefully guards his amour propre by assuming that his opponent is as decent a man as he is, and just as honest—and perhaps, after all, right."

The conclusions that the worldly reporters came to were often perverse, or could seem that way. Liebling crowned his career as a reporter with an affectionate book-length paean to Earl Long, a corrupt and half-crazy segregationist governor. But he saw that Long was a more interesting man and, in a complicated way, a greater force for good than the reformers who were his critics. (Long was a segregationist but not a hater; he kept the redneck vote from going overboard.) What the old dispensation, high and low, understood was that the world's work gets done, and always will get done, in the space between official pieties and human possibilities. The press used to recognize the human possibilities; today it sometimes seems to be the chief source of the official pieties. The old, worldly tradition in American newspapering now belongs almost exclusively to diehards like Murray Kempton, whose sometimes deliberately perverse judgments—that a gangster can display more honor than a mayor of New York, or that Richard Nixon had more character than Bill Clinton—often feel like a kind of final Flamboyant Gothic flourish placed by the one remaining craftsman on the peaked roof of the old church. . . .

The funny thing about a free press is that it is not really very good at its manifest role but is terrific at a lot of its latent roles. Journalism has been bad at history, since it can paint only quickly and in very broad strokes. (Historians spend decades clearing up confusions that journalists create in minutes; what actually happened during the Tet offensive in Vietnam, for instance, is hard to know for sure, but it was almost certainly not what was reported as happening at the time.) The press is also a poor tribunal and a worse department of justice—its standards of evidence are too low, and its amnesia is too sudden. But it can make a surprisingly good guardian of the public's compassion and sense of proportion. A free press, more than any other institution—more than schools or parliaments or scholars—protects public decency.

It does this, like it or not, by making a distinction between the middle and the margins (All the News That's Fit to Print). This task is often viewed with horror today, since the attempt to create a "middle" and an "other"—to say that there is a spectrum of rational views and a fringe of crazy ones—is supposed to be the pernicious work of the power structure. But no liberal society can function without the desire to distinguish between kinds of public speech that are acceptable and kinds that—because of their incivility, their inability to be modified, their blindness, their malice, or their potential for doing violence—do not belong in the conversation at all. All human groups have to try to make these distinctions, and they can make them on good principles or bad.

The nice thing about the press as a sorter-out of bourgeois liberal societies is that it has no power except the cumulative power of example— the power to make you want to sound worldly yourself. "A sense of style is the radical journalist's best friend," I. F. Stone once confided to a young reporter; it was the bedrock of independence, he thought, because nobody owned it but you. Style in journalism depends in part on worldliness, or judgment—on knowing which way is up, even when everyone else thinks it's down. That was true fifty years ago, and it is still true. But it's hard to know how you get more people who work in the media to understand that, as Michael Kinsley has written, our job is not to bring reality into line with appearances but to bring appearances into line with reality.

It's fun to imagine an Institute for Worldly Journalism set up on that imaginary campus which also harbors Liebling's famous School for Publishers (without which, he wrote, no school for journalists has meaning). The institute would need to have a bar, a fire bell, a clutch of lovable corrupt politicians, and the collected works of Trollope and Damon Runyon, among others. It might also conduct regular tours of the publishers' school next door, just so that the young reporters could be reminded which way is *really* up. Of course, the world itself isn't a bad institute, but by the time you've learned what the world has to teach it's usually too late to do anything about it.

## Media Power in American Politics

*See Lowi and Ginsberg, pp. 576–585*

*Public confidence in national institutions has dropped in recent years, and David Shaw notes that the media have not been immune. He traces the decline to a perception that members of the media—reporters, commentators, editors— are increasingly out of touch with "the everyday concerns of the average reader and viewer." National reporters have become part of the powerful elite about which they write (see Goldstein, "Term Limits for the Unelected"), and the increasing distance between reporters and readers (in terms of income, education, and tastes) injects a bias into how the media interpret events. Public reaction against these phenomena is one reason, Shaw argues, for the popularity of talk radio and other alternative media.*

# David Shaw
# "Distrustful Public Views Media as 'Them—Not Us' "*

By almost any reasonable measure, the mainstream news media in this country are more responsible and more ethical today than at any time in their history.

Gone—for the most part—are the days when editors and reporters accepted extravagant gifts and free meals from news sources, when reporters routinely masqueraded as police officers, doctors and others in pursuit of a story, when stories were featured or killed almost daily to accommodate the financial, political or social interests of the publisher—or his wife.

And yet public confidence in the news media is in steady decline. In a *Times* poll conducted last month, only 17% said the media, overall, are doing a "very good" job—down from 30% in 1985. Almost 70% agreed with the statement: "The news media give more coverage to stories that support their own point of view than to those that don't." Forty percent said they

* David Shaw, "Distrustful Public Views Media as 'Them—Not Us' " in the *Los Angeles Times* (April 1, 1993). Reprinted with permission.

have less confidence in the news media today than they did when they first began paying attention to news and current events.

Why?

One explanation may be that many members of the public feel a growing disenfranchisement from the news media, as they do from the government. Increasingly, they think, the people who report, edit and broadcast the news are elitist—well-paid, well-educated sophisticates who are more interested in (and have more in common with) the movers and shakers they cover than in the everyday concerns of the average reader and viewer.

Many in the responsible, mainstream news media—especially the print media—say there's another problem. They're paying, they say, for the sins of their less responsible, sensation-minded brethren, many of them in television.

Fact-based docudramas, tabloid TV shows such as "Hard Copy," "Inside Edition" and "A Current Affair," and local TV news shows that emphasize murder and mayhem—flash, crash and trash—have blurred the lines between substance and fluff, between journalism and hype, between news and entertainment. . . .

. . . [F]or many people the programs, "all have fundamentally the same perceived value."

As David Paletz, a professor at Duke University who writes about media and politics, puts it: "All the stuff on TV which is not news but is in some way close to news amplifies the diversity of what can be considered news, and people . . . ultimately equate them with regular news."

The result, Paletz says, is a kind of "news miasma."

But readers and viewers are not the only victims of this miasma. Reporters, editors and television news directors also seem at times to give news organizations with widely varying standards "fundamentally the same perceived value."

Jose Rios, news director at KTTV Channel 11, a Fox station, says the success of the tabloid TV programs has influenced the way traditional television newsrooms operate. "You look at what's on the air on some stations, just in terms of production, it would have been absolutely *verboten* five years ago," he says.

Mainstream newspapers have been similarly influenced by both tabloid television and the tabloid newspapers sold in supermarkets. . . .

. . . [A] supermarket tabloid, the *Globe*, was the first U.S. publication to name the Florida woman who accused William Kennedy Smith of raping her two years ago. (Smith was acquitted.) Despite policies against using the names of rape victims, NBC used the tabloid's story to justify its own broadcast of the woman's name—and the *New York Times* decided that if NBC News could do so, the *Times* should too. . . .

. . . Since the public tends to lump much of the news media together, it may not matter much which medium or which news organization is the silliest or most irresponsible. As Dan Rather says, "I don't think it helps anybody in journalism to point fingers and make accusations along the lines of, 'Your end of the boat is sinking.' There's no such thing as 'Your

end of the boat is sinking.' If the boat is sinking, then we're all sinking—
the boat in this case being our reputation, our credibility with the public."

Media credibility is not all that's sinking in contemporary society,
though. Public opinion polls reveal a growing disenchantment with all social institutions. The number of people saying they have a "great deal" or
"a lot" of confidence in Congress, organized religion, the Supreme Court,
public schools, big business and organized labor have all declined in those
polls over the last 20 or 25 years. . . .

. . . "The gnawing contrast between what life should be, according to
[the commercial] blandishments we see, and what it is increasingly . . . has
contributed to a pervasive hostility between the races, between men and
women, between people and their institutions, including the media," says
Mark Crispin Miller, a professor of media studies at Johns Hopkins University. . . .

In the case of the news media, the hostility may be especially virulent
because the role and visibility of the media have probably changed more
in recent years than have the role and visibility of any other major social
institution.

Historically, most of the news that people read and saw was prepack-
aged; reporters asked questions and wrote stories and when newspaper
and magazine editors and television news directors deemed them ready
for the public, they were published and broadcast. The journalistic process
itself was invisible—concealed.

Now CNN, C-SPAN and the major networks bring live news—press
conferences, troop landings, presidential debates—into the nation's living
rooms as they're happening; viewers often get to see reporters asking
rude, stupid, arrogant, insensitive questions, whether shouted at President
Ronald Reagan in the Rose Garden or directed at military leaders in press
briefings during the Persian Gulf War.

The actual process of journalism, like that of making sausage, is not
very attractive. Many people wouldn't eat sausage if they had to watch it
being made; it shouldn't be surprising that they often feel like throwing
up when they watch reporters at work. . . .

. . . Not only have the media become visible and ubiquitous but—perhaps most important—they have become substantially more powerful.
Mergers and monopolies have given individual news organizations more
power, and the decline of political parties and several other institutions
have given the news media overall more power.

Americans have traditionally been skeptical of powerful individuals
and institutions, and as the media have become more powerful—in effect,
replacing the political parties as kingmakers (and kingbreakers) on the
campaign trail, for example—growing public hostility was probably inevitable. The media, collectively, have simply become a bigger and more inviting target.

Along with increased power, however, has come a growing elitism in
the media and a concomitant sense in the public that the media no longer
represents the average person.

Alexis de Tocqueville, the French author and statesman, wrote in the late 1830s that American journalists, while "not great writers," nonetheless were the only American writers he would acknowledge because, "generally in a very humble position, with a scanty education . . . they speak the language of their country."

Most journalists remained—until relatively recently—"of the people, not above the people" and as a result, they were generally portrayed in popular culture as good men with "good values; they represented the common American," in the words of Roy Peter Clark of the Poynter Institute for Media Studies.

Real-life journalists were typically underpaid, unsophisticated, chain-smoking, hard-drinking "blue-collar, salt-of-the-earth types . . . [who] stood up for the little guy" and they were depicted accordingly on the silver screen, says Glenn Garelik, a longtime magazine journalist who teaches courses in "the media and society in the 1990s" at Georgetown University. . . .

. . . No more.

Over the past dozen years, in movies such as "Absence of Malice," "Die Hard," "Bob Roberts" and "The Bonfire of the Vanities"—and in such television series as "Hearts Afire" and "Love & War"—journalists have been variously depicted as superficial, callous, exploitative and possessed of overweening ambition and "values that much of their audience find inimical," as Garelik wrote in the *New York Times* early this year.

Back when reporters were "paid $9 a week and had just a high school education . . . [they] knew the streets . . . they could go where the rats could go," Garelik said in an interview.

Now, to many, the media are the rats. . . .

. . . It could be argued, of course, that this pop culture depiction of the journalist doesn't mirror reality so . . . much as it creates (or at least influences) reality—that people think ill of journalists because they're responding to recent movie and television portrayals that have made journalists look bad.

Which came first—the image or the reality? Do the two reinforce each other? Or do the images created by movies and television have such resonance with the public largely because they confirm what the public already thinks?

To be sure, today's better-educated, more sophisticated journalists bring a quality and range of knowledge and expertise to the job that makes today's newspapers, on balance, better and more comprehensive than they were 30 years ago, says Shelby Coffey, editor of the *Los Angeles Times*. But those improvements have come at a price—a growing gap between the news media and the people for whom they write and broadcast.

There's "a sense that we're elite," says Fancher of the *Seattle Times*. "We come off as thinking we're a whole helluva lot smarter than the people we [write] . . . for, and they don't like that."

[Van Gordon] Sauter, the Fox News president, worries that many in the media have become so "arrogant . . . so damned stuffy and self-important and self-righteous and, in effect, sort of removed from the daily concerns of people that it was easy for people to go to other sources [of news] that just seem a bit more real."

Too many traditional journalists these days, Sauter says, "think that they somehow have been anointed by some higher power to bring 'The Truth' to the peasantry—and the peasantry is saying, 'Up yours.' "

It's no wonder that during several controversies in recent years—the congressional pay raise in 1988, the House banking scandal in 1991–92, the nomination of Zoe Baird as U.S. attorney general this year—it was radio and TV talk shows, not the mainstream news media, that first connected with the anger and resentment many Americans felt.

The news media are "just not making the connections to the audience" that they once did, says Maxwell McCombs, a professor of communications at the University of Texas. "People simply aren't interested in what we have to say. . . . What's in newspapers, what's on television, just doesn't have much relevance to their daily lives."

Newspaper editors have been talking more in recent years about the need for "diversity" in the newsroom, in part to make their publications more relevant to many readers in our increasingly multicultural society. That's obviously an urgent need; for all the talk newspaper newsrooms remain 90% white—and 66% male. One reason there is growing public disenchantment with the news media is that there are growing numbers of ethnic minorities in our society—and growing numbers of very vocal critics among minorities and women—who do not see the reality of their daily lives reflected in news coverage.

But newsroom diversity must also include white ethnics and others from middle-class, non-Ivy League homes, people who drive Fords, not BMWs, people who—like their predecessors—can relate to the people they write for.

More than 80% of all U.S. journalists hold bachelor's degrees, compared with 21% in the general population. The median salary for a journalist is $31,000—compared with an average per capita income in this country of $19,000—and many top journalists in big cities make six-figure salaries; some of the most influential, especially in television, make more than $1 million a year.

Increasingly, these journalists-cum-entrepreneurs frequent fancy French restaurants, write books and go on lucrative lecture tours. Like the politicians, entertainers, athletes, Wall Street lawyers and titans of industry they write about, they've become celebrities in their own right.

A *Los Angeles Times* story listing celebrities who attended President Clinton's inaugural ball listed "media celebrities" Bob Woodward, Carl Bernstein and Peter Jennings *before* mentioning either the "Hollywood celebrities"—Warren Beatty, Jack Nicholson, Sigourney Weaver and Shirley MacLaine—or the "political celebrities"—George Stephanopoulos, the White House press secretary; Gov. Ann Richards of Texas, and Ron Brown, then Commerce secretary-designate.

Media celebrities routinely party and vacation with top government officials and other famous people; they also grace the covers of national magazines and appear regularly on the Sunday morning television talk shows, where they chat up—on a first-name basis—the very politicians the public has become disillusioned with.

In the recent *Times* poll, 65% of the people agreed with the statement, "The press looks out mainly for powerful people," 60% said people who work in the news media have little in common with people like them; 50% said they only "infrequently" see things that are relevant to their own lives reported in the news media.

"The top journalists move in packs with the affluent and powerful in Washington," says Hodding Carter, the columnist and television commentator. "They swarm with them in the summer to every agreeable spot on the Eastern Seaboard. When any three or four of them sit down together on a television talk show, it is not difficult to remember that the least well paid of these pontificators make at least six times more each year than the average American family."

Many journalists, it seems, have lost not only their traditional connection to the common man but their sense of being outsiders, their perspective, even, at times, their independence. They may still talk about the underdog, but their friends are often the "overdogs"; many journalist now have more in common, socially and financially, with the ruling class than the underclass. In a time of unprecedented public skepticism toward those in government, the most prestigious news media have virtually become part of government—the Fourth Estate in word and deed.

"The power structure has co-opted us, and . . . our egos were such that we allowed it to happen," says Dennis Britton, editor of the *Chicago Sun-Times.*

When Bill and Hillary Rodham Clinton decided to enroll their daughter, Chelsea, in the private Sidwell Friends school in Washington, a *New York Times* story on the school was headlined "Sidwell Is Often Chosen by Capital's Elite;" the first "elite" parents named in the story were Donald E. Graham, publisher of the *Washington Post*; Judy Woodruff, the PBS reporter, and Albert R. Hunt, Washington bureau chief of the *Wall Street Journal.* After these Washington elite came three U.S. senators. Then: David Brinkley of ABC News and Leslie Stahl of CBS News.

As Charles Peters, editor of the *Washington Monthly*, said in his March column, "This helps explain the lack of criticism from the Washington press about the Clintons' decision to send Chelsea to a private school."

Peters says these shared attitudes also help explain why the news media were "so slow to see the problem" presented by "another common practice among the elite"—hiring an illegal immigrant housekeeper and not paying Social Security taxes.

When it was disclosed that Baird, President Clinton's first choice for attorney general, had done just that, the Washington Post headlined a story, "Baird's Hiring Not Seen as a Major Block."

But the public was outraged, and a week later, the nomination was withdrawn.

It's not surprising that many in the public see the news media as part of "them" in the increasing "us" vs. "them" polarization of American society.

"I think we are elitist in that the people who are in my [newsroom] . . . and in . . . your newsroom aren't representative of the broader society that they cover," says William Woo, editor of the *St. Louis Post-Dispatch*. "I think we are out of touch in terms of associations.

"How many members of the *Los Angeles Times* and the *Post-Dispatch* belong to the American Legion, belong to Kiwanis, go to prayer breakfast? I can tell you that a helluva lot of people that we like to see the paper to go to those things. . . . I think we are disconnected," he says.

With that disconnect comes, inevitably, a certain insensitivity, even callousness. As a result, many members of the public say, the news media too often intrude into the private lives and private moments of non-public figures, people very much like themselves.

"They stick a microphone in front of accident victim and say, 'Hi, I'm from the news. How do you feel now that you're dying?' " Marian Dolan, 56, of Folkston, Ga., told a *Times* reporter in a follow-up interview to the *Times* poll.

"How do they think someone feels? Don't they know? Don't they care?" . . .

. . . This public disenchantment has given rise to a whole range of media critics as well as to several media watchdog groups. Accuracy in Media. Fairness and Accuracy in Reporting. The Media Research Center. The Center for Media and Public Affairs.

The very existence—and virulence—of their criticism has helped contribute to the perception that the media are more flawed than ever.

In an attempt to analyze this perception—and the underlying realities—news media executives in their annual meetings routinely feature speeches and panel discussions on what the press is doing wrong and how performance can be improved. Newspapers, magazines and, less often, television also carry occasional stories that examine media misconduct. Media companies like *Times Mirror*—and its subsidiary the *Los Angeles Times*—conduct polls on public attitudes toward the media. . . .

. . . But these remain the exceptions. There is little systematic examination in the media of how the media do their job, what their decision-making processes are, what their traditions, limitations, objectives and profit margins are.

"We pride ourselves on doing superficial looks at whether we wrote a story for the right reasons or not," says Geneva Overholser, editor of the *Des Moines Register*. "But we don't let it all hang out about whether the corporatization of American journalism is terrible for American democracy." . . .

. . . If the news media want to reverse their decline in public esteem, "We better start explaining ourselves more," Rather says. "I do not except myself from the criticism that we haven't done a very good job of it."

## DEBATING THE ISSUES: THE MEDIA— HOW INFLUENTIAL ARE THEY?

*See Lowi and Ginsberg, pp. 577–578 or brief edition, pp. 224–225*

*The way in which politics is reported and what journalists choose to cover both play critical roles in facilitating the deliberative process of democracy. It should not be surprising, therefore, that critics of the media abound. James Fallows, Washington, D.C., editor of the* Atlantic Monthly, *argues that Americans hate the media because reporters are more interested in the "inside baseball" of Washington intrigue than in issues and public policies that are important to people. President Clinton's policy on health care, for example, is portrayed as merely a strategic move in a political game, rather than an attempt to put forth public policy that should be debated and discussed as a means to better serve America's health care needs. Although the interest in the "game" of politics and the effort to predict political outcomes might engage reporters inside the Beltway (the highway that surrounds Washington, D.C.), Fallows argues that they are woefully out of touch with the interests and concerns of most Americans. The result is a loss of credibility for the media, and more worrisome, a weak link in the deliberative process of democracy.*

*Some critics have argued that the media don't provide voters with the information they need. They approve of an emerging trend called either "civic journalism" or "public journalism," in which newspapers in several cities are attempting to address the problems with political coverage and respond more directly to citizens' interests. Howard Kurtz, the Washington Post media critic, is less convinced of the merits of this movement. In his view, public journalism puts reporters and editors in the uncomfortable position of openly taking sides in political debates, and candidates themselves tend to dislike unscripted encounters that are the hallmark of the process. At the same time, readers and other members of the public appear to support efforts to make the political process more participatory.*

# James Fallows
# "Why Americans Hate the Media"*

### NOT ISSUES BUT THE GAME OF POLITICS

A generation ago political talk programs were sleepy Sunday-morning affairs. The Secretary of State or the Senate majority leader would show up to answer questions from Lawrence Spivak or Bob Clark, and after thirty minutes another stately episode of *Meet the Press* or *Issues and Answers* would be history.

Everything in public life is "brighter" and more "interesting" now. Constant competition from the weekday trash-talk shows has forced anything involving political life to liven up. Under pressure from the Saturday political-talk shows—*The McLaughlin Group* and its many disorderly descendants—even the Sunday-morning shows have put on rouge and push-up bras.

*Meet the Press*, moderated by Tim Russert, is probably the meatiest of these programs. High-powered guests discuss serious topics with Russert, who worked for years in politics, and with veteran reporters. Yet the pressure to keep things lively means that squabbling replaces dialogue.

The discussion shows that are supposed to enhance public understanding may actually reduce it, by hammering home the message that issues don't matter except as items for politicians to fight over. Some politicians in Washington may indeed view all issues as mere tools to use against their opponents. But far from offsetting this view of public life, the national press often encourages it. As Washington-based talk shows have become more popular in the past decade, they have had a trickle-down effect in cities across the country. In Seattle, in Los Angeles, in Boston, in Atlanta, journalists gain notice and influence by appearing regularly on talk shows—and during those appearances they mainly talk about the game of politics.

In the 1992 presidential campaign candidates spent more time answering questions from "ordinary people"—citizens in town-hall forums, callers on radio and TV talk shows—than they had in previous years. The citizens asked overwhelmingly about the *what* of politics: What are you going to do about the health-care system? What can you do to reduce the cost of welfare? The reporters asked almost exclusively about the *how*: How are you going to try to take away Perot's constituency? How do you answer charges that you have flip-flopped?

After the 1992 campaign the contrast between questions from citizens and those from reporters was widely discussed in journalism reviews and postmortems on campaign coverage. Reporters acknowledged that they should try harder to ask questions about things their readers and viewers seemed to care about—that is, questions about the differences that political choices would make in people's lives.

In January of 1995 there was a chance to see how well the lesson had sunk in. In the days just before and after Bill Clinton delivered his State of the Union address to the new Republican-controlled Congress, he answered questions in a wide variety of forums in order to explain his plans.

On January 31, a week after the speech, the President flew to Boston and took questions from a group of teenagers. Their questions concerned the effects of legislation or government programs on their communities or schools. These were the questions (paraphrased in some cases):

- "We need stronger laws to punish those people who are caught selling guns to our youth. Basically, what can you do about that?"

- "I notice that often it's the media that is responsible for the negative portrayal of young people in our society." What can political leaders do to persuade the media that there is good news about youth?

- Apprenticeship programs and other ways to provide job training have been valuable for students not going to college. Can the Administration promote more of these programs?

- Programs designed to keep teenagers away from drugs and gangs often emphasize sports and seem geared mainly to boys. How can such programs be made more attractive to teenage girls?

- What is it like at Oxford? (This was from a student who was completing a new alternative-school curriculum in the Boston public schools, and who had been accepted at Oxford.)

- "We need more police officers who are trained to deal with all the other different cultures in our cities." What can the government do about that?

- "In Boston, Northeastern University has created a model of scholarships and other supports to help inner-city kids get to and stay in college. . . . As President, can you urge colleges across the country to do what Northeastern has done?"

Earlier in the month the President's performance had been assessed by the three network-news anchors: Peter Jennings, of ABC; Dan Rather, of CBS; and Tom Brokaw, of NBC. There was no overlap whatsoever between the questions the students asked and those raised by the anchors. None of the questions from these news professionals concerned the impact of legislation or politics on people's lives. Nearly all concerned the struggle for individual advancement among candidates.

Peter Jennings, who met with Clinton as the Gingrich-Dole Congress was getting under way, asked whether Clinton had been eclipsed as a political leader by the Republicans. Dan Rather did interviews through January with prominent politicians—Senators Edward Kennedy, Phil Gramm, and Bob Dole—building up to a profile of Clinton two days after the State of the Union address. Every question he asked was about popularity or political tactics. He asked Phil Gramm to guess whether Newt Gingrich would enter the race (no) and whether Bill Clinton would be renominated by his party (yes). He asked Bob Dole what kind of mood the President seemed to be in, and whether Dole and Gingrich were, in effect, the new bosses of Washington. When Edward Kennedy began giving his views about the balanced-budget amendment, Rather steered him back on course: "Senator, you know I'd talk about these things the rest of the afternoon, but let's move quickly to politics. Do you expect Bill Clinton to be the Democratic nominee for re-election in 1996?"

The *CBS Evening News* profile of Clinton, which was narrated by Rather and was presented as part of the series *Eye on America*, contained no mention of Clinton's economic policy, his tax or budget plans, his failed attempt to pass a health-care proposal, his successful attempt to ratify NAFTA, his efforts to "reinvent government," or any substantive aspect of his proposals or plans in office. Its subject was exclusively Clinton's handling of his office—his "difficulty making decisions," his "waffling" at crucial moments. If Rather or his colleagues had any interest in the content of Clinton's speech as opposed to its political effect, neither the questions they asked nor the reports they aired revealed such a concern.

Tom Brokaw's questions were more substantive, but even he concentrated mainly on politics of the moment. How did the President feel about a poll showing that 61 percent of the public felt that he had no "strong convictions" and could be "easily swayed"? What did Bill Clinton think about Newt Gingrich? "Do you think he plays fair?" How did he like it that people kept shooting at the White House?

When ordinary citizens have a chance to pose questions to political leaders, they rarely ask about the game of politics. They want to know how the reality of politics will affect them—through taxes, programs, scholarship funds, wars. Journalists justify their intrusiveness and excesses by claiming that they are the public's representatives, asking the questions their fellow citizens would ask if they had the privilege of meeting with Presidents and senators. In fact they ask questions that only their fellow political professionals care about. And they often do so—as at the typical White House news conference—with a discourtesy and rancor that represent the public's views much less than they reflect the modern journalist's belief that being independent boils down to acting hostile.

## THE ONE-TRACK MIND

The limited curiosity that elite reporters display in their questions is also evident in the stories they write once they have received answers. They are interested mainly in pure politics and can be coerced into examining the substance of an issue only as a last resort. The subtle but sure result is a stream of daily messages that the real meaning of public life is the struggle of Bob Dole against Newt Gingrich against Bill Clinton, rather than our collective efforts to solve collective problems.

The natural instinct of newspapers and TV is to present every public issue as if its "real" meaning were political in the meanest and narrowest sense of that term—the attempt by parties and candidates to gain an advantage over their rivals. Reporters do, of course, write stories about political life in the broader sense and about the substance of issues—the pluses and minuses of diplomatic recognition for Vietnam, the difficulties of holding down the Medicare budget, whether immigrants help or hurt the nation's economic base. But when there is a chance to use these issues as props or raw material for a story about political tactics, most reporters leap at it. It is more fun—and easier—to write about Bill Clinton's "positioning" on the Vietnam issue, or how Newt Gingrich is "handling" the need to cut Medicare, than it is to look into the issues themselves.

Examples of this preference occur so often that they're difficult to notice. But every morning's newspaper, along with every evening's newscast, reveals this pattern of thought.

- Last February 1995, when the Democratic President and the Republican Congress were fighting over how much federal money would go to local law-enforcement agencies, one network-news broadcast showed a clip of Gingrich denouncing Clinton and another of Clinton standing in front of a sea of uniformed police officers while making a tough-on-crime speech. The correspondent's sign-off line was "The White House thinks 'cops on the beat' has a simple but appealing ring to it." That is, the President was pushing the plan because it would sound good in his campaign ads. Whether or not that was Clinton's real motive, nothing in the broadcast gave the slightest hint of where the extra policemen would go, how much they might cost, whether there was reason to think they'd do any good. Everything in the story suggested that the crime bill mattered only as a chapter in the real saga, which was the struggle between Bill and Newt.

- Last April, after the explosion at the federal building in Oklahoma City, discussion changed quickly from the event itself to politicians' "handling" of the event. On the Sunday after the blast President Clinton announced a series of new anti-terrorism measures. The next morning, on National Public Radio's *Morning Edition*, Cokie Roberts was asked about the prospects of the proposals' taking effect. "In some ways it's not even the point," she replied. What mattered was that Clinton "looked good" taking the tough side of the issue. No one expects Cokie Roberts or other political correspondents to be experts on controlling terrorism, negotiating with the Syrians, or the other specific measures on which Presidents make stands. But all issues are shoehorned into the area of expertise the most-prominent correspondents do have: the struggle for one-upmanship among a handful of political leaders.

- When health-care reform was the focus of big political battles between Republicans and Democrats, it was on the front page and the evening newscast every day. When the Clinton Administration declared defeat in 1994 and there were no more battles to be fought, health-care news coverage virtually stopped too—even though the medical system still represented one seventh of the economy, even though HMOs and corporations and hospitals and pharmaceutical companies were rapidly changing policies in the face of ever-rising costs. Health care was no longer political news, and therefore it was no longer interesting news.

\* \* \*

## POINTLESS PREDICTION: THE POLITICAL EXPERTS

On Sunday, November 6, 1994, two days before the congressional elections that swept the Republicans to power, *The Washington Post* published the results of its "Crystal Ball" poll. Fourteen prominent journalists, pollsters, and all-around analysts made their predictions about how many seats each party would win in the House and Senate and how many governorships each would take.

One week later many of these same experts would be saying on their talk shows that the Republican landslide was "inevitable" and "a long time coming" and "a sign of deep discontent in the heartland." But before the returns were in, how many of the fourteen experts predicted that the Republicans would win both houses of Congress and that Newt Gingrich would be speaker? Exactly three.

What is interesting about this event is not just that so many experts could be so wrong. Immediately after the election even Newt Gingrich seemed dazed by the idea that the forty-year reign of the Democrats in the House had actually come to an end. Rather, the episode said something about the futility of political prediction itself—a task to which the big-time press devotes enormous effort and time. *Two days* before the election many of the country's most admired analysts had no idea what was about to happen. Yet within a matter of weeks these same people, unfazed, would be writing articles and giving speeches and being quoted about who was "ahead" and "behind" in the emerging race for the White House in 1996.

## SPOON-FEEDING: THE WHITE HOUSE PRESS CORPS

In the early spring of last year [1995], when Newt Gingrich was dominating the news from Washington and the O. J. Simpson trial was dominating the news as a whole, *The Washington Post* ran an article about the pathos of the White House press room. Nobody wanted to hear what the President was doing, so the people who cover the President could not get on the air. Howard Kurtz, the *Post*'s media-writer, described the human cost of this political change:

Brit Hume is in his closet-size White House cubicle, watching Kato Kaelin testify on CNN. Bill Plante, in the adjoining cubicle, has his feet up and is buried in the *New York Times*. Brian Williams is in the corridor, idling away the time with Jim Miklaszewski.

An announcement is made for a bill-signing ceremony. Some of America's highest-paid television correspondents begin ambling toward the pressroom door.

"Are you coming with us?" Williams asks.

"I guess so," says Hume, looking forlorn.

The White House spokesman, Mike McCurry, told Kurtz that there was some benefit to the enforced silence: "Brit Hume has now got his crossword puzzle capacity down to record time. And some of the reporters have been out on the lecture circuit."

The deadpan restraint with which Kurtz told this story is admirable. But the question many readers would want to scream at the idle correspondents is *Why don't you go out and do some work?*

Why not go out and interview someone, even if you're not going to get any airtime that night? Why not escape the monotonous tyranny of the White House press room, which reporters are always complaining about? The knowledge that O.J. will keep you off the air yet again should liberate you to look into those stories you never "had time" to deal with before. Why not *read a book*—about welfare reform, about Russia or China, about race relations, about anything? Why not imagine, just for a moment, that your journalistic duty might involve something more varied and constructive than doing standups from the White House lawn and sounding skeptical about whatever announcement the President's spokesman put out that day?

What might these well-paid, well-trained correspondents have done while waiting for the O.J. trial to become boring enough that they could get back on the air? They might have tried to learn something that would be of use to their viewers when the story of the moment went away. Without leaving Washington, without going farther than ten minutes by taxi from the White House (so that they could be on hand if a sudden press conference was called), they could have prepared themselves to discuss the substance of issues that affect the public.

For example, two years earlier Vice President Al Gore had announced an ambitious plan to "reinvent" the federal government. Had it made any difference, either in improving the performance of government or in reducing its cost, or was it all for show? Republicans and Democrats were sure to spend the next few months fighting about cuts in the capital-gains tax. Capital-gains tax rates were higher in some countries and lower in others. What did the experience of these countries show about whether cutting the rates helped an economy to grow? The rate of immigration was rising again, and in California and Florida it was becoming an important political issue. What was the latest evidence on the economic and social effects of immigration? Should Americans feel confident or threatened that so many foreigners were trying to make their way in? Soon both political parties would be advancing plans to reform the welfare system. Within a two-mile radius of the White House lived plenty of families on welfare. Why not go and see how the system had affected them, and what they would do if it changed? The federal government had gone further than most private industries in trying to open opportunities to racial minorities and women. The Pentagon had gone furthest of all. What did people involved in this process—men and women, blacks and whites—think about its successes and failures? What light did their experience shed on the impending affirmative-action debate?

The list could go on for pages. With a few minutes' effort—about as long as it takes to do a crossword puzzle—the correspondents could have drawn up lists of other subjects they had never before "had time" to investigate. They had the time now. What they lacked was a sense that their responsibility involved something more than standing up to rehash the day's announcements when there was room for them on the news.

\*   \*   \*

## OUT OF TOUCH WITH AMERICA

In the week leading up to a State of the Union address White House aides always leak word to reporters that this year the speech will be "different." No more laundry list of all the government's activities, no more boring survey of every potential trouble spot in the world. This time, for a change, the speech is going to be short, punchy, and thematic. When the actual speech occurs, it is never short, punchy, or thematic. It is long and detailed, like all its predecessors, because as the deadline nears, every part of the government scrambles desperately to have a mention of its activities crammed into the speech somewhere.

In the days before Bill Clinton's address a year ago [1995] aides said that no matter what had happened to all those other Presidents, this time the speech really would be short, punchy, and thematic. The President understood the situation, he recognized his altered role, and he saw this as an opportunity to set a new theme for his third and fourth years in office.

That evening the promises once again proved false. Bill Clinton gave a speech that was enormously long even by the standards of previous State of the Union addresses. The speech had three or four apparent endings, it had ad-libbed inserts, and it covered both the details of policy and the President's theories about what had gone wrong with America. An hour and twenty-one minutes after he took the podium, the President stepped down.

Less than a minute later the mockery from commentators began. For instant analysis NBC went to Peggy Noonan, who had been a speechwriter for Presidents Ronald Reagan and George Bush. She grimaced and barely tried to conceal her disdain for such an ungainly, sprawling speech. Other commentators soon mentioned that congressmen had been slipping out of the Capitol building before the end of the speech, that Clinton had once more failed to stick to an agenda, that the speech probably would not give the President the new start he sought. The comments were virtually all about the tactics of the speech, and they were almost all thumbs down.

A day and a half later the first newspaper columns showed up. They were even more critical. On January 26 *The Washington Post*'s op-ed page consisted mainly of stories about the speech, all of which were withering. "ALL MUSH AND NO MESSAGE" was the headline on a column by Richard

Cohen. "AN OPPORTUNITY MISSED" was the more statesmanlike judgment from David Broder. Cohen wrote: "Pardon me if I thought of an awful metaphor: Clinton at a buffet table, eating everything in sight."

What a big fat jerk that Clinton was! How little he understood the obligations of leadership! Yet the news section of the same day's *Post* had a long article based on discussions with a focus group of ordinary citizens in Chicago who had watched the President's speech. "For these voters, the State of the Union speech was an antidote to weeks of unrelenting criticism of Clinton's presidency," the article said.

"Tonight reminded us of what has been accomplished," said Maureen Prince, who works as the office manager in her husband's business and has raised five children. "We are so busy hearing the negatives all the time, from the time you wake up on your clock radio in the morning. . . ."

The group's immediate impressions mirrored the results of several polls conducted immediately after the president's speech.

ABC News found that eight out of 10 approved of the president's speech. CBS News said that 74 percent of those surveyed said they had a "clear idea" of what Clinton stands for, compared with just 41 percent before the speech. A Gallup Poll for *USA Today* and Cable News Network found that eight in 10 said Clinton is leading the country in the right direction.

Nielsen ratings reported in the same day's paper showed that the longer the speech went on, the larger the number of people who tuned in to watch.

The point is not that the pundits are necessarily wrong and the public necessarily right. The point is the gulf between the two groups' reactions. The very aspects of the speech that had seemed so ridiculous to the professional commentators—its detail, its inclusiveness, the hyperearnestness of Clinton's conclusion about the "common good"—seemed attractive and worthwhile to most viewers.

"I'm wondering what so much of the public heard that our highly trained expert analysts completely missed," Carol Cantor, a software consultant from California, wrote in a discussion on the WELL, a popular on-line forum, three days after the speech. What they heard was, in fact, the speech, which allowed them to draw their own conclusions rather than being forced to accept an expert "analysis" of how the President "handled" the speech. In most cases the analysis goes unchallenged, because the public has no chance to see whatever event the pundits are describing. In this instance viewers had exactly the same evidence about Clinton's performance that the "experts" did, and from it they drew radically different conclusions.

In 1992 political professionals had laughed at Ross Perot's "boring" and "complex" charts about the federal budget deficit—until it became obvious that viewers loved them. And for a week or two after this State of the Union speech there were little jokes on the weekend talk shows about how out of step the pundit reaction had been with opinion "out there."

But after a polite chuckle the talk shifted to how the President and the speaker and Senator Dole were handling their jobs.


## TERM LIMITS

As soon as the Democrats were routed in the 1994 elections, commentators and TV analysts said it was obvious that the American people were tired of seeing the same old faces in Washington. The argument went that those who lived inside the Beltway had forgotten what it was like in the rest of the country. They didn't get it. They were out of touch. The only way to jerk the congressional system back to reality was to bring in new blood.

A few days after the new Congress was sworn in, CNN began running an updated series of promotional ads for its program *Crossfire*. (Previous ads had featured shots of locomotives colliding head-on and rams locking horns, to symbolize the meeting of minds on the show.) Everything has been shaken up in the capital, one of the ads began. New faces. New names. New people in charge of all the committees.

"In fact," the announcer said, in a tone meant to indicate whimsy, "only one committee hasn't changed. The *welcoming* committee."

The camera pulled back to reveal the three hosts of *Crossfire*—Pat Buchanan, John Sununu, and Michael Kinsley—standing with arms crossed on the steps of the Capitol building, blocking the path of the new arrivals trying to make their way in. "Watch your step," one of the hosts said.

Talk about not getting it! The people who put together this ad must have imagined that the popular irritation with inside-the-Beltway culture was confined to members of Congress—and didn't extend to members of the punditocracy, many of whom had held their positions much longer than the typical congressman had. The difference between the "welcoming committee" and the congressional committees headed by fallen Democratic titans like Tom Foley and Jack Brooks was that the congressmen can be booted out.

"Polls show that both Republicans *and* Democrats felt better about the Congress just after the 1994 elections," a Clinton Administration official said last year. "They had 'made the monkey jump'—they were able to discipline an institution they didn't like. They could register the fact that they were unhappy. There doesn't seem to be any way to do that with the press, except to stop watching and reading, which more and more people have done."


## LOST CREDIBILITY

There is an astonishing gulf between the way journalists—especially the most prominent ones—think about their impact and the way the public does. In movies of the 1930s reporters were gritty characters who instinctively sided with the common man. In the 1970s Robert Redford and Dustin Hoffman, starring as Bob Woodward and Carl Bernstein in *All the President's Men*, were better-paid but still gritty reporters unafraid to challenge big power. Even the local-TV-news crew featured on *The Mary Tyler Moore Show* had a certain down-to-earth pluck. Ted Knight, as the peabrained news anchor Ted Baxter, was a ridiculously pompous figure but not an arrogant one.

Since the early 1980s the journalists who have shown up in movies have often been portrayed as more loathsome than the lawyers, politicians, and business moguls who are the traditional bad guys in films about the white-collar world. In *Absence of Malice*, made in 1981, an ambitious newspaper reporter (Sally Field) ruins the reputation of a businessman (Paul Newman) by rashly publishing articles accusing him of murder. In *Broadcast News*, released in 1987, the anchorman (William Hurt) is still an airhead, like Ted Baxter, but unlike Ted, he works in a business that is systematically hostile to anything except profit and bland good looks. The only sympathetic characters in the movie, an overeducated reporter (Albert Brooks) and a hyperactive and hyperidealistic producer (Holly Hunter), would have triumphed as heroes in a newspaper movie of the 1930s. In this one they are ground down by the philistines at their network.

In the *Die Hard* series, which started in 1988, a TV journalist (William Atherton) is an unctuous creep who will lie and push helpless people around in order to get on the air. In *The Bonfire of the Vanities* (1990) the tabloid writer Peter Fallow (Bruce Willis) is a disheveled British sot who will do anything for a free drink. In *Rising Sun* (1993) a newspaper reporter known as "Weasel" (Steve Buscemi) is an out-and-out criminal, accepting bribes to influence his coverage. As Antonia Zerbisias pointed out in the *Toronto Star* in 1993, movies and TV shows offer almost no illustrations of journalists who are not full of themselves, shallow, and indifferent to the harm they do. During Operation Desert Storm, *Saturday Night Live* ridiculed American reporters who asked military spokesmen questions like "Can you tell us exactly when and where you are going to launch your attack?" "The journalists were portrayed as ignorant, arrogant and pointlessly adversarial," Jay Rosen, of New York University, wrote about the episode. "By gently rebuffing their ludicrous questions, the Pentagon briefer [on *SNL*] came off as a model of sanity."

Even real-life members of the Washington pundit corps have made their way into movies—Eleanor Clift, Morton Kondracke, hosts from *Crossfire*—in 1990s releases such as *Dave* and *Rising Sun*. Significantly, their role in the narrative is as buffoons. The joke in these movies is how rapidly the pundits leap to conclusions, how predictable their reactions are, how automatically they polarize the debate without any clear idea of what has really occurred. That real-life journalists are willing to keep appearing in such movies, knowing how they will be cast, says something about the source of self-respect in today's media: celebrity, on whatever basis, matters more than being taken seriously.

Movies do not necessarily capture reality, but they suggest a public mood—in this case, a contrast between the apparent self-satisfaction of the media celebrities and the contempt in which they are held by the public. "The news media has a generally positive view of itself in the watchdog role," wrote the authors of an exhaustive survey of public attitudes and the attitudes of journalists themselves toward the press. (The survey was conducted by the Times Mirror Center for the People and the Press, and was released last May.) But "the outside world strongly faults the news media for its negativism. . . . The public goes so far as to say that the press gets in the way of society solving its problems. . . ." According to the survey, "two out of three members of the public had nothing or nothing good to say about the media."

The media establishment is beginning to get at least an inkling of this message. Through the past decade discussions among newspaper editors and publishers have been a litany of woes: fewer readers; lower "penetration" rates, as a decreasing share of the public pays attention to news; a more and more desperate search for ways to attract the public's interest. In the short run these challenges to credibility are a problem for journalists and journalism. In the longer run they are a problem for democracy.

Howard Kurtz
"When News Media Go to Grass Roots,
Candidates Often Don't Follow"*

A few days before the New Hampshire primary in February, Robert J. Dole said he was surprised to learn that jobs and economic insecurity were such big issues in the presidential campaign.

Had he read a series in the Boston *Globe* last November, he would have learned that "it's still the economy," according to town meetings, focus groups and polling in one New Hampshire town. The "People's Voice" series is one of dozens of grass-roots efforts in this campaign season by newspapers, and television and radio stations, rising from a growing movement called public journalism.

It is, in essence, an attempt by news organizations to fashion a citizens' agenda by orchestrating meetings and task forces—and, in some cases, drafting volunteers and pushing for solutions to local problems. While critics say this amounts to an abandonment of objectivity, supporters from Maine to California say the approach weans journalists from their dependence on political insiders and helps them forge new connections with their communities.

"It's not that different than going door to door" and interviewing voters, said *Globe* Editor Matthew Storin. "There's a little bit of a marketing spin to it. But I like doing this part of public journalism, even if it's being packaged as something new and it's not quite new. I can live with that. We're all trying to sell newspapers."

It might seem a rather obvious exercise for reporters to try to discover what voters are thinking. But in the wake of the 1992 campaign, when candidates used talk shows to bypass the mainstream press, newspapers in particular are searching for ways to remain relevant. And, with foundations handing out money for that very purpose, public journalism has become a handy way to grab the spotlight.

The movement's advocates argue that much of the public is disgusted with the usual horse-race coverage of politics. Consider the responses of focus-group participants in New Hampshire and Massachusetts in a study for the Pew Center for Civic Journalism:

"I think the media and politicians are connected. They are tied together by money and power and they just don't know about people like me."—Kathy, a homemaker.

"Most reporters give the editor or publisher what they want to hear." —Tony, a law enforcement officer.

"They care more about asking questions than listening to the answers."—Charlie, a salesman.

"They get away from the real issues of the campaign and don't tell us what a person really thinks."—Joyce, an accounting clerk.

Still, the notion that the news media should foster unscripted encounters between the public and the politicians has not been embraced by the candidates themselves. When the *Globe* and a Boston television and radio station sponsored a citizens' forum in Derry, N.H., only GOP candidates Richard G. Lugar, Robert K. Doman and Alan Keyes showed up. The major candidates also pulled out one day before a Des Moines forum, staged by Iowa Public Television and several other news organizations, when Senate Majority Leader Dole refused to participate.

Noncandidates, though, can use such forums to score political points. Hillary Rodham Clinton received upbeat coverage in March for joining a citizens' conference on the family, sponsored by the *Minneapolis Star Tribune* and a public television station. These are ambitious ventures: The *Star Tribune*, which last week convened a gathering of 400 people, says the purpose is "to help the state imagine a new kind of politics."

As public journalism has gained momentum in the last half-dozen years, it has taken on a variety of forms. Some news organizations have merely offered free pizzas to entice readers to attend meetings or fill out questionnaires. Others have joined forces with local universities that they also must cover. Still others have stretched the boundaries of what journalists ordinarily do.

The *Akron Beacon Journal* persuaded 22,000 citizens to mail in coupons pledging to work for improved race relations. The *Charlotte Observer* held inner-city town meetings in a "Taking Back Our Neighborhoods" campaign that prompted the city to tear down dilapidated buildings and open parks and recreational facilities. The Huntington, W.Va., *Herald-Dispatch* helped solicit volunteers for a half-dozen task forces on economic development and sponsored a visit to the state legislature to lobby on the issue.

"People are less concerned about the issue of reporting news versus making news," said Robert Gabordi, the *Herald-Dispatch* editor. "That's an old argument that doesn't stand up anymore. The more important question to ask is, are you being as aggressive a watchdog on a project you may have had a part in? We took a pretty hard look at the successes and failures of the whole project."

But Leonard Downie Jr., *The Washington Post*'s executive editor and a leading critic of public journalism, questioned the practice of "forcing politicians to appear at a forum of our choosing and to focus only on those questions we want to ask." He said it is "beyond the pale" for news organizations to get involved in advocating solutions, or even urging people to vote.

"That is a great danger to the credibility of the newspaper . . . even when the cause is the best possible cause," Downie said, adding: "It is very seductive, particularly for the top editors involved, who become celebrities through this process."

Some journalists expressed mixed feelings. *San Francisco Chronicle* reporter John King was at the center of a "Voice of the Voter" project during last year's mayoral race. He said he was surprised by "how thoughtful a lot of people are about the city" and contrasted it with his usual reporting: "You talk to your seven or eight appointed experts and they all say funny things that you slap in the paper. The more ridiculous the charge, the more space you give it."

At the same time, King said of the paper's practice of publishing reader comments verbatim: "It was really the Voice of the Yahoo. Instead of writing a crazy letter, people would call the voice mail and we'd run a 100-word rant from someone."

Some recent public journalism ventures have taken on a cookie-cutter flavor, in part because they work with such organizations as the Pew center and the Poynter Institute for Media Studies, which provide funding and technical assistance. Pew alone is financing such efforts in 17 cities this year. These often feature a catchy logo ("We the People," "Voices of Florida," "Front Porch Forum") and some polls and focus groups, with the findings splashed across the front page.

"There are superficial versions and there are more substantial versions," said Jay Rosen, director of New York University's Project on Public Life and the Press. "To me, proclaiming that you are 'the people's voice' is a problem unless you have made some extraordinary effort at public listening, to understand not only their votes but their lives in depth. Simply throwing ordinary people's voices into the paper is not worth a helluva lot."

Some efforts during the 1996 campaign have been worthwhile but low-risk. The *Des Moines Register* used the state's new fiber-optic network to allow high school students to question Republican candidates such as Malcolm S. "Steve" Forbes. "It wasn't front-page stuff," said David Yepsen, the paper's political editor. "Most of the questions were fairly predictable —positions on issues, that sort of thing. But it helped engage a segment of the electorate that's just getting interested in politics."

The Derry project—launched by the *Globe*, WABU-TV and WBUR-FM —is among the more ambitious. Some participants say it strikes at the heart of what is wrong with the news business.

"To me, civic journalism is simply a return to the roots of what journalism was originally," said Ted O'Brien, news director of WABU, a UHF station owned by Boston University. "As you move into the larger markets, your life becomes very different from the mass of people who are watching. Since Watergate, you have a whole new group of reporters coming out of the upper middle class, and they're attracted by the glamour rather than the nitty-gritty."

The Derry effort zoomed in on the nitty-gritty, and that, for a business drawn to drama, was often a problem. "The challenge was trying to turn what we were hearing from people and learning about their lives into journalism," said Tara Murphy, project coordinator for WBUR, who conducted the Pew focus groups. "Some reporters feel kind of uncomfortable doing a story about something that has been organized. But these groups were not intended to be the story. They were listening posts for reporters."

Storin also found himself frustrated by the Derry participants. "They're not the clever, articulate people you're used to reading about in newspapers," he said. "We have to find a way to make them more interesting."

On separate occasions, Sens. Lugar (R-Ind.) and Phil Gramm (R-Tex.) and former Tennessee governor Lamar Alexander met with a half-dozen Derry residents at a local high school. Initially, the journalists said, the residents were a bit intimidated and did not ask follow-up questions. With some prodding from the reporters, that changed over time.

The basic, straightforward queries of ordinary citizens occasionally produced flashes of insight. When Priscilla Parten of Derry asked Alexander who would care for the elderly if the budget were cut, he spoke of "more personal responsibility in our own families." That drew a negative reaction, including a critical column by the *Globe*'s Ellen Goodman.

"It's easy to avoid a question from a reporter and not look bad, but you can't avoid a question from these people," O'Brien said. "You can't blow them off in the same way."

Months before Patrick J. Buchanan began surging in the polls with a populist economic message, the New Hampshire surveys found "that nearly 60 percent of potential voters felt they did not earn enough money, that 30 percent said they never will, and more than half worried that they might lose their homes and that their children will never have good jobs at good pay," the *Globe* reported.

In the focus groups, said Royal Ford, the *Globe*'s New Hampshire correspondent, "they didn't want to talk about moral issues. They wanted to talk about jobs, their future, their kids' future."

Ford found the exercise worthwhile, but added: "If the Boston *Globe* had said to me, 'Here's four months, roam around New Hampshire,' it probably would have produced the same thing." He also encountered skepticism within his own newspaper: "Some of the old Washington hands didn't think much of it. They asked how my obedient little voters were doing."

David Shribman, the Globe's Washington bureau chief, told Murphy that "most traditional reporters viewed it with dread and trepidation. . . . They were also repelled—not too strong a word—by the near-religious zeal of this new civic religion." But in the end, Shribman said, the project was viewed as "an absolute, bell-ringing, positive success."

Among Derry's 30,000 residents, the venture also drew rave reviews. "I thought it was wonderful," said Pat MacEachern, a volunteer teacher's aide, who expressed concern about education for her 5-year-old. "It focused more on what normal, everyday people are thinking about and what their concerns are. A lot of times, the global issues or what they're talking about in Washington isn't really relevant."

Vickie Buckley Chase, executive director of the Derry Chamber of Commerce, agreed. "It was an excellent opportunity to express our wants and desires without having the mass media coming down on us," she said. "It gave me an opportunity to see what might be in our future."

Some journalists say the movement's impact should not be oversold. "It's probably more effective as it gets more localized," King said. "The notion that it's going to affect the presidential race is pretty absurd."

But enthusiasts such as NYU's Rosen say it's no accident that public journalism has taken off in places such as Boston, Charlotte, Miami, Wichita, Madison and Norfolk.

"There's a growing breach between the national press corps and local and regional journalists who used to look upwards for their cues," he said. "I don't think people in the elite press quite understand this."

# 14

# Government and the Economy: An Introduction to Public Policy

### Making and Maintaining a National Market Economy

*See Lowi and Ginsberg, pp. 609–615*

*Should the government play a role in the economy? As Lowi and Ginsberg discuss in the text, the government has always played a role in the economy, providing property for development, enforcing contracts and prohibiting theft of private property, providing subsidies to encourage the growth of particular industries, and regulating trade. Yet should there be a limit to government involvement, particularly when the economy is depressed? This debate was central to the presidential election of 1932 between the Democratic candidate, Franklin D. Roosevelt, and the Republican president, Herbert Hoover. In Roosevelt's campaign address, printed here, he argues for vigorous government involvement in the economy to provide unemployment insurance, housing for the poor, and additional public works programs to deal with the hardship of the Great Depression. Hoover, on the other hand, was very much opposed to what he argued was the radical alteration of the relationship between government and the private sector which was "built up by 150 years of the toil of our fathers." It was the extension of freedom and the exercise of individual initiative which made the American economic system strong, and which would gradually bring about economic recovery, Hoover argued. While Roosevelt won the election and fundamentally altered the relationship between the government and the economy, the debate is by no means settled. Do you agree that the government is too involved in the economy? What should the government stop doing? Does the government do anything that is essential to the operation of the economy?*

## Franklin D. Roosevelt
## "Call for Federal Responsibility"*

The first principle I would lay down is that the primary duty rests on the community, through local government and private agencies, to take care of the relief of unemployment. But we then come to a situation

---

* Franklin D. Roosevelt, "Call for Federal Responsibility" in *The Public Papers and Addresses of Franklin D. Roosevelt*, comp. Samuel P. Rosenman (New York: Russell and Russell, 1969).

where there are so many people out of work that local funds are insufficient.

It seems clear to me that the organized society known as the State comes into the picture at this point. In other words, the obligation of government is extended to the next higher unit.

I practise what I preach. In 1930 the state of New York greatly increased its employment service and kept in close touch with the ability of localities to take care of their own unemployed. But by the summer of 1931 it became apparent to me that actual state funds and a state-supervised system were imperative.

I called a special session of the legislature, and they appropriated a fund of $20 million for unemployment relief, this fund to be reimbursed to the state through the doubling of our income taxes. Thus the state of New York became the first among all the states to accept the definite obligation of supplementing local funds where these local funds were insufficient.

The administration of this great work has become a model for the rest of the country. Without setting up any complex machinery or any large overhead, the state of New York is working successfully through local agencies, and, in spite of the fact that over a million people are out of work and in need of aid in this one state alone, we have so far met at least the bare necessities of the case.

This past spring the legislature appropriated another $5 million, and on November 8 the voters will pass on a $30 million bond issue to tide us over this winter and at least up to next summer. . . .

I am very certain that the obligation extends beyond the states and to the federal government itself, if and when it becomes apparent that states and communities are unable to take care of the necessary relief work.

It may interest you to have me read a short quotation from my message to the legislature in 1931:

What is the State? It is the duly constituted representative of an organized society of human beings, created by them for their mutual protection and well-being. One of the duties of the State is that of caring for those of its citizens who find themselves the victims of such adverse circumstances as make them unable to obtain even the necessities of mere existence without the aid of others.

In broad terms, I assert that modern society, acting through its government, owes the definite obligation to prevent the starvation or the dire want of any of its fellowmen and women who try to maintain themselves but cannot. To these unfortunate citizens aid must be extended by the government, not as a matter of charity but as a matter of social duty.

That principle which I laid down in 1931, I reaffirm. I not only reaffirm it, I go a step further and say that where the State itself is unable successfully to fulfill this obligation which lies upon it, it then becomes the positive duty of the federal government to step in to help.

In the words of our Democratic national platform, the federal government has a "continuous responsibility for human welfare, especially for the protection of children." That duty and responsibility the federal government should carry out promptly, fearlessly, and generously.

It took the present Republican administration in Washington almost three years to recognize this principle. I have recounted to you in other speeches, and it is a matter of general information, that for at least two years after the crash, the only efforts made by the national administration to cope with the distress of unemployment were to deny its existence.

When, finally, this year, after attempts at concealment and minimizing had failed, it was at last forced to recognize the fact of suffering among millions of unemployed, appropriations of federal funds for assistance to states were finally made.

I think it is fair to point out that a complete program of unemployment relief was on my recommendation actually under way in the state of New York over a year ago; and that in Washington relief funds in any large volume were not provided until this summer, and at that they were pushed through at the demand of Congress rather than through the leadership of the President of the United States.

At the same time, I have constantly reiterated my conviction that the expenditures of cities, states, and the federal government must be reduced in the interest of the nation as a whole. I believe that there are many ways in which such reduction of expenditures can take place, but I am utterly unwilling that economy should be practised at the expense of starving people.

We must economize in other ways, but it shall never be said that the American people have refused to provide the necessities of life for those who, through no fault of their own, are unable to feed, clothe, and house themselves. The first obligation of government is the protection of the welfare and well-being, indeed the very existence, of its citizens. . . .

The next question asks my attitude toward appropriations for public works as an aid to unemployment. I am perfectly clear as to the principles involved in this case also.

From the long-range point of view it would be advisable for governments of all kinds to set up in times of prosperity what might be called a nest egg to be used for public works in times of depression. That is a policy which we should initiate when we get back to good times.

But there is the immediate possibility of helping the emergency through appropriations for public works. One question, however, must be answered first because of the simple fact that these public works cost money.

We all know that government treasuries, whether local or state or federal, are hard put to it to keep their budgets balanced; and, in the case of the federal Treasury, thoroughly unsound financial policies have made its situation not exactly desperate but at least threatening to future stability if the policies of the present administration are continued.

All public works, including federal, must be considered from the point of view of the ability of the government Treasury to pay for them. There are two ways of paying for public works. One is by the sale of bonds. In principle, such bonds should be issued only to pay for self-sustaining projects or for structures which will without question have a useful life over a long period of years. The other method of payment is from current revenues, which in these days means in most cases added taxes. We all know that there is a very definite limit to the increase of taxes above the present level.

From this point, therefore, I can go on and say that, if funds can be properly provided by the federal government for increased appropriations for public works, we must examine the character of these public works. I have already spoken of that type which is self-sustaining. These should be greatly encouraged. The other type is that of public works which are honestly essential to the community. Each case must rest on its own merits.

It is impossible, for example, to say that all parks or all playgrounds are essential. One may be and another may not be. If a school, for instance, has no playground, it is obvious that the furnishing of a playground is a necessity to the community. But if the school already has a playground and some people seek merely to enlarge it, there may be a very definite question as to how necessary that enlargement is.

Let me cite another example. I am much interested in providing better housing accommodations for the poor in our great cities. If a slum area can be torn down and new modern buildings put up, I should call that almost a human necessity; but, on the other hand, the mere erection of new buildings in some other part of the city while allowing the slums to remain raises at once a question of necessity. I am confident that the federal government working in cooperation with states and cities can do much to carry on increased public works and along lines which are sound from the economic and financial point of view.

Now I come to another question. I am asked whether I favor a system of unemployment insurance reserves made compulsory by the states, supplemented by a system of federally coordinated state employment offices to facilitate the reemployment of jobless workers.

The first part of the question is directly answered by the Democratic platform which advocates unemployment insurance under state laws.

This is no new policy for me. I have advocated unemployment insurance in my own state for some time, and, indeed, last year six Eastern governors were my guests at a conference which resulted in the drawing up of what might be called an idea plan of unemployment insurance.

This type of insurance is not a cure-all but it provides at least a cushion to mitigate unemployment in times of depression. It is sound if, after starting it, we stick to the principle of sound insurance financing. It is only where governments, as in some European countries, have failed to live up to these sound principles that unemployment insurance has been an economic failure.

As to the coordinated employment offices, I can only tell you that I was for the bills sponsored by Senator Wagner of my own state and passed by the Congress. They created a nationally coordinated system of employment offices operated by the individual states with the advisory cooperation of joint boards of employers and employees.

To my very great regret this measure was vetoed by the President of the United States. I am certain that the federal government can, by furnishing leadership, stimulate the various states to set up and coordinate practical, useful systems.

# Herbert Hoover
## "Against the Proposed New Deal"*

This campaign is more than a contest between two men. It is more than a contest between two parties. It is a contest between two philosophies of government.

We are told by the opposition that we must have a change, that we must have a new deal. It is not the change that comes from normal development of national life to which I object but the proposal to alter the whole foundations of our national life which have been builded through generations of testing and struggle, and of the principles upon which we have builded the nation. The expressions our opponents use must refer to important changes in our economic and social system and our system of government, otherwise they are nothing but vacuous words. And I realize that in this time of distress many of our people are asking whether our social and economic system is incapable of that great primary function of providing security and comfort of life to all of the firesides of our 25 million homes in America, whether our social system provides for the fundamental development and progress of our people, whether our form of government is capable of originating and sustaining that security and progress.

This question is the basis upon which our opponents are appealing to the people in their fears and distress. They are proposing changes and so-called new deals which would destroy the very foundations of our American system.

Our people should consider the primary facts before they come to the judgment—not merely through political agitation, the glitter of promise, and the discouragement of temporary hardships—whether they will support changes which radically affect the whole system which has been builded up by 150 years of the toil of our fathers. They should not approach the question in the despair with which our opponents would clothe it.

Our economic system has received abnormal shocks during the past

* Herbert Hoover, "Against the Proposed New Deal" in *The State Papers and Other Public Writings of Herbert Hoover*, ed. William S. Myers (Garden City, NY: Doubleday, Doran, and Co., 1934).

three years, which temporarily dislocated its normal functioning. These shocks have in a large sense come from without our borders, but I say to you that our system of government has enabled us to take such strong action as to prevent the disaster which would otherwise have come to our nation. It has enabled us further to develop measures and programs which are now demonstrating their ability to bring about restoration and progress.

We must go deeper than platitudes and emotional appeals of the public platform in the campaign if we will penetrate to the full significance of the changes which our opponents are attempting to float upon the wave of distress and discontent from the difficulties we are passing through. We can find what our opponents would do after searching the record of their appeals to discontent, group and sectional interest. We must search for them in the legislative acts which they sponsored and passed in the Democratic-controlled House of Representatives in the last session of Congress. We must look into measures for which they voted and which were defeated. We must inquire whether or not the presidential and vice-presidential candidates have disavowed these acts. If they have not, we must conclude that they form a portion and are a substantial indication of the profound changes proposed.

And we must look still further than this as to what revolutionary changes have been proposed by the candidates themselves.

We must look into the type of leaders who are campaigning for the Democratic ticket, whose philosophies have been well known all their lives, whose demands for a change in the American system are frank and forceful. I can respect the sincerity of these men in their desire to change our form of government and our social and economic system, though I shall do my best tonight to prove they are wrong. I refer particularly to Senator Norris, Senator La Follette, Senator Cutting, Senator Huey Long, Senator Wheeler, William R. Hearst and other exponents of a social philosophy different from the traditional American one. Unless these men feel assurance of support to their ideas, they certainly would not be supporting these candidates and the Democratic Party. The seal of these men indicates that they have sure confidence that they will have voice in the administration of our government.

I may say at once that the changes proposed from all these Democratic principals and allies are of the most profound and penetrating character. If they are brought about, this will not be the America which we have known in the past.

Let us pause for a moment and examine the American system of government, of social and economic life, which it is now proposed that we should alter. Our system is the product of our race and of our experience in building a nation to heights unparalleled in the whole history of the world. It is a system peculiar to the American people. It differs essentially from all others in the world. It is an American system.

It is founded on the conception that only through ordered liberty, through freedom to the individual, and equal opportunity to the individual will his initiative and enterprise be summoned to spur the march of progress.

It is by the maintenance of equality of opportunity and therefore of a society absolutely fluid in freedom of the movement of its human particles that our individualism departs from the individualism of Europe. We resent class distinction because there can be no rise for the individual through the frozen strata of classes, and no stratification of classes can take place in a mass livened by the free rise of its particles. Thus in our ideals the able and ambitious are able to rise constantly from the bottom to leadership in the community.

This freedom of the individual creates of itself the necessity and the cheerful willingness of men to act cooperatively in a thousand ways and for every purpose as occasion arises; and it permits such voluntary cooperations to be dissolved as soon as they have served their purpose, to be replaced by new voluntary associations for new purposes.

There has thus grown within us, to gigantic importance, a new conception. That is, this voluntary cooperation within the community. Cooperation to perfect the social organization; cooperation for the care of those in distress; cooperation for the advancement of knowledge, of scientific research, of education; for cooperative action in the advancement of many phases of economic life. This is self-government by the people outside of government; it is the most powerful development of individual freedom and equal opportunity that has taken place in the century and a half since our fundamental institutions were founded.

It is in the further development of this cooperation and a sense of its responsibility that we should find solution for many of our complex problems, and not by the extension of government into our economic and social life. The greatest function of government is to build up that cooperation, and its most resolute action should be to deny the extension of bureaucracy. We have developed great agencies of cooperation by the assistance of the government which promote and protect the interests of individuals and the smaller units of business. The Federal Reserve System, in its strengthening and support of the smaller banks; the Farm Board, in its strengthening and support of the farm cooperatives; the Home Loan Banks, in the mobilizing of building and loan associations and savings banks; the Federal Land Banks, in giving independence and strength to land mortgage associations; the great mobilization of relief to distress, the mobilization of business and industry in measures of recovery, and a score of other activities are not socialism—they are the essence of protection to the development of free men.

The primary conception of this whole American system is not the regimentation of men but the cooperation of free men. It is founded upon the conception of responsibility of the individual to the community, of the responsibility of local government to the state, of the state to the national government.

It is founded on a peculiar conception of self-government designed to maintain this equal opportunity to the individual, and through decentralization it brings about and maintains these responsibilities. The centralization of government will undermine responsibilities and will destroy the system.

Our government differs from all previous conceptions, not only in this decentralization but also in the separation of functions between the legislative, executive, and judicial arms of government, in which the independence of the judicial arm is the keystone of the whole structure.

It is founded on a conception that in times of emergency, when forces are running beyond control of individuals or other cooperative action, beyond the control of local communities and of states, then the great reserve powers of the federal government shall be brought into action to protect the community. But when these forces have ceased, there must be a return of state, local, and individual responsibility.

The implacable march of scientific discovery with its train of new inventions presents every year new problems to government and new problems to the social order. Questions often arise whether, in the face of the growth of these new and gigantic tools, democracy can remain master in its own house, can preserve the fundamentals of our American system. I contend that it can; and I contend that this American system of ours has demonstrated its validity and superiority over any other system yet invented by human mind.

It has demonstrated it in the face of the greatest test of our history— that is the emergency which we have faced in the past three years.

When the political and economic weakness of many nations of Europe, the result of the World War and its aftermath, finally culminated in collapse of their institutions, the delicate adjustment of our economic and social life received a shock unparalleled in our history. No one knows that better than you of New York. No one knows its causes better than you. That the crisis was so great that many of the leading banks sought directly or indirectly to convert their assets into gold or its equivalent with the result that they practically ceased to function as credit institutions; that many of our citizens sought flight for their capital to other countries; that many of them attempted to hoard gold in large amounts. These were but indications of the flight of confidence and of the belief that our government could not overcome these forces.

Yet these forces were overcome—perhaps by narrow margins—and this action demonstrates what the courage of a nation can accomplish under the resolute leadership in the Republican Party. And I say the Republican Party, because our opponents before and during the crisis, proposed no constructive program; though some of their members patriotically supported ours. Later on the Democratic House of Representatives did develop the real thought and ideas of the Democratic Party, but it was so destructive that it had to be defeated, for it would have destroyed, not healed.

In spite of all these obstructions, we did succeed. Our form of government did prove itself equal to the task. We saved this nation from a quarter of a century of chaos and degeneration, and we preserved the savings, the insurance policies, gave a fighting chance to men to hold their homes. We saved the integrity of our government and the honesty of the American dollar. And we installed measures which today are bringing back recovery. Employment, agriculture, business—all of these show the steady, if slow, healing of our enormous wound.

I therefore contend that the problem of today is to continue these measures and policies to restore this American system to its normal functioning, to repair the wounds it has received, to correct the weaknesses and evils which would defeat that system. To enter upon a series of deep changes, to embark upon this inchoate new deal which has been propounded in this campaign, would be to undermine and destroy our American system.

## Maintaining a Capitalist Economy

*See Lowi and Ginsberg, pp. 615–627*

*The statistic is common to any American who watches the news or reads a paper: Gross Domestic Product, or GDP, is a measure of economic activity established in the 1930s by an economist in the Department of Commerce. It is widely used as an indicator of overall prosperity. As Cobb, Halstead, and Rowe point out, however, there are limits to what the GDP can tell us about economic well being. GDP is "simply a gross measure of market activity, of money changing hands"; it does not, the authors maintain, distinguish between desirable and undesirable growth and development. Furthermore, the GDP statistic does not take into account the status of the family, the community, or the environment —all of which have a dramatic impact on social and economic health—but actually records negative consequences in all three arenas as an indication of economic growth. For example, from a strictly economic perspective, divorce creates growth through legal bills and second households, and pollution registers a two-fold gain: first when it is measured as the by-product of production, and again when the national government pays for cleaning up toxic waste sites.*

*The problem, these authors argue, is that GDP is a statistic grounded in an economic theory that views any growth, regardless of the cost, as positive. They propose a broader measure of economic growth, one which recognizes that growth can have environmental and social costs.*

*Suppose you are an employee of the Commerce Department charged with finding new ways to measure the value of the U.S. economy. What kinds of things would you consider? How would you take into account the health of the family, communities, and the natural habitat? How would this broader measure influence government policies?*

## Clifford Cobb, Ted Halstead, and Jonathan Rowe
## "If the GDP Is Up, Why Is America Down?"*

Throughout the tumult of the elections last year [1994] political commentators were perplexed by a stubborn fact. The economy was performing splendidly, at least according to the standard measurements. Productivity and employment were up; inflation was under control. The World Economic Forum, in Switzerland, declared that the United States had regained its position as the most competitive economy on earth, after years of Japanese dominance.

The Clinton Administration waited expectantly, but the applause never came. Voters didn't *feel* better, even though economists said they should. The economy as economists define it was booming, but the individuals who compose it—or a great many of them, at least—were not. President Bill Clinton actually sent his economic advisers on the road to persuade Americans that their experience was wrong and the indicators were right.

This strange gap between what economists choose to measure and what Americans experience became the official conundrum of the campaign season. "PARADOX OF '94: GLOOMY VOTERS IN GOOD TIMES," *The New York Times* proclaimed on its front page. "BOOM FOR WHOM?" read the cover of *Time* magazine. Yet reporters never quite got to the basic question—namely, whether the official indicators are simply wrong, and are leading the nation in the wrong direction.

The problem goes much deeper than the "two-tiered" economy—prosperity at the top, decline in the middle and at the bottom—that received so much attention. It concerns the very definition of prosperity itself. In the apt language of the nineteenth-century writer John Ruskin, an economy produces "illth" as well as wealth; yet the conventional measures of well-being lump the two together. Could it be that even the upper tier was—and still is—rising on the deck of a ship that is sinking slowly into a sea of illth, and that the nation's indicators of economic progress provide barely a clue to that fact?

Ample attention was paid to the symptoms: People were working longer hours for less pay. The middle class was slipping while the rich were forging ahead. Commutes were more harried. Crime, congestion, and media violence were increasing. More families were falling apart. A *Business Week*/Harris poll in March imparted the not surprising news that more than 70 percent of the public was gloomy about the future.

Sounding much like the guidance department of a progressive New York grammar school, the Clinton Administration said that Americans were simply suffering the anxieties of adjustment to a wondrous new economy. Speaking in similar terms, Alan Greenspan, the chairman of the Federal Reserve Board, told a business gathering in San Francisco this past February that "there seemingly inexplicably remains an extraordinarily deep-rooted foreboding about the [economic] outlook" among the populace.

Those silly people. But could it be that the nation's economic experts live in a statistical Potemkin village* that hides the economy Americans are actually experiencing? Isn't it time to ask some basic questions about the gauges that inform expert opinion, and the premises on which those gauges are based?

Economic indicators are the main feedback loop to national policy. They define the economic problems that the political arena seeks to address. If the nation's indicators of economic progress are obsolete, then they consign us to continually resorting to policies that cannot succeed because they aren't addressing the right problems.

Today the two political parties differ somewhat in regard to means, but neither disputes that the ultimate goal of national policy is to make the big gauge—the gross domestic product—climb steadily upward. Neither questions that a rising GDP will wash away the nation's ills: if Americans feel unsettled despite a rising GDP, then clearly even more growth is needed.

This was clear in the months after the election, as the media continued to report economy up, people down stories that never quite managed to get to the crucial question: What is "up," anyway? In July, *Business Week* ran a cover story called "The Wage Squeeze" that got much closer than most. The article showed remarkable skepticism regarding the conventional wisdom. But the magazine's editorial writers retreated quickly. Why aren't workers doing better even as corporate profits and "the economy" are up? "America just may not be growing fast enough," they said.

Furthermore, the GDP and its various proxies—rates of growth, expansion, recovery—have become the very language of the nation's economic reportage and debate. We literally cannot think about economics without them. Yet these terms have increasingly become a barricade of abstraction that separates us from economic reality. They tell us next to nothing about what is actually going on.

The GDP is simply a gross measure of market activity, of money changing hands. It makes no distinction whatsoever between the desirable and the undesirable, or costs and gain. On top of that, it looks only at the portion of reality that economists choose to acknowledge—the part involved in monetary transactions. The crucial economic functions performed in the household and volunteer sectors go entirely unreckoned. As a result the GDP not only masks the breakdown of the social structure and the natural habitat upon which the economy—and life itself—ultimately depend; worse, it actually portrays such breakdown as economic gain.

Yet our politicians, media, and economic commentators dutifully con-

* From late-eighteenth-century Russian history. Potemkin created the look of prosperity in a village that Catherine the Great was visiting, hiding the actual deplorable conditions.

tinue to trumpet the GDP figures as information of great portent. There have been questions regarding the accuracy of the numbers that compose the GDP, and some occasional tinkering at the edges. But there has been barely a stirring of curiosity regarding the premise that underlies its gross statistical summation. Whether from sincere conviction or from entrenched professional and financial interests, politicians, economists, and the rest have not been eager to see it changed.

There is an urgent need for new indicators of progress, geared to the economy that actually exists. We are members of Redefining Progress, a new organization whose purpose is to stimulate broad public debate over the nature of economic progress and the best means of attaining it. Accordingly, we have developed a new indicator ourselves, to show both that it can be done and what such an indicator would look like. This new scorecard invites a thorough rethinking of economic policy and its underlying premises. It suggests strongly that it is not the voters who are out of touch with reality.

*   *   *

## THE GDP TODAY: HOW DOWN BECOMES UP

If the chief of your local police department were to announce today that "activity" on the city streets had increased by 15 percent, people would not be impressed, reporters least of all. They would demand specifics. Exactly *what* increased? Tree planting or burglaries? Volunteerism or muggings? Car wrecks or neighborly acts of kindness?

The mere quantity of activity, taken alone, says virtually nothing about whether life on the streets is getting better or worse. The economy is the same way. "Less" or "more" means very little unless you know *of what*. Yet somehow the GDP manages to induce a kind of collective stupor in which such basic questions rarely get asked.

By itself the GDP tells very little. Simply a measure of total output (the dollar value of finished goods and services), it assumes that everything produced is by definition "goods." It does not distinguish between costs and benefits, between productive and destructive activities, or between sustainable and unsustainable ones. The nation's central measure of well-being works like a calculating machine that adds but cannot subtract. It treats everything that happens in the market as a gain for humanity, while ignoring everything that happens outside the realm of monetized exchange, regardless of the importance to well-being.

By the curious standard of the GDP, the nation's economic hero is a terminal cancer patient who is going through a costly divorce. The happiest event is an earthquake or a hurricane. The most desirable habitat is a multibillion-dollar Superfund site. All these add to the GDP, because they cause money to change hands. It is as if a business kept a balance sheet by merely adding up all "transactions," without distinguishing between income and expenses, or between assets and liabilities.

The perversity of the GDP affects virtually all parts of society. In 1993 William J. Bennett, who had been the Secretary of Education in the Reagan Administration, produced a study of social decline. He called it "The Index of Leading Cultural Indicators," a deliberate counterpoint to the Commerce Department's similarly named regular economic report. His objective was to detail the social erosion that has continued even as the nation's economic indicators have gone up.

The strange fact that jumps out from Bennett's grim inventory of crime, divorce, mass-media addiction, and the rest is that much of it actually adds to the GDP. Growth can be social decline by another name. Divorce, for example, adds a small fortune in lawyers' bills, the need for second households, transportation and counseling for kids, and so on. Divorce lawyers alone take in probably several billion dollars a year, and possibly a good deal more. Divorce also provides a major boost for the real-estate industry. "Unfortunately, divorce is a big part of our business. It means one [home] to sell and sometimes two to buy," a realtor in suburban Chicago told the *Chicago Tribune.* Similarly, crime has given rise to a burgeoning crime-prevention and security industry with revenues of more than $65 billion a year. The car-locking device called The Club adds some $100 million a year to the GDP all by itself, without counting knock-offs. Even a gruesome event like the Oklahoma City bombing becomes an economic uptick by the strange reckonings of the GDP. "Analysts expect the share prices [of firms making anti-crime equipment] to gain during the next several months," *The Wall Street Journal* reported a short time after the bombing, "as safety concerns translate into more contracts."

Bennett cited the chilling statistics that teenagers spend on average some three hours a day watching television, and about five minutes a day alone with their fathers. Yet when kids are talking with their parents, they aren't adding to the GDP. In contrast, MTV helps turn them into ardent, GDP-enhancing consumers. Even those unwed teenage mothers are bringing new little consumers into the world (where they will quickly join the "kiddie market" and after that the "teen market," which together influence more than $200 billion in GDP). So while social conservatives like Bennett are rightly deploring the nation's social decline, their free-marketeer counterparts are looking at the same phenomena through the lens of the GDP and breaking out the champagne.

Something similar happens with the natural habitat. The more the nation depletes its natural resources, the more the GDP increases. This violates basic accounting principles, in that it portrays the depletion of capital as current income. No businessperson would make such a fundamental error. When a small oil company drains an oil well in Texas, it gets a generous depletion allowance on its taxes, in recognition of the loss. Yet that very same drainage shows up as a gain to the nation in the GDP. When the United States fishes its cod populations down to remnants, this appears on the national books as an economic boom—until the fisheries collapse. As the former World Bank economist Herman Daly puts it, the current national-accounting system treats the earth as a business in liquidation.

Add pollution to the balance sheet and we appear to be doing even better. In fact, pollution shows up twice as a gain: once when the chemical factory, say, produces it as a by-product, and again when the nation spends billions of dollars to clean up the toxic Superfund site that results. Furthermore, the extra costs that come as a consequence of that environmental depletion and degradation—such as medical bills arising from dirty air—also show up as growth in the GDP.

This kind of accounting feeds the notion that conserving resources and protecting the natural habitat must come at the expense of the economy, because the result can be a lower GDP. That is a lot like saying that a reserve for capital depreciation must come at the expense of the business. On the contrary, a capital reserve is essential to ensure the future of the business. To ignore that is to confuse mere borrowing from the future with actual profit. Resource conservation works the same way, but the perverse accounting of the GDP hides this basic fact.

No less important is the way the GDP ignores the contribution of the social realm—that is, the economic role of households and communities. This is where much of the nation's most important work gets done, from caring for children and older people to volunteer work in its many forms. It is the nation's social glue. Yet because no money changes hands in this realm, it is invisible to conventional economics. The GDP doesn't count it at all—which means that the more our families and communities decline and a monetized service sector takes their place, the more the GDP goes up and the economic pundits cheer.

Parenting becomes child care, visits on the porch become psychiatry and VCRs, the watchful eyes of neighbors become alarm systems and police officers, the kitchen table becomes McDonald's—up and down the line, the things people used to do for and with one another turn into things they have to buy. Day care adds more than $4 billion to the GDP; VCRs and kindred entertainment gear add almost $60 billion. Politicians generally see this decay through a well-worn ideological lens: conservatives root for the market, liberals for the government. But in fact these two "sectors" are, in this respect at least, merely different sides of the same coin: both government and the private market grow by cannibalizing the family and community realms that ultimately nurture and sustain us.

These are just the more obvious problems. There are others, no less severe. The GDP totally ignores the distribution of income, for example, so that enormous gains at the top—as were made during the 1980s—appear as new bounty for all. It makes no distinction between the person in the secure high-tech job and the "downsized" white-collar worker who has to work two jobs at lower pay. The GDP treats leisure time and time with family the way it treats air and water: as having no value at all. When the need for a second job cuts the time available for family or community, the GDP records this loss as an economic gain.

Then there's the question of addictive consumption. Free-market fundamentalists are inclined to attack critics of the GDP as "elitists." People buy things because they want them, they say, and who knows better than the people themselves what adds to well-being? It makes a good one-liner. But is the truth really so simple? Some 40 percent of the nation's drinking exceeds the level of "moderation," defined as two drinks a day. Credit-card abuse has become so pervasive that local chapters of Debtors Anonymous hold forty-five meetings a week in the San Francisco Bay area alone. Close to 50 percent of Americans consider themselves overweight. When one considers the $32 billion diet industry, the GDP becomes truly bizarre. It counts the food that people wish they didn't eat, and then the billions they spend to lose the added pounds that result. The coronary-bypass patient becomes almost a metaphor for the nation's measure of progress: shovel in the fat, pay the consequences, add the two together, and the economy grows some more.

So, too, the O. J. Simpson trial. When *The Wall Street Journal* added up the Simpson legal team ($20,000 a day), network-news expenses, O.J. statuettes, and the rest, it got a total of about $200 million in new GDP, for which politicians will be taking credit in 1996. "GDP OF O.J. TRIAL OUTRUNS THE TOTAL OF, SAY, GRENADA," the *Journal's* headline writer proclaimed. One begins to understand why politicians prefer to talk about growth rather than what it actually consists of, and why Prozac alone adds more than $1.2 billion to the GDP, as people try to feel a little better amid all this progress.

*   *   *

. . . [N]o field has grown more tightly shut than economics, whose basic orthodoxies have persisted for at least a hundred years. Unless history stops cold, these, too, will eventually yield, and the time is now propitious. The generation that developed the GDP, and for which the GDP distilled an entire world view, is now mainly retired. The students and disciples of that generation are well into their middle years, rumbling along on mental capital from long ago. For the generation that is replacing them, the defining traumas were not the Depression and the Second World War but rather the material glut and environmental and social disintegration of which many in the old guard served as unwitting boosters and engineers.

To be sure, the old order does not lack acolytes. But for a growing number of economists, the conceptual tools and measurements of the neoclassical model—Keynesian twists included—are no longer adequate. These economists are demanding that their profession start to take account of the larger economy in which the market is grounded—the natural and social spheres, which they have in the past dismissed as the netherworlds of externality. In a survey in the 1980s of economists at fifty major universities two thirds acknowledged a sense of "lost moorings" in the profession.

In recent decades this kind of critique has been associated mainly with the ecological camp. Herman Daly, Hazel Henderson, Kenneth Boulding,

and other writers have pointed out that in a world of finite physical resources the possibility of endless material expansion is not something we
should count on. What is new today is that a similar argument is coming
from certain quarters on the right: specifically that the pursuit of GDP has
been undermining traditional values and social cohesion, much as it has
been destroying the natural habitat.

Americans are conditioned to see ecology and social conservatism as
occupying opposite ends of the political spectrum. But that is largely an
optical illusion, reinforced by an antiquated national accounting system.
The fact is that adherents at both ends deplore the way the pursuit of GDP
can undermine the realm of their concern. Much as this pursuit turns ancient forests into lumber and beaches into sewers, so it turns families into
nodes of consumption and the living room into a marketing free-fire zone.
Both camps speak from the standpoint of *values* against the moral relativism and opportunism of the market. "If you read the New Testament or
the Pope's encyclical, it's no cheers for socialism and one and a half or two
for capitalism," William Bennett, who was Reagan's Secretary of Education, observes. "Socialism treats people as a cog in the machine of the
state; capitalism tends to treat people as commodities."

This strain of conservatism, partly rooted in traditional Christian teachings, was largely dormant during the Cold War, when the greater enemy
communism predominated. But with the fall of the Soviet bloc it has rea-
wakened, and the result has been a widening gap on the right between social conservatives and libertarian free-marketeers. This gap was easily
overlooked in the Republican triumph last November, but it may well become as important as the one between the Republicans and the Democrats they replaced.

It can be seen, for example, in the diverging views of that archetypal
Republican era, the Reagan eighties. Martin Anderson, who was Reagan's
domestic-policy adviser, gave the rapturous libertarian view in his book
*Revolution* (1988). "It was the greatest economic expansion in history," An-
derson wrote. "Wealth poured from the factories of the United States, and
Americans got richer and richer."

But does richer mean better—even assuming that all Americans
shared in this bounty, which they didn't? For libertarians, as for many
Keynesian liberals, the question isn't relevant. For social conservatives,
however, it is *the* question. Bennett does not disparage the economic
achievements of the Reagan years. Nor does he dispute that more family
income can mean better schooling, medical care, and the like. But recently he has been calling attention to the social decay that has continued
despite (and often in the name of) economic growth. "Would you rather
have kids raised by rich people with lousy values, or by good people who
just don't have much money?" he asks. "A lot of us would say we want the
values right."

What the right calls "family values" is one arena in which the latent
conflict between market and nonmarket values is coming out into the
open. In a long article in *The Washington Post* last November, Edward Lutt-

wak, of the Center for Strategic and International Studies, a conservative think tank in Washington, D.C., pointed out that much family disruption today arises from the "creative destruction" of the market that free-market economists adore. The failure to acknowledge this, Luttwak wrote, is "the blatant contradiction at the very core of what has become mainstream Republican ideology."

In an interview Luttwak argued that people need stability more than they need much of the new stuff that makes the GDP go up. Yet economists talk about stability "in entirely negative terms," he said. Conservation becomes a dirty word. One would think that conservatives would be the first to point this out; stability, after all, is what families and communities are for. But the political right is muzzled on these issues, Luttwak said, by the economic interests of its major funders. "Any conservative who wishes to conserve will not be funded."

This split has a distinct similarity to the tension that arose in the Democratic Party in the seventies between environmentalists and the growth-boosting Keynesian mainstream. It could betoken the beginning of a new politics in which the popular currents represented by social conservatives and environmentalists increasingly find common cause. Some writers have made the connection already. For example, Fred Charles Iklé, who was an undersecretary of defense in the Reagan Administration, wrote an article for the *National Review* in which he criticized the "growth utopians" of the right. "Citizens who fear for our vanishing patrimony in nature," Iklé wrote, "drink from a wellspring of emotions that nourishes the most enduring conservative convictions." (He also tweaked the magazine's right-wing readers by pointing out that economic growth almost invariably leads to bigger government.)

Just a few years ago a confluence of the environmental and social-conservative impulses would have seemed unlikely. But the political seas are changing rapidly. The coalition that came together to oppose NAFTA and GATT—environmentalists and anti-corporate populists like Ralph Nader on the one hand, and social conservatives like Pat Buchanan on the other—seemed an oddity to most pundits. But something similar happened when the Walt Disney Company proposed a new theme park near the Civil War battlefield in Manassas, Virginia. Buchanan and numerous other tradition-minded conservatives joined environmentalists in blasting the proposal. In his syndicated newspaper column Buchanan demanded, "Conservatives who worship at the altar of an endlessly rising GNP should tell us: What is it they any longer wish to conserve?"

The two camps have converged in opposing the so-called "takings" bills, which would require the taxpayers to compensate property owners for restrictions on the use of their property. The Reverend Donald E. Wildemon, the president of the American Family Association, in Tupelo, Mississippi, has called such a proposal in his state the "porn owners' relief measure," because it could restrict the ability of local governments to control such things as topless bars. Environmentalists of course worry about the implications for the protection of wetlands, open space, and the like.

The two camps agree that "growth" is not an end in itself but must serve larger values that are not economic in the usual sense.

We may be witnessing the opening battles in a new kind of politics that will raise basic questions about growth—questions that defy the conventional left-right divide. Where the old politics was largely concerned with the role of government—with the relation between public and private sectors—the emerging one will be more concerned with such issues as central versus local, market culture versus family and community culture, material accretion versus quality and values. The new politics will not be anti-growth, because to be categorically against growth is as nonsensical as to be categorically for it. Rather, it will begin with Luttwak's sane observation that when your goal is simply to increase GDP, then "what you increase isn't necessarily good." It will insist that growth—and economics generally—must be a means to an end, and not an end in itself.

This is not to suggest that such a new alliance is around the corner. But although the differences between the social-conservative and environmentalist camps are still large, they are probably etched more sharply among leaders in Washington than in the nation as a whole. These groups are converging on one crucial issue—namely, the ends of economic life. In their different ways they are expressing the feeling, widespread among the public, that the pronouncements from economic experts are fundamentally out of sync with the experience of their own lives; that economics must be about more than just the production and consumption of stuff; and that we need larger goals and better ways to measure our achievements as a nation.

Of course, this instinct could play out in many ways. But at least one thing is clear: boosting the GDP is no longer a sufficient aim for a great nation, nor one that America can continue to endure.

## DEBATING THE ISSUES: REGULATION: FOR AND AGAINST

*See Lowi and Ginsberg, pp. 618–619*

*"Get government off our backs" has long been the rallying cry from business, which argues that government regulatory burdens have increased dramatically since the 1970s. Regulations impose different demands in the pursuit of social and economic goals: regulations might require documentation of a business practice, mandate the purchase and installation of new equipment, impose safety and training requirements, or prohibit certain business practices altogether. These rules are enforced by hefty fines levied against business deemed out of compliance by a regulator. The question is, how much government regulation is legitimate? Since the Republicans assumed control in 1994, Congress has again begun considering ways to scale back the regulatory burdens for business, focusing on workplace safety, the environment, consumer product safety, mar-*

*keting practices, civil liability, and many other kinds of activity. Is the public interest better served by the liberalization of businesses, or through the existence and enforcement of government regulations? And if we can agree that some regulation is necessary, how do we decide what is essential and reasonable?*

*Sheila Moloney, assistant editor of a conservative journal,* Policy Review, *criticizes the scope of regulations imposed on small business and the ways in which they are enforced. Recounting events involving businesswomen in the home health care industry, child care and development, tourism, and real estate development, Moloney argues that the cost of regulations are inhibiting the development of small businesses (a significant number of which are owned and operated by women), particularly regulations imposing paperwork and those defining tax burdens. A solution, she argues, might involve regulators reorienting themselves toward cooperating with business to make workplaces safer, cleaner, and fairer, but she suggests that such a transition is unlikely.*

*Joshua Shenk looks at regulation from a different vantage point. If regulations are so stifling, he asks, is the solution to simply get rid of them? More specifically, what regulations would critics eliminate, and why? Shenk argues that the debate over regulation is intentionally shallow, couched in rhetoric about stifling and costly government regulations, but with very little detail about the particular regulations that should be eliminated. Moreover, critics fail to connect regulations to the public demands for workplace safety, pure food products, safe drugs and medical devices, clean air, and clean water. The problem, he argues, is that the regulatory "reform" effort taking place in Congress is not intended to facilitate more reasonable regulations and greater business efficiency, but is rather designed to stifle the regulatory process through multiple reviews and judicial appeals. Regulatory agencies have done many things right, Shenk argues. A genuine regulatory debate would examine the successes and the failures, and probe the rhetoric that currently passes for serious public policy discussion.*

# Sheila A. Moloney
## "The Lady in Red Tape"*

Judy Hooper has two passions in life: doughnuts and the Occupational Safety and Health Administration (OSHA).

Hooper loves doughnuts. That's one of the reasons she opened a bakery in Evanston, Illinois. It's a small shop, bringing in about $50,000 in profits annually. That's not enough to make her rich, but the challenge of running a small business and her talent for baking keep this 35-year-old Chicago native busy.

Ask Hooper about OSHA, however, and her face glazes over with disdain. A 1994 inspection of her 30-person bakery by OSHA officials left Hooper with $13,000 in frivolous fines. Her infractions included a failure to warn employees of the hazards of household dishwashing liquid. To re-

* Sheila A. Maloney, "The Lady in Red Tape" in *Policy Review* (September/October 1996). Reprinted with permission.

coup the cost of the fines, she would have to sell 260,000 doughnuts, or 10,400 cakes, or 1,040,000 cookies.

The national news media picked up her story, but OSHA refused to back down. So has Hooper. Though she paid the fine, she hopes to file a class-action suit against the federal agency, and is trying to enlist other OSHA victims to help her cause.

She will find plenty of recruits. The bakery owner joins millions of women entrepreneurs across the country who are finding out just how intrusive Big Government can be. Indeed, one of the most overlooked issues in this campaign season is how the rising number of women business owners—a third of all U.S. firms—are being beaten down by Washington's overbearing laws, inflexible regulations, and arcane tax policies.

If they mobilized, these women could be a potent force. The National Foundation for Women Business Owners (NFWBO) reports that the number of women-owned businesses in the United States will reach 8 million this year, employing more than 18.5 million people and generating more than $2.28 trillion in gross sales. Over the last nine years, NFWBO estimates, the number of women-owned firms has increased 78 percent. "The growth in the number of women-owned businesses continues to be dramatic across the nation," says Julie R. Weeks, NFWBO's director of research. But Sue Myrick, a first-term Republican congresswoman from North Carolina and a former small-business owner, knows first-hand how Big Government threatens this growth: "Most government-imposed regulations are duplicative, expensive, and time-consuming," she says. "If not checked, regulations can cripple a small-business owner's ability to compete in the marketplace."

## ATTACK ON NURSES

Consider Arlene Kaplan's Heart to Home, Inc., a New York company that provides skilled nurses for patients needing home health care. To accommodate their unpredictable hours, Heart to Home hires nurses as independent contractors. That means the nurses pay their own state, federal, and Social Security taxes.

For the 70 nurses working for Kaplan—and the thousands of others who labor as independent contractors in health care—their employment status buys them flexibility. They are free to schedule their work around their families and other commitments, working anywhere from 5-hour to 60-hour weeks as needed. For the home health-care industry, independent contractors deliver affordable, quality care on demand.

But to the IRS, the independent contractors who find jobs through Kaplan's company aren't independent enough. Based on a 20-point litmus test, IRS officials determined in a 1990 audit that Heart to Home's nurses legally were not independent contractors, but employees. Kaplan's business was assessed $250,000 in back taxes and fines for misrepresenting her workers to the IRS.

According to Sandra Abalos, a CPA, the test is "so vague and so subjective" that even tax law practitioners cannot determine who is an employee and who is an independent contractor. Heart to Home's lawyer Barry Frank believes the IRS is "targeting small businesses" by frequently auditing those who hire independent contractors. In the last seven years, the IRS reclassified 439,000 independent contractors as employees and collected more than $750 million in fines.

So far Kaplan's business has accrued $20,000 in legal fees and expects another $40,000 in court costs when she goes up against the IRS later this year. Unlike most people engaged in legal jousting with this federal agency, however, Kaplan is the plaintiff: Through a complicated financial maneuver, she managed to sue the IRS.

"If the government wins, they put me out of business," Kaplan says. "I don't own enough things in this entire world to pay off what they want from me." Even if Kaplan is successful, there is little hope she'll be reimbursed by the IRS for her legal fees. But forcing the agency to retreat would be a moral victory for her, and might make IRS agents a little less eager the next time around. Says Kaplan, "Maybe they will get off someone else's back in this business."


### TRIPPING UP TODDLERS

The IRS, of course, retains no monopoly on crippling regulation. A few years ago, Virginia resident Tanya Wallace started a small business called Toddlin' Time, a playgroup for stay-at-home moms and their kids. When she decided to franchise her idea, however, she ran up against Federal Trade Commission (FTC) regulations intended for larger companies.

The FTC's "franchise rule" requires all companies, regardless of their size, to meet the same franchising requirements. So Toddlin' Time, which simply brings mothers and children together at dance studios and karate centers to play games, must meet the same auditing requirements as McDonald's, a company with billions of dollars in sales and operating costs, expensive equipment, and trained staff.

With just a few hours a week in administrative work, Toddlin' Time franchise owners can earn around $14,000 per year by enrolling 50 kids for six-week sessions at $36 per child. Wallace sees her idea as an excellent opportunity to combine family and business in a way that "feels comfortable to home-based women." The business gives kids a regular time and place to play together while stay-at-home moms get to know each other.

It's an easy concept to market. But FTC franchising rules have stopped Wallace cold. To comply, she had to expend $15,000 in auditing and lawyers' fees just to become a licensed franchiser. But Wallace couldn't pass these high start-up costs along to the moms interested in Toddlin' Time, so she marketed her franchise below cost. That meant selling four franchising chains just to break even. Yet the fees did not end when her start-up was complete. The FTC requires franchise operators to update their financial statements every year and demands yearly audits to verify the changes.

"We're not a big company," Wallace explains. "We can't afford the two or three or four thousand dollars each year to [prepare] FTC financial statements."

After six years and 10 successful Toddlin' Time franchises, Wallace is putting the brakes on further expansion. She says she simply can't afford the fees and regulations. Despite these setbacks, Wallace has not totally given up on the idea of Toddlin' Time. She is pursuing a consulting practice to spread her idea, though not her logo, to moms around the nation.

"There is little that you can do when you're up against Big Government and government regulations," she says. "It's easier to walk away, unfortunately, than to deal with all the regulations and expectations they have for you."

## THE DISABLERS

When it comes to federal regulations like the Americans with Disabilities Act, however, walking away is not an option. Ask Karla Hauk.

She and her husband and business partner, Richard Hauk, opened a 32-room Days Inn franchise in Wall, South Dakota. That was on July 1, 1993, about six months after the ADA went into effect. They thought they were ready: Following their franchiser-approved plans, they made two of their 32 rooms accessible to handicapped patrons and made the entrance of their motel accessible to wheelchairs. When they opened their doors, they became the first motel in Wall to provide rooms with accommodations for the handicapped.

Their reward? Karla, Richard, their architect, their contractor, and their franchiser all are being sued by the U.S. Justice Department for failure to comply with ADA regulations. They are charged with "unlawful discrimination" toward individuals with disabilities.

It all started with a whirlpool. According to the Justice Department's suit, the Hauks' two-story motel became a three-story facility when they installed a whirlpool in the basement. ADA regulations require that their motel have an elevator so that handicapped customers can reach every floor, as well as a ramp leading to the whirlpool. According to Karla Hauk, installing the elevator alone would cost more than $100,000, not including the increase in property taxes. Even if the owners removed the whirlpool and left the basement empty, they would still be required to build an elevator for handicapped access, because the Justice Department has declared the basement "occupiable space."

In addition to the elevator, the ADA requires the Hauks to widen all of the bathroom doors in the nonhandicapped rooms. "If someone who uses a wheelchair . . . visits another guest in a non-accessible guest room, he or she will not be able even to enter the bathroom in that room," according to the suit.

Changing the building's design after the fact looks nearly impossible. "Structurally we don't know how you can do it," says Hauks' lawyer Kim Ruckdaschel-Haley. "What do you do, just knock the place down and start over?"

Karla Hauk says she believes there should be provisions for the handicapped, but that "a lot of this is unreasonable." She says if they had known then what they know now, they never would have built the motel. "We wish to God we never had. They will bankrupt us."

Because the Hauks' business is dependent upon the seasonal tourist traffic at nearby Badlands National Park, they bring in profits of only $20,000 to $25,000 a year. "If Karla and Richard have to fight this, they'll have to go out of business," says their lawyer. In addition to substantial costs to comply with the ADA regulations, the co-owners could each be fined $50,000 by the Justice Department. When the ADA went into effect, it was unclear how the law would be implemented, says Ruckdaschel-Haley. "Karla and Richard in good faith thought they were doing everything they could."

For ADA bureaucrats, it seems, everything is not enough. So says Debbie Shaffer, owner of an interior design firm in Walla Walla, Washington. Shaffer wanted to move her eight-year-old company, DGS Interiors, out of her home and into a downtown storefront to expand her business. The proposed Main Street site consisted of a 1,500 square-foot main floor for retail sales, with a raised mezzanine to serve as both a design studio and an administrative office.

The problem? Contractors familiar with ADA regulations informed Shaffer that she had two options in bringing the bi-level facility up to code: either build an elevator to make the second floor accessible to the handicapped, or illogically and wastefully duplicate the design studio on the showroom floor.

If a handicapped client wanted a design consultation, Shaffer says, she could easily accommodate their needs by bringing her portable decorating samples down to the lower level. But this was not good enough: According to the ADA, this special treatment would unfairly discriminate against the handicapped.

To comply with the ADA codes, Shaffer would have to spend $150,000 to install an elevator, build handicapped bathrooms, and widen all of the building entrances and doorways. These costs were in addition to her other remodeling expenses. "I have a great amount of support for people with any kind of disability," she says, having grown up with a sister who is deaf. "But the government steps in and takes it too far."

The results? "As a small business owner, it was black and white," Shaffer explains. "I couldn't afford it." Shaffer believes the downtown location could have increased her business by 50 percent, but because the regulations were "too overwhelming, with too many hoops to jump through," she was forced to scrap her plans to expand.

## DOUGHNUT HOLES

If the ADA's regulatory reach can be breathtakingly broad and intrusive, its rival in the universe of federal agencies is OSHA. Over the last two fiscal years, OSHA has recorded 234,409 violations and assessed over $158 million in fines.

Responding to complaints by a disgruntled employee, OSHA held a three-hour inspection of Judy's Bakery, the Illinois mom-and-pop operation cited above. Nothing could have prepared Judy Hooper for OSHA's report, which cited her for, among other things:

(1) Failing to have a written "Material Safety Data Sheet" for "hazardous" chemicals used at the bakery. The only chemicals used at Judy's Bakery are household bleach and the sort of pink dishwashing liquid used in many homes. Both "chemicals" have clearly marked warning labels. OSHA was unmoved. Fine: $2,500.

(2) Failing to have a written plan for emergencies such as a fire. Hooper's shop, which is on the first floor and has four clearly marked exits, is inspected twice a year by the Evanston fire department. Local fire officials had never found any potential safety problems. Fine: $2,500.

(3) Failing to have an accident log on the shop's wall. At the time, her company had never had an accident requiring a workmen's compensation claim. The officials said this was irrelevant and argued that even if the log contained all zeroes (one for each day without accidents), it must still be hung on the wall. Fine: $500.

At her informal settlement hearing with OSHA officials, Hooper was able to negotiate the fines down from $13,000 to $5,450. The catch was that Hooper was required to spend the balance of the fines due—approximately $7,500—on safety and health programs for her employees and to present proof that she had complied. Ironically, none of the citations was related to the employee's complaints, which were found to be baseless.

## THE GENTLE SCRUB JAY

It was not the safety of employees that concerned the government officials who intruded into Anita Cragg's business, but the safety of the Florida scrub jay.

Cragg, the owner and president of Space Coast Management Services, Inc., bought an existing subdivision in Country Cove, Florida, in 1992, with plans to expand and build new homes adjacent the previously developed site. Cragg's permits were in order and some buyers were waiting to build and settle in.

Enter the scrub jay. While surveying for waterline extensions in 1993, officials from the U.S. Fish and Wildlife Service (USFWS) noted two jays flying onto Cragg's lots. Under the Endangered Species Act, the scrub jay, a 12-inch-long, blue and gray crested jay, is listed as threatened. The officials claimed that Cragg's planned development posed a potential hazard to land "suitable for occupation by scrub jays" and suspended construction on the site.

According to Cragg, neither the USFWS, nor an independent environmental engineer hired by Cragg, could locate any scrub jay nests on her property. Her four-person company fought with officials from the USFWS for 18 months. Construction was frozen in the meantime, while Cragg's buyers had to continue paying real-estate taxes on the land.

The Fish and Wildlife Service pushed Cragg into a corner. The agency forced her firm to purchase four acres off-site for every one on-site to compensate for the loss of potential scrub jay habitat. That little bargain cost her more than $100,000. It "didn't really help the scrub jay," she says, "because we really weren't hurting it in the first place."

## An Irresistible Offer

From 1964 until 1979, most of the commercial garbage in Seattle was hauled to one landfill located on the Tulalip Indian reservation. The site was closed and cleaned up in 1979, getting a clean bill of health from the Environmental Protection Agency. For the next 16 years, there wasn't a whiff of trouble from Seattle's former commercial dump.

And then the EPA started talkin' trash: In 1995, the agency placed the Tulalip Landfill on the Superfund's National Priority List, a list reserved for the country's most serious hazardous waste sites. EPA Project Manager Cindy Colgate admitted that "sometimes we think a problem is taken care of when it's not."

Apparently, this was one of those times. Superfund legislation allows the EPA to retroactively assess liability for environmental clean-ups. So the agency is asking Seattle's commercial businesses for approximately $40 million to clean up the landfill a second time.

The EPA has made what it calls "settlement offers" to 208 Seattle companies, each of which hauled more than 200 tons of waste to the site. These offers allow companies the chance to "resolve their liability" by making payments of $11,070 to $185,497 to the EPA, according to Colgate. The official insists this "is not a fine," but instead an "agreement between the EPA and the parties which says we won't sue them regarding the site." It also protects the firms from third-party suits. Many attorneys are advising firms to pay the EPA and move on. So far, 187 parties have decided to settle rather than face EPA lawsuits.

For some women-owned firms, the experience has been a primer on the power of federal agencies to impose their will. One such firm in Seattle, an import-export company whose owners asked not to be identified, agreed to pay their $11,070 fine. In total, Seattle's business owners are forking over $8,130,610 to the EPA—at least $30 million short of its goal. Suzanne Burke, the president of the Fremont Dock Co., which was not named in the settlement, says she believes the 208 letters are "just the beginning," and fears her company may be next on the list. She says the $40 million Superfund cleanup is "an absolute horror for small businesses."

## FIGHTING BACK

There may be some legislative help on the way for business owners. Congress is seeking to clarify the ambiguity over the tax status of independent contractors versus employees, which bedeviled business owner Arlene Kaplan. Congressman Jon Christensen, a Nebraska Republican, is sponsoring a bill to simplify IRS rules for independent contractors. A spokesman for Christensen says the bipartisan bill could pass this year. Oklahoma Republican Don Nickles has introduced similar legislation in the Senate because, according to his spokesman, "hassle from the IRS" is the principal complaint from his constituents.

But as more women start their own businesses, they are becoming more cynical about government's helping hand. Forty-seven percent of the women business owners surveyed in 1995 by the United States Trust Company believed that government policies had made things "a little worse or much worse" for their businesses. When asked to rate specific government policies, almost all of the female respondents (91 percent) said they feel most threatened by government-required paperwork, while 90 percent feel threatened by taxes on businesses, raw materials, final products, or services.

The bureaucrats contend they're changing the system. Several officials separately claimed OSHA's new and improved agency has purged archaic enforcement procedures, yet all cited the same case to prove their reform: "Instead of fining someone for not hanging one of our posters about workers' rights," they say, "we offer them a poster to hang." While this may be a first step in dismantling the adversarial relationship between employers and OSHA, it demonstrates how federal agencies are not getting the message from business owners across the country. What happens, one might ask, if they don't hang the poster?

Women business owners are bumping against a ceiling all right. But it isn't made of glass—it's made of red tape.

# Joshua Wolf Shenk
# "The Case for (Some) Regulation"*

Jack Faris, president of the National Federation of Independent Business, has a simple message for the 104th Congress. "Our members want the federal government off their backs, out of their pockets, and off their land." Simple enough for you?

It is for Congressional Republicans. NFIB played a crucial role in beating back universal health coverage. Now the small business lobby—with 600,000 members—has a new target: federal regulations. They've asked for a freeze in all new rules, and they are likely to get it. The "Regulatory Transition Act of 1995," sponsored by Rep. Tom DeLay (R-Texas), would impose a six-month moratorium on federal regulations, retroactive to last election day.

But don't ask NFIB precisely what this will accomplish. Kim McKernan, the group's chief lobbyist for the House of Representatives, cannot even name a single regulation she'd like to see repealed. "That's what the moratorium is for," she says. "Stop the bleeding. Let's take a look at the landscape and re-evaluate."

Indeed, for opponents of regulation, vagueness is a powerful weapon. Polls show vigorous public support for federal controls on the environment, consumer safety, and food and drugs. Businesses, meanwhile, despise these regulations: They don't want to be told what to do, especially if it costs them money. "Regulatory reform" is the Republicans' magic bullet. Reducing excessive burdens on business, they argue, will create jobs and lower prices for consumer goods. Everyone, they say, ends up richer, safer, and healthier.

But there is no magic bullet. Real regulatory reform—making the process smarter and more efficient, paring out senseless rules and toughening others—would take hard work and political courage. The Republican agenda is old-fashioned laissez-faire capitalism in disguise. Rather than dismantle agencies and provoke a public outcry, they plan to hogtie the system with cumbersome new rules and restrictions. This is a boon to business owners and corporate managers; it's a disaster for the ordinary guy.

Take this moratorium. It's billed as an antidote to red tape, but the volume of paperwork, procedural rules, and sheer mayhem provoked by its implementation would be staggering. Civil servants would be stopped dead in their tracks—whether they explicate tax codes at the Treasury Department, review new medications at the Food and Drug Administration (FDA), or enforce recalls at the Consumer Product Safety Commission. Federal regulators would spend weeks compiling lists of current, past, and future regulations. Millions of Americans who depend on the existing rules will be thrust into a vacuum.

---

* Joshua Wolf Shenk, "The Case for (Some) Regulation" in the *Washington Monthly* (March 1995). Reprinted with permission from the *Washington Monthly*.

## REAGAN'S BLUEPRINT

Congressional Republicans lifted their blueprint for this wave of deregulation straight from Ronald Reagan. Upon taking office in 1981, Reagan banned new rules for 30 days and issued an executive order forbidding agencies from issuing regulations—large or small—without explicit approval from the Office of Management and Budget. In theory, OMB would amend or reject rules where the costs outweighed the benefits. In practice, wherever possible, it blocked civil servants from enforcing the law.

For example, in the fall of 1981—ten years after Reye's Syndrome was first linked to use of aspirin—the Centers for Disease Control found in four independent studies that children with viral illnesses, such as chicken pox or flu, risked contracting Reye's if treated with aspirin. The FDA commissioned its own study, and concluded similarly. On June 4, 1982, Health and Human Services Secretary Richard Schweiker announced a FDA educational campaign and a requirement that warning labels on aspirin products "be changed to advise against their use in 'children with flu and chicken pox.' " As required, he submitted the rule to OMB's Office of Information and Regulatory Affairs (OIRA). OIRA sent the rule back for further study, objecting that the risk of fatalities had not been conclusively proven. In 1983 *The Wall Street Journal* revealed that OIRA took its cues from the Aspirin Foundation of America, which thought the label would hurt business.

With the FDA paralyzed, public interest groups took the matter to court, a regular event in Reagan's first term, and the administration drew a stern rebuke. "All scientific evidence in the record points to a link between [aspirin] and Reye's Syndrome," the U.S. Court of Appeals for the District of Columbia wrote in 1984. "The pace of agency decision-making is unreasonably dilatory." The warning-label rule took effect in June 1986, but the four-year delay had taken its toll. The advocacy group Public Citizen estimates 3,000 children contracted Reye's Syndrome in that time, a third of whom died; many of the surviving children suffered permanent brain damage.

Disabling the full body of federal regulations was a big job. What couldn't be done through OMB, or with political appointees, was a job for the Task Force on Regulatory Relief. Directed by Vice President Bush, the task force directly solicited industry wish lists of regulations they wanted delayed or eliminated. Three months into the administration, it had already blocked 34 regulations on auto companies alone—on bumpers, pedestrian safety, fuel economy standards, and lead-reduction standards for fuel, among others. As Gareth G. Cook reports in this issue, Reagan was particularly solicitous of Detroit in thwarting air bag requirements. "Federal regulations," Reagan told a gathering of auto executives during the 1980 campaign, "are the cause of all your problems."

If Reagan had pushed regulators to be smarter, not slower, or more results-oriented, he might have left a legacy of real reform. Pragmatists might even have forgiven some excesses if he had rationalized the system, consolidated overlapping programs, and tightened loopholes. Instead, Reagan (and Bush after him) ignored real problem areas, sought political points with ignorant denunciations of the regulatory state, and took credit for new legislation while subverting it behind the scenes. By 1989, regulatory spending was at an all-time high and public confidence in the system was at an all-time low. According to a 1988 *Times-Mirror* poll, 67 percent of Americans agreed that government was "usually inefficient and wasteful."

## THE PAST IS PROLOGUE

Republicans aren't about to let a bad idea get in the way of good politics. And as with "Star Wars" and tax cuts, they're eager to mimic Reagan on regulatory reform. Same industry backscratching, same populist veneer, same half-baked solutions. But you won't hear the same anti-government rhetoric this time. "Of course we're going to protect people," says Rep. David McIntosh (R-Indiana), chairman of the Subcommittee on Economic Growth, Natural Resources, and Regulatory Affairs. "That's our job." "Let there be no mistake," echoes Sen. Bill Roth (R-Delaware), "we need a clean environment, safe workplaces, and safe medications." These men pay attention to the polls. In 1994, *Times-Mirror* found that 82 percent of Americans believe "there need to be stricter laws and regulations to protect the environment." Similar sentiments are found on regulations of medications, food and water, and consumer products.

But scrutinize the proposed "reforms" and you'll find nothing of the sort. It's sabotage in disguise. Take cost-benefit analysis, the core of their strategy. "To free Americans from bureaucratic red tape," the Contract With America states, "we will require every new regulation to stand a new test: Does it provide benefits worth the cost?" But cost-benefit analysis, an essential element in private sector strategic planning, is an empty concept in government regulation. "Benefits" and "costs" of any act depend entirely on the perspective of the analyst. In 1981, Bush sought repeal of a Department of Agriculture requirement for labels on meat products that contained crushed bone, arguing that it cost "the economy" $500 million a year. That figure was an industry estimate of lost revenue, the cost of throwing away meatless carcasses instead of grinding them up and adding them to the pile. But if informed consumers choose not to buy $500 million worth of crushed bone, is that the fault of the regulation or the virtue of a free market? The Department of Agriculture hadn't even banned this sketchy food-product; it simply insisted that Americans be aware that their "prime ground beef" was, in fact, "prime ground beef—with tasty bits of crushed bone."

Of course, in the hands of a dispassionate analyst, cost-benefit calculations can be a useful tool. Indeed, federal agencies already conduct them, and OMB still reviews regulations and haggles with agencies to make them as efficient as possible. But the Job Creation and Wage Enhancement Act, outlined in the Contract and now working its way through committees in the House, requires that such data be published, subject to judicial review, and approved by a peer review panel. This panel must consist of experts with "recent professional experience" in the area of regulation. "There is no prohibition," an OMB Watch report points out, "on industry scientists or representatives, or those with a financial interest in the regulation, serving on the peer review panel."

The real boondoggle is judicial review. Aggrieved businesses already have the right to challenge regulation. And a vast majority of regulatory decisions *are* appealed in courts—including 80 percent of the Environmental Protection Agency's and 96 percent of the Occupational Safety and Health Administration's. The Job Creation and Wage Enhancement Act would allow companies to bring lawsuits *before* agencies reach their decision—meaning all their data and analysis can be challenged in court. When regulators seek to act on an "emergency," this too becomes a question for the courts—a prescription for endless delay. While seeking tort reform that would dramatically decrease the rights of individuals to sue businesses, Republicans seek regulatory reform to enhance the hand of business in blocking measures for public health and safety.

The Republican agenda contradicts itself. It claims to seek efficiency, but would produce the opposite: more meaningless paperwork, more rigidity, more gridlock. Unless the public eases its demand for basic safeguards and quality-of-life measures (which it won't), politicians in the pocket of big-spending lobbies like the NFIB will face a contradiction that no amount of maneuvering can reconcile. Establishing community standards, by definition, involves infringing, at times, on individual interests. Of course small business wants government "off their backs, out of their pockets, and off their land." This simplistic demand can't—and won't—be met. If anti-regulatory politicians weren't so adept at masking their intentions with vague language and euphemisms, this would be abundantly clear.

## WHO'S TO BLAME?

When political leaders lie to the public, it is the fault of these leaders and the fault of those who let them get away with it. You can blame the Republicans for their scandalous dishonesty. But you must also blame the people who ought to know better. In a January 23 editorial, *The Washington Post* cautioned that Republicans were planning a "systematic assault on regulation" and that "sorting all through this is going to take a while." "Considering all that's at stake," they concluded, "it should." Considering all that's at stake, where has *The Post*'s coverage been? At press time, Cindy Skrzycki, the regulation beat reporter, had written fourteen stories since election day. Not one offered serious analysis of the effects of regulation. A 625-word profile of McIntosh, the upstart freshman representative leading the charge on regulatory reform, offered breezy assessments of his political style. The day before, McIntosh's subcommittee had held day-long hearings. "He used the hearing," Skrzycki reported, "to rail against the Clinton administration's 'insincerity' on regulatory reform. 'President Clinton is having a love affair with federal regulations,' he said." Thanks. But what about his proposals and their effects? And for background, how about his work on Dan Quayle's Council on Competitiveness, the Bush administration's equivalent of the Task Force on Regulatory Relief? McIntosh, the Council's executive director, developed a reputation as a fierce ideologue, fighting a worldwide treaty on rare species, as well as EPA limits on sulfur dioxide and lead battery incineration.

*The Post* isn't the only news source missing the story on regulations. There has been no shortage of committee hearings or new legislation in the last several months; still, none of the country's top newspapers or magazines have given this subject much attention. The stories that are written, for the most part, are vague and superficial. The *Los Angeles Times* compared the FDA to a pendulum—"either it swings too far in relaxing its standards . . . or it swings too far in the other direction by being too tough." And *The New York Times* offered this gem: "Critics [of a regulation bill] say the legislation would tie the regulatory process into knots of scientific review, economic analysis, legal challenge and political gridlock. But advocates say the bill would guarantee simplicity and common sense where now there is obfuscation and red tape." This is accurate so far as it goes, but without providing details—concrete examples of regulation's real-life benefits and real-life flaws—it's almost entirely without value.

Even after House Speaker Newt Gingrich labeled FDA chief David Kessler "a thug and a bully," the coverage was barely palpable. *The Wall Street Journal* reported Gingrich's ties to pharmaceutical companies and *The Post* probed the efficacy of the "Cardiopump," a device Gingrich chided the FDA for not having approved. But what about the efficacy of the agency itself? Gingrich called the FDA "America's leading job killer," with the EPA "a close second." He suggested replacing the agency with biomedical "entrepreneurs" (in other words, self-regulation). This is the Speaker of the House toying with abolishing the FDA. Isn't that time for a hard look at the agency? Why *does* it cost an average of $230 million to get a drug from the laboratory to the drugstore? Why can't terminal AIDS and cancer patients smoke marijuana without risking arrest? Do other countries manage drug regulation better? According to a recent study by Public Citizen, the FDA deserves some credit; over the last 22 years, the U.S. has been forced to recall dramatically fewer drugs (9) than France (31), Germany (30) and the United Kingdom (23). The point isn't that newspapers should rush to the FDA's defense, but that it should do whatever possible to keep this debate grounded in facts.

If newspapers fail in their neglect of this subject, other media overemphasize regulation. Network TV news, and news "magazines" in particular, sniff out malfeasance like blood hounds and ignore the bigger picture. They demonize regulators and turn flukes into scandals. ABC News's John Stossel built a career on this tabloid-style "consumer advocacy." Then, last year, he switched course and broadcast a special asking "Are We Scaring Ourselves to Death?" which not-so-subtly argued that the FDA, EPA, and Consumer Product Safety Commission caused more trouble than they were worth. Stossel trotted out horror story after horror story, but never put regulations into context and offered no practical suggestions. In recent speeches to libertarian groups, Stossel made his facile argument explicit, endorsing "self-regulation" of industry. Federal health and safety regulations, he said, "don't make life safer. They make life less safe." If his simplistic analysis didn't so closely resemble that of the Speaker of the House of Representatives, we might have less cause to worry. Indeed, Stossel's farce will likely be repeated in scores of committee hearings in the months to come.

The impulse to sensationalize regulation, on one hand, or to virtually ignore it on the other, is not hard to understand. Readers slogging through this article can attest to the subject's tediousness. And unlike financial affairs—an equally complicated subject that draws enormous attention in newspapers—the constituency for regulation stories is not as easily defined. But although the politics of regulation can be mind-numbing, their real-life implications are enormous. Casting stories about regulation as a struggle between anti-regulation reformers and pro-regulation defenders of the status quo is inaccurate and irresponsible. And educating the public has never been more essential.

What, then, should journalists be reporting? In three words: examples, examples, examples. The scope of federal health and safety regulations is enormous; it consists of thousands of employees spanning dozens of agencies. Some regulations set unrealistic goals and ought to be reined in. Other regulations are aimed in the right direction, but just don't get the job done. Still others are too feeble, held back by timid lawmakers wary of offending a powerful interest. The point is that only by elucidating the real benefits and drawbacks of specific regulation will we make progress toward what should be a universal goal: providing basic protections in the most efficient way possible. While expressing strong support of regulation, *Times-Mirror* found, 63 percent of respondents also think "government regulation of business usually does more harm than good." Americans don't dislike regulation; they just want it done more effectively.

## GETTING IT RIGHT

Regulatory reform, it is important to understand, is not an oxymoron. In his 1993 book, *Breaking the Vicious Cycle*, Stephen Breyer points to the illogic of a regulatory system that has been built, not by master plan, but by a series of responses to individual crises. Even if each regulation is sensible and well enforced, it may not make sense in the larger context. "Rules designed to limit zinc in water," Breyer offers for example, "raise the cost of using regular diapers, encouraging the use of disposable—and doubtfully 'recyclable'—diapers, which are a major contributor to landfills." While the National Highway Traffic and Safety Administration vigorously regulates safety, its fuel economy standards have been an incentive for automakers to build smaller cars, which are in fact less safe.

Often, poor communication within an agency, or between different agencies, lends the regulatory system a random quality. Breyer points out that, at one point, the EPA's Office of Solid Waste and Emergency Response had classified as hazardous waste certain elements found in chlorofluorocarbons (CFCs). Resulting rules severely discouraged the recycling of refrigerators, which contain CFCs. Meanwhile, another EPA department, the Office of Air and Radiation, was urging that refrigerators be recycled to save the ozone layer.

As another example, take meat supply oversight. The FDA checks live animals in farms or pens, but the Department of Agriculture assumes control once they reach the slaughterhouse. The two share oversight at retail outlets—with jurisdiction over different products—but only the FDA can conduct inspections. The EPA, meanwhile, determines "tolerance levels" for pesticide residues in food. But—the loop closes—the FDA checks for chemicals in the tissue of livestock. Even within individual agencies, as Breyer points out above, coordination among departments can be nonexistant. "I've been in meetings," says Gary Bass, director of OMB Watch, "where business comes into EPA and says, 'Look, we'll give you more information than what you're requesting, if you just get all your different offices—the air office, the water office—if you get your act together and collect it uniformly.' And you look around the room and you see the officials; they don't have the authority to talk cross-program."

The irony of Republican reforms is that they extol the values of the free market, competition, and common sense, but would make regulatory bureaucracies even more top-heavy, cumbersome, and inefficient. "What the legislation on Capitol Hill is designed to do," says Joan Claybrook, president of Public Citizen, "is to dismantle these programs through gridlock. To put forth so many costly, unnecessary red tape requirements that the decision maker could never make a decision." This worsens the bureaucratic snarl that drove 68 percent of Americans in 1994 to think "dealing with a federal government agency is often not worth the trouble," up from 58 percent in 1987.

Real reform often requires giving regulators *more* flexibility, more authority to set guidelines and to use common sense to judge whether they are being met. As opposed to "command and control," "performance standard" regulation is often far more effective. In 1985, the *Monthly* ran a story headlined, "Why Regulators Need a DON'T DO IT IF IT'S STUPID Clause." The reporter detailed a six-year, multi-million dollar battle over a harmless pile of lime in Minneapolis. The EPA had determined that any material with a pH higher than 12 is hazardous. And though the 75,000 tons of lime could have been useful in any number of ways—lime is commonly used in agriculture, construction, and even pollution control—its designation as hazardous meant no one could touch it. Republican measures would make the problem worse. When an agency is in perpetual threat of a lawsuit—not just over a decision it makes, but over any of the evidence it uses to make that decision—it will become sluggish, documenting each step with reams of paperwork, avoiding exposure to criticism. Agencies will become timid, afraid to make decisions. This strategy runs counter to public interest, but, in the long run, it hurts "special interests" (like small business owners) even more. Ask your local shopkeeper what he dislikes most: being told what to do, or not knowing what's legal or illegal. I suspect you'll find that it's not Orwell's world he fears, but Kafka's.

The last thing the system needs is another layer of checks and balances, analyses and judicial review. "The less his power," Woodrow Wilson wrote of the civil servant in 1883, "the more safely obscure and unnoticed does he feel his position to be, the more readily does he relapse into remissness." Although bureaucrats get the blame for this rigidity, often the fault is with the laws themselves. To assert authority, Congress often steps further than it should. The Delaney Clause of the 1958 Food Additive Amendments to the FDA legislation prohibits any carcinogenic additive to food, regardless of the concentration or risk involved. And the Solid Waste Disposal Act states that waste may contain "no migration of hazardous constituents." Both of these examples, Breyer writes, "seem to instruct the agencies not to permit addition, removal, or packaging of or by any substance that contains even a single molecule of an offending chemical, however large the cost or small the risk." The most egregious examples of this trend come from the Reagan years, when Congress was rightly suspicious that the executive branch would do as much as possible to subvert the intent of the law. The 1986 Safe Drinking Water Act requires all water to be purified, regardless of its initial level of safety, and that any synthetic substance in water, regardless of its concentration or health effects, be treated. In Anchorage, Alaska, city officials found themselves in violation of an Act provision that requires a 30 percent reduction of waste, because there wasn't enough waste in the water to remove. In other words, the water was too clean to comply with the law. Rather than spend $160 million on a new wastewater treatment plant, the city arranged for local fish-processing plants to dump fish entrails into city sewers so the city could remove them, and meet the standard.

Finding problem spots, though, is the easy part. Good regulations are often more difficult to identify, since their effectiveness gives the impression of normalcy. Regulators are easily blamed—either for being too cautious or too lax—and rarely receive credit for doing their job effectively. Manufacturers eagerly take credit for initiatives they've been forced into. Catalytic converters are a good example. Auto companies fiercely resisted pollution control devices, estimating they would cost about $3,000 per car. General Motors testified in 1973 that the requirement could lead to a "complete stoppage of the entire production . . . with the obvious tremendous loss to company shareholders, employees, suppliers and communities." When the EPA stood firm, General Motors introduced the converters, touting its technological prowess and environmental sensitivity. The year after the converters were made standard, hydrocarbon and carbon monoxide emissions from new cars were cut in half. In 1995, the typical new car emits about one percent of the pollution of 1970 models, made before the first real Clean Air Act, and the cost per car is several hundred dollars. Same with lead in gasoline. Industry fiercely resisted the restrictions initially, but the increase in cost per gallon of gas has proven to be merely one penny. Now, with lead effectively eliminated as an air pollutant, oil companies beat their breasts with pride.

In the late fifties and early sixties, the sedative thalidomide was licensed and marketed in several dozen countries. Between 1959 and 1961, pregnant women using the drug across 20 countries gave birth to 10,000 babies with serious, identical, and rare deformities. As the news began to spread, an American pharmaceutical company had an application pending with the FDA to market thalidomide in the U.S., but a skeptical FDA had not signed off. There are many variations on this story: isoproterenol inhalers, used to relieve asthma, caused 3500 deaths in England and Wales in the sixties; practolol, an anti-hyper-intensive, caused a number of cases of permanent or near-permanent blindness in England in the seventies. Of course, the tragedies that led to broadening the FDA's mandate are noticeable as well, providing proper reminder that a company's market incentive to test a product goes only so far. In 1976, the agency was given authority to regulate medical devices after the Dalkon Shield, an intrauterine contraceptive, was proven responsible for 18 deaths and 66,000 miscarriages.

Cars, drugs, and medical devices provide the most dramatic stories, but much of the success in regulation is in the commonplace. To appreciate the work of the Consumer Product Safety Commission, glance over the "recalls" page in *Consumer Reports* each month. In the January 1995 issue, you'll see that Krups blenders have blades that can break apart and embed slivers of metal in food. A new model of orthodontic pacifier can break apart and choke babies. And a new model of a wooden bunk bed can trap a child's head and lead to strangulation. Even when companies issue voluntary recalls, the pressure applied by the CPSC—and its authority to levy fines—is no small factor.

Although you're not likely to hear this from Republican "reformers," often the problem with regulation is that it's too weak, not too tough. The Federal Aviation Administration, for example, has been rightly chastised for its "tombstone mentality," failing to institute reforms until a tragedy—or series of tragedies—sparks public opinion. As early as 1980, for example, the National Transportation Safety Board was urging the FAA to require crash-resistant fuel lines and tanks on commuter aircraft, a precaution the agency postponed for nearly 15 years. And the need for tougher requirements for de-icing was evident as early as 1982, when 78 people died when an Air Florida jet with iced wings crashed just after takeoff from Washington, D.C. The FAA waited ten years—and for 23 more ice-related accidents—to take action. In both cases, administrative delay—due to un-necessary cost-benefit analyses and industry resistance—was at the heart of the inaction.

Although the first round of regulatory "reform" is well under way, the heartening news for citizens interested in honest dialogue on regulation is that much of the Republican agenda is long-term. In the next several years, committees in the House and Senate will go after regulation of food, drugs, air, water, and work safety. Journalists will have a peg, if they want it, for lengthy discussion of every link in the federal regulatory chain. And despite a less than auspicious start, the new majority party could translate their fervor into genuinely improving the system. Watch out, though. They could make it much, much worse.

# 15

## Government and Society

### The Welfare State

*See Lowi and Ginsberg, pp. 637–660*

*We often talk about social welfare policy as if it were distinct from economic policy. Social welfare policy is aimed at providing security, typically in the form of income or health care benefits, for people in need such as the elderly, the disabled, unemployed, and children from low-income households. Economic policy, on the other hand, typically deals with macroeconomic conditions such as inflation and the balance of trade, as well as with industry-specific regulatory issues. In practice, however, the distinction between the two policy areas is less clear. More than half of the federal budget is spent on social welfare programs (mostly Social Security and Medicare). Such an enormous federal outlay has significant consequences for the economy—it gives groups of individuals consumer buying power, it benefits major industries such as health care, and it is a primary contributor to the federal deficit each year. Nevertheless, for analytical purposes, these two categories of policy remain separate.*

*Much of what we consider to be the modern welfare state got its start during the 1930s when President Franklin Roosevelt responded to the Great Depression with a variety of social insurance and economic security programs. In 1934, Roosevelt sent Congress legislation that established Social Security, aid to families with dependent children, and unemployment insurance, and strengthened public health programs. In the message to Congress reproduced here, Roosevelt set out some principles that he believed should guide government action. The programs should start small, he argued. They should be self-sustaining insurance programs that do not require "the proceeds of general taxation." They should be managed by the states (except for Social Security); and the federal government should maintain control over program funds.*

*Roosevelt's proposal was controversial despite its small scale, and opponents immediately challenged parts of the program as an unconstitutional expansion of federal government power. (The Supreme Court upheld the legislation in 1937.) Even though Roosevelt proposed only modest spending—$100 million, or about $1.5 billion in today's dollars—funding levels grew quickly as organized constituencies fought to preserve and bolster the programs. In 1997, the federal government will spend more than $300 billion on Social Security alone.*

# Franklin D. Roosevelt
## "A Program for Social Security"*

In addressing you on June 8, 1934, I summarized the main objectives of our American program. Among these was, and is, the security of the men, women, and children of the nation against certain hazards and vicissitudes of life. This purpose is an essential part of our task. In my annual message to you I promised to submit a definite program of action. This I do in the form of a report to me by a Committee on Economic Security, appointed by me for the purpose of surveying the field and of recommending the basis of legislation.

I am gratified with the work of this committee and of those who have helped it: The Technical Board of Economic Security, drawn from various departments of the government; the Advisory Council on Economic Security, consisting of informed and public-spirited private citizens; and a number of other advisory groups, including a Committee on Actuarial Consultants, a Medical Advisory Board, a Dental Advisory Committee, a Hospital Advisory Committee, a Public Health Advisory Committee, a Child Welfare Committee, and an Advisory Committee on Employment Relief. All of those who participated in this notable task of planning this major legislative proposal are ready and willing at any time to consult with and assist in any way the appropriate congressional committees and members with respect to detailed aspects.

It is my best judgment that this legislation should be brought forward with a minimum of delay. Federal action is necessary to and conditioned upon the actions of states. Forty-four legislatures are meeting or will meet soon. In order that the necessary state action may be taken promptly, it is important that the federal government proceed speedily.

The detailed report of the committee sets forth a series of proposals that will appeal to the sound sense of the American people. It has not attempted the impossible nor has it failed to exercise sound caution and consideration of all of the factors concerned: the national credit, the rights and responsibilities of states, the capacity of industry to assume financial responsibilities, and the fundamental necessity of proceeding in a manner that will merit the enthusiastic support of citizens of all sorts.

It is overwhelmingly important to avoid any danger of permanently discrediting the sound and necessary policy of federal legislation for economic security by attempting to apply it on too ambitious a scale before actual experience has provided guidance for the permanently safe direction of such efforts. The place of such a fundamental in our future civilization is too precious to be jeopardized now by extravagant action. It is a sound idea—a sound ideal. Most of the other advanced countries of the

---

* Franklin D. Roosevelt, "A Program for Social Security" in the *United States Historical Record*, 74 Cong., 1 Sess., pp. 545–46.

world have already adopted it, and their experience affords the knowledge that social insurance can be made a sound and workable project.

Three principles should be observed in legislation on this subject. In the first place, the system adopted, except for the money necessary to initiate it, should be self-sustaining in the sense that funds for the payment of insurance benefits should not come from the proceeds of general taxation. Second, excepting in old-age insurance, actual management should be left to the states, subject to standards established by the federal government. Third, sound financial management of the funds and the reserves and protection of the credit structure of the nation should be assured by retaining federal control over all funds through trustees in the Treasury of the United States.

At this time, I recommend the following types of legislation looking to economic security:

First, unemployment compensation.

Second, old-age benefits, including compulsory and voluntary annuities.

Third, federal aid to dependent children through grants to states for the support of existing mother's pension systems and for services for the protection and care of homeless, neglected, dependent, and crippled children.

Fourth, additional federal aid to state and local public-health agencies and the strengthening of the federal Public Health Service. I am not at this time recommending the adoption of so-called health insurance, although groups representing the medical profession are cooperating with the federal government in the further study of the subject, and definite progress is being made.

With respect to unemployment compensation, I have concluded that the most practical proposal is the levy of a uniform federal payroll tax, 90 percent of which should be allowed as an offset to employers contributing under a compulsory state unemployment compensation act. The purpose of this is to afford a requirement of a reasonably uniform character for all states cooperating with the federal government and to promote and encourage the passage of unemployment compensation laws in the states. The 10 percent not thus offset should be used to cover the costs of federal and state administration of this broad system. Thus, states will largely administer unemployment compensation, assisted and guided by the federal government.

An unemployment compensation system should be constructed in such a way as to afford every practicable aid and incentive toward the larger purpose of employment stabilization. This can be helped by the intelligent planning of both public and private employment. It also can be helped by correlating the system with public employment so that a person who has exhausted his benefits may be eligible for some form of public work as is recommended in this report. Moreover, in order to encourage the stabilization of private employment, federal legislation should not foreclose the states from establishing means for inducing industries to afford an even greater stabilization of employment.

In the important field of security for our old people, it seems necessary to adopt three principles—first, noncontributory old-age pensions for those who are now too old to build up their own insurance; it is, of course, clear that for perhaps thirty years to come funds will have to be provided by the states and the federal government to meet these pensions. Second, compulsory contributory annuities, which in time will establish a self-supporting system for those now young and for future generations. Third, voluntary contributory annuities by which individual initiative can increase the annual amounts received in old age. It is proposed that the federal government assume one-half of the cost of the old-age pension plan, which ought ultimately to be supplanted by self-supporting annuity plans.

The amount necessary at this time for the initiation of unemployment compensation, old-age security, children's aid, and the promotion of public health, as outlined in the report of the Committee on Economic Security, is approximately $100 million.

The establishment of sound means toward a greater future economic security of the American people is dictated by a prudent consideration of the hazards involved in our national life. No one can guarantee this country against the dangers of future depressions, but we can reduce these dangers. We can eliminate many of the factors that cause economic depressions and we can provide the means of mitigating their results. This plan for economic security is at once a measure of prevention and a method of alleviation.

We pay now for the dreadful consequence of economic insecurity—and dearly. This plan presents a more equitable and infinitely less expensive means of meeting these costs. We cannot afford to neglect the plain duty before us. I strongly recommend action to attain the objectives sought in this report.

## Who Is Poor? Who Shall Be Poor?

*Lowi and Ginsberg, pp. 671–673*

*Who receives benefits from government? This question is central to discussions of public policy, as well as to the current debate over the deficit and who shall bear the burden of cutting back government programs. Howe and Longman argue that, contrary to widespread public perception, government benefits are tilted heavily in favor of the middle class and wealthy, not the poor. Social Security, government pensions, Medicare, and various tax deductions and credits provide benefits without regard to need. According to the authors, these programs distort social policy by diverting funding to the already well-off. In 1994, for example, $8 billion in Social Security payments went to households with incomes over $100,000. Their solution is to gradually phase out benefit payments and tax deductions as income rises, a controversial proposal given the political clout of the various groups, such as the American Association of Retired Persons (AARP), that will surely try to protect their favorite programs.*

# Neil Howe and Philip Longman
# "The Next New Deal"*

With the coming of the next New Deal, Americans will look back and marvel at what became of our old welfare state—that tangle of inequity and dysfunction once known as federal entitlements. Why did the public tolerate a system that wound up distributing most of its benefits to the well-off? And how did the economy survive its costs?

History books will no doubt concentrate on a few choice examples of the conditions that finally forced a wholesale reform. Readers may learn, for instance, that by 1991 the federal government's largest housing subsidy program was providing an average of $3,000 a year to each of the six million wealthiest households in America, while offering nothing to the 36 million Americans in poverty.

To qualify for this particular benefit, called the home-mortgage deduction, you had to borrow using your first or second home as collateral. And the more you borrowed, even if it was to finance a chalet in Aspen—or just a ski trip to Aspen—the more subsidy you would receive from other taxpayers. By 1991 the cost of the home-mortgage deduction had risen to $37 billion, of which 81 percent went directly to households with incomes over $50,000. Meanwhile, economists bemoaned the anemic U.S. personal savings rate, which in the late 1980s fell to its lowest level since the 1930s.

The U.S. health-care system a quarter century after the announcement of the Great Society will also provide future historians with rich examples of the conditions that led to the next New Deal. How to explain that the U.S. economy staggered under the highest per capita health-care costs on earth, and still 23 million Americans under the age of thirty-five were uninsured for any medical care at all?

Stranger yet was what happened to these uninsured Americans, and to everyone else, if they happened to live to be sixty-five. After that birthday a citizen, regardless of income, became entitled to take part in a program called Medicare, which would pay for everything from CAT scans to pacemakers, from chiropractic to orthopedic recliners. In 1991 Medicare spent nearly $19 billion subsidizing the health care of households earning $50,000 or more. That year government experts projected that the mounting cost of Medicare would cause the program to collapse within fifteen years, and that if current trends continued, total health-care spending would rise to an economy-shattering 44 percent of the gross national product by 2030. No one listened.

Gold-plated pensions for federal employees will also no doubt be held up by future historians as emblematic of the decadence of late-twentieth-century political culture. By what accident of history were military and civil-service retirees with incomes over $100,000 collecting $9.2 billion

* Neil Howe and Philip Longman, "The Next New Deal" in the *Atlantic Monthly* (April 1992). Reprinted with permission.

from the U.S. Treasury in 1991? For half this sum the official poverty rate for all American elderly could have been reduced to zero. At the very least, Congress could have done something about the $1.4 trillion in unfunded federal pension liabilities on the books. But the House of Representatives was busy with other business at the time—such as voting itself a controversial pay hike that would later be remembered for its explosive impact on pension costs. Retiring in 1991, a typical congressman looked forward to $1,098,735 in lifetime benefits; by 1993 the figure had risen to $1,523,263.

Finally, there was the program originally designed to offer all Americans what President Franklin Roosevelt's brain trusters called "a floor of protection" against destitution in old age. But over the course of more than half a century Social Security had evolved into something radically different. By 1991 the system was distributing more than $55 billion a year, or more than a fifth of its benefits, to households with incomes above $50,000 a year. For that much money the government could have provided every American with cradle-to-grave insurance against poverty—including the one American child in twenty who lived in a household reporting a cash income during 1991 of less than $5,000.

For many years the worsening inefficiency and inequity of the U.S. social-welfare system seemed to make little impression on American political opinion. Political leaders as diverse as Newt Gingrich, George Bush, Bill Clinton, and Daniel Patrick Moynihan expressed alarm at the moral hazard of providing welfare benefits to poor unwed mothers. But few political leaders worried about the moral hazard—and incomparably larger cost—of subsidizing home-equity loans for rising young stockbrokers, granting free medical care, PX cards, and half pay for life to ex-colonels at age forty-two, passing out farm payments to affluent agribusiness owners, or writing checks to globe-trotting senior citizens which got forwarded to Bermuda. It was convenient to assume that free lunches corrupted only the underclass.

As the 1990–1992 recession lingered, forcing local governments to cut teachers' pay, ignore the raving homeless, and fence off sagging bridges, state governors turned to Washington, where politicians shrugged their shoulders and pointed to a budget bursting with entitlement programs running on autopilot. Meanwhile, ordinary Americans wondered what was happening to their nation's public sector. It could afford neither to build for the future nor to care for the needy—despite unprecedented borrowing, a near-record level of taxation, and sinking defense outlays that by the fall of 1992 had reached their lowest share of GNP since Harry Truman ran for President. With the vaunted post-Cold War "peace dividend" evaporating, the United States found itself unable to invest adequately in either its infrastructure or its children. Eventually people began to talk of another Great Depression, before the coming of the next New Deal.

## A WELFARE STATE FOR THE AFFLUENT

Rudolf Goldscheid, the socialist economist, once observed, "The budget is the skeleton of the state stripped of all misleading ideologies." By now federal entitlement spending has become so pervasive in American life—not just among the poor but most notably among the middle class and the affluent—that one cannot make sense of our politics or the condition of our economy without considering how this spending rearranges the nation's resources and defines our choices as a society.

Ever since the early 1980s, when the United States lost control of its fiscal policy, the term "entitlements"—referring to all federal benefit payments to individuals—has been part of the American political lexicon. Today the twelve-digit numbers that first worried budget experts back in the late 1970s look positively quaint—although events have proved that the growth of entitlements is indeed the leading cause of the nation's long-term structural deficits. This year the cost of federal benefits is larger than was the entire federal budget when Ronald Reagan arrived in Washington with a mandate to slash the welfare state.

All told, entitlements have become a trillion-dollar river. The main current includes more than $700 billion in direct outlays, received by at least one member of roughly half the nation's households. These expenditures account for more than 45 percent of all federal spending, and are more than twice as large as the amount consumed by defense. Another flow of nearly $200 billion is distributed in the form of tax subsidies to individuals, such as the home-mortgage deduction and the exclusion for employer-paid health care. These explicit breaks in the tax code are the moral and fiscal equivalent of the government's simply mailing a check. To pay for them, other people's taxes have to be raised, other benefits have to be cut, or the deficit has to be increased.

The accumulating burden is not about to ease. Our economy shows no sign of "outgrowing" the cost of entitlements, as many partisans of Reaganomics, along with many liberals, once hoped. Though the relative cost typically rises and falls with the business cycle, it has always emerged from each new recession larger than it emerged from the last. In fiscal year 1992 federal benefit outlays alone will exceed 12 percent of GNP, the second highest level ever. Including tax benefits, the total cost of federal entitlements amounts to well over 15 percent of GNP, and Congress now projects that it will climb steadily through the late 1990s. For the first time, the economy should not expect any post-recession relief.

Who benefits from this spending? Until recently no one really knew. Budget experts, to be sure, have always pointed to a few eyebrow-raising numbers. Consider the fact that of all federal benefit outlays, only a quarter flows through programs that require any evidence of financial need—and that even this "means-tested" quarter includes such middle-class staples as student loans and VA hospital care. Consider also that only one of every eight federal benefit dollars actually reaches Americans in poverty. But reliable income figures for all recipient households have simply not been available. Cash-income surveys conducted by the Census Bureau are plagued by high rates of underreporting (especially by the wealthy). Tax-return data from the Internal Revenue Service are more accurate, but do not cover the entire population (especially the poor).

Several years ago, however, growing curiosity on Capitol Hill persuaded the nonpartisan Congressional Budget Office to try to unravel the mystery. By merging the Census and IRS data sources, CBO economists ultimately arrived at reliable and comprehensive estimates of benefits by household income. The estimates were circulated behind closed doors during the 1990 budget summit and have since been updated—though they have never yet been published. The benefit-income statistics we cite throughout this article are based on these CBO estimates, which cover about 80 percent of all federal benefit outlays.

These numbers destroy any ideological myths Americans may cling to about who gets what from government. They offer an accurate glimpse of that "skeleton of the state"—which has too long been locked in the political closet.

The CBO research demonstrates, in fact, that the most affluent Americans actually collect slightly more from the welfare state than do the poorest Americans. It shows that last year U.S. households with incomes over $100,000 received, on average, $5,690 worth of federal cash and in-kind benefits, while the corresponding figure for U.S. households with incomes under $10,000 was $5,560. Quite simply, if the federal government wanted to flatten the nation's income distribution, it would do better to mail all its checks to random addresses. The problem is not that poverty programs don't target the poor. More than 85 percent of the benefits from AFDC, SSI, and food stamps do indeed go to households with incomes under $20,000. But their impact is neutralized by all the other programs, which tilt the other way and are, of course, much greater in size.

The trend over time is also unsettling. Liberals sometimes attribute the growing disparity of income in America to Reagan-era cuts in targeted poverty programs. Among the very poorest households that is indeed one cause. From 1980 to 1991, in constant dollars, the average federal benefit received by households with incomes under $10,000 declined by seven percent. Yet liberals typically overlook the gentrification of America's untargeted nonpoverty programs, which has been pushing even more powerfully to widen the gap between rich and poor. During those same eleven years, among households with incomes over $200,000 the real value of average benefits received (mostly Social Security, Medicare, and federal pensions) fully doubled.

But thus far we have been considering only direct outlays. When we include the value of entitlements conveyed through the tax code, the bias in favor of the well-off becomes even more pronounced.

## TAX EXPENDITURES AND OTHER SUBSIDIES

Such tax subsidies date back to 1918, when patriotic fervor for U.S. troops in Europe was running high. Political leaders in Washington felt they should do something dramatic to reward the doughboys. Facing a tight budget, Congress hesitated to raise veterans' benefits directly. But then someone on Capitol Hill took a look at the five-year-old federal income-tax system and came up with a nifty idea: Why not "raise" veterans' benefits simply by exempting such benefits from the tax?

Over the years many more "tax expenditures" have followed, nearly all of them—like the first—created entirely off budget, without estimating eventual cost and far from the scrutiny that normally accompanies direct appropriations. Several, including the exemptions for Social Security benefits and for employer-paid health care, were created not by Congress but by offhand IRS rulings in the 1930s and 1940s. At the time, no one paid them much notice, because tax rates were low, Social Security benefits were modest, and company health plans were rare. But in fiscal year 1992 these two rulings alone are costing the federal government nearly $90 billion, which is more than the Pentagon's total budget for weapons procurement.

Though tax expenditures as a political art were invented during the First World War, the term itself dates back only to the mid-1960s, when it was coined by Stanley S. Surrey, a Harvard Law don who served as assistant secretary of the Treasury for tax policy in the Kennedy and Johnson Administrations. In the course of his battles with Congress over tax policy, Surrey was struck by the fact that Congress was increasingly using selective tax reductions for specific groups of people, rather than direct appropriations, as a means of distributing public resources.

Surrey's favorite example was the deduction for medical expenses. He explained that this tax provision had precisely the same impact, both on the budget and on the public, as a multibillion-dollar benefit program that heavily favored the very rich (because they pay taxes at the highest rates) and that entirely excluded the very poor (because they don't pay taxes at all). There was indeed only one big difference: the same Congress that created the tax provision would never dare to create the benefit program.

Although the tax-expenditure concept has been widely accepted by economists over the past thirty years, it strikes many Americans the wrong way. A common complaint is that the concept somehow assumes that government "owns" all your income before doing you the favor of letting you keep part of it. This is not the case. The concept simply assumes that each person owes the government according to a general rate schedule superimposed on every person's ability to pay. Whatever violates such equal treatment is deemed the equivalent of a benefit outlay—the same, that is, as a check in the mail.

From the dogmatic insistence that there is no such thing as a tax expenditure, any number of absurdities must follow: for instance, that a public policy exempting all circus clowns from paying income taxes would not be a public benefit to circus clowns—who would simply be keeping more of "their own" money. Who cares if keeping more of "their" money means taking more of someone else's? Or if it means bankrupting everyone's kids? The ultimate thrust of this line of reasoning is to deny that a society can consent to and act upon any equitable principle of public sacrifice. Accordingly, all taxation is inherently unjust, and though cheating on your taxes may be legally wrong, it cannot be morally wrong.

It is no surprise that many well-off Americans, uneasy about their nation's loss of fiscal discipline, find consolation in this pugnacious illogic. What is surprising is to hear conservatives leading the chorus. Back in the early 1970s, strange to say, many of these same intellectuals pushed Nixon's ill-fated "negative income tax," the very premise of which is that less tax is the precise equivalent of more income. But during the 1980s they have become the preachers of a selective civic virtue—austerity for targeted benefits to the poor and indulgence toward shotgun tax favors to the affluent.

Today, even though the government publishes estimates of the cost of different tax expenditures, this form of spending still attracts comparatively little attention. But by now the numbers involved, and their social and economic effects, are too large to ignore. Honest people can and do differ over what constitutes a genuine tax expenditure, as opposed to "equitable" treatment—say, for investment income or charitable donations. According to some, ability to pay should be measured by what a person earns; according to others, by what a person consumes. But even if we confine our list of tax expenditures to those that contradict any principle of ability to pay—that is, to those that nearly all economists can agree on—the total fiscal cost comes to at least $170 billion. Those tax expenditures arbitrarily reward millions of lucky people for such endeavors as financing a built-in sauna, hiring an au pair, or getting the boss to pay for the therapist.

This spending is regressive in the strictest sense of the word. Even when poorer households qualify for these benefits (and often they do not), what they receive is smaller, relative to their income, than what goes to the affluent. According to the congressional Joint Committee on Taxation, for example, last year the average value of the mortgage-interest deduction for taxpayers with incomes over $100,000 was $3,469. In contrast, the same deduction was worth an average of only $516 for taxpayers in the $20,000 to $30,000 bracket who qualified to take the benefit—and of course many, including renters and those who opted for the standard deduction, did not.

When we add together all the tax expenditures and all the direct outlays for which we have 1991 income data—and this is about 80 percent of each type of entitlement—an unambiguous picture emerges. On average, households with incomes under $10,000 collected a total of $5,690 in benefits. On average, households with incomes over $100,000 collected $9,280. In terms of total fiscal cost, moreover, the aggregate amounts received by the non-needy in 1991 were staggering. One half (at least $400 billion) of all entitlements went to households with incomes over $30,000. One quarter (at least $200 billion) went to households with incomes over $50,000. These are the facts—regardless of what our political folktales might say.

How did our entitlement system wind up delivering most of its benefits to people who are clearly not in need? Obviously, the overall spending pattern does not conform to any master plan. Congress never passed a "Comprehensive Welfare for the Well-Off Act." Rather, the system we see today is the inadvertent legacy of thousands of why-not-please-everybody votes on Capitol Hill—together with economic and demographic trends that no one anticipated.

Nor does any conspiracy lie behind the way Americans have chosen over the past decade to finance the growth of entitlements. They have done so through deficit spending—the result of a persistent ideological deadlock between cutting spending and raising taxes. Each side, unfortunately, has reason to regret the outcome. On the one hand, those who prevented significant reform in the welfare state have worsened any prevailing trend toward inequity by income and class. On the other hand, those who urged that it is better to finance the welfare state through debt than through taxes have burdened Americans with a new layer of inequity by age and generation.

These are the conditions leading to the coming of the next New Deal —a new deal that is needed to restore both fairness and efficiency to our trillion-dollar entitlement budget. The U.S. social-welfare system has by now come to resemble a ramshackle mansion on a hill, with squeaky back stairways and barren hallways leading to musty, sealed-off chambers.

Open this door and behold the federal railroad retirement system—a Christmas gift from Congress to the railroad industry in 1935, still chugging after all these years, at an annual cost of $7.8 billion. That crowing in the pantry is the sound of $50,000, on average, in direct federal payments being snatched up by each of the 30,000 biggest-grossing farmers in America. Not one of them looks like Pa Joad. And down this hall you'll find the bonanza-baby nursery, filled with Americans born from 1910 through 1916, whose Social Security benefit levels are higher than those of anyone born before or after. Can anyone remember why? What about that thumping noise? Maybe it's the so-called one-percent "kicker" from the 1970s, which still inflates civil-service pensions.

This is a structure, leaky and drafty and wildly expensive to heat, that was tolerably suited to its previous owners but now requires radical remodeling. What would FDR, architect of the original New Deal, have said if he had learned that by 1991 a fifth of American children would be living in poverty—still ill housed and ill nourished—while a fifth of the dollars spent by major federal benefit programs went to households earning $50,000 or more?

Fortunately, the system can be made to work again. But before the next New Deal can happen, Americans will have to start viewing entitlements as a whole, and debating comprehensive reforms.

## WELFARE FOR THE WELL-OFF

Even if our current entitlement system were sustainable well into the twenty-first century—and it is not—most Americans would still have good reason to demand a new deal. Consider how little we as a nation are getting back for the money we are spending: no national health-insurance plan, no maternity benefits or family allowances such as are available in Germany and France, no guarantee against falling into poverty or even becoming homeless—in old age or at any other time of life.

In 1990, for example, the federal government handed out an average of $11,400 worth of benefits to every American aged sixty-five or over—more than ten times what it gave to each child—yet 3.7 million senior citizens still languished below the poverty line. Many of the latter receive a "means-tested" benefit—Supplemental Security Income. But for an elderly person living alone in 1990 the federal SSI program offered a maximum cash benefit of 74 percent of the poverty level, or $4,632 annually. That same year, while 18 million Americans earning less than $15,000 at full-time, year-round jobs "contributed" their FICA dollars, a CEO and spouse could retire and expect to receive more than $24,000 annually in tax-sheltered Social Security and Medicare benefits, in addition to their corporate pension and "medi-gap" plan, and sundry forms of private investment income.

Why doesn't the welfare state do a better job of actually insuring against poverty? The bottom-line reason is that we divert too many resources to the affluent.

The most stunning illustrations of welfare for the well-off come in the form of entitlements conveyed through the tax code. Consider, for example, the exclusion from taxation of most Social Security income along with the insurance value of Medicare benefits, which together cost the Treasury about $34 billion last year. The households that receive the largest favor are those with the most income. In fact, both these tax expenditures may be regarded as especially insidious forms of back-door spending, since they simply add to the already top-heavy distribution of Social Security and Medicare benefits. For the 37 percent of senior citizens who regularly vacation abroad, these tax subsidies are enough to pay for a few extra days of shopping in tropical ports of call. But they do little for another 40 percent of senior citizens who owe no tax on their Form 1040 because they aren't as well off. This is why every other major industrial nation regards all or nearly all of its social-insurance benefits as taxable income.

The same point applies to the child-care credit, which cost the government more than $3 billion last year. Households with incomes below $10,000 received virtually no benefit from this tax subsidy. Those with incomes above $50,000, however, received $1.2 billion to help pay for nannies and other child-care expenses.

For the really big bucks, take a look at the exclusion for employer-paid health care. Under this provision, those Americans fortunate enough to receive health-care insurance from their employers are allowed to exclude the value of their insurance from both income and payroll taxation. Last year this single tax expenditure cost the U.S. Treasury $60 billion in forgone revenue.

Who benefited? Obviously, no one among the 35 million people not covered by any form of health insurance or among the 32 million people who pay for their plans out of their own pockets. These 67 million Americans are twice as likely to live in poverty as are all other Americans. But that is only part of the inequity. Among households that were covered by employer-paid health-care plans, the average benefit for those in the highest income brackets was many times larger than the average for those in the lowest income brackets. Moreover, most economists agree that such large subsidies encourage their beneficiaries to overconsume health-care services, and thus put even more inflationary pressure on a system already in crisis. Who will argue with an employer who offers a "Gold Plan" package that provides generous coverage for every medical contingency, from orthodontia to nose jobs to psychoanalysis, as long as it's tax-free?

It is much the same story with most other entitlements conveyed through the tax code. Not only are they inequitable in their distribution of benefits but also they contribute to gross distortions in how the U.S. economy allocates resources. In addition to overconsuming health care, for example, affluent Americans tend to overconsume powder rooms and swimming pools and vacation homes at the expense of more-productive investments—thanks to the mortgage deduction and other tax subsidies for owner-occupied real estate. One result of all these tax favors: the hospitals and homes of Grosse Point and other affluent suburbs of Detroit are far more luxurious than any to be found in, say, the suburbs of Yokohama or Stuttgart. But only in Detroit do the suburbs surround a burned-out, deindustrializing core. Not coincidentally, every major industrial society except the United States pays for little (or none) of its health care with tax-sheltered insurance, and tightly restricts (or prohibits) any deductions for interest on home mortgages.

To the rule that says most tax subsidies go to the wealthy, there is one exception: the Earned Income Tax Credit. First enacted in 1975, the EITC is the closest America has ever come to a negative income tax. But its effect on the overall picture is negligible. Even after including the EITC with all the other tax expenditures mentioned above, the bottom line is still that the rich receive by far the largest benefits.

Households with incomes below $10,000, for example, receive an average of $131 a year from all these tax-subsidy programs combined. Middle-class households do better: those with incomes in the $30,000 to $50,000 range receive tax benefits averaging $1,483. But it is the truly affluent who receive the greatest subsidy: the average benefit for households with incomes over $100,000 is $3,595 a year, or nearly thirty times what goes to households most in need.

## THE WEIGHT OF REALITY UPON IDEOLOGY

Why have Americans put up for so long with such flagrant malfunctioning of their social-welfare system? Part of the explanation must lie in today's political culture, which by the standards of FDR's crusading generation has remained exceptionally cautious in its thinking about the major institutions of the welfare state, and preoccupied with mere process issues. Meanwhile, as the decades have passed, the earth has been slowly shifting beneath the major monuments of the first New Deal. The old assumptions will not hold.

When Social Security first started paying out benefits, for example, the elderly were by far the most destitute age group in American society. As recently as 1969, 25 percent of American elderly were officially designated "poor"—as were only 14 percent of children under age eighteen. Today the relative positions of the very old and the very young are just about reversed: in 1990, 12 percent of the elderly and 21 percent of children were poor. Other indicators, such as noncash income, financial assets, and homeownership rates, also show that the typical elderly household is now considerably better off than the typical young family. At the same time, as we have seen, millions of the elderly continue to live in poverty. And yet Social Security continues to distribute none of its benefits on the basis of need.

We live in a world radically different from that of FDR's generation. How touching it is for the historian to read that New Deal planners once projected that Social Security's survivors' and unemployment benefits would steadily reduce means-tested family assistance. The assumption, of course, was that widows were the only single mothers struggling to raise children. That 13 million children would be living with single nonwidowed mothers in 1990 was simply unthinkable. And how maddening it is for today's married woman to learn that she won't receive Social Security benefits based on her earnings unless she makes at least half her husband's salary throughout her working life. It should come as no surprise that a social-welfare system designed to serve the America of Benny Goodman and Norman Rockwell now stands in need of serious structural repair.

We also live in a world radically different from that of the Johnson and Nixon presidencies, when the steepest increases in entitlement spending took place. In that era renowned economists wrote books about the "challenge of abundance" and testified before Congress about how Americans would soon enjoy a twenty-two-hour workweek. In 1972, on the eve of Social Security's largest single benefit hike, the system's actuaries projected that henceforth real U.S. wages would forever rise at the rate of 56 percent every two decades—an assumption that made almost anything affordable. Looking back, that sort of economic euphoria seems as dated as *2001: A Space Odyssey*. What has in fact happened over the twenty years since 1972 is that real wages, as defined by the actuaries, have grown by hardly more than four percent. Polls indicate that most Americans are no longer confident that today's children will do as well economically as their parents—

and indeed they will not, unless the country frees up the resources it needs to undertake wide-scale investments in improving productivity.

Sixty years after the New Deal there is virtually no connection between the pattern of entitlement spending and any coherent public purpose. So why is reform so often regarded as impossible?

Part of the reason is ideological. Throughout the Reagan years the allure of supply-side economics persuaded many conservatives that reforming entitlements was no longer necessary; with tax cuts and deregulation, the nation could simply "outgrow" them. The party that once fought losing battles against the New Deal could thereby dish the Whigs and painlessly rid itself of its plutocratic reputation. Liberals, meanwhile, have been slow to grasp how an ideal that was once taken as the nation's highest expression of community has evolved into a system that serves the interests of economic royalists at the expense of the common man.

Today reality is gradually wearing away these ideological misconceptions. Still, the reform of any single entitlement program is blocked by highly organized special-interest groups, from the gray-power and pension lobbies to the agribusiness, construction, and health-care industries. Even affluent beneficiaries who may be uncomfortable accepting government money don't like feeling singled out for sacrifice. The Palm Beach retiree, for example, won't go along with higher taxes on his Social Security benefits just so that the yuppie down the street can get another tax break.

What is needed is a comprehensive approach to entitlement reform— one that cuts not only direct spending but also tax expenditures for the well-off. In this way entitlement reform could avoid becoming a contest between generations. By putting every form of government spending on the table, America could also end that long-running, sterile debate between those who want to cut spending and those who want to cut taxes. Genuine reform could at last be what it should be: a more equitable and productive redirection of the nation's limited resources.

## THE PEACE DIVIDEND IS NOT ENOUGH

But couldn't we get by, many readers will ask, with just staying the course? Won't the end of the Cold War free up enough resources so that we won't need to take on entitlement reform?

The short answer is no. A world at peace won't be enough to right the nation's fiscal imbalance.

As we mentioned earlier, benefit outlays accounted for 45 percent of all federal spending in calendar year 1991. Yet this conventional measure of the cost of entitlements, large as it is, underestimates their practical importance. First, it includes only the benefits themselves, not the cost of administering them. Add on a minimal five percent overhead, and the total rises to 48 percent of the budget. Second, a fair measure would compare entitlements only with other types of spending that are adjustable, not with spending that is entirely beyond anyone's control. So let's subtract net interest payments on the national debt ($199.4 billion) and last year's payments on the S&L bailout ($101.8 billion). Both are obligations that must be met in order to avoid a devastating financial panic. Now the total rises to 60 percent of the budget. Finally, let's figure in the $170 billion in benefit-like tax expenditures. This pushes the total up to just over 65 percent of the budget.

The bottom line might be summarized this way: Entitlements, defined as the full cost of both direct and tax-code benefits, amount to two thirds of the federal spending over which government has some control.

A large part of the remaining third is defense spending. The cuts now scheduled will help, but alone they are clearly insufficient. Consider that even eliminating the entire Marine Corps would not defray the annual cost of military pensions. In fact, even if the Department of Defense were abolished and all the armed forces disbanded, the U.S. Treasury would still not be able to pay this year's bills without borrowing. As for the small corner of the budget still dedicated to "discretionary" civilian projects—everything from running parks, regulating polluters, and sheltering runaway children to building highways, testing superconductors, and arresting drug traffickers—as a share of GNP that corner has been smaller since the late 1980s than at any other time since the late 1950s. It is unlikely that Americans could achieve major savings in this catchall budget area without curtailing some of the vital core services they expect from government. Most policy discussions instead favor more of this type of spending, which no doubt would already be larger today were it not perpetually crowded out by the metastasizing of universal benefits.

Another question, still sometimes heard in post-Reagan America, is "Why reform entitlements or even worry about the deficit when we can always just raise taxes?" But the answer is clear enough: The revenue option won't work because it won't happen. One can find many polls showing that most Americans favor the concept of a means test for benefits. But one cannot find any poll showing that more than a small minority of Americans favor a large, general-purpose tax hike.

This anti-tax sentiment is linked to widespread cynicism about government, especially the federal government, which should make many liberals think twice before dismissing entitlement reform. Quite simply, those who want more taxes and bigger budgets must first demonstrate that government can apply commonsense priorities to the money it is already spending. Anyone waiting for public attitudes to change spontaneously should take a closer look at America's rising generation of voters under thirty—not just at their Republican sympathies, which incline them against taxes anyway, but at their intense distrust of unkeepable promises, breakable chain letters, and crocodile tears. What the typical new voter most distrusts, in short, is just the sort of rhetoric that still enshrouds our welfare state.

## UNFAVORABLE DEMOGRAPHICS

Each decade since the first New Deal, from the 1930s through the 1980s, entitlement spending has grown faster than the economy. Under our current system it is certain to do so in future decades as well, especially once the oldest members of the enormous postwar Baby Boom generation begin reaching retirement age, just sixteen years from now. Today more than 60 percent of all federal benefit spending flows to the 12 percent of Americans who are age sixty-five or older. As long as the welfare state allocates most benefits on the basis of seniority alone, the cost will grow geometrically as the size of the elderly population increases. In combination with the aging of the population, improvements in medical technology will likely cause per capita health-care costs to continue growing several times as fast as per-worker GNP.

Demographic data easily numb the mind, but one can gain an intuitive sense of what all this means for government spending by considering just how favorable demographic trends have been for the United States in recent years. During the 1980s the 76 million members of the Baby Boom generation moved into their prime productive years—old enough to have mastered job skills but too young to retire. The result was an automatic surge in federal revenue—especially since the women of this generation have been far more likely than their mothers to work for wages, and therefore to contribute taxes.

Meanwhile, demographics have also been favorable to the spending side of the budget. The growth rate of the retirement-age population has actually been slowing down since the mid-1980s, owing to the declining birth rates of the late 1920s. Yet the United States is still running enormous budget deficits. What will happen when these favorable demographic trends turn into unfavorable trends, beginning around 2010?

Since 1960, federal benefit outlays alone have grown from roughly five percent to 12 percent of GNP. No one knows, of course, what the future may bring. But if one adopts the economic, demographic, and medical assumptions used by the Social Security Administration and the Health Care Financing Administration, the total cost will rise much further over the next fifty years, perhaps to 21 percent of GNP (best case) or to 30 percent of GNP (most plausible case). And this assumes not a single new program or eligibility provision. Outlays of this magnitude would threaten to crowd out not only all forms of public and private investment but also any hope that government might respond to new social needs. Ultimately, even huge tax hikes would merely cover the growing cost of programs whose original intentions had long been forgotten.

Well before we reach such nightmare fiscal scenarios, moreover, the income inequity of the U.S. welfare state will become painfully obvious. Look ahead to the year 2000, when today's unusually affluent Americans in their fifties begin to retire. This is a cohort of lifelong upward mobility whose average household wealth in retirement (according to the economists Frank Levy and Richard Michel) is likely to exceed that of all living

Americans born either before or after them. Then consider the position of today's young adults—handicapped by unstable family backgrounds, an inferior education, and stagnating entry-level wages. By the year 2000, while raising families amid growing talk of yet another hike in the payroll tax, they will cast searching eyes at the abundance of their elders. In her recent book *Social Insecurity* the former Social Security commissioner Dorcas Hardy does not hesitate to link the issues of age, income, and race. "As we move into the next century," she asks, "will the minorities of this country—immigrants and otherwise—come to see the Social Security system as a mechanism by which the government robs their children of a better future, in order to support a group of elderly white people in a retirement that is both too luxurious and too long?"

Take it from someone who once ran the system: the entitlement crisis is not about to go away if we just ignore it.

## A COMPREHENSIVE REFORM

Overhauling the U.S. welfare state so that it serves our national goals will entail enormous changes, most likely including a wholesale restructuring of the U.S. health-care system. But in the meantime we Americans can make federal entitlements much more equitable, and free up the resources we need to cut our fiscal deficits and boost our national savings, by acting on a simple if far-reaching principle. The principle is that one's benefits should be proportional to one's need—whether the subsidy comes in the form of health insurance or a farm subsidy or a mortgage-interest deduction or a Social Security check.

How might such a principle be applied to the existing welfare state, and how much money would it save? Any reform package should satisfy the three most common objections to a cost-control effort. First, it should not reduce the income of any household that is anywhere near the poverty line. More precisely, the half of all U.S. households that report incomes over $30,000 should be asked to bear nearly all the extra burden.

Second, any reform package should adjust benefits according to a graduated scale, so that middle- and upper-income households do not become net losers just because they happen to rise a few dollars above a certain threshold. Nor should earning a high income become a disqualification for receiving any subsidy. To preserve the universal character of our major entitlement programs, members of every household, regardless of income, should still stand to gain some benefits, albeit in proportion to their needs.

Third, any comprehensive reform must take into account the quasicontractual nature of at least some entitlement programs. This last proviso is the toughest to accommodate, but not as tough as is sometimes thought.

Strongly rooted in American political folklore, for example, is the idea that Social Security recipients are only "getting their money back," that Social Security is an "inviolable contract," and so forth. But such claims have no financial or even legal basis, however much certain politicians and interest groups may claim otherwise. True enough, the original Social Security Act of 1935 included a "money back" guarantee (with some interest) on all employee contributions, and called for benefit levels to be calculated on the basis of the lifetime covered wages earned by each individual. But the guarantee was eliminated by Congress in 1939, and the link between benefit levels and years of participation, after being weakened in 1939, was entirely discarded in 1950.

Ever since, the U.S. Supreme Court has repeatedly ruled that no covered worker retains any right, contractual or otherwise, over taxes paid into the system. In fact, the Social Security Administration keeps no direct records of how much each person contributes. It just keeps records of each person's wage history, to which a politically determined benefit formula is applied when that person retires. Today's retirees, as it happens, receive benefits worth two to ten times what they would have earned had they invested all their lifetime Social Security taxes (both their own and their employer's) in Treasury bonds. Meanwhile, largely because of the very steep increases in Social Security taxes in recent years, most economists agree that under current law Social Security will not offer large categories of younger participants anything approaching a fair market return on what they paid into the system.

So there is no reason that Social Security benefits for the well-off cannot be reduced if a majority of Americans decide that their collective resources should be used for different purposes. The same is true for civil-service and military pensions, although here the case is much stronger that an implied contract exists between well-off pensioners and the government.

Before the 1970s federal employees worked for lower wages than their counterparts in the private sector. One reason they did so was the expectation of receiving government pensions far more generous than any offered by private-sector employers. Even today, no private pension offers benefits at such an early age, at such a high percentage of pay, with such lenient provisions for disability, or with such generous indexing. Moreover, because these government pension programs were never funded on an actuarially sound basis, current taxpayers are now unjustly stuck with a huge tab for yesterday's unwise policy. Still, these benefits are part of the compensation that was promised at the time—a distinction that makes a moral if not a legal difference and ought to limit benefit reductions even to the most affluent federal pensioner.

Applying our simple principle would not require a big new bureaucracy. All means-testing could be achieved exclusively through tax returns, much as we now handle the limited taxation of Social Security for households with adjusted gross incomes over $25,000. Each filer would be required to enter all benefits received, which could be checked against federal records. Above certain limits the total would trigger a "benefit-withholding" liability, which the filer would send back to the IRS along with any outstanding income-tax liability. As a practical matter, federal benefits could be withheld just as wages are withheld, based on a tax filer's previous experience.

How would benefit-withholding rates be set? Here are a few illustrative options, with estimates of how much money they would have saved in calendar year 1991 alone.

• For all cash and in-kind entitlement programs except federal-employee pension plans: Withhold 7.5 percent of any benefits that cause total household income to exceed $30,000, and withhold an additional five percent at the margin for each additional $10,000 in household income. The maximum reduction of benefits would be 85 percent, applicable to households with incomes of $190,000 or more. Total savings: $33.5 billion.

• For civil-service and military pensions: Same as above, but with a much lower maximum withholding rate, in deference to the quasi-contractual nature of these benefits. The maximum reduction of benefits would be 25 percent, for households earning $70,000 a year or more. Total savings: $7.6 billion.

• For all major entitlement benefits conveyed through the tax code except benefit exclusions: Limit the amount of such tax expenditures received by upper-income households to the average expenditure per household within the $30,000 to $50,000 bracket. In 1991, for example, this would have limited the total allowable mortgage-interest deduction to roughly $2,500. Total savings: $34.7 billion.

• For benefit tax exclusions: Get rid of all income thresholds and make Social Security just as taxable as any other cash income—except for 15 percent of pre-reform benefits. This untouched residual will offer, to even the wealthiest of today's retirees, at least a five percent tax-free return on all contributions they have personally paid into the system. Also, for households with incomes from $30,000 to $50,000, phase out half of the tax exclusion on the insurance value of Medicare (net of Medicare Part B premiums). Total savings: $16.9 billion.

Altogether, these provisions, if they had been in place in 1991, would have freed up $93 billion in the federal budget. To be sure, no one would advocate instituting all of them in one year, especially in a bad recession year. But imagine that they were phased in over four years—starting, say, in 1993. Assuming that income brackets were adjusted for inflation, and using official budget and revenue projections, total annual savings would rise to $149 billion by 1996. That would be enough to ensure that the next recovery is a genuine investment-led expansion, not another borrow-and-consume bacchanalia.

The budget savings could be considerably higher. The figures noted here reflect only about 80 percent of all federal entitlements and tax expenditures, those for which income distributions are known. The extra 20 percent included, total budget savings in 1996 could rise to more than $186 billion. Furthermore, trimming subsidies to the affluent reduces their incentive to take advantage of available benefits. Thus, to the extent that it would prompt middle- and upper-income Americans to forgo benefits altogether—for example, by retiring later, or by opting for less tax-sheltered health insurance and housing—the measure would clearly save taxpayers more than the amount a static calculation would indicate.

Because all the savings would be collected through the tax code, a single piece of legislation, falling under the jurisdiction of the tax committee in each house, would be sufficient to implement the reform. Imagine doing the same job by amending every benefits statute: the process would snake through dozens of committees, grind on for years if not decades, and ultimately be undone by interest groups.

This approach also has the virtue of treating all Americans fairly, according to their individual circumstances, unlike most other reform proposals—for example, limiting all cost-of-living adjustments (COLAS). Even a COLA freeze that discriminated against large monthly benefits would lead to obvious inequities. For a widow receiving no income other than one large Social Security check, a COLA may be essential to keep food on the table. For a triple-dipping federal pensioner receiving the minimum Social Security benefit, that same COLA may be just enough to cover the annual rise in greens fees at the club. An income-based approach takes account of the difference. Unlike most government agencies, moreover, the Internal Revenue Service is well trained in tracking dollars no matter how far they travel. Even the farm subsidy that filters down through five partnerships before appearing as personal income will have to show up, earmarked, on someone's Form 1040.

Politically, this approach balances the sacrifices asked of elderly and working-age Americans, without raising tax rates and without burdening the poor or even most of the middle class. Moreover, the plan would reduce specific programs in rough proportion to their overall size in the budget. Roughly half the savings would come from Social Security and Medicare and the related taxation of benefits. An additional 40 percent would come from other programs and tax expenditures, especially employer-paid health care and mortgage interest. Another eight to nine percent would come from federal pensions.

Would such a reform in and of itself constitute another New Deal? Hardly. The measures it would comprise are, however, the essential preconditions for the next New Deal. Without them the United States will simply see more and more of its options as a nation crowded out by the compounding costs of our subsidies to the well-off.

As always, every area of federal spending should be scrutinized. Missionless bombers must be cut. Pork-barrel waterways must be eliminated. Welfare programs targeting the poor must undergo further changes, to require the able-bodied to work and to reduce the cycle of dependency. But none of these areas is where the big money is, and it is not by reforming them that the United States will free up the resources it needs to build a more just and productive society in the next century.

Whenever one's vision of that new society—whether it includes a national health service or means-tested health vouchers, a negative income tax or a 15 percent flat tax, green cars running on hydrogen or mag-lev trains humming from city to city—to get something new, one must give up something old. A society that cannot find the resources to pay for sixty-cent tuberculosis vaccinations for ten-year-olds must ask itself why it is offering subsidized health care and housing to millionaires. Call it a rendezvous with destiny.

## DEBATING THE ISSUES: THE WELFARE REFORM DEBATE

See Lowi and Ginsberg, pp. 648–649 or brief edition, pp. 346–347

For all their policy differences, in 1996 the Republican and Democratic Parties agreed in principle on one thing: the welfare system was not working. The number of children living in poverty continued to rise, the number of people receiving welfare benefits grew, and the system generated a culture of dependency that perpetuated through generations of families. Yet the parties argued over how best to fix the system. In 1996 Congress passed, and President Clinton signed, a welfare reform bill that is a dramatic departure from the past system. The main federal program, Aid to Families with Dependent Children (AFDC), was changed from an "entitlement" program—in which spending automatically rose to provide benefits to all eligible people—to a system of replaced with "block grants" that states can use to develop their own welfare programs; states can now set spending caps for their welfare expenditures. The law also imposed work requirements, set time limits on benefits, and eliminated benefits for legal immigrants.

Peter Edelman, who was an assistant secretary for the Department of Health and Human Services during Clinton's first term, argues that signing the legislation was the "worst thing Bill Clinton has done." The time limits, which proponents argue will force people to find jobs, will in his view push more families, and especially children, into poverty and homelessness. There simply are not enough jobs for existing welfare recipients to be self sufficient, he argues. The law is mean spirited, and devoid of values representing individual responsibility and community responsibility for those in need. No one, he argues, enjoys receiving welfare, but making the transition to work can be facilitated by a properly designed program (child care subsidies, continued health care, incentives for savings), rather than mandated with support terminated regardless of employment success or failure.

Edelman also believes that allowing states to set their own policies will lead to a "race to the bottom" as states compete to lower benefits to avoid becoming welfare magnets. Mickey Kaus, however, sees the reliance upon the states as the strength of the legislation. Kaus takes Edelman head on, arguing that the states have been the source of innovation and even the reduction of welfare case loads in the past decade. Citing welfare reform efforts in several of the Great Lake states, Edelman points out the generosity of these states, and their creativity in reducing welfare case loads. Signing the bill, he argues, was rather "one of the *better things Bill Clinton has done." The debate parallels many of the ongoing debates over the proper location for public policy initiatives and implementation—the national level or the states? This debate between Kaus and Edelman originally appeared in* Slate, *an online journal edited by longtime political journalist Michael Kinsley.*

# Peter Edelman
## "The Worst Thing Bill Clinton Has Done"*

I hate welfare. To be more precise, I hate the welfare system we had until last August, when Bill Clinton signed a historic bill ending "welfare as we know it." It was a system that contributed to chronic dependency among large numbers of people who would be the first to say they would rather have a job than collect a welfare check every month—and its benefits were never enough to lift people out of poverty. In April of 1967 I helped Robert Kennedy with a speech in which he called the welfare system bankrupt and said it was hated universally, by payers and recipients alike. Criticism of welfare for not helping people to become self-supporting is nothing new.

But the bill that President Clinton signed is not welfare reform. It does not promote work effectively, and it will hurt millions of poor children by the time it is fully implemented. What's more, it bars hundreds of thousands of legal immigrants—including many who have worked in the United States for decades and paid a considerable amount in Social Security and income taxes—from receiving disability and old-age assistance and food stamps, and reduces food-stamp assistance for millions of children in working families.

When the President was campaigning for re-election last fall, he promised that if re-elected he would undertake to fix the flaws in the bill. We are now far enough into his second term to look at the validity of that promise, by assessing its initial credibility and examining what has happened since.

I resigned as the assistant secretary for planning and evaluation at the Department of Health and Human Services last September, because of my profound disagreement with the welfare bill. At the time, I confined my public statement to two sentences, saying only that I had worked as hard as I could over the past thirty-plus years to reduce poverty and that in my opinion this bill moved in the opposite direction. My judgment was that it was important to make clear the reasons for my resignation but not helpful to politicize the issue further during an election campaign. And I did want to see President Clinton re-elected. Worse is not better, in my view,

* Peter Edelman, "The Worst Thing Bill Clinton Has Done," in *The Atlantic Monthly* (March 1997). Reprinted with permission.

and Bob Dole would certainly have been worse on a wide range of issues, especially if coupled with a Republican Congress.

I feel free to speak out in more detail now, not to tell tales out of school but to clarify some of the history and especially to underscore the damage the bill will do and explain why the bill will be hard to fix in any fundamental way for a long time to come. It is also important to understand what is being done and could be done to minimize the damage in the short run, and what would be required for a real "fix": a strategy to prevent poverty and thus reduce the need for welfare in the first place.

[Three] questions are of interest now. How bad is it [the bill] really, and how can the damage be minimized as the states move to implement it? Can it be fixed in this Congress? What would a real fix be, and what would it take to make that happen?

\* \* \*

## THE BOTTOM, REACHED

This was *the* major milestone in the political race to the bottom. The President had said he was willing to sign legislation that would end a sixty-year commitment to provide assistance to all needy families with children who met the federal eligibility requirements. In the floor debate Senator Edward Kennedy, who voted against the bill, described it as "legislative child abuse."

In late 1995 and early 1996 the Republicans saved the President from having to make good on his willingness to sign a welfare block-grant bill by sending him versions of the bill that contained horrible provisions concerning food stamps, disabled children, and foster care, which he vetoed. The Republican strategy at the time was to run against the President as a hypocrite who talked welfare reform but wouldn't deliver when he had the chance.

But President Clinton was not finished. Perhaps he saw some threat to himself in the Republican strategy. Perhaps he did not see the entitlement as being quite so meaningful as others did. It is important to remember that he is not only a former governor but the former governor of Arkansas. AFDC benefits in Arkansas were so low that he might not have seen the entitlement as meaning what it does in higher-benefit states. He might have thought that as governor of Arkansas he would have been able to design a better program if he had received the federal money in the form of a block grant, without the restrictions, limited as they were, that were imposed by the federal AFDC program. And many people have remarked that he seems never to have met a governor he didn't like—an observation that appeared valid even after the 1994 elections reduced the number of Democrats in the gubernatorial ranks.

Whatever the reason, when the governors came to town for their winter meetings early last year, the President invited them to draft and submit new proposals on welfare and, for that matter, Medicaid. For a time it seemed to some observers that the President might even be willing to consider block grants for Medicaid, but it quickly became apparent that Medicaid block grants would have negative consequences for a much larger slice of the electorate than would welfare block grants. Large numbers of middle-income people had elderly parents in nursing homes whose bills were paid by Medicaid—to say nothing of the potential impact on hospitals, physicians, and the nursing homes themselves, all of which groups have substantial political clout. Welfare had no politically powerful constituency that would be hurt by conversion to block grants.

Hill Republicans, still pursuing the strategy of giving the President only bills that he could not sign, tied the governors' welfare and Medicaid proposals into a single bill. It was clear that the President would veto the combined bill, because by spring he had come out firmly against block grants for Medicaid.

As of late spring it looked as if a stalemate had been reached, and that 1996 might pass without enactment of a welfare bill. Behind the scenes, however, White House political people—Rahm Emanuel and Bruce Reed, in particular—were telling Hill Republicans almost daily that if they separated the welfare and Medicaid bills, they could get a bill that the President would sign. In early summer a new dynamic arose on the Hill. House Republicans, especially freshmen, began to worry that they were vulnerable to defeat on the basis that they had accomplished so little of what they had come to Washington to do. Thinking that Bob Dole was a sure loser anyway, they decided to save their own skins even though it would be to the detriment of the Dole candidacy. The Republicans decided to separate welfare and Medicaid, and began to move a freestanding welfare bill through Congress. The Senate and House bills were each roughly comparable to the respective Senate and House bills passed in 1995, but this time the conference outcome was very different: the conference produced a bill that was fairly close to what the Senate had passed. This time the Hill Republicans wanted the President to sign it.

The game was over. Now no one could ever say again with any credibility that this President is an old liberal.

## How Bad Is It, Really?

Before I begin my critique, I need to say something about the motivations of those who genuinely support this new approach. Some of them, anyway, had in my estimation gotten impatient with the chronicity of a significant part of the welfare caseload and the apparent intractability of the problem. I believe they had essentially decided that handing everything over to the states was the only thing left to try that didn't cost a huge amount of money. They may well understand that there will be a certain amount of suffering, and may believe that the bucket of ice-cold water being thrown on poor people now will result in a future generation that will take much more personal responsibility for itself and its children. I think they have made a terrible mistake, as I will try to show, but I respect the frustration that motivated at least some of them.

How bad, then, is it? Very bad. The story has never been fully told, because so many of those who would have shouted their opposition from the rooftops if a Republican President had done this were boxed in by their desire to see the President re-elected and in some cases by their own votes for the bill (of which, many in the Senate had been foreordained by the President's squeeze play in September of 1995).

The same de facto conspiracy of silence has enveloped the issue of whether the bill can be easily fixed. The President got a free ride through the elections on that point because no one on his side, myself included, wanted to call him on it. He even made a campaign issue of it, saying that one reason he should be re-elected was that only he could be trusted to fix the flaws in the legislation. David Broder wrote in *The Washington Post* in late August that re-electing the President in response to this plea would be like giving Jack the Ripper a scholarship to medical school.

Why is the new law so bad? To begin with, it turned out that after all the noise and heat over the past two years about balancing the budget, the only deep, multi-year budget cuts actually enacted were those in this bill, affecting low-income people.

The magnitude of the impact is stunning. Its dimensions were estimated by the Urban Institute, using the same model that produced the Department of Health and Human Services study a year earlier. To ensure credibility for the study, its authors made optimistic assumptions: two thirds of long-term recipients would find jobs, and all states would maintain their current levels of financial support for the benefit structure. Nonetheless, the study showed, the bill would move 2.6 million people, including 1.1 million children, into poverty. It also predicted some powerful effects not contained in the previous year's analysis, which had been constrained in what it could cover because it had been sponsored by the Administration. The new study showed that a total of 11 million families—10 percent of all American families—would lose income under the bill. This included more than eight million families with children, many of them working families affected by the food-stamp cuts, which would lose an average of about $1,300 per family. Many working families with income a little above what we call the poverty line (right now $12,158 for a family of three) would lose income without being made officially poor, and many families already poor would be made poorer.

The view expressed by the White House and by Hill Democrats, who wanted to put their votes for the bill in the best light, was that the parts of the bill affecting immigrants and food stamps were awful (and would be re-addressed in the future) but that the welfare-reform part of the bill was basically all right. The immigrant and food-stamp parts of the bill *are* awful, but so is the welfare part.

The immigrant provisions are strong stuff. Most legal immigrants currently in the country and nearly all future legal immigrants are to be denied Supplemental Security Income and food stamps. States have the option of denying them Medicaid and welfare as well. New immigrants will be excluded from most federal means-tested programs, including Medicaid, for the first five years they are in the country. All of this will save about $22 billion over the next six years—about 40 percent of the savings in the bill. The SSI cuts are the worst. Almost 800,000 legal immigrants receive SSI, and most of these will be cut off. Many elderly and disabled noncitizens who have been in the United States for a long time and lack the mental capacity to do what is necessary to become citizens will be thrown out of their homes or out of nursing homes or other group residential settings that are no longer reimbursed for their care.

The food-stamp cuts are very troubling too. Exclusive of the food-stamp cuts for immigrants, they involve savings of about $24 billion. Almost half of that is in across-the-board cuts in the way benefits are calculated. About two thirds of the benefit reductions will be borne by families with children, many of them working families (thus reflecting a policy outcome wildly inconsistent with the stated purposes of the overall bill). Perhaps the most troubling cut is the one limiting food stamps to three months out of every three years for unemployed adults under age fifty who are not raising children. The Center on Budget and Policy Priorities describes this as "probably the single harshest provision written into a major safety net program in at least 30 years"—although it turns out that more states than the drafters anticipated can ask for an exception that was written to accommodate places with disproportionate unemployment. One of the great strengths of food stamps until now has been that it was the one major program for the poor in which help was based only on need, with no reference to family status or age. It was the safety net under the safety net. That principle of pure need-based eligibility has now been breached.

Neither the cuts for immigrants nor the food-stamp cuts have anything to do with welfare reform. Many of them are just mean, with no good policy justification. The bill also contains other budget and benefit reductions unrelated to welfare. The definition of SSI eligibility for disabled children has been narrowed, which will result in removal from the rolls of 100,000 to 200,000 of the 965,000 children who currently receive SSI. Although there was broad agreement that some tightening in eligibility was warranted, the changes actually made will result in the loss of coverage for some children who if they were adults would be considered disabled. Particularly affected are children with multiple impairments no one of which is severe enough to meet the new, more stringent criteria. Child-nutrition programs have also been cut, by nearly $3 billion over six years, affecting meals for children in family day care and in the summer food program. Federal funding for social services has been cut by a six-year total of $2.5 billion. This is a 15 percent cut in an important area, and will hamper the states in providing exactly the kind of counseling and support that families often need if a parent is going to succeed in the workplace.

So this is hardly just a welfare bill. In fact, most of its budget reductions come in programs for the poor other than welfare, and many of them affect working families. Many of them are just cuts, not reform. (The bill also contains an elaborate reform of federal child-support laws, which had broad bipartisan support and could easily have been enacted as separate legislation.)

This brings us to welfare itself. Basically, the block grants mean that the states can now do almost anything they want—even provide no cash benefits at all. There is no requirement in the new law that the assistance provided to needy families be in the form of cash. States may contract out any or all of what they do to charitable, religious, or private organizations, and provide certificates or vouchers to recipients of assistance which can be redeemed with a contract organization. So the whole system could be run by a corporation or a religious organization if a state so chooses (although the latter could raise constitutional questions, depending on how the arrangement is configured). Or a state could delegate everything to the counties, since the law explicitly says that the program need not be run "in a uniform manner" throughout a state, and the counties could have varying benefit and program frameworks. For good or for ill, the states are in the process of working their way through an enormous—indeed, a bewildering—array of choices, which many of them are ill equipped to make, and which outside advocates are working hard to help them make well.

The change in the structure is total. Previously there was a national definition of eligibility. With some limitations regarding two-parent families, any needy family with children could get help. There were rules about participation in work and training, but anybody who played by the rules could continue to get assistance. If people were thrown off the rolls without justification, they could get a hearing to set things right, and could go to court if necessary. The system will no longer work that way.

The other major structural change is that federal money is now capped. The block grants total $16.4 billion annually for the country, with no new funding for jobs and training and placement efforts, which are in fact very expensive activities to carry out. For the first couple of years most of the states will get a little more money than they have been getting, because the formula gives them what they were spending a couple of years ago, and welfare rolls have actually decreased somewhat almost everywhere (a fact frequently touted by the President, although one might wonder why the new law was so urgently needed if the rolls had gone down by more than two million people without it).

Many governors are currently crowing about this "wind-fall" of new federal money. But what they are not telling their voters is that the federal funding will stay the same for the next six years, with no adjustment for inflation or population growth, so by 2002 states will have considerably less federal money to spend than they would have had under AFDC. The states will soon have to choose between benefits and job-related activities, with the very real possibility that they will run out of federal money before the end of a given year. A small contingency fund exists for recessions, and an even smaller fund to compensate for disproportionate population increases, but it is easy to foresee a time when states will have to either tell applicants to wait for the next fiscal year or spend their own money to keep benefits flowing.

The bill closes its eyes to all the facts and complexities of the real world and essentially says to recipients, Find a job. That has a nice bumper-sticker ring to it. But as a one-size-fits-all recipe it is totally unrealistic.

Total cutoffs of help will be felt right away only by immigrants and disabled children—not insignificant exceptions. The big hit, which could be very big, will come when the time limits go into effect—in five years, or less if the state so chooses—or when a recession hits. State treasuries are relatively flush at the moment, with the nation in the midst of a modest boom period. When the time limits first take effect, a large group of people in each state will fall into the abyss all at once. Otherwise the effects will be fairly gradual. Calcutta will not break out instantly on American streets.

To the extent that there are any constraints on the states in the new law, they are negative. The two largest—and they are very large—are the time limit and the work-participation requirements.

There is a cumulative lifetime limit of five years on benefits paid for with federal money, and states are free to impose shorter time limits if they like. One exception is permitted, to be applied at the state's discretion: as much as 20 percent of the caseload at any particular time may be people who have already received assistance for five years. This sounds promising until one understands that about half the current caseload is composed of people who have been on the rolls longer than five years. A recent study sponsored by the Kaiser Foundation found that 30 percent of the caseload is composed of women who are caring for disabled children or are disabled themselves. The time limits will be especially tough in states that have large areas in chronic recession—for example, the coal-mining areas of Appalachia. And they will be even tougher when the country as a whole sinks into recession. It will make no difference if a recipient has played by all the rules and sought work faithfully, as required. When the limit is reached and the state is unable or unwilling to grant an exception, welfare will be over for that family forever.

Under the work-participation requirements, 25 percent of the caseload must be working or in training this year, and 50 percent by 2002. For two-parent families 75 percent of the caseload must be working or in training, and the number goes up to 90 percent in two years. The Congressional Budget Office estimates that the bill falls $12 billion short of providing enough funding over the next six years for the states to meet the work requirements. Even the highly advertised increased child-care funding falls more than $1 billion short of providing enough funding for all who would have to work in order for the work requirements to be satisfied. States that fail to meet the work requirements lose increasing percentages of their block grants.

The states are given a rather Machiavellian out. The law in effect assumes that any reduction in the rolls reflects people who have gone to work. So states have a de facto incentive to get people off the rolls in any way they can, not necessarily by getting them into work activities.

The states can shift a big chunk of their own money out of the program if they want to. There is no matching requirement for the states, only a maintenance-of-effort requirement that each state keep spending at least 80 percent of what it was previously contributing. This will allow as much as $40 billion nationally to be withheld from paying benefits over the next six years, on top of the $55 billion cut by the bill itself. Moreover, the 80 percent requirement is a static number, so the funding base will immediately start being eroded by inflation.

Besides being able to transfer some of their own money out, the states are allowed to transfer up to 30 percent of their federal block grants to spending on child care or other social services. Among other things, this will encourage them to adopt time limits shorter than five years, because this would save federal money that could then be devoted to child care and other help that families need in order to be able to go to work. Hobson's choice will flourish.

The contingency fund to cushion against the impact of recessions or local economic crises is wholly inadequate—$2 billion over five years. Welfare costs rose by $6 billion in three years during the recession of the early nineties.

The federal AFDC law required the states to make decisions on applications within forty-five days and to pay, retroactively if necessary, from the thirtieth day after the application was put in. There is no such requirement in the new law. All we know from the new law is that the state has to tell the Secretary of Health and Human Services what its "objective criteria" will be for "the delivery of benefits," and how it will accord "fair and equitable treatment" to recipients, including how it will give "adversely affected" recipients an opportunity to be heard. This is weak, to say the least.

## FIFTY WELFARE POLICIES

Given this framework, what can we predict will happen? No state will want to be a magnet for people from other states by virtue of a relatively generous benefit structure. This is common sense, unfortunately. As states seek to ensure that they are not more generous than their neighbors, they will try to make their benefit structures less, not more, attractive. If states delegate decisions about benefit levels to their counties, the race to the bottom will develop within states as well.

I do not wish to imply that all states, or even most states, are going to take the opportunity to engage in punitive policy behavior. There will be a political dynamic in the process whereby each state implements the law. Advocates can organize and express themselves to good effect, and legislatures can frustrate or soften governors' intentions. There is another important ameliorating factor: many welfare administrators are concerned about the dangers that lie in the new law and will seek to implement it as constructively as they can, working to avoid some of the more radical negative possibilities.

Citizens can make a difference in what happens in their state. They can push to make sure that it doesn't adopt a time limit shorter than five years, doesn't reduce its own investment of funds, doesn't cut benefits, doesn't transfer money out of the block grant, doesn't dismantle procedural protections, and doesn't create bureaucratic hurdles that will discourage recipients. They can press for state and local funds to help legal immigrants who have been cut off from SSI or food stamps and children who have been victimized by the time limits. They can advocate an energetic and realistic jobs and training strategy, with maximum involvement by the private sector. And they can begin organizing and putting together the elements of a real fix, which I will lay out shortly.

## THE JOBS GAP

Even given effective advocacy, relatively responsive legislatures and welfare administrators, and serious efforts to find private-sector jobs, the deck is stacked against success, especially in states that have high concentrations of poverty and large welfare caseloads. The basic issue is jobs. *There simply are not enough jobs now.* Four million adults are receiving Aid to Families with Dependent Children. Half of them are long-term recipients. In city after city around America the number of people who will have to find jobs will quickly dwarf the number of new jobs created in recent years. Many cities have actually lost jobs over the past five to ten years. New York City, for example, has lost 227,000 jobs since 1990, and the New York metropolitan area overall has lost 260,000 over the same period. New York City had more than 300,000 adults in the AFDC caseload in 1995, to say nothing of the adults without dependent children who are receiving general assistance. Statistics aside, all one has to do is go to Chicago, or to Youngstown, Ohio, or to Newark, or peruse William Julius Wilson's powerful new book, *When Work Disappears*, to get the point. The fact is that there are not enough appropriate private-sector jobs in appropriate locations even now, when unemployment is about as low as it ever gets in this country.

For some people, staying on welfare was dictated by economics, because it involved a choice between the "poor support" of welfare, to use the Harvard professor David Ellwood's term, and the even worse situation of a low-wage job, with its take-home pay reduced by the out-of-pocket costs of commuting and day care, and the potentially incalculable effects of losing health coverage. With time limits these people will no longer have that choice, unappetizing as it was, and will be forced to take a job that leaves them even deeper in poverty. How many people will be able to get and keep a job, even a lousy job, is impossible to say, but it is far from all of those who have been on welfare for an extended period of time.

The labor market, even in its current relatively heated state, is not friendly to people with little education and few marketable skills, poor work habits, and various personal and family problems that interfere with regular and punctual attendance. People spend long spells on welfare or are headed in that direction for reasons other than economic choice or, for that matter, laziness. If we are going to put long-term welfare recipients to work—and we should make every effort to do so—it will be difficult and it will cost money to train people, to place them, and to provide continuing support so that they can keep a job once they get it. If they are to have child care and health coverage, that will cost still more. Many of the jobs that people will get will not offer health coverage, so transitional Medicaid for a year or two will not suffice. People who have been on welfare for a long time will too often not make it in their first job and will need continuing help toward and into a second job. Both because the private sector may well not produce enough jobs right away and because not all welfare recipients will be ready for immediate placement in a private-sector job, it will be appropriate also to use public jobs or jobs with nonprofit organizations at least as a transition if not as permanent positions. All of this costs real money.

For a lot of people it will not work at all. Kansas City's experience is sadly instructive here. In the past two years, in a very well-designed and well-implemented effort, a local program was able to put 1,409 out of 15,562 welfare recipients to work. As of last December only 730 were still at work. The efforts of Toby Herr and Project Match in Chicago's Cabrini-Green public-housing project are another case in point. Working individually and intensively with women and supporting them through successive jobs until they found one they were able to keep, Herr had managed to place 54 percent of her clients in year-round jobs at the end of five years. This is a remarkable (and unusual) success rate, but it also shows how unrealistic is a structure that offers only a 20 percent exception to the five-year time limit.

I want to be very clear: I am not questioning the willingness of long-term welfare recipients to work. Their unemployment is significantly related to their capacity to work, whether for personal or family reasons, far more than to their willingness to work. Many long-term welfare recipients are functionally disabled even if they are not disabled in a legal sense. News coverage of what the new law will mean has been replete with heartbreaking stories of women who desperately want to work but have severe trouble learning how to operate a cash register or can't remember basic things they need to master. A study in the state of Washington shows that 36 percent of the caseload have learning disabilities that have never been remediated. Many others have disabled children or parents for whom they are the primary caretakers. Large numbers are victims of domestic violence and risk physical retaliation if they enter the workplace. These personal and family problems make such people poor candidates for work in the best of circumstances. Arbitrary time limits on their benefits will not make them likelier to gain and hold employment. When unemployment goes back up to six or seven or eight percent nationally, as it will at some point, the idea that the private sector will employ and continue to employ those who are the hardest to employ will be even more fanciful than it is at the current, relatively propitious moment.

When the time limits take effect, the realities occasioned by the meeting of a bottom-line-based labor market with so many of our society's last hired and first fired will come into focus. Of course, a considerable number will not fall off the cliff. An increased number will have obtained jobs along the way. The time limits will help some people to discipline themselves and ration their years of available assistance. Some will move in with family or friends when their benefits are exhausted. The 20 percent exception will help as well.

But there will be suffering. Some of the damage will be obvious—more homelessness, for example, with more demand on already strapped shelters and soup kitchens. The ensuing problems will also appear as increases in the incidence of other problems, directly but perhaps not provably owing to the impact of the welfare bill. There will be more malnutrition and more crime, increased infant mortality, and increased drug and alcohol abuse. There will be increased family violence and abuse against children and women, and a consequent significant spillover of the problem into the already overloaded child-welfare system and battered-women's shelters.

## Can the Welfare Bill Be Fixed This Year?

I am amazed by the number of people who have bought the line that the bill was some little set of adjustments that could easily be done away with. Congress and the President have dynamited a structure that was in place for six decades. A solid bipartisan majority of Congress and the President himself have a stake in what they have already done. Fundamental change in the bill is therefore not possible this year. So the answer to the question is no, not in any fundamental way.

One possible area for adjustment is in the immigrant and food-stamp provisions. These occasioned the most hand-wringing from the President and some of the people who voted for the bill. They could be changed without redoing everything. The President has made some proposals for limited change on these items.

The bigger question is welfare. If there is going to be a short-term fix of the new law, it will be not in the fundamentals of the new structure but rather in some of the details. It might possibly include the following, although I hasten to say that even this list stretches credulity.

- *Jobs.* Congress could make extra funds available to the states for job creation, wage subsidies, training, placement, support and retention services, and so on. The President has proposed a fund of $3 billion over three years for this kind of activity, saying it would result in a million new jobs. As campaign rhetoric, this was pure spin. It amounts to $3,000 per job. There is simply no way in which $3,000 per job will get a million jobs for people who have been on the welfare rolls for extended periods of time. The President has also proposed a modest additional tax credit for hiring welfare recipients. This, too, will have little practical effect.

- *Time limits.* The Democrats tried very hard to create a voucher covering basic necessities for children in families that had run up against the time limit. The idea failed by a narrow margin in the Senate, and is worth pursuing. Another item worth advocating would be raising the 20 percent exception to the time limit to 25 or even 30 percent.

- *Work requirements.* The states are chafing under the requirements about the percentage of the caseload that has to be participating in work or related activities. It would help a little if people were permitted to receive vocational training for longer than the twelve months the law allows.

- *Limits on state flexibility in the use of funds.* The law is excessively flexible on what the states can do with the block-grant funds. A number of possible changes would be helpful: reducing the percentage that can be transferred out of the block; raising the requirement for states' contributions of their own funds; requiring states to comply with the plans they adopt; requiring states to process applications for assistance expeditiously; and clarifying the procedural protections for people denied or cut off from assistance.

- *Data.* It is vitally important that adequate data be gathered and reported on what happens under the new legislation. The new law contains some funding for research and some instructions about data to be gathered, but additional funds and specification would be helpful.

If reliable and affordable health care and child care were added to this list, and were available beyond a transitional period, it would help a lot. However, my crystal ball tells me that whatever is enacted in these areas will be modest at best, and the new structure will remain substantially in place. And of course not even these adjustments would solve the fundamental problems created when the previous structure was dynamited: the disappearance of the national definition of eligibility and of the guarantee that federal funds will be available for all eligible children.

## What Would a Real Fix Involve?

A real fix would involve, first, jobs, jobs, jobs—preferably and as a first priority in the private sector, but also in the public sector, where there is real work to be done. And then everything that enables people to be productive citizens. Schools that teach every child as well as they teach every other child. Safe neighborhoods. Healthy communities. Continuing health-care and day-care coverage, so that people can not only go to work but also keep on working. Ending the racial and ethnic discrimination that plagues too many young people who try to enter the job market for the first time.

When we discuss jobs, we need to be talking about opportunities for men and women both. That may seem obvious, but the welfare bill skews our focus. By allocating to long-term welfare recipients such a large share of the limited resources available for jobs and training, we may be draining funds and attention from others who deserve to be a higher priority. Inner-city young men come particularly to mind. We need to be promoting responsible fatherhood, marriage, and two-parent families. If young men cannot find work, they are far less likely to marry. They may have children, but economics and low self-esteem may defeat responsibility. Tough child-support enforcement is part of the solution, but genuine opportunity and clear pathways to opportunity are vital.

The outside world tends to believe that the inner city is hopeless. (I do not mean to neglect strategies to reduce rural poverty.) That is not the case. In the toughest neighborhoods, with all the dangers and pitfalls of street life, there are young people who beat the odds, stay in school and graduate, and go to college or get a job. These young people have exceptional strength and resiliency. But there are many more who could make it with a little extra support and attention. It is enormously important that we increase the number of young people who make it. We give a lot of lip service to prevention, whether of crime or drug abuse or teen pregnancy. But we will never prevent these negative outcomes as well as we could until we pursue a general strategy of creating opportunity and clear pathways to opportunity—a positive youth-development strategy.

Many of the jobs that welfare recipients and other low-income people get do not pay enough to pull them out of poverty. Continuing attention to the minimum wage and the Earned Income Tax Credit will be necessary. States should insist, as the city of Baltimore has, that all their contractors pay all their workers a sufficient wage to keep them out of poverty (or at least approximately enough to keep a family of four out of poverty), and should fund their contracts accordingly. Current child-care and health-care policies are insufficient to allow low-wage workers to stay out of poverty even if transitional subsidies let them escape temporarily when they leave the welfare rolls. Federal and state child-care subsidies should help all workers who would otherwise be poor, not just those who have recently left the welfare rolls. And at the end of the day we still have 40 million Americans, including 10 million children, who do not have health coverage. We still have to deal with that as part of a real antipoverty strategy.

We have been reduced to the politics of the waitress mom. She says, all too legitimately, "I bust my tail. I don't have decent child care. I don't have health coverage. Why should 'these people' get what I don't have?" We started to bring greater equity to the working poor but, except for the recent minimum-wage increase, progress was halted by the 1994 congressional elections. A real fix would help the waitress mom as well as those a rung below her on the income ladder.

We are not just talking policy; we are talking values. We are talking people, especially young people growing up, who understand that they have to take responsibility for themselves, both as earners and as parents.

Personal responsibility and community responsibility need to intersect. The community has a responsibility to help instill and nurture values. The community has a responsibility to offer support, especially to children and youths, so that everyone has an opportunity to acquire the tools necessary to achieve the personal responsibility that is such a vital element in the equation. The community has a responsibility to help parents do their job. And community means something different from programs, something larger, although programs are part of the equation. Liberals have tended to think in terms of programs. The community's taking responsibility is a much larger idea. But communities cannot succeed in isolation. National leadership and policy are essential as well.

Welfare is what we do when everything else fails. It is what we do for people who can't make it after a genuine attempt has been mounted to help the maximum possible number of people to make it. In fact, much of what we do in the name of welfare is more appropriately a subject for disability policy. The debate over welfare misses the point when all it seeks to do is tinker with welfare eligibility, requirements, and sanctions. The 1996 welfare law misses the point.

To do what needs to be done is going to take a lot of work—organizing, engaging in public education, broadening the base of people who believe that real action to reduce poverty and promote self-sufficiency in America is important and possible. We need to watch very carefully, and we need to document and publicize, the impact of the 1996 welfare legislation on children and families across America. We need to do everything we can to influence the choices the states have to make under the new law. We *can* ultimately come out in a better place. We should not want to go back to what we had. It was not good social policy. We want people to be able to hold up their heads and raise their children in dignity. The best that can be said about this terrible legislation is that perhaps we will learn from it and eventually arrive at a better approach. I am afraid, though, that along the way we will do some serious injury to American children, who should not have had to suffer from our national backlash.

# Mickey Kaus
## "[Response to Edelman]"*

Dear Peter,

In the cover article of the March Atlantic, you say that signing last year's Republican welfare-reform bill was "The Worst Thing Bill Clinton Has Done," something that will "hurt millions of poor children" while doing little to promote work. Indeed, you quit your position as an assistant secretary of health and human services to protest the president's action. (Be honest: Were you really going to stick around for his second term, even if he'd vetoed the bill?) Many of my friends have found your article a crystallizing summary of why they opposed the bill and consider Clinton an unprincipled opportunist. The Economist called it a "searing indictment." You have George Will and Anthony Lewis on your side, as well as Robert Reich, Sen. Edward Kennedy, and Sen. Daniel Patrick Moynihan (who anticipates "something approaching an Apocalypse").

I didn't find your article convincing at all, but then that's not surprising. My journalistic ego is heavily invested in the notion that Clinton's decision was, on balance, the right one. What is surprising is the way you ignore or underplay the evidence that has been accumulating since that decision. Neither of us, nor anybody else, knows whether the law will ultimately be a triumph or a disaster. There are too many uncertainties. But Clinton's reasoning is looking stronger and stronger, and yours weaker and weaker.

A note about what I won't argue. I won't claim that the new welfare law is wonderful. We could each imagine much better bills; they might not even be that dissimilar. (Like you, I favor a large program of public jobs.) The issue is only whether the result of the new law will be better than what would have happened if Clinton hadn't signed it. Second, we agree that parts of the bill really are terrible, specifically the cuts in assistance to elderly and disabled legal immigrants, and the gratuitous cuts in food-stamp aid. Clinton thinks these cuts are terrible too—he is said to have described the legislation as "a decent welfare bill wrapped in a sack of shit." The immigrant and food-stamp cuts are the sack of shit. He is trying to reverse many of them. But your article's point is precisely that it's not just those provisions that are disastrous. You also denounce the core of the bill: the replacement of the basic federal welfare program, Aid to Families with Dependent Children, with a "block grant" that states can spend on aid programs of their own devising. "The immigrant and food-stamp parts of the bill are awful," you argue, "but so is the welfare part."

Is it really? Here are three reasons why it's not:

1) The caseload is dropping. You say, "welfare rolls have actually decreased somewhat" over the past two years. That's a highly strategic

* Mickey Kaus, "[Response to Edelman]" from *Slate*, www.slate.com) (April 7, 1997). Reprinted with permission. *Slate* is a trademark of Microsoft Corporation.

understatement. In fact, as welfare reform has been debated and implemented, caseloads have been falling through the floor. Nationally, they've fallen about 8 percent since 1994, and they are still dropping. The magnitude of this drop wasn't clear when Clinton signed the law last year, though conservatives predicted it (liberals tended to discount the possibility). True, the drop might not necessarily be good news, if women with children are being forced off the rolls into degradation. But there is little evidence, as of now, that this is happening. Massachusetts surveyed those who left welfare during two months last year. About half went into jobs; another 9 percent no longer qualified for aid because of other income (primarily child support) or support from family and friends. Most of the remainder no longer had children young enough to receive aid, or else they had left the state.

And it's not just that people are leaving the rolls. Fewer are applying. In Wisconsin, new applications dropped almost 50 percent after the introduction of reforms encouraging (and ultimately requiring) work. This at least suggests that potential recipients are responding to the end of the welfare "entitlement" by making other, better choices with their lives—taking jobs, perhaps even avoiding out-of-wedlock births.

Note that even if those who have disappeared from the rolls haven't taken jobs, the caseload drop is probably still good news. Some erstwhile recipients may marry or live with a breadwinner. Others may be living with relatives who then have ways (and reasons) to encourage work or marriage that government caseworkers don't have.

Is welfare reform responsible for the caseload drop? A strong economy is certainly part of the explanation (though the big welfare increase of the late 1960s occurred in a booming economy). But reform has played a part. A USA Today survey discovered that the caseload began to drop especially rapidly in the four months of 1996 that followed Clinton's signing of the welfare bill. And, not surprisingly, caseloads have fallen most in the states that most diligently attempt to require recipients to work. Both Wisconsin and neighboring Minnesota have strong economies—in Minnesota unemployment averaged 3.9 percent from 1994 through 1996; in Wisconsin it averaged 4.0 percent. But Minnesota's caseload dropped only 4.9 percent last year. Wisconsin, which instituted a relatively strict work requirement, saw a drop of 28.4 percent. (Even in Milwaukee, which has a substantial inner-city ghetto, caseloads have fallen by 23 percent.)

The clearest implication of the caseload drop, which your article deliberately downplays, is that there will now be much more money available for reform—for providing jobs and child care, which costs more than just sending welfare checks. Under the old AFDC system, federal payments to the states varied with the caseload, and those payments would now have dropped automatically. Under the new block-grant system, the federal payment of $ 6.4 billion remains fixed at its record high 1994–95 level, despite the 8 percent smaller caseload. In effect there is at least an 8 percent boost in funding for welfare, compared with what would have happened if Clinton hadn't signed the bill. This extra money is there whether the caseload drop is due to the strong economy or due to welfare reform itself.

So it is wrong to say, as even the editor of SLATE has said, that the bill requires expensive work programs but "supplies less money" to do them. It supplies more money. And it's wrong for you to cite a Congressional Budget Office estimate that "the bill falls $ 2 billion short of providing enough funding over the next six years" to put recipients to work. That CBO estimate did not take into account the extra money freed up by the caseload drop. An 8 percent drop would almost certainly be enough to wipe out the $ 2 billion shortfall. (The crude math: 8 percent of $ 6.4 billion times six years is $ 7.7 billion.) None of this guarantees that states will use the extra money to provide work and child care—they could siphon it off into road building or tax cuts—but most states will have the money if they want to use it.

2) The bill's "draconian" provisions are phony. You cite two requirements of the law as especially onerous. The first is "an absolute lifetime limit of five years, cumulatively, that a family can be on welfare. . . . The big hit, which could be very big, will come when the time limits go into effect . . . [and] a large group of people in each state will fall into the abyss all at once." The mainstream press has played up the five-year limit as well, noting, as you do, that the law allows states to exempt a mere 20 percent of the caseload.

But, as you know, the law sets a time limit only on the use of federal dollars. States provide about 45 percent of welfare funding themselves, and nothing prevents them from using that money to keep families on the rolls past five years. That's the huge, eviscerating loophole in the "absolute" five-year limit. The "20 percent exemption" is just gravy. A recent Wall Street Journal article described the successful efforts of Mark Greenberg, a very smart lawyer at the Center for Law and Social Policy, to show states how to get around the time limits. "If a state doesn't want the time limit to run, it has substantial ability to do that," Greenberg notes.

Even crazier is your assertion that "the states are chafing under the requirements about the percentage of the caseload that has to be participating in work or related activities." In fact, states are discovering that the requirements are surprisingly easy to meet, or to evade. In 1998, for example, each state must nominally get 30 percent of its caseload into "work activities." But read the law's fine print and you see that states get to subtract the caseload drop since 1995—about 5 percent, on average, and growing. States also get to count the approximately 8 percent of the caseload that already works part time—so they are up to 23 percent before they even start. Add on various other exemptions and reductions (for vocational education, for example, or teens in high school) and you realize that any governor who thinks he can't easily meet the bill's work requirements through the end of the century just isn't paying attention.

3) Let 50 reforms compete. Basically the law lets states do what they want with welfare. If they want to spend money to provide public jobs and

child care (as we both hope they do), the money will most likely be there. If they prefer to keep welfare families on the dole, they will be able to do so, whatever the "absolute" limits and requirements seem to say. The overriding rationale for the law is precisely the freedom it gives the states: With 50 jurisdictions trying various reforms, we will find out soon enough which ones work and which ones don't.

That wouldn't have happened if Clinton had vetoed the bill. Your article suggests that without the bill states could still "experiment with reform under the existing law." But in fact state reforms had to be approved by the Department of Health and Human Services, for which you worked. One of the states that applied for such permission was Wisconsin. The Wisconsin proposal wasn't perfect, but it was mighty close. It required work of virtually all welfare recipients, but if private-sector jobs were unavailable, it proposed to provide tens of thousands of public "community-service" jobs. Wisconsin offered subsidized child care to single mothers who needed it —not just to mothers on welfare, but also (as you recommend in your Atlantic piece) to poor working mothers who have never gone on welfare. It even offered subsidized health care—again, not just to those on welfare, but to all low-income families.

What was the reaction of your department (HHS) to this promising, relatively liberal, well-funded proposal? Permission was never granted. Why? In part because Wisconsin didn't offer to pay community-service wages that increased with family size—as if private jobs pay wages that increase when you have another child. For me, at least, this was the final straw. If you and the other officials at HHS wouldn't allow the best welfare reform in the nation to proceed—at a time of maximum reformist pressure, with an election looming and the president himself praising Wisconsin's plan—then it was time to eliminate the HHS veto over reform.

Recently I debated you on the radio, and you actually boasted that HHS never granted Wisconsin permission to try its reform! But now that Clinton has signed the block-grant bill, Wisconsin doesn't have to ask you. Which is why, I think, signing the bill was one of the better things Bill Clinton has done.

# 16

# Foreign Policy and World Politics

## The Values in American Foreign Policy

*Lowi and Ginsberg, pp. 689–694 or brief edition, pp. 369–371*

*This article, which George Kennan wrote while serving as a State Department planner, set out the policy of containment which was to guide U.S. Cold War policy toward the Soviet Union. Kennan felt that contemporary thinking about the Soviet Union was caught between two unrealistic poles: hard core anti-communists who feared creeping Socialism within the United States, and ac-commodationists such as Henry Wallace who felt that the United States could induce the Soviets to pursue a more cooperative stance. Neither side accurately read Soviet intentions, Kennan felt. He argued that the Soviet leadership was authoritarian as well as pragmatic, and they were more concerned with power and control than any ideological purity. The Soviets would respond to consistent U.S. counter pressure: "firm and vigilant containment," he concluded, would keep the Soviets from expanding their influence too far beyond their borders. To Kennan's dismay, his article was widely interpreted as confirming a Soviet drive for global domination; this was not his intent.*

## "X" [George Kennan]
## "The Sources of Soviet Conduct"*

The political personality of Soviet power as we know it today [in 1947] is the product of ideology and circumstances: ideology inherited by the present Soviet leaders from the movement in which they had their political origin, and circumstances of the power which they now have exercised for nearly three decades in Russia. There can be few tasks of psychological analysis more difficult than to try to trace the interaction of these two forces and the relative role of each in the determination of official Soviet conduct. Yet the attempt must be made if that conduct is to be understood and effectively countered. . . .

Now the outstanding circumstance concerning the Soviet régime is that down to the present day this process of political consolidation has never been completed and the men in the Kremlin have continued to be

---

* "X" [George Kennan], "The Sources of Soviet Conduct" in *Foreign Affairs*, Vol. 25 (1947): 566–582. Reprinted by permission of *Foreign Affairs*. Copyright (1947) by the Council on Foreign Relations, Inc.

predominantly absorbed with the struggle to secure and make absolute
the power which they seized in November 1917. They have endeavored to
secure it primarily against forces at home, within Soviet society itself. But
they have also endeavored to secure it against the outside world. For ideology, as we have seen, taught them that the outside world was hostile and
that it was their duty eventually to overthrow the political forces beyond
their borders. The powerful hands of Russian history and tradition
reached up to sustain them in this feeling. Finally, their own aggressive in-
transigence with respect to the outside world began to find its own reaction. . . .

Now it lies in the nature of the mental world of the Soviet leaders, as
well as in the character of their ideology, that no opposition to them can
be officially recognized as having any merit or justification whatsoever.
Such opposition can flow, in theory, only from the hostile and incorrigible
forces of dying capitalism. As long as remnants of capitalism were officially
recognized as existing in Russia, it was possible to place on them, as an
internal element, part of the blame for the maintenance of a dictatorial
form of society. But as these remnants were liquidated, little by little, this
justification fell away; and when it was indicated officially that they had
been finally destroyed, it disappeared altogether. And this fact created one
of the most basic of the compulsions which came to act upon the Soviet
régime: since capitalism no longer existed in Russia and since it could not
be admitted that there could be serious or widespread opposition to the
Kremlin springing spontaneously from the liberated masses under its authority, it became necessary to justify the retention of the dictatorship by
stressing the menace of capitalism abroad. . . .

[T]he innate antagonism between capitalism and Socialism . . . has become imbedded in foundations of Soviet power. It has profound implications for Russia's conduct as a member of international society. It means
that there can never be on Moscow's side any sincere assumption of a community of aims between the Soviet Union and powers which are regarded
as capitalist. It must invariably be assumed in Moscow that the aims of the
capitalist world are antagonistic to the Soviet régime, and therefore to the
interests of the peoples it controls. If the Soviet Government occasionally
sets its signature to documents which would indicate the contrary, this is
to be regarded as a tactical manœuvre permissible in dealing with the enemy (who is without honor) and should be taken in the spirit of *caveat emp-
tor*. Basically, the antagonism remains. It is postulated. And from it flow
many of the phenomena which we find disturbing in the Kremlin's conduct of foreign policy: the secretiveness, the lack of frankness, the duplic-
ity, the wary suspiciousness, and the basic unfriendliness of purpose. These
phenomena are there to stay, for the foreseeable future. There can be variations of degree and of emphasis. When there is something the Russians
want from us, one or the other of these features of their policy may be
thrust temporarily into the background; and when that happens there will
always be Americans who will leap forward with gleeful announcements

that "the Russians have changed," and some who will even try to take credit for having brought about such "changes." But we should not be misled by tactical manœuvres. These characteristics of Soviet policy, like the postulate from which they flow, are basic to the internal nature of Soviet power, and will be with us, whether in the foreground or the background, until the internal nature of Soviet power is changed.

This means that we are going to continue for a long time to find the Russians difficult to deal with. It does not mean that they should be considered as embarked upon a do-or-die program to overthrow our society by a given date. The theory of the inevitability of the eventual fall of capitalism has the fortunate connotation that there is no hurry about it. . . .

This brings us to the second of the concepts important to contemporary Soviet outlook. That is the infallibility of the Kremlin. The Soviet concept of power, which permits no focal points of organization outside the Party itself, requires that the Party leadership remain in theory the sole repository of truth. For if truth were to be found elsewhere, there would be justification for its expression in organized activity. But it is precisely that which the Kremlin cannot and will not permit.

The leadership of the Communist Party is therefore always right, and has been always right ever since in 1929 Stalin formalized his personal power by announcing that decisions of the Politburo were being taken unanimously.

On the principle of infallibility there rests the iron discipline of the Communist Party. In fact, the two concepts are mutually self-supporting. Perfect discipline requires recognition of infallibility. Infallibility requires the observance of discipline. And the two together go far to determine the behaviorism of the entire Soviet apparatus of power. But their effect cannot be understood unless a third factor be taken into account: namely, the fact that the leadership is at liberty to put forward for tactical purposes any particular thesis which it finds useful to the cause at any particular moment and to require the faithful and unquestioning acceptance of that thesis by the members of the movement as a whole. This means that truth is not a constant but is actually created, for all intents and purposes, by the Soviet leaders themselves. It may vary from week to week, from month to month. It is nothing absolute and immutable—nothing which flows from objective reality. It is only the most recent manifestation of the wisdom of those in whom the ultimate wisdom is supposed to reside, because they represent the logic of history.

The accumulative effect of these factors is to give to the whole subordinate apparatus of Soviet power an unshakeable stubbornness and steadfastness in its orientation. This orientation can be changed at will by the Kremlin but by no other power. Once a given party line has been laid down on a given issue of current policy, the whole Soviet governmental machine, including the mechanism of diplomacy, moves inexorably along the prescribed path, like a persistent toy automobile wound up and headed in a given direction, stopping only when it meets with some un-answerable force. The individuals who are the components of this machine are unamenable to argument or reason which comes to them from outside sources. Their whole training has taught them to mistrust and discount the glib persuasiveness of the outside world. Like the white dog before the phonograph, they hear only the "master's voice." And if they are to be called off from the purposes last dictated to them, it is the master who must call them off. Thus the foreign representative cannot hope that his words will make any impression on them. The most that he can hope is that they will be transmitted to those at the top, who are capable of changing the party line. But even those are not likely to be swayed by any normal logic in the words of the bourgeois representative. Since there can be no appeal to common purposes, there can be no appeal to common mental approaches. For this reason, facts speak louder than words to the ears of the Kremlin; and words carry the greatest weight when they have the ring of reflecting, or being backed up by, facts of unchallengeable validity.

But we have seen that the Kremlin is under no ideological compulsion to accomplish its purposes in a hurry. Like the Church, it is dealing in ideological concepts which are of long-term validity, and it can afford to be patient. It has no right to risk the existing achievements of the revolution for the sake of vain baubles of the future. The very teachings of Lenin himself require great caution and flexibility in the pursuit of Communist purposes. Again, these precepts are fortified by the lessons of Russian history: of centuries of obscure battles between nomadic forces over the stretches of a vast unfortified plain. Here caution, circumspection, flexibility and deception are the valuable qualities; and their value finds natural appreciation in the Russian or the oriental mind. Thus the Kremlin has no compunction about retreating in the face of superior force. And being under the compulsion of no timetable, it does not get panicky under the necessity for such retreat. Its political action is a fluid stream which moves constantly, wherever it is permitted to move, toward a given goal. Its main concern is to make sure that it has filled every nook and cranny available to it in the basin of world power. But if it finds unassailable barriers in its path, it accepts these philosophically and accommodates itself to them. The main thing is that there should always be pressure, unceasing constant pressure, toward the desired goal. There is no trace of any feeling in Soviet psychology that that goal must be reached at any given time.

These considerations make Soviet diplomacy at once easier and more difficult to deal with than the diplomacy of individual aggressive leaders like Napoleon and Hitler. On the one hand it is more sensitive to contrary force, more ready to yield on individual sectors of the diplomatic front when that force is felt to be too strong, and thus more rational in the logic and rhetoric of power. On the other hand it cannot be easily defeated or discouraged by a single victory on the part of its opponents. And the patient persistence by which it is animated means that it can be effectively countered not by sporadic acts which represent the momentary whims of democratic opinion but only by intelligent long-range policies on the part of Russia's adversaries—policies no less steady in their purpose, and no less variegated and resourceful in their application, than those of the Soviet Union itself.

In these circumstances it is clear that the main element of any United States policy toward the Soviet Union must be that of a long-term, patient but firm and vigilant containment of Russian expansive tendencies. It is important to note, however, that such a policy has nothing to do with outward histrionics: with threats or blustering or superfluous gestures of outward "toughness." While the Kremlin is basically flexible in its reaction to political realities, it is by no means unamenable to considerations of prestige. Like almost any other government, it can be placed by tactless and threatening gestures in a position where it cannot afford to yield even though this might be dictated by its sense of realism. The Russian leaders are keen judges of human psychology, and as such they are highly conscious that loss of temper and of self-control is never a source of strength in political affairs. They are quick to exploit such evidences of weakness. For these reasons, it is a *sine qua non* of successful dealing with Russia that the foreign government in question should remain at all times cool and collected and that its demands on Russian policy should be put forward in such a manner as to leave the way open for a compliance not too detrimental to Russian prestige.

In the light of the above, it will be clearly seen that the Soviet pressure against the free institutions of the western world is something that can be contained by the adroit and vigilant application of counter-force at a series of constantly shifting geographical and political points, corresponding to the shifts and manœuvres of Soviet policy, but which cannot be charmed or talked out of existence. The Russians look forward to a duel of infinite duration, and they see that already they have scored great successes. . . .

It is clear that the United States cannot expect in the foreseeable future to enjoy political intimacy with the Soviet régime. It must continue to regard the Soviet Union as a rival, not a partner, in the political arena. It must continue to expect that Soviet policies will reflect no abstract love of peace and stability, no real faith in the possibility of a permanent happy coexistence of the Socialist and capitalist worlds, but rather a cautious, persistent pressure toward the disruption and weakening of all rival influence and rival power.

Balanced against this are the facts that Russia, as opposed to the western world in general, is still by far the weaker party, that Soviet policy is highly flexible, and that Soviet society may well contain deficiencies which will eventually weaken its own total potential. This would of itself warrant the United States entering with reasonable confidence upon a policy of firm containment, designed to confront the Russians with unalterable counter-force at every point where they show signs of encroaching upon the interests of a peaceful and stable world.

But in actuality the possibilities for American policy are by no means limited to holding the line and hoping for the best. It is entirely possible for the United States to influence by its actions the internal developments, both within Russia and throughout the international Communist movement, by which Russian policy is largely determined. This is not only a question of the modest measure of informational activity which this government can conduct in the Soviet Union and elsewhere, although that, too, is important. It is rather a question of the degree to which the United States can create among the peoples of the world generally the impression of a country which knows what it wants, which is coping successfully with the problems of its internal life and with the responsibilities of a World Power, and which has a spiritual vitality capable of holding its own among the major ideological currents of the time. To the extent that such an impression can be created and maintained, the aims of Russian Communism must appear sterile and quixotic, the hopes and enthusiasm of Moscow's supporters must wane, and added strain must be imposed on the Kremlin's foreign policies. For the palsied decrepitude of the capitalist world is the keystone of Communist philosophy. Even the failure of the United States to experience the early economic depression which the ravens of the Red Square have been predicting with such complacent confidence since hostilities ceased would have deep and important repercussions throughout the Communist world.

By the same token, exhibitions of indecision, disunity and internal disintegration within this country have an exhilarating effect on the whole Communist movement. At each evidence of these tendencies, a thrill of hope and excitement goes through the Communist world; a new jauntiness can be noted in the Moscow tread; new groups of foreign supporters climb on to what they can only view as the band wagon of international politics; and Russian pressure increases all along the line in international affairs.

It would be an exaggeration to say that American behavior unassisted and alone could exercise a power of life and death over the Communist movement and bring about the early fall of Soviet power in Russia. But the United States has it in its power to increase enormously the strains under which Soviet policy must operate, to force upon the Kremlin a far greater degree of moderation and circumspection than it has had to observe in recent years, and in this way to promote tendencies which must eventually find their outlet in either the break-up or the gradual mellowing of Soviet power. For no mystical, Messianic movement—and particularly not that of the Kremlin—can face frustration indefinitely without eventually adjusting itself in one way or another to the logic of that state of affairs.

Thus the decision will really fall in large measure in this country itself. The issue of Soviet-American relations is in essence a test of the over-all worth of the United States as a nation among nations. To avoid destruction the United States need only measure up to its own best traditions and prove itself worthy of preservation as a great nation.

Surely, there was never a fairer test of national quality than this. In the light of these circumstances, the thoughtful observer of Russian-American relations will find no cause for complaint in the Kremlin's challenge to American society. He will rather experience a certain gratitude to a Providence which, by providing the American people with this implacable challenge, has made their entire security as a nation dependent on their pulling themselves together and accepting the responsibilities of moral and political leadership that history plainly intended them to bear.

The first step toward a resolution in Bosnia should be to take all necessary steps for the fulfillment of the peace plan proposed earlier this year by the United States, Britain, France, Germany and Russia—and accepted by the Bosnian government. This means resolute rejection of the fatalistic arguments that it is too late to save the victims of aggression in Bosnia, or that domestic political constraints in the United States and the other NATO countries are insurmountable, or that the United States and Western Europe should not risk discord with Moscow, or that the United Nations is the problem and not the solution. Rejecting fatalistic arguments requires that leaders, parliaments and general publics be aware of how their counterparts in the 1930s behaved and with what consequences.

## Roles Nations Play

*See Lowi and Ginsberg, pp. 707–718 or brief edition, pp. 384–390*

*Why, in the immediate aftermath of Cold War victory, asks Edward Luttwak, a scholar at the Center for Strategic and International Studies, have the great powers become so unable to "cope with all manner of violent disorders?" The great powers are now reluctant to become involved in international crises, and they will not tolerate any casualties in combat situations: eighteen American deaths in Somalia, he notes, led to an immediate reversal in U.S. policy (and also indirectly led to the resignation of a Secretary of Defense, Les Aspin). Luttwak offers an unusual explanation. Our attitudes toward combat losses have changed, he argues, because of demographic and social changes that raise the "costs" of deaths. In the nineteenth century, he argues, families were large and death more common among the young. Now, families are smaller and parents have more invested in their children, so tolerance for casualties drops. Luttwak does not consider this squeamishness a positive development. Being a world power requires a willingness to intervene and has a cost in lives on its own, he concludes. Do you think he makes a good argument?*

# Edward N. Luttwak
# "Where Are the Great Powers?
# At Home with the Kids"*

During the Cold War as before it, local and regional conflicts were often instigated or at least encouraged and materially supported by rival great powers. Now, by contrast, the absence of functioning great powers is the cause of the world's inability to cope with all manner of violent disorders. The result is that not only groups of secessionists and aggressive small powers, such as Serbia, but even mere armed bands can now impose their will or simply rampage, unchecked by any greater force from without. Today there is neither the danger of great power wars nor the relative tranquillity once imposed by each great power within its own sphere of influence.

By the traditional definition, great powers were states strong enough to successfully wage war without calling on allies. But that distinction is now outdated, because the issue today is not whether war can be made with or without allies, but whether war can be made at all. Historically, there have been tacit preconditions to great power status: a readiness to use force whenever it was advantageous to do so and an acceptance of the resulting combat casualties with equanimity, as long as the number was not disproportionate.

In the past, those preconditions were too blatantly obvious and too easily satisfied to deserve a mention by either practitioners or theoreticians. Great powers normally relied on intimidation rather than combat, but only because a willingness to use force was assumed. Moreover, they would use force undeterred by the prospect of the ensuing casualties, within limits of course.

## NOT-SO-GREAT BEHAVIOR

The Somalia debacle, precipitated by the loss of 18 U.S. soldiers, and the Haiti fiasco, caused by the fear that a handful of U.S. troops might be killed while defeating that country's military dictatorship, sufficiently exposed the current unreality of the great power concept. In pride or shame, Americans might dispute any wider conclusion from those events. They would like to reserve for themselves the special sensitivity that forces policy to change completely because 18 professional soldiers are killed (soldiers, one might add, who come from a country in which gun-related deaths were last clocked at one every 14 minutes). But in fact the virtue or malady, as the case may be, is far from exclusively American.

* Edward N. Luttwak, "Where Are the Great Powers? At Home with the Kids" in *Foreign Affairs* (July 1994), Volume 73, Number 4. Copyright © 1994 by The Council on Foreign Relations. Reprinted with permission of *Foreign Affairs*.

Most recently, Britain and France (not to mention that other putative great power, Germany) flatly refused to risk their ground troops in combat to resist aggression in the former Yugoslavia. Overcoming the fear of reprisals against their own troops, it was only with great reluctance, after almost two years of horrific outrages, that the two countries finally consented to the carefully circumscribed threat of NATO air strikes issued in February 1994. To be sure, neither Britain nor France nor any other European power has any vital interests at stake in the former Yugoslavia. But that is the very essence of the matter: the great powers of history would have viewed the disintegration of Yugoslavia not as a noxious problem to be avoided but as an opportunity to be exploited. Using the need to protect populations under attack as their propaganda excuse and with the restoration of law and order as their ostensible motive, they would have intervened to establish zones of influence for themselves, just as the genuine great powers did in their time (even distant Russia disputed the Austro-Hungarian annexation of Bosnia-Herzegovina in 1908). Thus the power vacuum would have been filled, to the disappointment of local small power ambitions, and to the great advantage of local populations and peace.

As for why nothing of the kind happened in the former Yugoslavia in the face of atrocities not seen since the Second World War, the reason is not in dispute: no European government was any more willing than the U.S. government to risk its soldiers in combat. Of Japan, literally nothing need be said on this score.

The refusal to tolerate combat casualties is not confined to democracies. The Soviet Union was still an intact totalitarian dictatorship when it engaged in the classic great power venture of Afghanistan, only to find that even its tightly regimented society would not tolerate the resulting casualties. At the time, outside observers were distinctly puzzled by the minimal Soviet theater strategy in Afghanistan. After an abortive effort to establish territorial control, the Soviet strategy defended only the largest towns and the ring road that connected them, otherwise conceding almost the entire country to guerrillas. Likewise, knowledgeable observers were astonished by the inordinately prudent tactics of Soviet ground forces. Except for a few commando units, they mostly remained confined inside their fortified garrisons, often failing to sally out even when guerrillas were known to be nearby. At the time, the explanation most commonly offered was the reluctance of Soviet commanders to rely on their poorly trained conscript troops. But there is a better explanation: the Soviet headquarters was under constant and intense pressure from Moscow to avoid casualties at all costs because of the outraged reactions of families and friends.

This example also allows us to eliminate another superficial explanation for the novel refusal to accept even modest numbers of combat casualties: the impact of television coverage. The Soviet Union never allowed its population to see any television images of war like those shown in the United States, and still the reaction of Soviet society to the casualties of the

Afghan war was essentially identical to the American reaction to the Vietnam War. Although in both cases cumulative casualties over the span of many years did not reach the casualty figures of one day of battle in past wars, they were nevertheless deeply traumatic.


## THE WAR OF ALL MOTHERS

There is a more fundamental explanation that remains valid in cases with or without democratic governance, with or without uncontrolled war reportage by television: the demographic character of modern, post-industrial societies. The populations of the great powers of history were commonly comprised of families of four, five or six children; families of one, two or three were rarer than families of seven, eight or nine. On the other hand, infant mortality rates were also high. When it was normal to lose one or more children to disease, the loss of one more youngster in war had a different meaning than it has for today's families, which have two or three children, all of whom are expected to survive, and each of whom represents a larger share of the family's emotional economy.

As any number of historical studies have shown, death itself was a much more normal part of the familial experience when it was not confined mostly to the very old. To lose a young family member for any reason was no doubt always tragic, yet a death in combat was not the extraordinary and fundamentally unacceptable event that it has now become. Parents who commonly approved of their sons' and daughters' decisions to join the armed forces, thereby choosing a career dedicated to combat and its preparation just as a fireman's career is dedicated to the fighting of fires, now often react with astonishment and anger when their children are actually sent into potential combat situations. And they are apt to view their wounding or death as an outrageous scandal, rather than as an occupational hazard.

The Italians, perhaps more post-industrial than most in this sense, with Europe's lowest birthrate, have a word for these reactions: *mammismo,* which might be translated as "motherism." These attitudes have great political resonance nowadays, powerfully constraining the use of force. The Soviet experience in Afghanistan proves that the constraint can become operative even without a mass media eager to publicize private grief, members of Congress ready to complain at the instance of relatives, or pointed questions being asked in a parliament.

Present attitudes toward combat losses that derive from the new family demography are powerful because they are not confined to the relatives and friends of servicemen on active duty. They are shared throughout society—and were shared even within the Soviet elite, it turns out—generating an extreme reluctance to impose a possible sacrifice that has become so much greater than it was when national populations were perhaps much smaller but families were much larger.

What of the Gulf War, then, or for that matter Britain's war to reconquer the Falklands? Do they not suggest a much simpler explanation: that attitudes depend on the perceived importance of the undertaking, the objective value of what is at stake, or—more realistically—the sheer ability of political leaders to justify the necessity of combat? After all, even during World War II, soldiers greatly resented assignments to what were described as secondary fronts, quickly dubbing any theater that was less than highly publicized as "forgotten." The less immediately compelling the justification, the more likely combat and its casualties are to be opposed. It might therefore seem that the new 2.2-children-per-family demographics and the resulting *mammismo* are irrelevant, that what counts is only what has always counted, namely the importance of the interests at stake, the political orchestration of the event and plain leadership.

Those contentions undoubtedly have some merit, but much less than meets the eye. In the first place, if lives can only be placed at risk in situations already dramatically prominent on the national scene, hence on a larger rather than a smaller scale, and only in final extremities, that in itself already rules out the most efficient use of force—early and on a small scale to prevent escalation.

## CONSTRICTED VISIONS

In the past, there was no question of limiting the use of force to situations in which genuinely vital interests, that is, survival interests, were at stake. To struggle for mere survival was the unhappy predicament of threatened small powers, which had to fight purely to defend themselves and could not hope to achieve anything more with their modest strength. Great powers were different; they could only remain great if they were seen as willing and able to use force to acquire and protect even non-vital interests, including distant possessions or minor additions to their spheres of influence. To lose a few hundred soldiers in some minor probing operation or a few thousand in a small war or expeditionary venture were routine events for the great powers of history.

Great powers are in the business of threatening, rather than being threatened. A great power cannot be that unless it asserts all sorts of claims that far exceed the needs of its own immediate security, including the protection of allies and clients as well as other less-than-vital interests. It must therefore risk combat for purposes that may be fairly recondite, perhaps in little-known distant lands, but definitely in situations in which it is not compelled to fight but rather deliberately chooses to do so. And that is the choice now denied by the fear of casualties.

Even now, exceptional strivings by exceptionally determined leaders skilled in the art of political leadership can widen a great power's freedom of action, overcoming at least in part the effects of the new family demographics. That was obviously the case in the Persian Gulf intervention and the Falklands reconquest; both would have been impossible undertakings had it not been for the exceptional leadership of President George Bush and Prime Minister Margaret Thatcher, respectively. Their leadership was the decisive factor, not the undoubted significance of keeping Iraq from controlling Saudi and Kuwaiti oil, or the equally undoubted insignificance of the Falklands for any practical purpose whatsoever (another illustration of the irrelevance of the "objective" value of whatever is at stake).

Leadership is important, but that consideration cuts both ways, because the routine functioning of a great power cannot depend on the fortuitous presence of exceptional leadership. It will be recalled, moreover, that a very low opinion of Argentine military strength (indeed, a gross underestimate of Argentine air power) and the resulting belief that casualties would be very low were crucial to Britain's commitment to war in the Falklands. Likewise, the imperative of minimizing casualties was the leitmotiv of the entire Persian Gulf intervention, from the initial deployment, which was originally presented as purely defensive, to the sudden decision to call off the ground war. (To be sure, there were other considerations as well, notably the fear that Iran would become the next threat if Iraq's army were utterly destroyed.) In any case, it seems clear that the freedom of action gained by successful leadership was still very narrow; it is not hard to guess what would have happened to President Bush and his administration if the casualties of the Persian Gulf venture had reached the levels of any one day of serious fighting in either world war.

## NATIONS OF FAMILIES

If the significance of the new family demographics is accepted, it follows that no advanced low-birth-rate countries can play the role of a classic great power anymore, not the United States or Russia, not Britain, France or, least of all, Germany or Japan. They may still possess the physical attributes of military strength or the economic base to develop such strength even on a great scale, but their societies are so allergic to casualties that they are effectively debellicized, or nearly so.

Aside from self-defense and exceptional cases à la the Persian Gulf War, only such conflict as can take place without soldiers is likely to be tolerated. Much can be done by air power, with few lives at risk, especially if bureaucratic resistance to the use of air power alone can be overcome. Sea power too can be useful at times, and robotic weapons will be used increasingly. But Bosnia, Somalia and Haiti remind us that the typical great power business of restoring order still requires ground forces. In the end, the infantry, albeit mechanized, is still indispensable, although now mostly withheld by the fear of casualties. It is true of course that high-birth-rate countries can still fight wars by choice, and several have in recent years. But even those very few among them that have competent armed forces lack other key great power attributes, including any significant strategic reach.

In the absence of functioning great powers, the entire character of world politics has changed. Under the old *machtpolitik* rules, for example, the United States should have been eager to extend its military influence to the Russian border by granting full NATO membership to Poland and other former Warsaw Pact countries. Instead the United States opposed NATO's expansion. In the central arena of world affairs, only the commercial and industrial policies that I have elsewhere labeled "geo-economic" still have a recognizably conflictual flavor.

Unless the world is content to cohabit with chronic disorder and widespread violence, a synthetic version of law-and-order interventionism by great powers will have to be invented. The remedies we already have are certainly inadequate. To keep the armed forces of the United States as powerful as possible—the preferred military option, of course—is ineffectual when intimidation will not do it, yet the United States refuses to fight. And U.S. ability to intimidate cannot but decline as the word spreads.

## IMPROBABLE STAND-INS

Two rather improbable schemes are therefore left. Both satisfy the essential requirement of circumventing the intolerance of casualties. Both could be organized quite efficiently, given the will to do so. Yet both would be furiously opposed by the military establishment, and both undeniably have unpleasant moral connotations.

One scheme would be to copy the Ghurka model, recruiting troops in some suitable region abroad, if not in Nepal itself. They would be mercenaries, of course, but they would be of high quality, and a common ethnic origin would assure their basic cohesion. In practice, U.S. Ghurkas would provide the infantry units, with native U.S. forces providing the more technical forms of combat support involving smaller risks and fewer casualties.

The alternative is to copy the foreign legion model, with units that combine U.S. officers and nonnative volunteers who have renounced their national allegiance, perhaps attracted by the offer of U.S. citizenship after a given term of service. Under both schemes, political responsibility for any casualties would be much reduced, even if not eliminated. The United States, by the way, raised ethnic mercenary units in Indochina with rather good results, and it recruited individual foreign volunteers for Europe-based special forces. So neither scheme is as outlandish or unprecedented as it may seem. Still, one would not want to bet that they would be seriously considered, let alone adopted.

If no remedy can be found for the passing of the great powers and the conspicuous inability of the United States itself to play that role, both the United States and the world had better become habituated to the consequences. Violent disorders unchecked by effective great power interventions have both immediate and delayed effects, including disrupted export markets, refugees and new sources of international crime and terrorism. But Americans will also have to learn not to see, hear or feel much that would otherwise offend their moral sensibilities. Richer inhabitants of the poorest countries learn from childhood how to step politely over the quadruple-amputee beggar in their path without ever actually looking at him, and how not to see the starving mother and child, the waif and the abandoned elderly who try to beg from them as they walk into a restaurant or bank. Blindness can be learned, and Americans will have to learn how to passively ignore avoidable tragedies and horrific atrocities. The experience of Bosnia-Herzegovina shows that Americans have already made much progress in that direction.

# DEBATING THE ISSUES:
# AMERICAN FOREIGN POLICY
# —SELF INTEREST OR IDEALISM?

*See Lowi and Ginsberg, pp. 716–717 or brief edition, pp. 388–389*

*For more than 40 years U.S. military policy was built upon a single premise: contain communism. American weaponry, tactics, and geopolitical strategies were all designed to counter the military and political strength of the former Soviet Union and its satellite states. The Cold War is over, and the Soviet Union has vanished. Now, the U.S. defense community must develop a new paradigm upon which it can build a post–Cold War policy framework. In a recent review (May 1997) of its military policy—called the "Quadrennial Defense Review— the Department of Defense defined as the greatest threat to U.S. security so-called "rogue states," or Third World powers with modern armies (and, in some nightmare scenarios, nuclear weapons and ballistic missiles). The United States should be prepared to fight two major regional conflicts simultaneously against these countries. Given the enormous budgetary and political implications of such a policy, it is not surprising that it generated a great deal of controversy.*

*Michael Klare, the defense correspondent for* The Nation, *argues the rogue state doctrine is at best a flimsy basis for defense policy. Most of the nations targeted as threats have, in fact, flimsy, obsolete weaponry and spend a minute amount on defense in contrast to the United States. An alternative doctrine, focusing U.S. military attention on one of two "peer states"—China or Russia— is fraught with miscalculation and potential complications. In either case, Klare argues, the massive budget investments required to transform the U.S. military are unwarranted.*

*But are the threats to U.S. security, or lack thereof, so clear? According to Frederick Kagan and David Fautua, who teach at the U.S. Military Academy at West Point, history provides plenty of lessons for today's military planners. In the year 376 c.e., Rome was stretched thin to fight two "major regional contingencies," and when a challenge from the formerly peaceful Goths arose, the Roman army collapsed. The U.S. Army, they argue, is similarly spread quite thin. While all of the services have taken budget cuts in the past decade, the army has been hit the hardest. The army is essential for peace-keeping chores, as well as the fundamental military mission of deterrence. We must, they conclude, accept the premise that major regional conflicts are the challenge of the future military, and maintain a strong army.*

*What do you think motivates this debate over military policy? The self interest of the armed services, such as the army? Or ideology? Is Klare's argument motivated by ideology? If so, what is the premise of his debate?*

*Imagine you are a defense planner. How do you balance the arguments put forth by the branches (air force, army, navy) versus arguments made by outside experts such as Klare? Does the self interest of the individual services diminish their input? Why or why not?*

# Michael T. Klare
# "Beyond the Rogues' Gallery"*

The Quadrennial Defense Review (Q.D.R.), to be released by the Defense Department on May 19, is expected to reaffirm the Pentagon's anti-"rogue" doctrine, which calls for the capacity to fight and defeat two Iraq-like regional powers more or less simultaneously. A greater reliance on high-tech weaponry will allow the Pentagon to carry out this mission with fewer troops, the Q.D.R. maintains, but the basic plan will remain unchanged. This blueprint, first adopted by President Clinton in 1993, provides the basic rationale for a $250 billion-per-year military budget—for this year, next year and as far as we can see into the future.

The Q.D.R. rests on the assumption that the greatest threat to U.S. security in the current era—in the absence of a superpower challenger—is posed by hostile Third World powers (or "rogue states") equipped with modern armies and weapons of mass destruction. No so-called rogue can by itself pose a catastrophic threat to U.S. interests, the argument runs, but a combination of them might. Hence, the need for a military capability to fight two "major regional conflicts" at the same time.

The anti-rogue strategy was initially devised in early 1990, a few months after the Berlin wall's collapse, when it became apparent that the Soviet Union would no longer constitute a credible superpower enemy. Unwilling to contemplate a world free of major military conflict, the Pentagon leadership immediately began planning for an endless series of regional wars with emerging Third World powers. This posture was crafted before Iraq's 1990 invasion of Kuwait, but was made official U.S. policy after the Gulf War's conclusion [see Klare, "The New 'Rogue State' Doctrine," May 8, 1995].

The Pentagon's anti-rogue strategy proved to have great marketing appeal and continues to enjoy considerable popularity on Capitol Hill. Most Americans still view "outlaws" like Iran, Libya and North Korea as the likeliest U.S. adversaries in future conflicts. Nevertheless, it is evident to many military officials that the rogue-state theory has begun to lose its potency. None of the prominent rogues have made any move in recent years to

* Michael T. Klare, "Beyond the Rogues' Gallery" in *The Nation* (May 26, 1997). Reprinted with permission.

threaten U.S. interests seriously, and periodic claims of major break-throughs by these states in acquiring nuclear or chemical weapons have rarely amounted to much. Furthermore, North Korea—once viewed as the most menacing of the rogues—is suffering from a devastating famine and has agreed to dismantle its nuclear weapons program. Only Iran now appears as a credible enemy—a supposition given added weight in recent months by claims that Teheran is building up its navy and supporting ter-rorist networks in Europe. Still, Iran spends only about 1 percent of what the United States spends on defense, and its poorly equipped military is a mere shadow of the force assembled by Saddam Hussein in 1990.

The current U.S. focus on rogue regimes presents another significant problem for Pentagon officials: At this point, all the rogues are armed with largely obsolete Soviet weaponry (most of it based on sixties and seventies technology) and thus provide no justification for the acquisition of sophis-ticated twenty-first-century arms by the United States. As part of its plan to insure U.S. military supremacy for decades to come, the Defense Depart-ment seeks to spend $60 billion a year on new high-tech weapons, includ-ing the F-22 Stealth fighter and the equally sophisticated Joint Strike Fighter. "We want to dominate across the full spectrum of conflict," says Defense Secretary William Cohen, "so that if we ever do have to fight, we will win on our terms." But a new generation of high-tech weapons is not needed to defeat any of the rogues now or—given their inability to ac-quire modern weaponry—in the foreseeable future.

With the growing obsolescence of the rogue doctrine, the Pentagon is searching for an alternate scenario. Many Pentagon insiders think they have found it in the concept of a "peer state enemy"—that is, a major mil-itary power capable of challenging the United States on something ap-proaching equal terms. To date, the most explicit expression of this view can be found in the *1997 Strategic Assessment*, published in February by the Institute for National Strategic Studies of the National Defense University. In a section on "Potential Challenges for the U.S. Military," this study in-troduces the idea of a "potential theater peer," described as a nation with "sufficient power to be a peer with the U.S. in the theater of operations near them."

These states are not characterized as global superpowers like the United States. "Nevertheless," the N.D.U. declares, "the potential regional peers *are far more challenging threats than are the rogue regimes* which might involve the U.S. in major regional conflicts." [Emphasis added.] This is so because (1) "they are nuclear powers," capable of destroying U.S. cities and "inflicting unacceptable damage on the U.S."; (2) "they are space powers," capable of "throw[ing] a good deal of tonnage into space relia-bly"; and (3) "they are nations of enormous size and resources," and thus "cannot be overrun or occupied." Defeating a "peer state" adversary would obviously require a much greater effort than Operation Desert Storm—and would entail a larger and far more costly military establish-ment than the one now in place.

But what state can be cast in this role? There are only two plausible candidates: Russia and China. At present, it is not essential for advocates of the "peer threat" posture to choose between them, but as the rogue-state threat loses it edge, Pentagon officials are likely to find themselves under increasing pressure to single out either Russia or China as the most credible peer-state adversary.

For many U.S. strategists, the most obvious candidate is Russia. Despite significant cutbacks, Moscow maintains a very large military establishment and still possesses a huge supply of nuclear weapons. Russia also retains a strategic interest in a vast region stretching from East Central Europe to the northwest Pacific, providing plenty of opportunities for future clashes with U.S. interests. Furthermore, most older Americans are accustomed to viewing Russia in adversarial terms, and so it should be relatively easy to generate public support for a new anti-Russian crusade.

Still, the decline in Russian military power has been so rapid and so far-reaching it seems unlikely to be a credible peer-state enemy for some time to come. Stephen Caldwell of the General Accounting Office wrote in *Armed Forces Journal* that, despite its large military establishment,

Russia drifts further away from its former status as a military superpower. . . . [Its] conventional capabilities continue to be severely limited by a combination of short-falls in manning, training, readiness, and logistics. Russian defense spending has dropped about 75 percent since the late 1980s. Finally, Russian desires to improve the military will be tempered by a struggling economy that, for the foreseeable future, will not support significant increases in military spending.

Of course, Russia retains vast industrial and technological resources that could be harnessed for the reconstitution of military power. The domestic political environment is also likely to prove hospitable to ultranationalistic political forces. Nevertheless, the collapse of its army in Chechnya demonstrates all too clearly Russia's deep and continuing weakness.

That leaves China. At first glance, China would appear a less likely choice than Russia: It has far fewer nuclear weapons (China has about 500 warheads, Russia about 11,800), and its conventional arms are less sophisticated than Russia's. China also lacks a modern navy and air force. Finally, China is far more important than Russia to the U.S. economy, as both a trading partner and site of future investment.

But China also has significant qualifications for the role of major foreign threat: Its military strength is waxing, not waning; its army is the largest in the world; its booming economy allows for steady increases in military spending; and it is flexing its muscles in a region of growing economic and strategic significance. Whereas Russia has done very little to provoke the West, China has clashed with Washington on a variety of sensitive issues, including Taiwan, nuclear proliferation, human rights and foreign trade practices.

In their public statements, Pentagon officials do not portray China as an immediate threat to U.S. interests. Rather, they argue that China's continued economic growth—combined with a more assertive leadership—could make it a major military challenger by the first or second decade of the twenty-first century.

"Overall, China is one of the few powers with the potential—political, economic and military—to emerge as a large-scale regional threat to U.S. interests within the next ten to twenty years," said Lieut. Gen. Patrick Hughes, Director of the Defense Intelligence Agency, in recent testimony before the Senate Armed Services Committee. "Should China become more assertive and aggressive [as a regional power], the prospects for direct confrontation with other regional powers will increase accordingly. *In a worst-case scenario, China would view the United States as a direct military threat.*" [Emphasis added.]

A similar assessment was provided by George Tenet, President Clinton's choice to be the new Director of Central Intelligence. "With one-fifth of the world's population and the largest standing army," Tenet declared in February, "China stands poised to compete as a dominant regional military power, and it can aspire to be the first new great power since World War II." The belief that China is likely to emerge as a major U.S. adversary in the twenty-first century is also held among many military analysts in the think-tank community and among some pundits. A characteristic expression of this view is *The Coming Conflict With China,* a new book by Richard Bernstein of *The New York Times* and Ross Munro of the conservative Foreign Policy Research Institute in Philadelphia. As their title suggests, Bernstein and Munro believe that China's growing assertiveness in Asia will lead to increased friction and possibly war with the United States.

This is, of course, a minority outlook among U.S. policy-makers. Most senior government officials and much of the business community continue to view China as a major trading partner rather than a potential adversary. Vice President Al Gore's recent visit to Beijing—in which he presided over the signing of multimillion-dollar contracts between Chinese and U.S. companies—is an obvious expression of this outlook.

For now, the advocates of "engagement" with Beijing are in the driver's seat in Washington. But the perception of China as a future peer enemy is growing in the military and intelligence communities, and appears to enjoy strong support among Republicans in Congress. Should Beijing clash with Washington over some vital matter—say, Taiwan or ballistic missile proliferation—the proponents of a more confrontational stance could gain the upper hand. The designation of China as a future peer enemy would give the Pentagon the justification it seeks for increased spending on high-tech weapons and deployment of additional forces abroad.

An anti-China stance of this sort would undoubtedly provoke a vigorous response from the increasingly nationalistic leadership in Beijing—leading, in turn, to recurring crises over Taiwan, proliferation and other sensitive pressure points. In such an environment, it could prove all too easy for some future show of force by either side to trigger a militant reaction by the other leading to further challenges and possibly the outbreak of hostilities. President Clinton's 1996 decision to deploy two aircraft carrier battle groups in the western Pacific in response to China's missile tests off the coast of Taiwan is indicative of precisely the sort of scenario that could result in combat.

At present, the debate over military strategy and U.S.-China relations is being conducted among small and predominantly conservative policy elites and their associates in Congress. These people are making decisions involving the lives and well-being of all Americans. The debate must be opened up to a wider public discussion in which alternative views are heard—and this debate should focus not just on which weapons systems to buy and which to cancel (as most discussion of the Q.D.R. is likely to revolve around) but on the fundamental issues of war and peace in the twenty-first century.

# Frederick W. Kagan and David T. Fautua
# "Could We Fight a War If We Had To?"*

In 376 c.e., Rome did not know that it faced a deadly crisis. Although it had the best army in the world, its numbers were barely sufficient to meet the requirements of what we would now call two major regional contingencies (MRC's). With great difficulty, one army maintained the stability of the Rhine frontier against the Germanic tribes. Another was mobilizing for war with Persia. As a result, there were practically no Roman units on the Danube frontier facing the Goths, who were then peaceful. In 376, circumstances did not seem particularly dangerous.

The next year a third MRC arose: the Goths along the Danube rebelled, destroying the few Roman detachments there and sacking a critical province. The legions marching on Persia abandoned their campaign and raced for the Danube, leaving the frontier with Persia bare of troops and vulnerable to attack. When the army on the Rhine turned to meet the emergency, the Germans quickly overran Gaul. Under the weight of this third, unanticipated, contingency the Roman two-MRC capability collapsed, and shortly thereafter the Roman army was destroyed at Adrianople.

The parallels with America's current situation are ominous. Although it is extremely unlikely that American forces will suffer an "Adrianople," they are spread as thinly today as the Roman legions were in 376. Not only can the U.S. Army not conduct two MRC's simultaneously, unless it withdrew from most of its international commitments, it could not conduct even one.

The post-cold-war world is a much more disorderly place—if not a ma-

* Frederick W. Kagan and David T. Fautua, "Could We Fight a War If We Had To?" in *Commentary* (May 1997). Reprinted with permission.

terially more dangerous one—than was the cold-war world. During that
conflict, the Soviet Union was for the most part successful in restraining
its clients from aggressions which did not suit its purposes—and those
purposes were narrowly defined. But with the fall of the Soviet Union and
the collapse of Communism around the world, Soviet clients have run unchecked and former Communist states have fallen into civil war. From Bosnia to Iraq to Korea, not to mention within the boundaries of the former
Soviet empire itself, and also not to mention the rise of China, we are seeing the beginning, not the end, of the unrest generated by the fundamental transformation of the international balance of power.

The consequences for America have also been plain to see. During the
six years of the post-cold-war era, two very different U.S. administrations
have felt the need to respond rapidly and decisively to crises around the
world. President Bush sent troops to Panama, to Somalia, and to the Persian Gulf; President Clinton has sent forces to Haiti, to Bosnia, to the Gulf
again, and to the seas around Taiwan. Under these two administrations,
we have dispatched troops abroad more often than we did during the previous twenty years under Presidents Reagan, Carter, Ford, and Nixon. Although dispute still rages over the question of what America's role should
be in the post-Soviet era, by the most reliable measure of all—what we
have actually done—that role is as extensive as ever, and there is no reason to think it will soon diminish.

It was, indeed, this reality which brought senior civilian and military officials to decide to base post-cold-war U.S. strategy on the need to meet
two MRC's simultaneously. (During the cold war itself, the need was to
fight a war all along the Central European front, plus one other major
conflict at the same time.) Former Secretary of Defense William Perry defined an MRC as one in which American forces could expect to face enemies fielding armies of up to one million men with between 2,000 and
4,000 tanks. To cope with one such MRC would require "four to five Army
divisions, four to five Marine brigade-equivalents, and enhanced-readiness
brigades from the Army National Guard." To cope with two nearly simul-
taneous MRC's would require ten Army divisions, fifteen Army National
Guard brigades, and three Marine expeditionary forces reinforced by Marine reserves.

Of course, as the Roman example shows, a power with the vast global
interests of the United States cannot be sure that two MRC's are in fact the
worst-case scenario. In the summer of 1994, for instance, tensions between
North and South Korea rose dramatically, prompting the U.S. to send
troops to fill out units stationed along the boundary of the demilitarized
zone and to develop detailed contingency plans for large-scale deployments. Later that summer, with tensions in Korea still high, a supposedly
beaten Saddam Hussein massed his troops along the Kuwait border. The
U.S. responded with the fastest deployment in history of a brigade of soldiers, Air Force wings, and Navy battle groups. All this occurred at the very
time the Pentagon was finalizing plans for the invasion of Haiti by 20,000

soldiers. The inadequacy of even a two-MRC capability in this situation was apparent.

Today, defense cuts have made such a manifold response impossible. America's armed forces have been cut by about a third across the board since 1991. Overall military spending has decreased by 24 percent and active-duty military manpower by 27 percent.

The reductions have affected all services. For example, Air Force tactical squadrons have been cut by 28 percent since 1991; the number of planes in those squadrons has fallen by 42 percent; and the Air Force's ability to move forces rapidly between theaters has been reduced by about 22 percent. As for the Navy, it has lost 34 percent of its ships, among them 61 percent of the support ships critical for sustaining operations around the world.

But it is the Army that has been hit the hardest: spending has declined by 29 percent and active-duty manpower by 32 percent. The Army's capability to deploy forces, moreover, has actually dropped by 44 percent. There were eighteen divisions in 1991; today there are ten.

Taken together, these cuts significantly reduce America's ability to respond rapidly and with decisive force to two major regional contingencies, as well as to the many smaller crises and conflicts which currently occupy the armed forces. Acknowledging as much, some defense experts have begun to suggest that we make do with a one-and-a-half-MRC strategy. It appears, indeed, that the Quadrennial Defense Review scheduled to be released later this spring will recommend further cuts in the Army's force structure below the ten-division level which is the absolute minimum for maintaining a two-MRC capability—even though the contingencies which the two-MRC strategy was intended to meet have far from disappeared. (Neither Saddam Hussein nor the North Koreans, for example, have materially altered their belligerent stands.)

But the situation is in fact worse than this implies. The Army today could not field the force which won the Gulf war. It does not have, in other words, even a *one*-MRC capability. Whereas the American land component of the forces that defeated Saddam Hussein comprised seven divisions, five heavy and two light (out of our then-total of eighteen divisions), today, out of ten divisions, only six are heavy, and five of these are already committed to defending American interests elsewhere around the world.

Thus, the First Armored Division is in Germany recovering from a year's deployment to Bosnia, while the First Infantry Division now anchors the peacekeeping mission there. The Second Infantry Division guards the demilitarized zone in Korea. The Third Infantry Division, permanently headquartered in Fort Stewart, Georgia, has sent a reinforced brigade to Saudi Arabia, now replaced by a similar brigade from the First Cavalry Division, based in Fort Hood, Texas. Lastly, the Fourth Infantry Division has one of its three brigades fully committed to a military modernization campaign; because its equipment is experimental, this brigade is not easily deployable. The other two brigades are designated to train reserve and National Guard units called up in time of war and so are also not immediately deployable.

What this means is that in order to send five heavy divisions as we did in 1991, we would have to withdraw entirely our heavy divisions from Bosnia and Korea and also send all those now stationed in the U.S., save the one that would have to train the National Guardsmen called up to fight. But withdrawing from either Bosnia or Korea, let alone from both, would itself entail large costs, undermining the credibility of America's commitments around the world and inviting instability and possibly war.

And this again is not all. Saddam allowed us six months in which to deploy, refit, and, most importantly, train for the Gulf war. We cannot assume that any future regional aggressor will move so slowly or so ineptly.

Here, indeed, is where the full extent of the predicament facing the Army becomes manifest. In order to grasp it, one needs to consider the new sorts of missions it is being required to carry out in the world, and their effects on its training programs.

As a fighting force, the Army's predominance today results less from its technological superiority than from the extremely high level of training undergone by its soldiers and officers. The importance of this advantage was made clear during the Gulf war. At the battle of 73 Easting on February 26, 1991, for example, an American cavalry unit consisting of 9 M1A1 tanks, 12 Bradley armored-personnel carriers, and 140 soldiers encountered a much larger tank brigade of the elite Republican Guards and in 23 minutes destroyed almost all of it, sustaining no casualties and taking over 200 prisoners. The Iraqi brigade had been dug-in in a perfect defensive position and actually surprised the American troops. So well-trained were the latter, however, that with a single command, every soldier was able to deploy and bring to bear the unit's firepower while on the move, engaging and destroying the Iraqi force without further orders.

This sharp warfighting edge was born of tough collective training in heavy-maneuver warfare. The skill demonstrated at 73 Easting resulted in the first place from cohesion within each tank and Bradley crew. To achieve such cohesion, a tank crew requires five weeks to practice loading, maintaining, aiming, and firing. At the end of that period, a crew can load and fire its main gun in three seconds, on the move, against a moving target, and almost never miss.

At the completion of crew training, each tank and Bradley crew must then integrate its skills and efforts into the unit as a whole. Thus, for another four weeks, crews practice maneuvering and firing as platoons, and then as battalions. During this time they rehearse responses for likely combat situations until those responses become second nature. And even when the battalion's skills have been honed to this level, training is still not complete, for battalions must practice fighting together in brigades— a process which occupies the remaining two months of the standard four-month training cycle.

This edge is now being lost. The Army today is heavily engaged in overseas missions, but none of them involves direct combat. They are, instead, deterrence missions (in Korea and Kuwait), peacekeeping missions (in Bosnia, Macedonia, and the Sinai), and humanitarian missions (Bosnia again and recently Somalia and Haiti). Training for such missions differs dramatically from training for conventional combat. There is no time in the training cycle to prepare adequately for both, and there are not enough units in the Army to maintain both our peacekeeping-and-deterrence commitments and the capability to fight a major regional conflict.

Consider the forces involved in Bosnia. For the past year, the First Armored Division has patrolled that war-torn land with skills gained from training not in combat but in Operations Other Than War (OOTW) in Hohenfels, Germany. There, units learn to police urban areas, establish check-points, conduct search-and-seizure and disarming operations, detect and clear minefields, and resolve conflicts among local inhabitants of different ethnicities. In addition to learning about the military threat in Bosnia, they also receive detailed briefings on the geography, climate, people, history, politics, government, economy, and infrastructure of the region to which they will be deployed.

The Army's success in establishing and maintaining peace and stability in Bosnia results directly from this extensive and innovative training program. In the process, however, and in an environment of reduced budgets, it has had to short-change training to develop combat skills of the sort demonstrated at 73 Easting.

Thus, the First Armored Division has just been relieved by the First Infantry Division. If, as seems likely, the two divisions continue to swap places every six months, each will have only a half-year in which to complete its normal training-and-maintenance pattern—a pattern that previously took, and needed, a full year. From that half-year, moreover, it will be necessary to deduct at least two months for the unit to enter and exit the theater of operations and to conduct maintenance of its equipment. On paper, that leaves exactly three months for training and one month for recuperation.

That training will necessarily be in the skills suited to a peacekeeping mission and not to combat. It cannot be otherwise. Given the amount of time available in the six-month period between deployments, one can train either to conduct policing operations or to conduct maneuver warfare, but not both. Indeed, it would be as disastrous to deploy troops trained in maneuver warfare to peacekeeping operations as to deploy peacekeeping units to a Gulf war scenario. The commitment of these two divisions to Bosnia, therefore, will effectively prevent them from responding immediately to any contingency in which maneuver warfare is being conducted. And so it goes.

To be sure, the First Armored Division and the First Infantry Division are gaining valuable experience in missions that seem destined to be an important part of our national-security involvement around the world. But we have simultaneously put at risk the Army's fundamental competence to fight wars.

Peacekeeping and peacemaking missions have not only reduced the time available to heavy divisions for training in war-fighting—after all, the Army's primary mission and reason for being—they have also encroached upon funding for such training. In 1994, for instance, Army units found themselves reacting to a host of OOTW and deterrence missions in Rwanda, Bosnia, Somalia, Cuba, Saudi Arabia, Northern Iraq, Korea, Haiti, and even in California to fight forest fires. The deployments to Korea alone cost nearly $2 billion, drawn from budgets which normally support training. Together with the diversion of soldiers, the net result of this loss of dollars was that three Army divisions reported slippages in their readiness ratings.

Finally, still another set of problems bedevils the Army in its reduced state. This one concerns the logistics units (known as below-the-line units or BTL's) which support combat—and, now, peacekeeping—forces with everything from medical supplies to fuel, ammunition, food, and potable water, and thus make all movement and activity possible. There are simply not enough of these essential units to go around, and so when any single brigade is deployed on a mission, the rest of the division—along with other divisions within the corps—is essentially immobilized, able neither to train collectively at home nor to deploy elsewhere.

This, for instance, was the dilemma facing the XVIII Airborne Corps, whose logistical elements supported the fielding of the Tenth Mountain Division to Haiti in September 1994. So great were the requirements of that operation that within two weeks the XVIII Airborne Corps had run out of BTL units; it was forced not only to activate Reserve and National Guard replacements for its own missing units at home but to send additional support to Haiti in the form of BTL's from other sectors of the Army.

Even when the Tenth Mountain Division was relieved in January 1995 by a single brigade of the 25th Infantry Division, the headaches remained severe. That one brigade required about half the logistical support of division and corps alike, which left the division's other two brigades without sufficient back-up even for routine training. For the duration of the Haiti deployment, those brigades were not deployable and could not be trained to become so.

BTL's maintain perhaps the highest operational tempo of any in the Army. For example, while the First Infantry Division and the First Armored Division rotate into and out of Bosnia every six months, their BTL support groups remain there year 'round. In the case of Haiti, logistics units were deployed a month before combat forces and remained for two months after those forces had withdrawn. What is more, about three-quarters of the BTL's are drawn from the Reserves, forcing the few in the active Army to be constantly on the go. Soldiers in one military-police unit, for instance, found themselves deployed to Operation Just Cause in Panama, Desert Storm in Saudi Arabia, and Operation Restore Hope in Somalia—all in one tour of duty. This operational tempo cannot be sustained indefinitely, and the scarcity of available units of this kind could well hinder attempts to deploy a force to another Haiti or Bosnia tomorrow—even if we could find the soldiers.

Advocates of spending cuts have an answer to all these problems. American technological superiority, they say, can overcome any numerical deficiencies, and in today's world with its new military realities it is more important to develop and procure new technologies than to maintain sizable ground forces. Some have even argued that the Air Force's high-performance aircraft and "smart" weapons, or the Navy's long-range cruise-missile system, can replace the Army in many if not all MRC's and lesser crises.

This view rests, in part, on the false assumption that armed force is mainly for killing people. As we have seen, however, the Army is now mostly otherwise engaged. Only ground forces (supported by air and naval assets) can perform peace-keeping chores—separating belligerents, establishing and protecting supply lines, and assuring orderly elections—and ground forces are similarly essential in what is today perhaps the Army's most important role: deterrence. The deployment of ground forces to a region unmistakably signals American resolve; they are much more salient than carrier battle groups (which usually remain invisible over the horizon) or Air Force wings (which can depart as quickly as they arrived), and their presence demonstrates a clear readiness to take casualties if necessary.

But the high-tech view is no less misleading when it comes to actual warfare. The high-performance aircraft and precision weapons systems touted by the techno-advocates can indeed degrade an enemy's combat power. But they cannot force an end to the conflict. For more than a month the most advanced weaponry pummeled Iraq from the air and sea, leaving Saddam battered but still defiant. It took 100 hours of ground combat to destroy his army physically and seize the territory at issue. This is the way of the world.

Today's Army has reached its breaking point. A force structure of ten divisions is barely adequate to handle even the peacekeeping, stability, and deterrence operations which face it now, let alone those likely to arise as instability continues or flares into war in regions of vital concern to the United States. Crises, moreover, can arise quickly and without warning. In the summer of 1994, we were able to deter Saddam and North Korea and still invade Haiti. True, we may not have been able successfully to fight both Saddam and North Korea at the same time, as called for in our two-MRC strategy. But whether we could have done so or not in 1994, we would find it almost impossible to do so today.

Just as the Roman empire in 376 did not foresee the crisis that befell it the following year, we may yet encounter a situation for which we are not prepared. Fortunately, Americans can still choose to pay for an Army large enough to maintain and restore stability in regions of critical interest and still be able to face major regional contingencies as they arise. If we decline to do so, a threat may emerge without warning one day, and we will find ourselves without the legions to confront it.

# 17

# Can the Government Govern?

*America heads into the twenty-first century with its citizens uneasy about government's ability to cope with modern problems. Most people think that government responds more to narrow special interests than to the public good, and political leaders seem unable to come up with solutions to long term problems like health care, economic pressure on the middle class, and civil rights. Public confidence in national institutions is at historic lows, and citizens seem to hold the very idea of "politics" in contempt: it is the process itself that is the problem, the thinking goes, and the public is increasingly turning to automatic governing mechanisms (referenda, term limits, balanced budget amendments) that bypass political institutions altogether. The readings in this section help put these attitudes in perspective. Political tension, far from being a new development, is endemic to democratic systems. More importantly, concerns about "gridlock" must be viewed in context. Our system of government was designed to obstruct: separation of powers, to give one example, requires that different branches of government, each with its own independent sources of power, reach consensus before decisive action is possible. In this regard, government gridlock can be viewed as a sign that the public is divided about the appropriate course of action. "Politics," which is just another way to describe negotiation, compromise, and the struggle for power, is how those divisions are resolved.*

## Can the Government Govern?

*Lowi and Ginsberg, pp. 725–728 or brief edition, pp. 397–400*

Thomas Jefferson, who was in Paris during the Constitutional Convention, corresponded at length with James Madison concerning the structure of the proposed government. In the letter reprinted here, Jefferson expresses his hope that the "troubles in the Eastern States," referring to Shay's Rebellion, will not lead to an overly harsh response by the state governments. Jefferson notes that democratic governance can only be achieved at the cost of turbulence and instability, and that only governments based on force can achieve total stability. "I hold it, that a little rebellion, now and then, is a good thing" he wrote in an often-cited passage. Jefferson was not suggesting that armed rebellion should be encouraged; rather, he felt that it was the price of a democratic government and active citizenry.

# Thomas Jefferson
# A Letter to James Madison*

Paris, January 30, 1787.

Dear Sir,

My last to you was of the 16th of December; since which, I have received yours of November the 25th, and December the 4th, which afforded me, as your letters always do, a treat on matters public, individual and economical. I am impatient to learn your sentiments on the late troubles in the Eastern States. So far as I have yet seen, they do not appear to threaten serious consequences. Those States have suffered by the stoppage of the channels of their commerce, which have not yet found other issues. This must render money scarce, and make the people uneasy. This uneasiness has produced acts absolutely unjustifiable; but I hope they will provoke no severities from their governments. A consciousness of those in power that their administration of the public affairs has been honest, may, perhaps, produce too great a degree of indignation; and those characters, wherein fear predominates over hope, may apprehend too much from these instances of irregularity. They may conclude too hastily, that nature has formed man insusceptible of any other government than that of force, a conclusion not founded in truth nor experience. Societies exist under three forms, sufficiently distinguishable. 1. Without government, as among our Indians. 2. Under governments, wherein the will of every one has a just influence; as is the case in England, in a slight degree, and in our States, in a great one. 3. Under governments of force; as is the case in all other monarchies, and in most of the other republics. To have an idea of the curse of existence under these last, they must be seen. It is a government of wolves over sheep. It is a problem, not clear in my mind, that the first condition is not the best. But I believe it to be inconsistent with any great degree of population. The second state has a great deal of good in it. The mass of mankind under that, enjoys a precious degree of liberty and happiness. It has its evils, too; the principal of which is the turbulence to which it is subject. But weigh this against the oppressions of monarchy, and it becomes nothing. *Malo periculosam libertatem quam quietam servitutem.* *[I prefer freedom with danger to slavery with ease.]* Even this evil is productive of good. It prevents the degeneracy of government, and nourishes a general attention to the public affairs. I hold it, that a little rebellion, now and then, is a good thing, and as necessary in the political world as storms in the physical. Unsuccessful rebellions, indeed, generally establish the encroachments on the rights of the people, which have produced them. An observation of this truth should render honest republican governors so mild in their punishment of rebellions, as not to discourage them too much. It is a medicine necessary for the sound health of government. . . .

* From "The Writings of Thomas Jefferson" in *The Papers of Thomas Jefferson,* Julian P. Boyd, ed. (Princeton: Princeton University Press, 1955). Copyright © 1955. Reprinted with permission.

*[Jefferson continues with a discussion of unrelated political affairs.]*

I am, dear Sir, with sincere esteem and affection, your most obedient humble servant.

## DEBATING THE ISSUES: WHAT ARE THE CONSEQUENCES OF DIVIDED GOVERNMENT?

*See Lowi and Ginsberg, pp. 736–737 or brief edition, pp. 408–409*

*Conventional political wisdom, as both of the authors in this section note, holds that a government divided between two political parties inhibits effective governance. The current control of the House and Senate by the Republican Party, and the Democratic Party's control of the White House is an obvious example, well illustrated by budget battle stalemates that resulted in federal government shutdowns—no passport services, no calls or visits to the Social Security Administration offices, and no tourist visits to Washington's famous memorials. But is the problem necessarily divided government?*

*In the following debate, political scientists Sean Kelly and Morris Fiorina focus on this question. Sean Kelly is primarily concerned with the significance of the political parties, themselves, in generating stalemate between the two branches, as opposed to an inherent tension that might exist between the executive and legislative branches regardless of party control. He argues that the performance of the executive and legislative branch is dependent upon the dynamics of the two parties. Under unified government, the level of agreement between the White House and Congress and their capacity for cooperating on "innovative" public policy are increased. Moreover, he suggests a strengthening of the political parties as a governing force within Washington, forcing elected officials to be more partisan in their politics, and suggesting a strengthening of partisan identification within the electorate as a result. As an exercise, you might want to critique his argument and his projections for Democratic Party governance following the 1992 elections.*

*Morris Fiorina argues that split political party control of the government is, for the most part, irrelevant for government performance. What matters is the consensus of American voters for government policies. A divided citizenry will stalemate the government, whether the government is unified or divided by party control. Despite unified government in 1993, Clinton's health care initiative failed because, Fiorina argues, the American public was not sure this was the right thing to do. Under this explanation, divided government is a "symptom" of deeper problems. And if divided political party control does not matter for performance, does unified control have any benefits? Yes, Fiorina argues: it presents the ruling party an "opportunity" to govern in a dramatically different direction, but opportunities can be squandered, as well.*

# Sean Kelly
# "The Policy Consequences of Divided Government"*

In the American constitutional system there is a natural rivalry between Congress and the president. It divides the power to govern in a conscious attempt to debilitate the exercise of power at the national level. Most important, the Constitution divides the power to legislate between Congress and the president, granting the power to legislate to the former, and to the latter the power to veto. The logic of "separate institutions sharing power" thrusts Congress and the presidency into an eternal struggle for institutional advantage and for predominance in the policy-making process.

The conventional wisdom in political science, fashioned by authors such as Woodrow Wilson, E. E. Schattschneider, and others, holds that partisan control of distinct political institutions shapes the contours of the interbranch relationship. According to the conventional wisdom, political parties bridge these institutional fissures, helping to hold together an otherwise hopelessly fragmented institutional system. Cooperation across institutional divides is encouraged by common programmatic interests, as well as shared political fortunes, when a single party controls both Congress and the presidency.

When the majority party in Congress faces a minority party president, natural institutional rivalries are exacerbated. First, under divided government members of Congress and the president do not share a common electoral fate. Therefore, they feel no compunction to cooperate with one another on many issues. The majority party in Congress fears the president will benefit electorally from their cooperation and will therefore refuse to follow the lead of the president. Similarly, the president will not want the Congress to capitalize on its own successes, and will not cooperate with congressional initiatives. Second, institutional conflict will increase because the majority party in Congress controls the levers of congressional power: the committee system, the nature and flow of the legislative agenda, and so forth. The majority party will use these powers to pursue its own interests, which are often opposed to those of the minority party president. Although conflict is inherent and desirable in democratic political systems, divided government leads programmatically opposed parties to feud across institutional boundaries, resulting in institutional conflict, delay, and inaction. Divided government, then, represents a qualitative shift in the relationship between Congress and the president.

Revisionist scholars argue that divided government does not qualitatively alter the relationship between the branches, largely dismissing the importance of political parties in contemporary American politics. They

* Sean Kelly, "The Policy Consequences of Divided Government" from *New Perspectives on American Politics*, edited by Lawrence C. Dodd and Calvin Tillson (Washington, D.C.: CQ Press, 1994). Reprinted with permission.

further contend that parties do not serve as mechanisms for overcoming the institutional rivalry between Congress and the president. Parties fail on this count because individual members of Congress have no incentive to adhere to their party's policy agenda. Given electorally weak political parties, members of Congress concerned with reelection must pursue party-neutral strategies for gaining reelection. Thus, parties will be ineffective institutions for shaping the collective behavior of individual members of Congress.

Recent scholarship to the contrary suggests that congressional political parties have enjoyed a renaissance over the last two decades. David Rohde demonstrates that majority party leaders in the House have become increasingly influential over the last two decades, and that partisan voting patterns have become much more pronounced. Similarly, Barbara Sinclair argues that the House majority party leadership has become more willing to use its powers to shape the legislative agenda and influence legislative outcomes. According to David Price, "the congressional parties over the last twenty years have become more active and their operations more extensive than at any other time in American history [and] the parties retain a central role in the present functioning of the Congress." And Bond and Fleisher identify party as a central variable in predicting a member's support of presidential initiatives.

Without question American political parties are relatively weak electoral organizations. In fact, weak political parties, I have argued, are a central cause of divided government. But this weakness in the electorate has not incapacitated the parties in government. If anything, the past two decades have been characterized by the continued, and perhaps increasing, importance of partisan loyalties in the Congress. This presents the analyst of American politics with an important paradox: in an era of weakening parties in the electorate, political parties remain important forces within government and play a strong role in shaping policy outcomes.

This paradox can be partly explained by the electoral dynamics of the era of divided government. The shift in the electoral context of the era of divided government has prompted office seekers to adopt new strategies within government that reinforce partisanship, in order to maintain electoral support.

Members of both parties have a primary interest in maintaining the symbolic importance of their party labels: the Democrats as the party of social and economic liberalism, and the Republicans as the party of social and economic conservatism. Within the electoral context of divided government, these symbolic positions impart to each party an electoral advantage, at the congressional level for the Democrats, and at the presidential level for the Republicans. Each party has an intense interest in maintaining the "value" of this label because of the electoral payoff it holds for members of each party. This electoral incentive will lead members of the two parties to behave in a more partisan fashion than we would otherwise expect given electorally weak parties, and in turn help to shape policy outcomes and reinforce public perceptions of the two parties. Parties, then, may function in a manner that is consistent with the conventional wisdom and its expectations.

Thus, political parties can and do play a central role in shaping the relationship between Congress and the president. Unlike previous political eras, which were marked by united party government, however, political parties will be unable to provide a means for establishing a focused and coherent policy agenda. Programmatic differences between the parties and sustained institutional conflict will stifle policy innovation and prevent a coherent policy agenda from emerging.

## POLICY AGREEMENT

The conventional wisdom suggests that divided government will lead, in part, to less institutional cooperation between the branches. Partisan competition laid on top of natural institutional rivalries will heighten conflict between the branches over matters of public policy. A simple way to test this hypothesis is to examine Congressional Quarterly's "presidential success" scores. These scores reflect the percentage of policy issues on which a majority in Congress supported the expressed policy position of the president, thus representing the level of policy agreement between the branches. Despite its flaws, the CQ system provides a fairly accurate measure of the "state of the relationship" between Congress and the president.

Mean policy agreement scores are given in Table 9-2. The first thing to note is that mean policy agreement scores under united government hover around 82 percent in all three interbranch relationships, and between 57 percent and 66 percent under divided government. The difference between these means ranges from 15.6 percent for the Senate-president and 25.8 percent for the House-president data. These are important differences, which are dismissed by revisionist scholars Petracca and Thurber.

Equally enlightening is an examination of the Eisenhower and Reagan administrations. The Republican party controlled the Congress during the first two years of the Eisenhower administration; it controlled the Senate for the first six years of the Reagan administration. The differences between policy agreement under united and divided government are truly striking under Eisenhower: 19.3 percent, 26.3 percent, and 17.3 percent, respectively. Under Reagan, the switch from a Republican to a Democratic Senate resulted in a drop of more than 20 percent in policy agreement between the Senate and the president.

These results lend some insight regarding the consequences of divided government for interbranch policy agreement, suggesting that the contentions of traditional scholars have empirical support. Divided government represents a qualitative shift in the relationship between Congress and the president. Interbranch policy agreement is increased when a single party

**Table 9-2**   Policy Agreement in the Era of Divided Government

| President | Congress-President | | House-President | | Senate-President | |
|---|---|---|---|---|---|---|
| | Uni | Div. | Uni. | Div. | Uni. | Div. |
| Eisenhower | 86.00 | 67.70 | 91.20 | 64.95 | 87.80 | 70.53 |
| Kennedy | 84.67 | — | 83.73 | — | 85.27 | — |
| Johnson | 82.64 | — | 86.54 | — | 79.82 | — |
| Nixon | — | 68.68 | — | 73.70 | — | 64.80 |
| Ford | — | 56.67 | — | 51.00 | — | 64.20 |
| Carter | 76.40 | — | 73.15 | — | 78.90 | — |
| Reagan | — | 61.86 | — | 46.64 | 82.65 | 60.60 |
| Bush | — | 54.70 | — | 41.20 | — | 68.35 |
| Mean | 81.77 | 62.43 | 82.78 | 57.33 | 81.59 | 66.35 |

*Source:* Calculated by the author from Congressional Quarterly presidential success scores.

controls both Congress and the presidency; conversely, interbranch policy agreement declines during periods of divided government.

United government will not necessarily result in a harmonious relationship between the branches. Our last period of united government, 1977 to 1981, is illustrative. President Jimmy Carter often found himself at loggerheads with the Congress, and the public perception of his travails no doubt contributed to his unsuccessful bid for reelection in 1980. Nevertheless, the existence of united government creates the conditions under which cooperation between the branches may emerge. The level of policy agreement between President Carter and the Congress was higher than that of his Republican counterparts.

In the absence of united government the conditions for a stable, cooperative relationship between the branches are nonexistent. Persistent divided government may encourage the Democrats in Congress and the Republican president to engage in what Ginsberg and Shefter call "institutional combat." Attempting to gain institutional and electoral advantage, the parties will use the institution they control to attack the other institution and, thereby, the other party. As domestic and international concerns intensify, such behavior may ultimately subvert attempts to cope with pressing policy issues at home and abroad.

## INNOVATIVE LEGISLATION

Although an examination of broad patterns of interbranch policy agreement can further our understanding of the institutional dynamics of divided government, our ultimate interest is in policymaking. Previous political eras provided a partisan and institutional context within which significant public policy could emerge. The conventional wisdom suggests that divided government hinders the ability of the American political system to respond to the pressing issues of the day through innovative legislation.

Contrary to the conventional wisdom, Mayhew presents evidence that partisan control of government has little effect on the formulation of innovative legislation. His analysis of data collected from various primary and secondary sources leads him to conclude that innovative legislation is more directly linked to timing (it is more likely to be enacted in the first two years of a presidential term) and the "public mood" (it is more likely to emerge when there is a public demand for an activist government). Mayhew concludes that "unified versus divided control has probably not made a notable difference during the postwar era."

Mayhew fails to provide a framework for distinguishing innovative policies from ordinary legislation. Innovative legislation is both *timely* and *enduring*. It addresses salient problems. For instance, New Deal programs were aimed at alleviating the burden of the Great Depression on the poor and the elderly, thus addressing a salient political need. Innovative legislation is enduring in that the impact of the policy remains evident across time and can be identified as having been successful in addressing a policy concern. New Deal programs such as Social Security and medical aid for the poor have endured; the public expects the government to continue them. Such legislation may therefore be considered innovative.

The most innovative pieces of legislation in Mayhew's database, then, are those viewed as innovative at the time of their passage and since judged to have been important. When taken as a group, these innovative policies comprise 147 of Mayhew's original 267 laws, or 55 percent of the original list of legislation.

The most straightforward test of the divided government hypothesis is to examine the mean number of innovative policies generated under divided and united government (see Table 9-3). When Mayhew's original data are used, divided government does not seem to hinder the passage of innovative legislation. Under united government, 12.8 pieces of innovative legislation were passed; under divided government, the figure is 11.7. Using a more stringent definition, however, a significant difference emerges. Periods of united government average 8.8 acts, with divided government producing about 6 acts. In more concrete terms, about 30 percent fewer innovative policies are passed in Congress under divided government than under a united one.

Of course a more sophisticated analysis of the data is in order so that alternative causes of this difference may be ruled out. Mayhew provides a model for a multivariate test. He argues that there are three possible other causes, beyond partisan control of government, of variation in innovative policy. When Mayhew's model is applied to the more restrictive list of innovative policy, divided government has the significant negative impact that is expected. All other things being equal, under divided government two fewer innovative policies are passed in every Congress. In more substantive terms, over the twelve periods of divided government accounted

**Table 9-3**   Mean Innovative Policy in the Era of Divided
Government

|  | Mayhew Measure 1946-1990 | | Kelly Measure 1946-1986 | |
|---|---|---|---|---|
|  | Uni. | Div. | Uni. | Div. |
| Mean | 12.78 | 11.69 | 8.78 | 6.09 |
| S.D. | 4.60 | 5.48 | 3.83 | 2.84 |
| N | 9 | 13 | 9 | 11 |

for in this data, perhaps twenty-four innovative policies were not passed because of divided government. Reassessed in this way, Mayhew's data reveals that divided government *matters*.

Does the era of divided government have a unique policy dynamic? The evidence presented here suggests that it does; it increases policy conflict between the branches. Perhaps more important, divided government inhibits passage of innovative legislation, which in turn hampers the ability of policymakers to establish a coherent policy agenda aimed at addressing the country's ills. During previous periods of "punctuated change," persistent united government allowed a stable policy agenda to emerge; under persistent divided government we should have no such expectation.

CONCLUSION

Over the past four decades divided government has become the primary means for organizing national and state politics. At the national level Republicans have controlled the White House, and Democrats have controlled the Congress. Likewise, most states had Republican governors and Democratic legislatures. Although the 1992 elections maintained divided government in the states, united government returned at the national level for the first time in twelve years. With the inauguration of Bill Clinton as president and solid Democratic majorities in the House and the Senate, the question becomes, why the return to united government at this point in history?

We need to reexamine one of the central causes of divided government. In contemporary American politics the Republic party has become associated with economic management, command over foreign affairs, and fiscal conservatism. The Democratic party has become associated with the maintenance of the modern service state and social liberalism. Given unique historical and institutional conditions, a politically significant minority of voters makes electoral choices based on the symbolic roles of the parties.

The 1992 presidential election was the first post-Cold War election. Significant arms control agreements, engineered by Ronald Reagan and George Bush, with the Soviets in the late 1980s and early 1990s decreased the perceived military threat of a large-scale nuclear war with the Soviets. The subsequent disintegration of the Soviet Union into the Commonwealth of Independent States further reduced the specter of Communist aggression around the world.

As the historically isolationist American electorate turned inward after an unprecedented, six-decade period of intense international involvement, one of the Republican party's major advantages in presidential politics was neutralized. Although foreign policy brushfires flared in the Balkans, East Africa, and elsewhere, they hardly rivaled the immediate dangers represented in the past by the Soviet Union. The new foreign policy map, although more complex—and for that reason perhaps more difficult to read—is not the bipolar map of the Cold War period. Without a powerful or well-defined enemy, U.S. foreign policy was eclipsed as an electoral concern, to the disadvantage of the Republican party. Paradoxically, then, Republican success in confronting and taming the Soviet threat undermined one of the party's primary electoral advantages.

When the American public focused on domestic concerns, it found a country in economic disarray. The economic dislocation prompted by the transition to a post-Cold War economy had spurred a recession; and the Republican president, seemingly preoccupied with foreign policy, appeared strangely out of touch with the widespread dissatisfaction of the American public. With the encouragement of independent candidate Ross Perot, domestic economic concerns focused more closely on the immense federal budget deficit and the national debt—all of which had emerged on the Republicans' watch.

Since the New Deal the American public has come to expect that the national government will take a proactive role in controlling the economy, especially during economic downturns, and will help to relieve the suffering of the economically disadvantaged. In particular, it has become the president's responsibility to respond to economic crises. The reliance of the contemporary Republican party on a philosophy of laissez-faire economics makes it ill-prepared to *actively* confront domestic economic concerns. Since the depression the Republican party has advanced a "ride it out" approach to the economy. This approach may have worked if the economy recovered before the presidential election, but a weak economy during the election undermined the electoral appeal of the Republican emphasis on economic conservatism.

National forces during 1992 thus favored the Democratic party at the presidential level. Republican successes abroad largely removed foreign policy from the national agenda, and the public subsequently focused on economic issues that the Republican president seemed reluctant to address. The Democratic party is symbolically and philosophically better prepared to offer programmatic solutions such as infrastructure development (roads, bridges, mass-transit, and so forth), development of a national health care reform, national service, and the like. As the public mood shifted to domestic social issues, Clinton was therefore better able to capitalize on the perceived social liberalism of the Democratic party, stressing its prochoice stance on abortion, and support of family medical leave, expanded voter registration, and so forth.

What should we expect from this period of united government? Based on previous experience with united government in the post-World War II period, the Clinton administration should enjoy high levels of cooperation with the Congress. Clinton and the Democratic Congress seem especially sensitive to their majority party status and are consciously seeking to build a relationship of trust between the two institutions. Despite early press coverage to the contrary, congressional Democrats have exhibited a willingness to cooperate with Clinton, and the White House has taken great pains to coordinate its policy agenda with the leadership in both chambers. Based on the CQ measure of policy agreement, Clinton should experience an overall "success" rate of between 76 and 83 percent, well above the historical average of 62 percent under divided government (see Table 9-2).

In addition, I suspect that united government will result in a flurry of innovative legislation aimed at turning back the Reagan-Bush social "revolution." Early in the Clinton administration Congress passed, and Clinton signed, the Family and Medical Leave Act and the National Voter Registration Act, both of which were vetoed by George Bush. Clinton and the Democrats in Congress will also seek to codify abortion rights through passage of the Freedom of Choice Act.

United government and the current political context suggest that the most promising area for significant progress is on the national budget deficit. As the public has focused on the domestic economy, it has demonstrated a new willingness to deal substantively with the deficit. President Clinton may be able to use his majority party status to raise taxes and cut spending in a manner that could not be conceived under divided government. Under divided government, Republican presidents resist tax increases and insist on spending cuts that impact traditional Democratic constituencies and hence meet congressional resistance. The Democratic Congress insists on tax increases that impact traditional Republican constituencies and resist spending cuts. United party government provides a context in which balanced tax increases and spending cuts may be enacted as the majority party keeps one eye on its future electoral fortunes. That old chestnut "only Nixon could go to China" may develop a contemporary analogue: "only Clinton could cut the deficit."

Although united government is likely to continue for at least four years, the electoral context that undergirds the era of divided government is still present. Parties remain a weak force in the electorate, split-ticket voting is still prevalent, the institutional and symbolic expectations of the American electorate are intact, and so forth. Bill Clinton may very well represent the exception to the rule of divided government rather than a harbinger of a return to normalcy, to united government. There is little reason to believe that the election of Bill Clinton represents an enduring shift toward the Democratic party, or even that Clinton will be successful in securing a second term; recent history suggests that he will not.

Given that these underlying dynamics are still present, and that the 1992 election was not a realigning event that will return us to a pattern of united party government, this period of united government should only further encourage us to seek more refined approaches and answers to the puzzle that divided government offers students of American politics.

# Morris Fiorina
# "The Consequences of Divided Government Revisited"*

\* \* \*

Chapter 6 concluded that the stronger claims for the negative effects of divided government had little empirical support. Four years of additional experience and research does not markedly change that conclusion. At the national level, in particular, there is little evidence that divided government alone can account for the perceived failings of the federal government. Some recent work does suggest that divided government may affect the substance of policy in undesirable ways, but studies of many more policy areas need to be done before a general conclusion to that effect can be sustained, and the degree of undesirability measured.

At the state level, there is less research, but it is more suggestive. When the experiences of the states are pooled, there is sufficient data to generate statistically significant differences in the direction predicted by critics of divided government: divided control, at least of the legislature, appears to exacerbate budgetary difficulties. Still, many factors other than divided control play a role, and there is no evidence that split branch government (one party controls both legislative chambers but not the governor's office) performs any worse than unified government.

## ACCOUNTABILITY UNDER UNIFIED CONTROL: THE LESSONS OF 1993–94

Chapter 6 noted that, over and above the disputable claim that divided government detracts from the efficiency and productivity of government, there is a more compelling argument that divided control confuses the

\* Morris Fiorina, "The Consequences of Divided Government Revisited" from *Divided Government.* Copyright © 1966. All rights reserved. Reprinted/adapted by permission of Allyn & Bacon.

lines of responsibility in American politics. With different institutions controlled by different parties, how can voters hold parties collectively responsible for their performance? Moreover, knowing that it is difficult for voters to assess responsibility, elected officials have less reason to worry about their performance. Even if they have nothing to show by way of tangible accomplishments, they can resort to the "blame game"—posture about what you support and blame the other party for your inability to deliver.

Certainly, the 1994 congressional elections are consistent with the notion that unified control enhances electoral accountability. For two decades election observers marvelled at the ability of Congressional incumbents to insulate themselves from larger issues of national policy and performance, but many of these incumbents evidently found their insulation insufficient in 1994. Speaker of the House Tom Foley, Judiciary Chair Jack Brooks, Senate Majority Leader heir-apparent Jim Sasser—these and many others found themselves too closely tied to the policies and performance of the Clinton administration for a majority of their constituents. As usual they ran, but this time they couldn't hide. Unified Democratic control may well have been the difference.

Still, it is easy to exaggerate the extent to which the election was dominated by an angry electorate exacting its revenge on the Democrats. That image takes too literally the earthquake, tidal wave, and tsunami metaphors that dominated post-election commentary. As noted in Chapter 9, a variety of important considerations underlay the election results. Certainly I will not be surprised if subsequent research shows that national issues and presidential performance affected the Congressional voting in 1994 to a greater extent than in other recent elections. But that still leaves open the question of *why?* Why were the Republicans able to "nationalize" the 1994 elections? Was the answer simply "unified Democratic control?" If so, why were they were not able to nationalize the 1978 elections against a floundering Carter administration? Do the 1994 results indicate that collective accountability was there all along, just lying dormant and waiting for unified control to revive it—despite the Republican's inability to capitalize in 1978—or was 1994 an aberration? If unified control has revived collective responsibility, then we might see an older pattern of politics reassert itself, a pattern wherein one party or the other expects to gain unified control in the presidential elections, and divided government occurs as a consequence of losing one or both Houses of Congress at the mid-term. If this were to happen, proponents of unified government will have the chance to test their beliefs against contemporary reality. As citizens, we can only hope that in such an eventuality the optimism of the advocates of unified government is justified. But for analysts, it is much too early to conclude either that the era of candidate-centered elections has reverted to an older party-centered era, or that, if it has, conditions will necessarily improve.

CONCLUSION: DIVIDED GOVERNMENT OR DIVIDED CITIZENRY?

All-in-all there is little in either the political experience or the scholarly literature of the mid-1990s that supports the stronger claims of the critics of divided government. To the extent that effects can be identified at all, the effects of divided government appear to be quite limited. Critics and commentators have been overly quick to lay the blame for the perceived failings of governments on split party control, while ignoring other, more important factors.

Prominent among those other factors are the preferences of the U.S. people. If citizens overwhelmingly condemn budget deficits, but just as overwhelmingly oppose cuts in entitlements and/or increases in taxes, there is not much that even a unified government can do to reduce the deficit. If citizens want government to insure a zero-risk society, but resent bureaucratic intrusion and red-tape, they are unlikely to be satisfied with the regulatory process. If citizens want guaranteed health care for all, un-restricted choice of doctors and facilities, and lower premiums than they currently pay, they are unlikely to be happy with any conceivable national health care plan. Does it make sense to blame political-institutional pro-cesses for failing to satisfy incompatible wants?

Of course, the fault may lie with our leaders. After all, if we had knowl-edgeable, public-spirited, charismatic leaders who could educate voters, inform their preferences, and dispel the illusions and contradictions, then the political process would work better. Perhaps that is the case, but I will not hold my breath waiting for such leaders, and I suspect that there have been few of them in the past. Such demigods typically are created after-the-fact in the panegyrics of palace historians. The times make the leader as much as the leader makes the times.

The electoral politics of the early 1990s have firmed up my belief that the prevailing dissatisfaction of Americans with their governments largely reflects their lack of agreement on what, if anything, should be done. If most people dislike the status quo, but different groups strongly disagree over what direction policy should move in, no one is going to be very happy with how government performs. Consider the suggestive data in Ta-ble 11-1. Over the course of the past generation, Americans' views of the power of the federal government have polarized. When Lyndon Johnson and the 89th Congress were adopting "Great Society" initiatives, a plural-ity of the electorate expressed satisfaction with the level of activity of the federal government, and a significant minority favored additional activity. In contrast, when Bill Clinton and the 103rd Congress were trying to pass a National Health Care plan, only a tiny minority were satisfied with the federal government as is, while large and equal-sized pluralities wanted to go in opposite directions. In both cases government was unified, but it acted in the former case and gridlocked in the latter. Probably an impor-tant difference was the size of the center relative to the opposed extremes in the 1960s versus the 1990s.

**Table 11-1**    The Disappearing Center

| Which one of these statements comes closest to your own views about governmental power today? | | |
| --- | --- | --- |

1. The federal government has too much power.

2. The federal government is using about the right amount of power for meeting today's needs.

3. The federal government should use its powers more vigorously to promote the well-being of all segments of the people.

|  | 1964 | 1992 |
| --- | --- | --- |
| Too much | 26% | 39 |
| About Right | 36 | 12 |
| More vigorously | 31 | 40 |

Those who yearn for energetic, effective government might do well to shift their focus away from the simple question of party control to the more complicated question of how to build majorities for the ends they support. If both divided control and lack of government action reflect the absence of popular consensus, attention should shift toward explaining the lack of consensus. Does it reflect the waning of consensus-building actors such as parties and the waxing of consensus-destroying actors such as single-issue groups? Does it reflect the divisive effects of a conflict-obsessed media and the polarizing effects of ideologically extreme political elites? Or are these developments too, just symptoms, not causes? Or as typically is the case, both? In the final analysis we are talking about the ability of a heterogeneous nation to govern itself, and no single factor operating in simple, straightforward fashion will determine how well or poorly we do. Future research may yet show that unified party control has some positive effects on government performance, but I doubt that it will turn out to be a "magic bullet" that will solve the vexing problems facing the nation.

Should we abandon the study of divided government then? Is it just another perspective that at first seemed to illuminate the political world, but in the end proved to obscure more than it enlightened? Despite the existing evidence, I hesitate to go that far. For one thing, the evidence on the limited effects of divided government is itself limited by the context in which it was produced. With the exception of some budgetary data from the 19th Century, virtually all the evidence comes from the post-World War II period, a period in which the New Deal party system gradually decayed into the era of divided government. Perhaps in this period of weakening party loyalties, declining parties, and the rise of new issues and problems, unified versus divided control made no difference. But is it simply an accident that the great political realignments identified by historically oriented scholars are all associated with unified government?

Jackson's Democracy captured the federal government in 1828 and held it for 12 years, setting a new policy direction after the political disarray of the 1820s. The gridlock of the 1850s was broken by Lincoln and the Republicans who took full control of the federal government in 1860 and maintained unified control for 14 years, while redefining the Union and charting a new course of economic development. The "era of no decision" came to an end with Republican capture of the federal government in 1896. They held it for 14 years, lost control for 8, then held it another 10, completing the alliance of government with business. Finally, FDR and the Democrats gained full control in 1932, held it for 14 years, and led the country into the modern world.

In each of these cases, unified control provided the political power to implement the mandate that the fact of unified control was thought to represent. There is little or no historical evidence that the development of a popular consensus preceded unified control. Quite on the contrary, Lincoln received only 40 percent of the popular vote (in a four-way election). FDR ran on a rather conservative platform, even promising to balance the budget. He struck out in a new direction only after his election. In these historical cases it appears that unified control provided an opportunity for the victorious political party to forge a new consensus, acting first, then taking its record to the electorate. The only consensus before the election was that the existing leadership should be changed.

From this perspective, divided government is important, but it is not an independent variable in a simple causal chain, as many contemporary analysts have conceived it. Rather, its place in a causal argument is more complex. It is a facilitating factor, one that helps the country lurch through one of the transformations that history periodically requires of us. Would the South have seceded if the Democrats had maintained blocking power in the Senate in the 1850s? Would FDR have had his famous 100 days if he had continued to face a Republican House majority led by Speaker Nicholas Longworth? No one can answer such counter-factual questions conclusively, but surely one could defend negative answers to questions like these.

Thus, there are at least two distinct possibilities. The first holds that divided government is only a symptom not a cause; where popular consensus exists both unified and divided governments will act on it. The second holds that unified government provides an opportunity for similarly unified political leadership to forge a popular consensus—not a guarantee, but an opportunity.

Looking ahead, the 1996 elections might shed some light on these alternative possibilities. At the present time, most observers expect the Republicans to gain seats in the House as a result of the continuing erosion of southern support for the Democrats, and retirements of Democratic incumbents in the Senate make regaining control of that body an uphill fight for the Democrats. If the Republicans were to cap off their 1994 resurgence with continued Congressional gains and capture of the Presidency, one might expect an emboldened party with unified control to move policy rightward. If the electorate were to register its approval by re-electing Republicans and maintaining unified control, their behavior would support the notion of unified control as facilitator of political change.

On the other hand, if the electorate were to reelect Bill Clinton in 1996, or elect a Republican president but get little by way of policy change, or get significant policy change but strip the Republicans of unified control in 1998 or 2000, their behavior would support the notion of divided government as symptom of popular dissensus.

As political scientists we should continue to observe and record. Our task is to analyze the evidence, refine the theoretical arguments, and construct the accounts that will inform our understanding of U.S. politics at the dawn of the new millennium.

## The Decline of Voting and the Rise of "Politics By Other Means"

*See Lowi and Ginsberg, pp. 746–756 or brief edition, pp. 415–422*

*A great frustration for many Americans is the influence wielded by rich individuals, organizations, and businesses in the governing process. The recent congressional hearings into the Democratic Party's fund-raising practices for the 1996 election revealed large contributions raised in questionable ways with possible links to public policy decisions by the White House. Why does our system operate this way? Why do the opportunities exist for what economist Paul Krugman calls, "so brazen" behavior? The answer, he argues, is simple. Average citizens, elected officials, and groups with strong interests at stake in the political process are all "rational." In the language of "rational choice" theory, people simply make decisions in a way that maximizes their self interest. Applied to politics, people will calculate the benefit to themselves of voting, contributing to the public policy debate, organizing, and contributing monetarily to elections. The theory predicts that the average citizen, when faced with the costs of participation, will choose not to, while those with a large stake in the outcomes of public policy decisions—such as corporations concerned about their tax status, or their ability to trade overseas—will gladly make monetary investments in politicians for projected returns far greater.*

*What do you think? Does the "free rider" problem explain the prominence of large financial contributors in the electoral process, and the absence of average Americans? If rational choice theory is correct, what kind of individual incentives might prompt more Americans to participate in the political process?*

# Paul Krugman
## "Rat Democracy: Economics Explains a Political Scandal"*

Like most people who once hoped for better, I have become resigned to the accumulation of tawdry detail about how President Clinton financed his re-election campaign. But condemning Clinton's brazen opportunism begs the question: Where did the opportunities to be so brazen come from?

This may seem to be a question for a political analyst, not an economist. But there is an approach to political analysis known as "rat choice" (rat as in "rational"—it's not a comment on the candidates) that flourishes along the border of the two fields. The working hypothesis of rat choice is that voting behavior reflects the more or less rational pursuit of individual interests. This may sound obvious, innocuous, and even excessively optimistic. But if you really think its implications through, they turn out to be quite subversive. Indeed, if you take rat choice seriously, you stop asking why democracy works so badly and start asking why it works at all.

What is the problem? Won't rational voters simply choose politicians who promise to serve their interests? Well, in a rough sense they do. The logic of democratic politics normally pushes both parties toward the center—more precisely, toward policies that serve the interests of the median voter. Consider, for example, the question of how big the government should be. In general, people with low incomes prefer a government that imposes high taxes in order to provide generous benefits. Those with high incomes prefer a government that does no such thing. The Democrats are, by inclination, the party of outstretched palms, the Republicans the party of tight fists. But both are forced to move away from those inclinations toward actual policies that more or less satisfy the voters in the middle, who don't like paying taxes but do like knowing that they won't be stuck with Grandma's medical bills.

But there are lots of issues that are not so big—issues that only involve, say, $10 or $20 billion a year—like who profits from electricity deregulation, or how much the government spends subsidizing irrigation water for Western farmers. Although these issues, cumulatively, are important to the electorate, the electorate doesn't vote—individual voters do. And it is rarely in the interest of the *individual* voter to take the trouble to track the details of public policy. After all, how much difference will one vote make?

Bells have just started going off in the head of any reader who remembers Econ 1. What I have just said is that the duties of a good citizen—

* Paul Krugman, "Rat Democracy: Economics Explains A Political Scandal" from *Slate*, www.slate.com (May 15, 1997). Reprinted with permission. *Slate* is a trademark of Microsoft Corporation.

such as becoming well informed before voting (and for that matter bothering to vote at all)—are subject to the dreaded *free-rider problem*. The free-rider problem arises whenever some valuable good or service is not "excludable"—that is, whenever the benefit cannot be restricted only to those who pay for it. It is clearly in the interest of all boaters to have a rescue service. But no individual boater has any incentive to pay for the service if others are willing to do so. If we leave provision of a lifesaving service up to individual decisions, each individual will try to free-ride on everyone else, and the service will be inadequate or worse.

The solution is government. It is in the collective interest of boaters that each boat owner be required to pay a fee, to support a Coast Guard that provides those nonexcludable benefits. And the same is true of police protection, public sanitation, national defense, the Centers for Disease Control, and so on. The free-rider problem is the most important reason all sane people concede that we need a government with some coercive power—the power, if nothing else, to force people to pay taxes whether or not they feel like it.

But there is a catch: The democratic process, the only decent way we know for deciding how that coercive power should be used, is itself subject to extremely severe free-rider problems. Rat-choice theorist Samuel Popkin writes (in his 1991 book, *The Reasoning Voter*): "Everybody's business is nobody's business. If everyone spends an additional hour evaluating the candidates, we all benefit from a better-informed electorate. If everyone but me spends the hour evaluating the candidates and I spend it choosing where to invest my savings, I will get a better return on my investments as well as a better government." As a result, the public at large is, entirely rationally, remarkably ill-informed about politics and policy. And that leaves the field open for special interests—which means people with a large stake in small issues—to buy policies that suit them.

For example, not many voters know or care whether the United States uses a substantial amount of its diplomatic capital to open European markets to Central American bananas. Why should they? (I only keep track of the dispute because I have to update my textbook, which includes the sentence: "Efforts to resolve Europe's banana split have proved fruitless.") But Carl Lindner, the corporate raider who now owns Chiquita Brands, has strong feelings about the issue; and thanks to his $500,000 in contributions, so does President Clinton. It's not that Clinton believed that money alone could buy him the election. But money does help, and any practical politician comes to realize that betraying the public interest on small issues involves little political cost, because voters lack the individual incentive to notice.

So what is the solution?

One answer is to try to change the incentives of politicians, by making it more difficult for special interests to buy influence. It is easy to be cynical about this, but the truth is that legal limits on how money can be given do have considerable effect. To take only the most extreme example: Outright bribes do not, as far as we can tell, play a big role in determining federal policies—and who doubts that they would if they were legal? So by all means let us have campaign-finance reform; but let us not expect too much from it.

Another answer is to promote civic virtue. There are those who believe that if only the media would treat the public with proper respect, people would respond by acting responsibly—that they would turn away from salacious stories about celebrities and read earnest articles about the flat-panel-display initiative instead. Well, never mind. But it is probably true that the quality of politics in America has suffered from the erosion of public trust in institutions that used to act, to at least some degree, as watchdogs. Once upon a time a politician had to worry about the reactions of unions, churches, newspaper editors, even local political bosses, all of whom had the time and inclination to pay attention to politics beyond the sound bites. Now we have become an atomized society of individuals who get their news—if they get it at all—from TV. If anyone has a good idea about how to bring back the opinion leaders of yore, I am all for it.

Finally, we can try to remove temptation, by avoiding policy initiatives that make it easy for politicians to play favorites. This is one reason why some of us cringed when Ron Brown began taking planeloads of businessmen off on sales trips to China and so on. Whether or not those trips did any good, or gave the wrong impression about how foreigners might influence American foreign policy, they obviously raised the question of who got to be on the plane—and how.

But there is ultimately no way to make government by the people truly be government for the people. That is what rat choice teaches, and nobody has yet proved it wrong—even in theory.

# APPENDIX OF SUPREME COURT CASES

# Appendix of
# Supreme Court Cases

*See Lowi and Ginsberg, pp. 47–48 or brief edition, pp. 45–47*

*As the text points out, early in the nation's history, the United States Supreme Court interpreted the powers of the national government expansively. The first Supreme Court case to directly address the scope of federal authority under the Constitution was McCulloch v. Maryland (1819). The facts, recited in the text, were straightforward: Congress created the Bank of the United States—to the dismay of many states who viewed the creation of a national bank as a threat to the operation of banks within their own state borders. As a result, when a branch of the Bank of the United States was opened in Maryland, that state attempted to limit the bank's ability to do business under a law that imposed taxes on all banks not chartered by the state.*

*In an opinion authored by Chief Justice Marshall, the Court considered two questions: whether Congress had the authority to create a national bank; and whether Maryland could in turn tax it. Marshall's answer to these two questions defends an expansive theory of implied powers for the national government and propounds the principle of national supremacy with an eloquence rarely found in judicial decisions.*

## *McCulloch v. Maryland* (1819)*

CHIEF JUSTICE JOHN MARSHALL delivered the opinion of the Court.

The first question made in the cause is, has Congress power to incorporate a bank? The power now contested was exercised by the first Congress elected under the present constitution. The bill for incorporating the Bank of the United States did not steal upon an unsuspecting legislature, and pass unobserved. Its principle was completely understood, and was opposed with equal zeal and ability. . . . In discussing this question, the counsel for the state of Maryland have deemed it of some importance, in the construction of the constitution, to consider that instrument not as emanating from the people, but as the act of sovereign and independent

* McCulloch v. Maryland, 17 U.S. 316, 1819.

states. The powers of the general government, it has been said, are delegated by the states, who alone are truly sovereign; and must be exercised in subordination to the states, who alone possess supreme dominion. . . . No political dreamer was ever wild enough to think of breaking down the lines which separate the states, and of compounding the American people into one common mass. Of consequence, when they act, they act in their states. But the measures they adopt do not, on that account, cease to be the measures of the people themselves, or become the measures of the state governments.

From these conventions the constitution derives its whole authority. The government proceeds directly from the people; is "ordained and established" in the name of the people; and is declared to be ordained, "in order to form a more perfect union, establish justice, insure domestic tranquility, and secure the blessings of liberty to themselves and to their posterity." The assent of the states, in their sovereign capacity, is implied in calling a convention, and thus submitting that instrument to the people. But the people were at perfect liberty to accept or reject it; and their act was final. It required not the affirmance, and could not be negatived, by the state governments. The constitution, when thus adopted, was of complete obligation, and bound the state sovereignties.

The government of the Union, then (whatever may be the influence of this fact on the case), is, emphatically, and truly, a government of the people. In form and in substance it emanates from them. Its powers are granted by them, and are to be exercised directly on them, and for their benefit.

This government is acknowledged by all to be one of enumerated powers. The principle, that it can exercise only the powers granted to it, is now universally admitted. But the question respecting the extent of the powers actually granted, is perpetually arising, and will probably continue to arise, as long as our system shall exist. The government of the United States though limited in its powers, is supreme; and its laws, when made in pursuance of the constitution, form the supreme law of the land, "anything in the constitution or laws of any state to the contrary notwithstanding." . . .

A constitution, to contain an accurate detail of all the subdivisions of which its great powers will admit, and of all the means by which they may be carried into execution, would partake of the prolixity of a legal code, and could scarcely be embraced by the human mind. It would probably never be understood by the public. Its nature, therefore, requires, that only its great outlines should be marked, its important objects designated, and the minor ingredients which compose those objects be deduced from the nature of the objects themselves. . . . in considering this question, then, we must never forget, that it is a constitution we are expounding.

Although, among the enumerated powers of government, we do not find the word "bank" or "incorporation," we find the great powers to lay and collect taxes; to borrow money; to regulate commerce; to declare and conduct a war; and to raise and support armies and navies. The sword and the purse, all the external relations, and no inconsiderable portion of the industry of the nation, are entrusted to its government. . . . [I]t may with great reason be contended, that a government, entrusted with such ample powers, on the due execution of which the happiness and prosperity of the nation so vitally depends, must also be entrusted with ample means for their execution. The power being given, it is the interest of the nation to facilitate its execution. It can never be their interest, and cannot be presumed to have been their intention, to clog and embarrass its execution by withholding the most appropriate means. . . . It is, then, the subject of fair inquiry, how far such means may be employed.

The government which has a right to do an act, and has imposed on it the duty of performing that act, must, according to the dictates of reason, be allowed to select the means. . . .

But the constitution of the United States has not left the right of Congress to employ the necessary means, for the execution of the powers conferred on the government, to general reasoning. To its enumeration of powers is added that of making "all laws which shall be necessary and proper, for carrying into execution the foregoing powers, and all other powers vested by this constitution, in the government of the United States, or in any department [or officer] thereof."

The counsel for the state of Maryland have urged various arguments, to prove that this clause . . . is really restrictive of the general right, which might otherwise be implied, of selecting means for executing the enumerated powers.

. . . [Maryland argues that] Congress is not empowered by it to make all laws, which may have relation to the powers conferred on the government, but such only as may be "necessary and proper" for carrying them into execution. The word "necessary" is considered as controlling the whole sentence, and as limiting the right to pass laws for the execution of the granted powers, to such as are indispensable, and without which the power would be nugatory. That it excludes the choice of means, and leaves to Congress, in each case, that only which is most direct and simple.

Is it true, that this is the sense in which the word "necessary" is always used? . . . We think it does not. If reference be had to its use, in the common affairs of the world, or in approved authors, we find that it frequently imports no more than that one thing is convenient, or useful, or essential to another. To employ the means necessary to an end, is generally understood as employing any means calculated to produce the end, and not as being confined to those single means, without which the end would be entirely unattainable.

Let this be done in the case under consideration. The subject is the execution of those great powers on which the welfare of a nation essentially depends. It must have been the intention of those who gave these powers, to insure, as far as human prudence could insure, their beneficial execution. This could not be done by confiding the choice of means to such narrow limits as not to leave it in the power of Congress to adopt any which might be appropriate, and which were conducive to the end. This provision is made in a constitution intended to endure for ages to come, and consequently, to be adapted to the various crises of human affairs. To have prescribed the means by which government should, in all future time, execute its powers, would have been to change, entirely, the character of the instrument, and give it the properties of a legal code. It would have been an unwise attempt to provide, by immutable rules, for exigencies which, if foreseen at all, must have been seen dimly, and which can be best provided for as they occur. To have declared that the best means shall not be used, but those alone without which the power given would be nugatory, would have been to deprive the legislature of the capacity to avail itself of experience, to exercise its reason, and to accommodate its legislation to circumstances. If we apply this principle of construction to any of the powers of the government, we shall find it so pernicious in its operation that we shall be compelled to discard it. . . .

We admit, as all must admit, that the powers of the government are limited, and that its limits are not to be transcended. But we think the sound construction of the constitution must allow to the national legislature that discretion, with respect to the means by which the powers it confers are to be carried into execution, which will enable that body to perform the high duties assigned to it, in the manner most beneficial to the people. Let the end be legitimate, let it be within the scope of the constitution, and all means which are appropriate, which are plainly adapted to that end, which are not prohibited, but consist with the letter and spirit of the constitution, are constitutional. . . .

It being the opinion of the court that the act incorporating the bank is constitutional, and that the power of establishing a branch in the state of Maryland might be properly exercised by the bank itself, we proceed to inquire: Whether the state of Maryland may, without violating the constitution, tax that branch?

That the power of taxation is one of vital importance; that it is retained by the states; that it is not abridged by the grant of a similar power to the government of the Union; that it is to be concurrently exercised by the two governments; are truths which have never been denied. But, such is the paramount character of the constitution that its capacity to withdraw any subject from the action of even this power, is admitted. . . . [T]he paramount character [of the Constitution] would seem to restrain, as it certainly may restrain, a state from such other exercise of this power as is in its nature incompatible with, and repugnant to, the constitutional laws of the Union. A law, absolutely repugnant to another, as entirely repeals that other as if express terms of repeal were used. . . .

This great principle is, that the constitution and the laws made in pursuance thereof are supreme; that they control the constitution and laws of the respective states, and cannot be controlled by them. From this, which may be almost termed an axiom, other propositions are adduced as corollaries, on the truth or error of which, and on their application to this case, the cause has been supposed to depend. These are, 1st. That a power to create implies a power to preserve. 2d. That a power to destroy, if wielded by a different hand, is hostile to, and incompatible with, these powers to create and to preserve. 3d. That where this repugnance exists, that authority which is supreme must control, not yield to that over which it is supreme.

. . . [T]axation is said to be an absolute power, which acknowledges no other limits than those expressly prescribed in the constitution, and like sovereign powers of every other description, is trusted to the discretion of those who use it. But the very terms of this argument admit that the sovereignty of the state, in the article of taxation itself, is subordinate to, and may be controlled by the constitution of the United States. How far it has been controlled by that instrument must be a question of construction. In making this construction, no principle not declared can be admissible, which would defeat the legitimate operations of a supreme government. . . .

All subjects over which the sovereign power of a state extends, are objects of taxation; but those over which it does not extend, are, upon the soundest principles, exempt from taxation. . . . The sovereignty of a state extends to everything which exists by its own authority, or is introduced by its permission; but does it extend to those means which are employed by Congress to carry into execution—powers conferred on that body by the people of the United States? We think it demonstrable that it does not. Those powers are not given by the people of a single state. They are given by the people of the United States, to a government whose laws, made in pursuance of the constitution, are declared to be supreme. Consequently, the people of a single state cannot confer a sovereignty which will extend over them.

If we apply the principle for which the state of Maryland contends, to the constitution generally, we shall find it capable of changing totally the character of that instrument. We shall find it capable of arresting all the measures of the government, and of prostrating it at the foot of the states. The American people have declared their constitution, and the laws made in pursuance thereof, to be supreme; but this principle would transfer the supremacy, in fact, to the states. If the controlling power of the states be established; if their supremacy as to taxation be acknowledged; what is to restrain their exercising this control in any shape they may please to give it? Their sovereignty is not confined to taxation. That is not the only mode in which it might be displayed. The question is, in truth, a question of supremacy; and if the right of the states to tax the means employed by the general government be conceded, the declaration that the constitution, and the laws made in pursuance thereof, shall be the supreme law of the land, is empty and unmeaning declamation. . . .

We are unanimously of opinion, that the law passed by the legislature of Maryland, imposing a tax on the Bank of the United States, is unconstitutional and void. This opinion does not deprive the states of any resources which they originally possessed. It does not extend to a tax paid by the real property of the bank, in common with other real property within the state, nor to a tax imposed on the interest which the citizens of Maryland may hold in this institution, in common with other property of the same description throughout the state. But this is a tax on the operations of the bank, and is, consequently, a tax on the operation of an instrument employed by the government of the Union to carry its powers into execution. Such a tax must be unconstitutional.

Reversed.

> *See Lowi and Ginsberg, pp. 115–116 or brief edition, pp. 73–76*
>
> *The declaration made in* Barron v. Baltimore *(1833) that citizenship had a dual aspect—state and national—set the terms of the Supreme Court's interpretation of the Bill of Rights for nearly 150 years. The reasoning of the case proved persuasive even after the adoption of the Fourteenth Amendment, as the federal courts refused to extend the protections of the federal Constitution to citizens aggrieved by the actions of state or local governments.*

## *Barron v. Baltimore* (1833)\*

[*Barron brought suit in a federal court claiming that the city of Baltimore had appropriated his property for a public purpose without paying him just compensation. He asserted that the Fifth Amendment to the Constitution operated as a constraint upon both state and federal governments.*]

CHIEF JUSTICE JOHN MARSHALL delivered the opinion of the Court.

. . . The question presented is, we think, of great importance, but not of much difficulty. The constitution was ordained and established by the people of the United States for themselves, for their own government, and not for the government of the individual states. Each state established a constitution for itself, and in that constitution, provided such limitations and restrictions on the powers of its particular government, as its judgment dictated. The people of the United States framed such a government for the United States as they supposed best adapted to their situation and best calculated to promote their interests. The powers they conferred on this government were to be exercised by itself; and the limitations on power, if expressed in general terms, are naturally, and, we think, necessarily, applicable to the government created by the instrument. They are limitations of power granted in the instrument itself; not of distinct governments, framed by different persons and for different purposes.

If these propositions be correct, the fifth amendment must be understood as restraining the power of the general government, not as applicable to the states. In their several constitutions, they have imposed such restrictions on their respective governments, as their own wisdom sug-

\* Barron v. Baltimore, 32 U.S. 243, 1833.

gested; such as they deemed most proper for themselves. It is a subject on which they judge exclusively, and with which others interfere no further than they are supposed to have a common interest. . . .

Had the people of the several states, or any of them, required changes in their constitutions; had they required additional safe-guards to liberty from the apprehended encroachments of their particular governments; the remedy was in their own hands, and could have been applied by themselves. A convention could have been assembled by the discontented state, and the required improvements could have been made by itself.

. . . Had congress engaged in the extraordinary occupation of improving the constitutions of the several states, by affording the people additional protection from the exercise of power by their own governments, in matters which concerned themselves alone, they would have declared this purpose in plain and intelligible language.

But it is universally understood, it is a part of the history of the day, that the great revolution which established the constitution of the United States, was not effected without immense opposition. Serious fears were extensively entertained, that those powers which the patriot statesmen, who then watched over the interests of our country, deemed essential to union, and to the attainment of those unvaluable objects for which union was sought, might be exercised in a manner dangerous to liberty. In almost every convention by which the constitution was adopted, amendments to guard against the abuse of power were recommended. These amendments demanded security against the apprehended encroachments of the general government—not against those of the local governments. In compliance with a sentiment thus generally expressed, to quiet fears thus extensively entertained, amendments were proposed by the required majority in congress, and adopted by the states. These amendments contain no expression indicating an intention to apply them to the state governments. This court cannot so apply them.

We are of opinion, that the provision in the fifth amendment to the constitution, declaring that private property shall not be taken for public use, without just compensation, is intended solely as a limitation on the exercise of power by the government of the United States, and is not applicable to the legislation of the states. We are, therefore, of opinion, that there is no repugnancy between the several acts of the general assembly of Maryland, given in evidence by the defendants at the trial of this cause, in the court of that state, and the constitution of the United States. This court, therefore, has no jurisdiction of the cause, and it is dismissed.

This cause came on to be heard, on the transcript of the record from the court of appeals for the western shore of the state of Maryland, and was argued by counsel: On consideration whereof, it is the opinion of this court, that there is no repugnancy between the several acts of the general assembly of Maryland, given in evidence by the defendants at the trial of this cause in the court of that state, and the constitution of the United States; whereupon, it is ordered and adjudged by this court, that this writ of error be and the same is hereby dismissed, for the want of jurisdiction.

*See Lowi and Ginsberg, pp. 134–139 or brief edition, pp. 76–77*

Brown v. Board of Education *(1954) was a momentous opinion, invalidating the system of segregation that had been established under* Plessy v. Ferguson *(1896). As the text points out, however, the constitutional pronouncement only marked the beginning of the struggle for racial equality, as federal courts got more and more deeply involved in trying to prod recalcitrant state and local governments into taking steps to end racial inequalities. The* Brown *decision follows.*

# Brown v. Board of Education (1954)*

[ *The* Brown *case involved appeals from several states. In each case, the plaintiffs had been denied access to public schools designated only for white children under a variety of state laws. They challenged the* Plessy v. Ferguson *(1896) "separate but equal" doctrine, contending that segregated schools were by their nature unequal.*

*Chief Justice Warren first discussed the history of the Fourteenth Amendment's equal protection clause, finding it too inconclusive to be of assistance in determining how the Fourteenth Amendment should be applied to the question of public education.*]

CHIEF JUSTICE WARREN writing for the majority.

. . . The doctrine of "separate but equal" did not make its appearance in this Court until 1896, in the case of Plessy v. Ferguson, involving not education but transportation. American courts have since labored with the doctrine for over half a century. In this Court, there have been six cases involving the "separate but equal" doctrine in the field of public education. . . .

In the instant cases, [the question of the application of the separate but equal doctrine to public education] is directly presented. Here, . . . there are findings below that the Negro and white schools involved have been equalized, or are being equalized, with respect to buildings, curricula, qualifications and salaries of teachers, and other "tangible" factors. Our decision, therefore, cannot turn on merely a comparison of these tangible factors in the Negro and white schools involved in each of the cases. We must look instead to the effect of segregation itself on public education.

In approaching this problem, we cannot turn the clock back to 1868 when the [Fourteenth] Amendment was adopted, or even to 1896 when Plessy v. Ferguson was written. We must consider public education in the light of its full development and its present place in American life throughout the Nation. Only in this way can it be determined if segrega-

* *Brown v. Board of Education of Topeka, Kansas,* 347 U.S. 483, 1954.

tion in public schools deprives these plaintiffs of the equal protection of the laws.

Today, education is perhaps the most important function of state and local governments. Compulsory school attendance laws and the great expenditures for education both demonstrate our recognition of the importance of education to our democratic society. It is required in the performance of our most basic public responsibilities, even service in the armed forces. It is the very foundation of good citizenship. Today it is a principal instrument in awakening the child to cultural values, in preparing him for later professional training, and in helping him to adjust normally to his environment. In these days, it is doubtful that any child may reasonably be expected to succeed in life if he is denied the opportunity of an education. Such an opportunity, where the state has undertaken to provide it, is a right which must be made available to all on equal terms.

We come then to the question presented: Does segregation of children in public schools solely on the basis of race, even though the physical facilities and other "tangible" factors may be equal, deprive the children of the minority group of equal educational opportunities? We believe that it does.

In Sweatt v. Painter, in finding that a segregated law school for Negroes could not provide them equal educational opportunities, this Court relied in large part on "those qualities which are incapable of objective measurement but which make for greatness in a law school." In McLaurin v. Oklahoma State Regents, the Court, in requiring that a Negro admitted to a white graduate school be treated like all other students, again resorted to intangible considerations: ". . . his ability to study, to engage in discussions and exchange views with other students, and, in general, to learn his profession." Such considerations apply with added force to children in grade and high schools. To separate them from others of similar age and qualifications solely because of their race generates a feeling of inferiority as to their status in the community that may effect their hearts and minds in a way unlikely ever to be undone. The effect of this separation on their educational opportunities was well stated by a finding in the Kansas case by a court which nevertheless felt compelled to rule against the Negro plaintiffs:

"Segregation of white and colored children in public schools has a detrimental effect upon the colored children. The impact is greater when it has the sanction of the law; for the policy of separating the races is usually interpreted as denoting the inferiority of the Negro group. A sense of inferiority affects the motivation of a child to learn. Segregation with the sanction of law, therefore, has a tendency to [retard] the educational and mental development of Negro children and to deprive them of some of the benefits they would receive in a racial[ly] integrated school system." Whatever may have been the extent of psychological knowledge at the time of Plessy v. Ferguson, this finding is amply supported by modern authority. Any language in Plessy v. Ferguson contrary to this finding is rejected.

We conclude that in the field of public education the doctrine of "separate but equal" has no place. Separate educational facilities are inherently unequal. Therefore, we hold that the plaintiffs and others similarly situated for whom the actions have been brought are, by reason of the segregation complained of, deprived of the equal protection of the laws guaranteed by the Fourteenth Amendment. This disposition makes unnecessary any discussion whether such segregation also violates the Due Process Clause of the Fourteenth Amendment.

Because these are class actions, because of the wide applicability of this decision, and because of the great variety of local conditions, the formulation of decrees in these cases presents problems of considerable complexity. On reargument, the consideration of appropriate relief was necessarily subordinated to the primary question—the constitutionality of segregation in public education. We have now announced that such segregation is a denial of the equal protection of the laws.

*See Lowi and Ginsberg, pp. 78 and 82 or brief edition, p. 122*

*One of the most significant changes in constitutional interpretation in the last twenty-five years has been the Court's willingness to look beyond the explicit language of the Bill of Rights to find unenumerated rights, such as the right to privacy. In discovering such rights, the Court has engaged in what is known as substantive due process analysis—defining and articulating fundamental rights—distinct from its efforts to define the scope of procedural due process, when it decides what procedures the state and federal governments must follow to be fair in their treatment of citizens. The Court's move into the substantive due process area has generated much of the political discussion over the proper role of the Court in constitutional interpretation, as discussed in further detail in Chapter 8 of your textbook.*

*The case that has been the focal point for this debate is* Roe v. Wade, *the 1973 case which held that a woman's right to privacy protected her decision to have an abortion. The right to privacy in matters relating to contraception and childbearing had been recognized in the 1965 decision of* Griswold v. Connecticut, *and was extended in subsequent decisions culminating in* Roe. *The theoretical issue of concern here relates back to the incorporation issue: Should the Supreme Court be able to prohibit the states not only from violating the express guarantees contained in the Bill of Rights, but its implied guarantees as well?*

# *Roe v. Wade* (1973)*

[*Texas law prohibited abortions except for "the purpose of saving the life of the mother." Plaintiff challenged the constitutionality of the statute, claiming that it infringed upon her substantive due process right to privacy.*]

* *Roe v. Wade,* 410 U.S. 113, 1973.

JUSTICE BLACKMUN delivered the opinion of the Court.

. . . [We] forthwith acknowledge our awareness of the sensitive and emotional nature of the abortion controversy, of the vigorous opposing views, and the deep and seemingly absolute convictions that the subject inspires. One's philosophy, one's experiences, one's exposure to the raw edges of human existence, one's religious training, one's attitudes toward life and family and their values, and the moral standards one establishes and seeks to observe, are all likely to affect one's thinking [about] abortion. In addition, population growth, pollution, poverty, and racial overtones tend to complicate and not to simplify the problem. Our task, of course, is to resolve the issue by constitutional measurement, free of emotion and of predilection. We seek earnestly to do this, and, because we do, we have inquired into, and in this opinion place some emphasis upon, medical and medical-legal history and what that history reveals about man's attitudes toward the abortion procedure over the centuries. . . .

[*The Court here reviewed ancient and contemporary attitudes toward abortion, observing that restrictive laws date primarily from the late nineteenth century. The Court also reviewed the possible state interests in restricting abortions, including discouraging illicit sexual conduct, limiting access to a hazardous medical procedure, and the states' general interests in protecting fetal life. The Court addressed only the third interest as a current legitimate interest of the state.*]

. . . The Constitution does not explicitly mention any right of privacy. In a line of decisions, however, . . . the Court has recognized that a right of personal privacy, or a guarantee of certain areas or zones of privacy, does exist under the Constitution. . . . This right of privacy, whether it be founded in the Fourteenth Amendment's concept of personal liberty and restrictions upon state action, as we feel it is, or, as the District Court determined, in the Ninth Amendment's reservation of rights to the people, is broad enough to encompass a woman's decision whether or not to terminate her pregnancy. The detriment that the State would impose upon the pregnant woman by denying this choice altogether is apparent. Specific and direct harm medically diagnosable even in early pregnancy may be involved. Maternity, or additional offspring, may force upon the woman a distressful life and future. Psychological harm may be imminent. Mental and physical health may be taxed by child care. There is also the distress, for all concerned, associated with the unwanted child, and there is the problem of bringing a child into a family already unable, psychologically and otherwise, to care for it. In other cases, as in this one, the additional difficulties and continuing stigma of unwed motherhood may be involved. All these are factors the woman and her responsible physician necessarily will consider in consultation.

On the basis of elements such as these, appellants and some amici argue that the woman's right is absolute and that she is entitled to terminate her pregnancy at whatever time, in whatever way, and for whatever reason she alone chooses. With this we do not agree. Appellants' arguments that Texas either has no valid interest at all in regulating the abortion decision, or no interest strong enough to support any limitation upon the woman's sole determination, is unpersuasive. The Court's decisions recognizing a right of privacy also acknowledge that some state regulation in areas protected by that right is appropriate. As noted above, a State may properly assert important interests in safeguarding health, in maintaining medical standards, and in protecting potential life. At some point in pregnancy, these respective interests become sufficiently compelling to sustain regulation of the factors that govern the abortion decision. The privacy right involved, therefore, cannot be said to be absolute. In fact, it is not clear to us that the claim asserted by some amici that one has an unlimited right to do with one's body as one pleases bears a close relationship to the right of privacy previously articulated in the Court's decisions. . . .

We therefore conclude that the right of personal privacy includes the abortion decision, but that this right is not unqualified and must be considered against state interests in regulation.

Where certain "fundamental rights" are involved, the Court has held that regulation limiting these rights may be justified only by a "compelling state interest," and that legislative enactments must be narrowly drawn to express only the legitimate state interests at stake.

. . . The District Court held that the appellee failed to meet his burden of demonstrating that the Texas statute's infringement upon Roe's rights was necessary to support a compelling state interest. . . . Appellee argues that the State's determination to recognize and protect prenatal life from and after conception constitutes a compelling state interest. As noted above, we do not agree fully with either formulation.

The appellee and certain amici argue that the fetus is a "person" within the language and meaning of the Fourteenth Amendment. In support of this they outline at length and in detail the well-known facts of fetal development. If this suggestion of personhood is established, the appellant's case, of course, collapses, for the fetus' right to life is then guaranteed specifically by the Amendment. The appellant conceded as much on reargument. On the other hand, the appellee conceded on reargument that no case could be cited that holds that a fetus is a person within the meaning of the Fourteenth Amendment.

The Constitution does not define "person" in so many words. Section 1 of the Fourteenth Amendment contains three references to "person." The first, in defining "citizens," speaks of "persons born or naturalized in the United States." The word also appears both in the Due Process Clause and in the Equal Protection Clause. "Person" is used in other places in the Constitution. . . . But in nearly all these instances, the use of the word is such that it has application only postnatally. None indicates, with any assurance, that it has any possible pre-natal application.

All this, together with our observation, that throughout the major portion of the 19th century prevailing legal abortion practices were far freer than they are today, persuades us that the word "person," as used in the Fourteenth Amendment, does not include the unborn.

. . . The pregnant woman cannot be isolated in her privacy. She carries an embryo and, later, a fetus, if one accepts the medical definitions of the developing young in the human uterus. . . . The situation therefore is inherently different from marital intimacy, or bedroom possession of obscene material, or marriage, or procreation, or education, with which [earlier cases defining the right to privacy] were concerned. As we have intimated above, it is reasonable and appropriate for a State to decide that at some point in time another interest, that of health of the mother or that of potential human life, becomes significantly involved. The woman's privacy is no longer sole and any right of privacy she possesses must be measured accordingly.

Texas urges that, apart from the Fourteenth Amendment, life begins at conception and is present throughout pregnancy, and that, therefore, the State has a compelling interest in protecting that life from and after conception. We need not resolve the difficult question of when life begins. When those trained in the respective disciplines of medicine, philosophy, and theology are unable to arrive at any consensus, the judiciary, at this point in the development of man's knowledge, is not in a position to speculate as to the answer.

. . . In view of all this, we do not agree that, by adopting one theory of life, Texas may override the rights of the pregnant woman that are at stake. We repeat, however, that the State does have an important and legitimate interest in preserving and protecting the health of the pregnant woman, whether she be a resident of the State or a nonresident who seeks medical consultation and treatment there, and that it has still *another* important and legitimate interest in protecting the potentiality of human life. These interests are separate and distinct. Each grows in substantiality as the woman approaches term and, at a point during pregnancy, each becomes "compelling."

With respect to the State's important and legitimate interest in the health of the mother, the "compelling" point, in the light of present medical knowledge, is at approximately the end of the first trimester. This is so because of the now established medical fact . . . that until the end of the first trimester mortality in abortion is less than mortality in normal childbirth. It follows that, from and after this point, a State may regulate the abortion procedure to the extent that the regulation reasonably relates to the preservation and protection of maternal health. Examples of permissible state regulation in this area are requirements as to the qualifications of the person who is to perform the abortion; as to the licensure of that person; as to the facility in which the procedure is to be performed, that is, whether it must be a hospital or may be a clinic or some other place of less-than-hospital status; as to the licensing of the facility; and the like.

This means, on the other hand, that, for the period of pregnancy prior to this "compelling" point, the attending physician, in consultation with his patient, is free to determine, without regulation by the State, that in his medical judgment the patient's pregnancy should be terminated. If that decision is reached, the judgment may be effectuated by an abortion free of interference by the State.

With respect to the State's important and legitimate interest in potential life, the "compelling" point is at viability. This is so because the fetus then presumably has the capability of meaningful life outside the mother's womb. State regulation protective of fetal life after viability thus has both logical and biological justifications. If the State is interested in protecting fetal life after viability, it may go so far as to proscribe abortion during that period except when it is necessary to preserve the life or health of the mother.

Measured against these standards, the Texas Penal Code, in restricting legal abortions to those "procured or attempted by medical advice for the purpose of saving the life of the mother," sweeps too broadly. The statute makes no distinction between abortions performed early in pregnancy and those performed later, and it limits to a single reason, "saving" the mother's life, the legal justification for the procedure. The statute, therefore, cannot survive the constitutional attack made upon it here. . . .

Reversed.

> *See Lowi and Ginsberg, p. 91*
>
> *The Supreme Court has had few occasions to rule on the constitutional limits of executive authority. As discussed in Chapters 4 and 8 of the text, the Court is understandably reluctant to articulate the boundaries of presidential and legislative power, given the Court's own somewhat ambiguous institutional authority. In the case that follows, however, the Court looked at one of the ways in which the Constitution circumscribes the exercise of presidential prerogative.*
>
> *United States v. Nixon (1974) involves claims to executive authority. President Richard Nixon had been implicated in a conspiracy to cover up a burglary of the Democratic Party Headquarters at the Watergate Hotel in Washington, D.C., during the 1972 re-election campaign. The Special Prosecutor assigned to investigate the break-in and file appropriate criminal charges asked the trial court to order the President to disclose a number of documents and tapes related to the cover-up in order to determine the scope of the President's involvement. The President produced edited versions of some of the materials, but refused to comply with most of the trial court's order, asserting that he was entitled to withhold the information under a claim of "executive privilege."*

# United States v. Nixon (1974)*

CHIEF JUSTICE BURGER delivered the opinion of the Court.

In the District Court, the President's counsel argued that the court lacked jurisdiction to issue the subpoena because the matter was an intra-branch dispute between a subordinate and superior officer of the Executive Branch and hence not subject to judicial resolution. That argument has been renewed in this Court with emphasis on the contention that the dispute does not present a "case" or "controversy" which can be adjudicated in the federal courts. The President's counsel argues that the federal courts should not intrude into areas committed to the other branches of Government. He views the present dispute as essentially a "jurisdictional" dispute within the Executive Branch which he analogizes to a dispute between two congressional committees. Since the Executive Branch has exclusive authority and absolute discretion to decide whether to prosecute a case, it is contended that a President's decision is final in determining what evidence is to be used in a given criminal case.

. . . Although his counsel concedes the President has delegated certain specific powers to the Special Prosecutor, he has not "waived nor delegated to the Special Prosecutor the President's duty to claim privilege as to all materials which fall within the President's inherent authority to refuse to disclose to any executive officer." The Special Prosecutor's demand for the items therefore presents, in the view of the President's counsel, a political question since it involves a "textually demonstrable" grant of power under Art. II. . . .

The demands of and the resistance to the subpoena present an obvious controversy in the ordinary sense, but that alone is not sufficient to meet constitutional standards. In the constitutional sense, controversy means more than disagreement and conflict; rather it means the kind of controversy courts traditionally resolve. Here at issue is the production or non-production of specified evidence deemed by the Special Prosecutor to be relevant and admissible in a pending criminal case. It is sought by one official of the Government within the scope of his express authority; it is resisted by the Chief Executive on the ground of his duty to preserve the confidentiality of the communications of the President. Whatever the correct answer on the merits, these issues are "of a type which are traditionally justiciable." . . .

. . . We turn to the claim that the subpoena should be quashed because it demands "confidential conversations between a President and his close advisors that it would be inconsistent with the public interest to produce." The first contention is a broad claim that the separation of powers doctrine precludes judicial review of a President's claim of privilege. The second contention is that if he does not prevail on the claim of absolute

* United States v. Nixon, 418 U.S. 683, 1974.

privilege, the court should hold as a matter of constitutional law that the privilege prevails over the subpoena *duces tecum.* . . .

[*The Court discussed its authority to interpret the Constitution, concluding that it had full power to interpret a claim of executive privilege.*]

In support of his claim of absolute privilege, the President's counsel urges two grounds one of which is common to all governments and one of which is peculiar to our system of separation of powers. The first ground is the valid need for protection of communications between high government officials and those who advise and assist them in the performance of their manifold duties; the importance of this confidentiality is too plain to require further discussion. Human experience teaches that those who expect public dissemination of their remarks may well temper candor with a concern for appearances and for their own interests to the detriment of the decisionmaking process. Whatever the nature of the privilege of confidentiality of presidential communications in the exercise of Art. II powers the privilege can be said to derive from the supremacy of each branch within its own assigned area of constitutional duties. Certain powers and privileges flow from the nature of enumerated powers; the protection of the confidentiality of presidential communications has similar constitutional underpinnings.

The second ground asserted by the President's counsel in support of the claim of absolute privilege rests on the doctrine of separation of powers. Here it is argued that the independence of the Executive Branch within its own sphere, insulates a president from a judicial subpoena in an ongoing criminal prosecution, and thereby protects confidential presidential communications.

However, neither the doctrine of separation of powers, nor the need for confidentiality of high level communications, without more, can sustain an absolute, unqualified presidential privilege of immunity from judicial process under all circumstances. The President's need for complete candor and objectivity from advisers calls for great deference from the courts. However, when the privilege depends solely on the broad, undifferentiated claim of public interest in the confidentiality of such conversations, a confrontation with other values arises. Absent a claim of need to protect military, diplomatic or sensitive national security secrets, we find it difficult to accept the argument that even the very important interest in confidentiality of presidential communications is significantly diminished by production of such material for *in camera* inspection with all the protection that a district court will be obliged to provide.

The impediment that an absolute, unqualified privilege would place in the way of the primary constitutional duty of the judicial branch to do justice in criminal prosecutions would plainly conflict with the function of the courts under Art. III. In designing the structure of our Government and dividing and allocating the sovereign power among three coequal branches, the Framers of the Constitution sought to provide a comprehensive system, but the separate powers were not intended to operate with absolute independence. To read the Art. II powers of the President as providing an absolute privilege as against a subpoena essential to enforcement of criminal statues on no more than a generalized claim of the public interest in confidentiality of nonmilitary and nondiplomatic discussions would upset the constitutional balance of "a workable government" and gravely impair the role of the courts under Art. III.

Since we conclude that the legitimate needs of the judicial process may outweigh presidential privilege, it is necessary to resolve those competing interests in a manner that preserves the essential functions of each branch. The right and indeed the duty to resolve that question does not free the judiciary from according high respect to the representations made on behalf of the President. The expectation of a President to the confidentiality of his conversations and correspondence, like the claim of confidentiality of judicial deliberations, for example, has all the values to which we accord deference for the privacy of all citizens and added to those values the necessity for protection of the public interest in his responsibilities against the inroads of such a privilege on the fair administration of criminal justice. The interest in preserving confidentiality is weighty indeed and entitled to great respect. However we cannot conclude that advisers will be moved to temper the candor of their remarks by the infrequent occasions of disclosure because of the possibility that such conversations will be called for in the context of a criminal prosecution.

On the other hand, the allowance of the privilege to withhold evidence that is demonstrably relevant in a criminal trial would cut deeply into the guarantee of due process of law and gravely impair the basic function of the courts. A President's acknowledged need for confidentiality in the communications of his office is general in nature, whereas the constitutional need for production of relevant evidence in a criminal proceeding is specific and central to the fair adjudication of a particular criminal case in the administration of justice. Without access to specific facts a criminal prosecution may be totally frustrated. The President's broad interest in confidentiality of communications will not be vitiated by disclosure of a limited number of conversations preliminarily shown to have some bearing on the pending criminal cases.

We conclude that when the ground for asserting privilege as to subpoenaed materials sought for use in a criminal trial is based only on the generalized interest in confidentiality, it cannot prevail over the fundamental demands of due process of law in the fair administration of criminal justice. The generalized assertion of privilege must yield to the demonstrated, specific need for evidence in a pending criminal trial. . . .

In this case the President challenges a subpoena served on him as a third party requiring the production of materials for use in a criminal prosecution on the claim that he has a privilege against disclosure of confidential communications. He does not place his claim of privilege on the ground they are military or diplomatic secrets. As to these areas of Art. II duties the courts have traditionally shown the utmost deference to presidential responsibilities. No case of the Court, however, has extended this high degree of deference to a President's generalized interest in confidentiality. Nowhere in the Constitution, as we have noted earlier, is there any explicit reference to a privilege of confidentiality; yet to the extent this interest relates to the effective discharge of a President's powers, it is constitutionally based. . . .

[*The Court distinguished this case from cases involving claims against the president while acting in an official capacity.*]

Mr. Chief Justice Marshall sitting as a trial judge in the *Burr* case was extraordinarily careful to point out that: "[I]n no case of this kind would a Court be required to proceed against the President as against an ordinary individual." Marshall's statement cannot be read to mean in any sense that a President is above the law, but relates to the singularly unique role under Art. II of a President's communications and activities, related to the performance of duties under that Article. Moreover, a President's communications and activities encompass a vastly wider range of sensitive material than would be true of any "ordinary individual." It is therefore necessary in the public interest to afford presidential confidentiality the greatest protection consistent with the fair administration of justice. The need for confidentiality even as to idle conversations with associates in which casual reference might be made concerning political leaders within the country or foreign statesmen is too obvious to call for further treatment. We have no doubt that the District Judge will at all times accord to presidential records that high degree of deference suggested in *United States v. Burr*, and will discharge his responsibility to see to it that until released to the Special Prosecutor no *in camera* material is revealed to anyone. This burden applies with even greater force to excised material; once the decision is made to excise, the material is restored to its privileged status and should be returned under seal to its lawful custodian.

Affirmed.

*See Lowi and Ginsberg, pp. 126–127 or brief edition, pp. 80–82*

In Roe v. Wade *(1973), the Court held that the right to privacy encompassed a woman's right to choose to have an abortion. In the twenty years since* Roe *was decided, a number of states have passed statutes attempting to limit that right and the Court indicated that it would uphold regulations on abortions so long as they did not place an "undue burden" upon a woman's right to choose an abortion, which was a less restrictive test for evaluating the constitutionality of the regulations than might have been applied, and which allowed for a broad interpretation by the states. Therefore, when a Pennsylvania law imposing significant restrictions on abortion "on demand" was passed in the early 1990s,* Planned Parenthood of SEPA *sued the state's Governor, Tom Casey, for violating a woman's right to an abortion.*

The Court in Planned Parenthood v. Casey *reaffirmed* Roe *by a bare majority.*

> A prominent factor in the majority's opinion was the extent to which the Court should be willing to upset a prior holding. The majority opinion discussed in detail the conditions under which a departure from a settled interpretation ought to be considered, and expressed concern about perceptions of institutional legitimacy that might result if it acted too precipitously to overturn a prior decision. The dissent argued just as strongly that the Court was not compelled to save Roe, since the initial decision was ill-considered.

## Planned Parenthood of Southeastern Pennsylvania v. Casey (1992)*

JUSTICE O'CONNOR, JUSTICE KENNEDY, and JUSTICE SOUTER announce the judgment of the Court.

### I

After considering the fundamental constitutional questions resolved by *Roe* [*v. Wade,* . . . ], principles of institutional integrity, and the rule of *stare decisis*, we are led to conclude this: the essential holding of *Roe v. Wade* should be retained and once again reaffirmed.

It must be stated at the outset and with clarity that *Roe*'s essential holding, the holding we reaffirm, has three parts. First is a recognition of the right of the woman to choose to have an abortion before viability and to obtain it without undue interference from the State. Before viability, the State's interests are not strong enough to support a prohibition of abortion or the imposition of a substantial obstacle to the woman's effective right to elect the procedure. Second is a confirmation of the State's power to restrict abortions after fetal viability, if the law contains exceptions for pregnancies which endanger a woman's life or health. And third is the principle that the State has legitimate interests from the outset of the pregnancy in protecting the health of the woman and the life of the fetus that may become a child. These principles do not contradict one another; and we adhere to each. . . .

### II

Our law affords constitutional protection to personal decisions relating to marriage, procreation, contraception, family relationships, child rearing, and education. Our cases recognize "the right of the individual, married or single, to be free from unwarranted governmental intrusion into mat-

* *Planned Parenthood of Southeastern Pennsylvania v. Casey,* 112 S.Ct. 2791.

ters so fundamentally affecting a person as the decision whether to bear or beget a child." *Eisenstadt v. Baird,* . . . Our precedents "have respected the private realm of family life which the state cannot enter." *Prince v. Massachusetts,* . . . These matters, involving the most intimate and personal choices a person may make in a lifetime, choices central to personal dignity and autonomy, are central to the liberty protected by the Fourteenth Amendment. At the heart of liberty is the right to define one's own concept of existence, of meaning, of the universe, and of the mystery of human life. . . .

While we appreciate the weight of the arguments made on behalf of the State in the case before us, arguments which in their ultimate formulation conclude that *Roe* should be overruled, the reservations any of us may have in reaffirming the central holding of *Roe* are outweighed by the explication of individual liberty we have given combined with the force of *stare decisis.* We turn now to that doctrine.

# III

*A* [W]hen this Court reexamines a prior holding, its judgment is customarily informed by a series of prudential and pragmatic considerations designed to test the consistency of overruling a prior decision with the ideal of the rule of law, and to gauge the respective costs of reaffirming and overruling a prior case. Thus, for example, we may ask whether the rule has proved to be intolerable simply in defying practical workability; whether the rule is subject to a kind of reliance that would lend a special hardship to the consequences of overruling and add inequity to the cost of repudiation; whether related principles of law have so far developed as to have left the old rule no more than remnant of abandoned doctrine; or whether facts have so changed or come to be seen so differently, as to have robbed the old rule of significant application or justification[.]

Although *Roe* has engendered opposition, it has in no sense proven "unworkable," representing as it does a simple limitation beyond which a state law is unenforceable[.]

We have seen how time has overtaken some of *Roe*'s factual assumptions: advances in maternal health care allow for abortions safe to the mother later in pregnancy than was true in 1973, and advances in neonatal care have advanced viability to a point somewhat earlier. But these facts go only to the scheme of time limits on the realization of competing interests, and the divergences from the factual premises of 1973 have no bearing on the validity of *Roe*'s central holding, that viability marks the earliest point at which the State's interest in fetal life is constitutionally adequate to justify a legislative ban on nontherapeutic abortions. The soundness or unsoundness of that constitutional judgment in no sense turns on whether viability occurs at approximately 28 weeks, as was usual at the time of *Roe*, at 23 to 24 weeks, as it sometimes does today, or at some moment even slightly earlier in pregnancy, as it may if fetal respiratory capacity can somehow be enhanced in the future. Whenever it may occur, the attainment of viability may continue to serve as the critical fact, just as it has done since *Roe* was decided; which is to say that no change in *Roe*'s factual underpinning has left its central holding obsolete, and none supports an argument for overruling it.

*B* In a less significant case, *stare decisis* analysis could, and would, stop at the point we have reached. But the sustained and widespread debate *Roe* has provoked calls for some comparison between that case and others of comparable dimension that have responded to national controversies and taken on the impress of the controversies addressed. . . .

[*The Court reviewed two earlier lines of cases involving major reversals of doctrine, holding that there had been no similar changes in the factual assumptions underpinning the decision here.*]

. . . In constitutional adjudication as elsewhere in life, changed circumstances may impose new obligations, and the thoughtful part of the Nation could accept each decision to overrule a prior case as a response to the Court's constitutional duty.

Because the case before us presents no such occasion it could be seen as no such response. Because neither the factual underpinnings of *Roe*'s central holding nor our understanding of it has changed (and because no other indication of weakened precedent has been shown) the Court could not pretend to be reexamining the prior law with any justification beyond a present doctrinal disposition to come out differently from the Court of 1973[.]

. . . In the present case, . . . as our analysis to this point makes clear, [a] terrible price would be paid for overruling. Our analysis would not be complete, however, without explaining why overruling *Roe*'s central holding would not only reach an unjustifiable result under principles of *stare decisis*, but would seriously weaken the Court's capacity to exercise the judicial power and to function as the Supreme Court of a Nation dedicated to the rule of law[.]

The underlying substance of [the Court's] legitimacy is . . . expressed in the Court's opinions, and our contemporary understanding is such that a decision without principled justification would be no judicial act at all. But even when justification is furnished by apposite legal principle, something more is required. Because not every conscientious claim of principled justification will be accepted as such, the justification claimed must be beyond dispute. The Court must take care to speak and act in ways that allow people to accept its decisions on the terms the Court claims for them, as grounded truly in principle, not as compromises with social and political pressures having, as such, no bearing on the principled choices that the Court is obliged to make. Thus, the Court's legitimacy depends on making legally principled decisions under circumstances in which their principled character is sufficiently plausible to be accepted by the Nation. . . .

The Court's duty in the present case is clear. In 1973, it confronted the already-divisive issue of governmental power to limit personal choice to undergo abortion, for which it provided a new resolution based on the due process guaranteed by the Fourteenth Amendment. Whether or not a new social consensus is developing on that issue, its divisiveness is no less today than in 1973, and pressure to overrule the decision, like pressure to retain it, has grown only more intense. A decision to overrule *Roe's* essential holding under the existing circumstances would address error, if error there was, at the cost of both profound and unnecessary damage to the Court's legitimacy, and to the Nation's commitment to the rule of law. It is therefore imperative to adhere to the essence of *Roe's* original decision, and we do so today.

## IV

From what we have said so far it follows that it is a constitutional liberty of the woman to have some freedom to terminate her pregnancy. We conclude that the basic decision in *Roe* was based on a constitutional analysis which we cannot now repudiate. The woman's liberty is not so unlimited, however, that from the outset the State cannot show its concern for the life of the unborn, and at a later point in fetal development the State's interest in life has sufficient force so that the right of the woman to terminate the pregnancy can be restricted.

That brings us, of course, to the point where much criticism has been directed at *Roe*, a criticism that always inheres when the Court draws a specific rule from what in the Constitution is but a general standard. . . . And it falls to us to give some real substance to the woman's liberty to determine whether to carry her pregnancy to full term.

We conclude the line should be drawn at viability, so that before that time the woman has a right to choose to terminate her pregnancy. We adhere to this principle for two reasons. First, as we have said, is the doctrine of *stare decisis*. Any judicial act of line-drawing may seem somewhat arbitrary, but *Roe* was a reasoned statement, elaborated with great care. We have twice reaffirmed it in the face of great opposition. Although we must overrule those parts of *Thornburgh* and *Akron I* which, in our view, are inconsistent with *Roe's* statement that the State has a legitimate interest in promoting the life or potential life of the unborn, the central premise of those cases represents an unbroken commitment by this Court to the essential holding of *Roe*. It is that premise which we reaffirm today.

The second reason is that the concept of viability, as we noted in *Roe*, is the time at which there is a realistic possibility of maintaining and nourishing a life outside the womb, so that the independent existence of the second life can in reason and all fairness be the object of state protection that now overrides the rights of the woman. Consistent with other constitutional norms, legislatures may draw lines which appear arbitrary without the necessity of offering a justification. But courts may not. We must justify the lines we draw. And there is no line other than viability which is more workable. . . .

The woman's right to terminate her pregnancy before viability is the most central principle of *Roe v. Wade.* It is a rule of law and a component of liberty we cannot renounce. . . .

Though the woman has a right to choose to terminate or continue her pregnancy before viability, it does not at all follow that the State is prohibited from taking steps to ensure that this choice is thoughtful and informed. Even in the earliest stages of pregnancy, the State may enact rules and regulations designed to encourage her to know that there are philosophic and social arguments of great weight that can be brought to bear in favor of continuing the pregnancy to full term and that there are procedures and institutions to allow adoption of unwanted children as well as a certain degree of state assistance if the mother chooses to raise the child herself. "The Constitution does not forbid a State or city, pursuant to democratic processes, from expressing a preference for normal childbirth." *Webster v. Reproductive Health Services* [(1989)]. It follows that States are free to enact laws to provide a reasonable framework for a woman to make a decision that has such profound and lasting meaning. This, too, we find consistent with *Roe*'s central premises, and indeed the inevitable consequence of our holding that the State has an interest in protecting the life of the unborn.

We reject the trimester framework, which we do not consider to be part of the essential holding of *Roe.* . . . The trimester framework suffers from these basic flaws: in its formulation it misconceives the nature of the pregnant woman's interest; and in practice it undervalues the State's interest in potential life, as recognized in *Roe.* . . .

Because we set forth a standard of general application to which we intend to adhere, it is important to clarify what is meant by an undue burden.

A finding of an undue burden is a shorthand for the conclusion that a state regulation has the purpose or effect of placing a substantial obstacle in the path of a woman seeking an abortion of a nonviable fetus. . . . [W]e answer the question, left open in previous opinions discussing the undue burden formulation, whether a law designed to further the State's interest in fetal life which imposes an undue burden on the woman's decision before fetal viability could be constitutional. The answer is no.

Some guiding principles should emerge. What is at stake is the woman's right to make the ultimate decision, not a right to be insulated from all others in doing so. Regulations which do no more than create a structural mechanism by which the State, or the parent or guardian of a minor, may express profound respect for the life of the unborn are permitted, if they are not a substantial obstacle to the woman's exercise of the right to choose. Unless it has that effect on her right of choice, a state measure designed to persuade her to choose childbirth over abortion will be upheld if reasonably related to that goal. Regulations designed to foster the health of a woman seeking an abortion are valid if they do not constitute an undue burden.

Even when jurists reason from shared premises, some disagreement is inevitable. . . . We do not expect it to be otherwise with respect to the undue burden standard. We give this summary:

(a) To protect the central right recognized by *Roe v. Wade* while at the same time accommodating the State's profound interest in potential life, we will employ the undue burden analysis as explained in this opinion. An undue burden exists, and therefore a provision of law is invalid, if its purpose or effect is to place a substantial obstacle in the path of a woman seeking an abortion before the fetus attains viability.

(b) We reject the rigid trimester framework of *Roe v. Wade*. To promote the State's profound interest in potential life, throughout pregnancy the State may take measures to ensure that the woman's choice is informed, and measures designed to advance this interest will not be invalidated as long as their purpose is to persuade the woman to choose childbirth over abortion. These measures must not be an undue burden on the right.

(c) As with any medical procedure, the State may enact regulations to further the health or safety of a woman seeking an abortion. Unnecessary health regulations that have the purpose or effect of presenting a substantial obstacle to a woman seeking an abortion impose an undue burden on the right.

(d) Our adoption of the undue burden analysis does not disturb the central holding of *Roe v. Wade*, and we reaffirm that holding. Regardless of whether exceptions are made for particular circumstances, a State may not prohibit any woman from making the ultimate decision to terminate her pregnancy before viability.

(e) We also reaffirm *Roe*'s holding that "subsequent to viability, the State in promoting its interest in the potentiality of human life may, if it chooses, regulate, and even proscribe, abortion except where it is necessary, in appropriate medical judgment, for the preservation of the life or health of the mother."